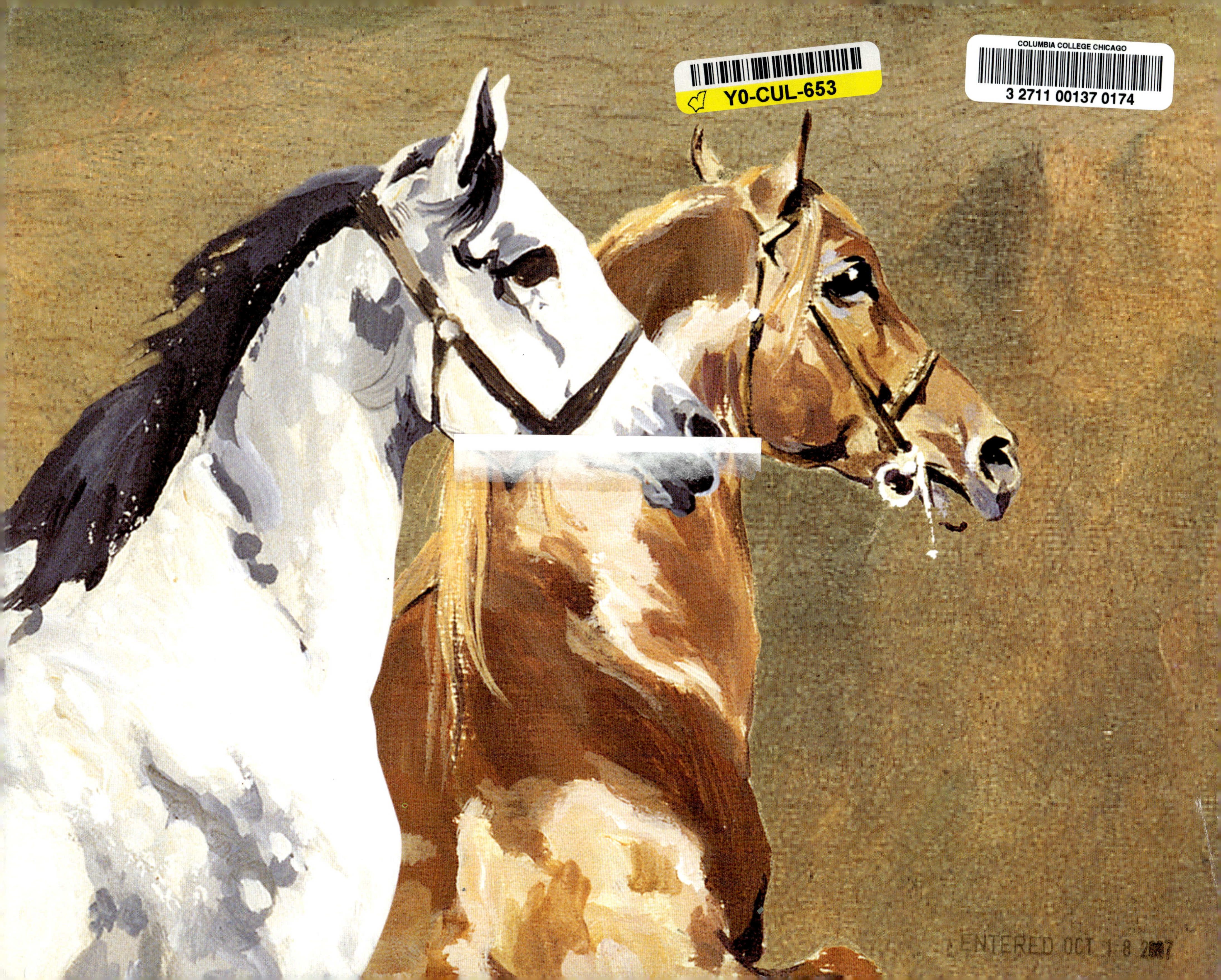

THE ARAB HORSE

THE ARAB HORSE

*A Complete Record of the Arab Horses
Imported into Britain from the Desert of Arabia from the 1830s*

Peter Upton

barzan

The Arab Horse

Barzan Publishing Ltd
Windrush Millennium Centre
Alexandra Road
Manchester M16 7WD
www.barzanpress.com

First published in 1989 by
The Crowood Press
Ramsbury, Marlborough,
Wiltshire SN8 2HE

Revised edition published 2006 by
Barzan Publishing Ltd

© Peter Upton 2006

All rights reserved. No part of this publication may be reproduced or transmitted in any form or by any means, electronic or mechanical, including photocopy, recording, or any information storage and retrieval system without permission in writing from the publishers.

ISBN: 095497 0 187
ISBN: 095497 0 195 (quarter-bound edition)

CIP Data A catalogue record for this title is available from the British Library

Designed by Kitty Carruthers
Printed and bound by SNP Leefung Printers Ltd

CONTENTS

Acknowledgements	7
Foreword By HRH Princess Alia al Hussein of Jordan	9
A History of the Desert Imports	11
Lists of the Horses Imported by the Blunts, 1878 – 1910	107
Mares	108
Stallions	110
Lists of the Horses Imported by Other Persons, 1830 – 1960	111
Mares	112
Stallions	115
The Existing Lines	125
The Blunts' Original Mares	127
The Blunts' Original Stallions	167
Other Original Mares	193
Other Original Stallions	223
Tables of Descent	265
The Blunts' Mares	267
The Blunts' Stallions	285
Other Mares	288
Other Stallions	296
Appendix 1: Origins and Strains	307
Appendix 2: The Tribes and their Horses	314
Glossary	319
Bibliography	320
Index of Horses' Names	323
General Index	332
Maps	
Bedouin Tribes of Arabia *c.* 1880	315
Desert Journeys in Northern Arabia	316
India in 1860	318

*Dedicated to W.S.B. and A.I.N.B., their
granddaughter Lady Anne Lytton and to all,
who by bringing Arab horses from the Desert of Arabia,
have played some part in the Arabian story.*

ACKNOWLEDGEMENTS

The author would like to record his thanks to all who generously provided him with information and material for this book. I would especially mention the late Lady Anne Lytton, friend and mentor, still greatly missed. To her I owe the suggestion that I should write this book. My thanks too, to the Earl of Lytton, who now lives with his wife and daughter at Blunt's old home, Newbuildings Place. He and members of his family have shown me great kindness in giving access to, and permission to quote from, family papers, diaries and journals.

To HRH Princess Alia al Hussein, I owe a special thanks for writing the foreword. Her words give authority to my endeavours. The history of the Arab horse is closely linked with that of the Hashemite Kingdom of Jordan. Emir Abdullah and Faisul rode north from the Hejaz on Arab Horses and today Princess Alia is director of the Royal Stud in Jordan. I am fortunate to have had many opportunities to visit that beautiful country and its famous stud, and to journey to the black tents of the Bedouin.

I wish to thank Rachel Kydd who opened my eyes with her own enthusiasm and knowledge, to a true understanding of the reward and satisfaction of thorough research and plain words. I hope I am not found wanting. I have enjoyed my eight years of intermittent study in the Manuscript Room at the British Library and I would wish to acknowledge the help of Miss J.M. Backhouse of the Department of Manuscripts.

Many thanks also to many friends abroad – Mary Jane Parkinson, Charles and Jeanne Craver, Gladys Brown-Edwards, Betty Finke, Robert Cadranell, Izabella Pawelec-Zawadzka, Anita Tolley and Mrs Sheila Stump, some of whom I have yet to meet but whom I feel I know, following long and rewarding correspondence on the trail of 'lost' horses, pictures and persons.

Sir Martin Gilliat assisted me considerably when I was researching Arab horses in the Royal Archives. There I found many interesting records and I gratefully thank him, Sir John Miller, Master of Horse (retired), Lieutenant-Colonel S.V. Gilbart-Denham, and Marcus Bishop MVO.

This book has also benefited greatly from the specialised knowledge of the late Colin Pearson, Ronald Kydd, Rosemary Archer, Dr Pesi Gazder and I should also like to express my thanks to Sir Henry and Lady May Abel-Smith, the Marquis of Tavistock, Count and Countess Lewenhaupt, Sir Dudley Forwood, Mrs M. Cousins, the late Santiago López and Ursula López, Pamela du Boulay, Mr and Mrs John Coward, Fiona Murray, Mrs Pat Robinson, Deirdre Hyde, Miss P.T. Sword, Mr and Mrs Derek Musgrave-Clark, Colonel Whent of the NPS, Mr T. Fraser from Brightwell Baldwin, Mr and Mrs Eric Parker owners of Blankney Hall, Mrs Gill Trimingham, Rohaise Thomas-Everard, Brian McDermot at the Mathaf Gallery, Mrs Pat Slater and Mr and Mrs Egerton, Mrs W.B.R.B. Somerville of Dargle Hill, Ireland, the Honourable Finn Guinness and Tamara el Dhagestani, whose family bred the old desert stallion Mehrez.

My thanks also for brotherly advice from my twin Roger and help from his artist son, Mark. Some of the photographs of the desert which appear in the book are by my son Simon who also undertook to reproduce the majority of the black and white pictures that accompany the text. Many of these reproductions were photographed from poor and faded originals or paintings dark with age, and they varied in size from one of twelve by nine feet to a newspaper photograph no bigger than a postage stamp. Many galleries were most helpful and provided me with copies of paintings – to them my thanks.

I have no doubt failed to mention others who have helped me in my task and to them I apologise. Their help was no less valuable and I am grateful. Lastly, to my wife Jay and our family, a personal debt. They have with great patience, not only accepted, but even approved my passion for the Arab horse.

Finally, I should like to thank the following for their kind permission to reproduce photographs, engravings and paintings: p.13 Sotheby's and The Tower of London; pp.14, 17, 26, 38, 40, 92 The Bridgeman Art Library; p.16 Mr and Mrs David Egerton; p.15*bl* Frost and Reed Ltd; p.15*r* Kimbell Art Museum, Fort Worth, Texas; p.18 The British Library; p.21 the Syndics of The Fitzwilliam Museum, Cambridge; p. 23 Her Majesty the Queen; p.25 Tate Britain; pp.27*b*, 26*l*, 88*r* The Director, National Army Museum; pp.31*tl*, 32*l* The National Pony Society; pp.37*r*, 50*bl*, 85, 90*bl* Simon D. Upton; p.50*tl* The Ashmolean Museum, Oxford; p.64, The National Gallery of Scotland; p.82 the Marquess of Tavistock and The Trustees of the Bedford Estates, Woburn Abbey; p.83 Musgrave Clark; p.91*tr* and *br*, The Arab Horse Society; p.93*bl* The Field; pp.94-5*b*, 97*r*, 99*r*, 102*l&r*, The Royal Archives, Jordan; p.98 The Trustees of the Imperial War Museum; p.101*tl* Tamara al Dhagestani.

The new revised edition of this book owes much to the help and encouragement given by Barzan Publishing Ltd. In particular I would like to thank Lionel Kelly, a man with an eye for detail and a new-found enthusiasm for Arab horses. I would also like to thank Kitty Carruthers for her hard work and artistic approach to the text and format of the book.

FOREWORD

Peter Upton is one of the greatest authorities known to me on the history of the Arabian horse in the United Kingdom – in fact, his knowledge of the history of the Arabian horse world-wide is quite unique. This, combined with his remarkable qualities as an artist and his special ability to portray true likenesses of individuals – both equine and human – make this book a valuable open window on the background of the Arabian horse in England, and indeed the world. This revised edition, substantially enlarging on the history of Arab horse importations to the United Kingdom, is splendidly enriched by the addition of many new full-colour and sepia images.

Alia al Hussein

A History of the Desert Imports

INTRODUCTION

This book has grown out of *Desert Heritage: An Artist's Collection of Blunt's Original Horses*, published in 1980. These original horses were those imported to England from the Desert of Arabia by Wilfrid Scawen Blunt and Lady Anne Blunt, between the years 1878 and 1910. Most people who have more than a passing interest in the Arab horse, will have read of the Blunts, their daughter Lady Wentworth and the world-famous Crabbet Stud. Further study into the history of the Arab horse in England, soon begins to reveal more dramatis personae, human and equine – Major Roger Upton, who travelled to the desert in search of the Arab horse and brought back six including the mare Kesia*[1], the Honourable Miss Dillon and her favourite stallion El Emir*, and Dwarka*, the desert stallion at one time owned by the Prince of Wales.

By searching diligently among old records, both in Britain and abroad, for those Arab horses bred in the Desert of Arabia and imported to England, it soon became obvious that they numbered far more than is generally realised. This book, therefore, aims to provide a complete record of all the desert-bred horses imported to England from whom present-day pure-bred Arabs descend. The earliest of these imports was, I have found, the stallion Padischah* foaled in 1826 and imported *c.* 1830.

▼ The Shamal, *etching by Charles W. Cain.*

▼ *Equestrian portrait of General Alexander Popham c. 1667, The Tower of London – an Arab stallion.*

Early Imports of Arab Horses

Many Arabs had arrived in this country prior to that date. Indeed the stallion Arundel*, and Truncefice*, a mare who came from Bradmound, King of Damascus, were brought to London by Sir Bevys of Hampton as early as the tenth century, and in 1624 the Royal Stud at Tutbury lists an Arabian colt, used to cover mares in hand. Later, Cromwell was eager to import some Arab horses:

> The Levant Company to Sir Thomas Bondyshe. Ambassador at Constantinople, 10 September, 1657, London.
> Upon intimation from his Highness the Lord Protector of his desire to be accommodated with some good Arabian horses, as a means to furnish England with a breed of that kind; We have now written to Aleppo (where heretofore there have bin some, and possible some may now be) to supply us with two of that sort, if it may be …

During the intervening years more than three hundred stallions and mares are recorded as having been imported to England. To be more exact is difficult, for many horses went by a number of names, often the result of a change of ownership and others were probably never recorded. The Alcock Arabian*, for example, imported in 1704 by Sir Robert Sutton via Constantinople and bought by the 2nd Duke of Ancaster, was also known as the Ancaster Turk, the Dorchester Turk, Brownlow Turk, Pelham's Grey Arabian, Holderness Turk and Sutton Turk and he was probably the same horse as the one known as the Honeywood Arabian, also called Sir J. William's Turk and Sir C. Turner's White Turk. From the Alcock Arabian* descend such famous grey Thoroughbred horses as the Tetrarch, Mumtaz Mahal and Mahmoud.

▶ Arabs Chasing a Loose Arab Horse in an Eastern Landscape, *oil painting by John F. Herring senior (1795-1865).*

▲ Royal Mares, *oil painting by F. Sibrechts, 1685.*

▶ Lord Grosvenor's Arabian with a Groom, *oil painting by George Stubbs, c. 1765. (Reproduced with kind permission of the Kimbell Art Museum, Forth Worth, Texas.)*

▼ Languish and Pantaloon *oil painting by John F. Herring senior, 1840.*

▼ The Godolphin Arabian, *oil painting by John Wootton, 1731.*

Considering what a difficult undertaking it must have been to obtain high-bred Arabians from the desert, it is surprising that so many were imported and reflects the high regard in which they were held. Few mares were allowed to leave Arabia, but Sir Robert Sutton, the Ambassador at Constantinople and importer of the Alcock Arabian*, sent one to the Duke of Newcastle in May 1709. Gervase Markham who sold a desert horse of his, the Markham Arabian*, to James I in 1616, considered the true stallion to be, 'The horse of Arabia, he is peerelesse, for he hath in him the purity and vertue of all other horses.'[2]

It was the restoration of the monarchy in 1660 which heralded the greatest period of Arab importation. Outstanding among these horses are the renowned stallions, the Byerley Turk*, the Darley Arabian*, the Leedes Arabian* and the Godolphin Arabian*, progenitors of the British Thoroughbred. Many other stallions from the Middle East also appear as ancestors of the Thoroughbred and it is more than probable that the 'Royal Mares' of Charles II were mostly of Arab blood too, for 'Charles II sent abroad the Master of the Horse [which some say was a late Sir Christopher Wyvil, others, the late Sir John Fenwick] in order to procure a number of foreign high-bred horses and mares for breeding; and the mares, thus procured by the said King's Interest, and brought to England… have, for that reason, been called Royal Mares.'[3]

▼ The Grey Arab, *oil painting by Sawrey Gilpin RA (1733-1807).*

The General Stud Book (GSB) was started in 1793 with a foundation of one hundred oriental stallions and forty-three mares.[4] It becomes evident that the Arab or oriental horse was considered as the pure breed and that only horses who descended from this breed were worthy to be acknowledged 'thoroughbred'. The GSB first published an Arabian Section in 1877, with the publication of Volume 13. This included the Sandeman purchases and Major Roger Upton's imports for the Honourable Henry Chaplin.

Although eastern horses were eagerly acquired by the princes and gentry of Europe throughout the sixteenth, seventeenth and eighteenth centuries, none of these early imports, it appears, were used for breeding pure Arabs. Matters were to change in the early nineteenth century, however, though not at first in England. In 1838, the 12-year-old grey desert-bred stallion Padischah*, who had been a gift from the Sultan of Turkey, was exported from England to Germany, there to stand at stud at Weil.[5] This Royal Stud, founded by King William I of Württemberg, already owned such famous Arabs as Bairaktar and Sultan*, the black stallion bought in 1837 at the Hampton Court Stud sale for 580 guineas.[6] Padischah* was to found a very strong line through his daughter Czebessie V, and her granddaughter Hamdany VI, by another desert horse Zarif. Sadly, Sultan* proved not to be a great success at stud and his line died out.

THE ARAB HORSE

▲ **The Black Arab,** *presented to His late Majesty William IV by the Imaum of Muscat, engraving by Paterson after a painting by Laporte.*

▼ **The Bay Arab,** *presented to His late Majesty William IV by the Imaum of Muscat, engraving by Scot after a painting by Laporte.*

Royal Gifts

Sultan*, had been one of four Arabs, the second gift of horses by the Imaum of Muscat to HM King William IV.[7] They had arrived in June 1837 and soon created a good deal of interest.

The Royal Stud at Hampton Court. Few who take any interest or aspire to any taste in horses when in the Metropolis, would neglect an opportunity, should it offer, to visit this celebrated stud… One of the most elegant of oriental customs is the habit of giving expression to the feelings through the agency of a typical vocabulary. Suiting the practice to the language of compliment, could there have been employed a more finished oratory of symbols than that lately adopted by the Imaum of Muscat? Could the most eloquent Demosthenes in the figurative have selected one of more expressive respect towards a British Monarch than the presentation of a line-of-battle ship and the purest bred courser of Araby?… We proceeded to a survey of the lions of the Stud Farm at the present moment, the Arabian horses, which have been recently received there as a present to His Majesty from the Eastern Prince before named. These are four in number, two stallions and two mares.

The first that was shown to me was a black stallion [Sultan*], standing 14 [hands], 3 [inches], branded 'M' on the off quarter. This horse is the most esteemed of the two, the colour in Arabs of the highest class being rarely if ever met with. Years, I was given to understand, were consumed in selecting the pair now at Hampton Court, and no limit put upon the price. Great as the difficulty has been to convey a just idea of the horse with a pencil, to put upon paper words to effect such a purpose is ten times a more hopeless affair. The first impression that the sight of this little unpretending animal made on me was anything save in accordance with my anticipations as I entered his box. The issue was precisely as we experience in contemplating a highly-finished picture – the more you gaze upon it, the more its beauties are developed. In this country we are by no means familiar with the Arab; many have not even seen one: I do not think above a score have come within my own notice; but I must say, that if the portraits with which every sportsman is acquainted of the Darley or Godolphin Arabians be faithful delineations of the animals they profess to represent, the whole model of the Arab horse, as I have seen it, differs *tolo coelo* from them. Here I had before me one, selected by a Prince whose subjects have ever been celebrated for trafficking in the purest blood of the Desert. I could not doubt his claim to legitimacy.

I have said his height is 14 [hands] 3 [inches], his form so angular that at fist glance it seems to defy all claim to symmetry. The whole character of shape and bearing is closely allied to that of the deer. When you come to a minuter examination of the parts, individually, then you are convinced how pure the fountain must have been whence such blood was obtained. The head of this horse can be likened to nothing but exquisitely chiselled marble; there is literally no flesh upon it; it is marble too to the touch. The eye is small, but clear to transparency; the cheek bones are prominent; and there is a fixedness about the ears that helps you to think you are really looking upon the work of a sculptor. The jaws stand very far asunder; the nostrils are large and high; and the windpipe is of an extraordinary size. The neck is light, and set on similar to the deer's; the shoulders more fleshy and upright than suits our taste; but below the knee the legs are perfection: you find quite as much bone as in the largest-sized English blood-horse, and the tendons are in your grasp like iron. His carcase, without being very full of substance, is round and tolerably deep; his quarters what we express by vulgar. His thighs are very thin and sinewy, his loins narrow, the hocks perfectly clean and slightly inverted; he is what we call 'cat-ham'd'. The tail is well set on, the dock small, the hair fine and scant, giving it the appearance of a mule's more than that of a horse. His shanks are short, and hard as adamant, the pasterns flexible, the hoofs singularly hard, but healthy and the feet open and roomy. You read his temper in his eye – he is a light-hearted animal, without the slightest taint of vice… they are crystal streams fresh, drawn from the spring whence it is acknowledged we derived the fertilisation of our Turf… The other stallion, a bright bay …

His head is less perfect, and his bone smaller, but his quarters are fuller… His back, which, like the other, is rather inclined to be hollow, is not more than 8 or 10 inches from hip to shoulder: I never saw a pony's so short… They were both brought out for me, and I saw them in all their paces. In their action, as in their lean spare forms, you detect nothing superfluous; it is quiet and graceful, and entirely without any expression of exuberant exertion. Utility is the characteristic of the Arab horse. I can imagine them going for days without fatigue. Nature intended them, and she has fitted them for endurance.

Of the two Arab mares (both grey) one produced a foal on her

▲ Grey Arab Mare, *presented to His late Majesty William IV by the Imaum of Muscat, engraving by Engleheart after a painting by Laporte.*

▼ Fleabitten Arab Mare, *presented to His late Majesty William IV by the Imaum of Muscat, engraving by Engleheart after a painting by Laporte.*

◀ *The Squire's Pets, oil painting by John F. Herring senior, 1852 – Imaum, the artist's Arabian (Imaum II).*

Study of a Horse, water-colour with chalks by Sir Edwin Landseer RA (1802-1873). ▶

passage and is now stinted to Actaeon. In her we have all the characteristics of the hind; in head, neck and limbs, as graceful and as fragile. The second a flea-bitten grey is the best in favor with the Sarans…[8]

The Imaum of Muscat was to continue this charming habit of sending gifts of Arab horses to our Royal Family, including six, the year after Sultan. In a letter to HM Queen Victoria, dated 26 August 1838, Lord Palmerston says, '…that an envoy is arrived from the Imaum of Muscat with a letter and presents to your Majesty'. He goes on to say that, '… the Imaum of Muscat is the independent sovereign of a considerable territory [who] about three years ago… sent His late Majesty as a present a 74-gun ship [so it was not always horses!] but that… The horses are not yet come. Having been sent to Bombay to be forwarded to England … Viscount Palmerston would humbly submit that it might perhaps be best that this envoy should not be received by Your Majesty on the same day as the Turkish Ambassador, lest any jealousy should be excited between them.' Not to be outdone, the Sultan of Turkey was also to send Arab horses as gifts to the Royal family!

In September 1839, more horses arrived for Queen Victoria from the Imaum and again in October 1840. Earlier that year, the Prince Consort had received two of his own – a white stallion named Imaum* and a bay called Mustapha*. In 1840, Queen Victoria decided to give the Arab horses to Prince Albert and he started a stud at Windsor, 'of all the Arab horses presented to Victoria by the Imaum of Muscat, the Shah of Persia and the King of Oude'.[9] Was this the very first English Arab stud?[10]

Seven years later, in April 1847, the Queen was to receive a further eight horses and she noted in her journal on 18 April 1847: 'We went to the stables and saw eight Arab horses sent me by the Imaum of Muscat, which are in a terrible condition.' The Imaum's gift, which arrived in July 1849, was of four stallions – Imaum*, a grey 5-year-old who was sent to Tattersall's on 18 March 1850 and sold for 12 $\frac{1}{2}$ guineas, Ibrahim* and Zanzibar*, also grey 5-year-olds who went to Tattersall's at the same time, realising 31 and 19 guineas respectively, and an aged chestnut named Muscat*. This last horse was given to Edwin Landseer, the Queen's favourite artist, on 22 March 1850. Imaum* appeared later as a model in many paintings by his new owner, John Frederick Herring senior.

Perhaps the reason for parting with these horses was that four more grey stallions had already arrived from the Imaum in February 1850. Two stallions which the Prince Consort received early in 1852 were described by the Queen on 2 May.

> We went to the stables, where we saw two fine horses which Albert has received from the Imaum of Muscat – the one, white, or rather grey and a bay. The first one is rather out of condition, and quite young but is sure to turn out handsome, but the second one is the greatest little beauty I ever saw, a perfect little animal in every detail, but is too small for Albert to ride, being only 14 hands high. It is a darling little creature, such a head and crest, carrying his tail so beautifully, and when he steps he seems hardly to touch the ground. Albert is quite delighted with him, and wishes him to be petted and taken the greater care of. I think there is nothing more beautiful than a beautiful horse!

This stallion, which excited such enthusiasm, was probably Said* foaled in 1846 who, in 1857, was also exported to Germany.

The last gift of horses from Muscat appears to have been five stallions in 1886 – Abeyan*, later given to Sir E. Wood, Terrafi*, Shoo-af-an*, Jesscan* (all who died at Hampton Court), and Terrassan*, a bay stallion foaled in

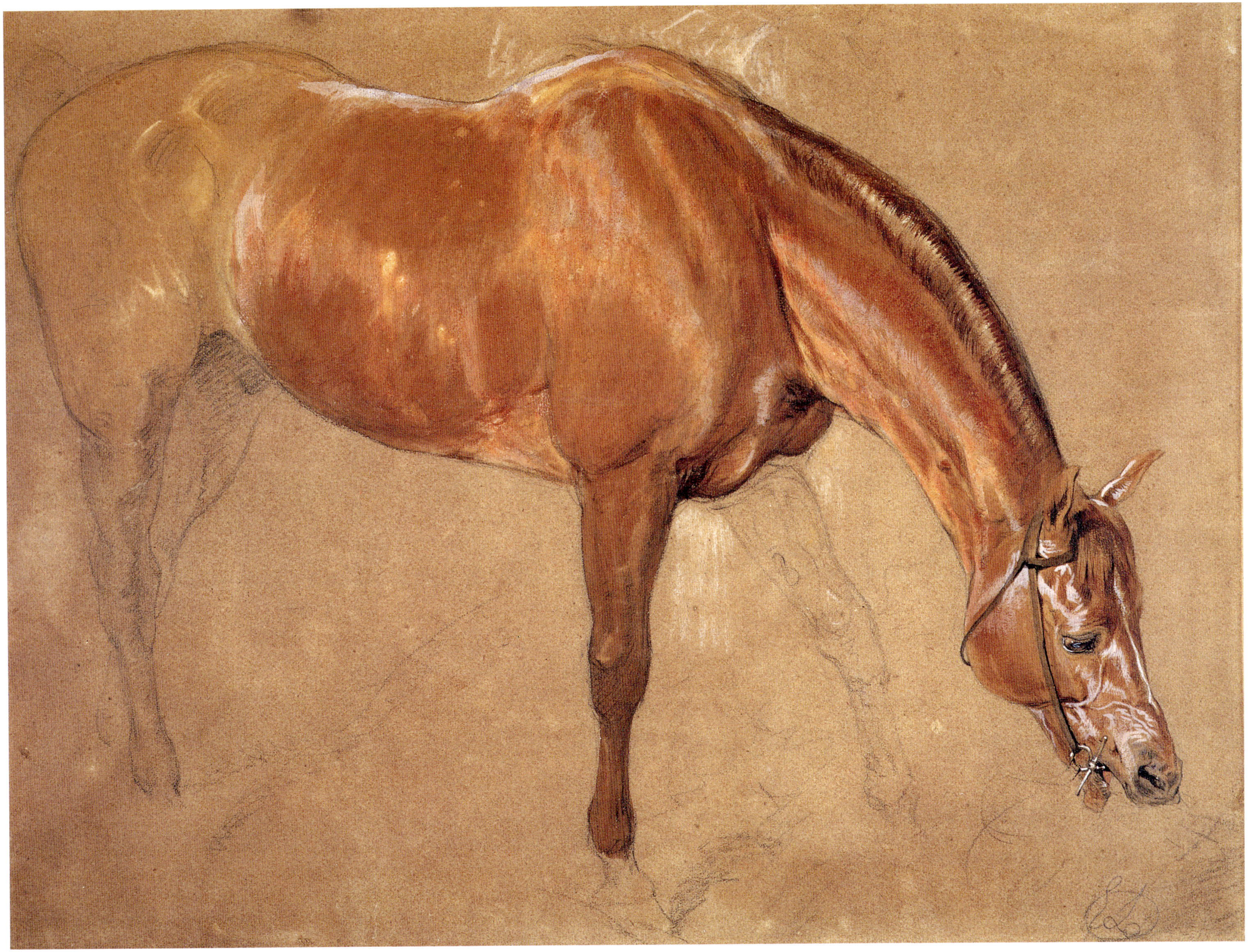

▲ The Queen viewing the Arabian horses presented to Her Majesty by Sir Jamsetjee Jejeebhoy, in the Riding House at Pimlico, *engraving by Landell, 1846.*

1879, presented by the Queen to the 'Congested Districts Board' in Dublin. He is registered in Volume 1 of the Polo Pony Stud Book published in 1894. Other horses arrived from Egypt, Morocco, Turkey and India during the nineteenth century.

In October 1845, 'Four high-bred Arabs [were sent] as a present to Her Majesty by Sir Jamsetjee Jejeebhoy of Bombay.' Queen Victoria wrote in her journal on 16 March 1846: 'We were presented with four beautiful Arab horses in magnificent cashmere horse cloths and trappings… They were all grey and very gentle.' One of the greys was named Khorseed*, another Serab* and a third Jemscheed*, a horse foaled in 1840 and exported to Germany in 1847. The Sultan of Turkey sent four stallions as a gift to the Prince of Wales in 1867. For some reason only one of these horses was entered in the GSB, namely Kouch*, a grey foaled c. 1860 and of the Seglawi Jedran strain. Wilfrid Blunt states that Kouch* rather than Kars* was the sire of Gomussa.[11]

Indjanin* was another desert horse to leave some mark on the Arab breed in Europe. He had been shipped to London from Calcutta, by the Viceroy of India, but was bought by Count Branicki in 1855 for his stud at Bialocerkiev in Poland.

[For] seven years [Indjanin] was used successfully in the stud. He proved to be such a good stallion that he spread the good reputation of the Branicki horses far beyond the borders of the Ukraine, so that Bialocerkiev became renowned for the breeding of oriental blood. So much so that the Sultan Abdul-Ajiz thought them worthy enough to form the basis of a new stud of oriental horses in the Imperial Stable in Constantinople. The Turkish Purchasing Commission chose from the Branicki stud 92

▲ *Saîd,* oil painting by John F. Herring senior, 1856.

horses of different sex and age. The two sons of Indjanin, Jarzmo and Inak became the founders of the Imperial Stud in Constantinople. They had both already shown themselves to be good stallions in their native stable. Among the younger horses purchased there were many children of theirs. The Purchasing Commission of the Sultan furnished a glowing testimony to the Branicki horses [1864].

Shortly after this date, the Prince of Wales received a horse from India, who was to prove another important sire for the Branicki stud, having been exported to Poland in 1878. This horse, Hussar*, whose descendants Wandyk and Ursus went to Spain in the early 1900s, has left many great names among the Arabians of Iberia.[12]

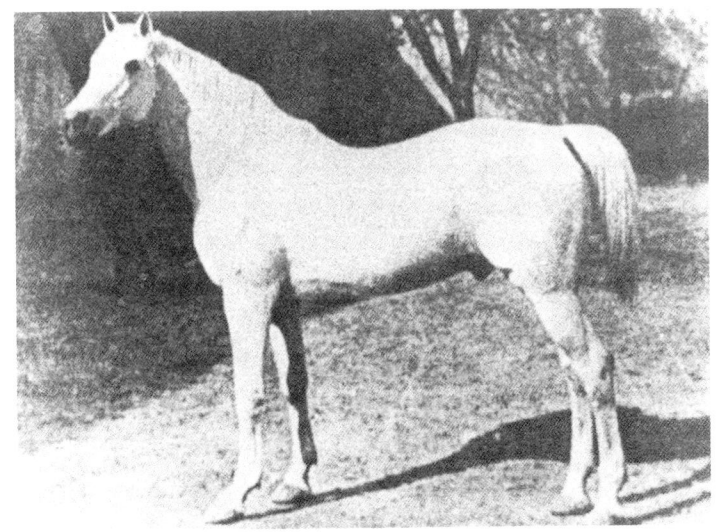

Wandyk, 1898. ▶

THE ARAB HORSE

Officers' Chargers and Indian Racehorses

The fashion of sending Arab horses as gifts to our Royal Family was to continue well into the twentieth century, but of those more will be recorded later.

Even without the Royal gifts, a surprisingly large number of Arab horses have been imported since Padischah's* arrival in the 1830s, and in this book you will find listed more than four hundred horses.[13] The larger number of stallions can be easily explained since the bedouin and Arab princes were loath to part with their precious mares – 'Guard your mares – their bellies are your treasure; their backs your safety and God will help their owners' (The Prophet Mohamed). Colts however, were surplus to requirements and a good market had existed for many years, supplying India with horses for racing and as officers' chargers. Concerned about the loss of horses abroad, the Turkish Porte was later to severely limit exports.

Many of the Arab horses imported to England during the nineteenth century, were naturally officers' chargers and racehorses, brought back from campaigns in India and Egypt.[14] Famous among these is Vonolel*, a grey horse foaled in the Nejd in 1875 and purchased in Bombay from Abdul Rahman by Lord Roberts in 1877. After serving as a charger for thirteen years, which included the forced march of some 313 miles from Kabul to Kandahar in August 1880, Vonolel* came back to England in 1893. Shalufzan*, Lord Roberts' bay Arab, accompanied Vonolel* on his return. In 1897, Lord Roberts took part in Queen Victoria's Diamond Jubilee Procession, mounted on his favourite charger, Vonolel*, who had been decorated by special permission of Her Majesty the Queen with the Kabul Medal with Four Clasps and the Kabul-Kandahar star.[15] Blitz* was another remarkable little horse, imported from India by Lord

◀ Lord Roberts on Vonolel Reviewing his Troops, *engraving after an oil painting by Charles W. Furse (1868-1904).*

William Beresford, after an almost unbeaten career as a racehorse spanning the years 1886 to 1889. The sum of 30,000 rupees (about £3,000), was offered and refused for him, although bought for only £70. Colonel T.A. St Quintin was to write of him in 1882:

> There was an absolute equine marvel in India at that time, rightly named 'Blitz' (lightning), a long, low grey Arab with a marvellous back and loin, 13 hands and $1/2$ inch in height. He had won the Civil Service Cup the year before with a lightweight, but now he had to carry top weight 9 [stone] 7 [pounds] and against a better class, which was thought quite impossible for him to do. [The race started] … and when the ponies came in sight Bob [a bay 4-year-old stallion belonging to Colonel St Quintin] was away by himself leading 5 or 6 lengths and people put down their glasses… But half-way little Blitz began to steal out of the ruck, and ridden hard from the quarter-mile post, gradually but surely made up his leeway and in spite of his heavy impost, closed nearer and nearer, until within 30 yards of the winning post he got alongside of Bob, and after an apparently great struggle, beat him half a length in 1 minute 22 $1/2$ seconds, with the rest of the

Field-Marshal Earl Roberts on his Charger, Vonolel, *oil painting by Charles W. Furse. (Courtesy of Tate London.)*

field nowhere. It was a marvellous and magnificent performance on his part… Think of him carrying 9 [stone] 7 [pounds] for three-quarters of a mile in 1 minute 22½ seconds, fighting it out inch by inch to the bitter end, untouched by whip or spur, and beating all the then records of pony racing in India… Picture him, a true Arab with his beautiful gazelle-like head, full-liquid eye, broad forehead, tapering muzzle and large nostril, a coat like satin and mane and tail like the finest silk. Beautiful and gallant little soul. He was a quiet, idle, gentle little fellow too… but put the colours on him in a ruck of horses and the gallant spirit and unequalled blood of his illustrious ancestors asserted itself at once, and he would race and struggle to the death. All glory to him![16]

Although used at stud in England, Blitz* eventually returned to India in the ownership of the Maharajah of Patiala, for whom he won seven races, again carrying off the three-quarters of a mile at Lucknow, by then known as the Eclipse Stakes.

Other leading racehorses to come out of India, include Rataplan*, Kismet*, Dictator*, Umpire* and Maidan* and no doubt all had interesting careers, but Maidan's* story is perhaps the most remarkable of all. As is so often the case, conflicting reports exist, but at least there is general agreement that Maidan* was a chestnut horse foaled c. 1869, who came out of Arabia to Bombay in 1871. Of those who knew him, we have the following notes. Lady Anne Blunt wrote in 1888: 'Maidan is a fine horse brought to England by Lord Airlie and was well-known and still remembered though it is years ago for he is 19 or 20.' Abdul Rahman vouched for his origin and gave a certificate, '… but the certificate had disappeared… so there is no proof or record, not even a name of breed [strain] … I should think he was all right. He has, however, been woefully knocked about so that the legs are filled…' On 29 September 1890, Lady Anne wrote again: 'His jaw deep and very good, head good, girth and shoulder good too. He is chestnut like Ashgar and not altogether unlike him, resembling also Tamarisk but less beautiful.'

In an article in *The Livestock Journal* of 1890 it states of Maidan*: 'Fresh and well with 8-inch bone and as clean in the legs as a 4-year-old, not withstanding the fact that he was hunted in Suffolk last year.' He would have been at least 21 years old – but can it be the same horse as regards the legs that Lady Blunt describes? Spencer Borden says in his book *The Arab Horse*, that, '… At 5 years of age (1874) he was sold to Lieutenant-Colonel Brownlow as a charger [Captain

◀ Lt. General Sir Charles Napier with his Arab Charger, Red Rover, *oil painting by Edwin Williams.*

THE ARAB HORSE

Umpire, an Arab Pony of the Keheilan Strain drawing *by F. Dodd.*

Blitz, a famous Arab pony.

Johnstone having bought him of Abder Rahman in 1871]. Brownlow rode at 19 stone with his equipment… yet Maidan carried him for twelve years in campaigns [through] India and Afghanistan, until [he] was killed in the fight at Kandahar', at the end of the famous forced march from Kabul.17 'At 17 years of age… Maidan was bought by Lord Airlie who again put him to racing.' In 1884 Maidan won the Ganges Hog Hunt Cup and also a 4-mile steeplechase. 'He was then sold to Captain the Honourable Eustace Vesey.'

Vesey bought him to take to England. Leaving India on a troopship *Jumna*, Maidan* got as far as Suez, where the ship met the expedition going to the relief of Suakim … and was pressed into service as a transport for troops to Massawah [near the southern end of the Red Sea].18 So it happened that the old racehorse and charger had his journey lengthened [he stood on his feet for one hundred days]… before he reached Marseilles.' Shortly after, he won a race for his owner at Pau and later, was raced successfully in England.

In a letter dated 1904, Randolph Huntington, gives a slightly different version, in that, 'Lord Airlie took him into the South of France where he won many races with him, then sold him to Captain the Honourable Eustace Vesey who, being retired, took him to England, then 19 years old, and the first mare he was ever known to cover was the mare Naomi and she produced the chestnut mare Nazli on 17 May 1888. I bought Naomi carrying the foal in February 1888.'19 Whatever the actual sequence of events, Maidan* must have been a very special horse. Purchased by the Honourable Miss Dillon, on the death of the Honourable Vesey, Maidan* now no youngster was to win yet another steeplechase at the age of 22 or 23 years. He slipped and broke a leg whilst out at exercise in 1892, and had to be destroyed.

▼ *British and Egyptian Army officers in the Sudan, 1898.*

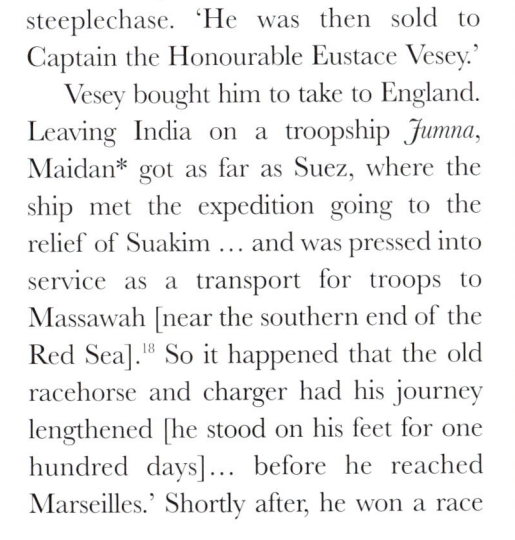

Many of the officers' chargers who took part in the Egyptian and Sudan campaigns of the 1880s and 1890s were Arabs, and of these some were to return to England. But how many horses and men were to die in the battles at El Obeid, Soukim, Omdurman and Khartoum! Bashom*, known as 'The Fox', survived although wounded at Omdurman and he was imported from Egypt in August 1901 by Captain W. Smythe VC of the Queen's Bays. It is recorded that he galloped fifty miles in one afternoon with dispatches. Bashom* had been born in the camp of the Roala tribe in the Northern Desert in 1892, and stood only 14 hands 1 inch – but he had a big heart. Sir W. Gateacre rode Khalifa*, a grey Arab, during the Egyptian campaign and Captain Honouré de Montmorency, later killed in South Africa, won his VC in the Sudan, his charger a 14 hands Arab named Parahk*

27

THE ARAB HORSE

◀ *Captain P.A. Kenna of the 21st Lancers in the Sudan in 1898. He was awarded the VC for his part in the charge at Omdurman.*

▼ *Kumwar Dokhul Singh on an Arab pony presented to Captain Douglas Haig by Sir Pertab Singh.*

The Polo Pony Society

Some of these horses from Egypt and India, took up the pursuit of the fox with the distinction and courage which they had once displayed in the face of the enemy, and many turned out to be excellent polo ponies. The well-known polo player T.B. Drybrough wrote in 1898 that:

> Among Arab ponies now playing in England are Mr T.E. Brandt's chestnut horse Huzzor, which is a winner of several first prizes and is somewhat remarkable for being occasionally used on the same day for stud purposes and polo… Mr W.H. Walker's Magic, is a Nejd who was imported by Captain Hayes, for whom he won some races in India. He was a wonderful polo pony [he played in the winning team for the County Cup at Hurlingham in 1889] and is now at stud… the sire of over 200 ponies.[20]

Drybrough also mentions a Mr A.M. Tree of Ashorne Hill, Leamington who had a stud of Arab horses and J.H. Munro Mackenzie of Calgary, Tobermory, Isle of Mull, Argyllshire, who was successful in breeding good ponies by a nice bay Arab 'The Syrian'*. Ameer*, a very well bred Arab, imported from India by Captain Little of the 9th Hussars, was a celebrated polo pony and C.D. Miller played on two good specimens of Arab ponies, Mecca and Modena. Nejdran*, imported from the desert by Captain Gainsford in 1902, played in the International Polo Match in Ireland 1903, only to be exported to the USA a year later.

In the Stud Books of the Polo Pony Society (PPS), who published Volume 1 in 1894, there are recorded a large number of Arab horses imported to this country.[21] Later renamed The Polo and Riding Pony Society (P&RPS), it was established, 'to promote the breeding of ponies for polo, riding and military purposes; and for the encouragement of the native breeds'. At their London shows they held classes for 'Eastern Sires', not exceeding 14 hands 2 inches. In 1905, Mootrub* won First Prize – £10 in those days! By 1912 the height limit for the Eastern Sires class had been raised to 15 hands. Then in 1913 the National Pony Society (NPS) was formed out of the old P & RPS and in 1918 the Arab Horse Society took over the organisation of classes for Arabs. The Eastern Sires remained, though now it was for 4-year-olds and upwards entered in the Arab-bred register and those of 50 per cent pure Arab blood – a far cry from the original concept, when all entries were imported desert horses, or the offspring of such.

▼ *Facsimile of The Polo and Riding Pony Society Show Catalogue, Eastern Sires Class, 1905.*

THE ARAB HORSE

▲ *The 11th Hussars' polo team in Jodhpore, 1899.*

▼ *T.E. Brandt's Arab pony, Huzzor.*   ▼ *W.H. Walker's Arab pony, Magic.*

30

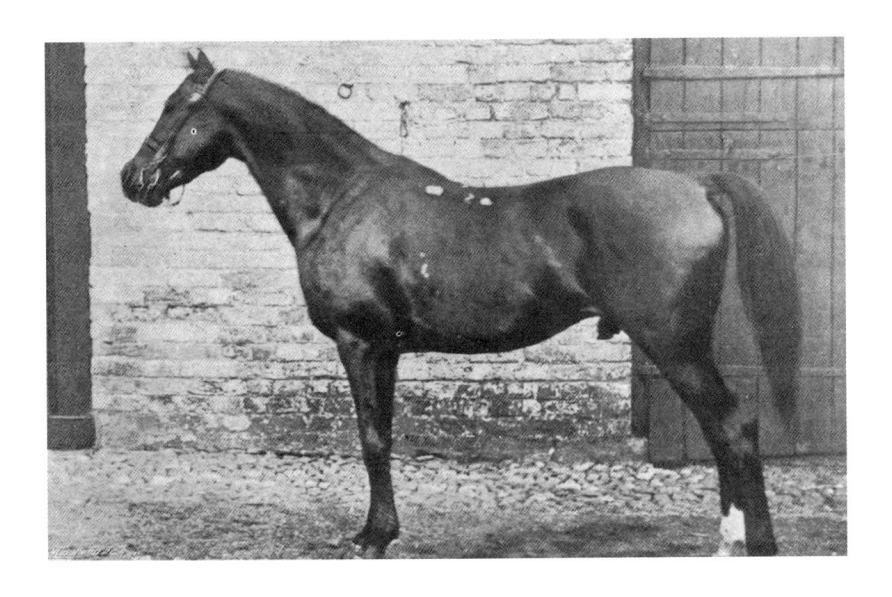

▲ G. Norris Midwood's The Bey.

▼ C.D. Miller on his Arab pony, Modena.

▲ The Leat, Dartmoor stallion bred by HRH The Prince of Wales, foaled in 1918. Sire – Dwarka.

▼ Dwarka.

As will be seen by perusing the lists of Imported Horses, many (too many), have been lost to the breed and it is but a small percentage of the Original Horses whose lines exist to this day. With the exception of those horses imported by the Blunts, who may claim to be the major influence, most of the other horses have played very little part in the Arabian story and their hold is tenuous. No horse can compare with the impact of the Blunts' original imports, like Mesaoud* or Rodania*, but nevertheless their role is significant and has helped to ensure a wider genetic pool at source. Some have left no direct lines in England, but have made their mark abroad, most notably Padischah*, Indjanin*, Hussar*, Yatagan*, Nejdran*, Haidee*, Noura*, Muha* and Turfa*. Others have played a considerable role in the improvement of our native breeds. Dwarka's* blood is to be found in Dartmoor ponies through his famous son, 'The Leat', bred by the Prince of Wales in 1918, and Chandi*, sired the beautiful hack 'Arabian Night', the mount of HM King George V.

▼ *Arabian Night as a yearling, a part-bred Arab. Sire – Chandi.*

Chandi.
▼

◄ *HM King George V riding Arabian Night in Rotten Row.*

▼ *Sahara, one of the last desert horses to be registered with the NPS.*

Major Roger Upton

The first Englishman to go to the Desert of Arabia for the express purpose of collecting pure-bred Arabs, with the desire to establish a stud of the same, was, of course, Major R.D. Upton.[22] He is a fascinating and elusive figure in the story of the Arab Horse, whose role may well be greatly underrated, being overshadowed by the bright star of Wilfrid Scawen Blunt.

Upton's second book, written in 1872, entitled *Newmarket and Arabia*, is a serious study relating to the history and breeding of the Thoroughbred, but examines its relationship with the Arab horse as well. His knowledge was such that it is difficult to believe that he had, at that time, not even visited the desert. He acknowledges earlier writers such as Palgrave, Gifford, Abd-el-Kader and General Daumas in the book, along with the assistance given him by, '…an Arab gentleman of a Nejdean family'. His conclusion, almost a plea, is best told in his own words:

▼ The Kal'a, Aleppo, *engraving by Peter Upton.*

The course to pursue is the attainment of a certain number of pure-bred Arabian horses and mares: The latter would most likely be in foal. It would be better if the Government would undertake this, and indeed engage to form such a national stud, as it could then be carried on in its integrity, without let or hindrance from whims or fancies of private individuals. A few well selected persons with knowledge of the Arabian horse and where to seek him, would be the first thing needful.

Was he offering his own services?

Should the Government not feel able to undertake it as a national scheme, there is a grand opening for private enterprise or for a combination of gentlemen who have the welfare of the horse at heart.

It is probable that Upton's subsequent desert journeys, given the backing of the Honourable Henry Chaplin and the Dangars, were the direct outcome of his book.

Major Upton's first desert journey started in October 1874. Earlier that year he had travelled back from Australia, for on 18 January he had painted a water-colour of the coast between Melbourne and Sidney. His eldest son, only 18 years old, may well have been on board ship too, for he was to accompany his father on his journeys to the desert. By 24 October they were at the Turkish port of Smyrna (Izmir) on their way to Aleppo, where they met J.H. Skene, HM Consul General. Skene had been Consul at Aleppo since 1855. He had travelled extensively among the Anazeh tribes and knew something of their horses. Upton and his son stayed with Mr and Mrs Skene in Aleppo, but some days after Christmas 1874, they set out eastwards across the desert to the Euphrates.

Skene was mounted on a 6-year-old Jelfan and Major Upton and his son on some 3-year-old colts they had bought. They were escorted by an old sheikh, with whom they spent their first night, in a village named Spheri. Here they saw some horses including a fine old mare of the Ras-el-Fedawi strain. Travelling on past the lake of Jubul to Dar Hafar, they met Sheikh Narhar of the Mowali tribe, then pressed on to the Euphrates River at Shass where they found the tents of the Weldi. Eventually turning south, the party followed the right bank of the river, spending one night at the Turkish barracks at Messkene. A little beyond there they headed northwards once again, for Aleppo.

They had seen several horses and mares and, indeed, had bought a 2-year-old colt of great promise – Alif. So what of the horses who were purchased for Albert Glas Sandeman, and who are listed in the General Stud Book, Volume 13 (1877), the first time that an Arabian section was included in this publication.

The following Arabian Horses, purchased by Skene, HM Consul at Aleppo, were imported by A. Sandeman in 1874:

Yatagan, a chestnut horse, now 7 years old, foaled 1870, a Greban, his dam of the Greban family, his sire of the Hellawee family; Zuleika, a bay mare, now 7 years old [foaled 1870] of the Maneghi Hedraj family, both her dam and sire were of that family; Haidee, a chestnut mare, now 8 years old [foaled 1869] of the Maneghi Hedraj family, both dam and sire of that family.

Many consider that Major Upton was instrumental in procuring and importing these horses for Sandeman and a note of Upton's which is quoted by the Reverend F. Furze Vidal in a letter to Randolph Huntington, dated 15 May 1896, would seem to support this view:[23]

Mrs Upton cannot remember the date of the arrival – but she thinks it must have been in March or April 1875 or 1876. The latter date would tally with Naomi's age and with what Mr Sandeman told me. In a note he, Upton, says: 'I have tried to get a Managhi Hedrudj of the family of Ibn Sbeyel of the Gomussa tribe of Sebaa Anezeh which I hold to be the best breed in the Desert. I have succeeded and one of them is now in my stable. I had enquired at the same time about mares; and two have come of the same family. The four are as follows:

No. 1. Chestnut stallion 4 years old, 14 hands 2 inches. His dam a Keheilet Jeabeh taken from the Heissa Anezeh, and his sire the famous Keheilan Hellawi of the Shammar tribe.

No. 2. Pearl grey stallion with black mane and black tail tipped with white, 4 years old, 14 hands 2 inches. His dam 'Managhi Hedrudj' of Ibn Sbeyel family of Gomussa Anezeh, and his sire of the same breed, now in the stud of the King of Italy.

No. 3. Bay mare 5 years old, 14 hands 1 1/2 inches. Same breed as No. 2, but dam and sire not the same.

No. 4. Chestnut mare 4 years old, 14 hands 3 inches. Same breed as Nos. 2 and 3, but dam and sire not the same. Noted for speed and bottom.'[24] Again in another note: 'In this country (Arabia) mares are never so handsome as stallions and these are the best looking I could get. The chestnut mare, however, was not selected for her shape – but for her speed and bottom.' I also send you a facsimile of a translation made by Upton of the delivery note and description of my old mare Zuleika (the No. 3 I presume).

The frontispiece to Major Roger Upton's book Newmarket and Arabia, *drawn on wood by the author after Adam.*

No. 1 is Yatagan*, No. 3, Zuleika* and No. 4, Haidee*, the three imported horses registered in GSB Volume 13, so it would appear that Upton was involved in procuring these horses. This is supported by a further note in one of his sketch books: '1874, chestnut horse purchased by Skene through Captain Upton for A.G. Sandeman.' The statement, '… one of them is now in my stable' [probably Skene's stable], must refer to No. 2, the pearl grey stallion, who for some reason was never registered. The Reverend F. Furze Vidal makes some errors in his letter, for the facsimile of the certificate he says is Zuleika*, is really that of the mare Kesia*, imported by Upton in 1875, and of a different strain. There can be little doubt that Major Upton had been closely associated with the horses of A. Sandeman, but it seems likely that Skene was actually commissioned to buy them and they were imported in 1874.

Major Upton had been commissioned to procure a stallion for the stud of Messrs W.J. and A.A. Dangar in Australia.[25] He was able to purchase the tall brown 3-year-old colt, who they named Alif (the first letter of the Arabic alphabet). This colt was taken to Aleppo and there ridden by Major Upton's son, until it was time to travel the ninety miles to Alexandretta, there to be loaded on board ship. Arriving at Marseilles, the horse was taken through France and thence to England. Alif was to remain in London for four weeks before taking passage to Australia. Whilst there, both Mr Tattersall and the Honourable Henry Chaplin saw the horse and declared him a very good Arab, but this view was not at first shared by the Australians.

However, by 1877, an extract from a report of the Agricultural Exhibition states that:

One of the gems of the show was without doubt Mr W.J. Dangar's Alif, a horse the like of which I never saw before. He's the most beautiful brown conceivable, perfectly free from white, with a wonderful set of legs and as much muscle as could well be got into one hide; he's splendid to stand behind with most astonishing length from hip to hock; and I fancy him getting first-class stock… some people affect to disbelieve that Alif is an Arab, but why I'm sure I can't see.

By early 1876, Sandeman had taken a lease on Brightwell Park in Oxfordshire and there in May, Zuleika* produced 'Symmetry', a colt foal by Yataghan* registered in the GSB. It is possible that Haidee* also foaled a colt by Yataghan* in the same year.[26] In 1877, a chestnut filly was born to Haidee* and Yataghan*, named Naomi. It was to be through this last foal that the Sandeman imports were to leave their mark on the Arab breed.

In Volume 15 of the GSB, Zuleika* and Haidee* both appear as being in the stud of J.C. MacDona, having been with him since 1882 or perhaps 1881. Haidee* had no further produce and died in 1884, whereas Zuleika* produced at least one more foal – a brown filly – by Bend Or in 1883 before she passed into the ownership of the Reverend F. Vidal c. 1886. He had already bought the mare Naomi from Sandeman, possibly some time in 1881 when he took the living at Creeting St Mary, near Needham, Suffolk.[27] The mare produced four foals between 1884 and 1888. She was sold to Randolph Huntington and sent to New York in August of 1888.[28] In 1893, Huntington also bought Naomi's daughter, Nazli, and her grandsons, Nimr and Garaveen, from Vidal, who travelled with them to New York. Whilst in America, Vidal went to the Chicago Exposition to judge the Arab and other classes and so undoubtedly saw the 'Hamidie Horses'.

In this way, the descendants of the Sandeman imports, Yataghan* and Haidee* were to cross the Atlantic, there to exert some considerable influence on Arab breeding in America. As the Reverend Vidal wrote on 20 May 1893:

'Dear Mr Huntington, you are now receiving the fruits of 35 years of careful study, expenditure and experience. Alas! Alas! That it should come to this. One soweth, but another reapeth.'

By June 1875, Major Upton and his son were once again on their way to the Desert of Arabia, this time with a commission to secure horses for the Honourable Henry Chaplin and a mare for A.A. Dangar. Leaving Marseilles on 11 June on board the steamship *Alphee*, they arrived at Smyrna after six days at sea. From there, the ship steamed down to Beirut, where they disembarked and rode through the Bakkah Valley to Damascus, there to meet with Consul Skene. In his twenty years as HM Consul of Aleppo, Skene had been able to make contact with many of the Bedouin tribes, and on this visit he was to introduce Major Upton to the Anazeh sheikhs, Suleyman Ibn Mirshid, Supreme Sheikh of the Gomussa Sebaa, and Jedaan Ibn

Brightwell Park, Oxfordshire. ▼

THE ARAB HORSE

Mahaid of the Fedaan.

They were eager to leave Damascus, where cholera raged, and accompanied by Ghudda, brother-in-law to Suleyman, they set off into the fierce midsummer sun. After sixteen hours in the saddle, they rested for a while in the shadow of some rocks at the end of a vast gorge, before riding on again across a wide plain. Only as the sun began to set did they near the Sebaa camp, and passing by herds of camels and numerous black tents, they arrived at last at the Sheikh's tent:

> … a man is seen to jump on the back of a mare, and rides forward to meet us… He is Suleyman Ibn Mirshid 'Shaykh of Shaykhs' – such was his title in the desert. Springing from his mare, he bids us welcome and brings us into his tent … Seated on a mat is Jedaan Ibn Mahaid, Shaykh of the Fadan Anazeh, with several others;

▼ *Naomi. Sire – Yataghan; dam – Haidee.*

Bedouin riders. ▶

▼ Chestnut Arab Stallion, *oil painting by John E Ferneley senior (1782-1860).*

THE ARAB HORSE

◄ *Facsimile of a translation of Kesia's certificate of authenticity* (hojja) *made by Major Roger Upton.*

> Translation in English by R. D. Upton.
>
> race
>
> A Kheilet of the Nowak
>
> her colour red (bay)
>
> race of her father
>
> Daba Nowak
>
> Saticated by (that is in foal by) the hedud Seklawy
> at abd   his tribe
>
> Roualla Anazah
>
> 17 July 1875 Christian year.
> Go mitter
> The Shaykh Suleyman ibn Murschud ×ʃ which are these signs
>
> [seal: Servant of God Suleyman ibn Murschud]

▼ *Bedouin.*

▼ A Grey Arab Stallion in a Wooded Landscape, *oil painting by Jacques-Laurent Agasse (1767-1849).*

he, recognising our effendi [Skene] starts to his feet, saying, 'Yes, it is he', and hastens to salute him … coffee is at once prepared.

Days were spent examining horses, mares, colts and fillies which were brought for them to see, but at first they had difficulty in finalising any purchase. Only the direct intervention of Sheikh Suleyman and Jedaan enabled Major Upton to be successful in the purpose of his desert journey.

Some three years after Upton's visit, Skene was to help Lady Anne and Wilfrid Scawen Blunt in much the same way. Indeed, he selected and purchased a number of Original Horses who were to become the foundation of Crabbet Stud, and without his experience and connections, it is conceivable that they would have had less success. Some of the horses described by Upton so vividly, were later seen by the Blunts. We know that Upton tried hard to purchase the white Hamdanieh, Sherifa*, but the price asked by Sheikh Takha, Chief Ulema of Aleppo, was too high. He, Upton, did, however, take a drawing of her back to show Chaplin. The Blunts were more fortunate. By 1878, Skene was able to purchase the mare for them for just £38, as the Ulema had just died and his family were eager to sell.

The horses that Major Upton succeeded in buying are described in some detail in his book, *Gleanings from the Desert of Arabia*:

Towards the close of a long and trying day, we made repeated offers for a bay mare, 5 years old and unblemished; she was a beautiful creature, just under 15 hands in height, very blood-like, but wildly excitable, glared at us like a tigress, and resented our approach even… It was Suleyman Ibn Mirshid who put the halter rope in my hands; her price was told out on the table, exactly that which I had offered and handed over to her former owner and the mare picketed at our tent. A very simple certificate of the mare's breeding and family was written out at my request in the presence of two sheikhs to which they placed their seals.

A bay mare [Jemima*].
Breed – Keheilet Nowak.
Breed of dam – Keheilet Nowak; breed of sire – Keheilan Nowak.
Her family from Keheilan Nowak; her owner Dabah Nowak of the Gomussa tribe Sebaa Anazeh.
16th Tammuz [July] of the Christian Year 1875.
The testifier of this writing is: Suleyman Ibn Mirshid and Jedaan Ibn Mahaid.

Another man brought up his mare with a colt at her foot… she became mine, but he led away the little foal in sullen silence… I could not get the little colt; but the mare was in foal and dropped in the following spring a bay filly, own sister to the colt.

Breed – a Keheilet of Nowak [Kesia*].
Her colour bay (red).
Breed of her sire – Dabah Nowak.
In foal by the hudud horse Seklawi-al-Abd. His tribe, i.e. the tribe of the horse – Roalla Anazeh.
17th Tammuz [July] of the Christian Year 1875. The testifier of this writing is: The Sheikh Suleyman Ibn Mirshid.

A dark bay colt of the celebrated Seklawi-Jedran strain, and of that in the family of Ibn Nederi, to some might appear small and unpretending in appearance, but we thought him a colt of promise. He was 2? years old and stood 14 hands 1? inches, but looked of less height. He had a beautiful head, showing much intelligence and much form, a perfect jibbah [prominent forehead]… good ears, a full eye, a very fine nostril and the nasal bones considerably depressed; a perfect neck and mitbeh [throat-line]. He had long sloping shoulders well developed at the base of the scapulae; withers high and running well back. His arms were long and muscular.

Breed – Seglawi Jedran Ibn Nederi [Ishmael*].
His colour bay (red).
Breed of his sire – Dahman abu Amr of the Gomussa tribe of Sebaa Anazeh.
His age 2 years and a half.
17th Tammuz [July] of the Christian year 1875.
The testifier of this writing is: The Sheikh Suleyman Ibn Mirshid.

Another Abayeh Sharrackieh, a chestnut mare, can only be described by the word magnificent. She was 14 hands and 2 inches in height, of great length, size and substance, of good bone and wonderfully handsome. Her head might be said to be of exaggerated beauty, and we both exclaimed, 'Had such a head and so fine a muzzle been depicted truthfully on canvas, it would have been pronounced to be most unnatural.' Her ears were good, and of the mare type; the jibbah developed to excess; the eye fine and prominent… the jaws deep and the muzzle excessively fine. She had a splendid neck, with great development of the splenius muscle; her chest was deep and very capacious. She had a fine barrel; she had large and powerful shoulders, fine quarters, a grand haunch, and the sacral bones so high that the setting on of the tail appeared to be almost the highest part of her body. Her withers were elevated; her arms were long, very large and muscular; knees large, square and deep; good thighs and hocks; short legs, clean, hard and of good bone. She was very slightly stag-kneed, but the hock sinews were not inclined forward, but perfectly upright; her pasterns of a moderate length; her feet were large and strong, and rather higher than is usual among desert horses. She stood over a great deal of ground; she had a free, grand, long stepping walk. Her formation indicated very high speed, and she had great substance and a powerful frame. She had a very full tail, which she carried when moving to a degree. I have seen her when she was galloping, with her loins and quarters covered and hidden by her widely spread and high carried tail. She was a mare of the highest courage, easily excited and full of fire.

The chestnut mare [Keren-Happuch*].
Breed – Abayeh Sherakieh.
Breed of sire – Keheilan Ajuz.
A mare of the Sheikh Jedaan Ibn Mahaid, a mare of the Gomussa tribe of the Sebaa.
16th Tammuz [July] of the Christian Year 1875.
The testifier of this writing is : Jedaan Ibn Mahaid.

We saw a family of the beautiful Tamri strain – mother, daughter, and son, all bay… The son was a bay colt of a beautiful colour, between 3 and 4 years of age; he was 14 hands 3 inches. He had a fine head, an eye of peculiar beauty, fine nostrils, and sharp, finely cut, and very handsome ears; a strong, light, muscular neck. He was deep in the chest, had a good barrel, a back of great width with arched ribs; his loins, croup, and haunch were very grand; his well-formed thighs were well let down, his hocks were finely formed, and his legs the hardest, cleanest and blackest I think I had ever seen. He stood back at the knees… He was considered to be a perfect animal, and was much thought of by his tribe.

Talkat, the owner of a fine bay horse I selected, walked behind his horse, which was led by the Sheikh to our tent.

Breed – a Keheilan horse of the Keheilans of Tamer [Joktan*].
Breed of his sire – Dahman abu Amr of the Gomussa tribe of the Sebaa [see Ishmael].
The name of his owner, Talkat.
16th Tammuz [July] of the Christian Year 1875.
The testifier of this writing is: Suleyman ibn Mirshid.

The Honourable Henry Chaplin.

Blankney Hall, Lincolnshire.

Kesia*, Ishmael*, Keren-Happuch* and Joktan* were all purchased for the Honourable Henry Chaplin.[29] A sportsman, politician and friend of the Prince of Wales, Chaplin is listed in *Burke's Peerage and Baronetage* as having, 'His fortune impaired by his hospitality and the cost of stables and kennels.'

It was to his property at Blankney Hall, Lincolnshire, that the new imports went, and where Kesia's* bay filly, named Kesia II*, was foaled in April 1876. Her line runs strongly in many present-day Arab horses throughout the world, but she was the only one of the Chaplin imports to have any influence. Keren-Happuch* died at Blankney leaving no produce and Kesia*, having had three more foals, was destroyed in 1881.[30] Lord Arthur Cecil, bought Kesia II* and bred two foals from her, both sired by the desert stallion Mameluke*.[31] The mare spent her last years at the stud of the Honourable Miss Ethelred Dillon, where, in August 1894, Wilfrid Scawen Blunt saw her, by then 18 years old, and wrote: 'Kesia [II] – a fine old ruin'. Jemima*, the desert mare, procured for the Dangars, was shipped to Australia, probably accompanied by Major Upton's son.

There are two last comments regarding the horses imported from the desert by Major Upton. It is strange indeed that Upton should make no mention of the Sandeman horses in *Gleanings from the Desert of Arabia*, the book he wrote after his desert journeys, particularly as he describes in great detail the horses he saw in the Gomussa camp, including those procured by him for the Honourable Henry Chaplin and the Dangars. In *Fraser's Magazine* for September 1876, in an article entitled, 'Arabian Horses studied in their native country 1874-5' written by Upton, he states: 'Of the six horses and mares we [Upton and his son] obtained from the Anazeh, two colts and two mares and a foal are now in England.' The six must be Ishmael*, Joktan*, Kesia* and Keren-Happuch* for Chaplin and the two horses for the Dangars, namely Alif and Jemima*. The foal now in England is, of course, Kesia II*. It seems as if Major Upton does not consider himself the purchaser or importer of the Sandeman horses.

With his death, in 1881, Major Roger Upton now fades from the scene – like a desert mirage. All we have to remind us of his small but significant contribution to the Arab story, are his books, some water-colour sketches, the precious blood of the horses he brought back from the Desert of Arabia and the idea of establishing a stud of pure-bred Arab horses.

The Desert Journeys of Wilfrid Scawen and Lady Anne Blunt

On 20 November 1877, Wilfrid Scawen Blunt and Lady Anne, were to set out for the Desert of Arabia.[32] Both were destined to play an epic role in the story of the Arab Horse. Indeed, theirs has been the major contribution, for they procured many fine horses from the desert tribes and Lady Anne was instrumental in preserving for posterity the majority of the precious horses of the stud of Ali Pasha Sherif. Their first two desert journeys are well documented in the books, *Bedouin Tribes of the Euphrates* and *A Pilgrimage to Nejd*, by Lady Anne Blunt, and much has been written about both of them and their world-famous Crabbet Stud.

The Blunts first travelled in the footsteps of Major Upton – to Aleppo, there to meet the Consul, J.H. Skene. Lady Anne wrote on 14 December:

> … we sat talking to Mr Skene about horses… [He had] come to the conclusion that the Arab blood should be kept pure and that the only way to improve the breed of horses in England would be to breed pure Arabs there. We have a plan…

This was, of course, much the same as that Major Upton had written of so passionately, four years earlier, in his book,

Wilfrid Scawen Blunt. ▶

Newmarket and Arabia, and no doubt had discussed with Skene, whilst staying with him in Aleppo. The plan that Lady Anne alludes to was that they and Skene should form a partnership to import to England two stallions and four fillies – later changed to in-foal mares – for the purpose of establishing a stud of pure Arab horses.[33]

On Christmas Day 1877, the Blunts purchased their first Arab horse. 'Among the mares and horses Seyd Akmet brought, was a filly come from the Gomussa tribe Kehilet Dajanieh and lovely. We soon settled on her.'[34] She was to be named Dajania*. Other horses arrived at the Consul's stables. On 4 January 1878, 'Seyd Akmet [arrived] mounted on a dark bay mare of distinguished appearance. The mare we now looked at, she is the best looking I have seen (except the Kehilet filly). Rising 5, 15 hands, a beautiful head, and in addition to her other good points… A bargain was made [Hagar*]. On 5 January, '[Kars*] was a picture of distinction and beauty though in very poor condition and all our eyes seemed fixed on him. He is the horse Seyd Ahmet mentioned ten days ago as having just returned from Kars with his owner, a Turkoman chief of irregular cavalry… He is rising 4. When he returned home he did not feed well and to make him do so he was fired on the stomach.[35] His breed is Seglawi Jedran and his owner bought him from the family of Ibn Sbeyni of the Mehed Fedaan.'

Early in the New Year, Wilfrid and Lady Anne Blunt, left Aleppo for the town of Deyr, situated on the River Euphrates, accompanied by Skene. On their third night out, they camped close to the now empty fort at Mesquineh (Meskene). It was just beyond this point that Upton and Skene had turned back for Aleppo in 1875. Seven days later, on 18 January, the travellers reached Deyr. There the Blunts purchased a number of mares, including a chestnut Saadeh Togan, Tamarisk*, a 3-year-old bay Managhieh, Jerboa*, and a grey Saadeh Togan 'Ferha' (the Gay) who they renamed Francolin*. Lady Anne wrote of the Managhieh filly: '… Wilfrid and Skene both liked her, I fancy her particularly – she gallops well and in a few minutes the matter was settled, we got her for £71.'

Being told by the Governor of Deyr, Huseyn Pasha, that a visit to the Anazeh was quite out of the question, plans were made to visit the Shammar in Mesopotamia. The went alone, as Skene was to return to Aleppo, taking with him the three new mares, though an arrangement was made that they should meet again at Deyr. Basilisk*, the first mare of the Seglawieh Jedranieh strain to be purchased for the Blunts, was obtained by Skene from her breeder, Abd el Jadir of Deyr, in February of 1878. This sale

◀ *Lady Anne Blunt in 1886.*

▲ Francolin, *oil painting by Lady Anne Blunt.*

▼ *Kars at Crabbet.*

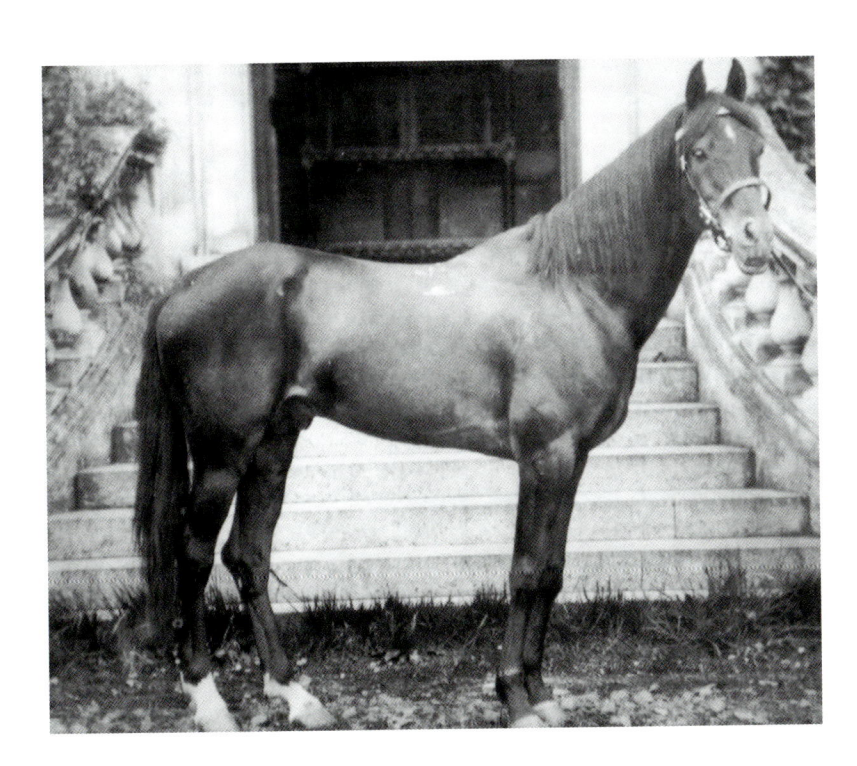

▲ Basilisk, *water-colour by Lady Anne Blunt, 1884.*

▼ *Tamarisk.*

THE ARAB HORSE

▲ Downstream River Tigris, *etching by Charles W. Cain.*

▼ Water Wheels – Hit, *etching by Charles W. Cain.*

◀ The Tower of Nimrod, *sketch by Charles W. Cain.*

Baghdad, *etching by Charles W. Cain.* ▶

was possibly concluded before the Consul left Deyr, although a Managhieh 6-year-old, that had been purchased in Aleppo before they left that town, changed hands in part exchange.

Wilfrid and Lady Anne Blunt set off for Baghdad on 27 January and they crossed the River Euphrates below Hit near Rumady on 9 February. The next day they came upon a large camp of Bedouin, not far from the Tower of Nimrod, who turned out to be of the Al-Zoba tribe.[36] They rode into Baghdad on 11 February in pouring rain, and after a stay of some days with Colonel Nixon, the Consul General, and a visit to the King of Oude, now in exile, they travelled north, following the River Tigris upstream. Then, turning west, south of Mosul, to cross the country between the rivers, they eventually met with Faris, Sheikh of the northern branch of the Shammar. Lady Anne was to note: 'They had but few fine horses'.

On 20 March, the Blunts were ferried across the Euphrates again and arrived at Deyr, only to find that Skene was not there. Once more in the desert, despite attempts by the Pasha to stop them going to visit the Anazeh, at last news was received of Skene, who had been detained in Aleppo by the arrival of his successor as Consul, Mr Henderson. He was only some fifteen miles away at Arak, so at dawn the next day, Wilfrid and Lady Anne mounted their mares and set off at a gallop to meet him. Lady Anne described the ride: 'I rode Palmyra [Hagar*] … pulling only just enough to make it a pleasure to let her go with her smooth long striding gallop, but after three or four miles she began to run away with me.' She soon left Wilfrid far behind and, 'It was only when we came to the hills and very broken ground fully 12 miles from where we started, that I got a pull at her and at last stopped her … we were just 45 minutes doing these 12 miles.'

Skene had brought with him the chestnut Saadeh Togan, Tamarisk*, and a beautiful white Hamdaniyah Simrieh, Sherifa*, which he had purchased for the Blunts in Aleppo. This was the mare that Upton had tried to buy in 1875 (without success). At first they called her Mecca, and only later changed her name to Sherifa*.[37] Travelling south once more, the Blunts and Skene at last met up with the Anazeh near Jebel Ghorab. In *Bedouin Tribes of the Euphrates*, Lady Anne describes their introduction to Jedaan, the Akid or great warrior Skeikh of the Sebaa Anazeh. She was distinctly unimpressed by his appearance and manner, which she found off-hand, particularly as Consul Skene was an old acquaintance and his 'blood brother'. It was Skene who had also introduced

THE ARAB HORSE

▲ *Hagar at Crabbet.*

▼ *Desert Caravan, etching by Charles W. Cain.*

Major Upton to Jedaan Ibn Mehed at the camp of Sheikh Suleyman Ibn Mirshid of the Gomussa. However, when Jedaan rode in a fantasia, Lady Anne did admire his horsemanship and wrote:

He is the most celebrated horseman of the desert, and mounted as he is today on his big horse, he certainly gives one a fine idea of Bedouin prowess… He was riding a horse celebrated in the tribe, a powerful 4-year-old of at least 15 hands, of which we had already heard, and showed it off admirably, but I was disappointed in the animal. He is a bay Kehilan Akhras with 3 white feet (mutlak es shemal) and a great splotch of white down his nose. He has a fine sloping shoulder and powerful quarters, but the neck is heavy and the hocks set too high.

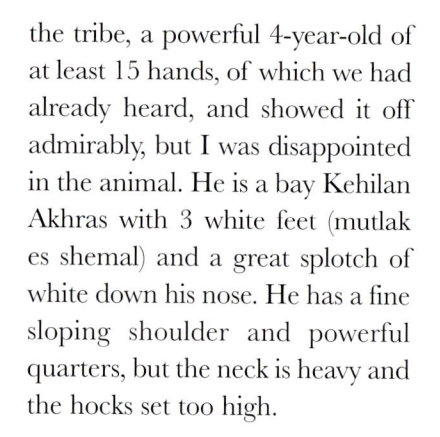

Later they were to think better of this horse, for in 1884 they bought him in India and named him Proximo*.

During their days spent with the Sebaa, the Blunts saw numerous horses and whilst staying in the camp of the Welled Ali they noted, in particular, a pretty grey Seglawi Jedran and a big bay Samhan el Gomea.

Then on the afternoon of 7 April, 'Beteyen Ibn Mirshid, Sheikh of the Gomussa came to Ibn Smeyr's tent at the Welled Ali camp'.[38] Tied to one of the tent pegs, was the mare of which he had just bought the bridle half.[39] 'She is Abeyeh Sherrak, 3 years old, dark bay, 15 hands or over, everything perfect… Her head good though not very fine. We should do a good thing if we got this mare.'

A more comprehensive description of Beteyen's mare (the Queen of Sheba*), appears in *The Bedouin Tribes of the Euphrates*, but, 'all agreed that she is incomparably superior to anything we have seen here or elsewhere, and would be worth a king's ransom if kings were still worth ransoming.' On 8 April, more

◀ *Queen of Sheba.*

Proximo, Jedaan's horse. ▶

mares were brought for them to look at. 'The next was a dark bay filly, black legs and four white feet, a fine shoulder and good quarters and beautiful head, rising 3 and already nearly 14 hands 3 inches. Her breed Dahmeh om Amr [Dahma*]'.⁴⁰

Whilst with the Gomussa, the Blunts met a young man, the son of Mijuel the Mesrab, husband of Mrs Digby, still living in Damascus and who they were later to meet.⁴¹ Wilfrid also became a close friend with Meshur Ibn Mirshid, nephew of Suleyman Ibn Mirshid, the Sheikh of Sheikhs, who had helped Major Upton considerably when he had visited the Gomussa to buy the horses for the Honourable Henry Chaplin. More days were spent at the Gomussa camp looking at horses and on 9 April, Lady Anne noted that: 'We have been talking about the mares that attracted our attention and these were not a few. I have never before seen such a collection of well-bred mares although, of course, even here there were only a few 'first class'… the dam of the Abeyeh [Queen of Sheba*] we want was here … a fine old brood mare though less handsome than her daughter.'

There was much talk of a ghazu (raid), by the Roala, and as the Blunts had agreed to undertake a diplomatic mission at the request of Jedaan, to visit Ibn Shaalan and propose an end to war, they took their leave of the Gomussa. Their small party was soon overtaken by a lone horseman, who turned out to be Meshur, come to wish them a last goodbye. He offered them his grey Hadbeh mare, for she was all he had worthy of giving, but Wilfrid declined the gift, as the mare and the boy had grown up together. On 14 April the Blunts at last reached the camp of the Roala — in the words of Lady Anne: 'The most wonderful spectacle the desert has to show…', and met Sheikh Sotamm Ibn Shaalan. They were not successful in their mission on behalf of Jedaan, though they were to hear later that a truce had been concluded.

Three days later they rode into Damascus. Here the Blunts saw more horses and on 22 April they purchased the chestnut mare, Damask Rose*: 'we liked [her] better than any of the others seen here. She is a Seglawich el Abd from the Welled Ali… altogether an air of distinction.'

Skene started for Aleppo once again, by Homs and Hama, and took with him five mares — Palmyra (Hagar*), Mecca (Sherifa*), the chestnut (Tamarisk*), Damask Rose* and a bay mare named Tamarisk. This last mare was exchanged by Skene at Hama for a chestnut of the Kehilet el Krush strain, to be named Burning Bush*, plus 60 Turkish pounds. Further purchases were made by Skene on behalf of the Blunts, once back in Aleppo. These included a bay Kehilet Ajuz, Purple Stock* and the Darley filly, so called as she was of the Ras-el-Fedawi strain, which the Blunts had been informed, mistakenly, was the strain of the Darley Arabian*. This Darley filly, named Wild Thyme* came from the Baggara tribe and cost 86 Napoleans.

THE ARAB HORSE

▲ *Jane Digby, drawing by W. Slater, 1827.*

▼ *Bedouin of the Roala.*

50

The Crabbet Stud is Founded

Throughout June and July, telegrams were exchanged between the Blunts (now back in England), and Skene in Aleppo. New purchases were listed and the Blunts worried about there being no news of Beteyen's mare, or the whereabouts of the first shipment of horses. Then, on 2 July, the horses arrived and the Crabbet Stud was founded.[42] 'Kars is beautiful, Palmyra [Hagar*] rather thin, Dajania very pretty as ever, the Darley filly [Wild Thyme*] disappointed us, she is leggy and light without any particular air. Zenobia [Burning Bush*] was rather less of a disillusion… She is,, however, not good looking… but is probably fast.' By the next day, Lady Anne felt that: 'Zenobia [Burning Bush*] is a really fine mare', and records that: 'Jerboa is fat and well, Dajanieh a lovely little thing, not so very small either, and of the Darley filly [Wild Thyme*] in her looks we are certainly disappointed.'

A telegram sent to Skene says: 'Mares safe. Kars, Jerboa and Palmyra much admired, Zenobia, opinion divided. Darley disappointing…' Another telegram to Skene, sent on 10 July reads: 'Approve plans but we want Beteyen's and Jirro's.'[43] On 11 August, the second group of horses were disembarked:

◀ *Damascus – The Return, etching by Charles W. Cain*

The chestnut Tamarisk we bought at Deyr, then the Darley [next]… an insignificant small bay filly – could that be the Managhieh Hedruj with such a name as Babylonia? Then Damask Rose the chestnut Seglawieh el Abd, thin but lively, and lastly the Kehilet Ajuz [Purple Stock*] – a great beauty. Then… Sherifa and her foal – both well… the foal appears perfect in shape although I regret to say he is turning grey.[44]

Lady Anne notes in her journal that Skene had left for the desert on 19 September, and in a letter received that month from Mrs Skene, she mentions the news that Chaplin had asked Henderson to buy mares for him, which shows that Chaplin thought a good deal of his Arabians purchased by Major Upton, for he would not otherwise be wanting more. In October, the Blunts received another telegram from Skene: 'Writing this in Beteyen's camp near Palmyra… Buying Beteyen's [Queen of Sheba*] and Rish. Exchanging Basilisk and Mesopotamia for Nigm's sons own brother and sister [Pharaoh* and Meshura*]. Samhan beyond reach.'

Wilfrid and Lady Anne Blunt left for their second journey to the desert on the morning of 16 November 1878. They, therefore, missed the telegram which

▲ Crabbet Park, *engraving by E.H. Delt.*

arrived later that day from Skene, announcing his success in concluding the purchase of not just Beteyen's mare, but the Seglawi Jedran colt as well. The purchase of the Queen of Sheba* and Pharaoh* for the Blunts was one of Consul Skene's last and most important achievements. An enigmatic figure, often (in my opinion) unfairly criticised, J.H. Skene played a significant role in the Arab story. Not only did he introduce Major Upton and Wilfrid and Lady Anne Blunt to the leading sheikhs of the Anazeh tribes and assist in buying such valuable horses as Queen of Sheba*, Pharaoh*, Sherifa*, Basilisk* and Wild Thyme*, he was also instrumental in proposing to the Blunts the idea (originally Major Upton's), of the foundation of a stud of pure-bred Arabs, which led to the formation of Crabbet.

From Beirut, Wilfrid and Lady Anne Blunt travelled to Damascus, as Major Upton had done. Here they visited Mrs Digby again, who told them that: 'our having bought Beteyen's mare and that colt of Ibn Nederi had caused "quite a sensation in the desert", it being talked about in all the tribes, the mare being the best in the desert and the colt as the finest horse among the Anazeh.' Skene had also sent two mares from Aleppo to Damascus, a chestnut Ras-el-Fedawi, 'very handsome and powerful' [Ariel] and the other, 'a bay 3-year-old Abeyeh Sherrak, with pretension to good looks [Ayesha]'. However, for this desert journey they were to rely more on their camels – four deluls (riding camels), and four big baggage camels.

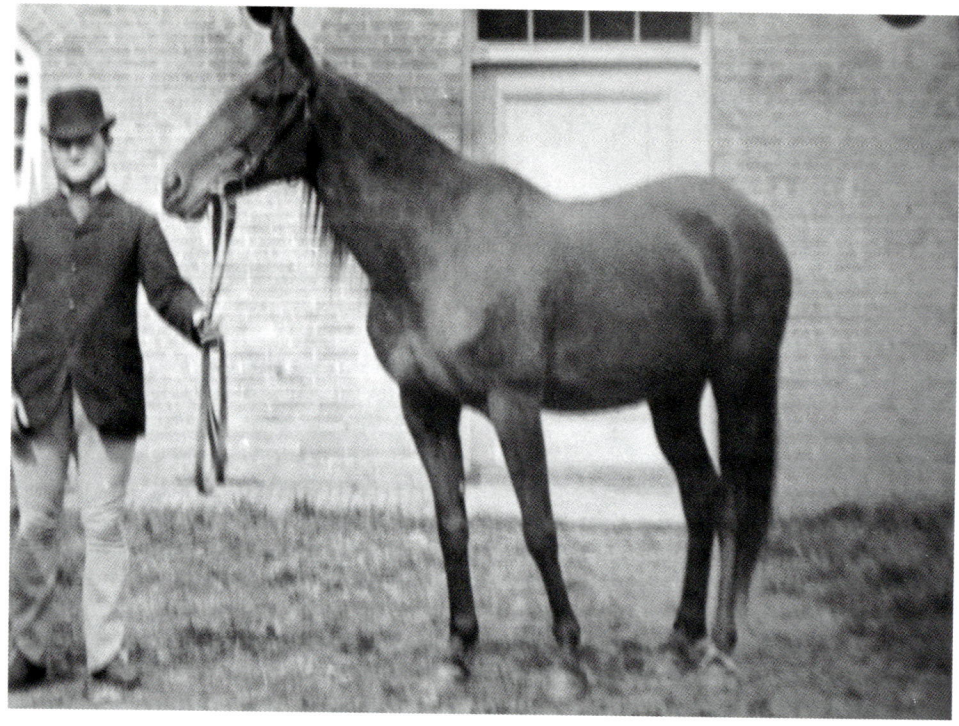

▲ *Darley.* ▼ *Sherifa and filly foal Shelfa, 1887.* ▲ *Purple Stock.*

On 13 December, the Blunts set off southwards to the Nejd and Hail, on a journey of some 1,300 desert miles, before arriving at Baghdad. This arduous ride is eloquently described in Lady Anne Blunt's second book, *A Pilgrimage to Nejd*. They entered the town of Hail on 24 January 1880 and whilst there, they took the opportunity of visiting the stud of the Emir Mohammed Ibn Rasheed. Lady Anne's first impression was one of disappointment, the horses being tethered in open yards and in the roughest possible condition but, as she admits later, they had made the all too common mistake of judging horses by condition, for, mounted and in motion, they at once became transfigured. It is interesting that Lady Anne should note that: 'In their heads, however, there is certainly a general superiority to the Anazeh mares.' This impression was no doubt supported by their misconception that there were two distinct breeds – one from the Anazeh and the other from the Nejd. However, they soon discovered that the horses were one and the same breed. Possibly Ibn Rasheed, unlike the Anazeh, but like many since, held those horses with pretty heads in the highest esteem.

▲ Ariel, water-colour by Lady Anne Blunt, painted at Hail, 26 January 1897.

▲ The Caravan Outside the Walls of Nejd, etching by Charles W. Cain.

Lady Anne made notes on some of the hundred horses in Ibn Rasheed's collection (see page 86). The majority were grey, though the Emir told them that, 'nearly all Arabs prefer bay with black points, though pure white with a very black skin and hoofs is also liked… but as a rule, colour is not much regarded at Hail, for there as elsewhere in Arabia, a fashionable strain is all in all'. The Blunts also heard that every spring a hundred yearlings were sent from Hail to Kuwait on the Persian Gulf to be sold at Bombay for £100 apiece.

In March, they at last reached Baghdad and whilst there received a telegram from Lord Lytton, Viceroy of India, inviting them to stay. Another telegram arrived from Consul Henderson in Aleppo in answer to their enquiries, saying that four horses, Pharaoh*, Queen of Sheba*, Basilisk* and Francolin* had reached Egypt safely. The Blunts bought two new horses in Baghdad, as Ariel had been badly wounded in a boar hunt. These were a chestnut Kehileh Nowak from the Fedaan, who they named Canora*, as they first saw her under a Kanora tree in the Residency courtyard, and Job, a grey horse purchased from the Consul, Colonel Nixon.

Wilfrid and Anne arrived back at Crabbet on 1 August 1880, after their stay in India. They had been away for almost nine months. Much had happened in their absence, including the safe arrival of the four horses shipped from Cairo. On 4 August, Wilfrid and Lady Anne rode out on Kars* and the new Seglawi Jedran Ibn Nederi named Pharaoh*. In her journal Anne criticised Pharaoh*: 'His defects are, however, such that we would not breed from him and had better sell him. [And this was the finest horse among the Anazeh!] His knees are those of a calf standing back a great deal, and his shoulder, though not bad, not good. I shall ride him a good deal and see how he goes and be able to recommend him as "carries a lady".'[45]

'Impecuniosus' of The Field write about the Crabbet Park Arabs on 23 July 1881 and described Pharaoh* thus:

A brown horse 5 years old; he is half brother to Meshura, and the family

Baghdad – Homage, *etching by Charles W. Cain.*

likeness is very striking, the mare having the better shoulders of the two. Pharaoh's shoulders lie well back, but are a trifle heavy. Time will improve him in this particular, the rather as he uses them to perfection, both on the lunge and under the saddle.

Later in the same article he does say that one or two stand back a bit at the knee. The horses at Crabbet were ridden a good deal and hunted. 'Impecuniosus' tells of Kars*:

Francolin, Purple Stock and Canora, 1882.

Baghdad – Entrance to Bazaar, *etching by Charles W. Cain.*

A performance worthy of chronicle was his seeing out all the second horses in a run with the Southdown, which was estimated at 20 miles in distance, and at the end of this pursuit clearing a piece of timber of over five feet in height, and all this with his master, who rides 13 stone, on his back.

Wilfrid also hunted Pharaoh* and used him as a leader in a four-in-hand. On occasions the Arabs were driven extremely long distances, especially when Blunt was visiting his friends among 'the Souls'.

The Blunts' family and friends on the steps at Crabbet.

▲ *Canora,* water-colour by Lady Anne Blunt, painted at Simla, 3 July 1879.

◀ *Wilfrid Scawen Blunt on Pharaoh (detail of a life-size oil painting by Lady Anne Blunt, 1881).*

To Egypt

On 9 November 1880, Wilfrid and Lady Anne Blunt were once again away on their travels, this time to Egypt. They planned to visit Jeddah from there, and then to go to Damascus and the desert to seek more Arab horses among the Anazeh. Whilst in Cairo, the Blunts met Ali Pasha Sherif, who invited them to see his Arab stud. This they did on 25 November and Lady Anne wrote of their visit:

> By appointment we were at Ali Pasha's house at 2 p.m. He received us and showed us his horses first, then a few mares and half a dozen foals, and afterwards directed us to go to see the remaining mares at Abassieh. Of the horses most were white or grey. The first, Shueyman and of that breed – handsome with fine head, not very good shoulder. The second called Vizier, a Seglawi Jedran of Ibn Soudan, fine all round, 18 years old but with no appearance of age. His head in shape reminded me of both Kars and Basilisk. The third, a young horse and still darkish grey Wadnan Khursan. There were about 5 more, one white Seglawi Jedran of either Ibn Sbeni or Ibn Soudan, very good, a fine shoulder – all the horses have splendid legs except a handsome chestnut (Dahman Shahwan) [Aziz]

◄ *Lady Anne and Wilfrid Blunt at Crabbet, 1887.*

▲ *A stallion at the stud of Ali Pasha Sherif.*

Ali Pasha Sherif stallion – possibly Shueyman. ▶

THE ARAB HORSE

with 4 white stockings who has badly curbed hocks. 4 years old only and used for breeding despite this defect... a splendid Seglawieh Jedran mare Hora, own sister to Vizir... In the desert at Abassieh we saw 2 bay Doheymeh Nejib mares difficult to choose between. The more interesting at first is a 5-year-old bright full bay (like Kars) ... Her crest, wither and shoulder exaggerated like the portraits of the Godolphin Arabian. She is a picture and at a little distance, very like Kars. The other mare was darker bay and altogether, I think, the best ... she is 6 or 7 years, a daughter of a celebrated Doheymeh Nejib mare called Norah, who died of the disease when this mare was 2 years old. The first bay is a granddaughter of Norah. Both of these are daughters of Vizir. The younger one has a head like Jasmine [Dajania*] and Kars.

Since our visit to the stud Ali Pasha has promised to let us have in writing a list of his different strains, those he now possesses and those he lost at the time of the disease. Several of them are probably quite extinct as he got them from Abbas Pasha, who had swept the whole of Arabia for specimens of the particular breeds he fancied.

On their visit to Jeddah, the Blunts looked at some mares and heard that many horses were dying of the sickness at Makkah.

◀ *Godolphin Arabian, engraving after Stubbs, by Joseph B. Pratt, 1894.*

Back in Cairo, they visited Ali Pasha Sherif and his stud again on 14 January 1881 and a month later they were on the road to Damascus. After spending some days in Jerusalem, Wilfrid and Lady Anne Blunt left on 6 March, crossed the River Jordan on 10 March and five days later, arrived in Damascus, where they had bought a house of their own. On 24 March, they started on their third desert journey. Travelling north-east, they reached Karieteyn in four days, then on 2 April they arrived at the camp of Beteyen Ibn Mirshid, south of Tudmur, and were most cordially received. Here they looked at horses, but Lady Anne noted: 'On the whole I have seen fewer and less good mares then three years ago.' Perhaps, with the horses in the stud of Ali Pasha Sherif still fresh in her mind, her judgement was more critical. They saw ten mares at Beteyen's camp, including the Abeyeh Sherrak, mother of Queen of Sheba*, 'bay ... 4 white feet, blaze, magnificent style of going just like the Queen of Sheba*. But this mare, seen close to, is quite small and narrow quartered', and a sister to the Queen – a very fine mare. Another they saw and eventually bought was Kubuysheh, taken from the Roala, very

◀ *Jedrania.*

▲ Zefifia, 1887.

handsome, who the Blunts called Ghazu, though later they changed her name to Zefifia*.

Taking leave of Beteyen, Wilfrid and Lady Anne rode on to the camp of Ibn Ernan, where they looked at several mares, and whilst on their way to visit Meshur they stopped with Afet. The Blunts saw the white Nowagieh mare Nura* at his tent, who looked much like Sherifa* and was last seen three years previously in Damascus, when she had belonged to Mrs Digby. They saw also a very small chestnut Seglawieh Obeyreh owned by Neddi Ibn ed Derri, and her bay yearling colt, going grey. He was extremely handsome, and Lady Anne noted: '[He] will be a wonderful horse.'

The Blunts were not to forget this colt and, in March 1887, they sent Zeyd Saad el Muteyri to buy him. They named him Azrek*. Of the other horses seen at Afet's they liked a grey Seglawi 3-year-old (Azrek's* brother), a bay Maneghieh by the same sire as Meshura* and a bay Abeyeh. Lady Anne also took the opportunity to enquire about the breeding of Pharaoh* and Basilisk* and Neddi Ibn ed Derri told her that eight years previously, a white mare of his Seglawiehs had been stolen by people from Aleppo, from a Sebaa – one of the Abadat to whom Neddi had sold her on shares, and there seemed to be no doubt that Basilisk*, was her daughter. Further

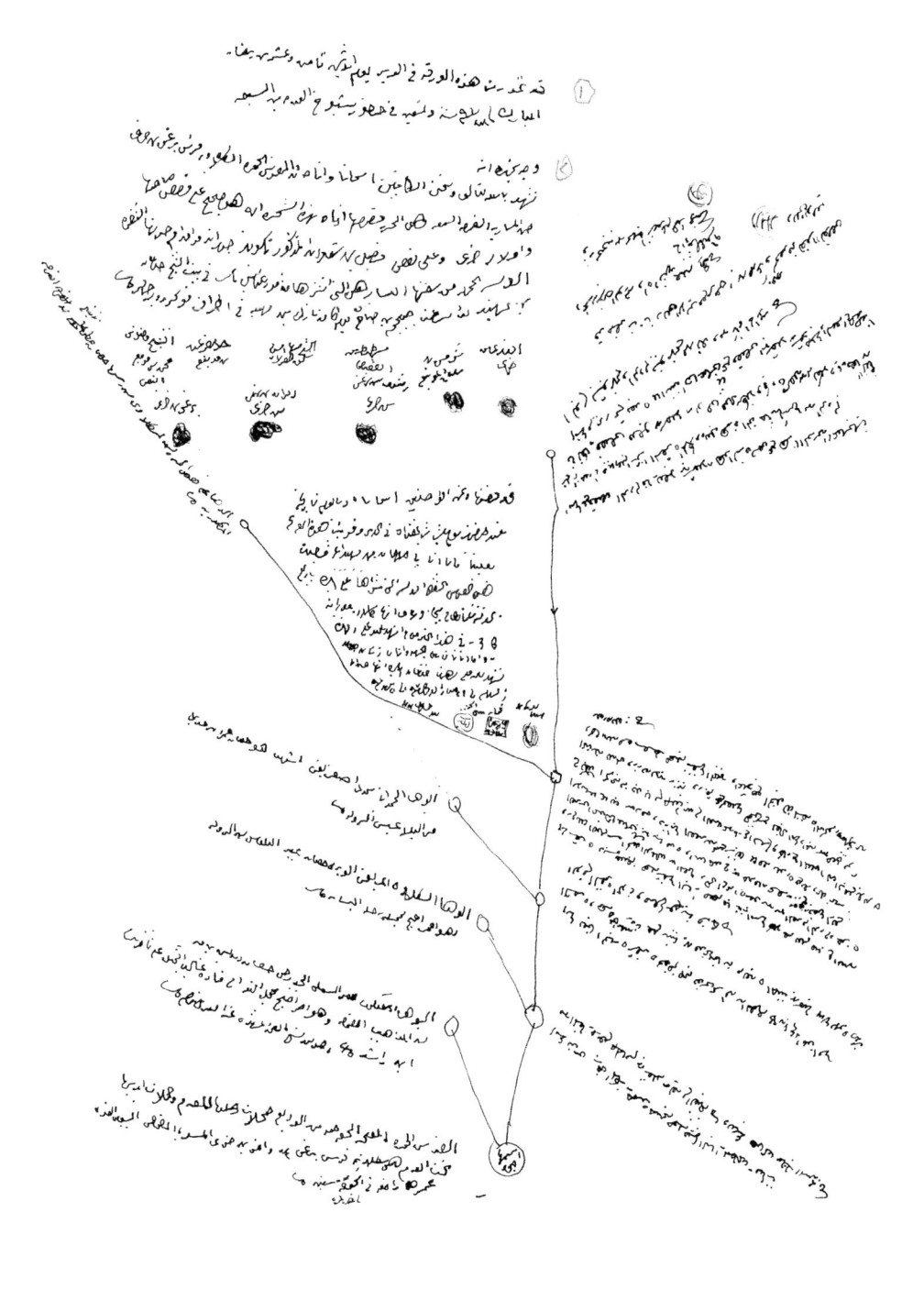

▲ *Facsimile of Meshura's certificate of authenticity* (hojja).

THE ARAB HORSE

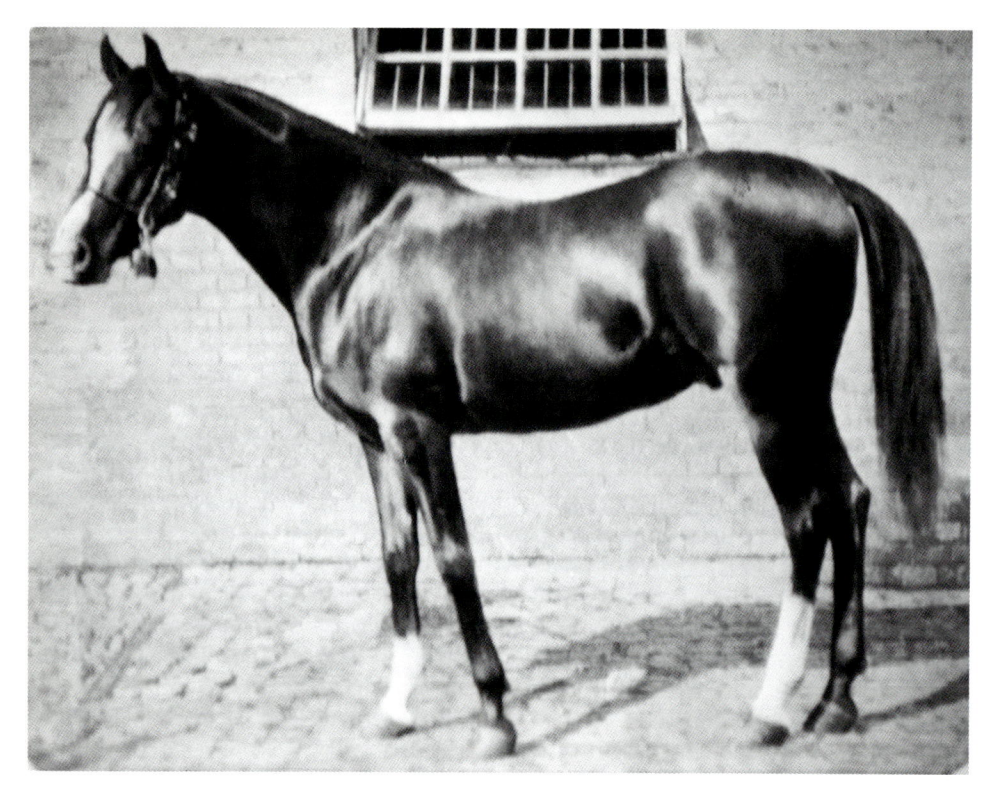

Jeroboam, son of Pharaoh ex Jerboa.

enquiries were made about Meshura* and Jirro's mare and after much discussion the Blunts purchased three mares – Nura, the bay Managhieh and the bay Abeyeh.

On 10 April, whilst on their way to Meshur's camp, they were joined by Abtan, on a chestnut Managhieh and her style was so fine that Wilfrid bought her. At Meshur's they saw many more good horses, including the Dahmeh om Amr (Dahma*), a dark chestnut mare (Rodania*) and a Meleyeh filly, daughter of the parrot-mouthed mare seen by Major Upton in 1875. Meshur insisted on giving them his grey mare, a 5-year-old ridden by him on ghazus, who was related to the bay horse of Jedaan's. The Blunts did not keep her though a good mare, for as Lady Anne noted: 'There seems to be an inexhaustible supply of really good ones [mares]. If we could stay another day we should see a hundred more, besides those already seen and we are delighted to see that the Gomussa do really still possess such numbers.'[46] They purchased Dahma* and Rodania* before leaving for Aleppo on 13 April. At a large camp of Fedaan they bought another Managhieh (their third), and at Ibn Sbeyni's tent they were shown, among others, a chestnut Shueymeh,

Sheykh Obeyd.

'head remarkably fine, tail well held, but something is wanting.' She was their final purchase, making nine in all.

Travelling north, the Blunts stopped at the house of Seyd Ahmed, the Sheikh of the Hannadi, in the village of Haggla. It was he who had got many of their earlier purchases for them and they were eager to gain further information regarding Kars*, Hagar* and others. Arriving at Aleppo, they found that Henderson was not at the Consulate, and learnt that there were problems over the export of horses. Seyd Ahmed brought the cousin of Mahmud Aga (the previous owner of Kars*), to see them and he told them that 'Mahmud Aga bought Kars* from an Arab of the Fedaan and that he *is* a Seglawi Ibn Sbeyni.' The following day, the Blunts went to view another Seglawi Jedran from Ibn Sbeyni, a 3-year-old colt, then they walked to the garden of Senor Mûsa, the Austrian Consul and owner of the well-known flea-bitten grey Kehilan Nowag horse, who had such a reputation among the Arabs.

The most worrying matter was, of course, that of export permits, with eight horses bought though some were still in the desert. However, the Blunts bought two more mares, for on 20 April Seyd Ahmed returned to Aleppo with the Seglawieh, who they named Jedrania*, with her colt foal and four days later they purchased the half-sister to Pharaoh* of whom they had heard so much (Meshura*). Eventually, the decision was made to bring Dahma* and Rodania* in from the desert, whilst the other mares, except for Zefifia*, were returned hence. With little time to spare, the Blunts left Aleppo, Wilfrid riding Rodania* and Lady Anne, Dahma.* On the last day of April they embarked with the five mares and the foal, to travel home by way of Smyrna, Palermo and Marseilles.

In the summer of 1881, Lady Anne Blunt went to the Horse Show at Islington and saw Lady Wilson's grey Egyptian horse win. Among the many visitors who came to Crabbet to look at the Arab horses were Captain Machell who trained for the Honourable Henry Chaplin, Lord Calthrop and the Honourable Miss Dillon who brought with her, her Managhi horse, Amir (El Emir*). He, Amir, had a gallop with Pharaoh* and the latter came in an easy winner. In November the Blunts left to spend the winter in Egypt, an arrangement which was to become an annual event. On 3 December they went again to see Ali Pasha Sherif and his horses. He had sold several and given some away, but Vizier was still there and the best, though the flea-bitten grey Shueyman was also well and a good horse. Lady Anne described several other horses but felt certain that Ali Pasha would ruin his stud with the chestnut Dahman Shahwan horse, Aziz. It is worth noting that the Blunts were eventually to buy twelve horses by Aziz, including Mesaoud*, Bint Helwa* and Bint Nura II* and they bred a filly at Sheykh Obeyd by him too.

In all it seems that they saw only three stallions at Ali Pasha Sherif's and fifteen mares out at Abassyeh. Four days later, the Blunts had the opportunity to see the horses of Prince Ibrahim. He had about sixty, but all except for two or three mares were Kadish (not Arabs), and Lady Anne noted that it was obvious that the only stud of Arab horses in Cairo was that of Ali Pasha Sherif. In February 1882, Wilfrid and Lady Anne bought Sheykh Obeyd, the pomegranite garden near Ein Shems. Here they were to establish another Arab stud and Lady Anne was to spend the last years of her life.

At Crabbet, eight of the mares were due to foal to Pharaoh* and the Blunts were particularly pleased with Jerboa's* splendid colt, who they named Jeroboam. Then, on 22 July 1882, the first Crabbet Sale was held and a number of the imports found buyers, including the mares Purple Stock* and Francolin*, sold to A.A. Dangar in Australia, Damask Rose*, Wild Thyme* and Canora*. Sold also, were the young horses, Purple Emperor*, Faris*, Saoud* and Darley*, but the biggest loss was undoubtedly Pharaoh*, bought by Count Potocki. The Blunts were to regret this sale later.

Rataplan, 1887. ▶

To India

In the autumn of 1883, Wilfrid and Lady Anne set out for India. Wilfrid had arranged with Mr Weatherby for an Arab race to take place at Newmarket the following year, and it is likely that this journey was undertaken to study racing in India and perhaps to buy some Arab horses. They were aware of the market in horses sent from Arabia to India and, indeed, Lady Anne had been told by Zeyd, a bedouin of the Muteyr tribe who they met in Cairo, that among others, the dealer Abder Rahman ed Teminni bought colts to take to Bombay from the Harb, Kahtan, Muteyr and Ateybeh.

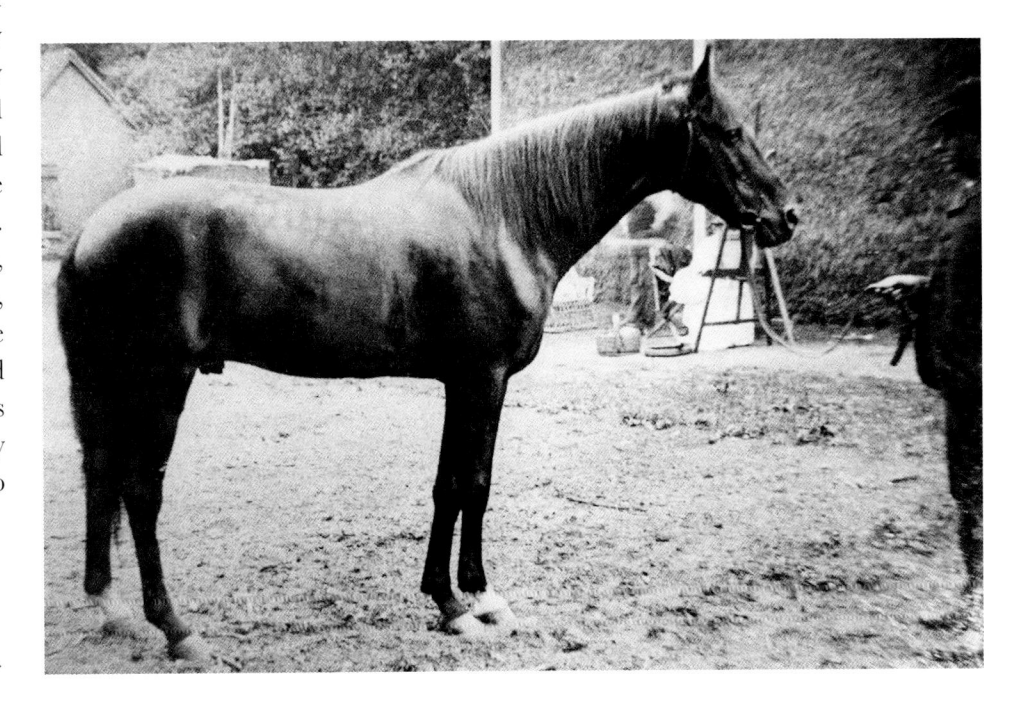

The Blunts went to the races at Hyderabad and visited many of the stables. They also met with Miss Dillon, who travelled with them to Bombay where Wilfrid and Lady Anne went to the stables of Abder Rahman. Here they saw 'Young Revenge' and Jedaan's bay horse (Proximo*), also several colts and horses from the Ateybeh, including a splendid Hadban Enzeyhi (Hadban*), who they bought. Wilfrid discussed a proposed Arab race in England, but found few owners willing to enter their horses and in Calcutta he urged the Maharajah of Johdpore and others to send horses over to Newmarket. Whilst in Calcutta, the Blunts watched Kismet* finish fourth in the Derby on 22 December. Back in Bombay, they once again visited the stables of Abdur Rahman who showed them a brown (Rataplan*), who Lady Anne preferred to any of the other horses. They settled to buy Proximo* and Rataplan* as well as Hadban* and happily both Abdur Rahman and Lord Beresford agreed to enter a horse each for the Arab race at Newmarket.

On 1 March 1884 the Blunts boarded the steamer bound for England and with them were their three horses, Abdur Rahman's Dictator* and Lord Beresford's Reformer. The horses suffered a great deal on the journey and Reformer died before they arrived back in England after twenty-eight days' travel.[47] The Arab race held at Newmarket is described more fully later in this short history. Suffice to note here that Dictator* ran second and Rataplan* third. A second Crabbet Sale in July 1884 saw Tamarisk* sold, and later the Duke of Westminster bought Basilisk*. Burning Bush* was given away to Miss Dillon. Meanwhile, a new horse, Abeyan*, arrived from the desert, presented to Lady Anne Blunt by Mr Henderson, Consul of Aleppo.

In September 1884, the Blunts travelled east again, but on this occasion it was to visit Count Joseph Potocki at

▲ *Nefisa, daughter of Hadban.*

▼ *Rose of Sharon, daughter of Hadban.*

▼ *The Crabbet Stud Book – Nefisa, dam of twenty-one foals.*

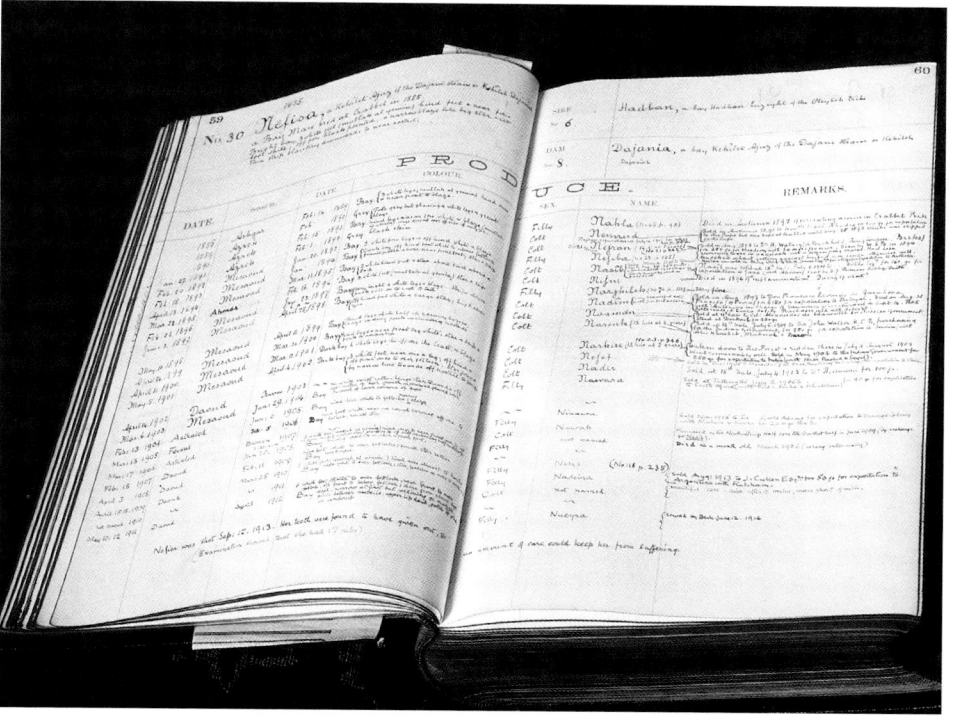

Antoniny in Poland. There they saw Pharaoh* looking splendid and Lady Anne considered that he was probably the only pure-bred Arab in the stud. Later, they were shown two very good grey colts, both by the old horse Hussar*, imported from England c. 1875. The year 1885 was to see the arrival of two foals by Hadban*, both of them, Nefisa and Rose of Sharon, were to become leading brood mares at Crabbet. However, it appears that the 'Indian Horses' as Francis the groom described them, were not very fertile and he lamented that they would not attend or take an interest! Francis had been sent to look at Mr Vidal's mare Naomi, in March, but although he reported that she was a fine mare with action, he considered her head very plain and Lady Anne noted that, 'this would put her out of the question'.[48] It seems surprising that the Blunts should part with Kars* and Hadban*, considering the quality of their foals, but both were sold to Australia in 1885. But for some home-bred colts, there was a real need of a good stallion for the stud. Before the departure of the two horses on 22 June, Lady Anne completed the painting of

▼ *Ashgar.*

▲ *Azrek, 1888.*

▼ *Kars, engraving by Peter Upton after an oil painting by Lady Anne Blunt, 1885.*

THE ARAB HORSE

Kars* she had begun two or three years earlier and she noted in her journal: 'With Kars the central figure in the stud has disappeared, the glory of it seems to be put out with Kars' absence. Goodbye Kars.' Lady Anne's present to Wilfrid for his 45th birthday was another painting, this time of Sherifa*, painted by Stephen Pearce. This oil-painting still hangs in the hall at Newbuildings, Blunt's old home. In September, two more stallions were sold – the old racehorse Dictator*, still owned by Abdur Rahman but who the Blunts had considered using at stud, and Abeyan who went to the Earl of Antrim.

The following autumn Wilfrid and Lady Anne set off once more for Egypt and Sheykh Obeyd. With thoughts of a new stallion much on their minds, in March of 1887 they sent Zeyd Sadd el Muteyri to the desert to buy the Ibn ed Derri Seglawi Jedran horse, who they had seen and so much admired in 1881. Zeyd's commission included the purchase of two more horses, if good enough. On 18 May, they received a letter from Consul Henderson: 'he [Zeyd] has bought the Seglawi horse, the grey of Ibn ed Derri, and a filly Jilfeh Stam el Bulad.' Meanwhile, Rataplan*, the last imported stallion still at Crabbet was shipped to Egypt in October 1887, together with the home-bred Jeroboam – both perished at sea. Not until September of 1888 did Azrek*, the Seglawi Jedran of Ibn ed Derri, arrive at Crabbet, accompanied by the mare Jilfa* and another stallion, Ashgar*, a Seglawi Obeyran from the Shammar.

THE ARAB HORSE

Purchase of Horses From the Stud of Ali Pasha Sherif

▲ *Sobha at Newbuildings, 1898.*

◀ *The Marquess of Rockingham's Arabian Stallion, with a Groom, oil painting by George Stubbs, 1766. (Courtesy of The National Gallery of Scotland.)*

▼ *Sherifa, engraving by Peter Upton after an oil painting by Stephen Pearce, 1885.*

Once again in Egypt for the winter of 1888, the Blunts visited the stud of Ali Pasha Sherif on 19 December, having heard on 15 December that he would perhaps be selling part of his stud. They found the palace rather dilapidated, but the horses well. Of the stallions, Lady Anne noted that, "No. 1, a 5-year-old bay by Aziz was ex the bay Dahmeh Nejiba, something like Kars; No. 2, was a bay 2-year-old brother; No. 3, 'Aziz', now described as a handsome very showy horse, the hocks much improved, who Lady Anne no longer regretted so much his having been bred from. No. 4 was 'Shueyman', the flea-bitten grey; No. 5, 'Ibn Nadir', a white Seglawi Jedran and a splendid horse; No. 6, a grey Dahman with very beautiful head; No. 7 a white horse, like Basilisk*, by Ibn Nadir – the pick of the whole (Ibn Sherara) – and No. 8, a young chestnut by Aziz. Of the mares, the first they saw was No. 9, a brown resembling the Queen of Sheba*; No. 10, Nura* the bay Dahmeh; No. 11, a lovely chestnut Dahmeh Nejiba; No. 12, a small chestnut daughter of Aziz; No. 14, 'Horra', the old Seglawieh Jedranieh and a beautiful mare she must have been. No. 15 was a grey yearling of Horra's and No. 16, an older grey daughter. No. 17, a flea-bitten grey mare, had a foal by No. 1. Nos. 18 and 19 were Jellabiehs and No. 20, 'Wazir', now 26 years old – his head very like Sherifa's*."

They saw little more than twenty horses during their visit. Then on 15 January, Lady Anne was given a list of ten horses and mares that Ali Pasha Sherif intended to sell. Of these, "No. 2 was the daughter of 'Makbûlah', the chestnut (Jelabieh), sire Aziz, 2 years (Khatila*), No. 4, the son of 'Yemameh' the younger, sire Aziz, chestnut Seklawi Soudani, 2 years (Mesaoud*), and No. 9, the son of the Jelabieh the chestnut son of 'Wazir', very handsome, 2 years (Merzuk*)." The prices asked for these three were: No. 4, £60 and No. 9, £100, and if they took more a reduction might be made. Lady Anne wrote that Ali Pasha Sherif's stud would soon be a thing of the past for it seemed to her that once he began to break it up and was in the hands of creditors, it could not last long. She was to be proved right. On 27 January, the Blunts bought the three young chestnuts for £220, and around midday on 29 January, the colts, as Lady Anne called them, arrived at Sheykh Obeyd. Two years later Mesaoud*, Merzuk* and Khatila* were imported to England and in the same year Azrek* was sold to the Honourable Cecil Rhodes for exportation to the Cape. Lady Anne wrote in the Crabbet Stud Book: 'Impossible not to regret his departure.'

Mesaoud*, the chestnut Seglawi Jedran of Ibn Sudan's strain, was to become the most important of the imported sires at Crabbet and nearly all their best mares descended from him.

65

THE ARAB HORSE

Wilfrid Blunt wrote that, 'he [Mesaoud*] may be considered as the foundation in the male line of our stud, for neither Kars nor Pharaoh nor Azrek were at all to be compared to him as a sire. His sons are too numerous to be counted here and have gone to every quarter of the globe. His best sons remaining with us are Astraled and Daoud.' In 1903 Mesaoud* was sold for exportation to Russia. It appears that 1887 was a vintage year for good foals, for not only were Mesaoud*, Merzuk* and Khatila* born that year, so were Shahwan* and Bint Helwa*, both of whom are mentioned later.

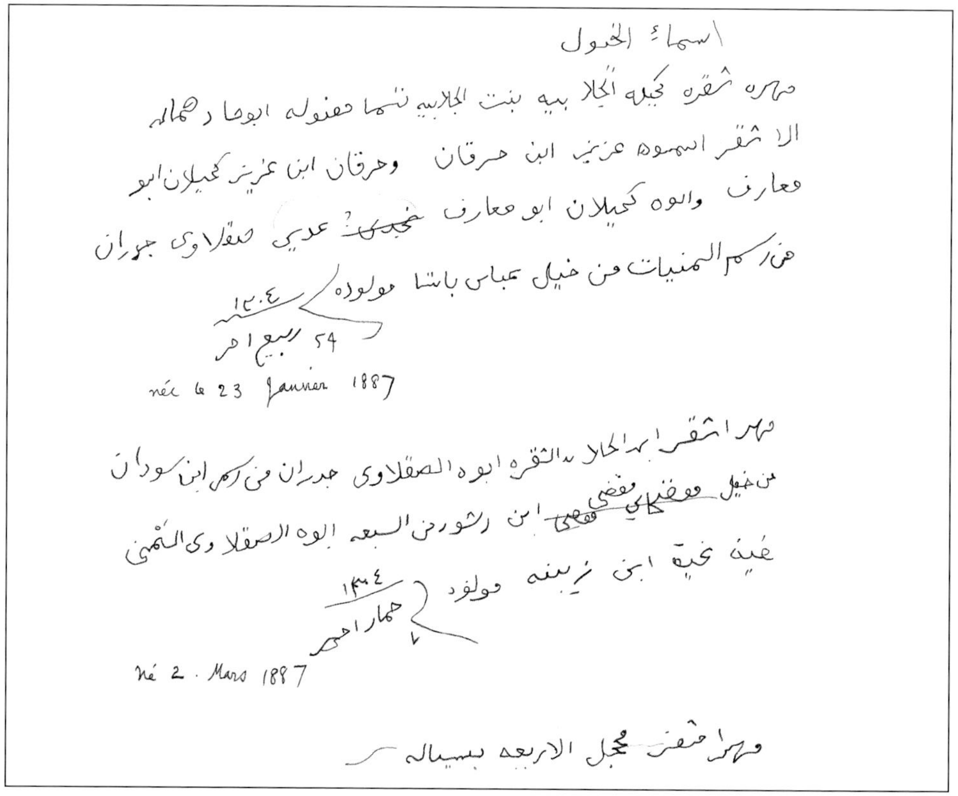

In March 1890, whilst looking at the Ali Pasha Sherif horses at bersim, Wilfrid and Lady Anne saw a white Hamdanieh of Mahmud Beg's with her 'blue' daughter, possibly for sale. They made enquiries, and the following

▲ *Daoud, son of Mesaoud.*

▶ *Facsimile of Mesaoud's pedigree, 1 February 1889 and, above, Mesaoud.*

month, Flemetomo, the man who had helped the Blunts to procure their first Ali Pasha Sherif horses, went to look for Mahmud Beg. The prices proposed were £140 for the old mare, Sobha*, and her colt of 3 months, Antar, and £120 for the young mare, Safra* with her colt of 30 days. Wilfrid made an offer of £200 for the four and Mahmud Beg to keep them until the next autumn. A year later, in 1891, the Blunts drove over to see Mahmud Beg's mares again, the price now being £220. Lady Anne wrote:

> I like the mares better than I expected and both the foals are remarkably fine ones. The young mare has improved but has not much of a shoulder… The old mare is very like Sherifa [both were of the Hamdanieh Simrieh strain], less fine head and less good shoulder, also I hope less in age – we think 20, they say 15 [in fact c. 12]. If she has foals age does not matter. At any rate, these two mares and Khatila are mazbût of mazbût (pure). The two colts are splendid, both, however, without fail intend to be greys.

They purchased the four, and the following day Wilfrid and Lady Anne rode out on Sobha* and Safra*. It was following this ride that Lady Anne wrote:

> I don't know what it is, or rather I don't know how to put it into words, that indescribable air of distinction which marks the horses and mares of Abbas Pasha's breeds, the breeds collected by him, for in the case of our two mares their dam [the dam of Sobha*] was never actually Ali Pasha's property, she having been bought by Mahmud Beg at the Sale by Auction in 1875, I think at hands of Ismael Pasha, but who had formed part of Abbas Pasha's stud. So it is, however. The moment one sees other horses beside them, when moving, one sees the style of the Abbas Pasha Collection.

Early in 1892 Lady Anne wrote enthusiastically about a stallion of Abbas Pasha blood which they had first seen on 15 January:

> Oh!!! Hope to get him though he has off knee marked. The horse, the horse at last came [Shahwan*]. The one Tomo promised, one sees his breeding, the unmistakable Ali Pasha Sherif stamp of horse. He is white, 5 years old, Dahman Shahwan… he is so fine in all ways – beautiful shoulders with excellent action, tail erect in the air… The price he says the Bey asks for the horse is £100.

They bought Shahwan* on 23 January for £62 and imported him to Crabbet in April 1892.⁴⁹ Shahwan* and Sobha* were both by the superb old Seglawi stallion, Wazir, as indeed was

▲ *Antar, son of Sobha, with Mutlak, 1907.*

▼ *Safra, oil painting by Lady Anne Blunt.*

Merzuk*. Wazir, much admired by the Blunts, had died in 1890 at the age of 28.

Only four years after purchasing Shahwan*, Wilfrid and Lady Anne had the opportunity to buy some more horses from Ali Pasha Sherif. In December 1895, Mutlak had brought a letter with a list of eight Ali Pasha Sherif horses for sale. It included Ibn Nadir, Ibn Nura, two colts – a chestnut and his grey half-brother – and four fillies. They had heard that Aziz might also be for sale. Just before the end of the year, the Blunts visited Ali Pasha Sherif's stud to see those for sale. The list now included Mes'ad and not Ibn Nura and the four horses were £50 each. On 6 January 1896, they bought the chestnut colt, (Ibn) Mahruss*, by Mahruss ex Bint Nura, who they first thought was of the Seglawi Semmeh strain, but later learnt that he was a Dahman Nejib.

When the Blunts arrived back at Sheykh Obeyd the following autumn, the news from Mutlak was that Ali Pasha Sherif's horses were to be sold off, though the Pasha meant to keep two, the beautiful chestnut filly, half-sister to (Ibn) Mahruss*, and Aziz.[50] As Lady Anne noted in her journal: 'The break up of this, the only *pure-bred* stud except ours is sad and I can't help pitying the unfortunate owner whatever his faults may be.' On 11 December 1896 the Blunts viewed the remaining Ali Pasha Sherif horses:

1. Ibn Nura – flea-bitten grey Seglawi Sudan, fine but very old, magnificent head.
2. Ibn Sherara – white Kehilan Jellabi, also fine and very old.
3. Bint 'Azz – flea-bitten grey Dahmeh Shahwanieh, fine, very old, beautiful head.
4. Makbula – white Kehileh Jellabieh in foal to Aziz.
5. Bint Fereyha – flea-bitten grey Dahmeh Shahwanieh (really Seglawieh Sbyeni), old but fine mare, in foal to Ibn Nura.
6. Bint Mumtaza (Badiaa) – chestnut Dahmeh Shahwanieh (really Dahmeh Nejiba), fine mare by Aziz, lovely head, in foal to Ibn Nura.
7. Bint Bint Fereyha (Fulana) – brown Dahmeh Shahwanieh (really Seglawieh Sbeyni), by Ibn Nura, great depth, head moderately good.
8. Bint Bint Mahroussa – bay, 1893 by Nasr.
9. Bint Makbula (Manokta) – grey Kehileh Jellabieh.
10. Iron grey filly – fine head.
11. Bint Bint Jamila – grey Seglawieh, 1894, by Aziz.
12. Bint Bint Jamila (II) – chestnut, 1895.
13. Ibn Bint Horra – grey Seglawi Sudan by Ibn Nura.
14. Ibn Bint Nura (Abu Khasheb) – grey Seglawi Sudan (really Dahman Nejib), 1893 by Mahruss.
15. Ibn Mumtaza – grey Dahman Shahwan (really Dahman Nejib), by Ibn Sherara.
16. Bint Bint Jellabiet-Feysul – grey Kehileh Jellabieh, 1896, by Ibn Nura, hand reared as dam died.
17. Bint Helwa – white Seglawieh Sudanieh, rather old but a beautiful mare in spite of rather weak back, fine head and style – with miserable foal (Ghazala).[51]

Next day, a note was sent to Ali Pasha Sherif asking for particulars of breed, age and price of nine of the horses seen, namely Bint'Azz, Makbula, Bint Fereyha, Bint Mumtaza, Bint Bint Fereyha, Bint Bint Mahroussa, Bint Bint Jamila (II), Ibn Bint Nura and Bint Helwa.

Through Mutlak the Blunts then heard on Sunday 13 December, that the horses were to be sold by auction the following Thursday, so word was sent to enquire about the possibility of buying prior to the sale. The following day a list of prices arrived and it was decided to buy Makbula*, Bint Fereyha, Bint Helwa*, Bint Bint Fereyha (Fulana*) and Ibn Bint Nura es Shakra (Abu Khasheb*) (the full brother to (Ibn) Mahruss*), for the sum of £350. When the horses arrived, a mistake had been made as Bint Mumtaza (Badiaa*) had come in place of Bint

▼ *Lady Anne and Wilfrid Blunt in the*

Helwa*. They decided to take Badiaa* as well, but it was not until the first auction that they were able to buy her.

On 30 December, Lady Anne went with Mutlak to see the Ali Pasha Sherif horses who were being kept in the garden and yard of the Old Palace near to the 'Continental' in Cairo. The horses looked woefully neglected and were without food and water. Lady Anne found the four old stallions – Mes'ad DB, Ibn Nura, Ibn Sherara and Ibn Nadir about twelve mares and youngstock including the old white mare Bint 'Azz, the grey orphan, Bint Bint Jellabiet-Feysul and Badiaa. The remnants of the stud of Ali Pasha Sherif were put up for public auction on 15 January 1897 – sixteen horses in all. Lady Anne bought the magnificent 20-year-old Ibn Nura for £E30 and Badiaa* for £E70. She missed getting the orphan, the chestnut Bint Bint Jamila and old Bint 'Azz. The last was bought by the dealer Amato for £E40 and exported to Russia, where she met with an accident and died without leaving any produce.

Two days after the sale, Lady Anne was able to purchase the grey Bint Bint Jamila el Kebira, for £E27 and three days later, Bint Bint Fereyha (Fasiha), another grey by Aziz and half-sister to Fulana*, for £50, from Abd el Hamid Bey, one of the many sons of Ali Pasha Sherif. On the day she bought Fasiha, Lady Anne wrote: 'We have now, therefore, secured the larger part of what remained of this famous stud.'

However, on 26 January she learnt from the Wakib of Ali Pasha Sherif that there were a further fifteen horses still to be sold. These included Aziz, Ibn Sherara, Ibn Nadir, Bint Bint Horra, Bint Makbula and some colts. One colt, the full brother to Badiaa, was looked at on 30 January 1897, but not considered equal to her. On 17 February, Lady Anne and Mutlak went to Cairo once again to see the Ali Pasha Sherif horses. Aziz looked glorious when he was ridden out by a boy. Next they saw a 4-year-old chestnut colt by Aziz ex Jellabieh and a 2 1/2-year-old grey colt by Mahruss. Then the mares – Bint Horra, very fine with good foal by Ibn Nura, Bint Nura es Shakra*, chestnut and fine, Bint Bint Azz (Azz*), Bint Jamila, white with chestnut colt (Jamil), and Bint Helwa es Shakra (Johara*), a fine chestnut mare.[52]

Later, Lady Anne noted in her journal: 'We *must* get one or two more Ali Pasha Sherif mares, we cannot let others take them…', and then again: 'the mare I really want is Bint Horra, but two or three others may be worth getting at moderate prices and Aziz at a small price.' On the 26 March 1897 the 2nd Sale took place and the following is a list of the horses and prices:

1. Aziz, £20, not sold.
2. Bint Bint Azz, grey, 1895, sold for £E29.
3. Ibn Johara, £32, splendid colt.
4. Ibn Zarifa Saghir (younger), £27.
5. Ibn Zarifa Kebir (older), £26.

▼ *Shahwan, 1887.*

▼ *Ibn Nura with Mutlak, 1898. (22 years old)*

▲ *Kasida.*

▲ *Bint Helwa.*

▲ *Mahruss, a stallion in Ali Pasha Sherif's stud.*

6. Ibn Bint Nura Saghir (younger), £56.
7. Ibn Bint Nura Kebir (older), £43.
8. Ibn Bint Jellabiet Feysul, chestnut, 1893, very beautiful, £55 [Feysul*].
9. Ibn Bint Nura es Shakra, £44.
10. Ibn Makbula, £63.
11. Ibn Azz Saghir (younger), £60.
12. Johara (Bint Helwa), Seglawieh, £80.
13. Bint Horra and Foal, £125.
14. Bint Nura es Shakra (chestnut), £106.
15. Bint Makbula, £225 [Kasida*].

Lady Anne bought Bint Horra and foal, and Bint Nura es Shakra. She bid for and regretted not buying Ibn Johara and Ibn Bint Jellabiet-Feysul.

Now she said: 'We really have the pick', but she went on buying. On 5 April, Lady Anne was offered Ibn Bint Jellabiet-Feysul (Feysul*), by Saleh Bey who had bought him at the auction and wanted to sell him and probably the Bint Jamila mare with her colt also. On 8 April, she went to see the horses offered. Bint Jamila had already been sold to Suares, the buyer of old Aziz and Lady Anne did not like or want the chestnut Jellabi colt (Feysul*), at any price!⁵³ She did, however, make an offer of £100 for Johara*, own sister to Bint Helwa*, and purchased the mare from Ibrahim Bey Sherif, son of Ali Pasha Sherif for £120 on 18 April. Lady Anne now considered the stud complete, but at the same time was concerned at the thought of leaving the horses to Judith, who as she put it, 'does not value them'.

On the last day of May 1897, six Ali Pasha Sherif horses arrived at Newbuildings – the Mahruss colt, Bint Helwa*, Badiaa*, Johara*, Bint Nura II* and Fulana*. Bint Helwa met with a terrible accident on Friday 13 June, getting her off foreleg broken in two places. This happened in the small meadow opposite Newbuildings entrance gate. She was found by Webb and with great difficulty got up the hill, into the yard, where a sling was arranged. By the following spring, she was gradually deprived of the sling and on the 28 April she foaled. Although able

▼ *Azz with Mutlak.*

THE ARAB HORSE

▼ *The Sheykh Obeyd Stud Book – No. 6. Feysul.*

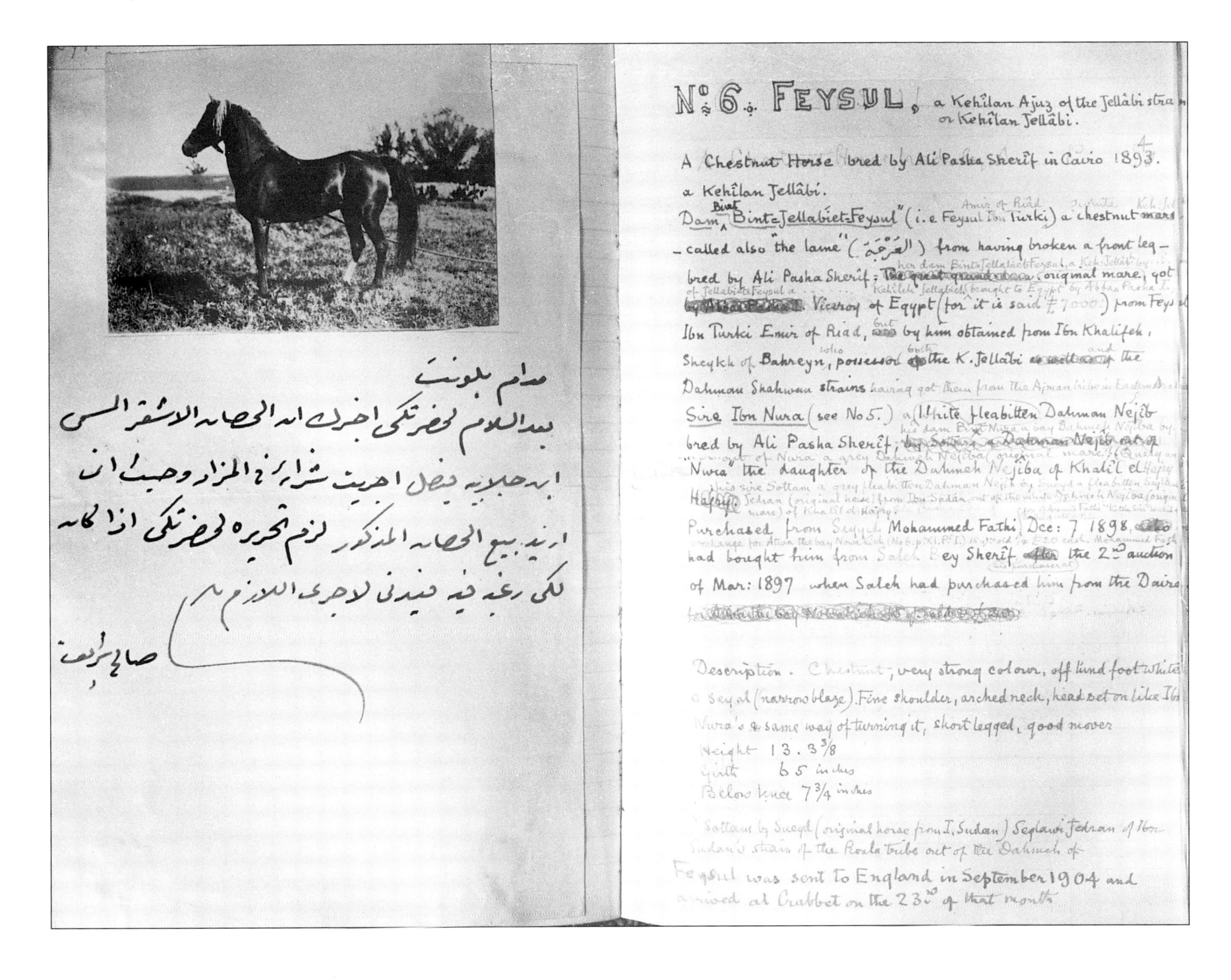

No 6. FEYSUL, a Kehîlan Ajuz of the Jellâbi strain
or Kehîlan Jellâbi.

A Chestnut Horse bred by Ali Pasha Sherif in Cairo 1893.
a Kehîlan Jellâbi.
Dam "Bint-Jellabiet-Feysul" (i.e Feysul Ibn Turki) a chestnut mare
– called also "the lame" (الْعَرْجَة) from having broken a front leg –
bred by Ali Pasha Sherif; her dam Bint Jellabiet Feysul, a Keh. Jellâbi by
of Jellabiet Feysul a Kehîleh Jellabieh brought to Egypt by Abbas Pasha I.
Viceroy of Egypt (for it is said £7000) from Feysul
Ibn Turki Emir of Riad, but by him obtained from Ibn Khalifeh,
Sheykh of Bahreyn, possessor who the K. Jellâbi as well as the
Dahman Shahwan strains having got them from the Ajman tribe in Eastern Arabia
Sire Ibn Nura (see No 5.) a White fleabitten Dahman Nejib
bred by Ali Pasha Sherif; his dam Bint Nura a bay Dahmeh Nejiba by
Sottam a Dahman Nejib out of
Nura the daughter of the Dahmeh Nejiba of Khalil el Hafey
his sire Sottam a grey fleabitten Dahman Nejib by Sueyd a fleabitten Seglawi
Jedran (original horse from Ibn Sudan out of the White Dahmeh Nejiba (original
mare) of Khalil el Hafey
Purchased from Seyyd Mohammed Fathi Dec. 7 1898.
had bought him from Saleh Bey Sherif after the 2nd auction
of Mar: 1897 when Saleh had purchased him from the Daira

Description. Chestnut, very strong colour, off hind foot white
Seyal (narrow blaze). Fine shoulder, arched neck, head set on like Ibn
Nura's & same way of turning it, short legged, good mover
Height 13. 3⅜
Girth 65 inches
Below knee 7¾ inches

Sottam by Sueyd (original horse from I. Sudan) Seglawi Jedran of Ibn
Sudan's strain of the Roala tribe out of the Dahmeh of
Feysul was sent to England in September 1904 and
arrived at Crabbet on the 23rd of that month

to limp about, the leg remained frightfully misshapen and the near leg suffered from the extra weight it had to support. When left in her box, the mare would lie down a great deal, which she would not do outside and also, when standing, she rested her head on the sill of the window opening, leaning her weight upon it, so easing the front legs. She lived to bear a further seven foals, the last in 1906 when she was 19 years old.

In November 1897, Lady Anne received a report from Nasr el Mizrab, son of a brother to Mijuel, who said that only three horses worth breeding from at that time could be found amongst the Sebaa and Fedaan; the same tribes among whom, only sixteen years earlier, the Blunts had seen an 'inexhaustible supply of really good mares'. During December, Mutlak saw the Bint Jamila colt (Jamil) again and described him as beautiful. Lady Anne noted: 'we should have bought him but for the obstruction of Wilfrid and Judith.' When Ayub Bey brought the Kehileh Jellabieh filly (Jellabieh) for them to see – white and very small but strong, Lady Anne bought her for £E60. Then in March 1898, she was also able to buy Bint Makbula es Shakra (Kasida*) from M. Léon Cléry.[54] In December of that year Lady Anne did, after all, purchase the Jellabi colt (Feysul*), whom she had written off the year before. She noted that Feysul* was own brother to their Jellabieh*, being by Ibn Nura and from the lame Jellabieh (El Argaa).[55]

Kasida*, Jellabieh* and Makbula* were shipped to England in 1898 and Feysul* followed six years later, in 1904, accompanied by his two sons, Ibn Yashmak* and Ibn Yemama*. Not until April 1901 did Lady Anne at last purchase Jamil, from M. Jacques Valensin, acting for Suares who had bought Jamil, together with his dam Bint Jamila, in March 1897, from the Daira of Ali Pasha Sherif. At the same time Lady Anne bought Bint Jamila and her two fillies, Aziza and Jamila. The last horse bred by Ali Pasha Sherif to be purchased by Lady Anne Blunt, was Bint Bint Azz (Azz*), a white Dahmeh Shahwanieh, for whom she paid Othman Bey Sherif the large sum of £300 on 11 May 1906. He had bought her after the 2nd Auction from the Daira of his father. Although Azz* had had some foals, including the white stallion Sahab in 1903, she produced no foals at Sheykh Obeyd, nor at Crabbet where she was sent in April 1910.[56]

In the seventeen years between 1889 and 1906 the Blunts bought thirty-four horses[57] of Ali Pasha Sherif breeding, all descending from the horses of the Collection of Abbas Pasha I, and of these, six stallions and thirteen mares were imported to England. The credit for saving and preserving these precious blood lines must be given to the Blunts, and to Lady Anne in particular. Indeed, most of the knowledge we now have regarding the original Abbas Pasha I horses is due to her careful research and diligent enquiry, which she recorded in her journals and stud books.

◀ *Azrek.*

Crabbet – A World Influence

Lady Anne wrote of the Crabbet Stud on 19 September 1908:

> The stud I want to perpetuate as a beautiful thing, or 'thing of beauty' in itself, not as a speculation, although I must keep it on strict business lines, but this without expectation of its paying – horsebreeding will not pay now with the human race intent on machine-made locomotion, not to mention flying!

In October 1909, the mare Ghazala* arrived in England. This daughter of Bint Helwa* had been sold by Lady Anne to Colonel Spencer Borden of Fall River, Massachusetts for 200 guineas, and was shipped from Liverpool on board the White Star *Cymric* to America. Ghazala* was entered in Volume 22 of the GSB, as, 'imported by Lady Anne Blunt, and in foal to Jamil'. This mare, who had already produced two outstanding daughters in Ghadia and Jemla at Sheykh Obeyd, was to found a second dynasty in America.

By the beginning of the twentieth century, Crabbet was recognised, both at home and abroad as the major source of pure-bred Arab horses. Sales to Arabian studs throughout the world had further extended the influence of Crabbet and this domination was to continue right up until the 1950s. Even in today's international world of the Arabian horse, Crabbet is synonymous with authenticity – a claim few others can support with absolute certainty. Of the sixteen stallions imported by the Blunts, except for Feysul*, all were eventually exported. Kars* and Hadban* were sold to Australia, Pharaoh* and Mesaoud* to Russia, Azrek* and Merzuk* to South Africa, Shahwan* to USA and Ibn Yashmak* back to Egypt. Indeed, if one checks the records of the first fifty stallions listed in the Crabbet Stud Book, 78 per cent were sold abroad – many to play important roles in perpetuating the breed, like Astraled, Nasik, Berk and Mirage* in the USA, Rasim, Naseem and Shareer in Eastern Europe and Nejran and Raouf in Australia. However, other superb stallions, sadly, were sold into oblivion such as Azrek's* bay son Ahmar who went to Java, and the grey, Seyal by Mesaoud* and Narkise, both shipped to India.

With the stud so well established, its future seemed secure, but increasing family problems led inexorably to conflict which very nearly spelt disaster for Crabbet. Lady Anne, who had lived alone at Sheykh Obeyd in Egypt since 1915, grew more and more concerned about the fate of the stud after her death. Her final solution, to leave the stud to her granddaughters – Lady Anne and Lady Winifrid – whilst understandable considering her distrust of her daughter

▲ *Ahmar, son of Azrek.*

▼ *Seyal, water-colour by Lady Anne Blunt.*

THE ARAB HORSE

◀ *Lady Anne Blunt*

▼ *Lady Anne Blunt's daughter, Judith, The Baroness Wentworth, on the front cover of* The Field, *1930.*

Lady Anne Blunt on Kasida, water-colour by Peter Upton. ▶

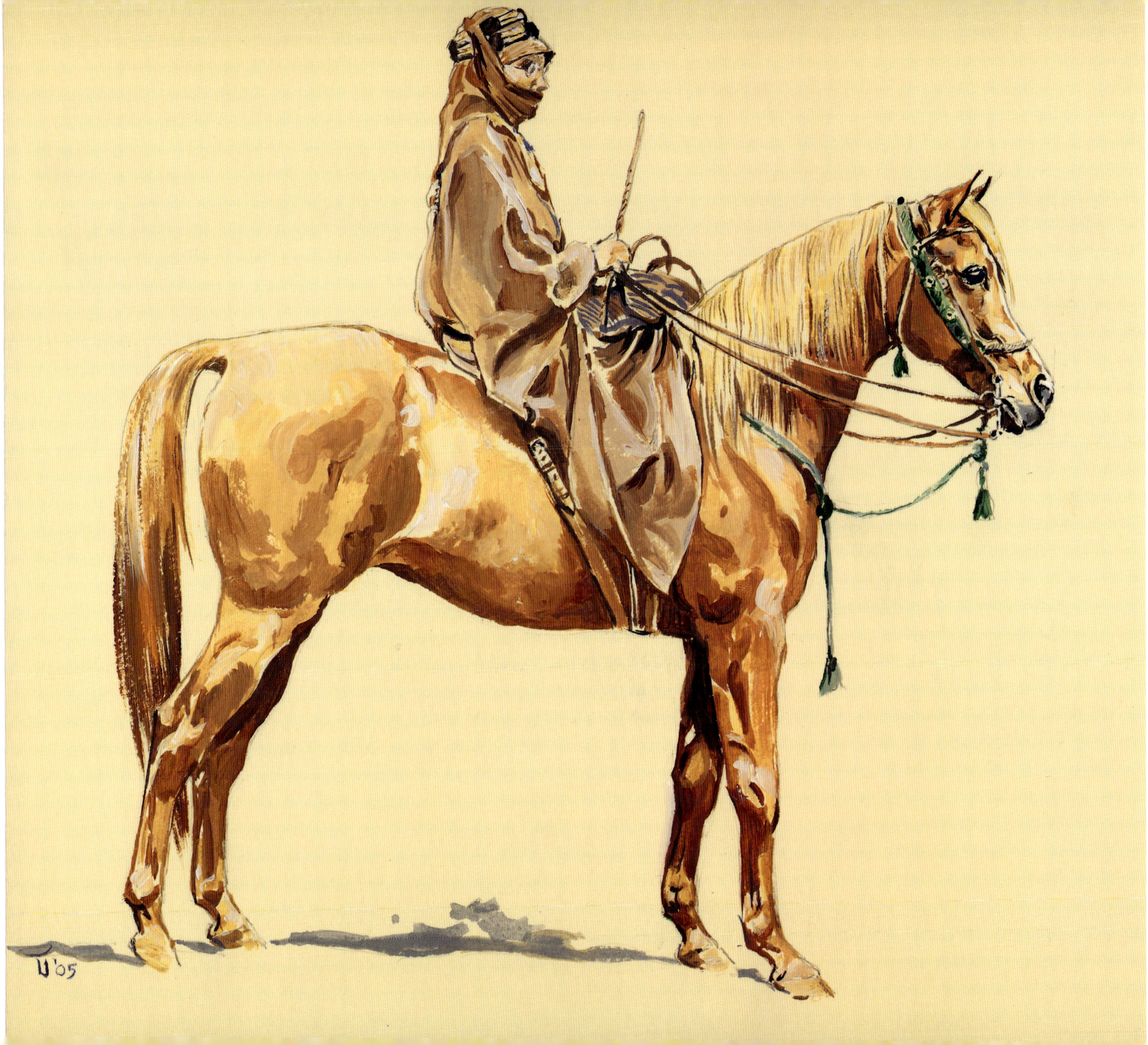

Wilfrid Scawen Blunt, in the desert. ▶

– solved nothing. Claims and counter-claims between Wilfrid and Lady Wentworth finally ended in a lawsuit, which Wilfrid – now old and ill – lost in 1920. His daughter, triumphant, led all the horses back to Crabbet.

So began a new chapter in the life of the stud, during which its fame and influence was to grow still further. In 1920, The Egyptian Royal Agricultural Society bought nineteen horses for their new Arab stud. The purchase of these Crabbet horses was to augment their foundation stock with ones rich in the blood of the horses of the Collection of Abbas Pasha I. Kazmeyn, one of these horses, must be considered one of the most influential stallions in modern Egyptian breeding. The acquisition of the white Polish stallion, Skowronek*, by Lady Wentworth, in 1920, was to prove more important than even she possibly imagined. His influence on the breed must come next to that of Mesaoud* and today it is no longer possible to find Crabbet lines in England without Skowronek* blood. The last stallion to stand at Crabbet, who contained no lines to Skowronek*, was Oran, foaled in 1940.[58]

The Arab Horse Society (AHS), had been founded in 1918, 'to promote the

THE ARAB HORSE

◀ Lady Wentworth, *tempera painting by the Honourable Neville Lytton.*

▼ Lady Wentworth with the famous stallion, Skowronek.

breeding and importation of pure-bred Arabs and to encourage the re-introduction of Arab blood into English light horse breeding'. Its first President was Wilfrid Scawen Blunt. Volume I of the Stud Book, published in 1919, listed one hundred stallions and mares, fourteen of whom were imported, thirty-seven bred by the Blunts and the majority of the rest bred from Crabbet stock. The imports include Ibn Yashmak*, Jellabieh*, Skowronek* and the desert-bred Dwarka*. On 10 September 1922, Wilfrid Blunt died, the old romantic and adventurer laid to rest close to his beloved Newbuildings Place.

THE ARAB HORSE

Now came the age of the Wentworth superhorse and visitors flocked from around the world to view, admire and buy. In March 1926, Kellogg commissioned Carl Schmidt to select Crabbet horses for his stud in America. Later that year, Prince Faisal Ibn Saud visited Crabbet and following this, Lady Wentworth received a gift of the desert mare Dafina* from Saudi Arabia. The Duke of Veragua chose four Crabbet mares for Spain and Roger Selby bought a number of the finest horses from Lady Wentworth, including the stallions Raffles, Nureddin II and Mirage*. He, incidentally, was the last desert horse to be acquired by the Crabbet Stud. By the 1930s the number of Arab breeders in England had increased significantly and most, including H.V.M. Musgrave Clark, Miss Lyon and Lady Yule, had founded their studs with horses purchased from Crabbet.

A very important sale for Lady Wentworth was that of six stallions and nineteen mares to Russia in 1936. There they founded some of the major family lines at Tersk. Most so-called 'straight Russian' Arabs contain at least 25 per cent Crabbet blood. Lady Wentworth wrote some scholarly works, her two most important books being *Thoroughbred Racing Stock and its Ancestors*, published in 1938 and *The Authentic Arabian and its Descendants*, which contains much of the historical material researched and collected by Lady Anne Blunt.

Mirage and Prince Faisal Ibn Saud, engraving.

During these vintage years, many were the horses bred at Crabbet who became famous names in the world of the Arabian. Lady Wentworth would acquire other top-class horses from other breeders, though naturally almost all were of Crabbet blood lines. However, one stallion who she bought in 1947 was Dargee, and he introduced the blood of other old English imports into Crabbet, such as Dwarka*, El Emir*, Mootrub, Ishtar* and Kesia*. With the death of Lady Wentworth in 1957, the world-famous Crabbet Stud passed from the ownership of the family to Cecil Covey, the Stud Manager. The old era was over. Covey found it necessary to sell many of the horses but continued with a much reduced stud until 1971, when the remaining stock was sold off, all except for the old white stallion Indian Magic.

Happily, Lady Anne Lytton, Lady Wentworth's daughter had moved to Newbuildings in 1955 and took with her the Arab mare Mifaria. There she continued to breed Arab horses until her death in 1979, over one hundred years since her grandparents bought their first desert horses and founded a stud of pure-bred Arabians. The Blunts were a remarkable family who will forever be associated with the long saga of the Arab horse.

NEWBUILDINGS PLACE · SUSSEX

▲ Newbuildings Place, *engraving*.

Lady Anne Lytton, *oil painting by the Honourable Neville Lytton.* ▶

▼ *Dargee.*

The Honourable Miss Ethelred Dillon

The Honourable Miss Dillon's stud, started about the same time as the Blunt's Crabbet Stud, was the only other stud of real importance during the early years. Its fortunes were to vary according to the uneasy financial situation of its owner and her ideas on Arabian type, which differed somewhat from those held by the Blunts.

El Emir*, the stallion imported by her in 1880, was her favourite, although she bought most of her mares from Crabbet, including the two desert mares Hagar* and Jedrania*. Another mare, purchased by Miss Dillon, in 1884, was Sir William Clay's Ishtar*, then 13 years old and described by Lady Anne Blunt as, 'undoubtedly pure-bred, but her pedigree has been lost through frequent changes of ownership'.[59] Sold at the 5th Crabbet Sale in 1889, Lady Wentworth wrote: 'Miss Dillon's underbred (pretended Arab) mare has been bought by old Mr Weatherby [for 110 guineas].' Spencer Borden states in his book, *The Arab Horse*, that Ishtar* was one of the first horses bought in the desert by the Blunts!

In the autumn of 1883, Miss Dillon had El Emir* shipped out to join her in India. Lady Anne Blunt wrote on 10 December 1883 from Bombay: 'Miss Dillon was there to welcome us... Viewed the horses, the bay Amir [El Emir*] who travels the world with his mistress and a chestnut... at last we mounted the horses. I had the chestnut, Wilfrid the favourite Amir who was tiresome and pulled and fretted, and Miss Dillon, a grey Arab evidently well bred, lent by Mr Gonne.' The horses imported by Miss Dillon have been criticised for their lack of quality. Lady Anne described El Emir* on 29 September 1890: 'his want of quality is so apparent, moreover he is very narrow in the quarter, does not hold his tail and has an extremely plain head.' Others question the authenticity of his breeding. However, if one studies the details of his breeding given in the GSB, Volume 15, they ring true. 'His sire a grey Kohel Cheyti. His dam a bay Managhieh Ibn Sbeyali. Bred by Dehmedi Alzoba Ibn Amoud of the Shammar.' Kohel Cheyti is Keheilan Sueyti – a recognised strain. The Al-Zoba tribe were allies of the Shammar, owning camels and carrying the lance, who occupied that area of southern Mesopotamia between the rivers – their sheikh, one El Hamoud. The Blunts, incidentally, met with the Al-Zoba tribe, south of Ramady on 10 February 1878.

Miss Dillon's enthusiasm for the Arab involved her in much correspondence. A letter to *The Field*, regarding the Blunts' desert stallion Kars*, received the following reply from H.A. Thompson, dated Sydney, 13 May 1893:

...sometime since I saw a query in The Field signed E. Dillon, which I presume came from you, asking where there was a son of Kars at stud. Kars, as perhaps you are aware, came out here together with several mares from the Crabbet Park and I know of two pure-bred horses by Kars, from these mares. One, a bay rising 5 years, dam Lady Alice by Pharaoh out of Francolin, imported; another by Kars, dam Judith by Farhan, imported, granddam Jemima, purchased in Arabia by Major Upton. He is 5 years, dark bay, height – 14 hands $3^{3}/_{4}$ inches, girth – 5 feet 9 inches, cannon bone - $8^{3}/_{4}$ inches. Very quiet. Jemima is described by Major Upton (when sent out here). A Kehileh Nowagieh of the Debbe Nowag family, bred in the Gomussa tribe of Sebaa Anazeh. She arrived here in 1875. I have never seen this last horse but the first I know well, as he belongs to my brother-in-law, and would be put on board a steamer here at 1150 guineas [?] – he is, I should say, about 15 hands.

Francolin, Lady Alice and Lady Anne (Kars, Purple Stock imported from Mr Blunt) are all in N.S. Wales, as I believe is Purple Stock, but I don't know exactly where the latter is. Francolin is old [18] but Lady Alice and Lady Anne are only 10 years old and could be bought.

A number of the horses bred by Miss Dillon were exported to USA, and most of the desert-bred horses which she imported or owned are to be found in the pedigrees of present-day Arabs.

▼ *An Arab in racing – India.*

The Indian Connection

Of the desert-bred imports to this country, many were shipped from India.[60] As mentioned earlier, Arab colts had been bought out of the desert by dealers to supply the Indian market and the best known of these dealers was Abdul Rahman Minnee of Bombay.[61] He came from a well-known family of Shagra in Kasim and the certificates of authenticity which he provided with the horses he sold were completely trustworthy, for he dealt directly with the tribes. The Blunts, as recorded earlier, bought from him and many others too for Maidan*, Dictator*, Vonolel* and Kismet* came from his stables.

Whilst on their first visit to India in 1879, Lady Anne was to write on 9 July:

> The chief interest to us in Bombay was the stables… we made a point of going both to Abd er Rahman's and the Parsee Jamsetjee's stables… The other stable kept by Parsee Jamsetjee was… better worth seeing these being, on average, better class – several bay, that might be asil [purebred], one very handsome grey of charger style… people don't come to deal with Jamsetjee so much as with Abder Rahman, who is said to be more honest. The third dealer Ali Abdullah is, I understand, the favourite with the English purchasers. Jamsetjee, the very old man, was sitting on a sofa near the gate to his premises and civilly let us look at everything he had … Jamsetjee's man told us that his agent buys chiefly in the neighbourhood of Mosul.[62]

The most general price for a horse was around R5000 and Lady Anne felt that the Arab dealers must make enormous profits: '… when it is considered that better and better looking horses could be got at Baghdad for £7 to £10 (at least four years ago). The cost of transport was mentioned to me and I think it came to £2 or £3. Grant £5 to cover expenses, the very least profit must by 100 per cent.' In all, about forty of the imported horses came from India, and of these at least ten were from the stable of Abd er Rahman.

Wilfrid Blunt was very enthusiastic about a projected Arab race to be held at Newmarket and he persuaded others, including Abd er Rahman, to enter horses. A list of possible runners from India included, Lord Beresford's Reformer, Abder Rahman's Dictator*, HH Aga Khan's Kuchkolla, Mr Broadwood's Kismet*, Ali Ibn Amr's Shere Ali,[63] Rabalain to be bought by Mohamed A Rogay from Dr Gaye and Jedaan (Proximo*) and Ambar (Rataplan*), two of the Blunts' purchases. In fact, Kuchkolla, Shere Ali and Rabalain didn't make the journey to England, but Kismet* did arrive in time for the race by a later ship. The Blunts took five horses with them back to England – Reformer, Dictator*, Proximo*, Rataplan* and Hadban*, but before leaving they went to see Kismet* again on 18 February 1884: 'We looked at Mr Broadwood's Kismet, whose jockey (Gerard) was there and showed him to us and said he had been talking to the owner about running him at Newmarket. I wish he would. It seems Mr Broadwood who is going home, is selling most of his horses.'

The Race took place on 2 July:

Newmarket: Racecard [Arab Race].

4.30 A Sweepstake of 25 sov. each with 300 added. 200 by The Jockey Club and 100 by W.S. Blunt Esq., for Arabian horses; 3-year-olds 7st 10lb, four 9st 5lb and upwards 9st 3lb. Two miles (15 subs). The race will be restricted to Arabs registered in the Stud Book, their produce or imported horses having such a guarantee of their authentic breeding as shall be deemed sufficient by the stewards. (The stewards of the Jockey Club will consider as Arab all horses sent from India which have won a public race there of the value of 1,000 rupees, under the rules of the Western Indian or Calcutta Turf Clubs, or have a certificate signed by the Secretary of either of these Clubs as Arabs, without objection having been raised to them on account of their breeding; also, all horses sent from the principle Arab Studs of the European Continent, if accompanied by a certified pedigree showing them to be of Arabian descent uncrossed with other blood; also, all horses of ascertained Arab blood, imported from Arabia, Syria, Egypt or the Persian Gulf, and accompanied with a Certificate of Exportation from the English Consul of the district).

1. Mr Wilfrid Blunt's ch.f. Halfa. Kars-Hagar, 3 yrs.
2. Mr Wilfrid Blunt's br.h. Rataplan, aged.
3. Mr A. Bourke's br.c. King Soloman. Kars-Queen of Sheba, 3 yrs.
4. Mr Broadwood's ch.h. Kismet, aged.
5. Major Meysey Thompson's b.c. Hadramaut. Kars-Hagar, 4 yrs
6. Mr Abdul Rahman Minni's b.h. Dictator, aged.
7. Mr Stephens' b.h. Purple Emperor by a horse unknown to importer (Mr Blunt) out of Purple Stock, 5 yrs.
8. Lord Strathnairn's bl.h. Kara Kouch of the Sultan's breed, aged. [Scratched]
9. Lord Strathnairn's Gr.h. Abd-el-Azaiz by Hermit (Arabian) out of Loo-el Nejdi, aged.lxiv [Scratched]
10. Admiral G. Tryon's b.c. Asil by an Abeyan Sherak horse out of Belkis, 3 yrs.
11. Mr A. Baird's b.c. Hadeed by Posta-Aida, 3 yrs.lxv [Scratched]
12. Major McCall's b. or br.h. Wanderer, aged. [Scratched]

Lady Anne Blunt noted in her journal:

> To sum up what I saw. We were near the turn when we saw the horses coming at what seemed a tremendous pace… Then we cantered up to see the finish… and I only saw … that Asil and Dictator were in front, Rataplan, third Kismet, fourth and Halfa last but one… Rataplan made the running all the way but was beaten before the finish.

Asil was described by Lady Blunt as, 'a very strong horse with a plain head, not at all like the Abeyan sire in Aleppo'. The Abeyan was the chestnut stallion of that name acquired for the Blunts by Consul Henderson and imported to Crabbet from Aleppo in 1884. A second race for Arabs took place at Sandown on 22 July. This time the result over one mile was: first, Hadramaut; second, Asil; third, Halfa; fourth, Dictator*; fifth, Rataplan* and sixth, Kismet*. The following day, the tables were turned when Asil won again, with Hadramaut second and Dictator* third. After 1886, no races for Arabs were to be run under the auspices of the Jockey Club until nearly a hundred years later.

Before we leave the Indian connection, Kismet* and two other horses are worthy of further discussion. In July 1886, Kismet* got his own back by winning a two-mile race for Arabs at Sandown Park. Second to him was Asil! Kismet*, a dark chestnut stallion was to see four countries before his untimely death on 11 November 1891. He was bred by the Muntifiq in the desert in 1879.[66] As a 5-year-old he went to Bombay and was purchased of Abdul Rahman by Lieutenant R.S. Broadwood of the 12th Lancers.[67] Over the next two years he had an unbeaten record in racing and his winnings amounted to £30,000:

Date		Location	Race
1883	12 July	Bangalore	The Mysore Cup, 1¹/₂ miles.
	14 July	Bangalore	The Mysore Purse, 1¹/₂ miles.
	19 July	Bangalore	Aga Khan's Purse, 1¹/₂ miles.
	8 September	Poonah	Aga Khan's Plate, 1¹/₂ miles.
	11 September	Poonah	Aga Khan's Purse, 1¹/₂ miles.
	22 November	Hyderabad	Deccan handicap, 1¹/₂ miles.
1884	12 February	Bombay	The Derby, 1¹/₂ miles.
	14 February	Bombay	Aga Khan's Purse, 1¹/₂ miles.

His top weight in the Mysore Cup was 9 stone 13 pounds and in the Derby he carried 9 stone 10 pounds. He was imported in April 1884 and sold after that year's Newmarket and Sandown Races to Sir R.D. Cunyngham. The Honourable John Corbett, his next owner, sold him on at a loss at the 1890 Crabbet Sale to the Reverend F.F. Vidal for £30. The next year Vidal leased him to Randolph Huntington of USA. Kismet* arrived at Long Island, New York by SS *Canada* on 11 November 1891 but died of pneumonia just two hours after completing his voyage. Huntington based his breeding programme on horses of the Muniqieh strain. He had already purchased the Muniqieh, Naomi, in 1888 and was to obtain two sons of Kismet* in 1893 – Nimr and Garaveen. No records exist, however, which claim that Kismet* is of the Muniqi strain.

Little is known of Mameluke*, except that he was a high-caste

Lord Herbrand Russell, oil painting by Sir George Reid

▲ *Garaveen. Sire – Kismet, dam – Kushdil.*

▼ *Dwarka, oil painting by G. Paice.*

▼ *Aldebaran. Sire – Dwarka ex Amida.*

Arabian, from the desert and imported from India by Lord Herbrand Russell, later the 11th Duke of Bedford. Records at Woburn tell us little more, but it seems probable that the date of importation can be identified as 1888. In that year, Lord Russell returned to England with his wife after four years spent in India as aide-de-camp to the Viceroy, Lord Dufferin. His interest in Arab horses then took him to the 4th Crabbet Sale on 28 July 1888, where he bought Halfa*, a chestnut mare, 7 years old, by Kars* ex Hagar*, for £80. She was noted in the Sales Catalogue as 'Quiet to ride and drive'.

The 11th Duke's cousin, Lord Arthur Cecil, used Mameluke* at stud in 1893 and 1894, for, he, at that time owned Kesia II*.[68] The result of the 1893 covering was Shabaka, who, exported to USA, founded a most successful family which includes such horses as Fadjur, Khemosabi and Ferzon.

No mention of Arab horses from India would be complete without Dwarka*. He was to earn himself the title of the 'Marvel'. He raced successfully in the East and 'then [carried] his importer and first owner for many seasons with the Burghley and Fitzwilliam packs. His stud work was carried on in the intervals between the last day's hunting and the first day's cub hunting each year.' He was bred by the Anazeh and chosen especially by a friendly Arab sheikh for General Ralph Broome who took him to India in 1897. Imported in 1901 by Mrs Atkinson, then leased or sold in 1916 to the Prince of Wales who stood him at stud at Tor Royal, Devonshire, he lived to be 20 years old and sired many horses including the important stallion Aldebaran.

Dwarka* was to be the last Arab horse imported from the desert to be accepted for entry in the GSB. In 1921, Messrs Weatherby and Sons, decided that the conditions of entry for the GSB must be the same for Arabs as for Thoroughbreds. So because of this decision, Volume 25, issued in 1925, is the last to include imported Arabs, unless they can be traced to horses already accepted in earlier volumes.

Egyptian Horses

As early as November 1846, Mohamed Ali had sent some Arab horses from Egypt to HM Queen Victoria and a year later the Pasha sent the grey stallion, Abdullah*. Well known is the story of Abbas Pasha's gift of the desert-bred grey stallion Mesenneh, who, so the tale goes, was sold to India, not being esteemed by the Queen. Whereupon the Pasha, hearing of this, sent a trusted Bedouin to buy him back again. No horse answering to the name Mesenneh appears in the *Royal Horse Book 1830 – 1865* and Abdullah* who could possibly have been the same horse, was destroyed on 13 March 1860. Noted in the book against his name is 'worn out'!

A small number of Arabs tracing to Abbas Pasha I's Collection did come to England. That is as well as the important group procured by Lady Anne Blunt from the stud of Ali Pasha Sherif. Aida*, a bay Hamdanieh Simrieh, imported by Mr Baird in 1880, had been bought by him from Ali Pasha Sherif. Her sire was the famous white Seglawi Wazir and her dam, Mahroussa. Having been sold on, her line unfortunately died out. Another Hamdanieh Simrieh, imported in 1881, but not named, had been bought in Cairo from a eunuch of Halim Pasha's. Lady Anne Blunt noted on 24 June 1881: 'Saw Mr Oppenheim who came… to ask about an Arab mare given as a wedding present to Baron Leopold de Rothschild by Mrs Oppenheim. The mare, a chestnut Hamdanieh Simrieh (vouched for by Ali Pasha Sherif)… She is to have a foal by Vizier.'[69] Again, on 4 May 1882, Lady Anne writes: 'Mr Leopold de Rothschild sent his mare and the stud groom who brought her chose Kars. This mare is beautiful, very small, however, very dark chestnut. Head something like Basilisk's.'

The Khedive seems to have been rather keen on the ladies, for he presented Mahomet* to Lady Rivers Wilson and, in 1881, an Arabian mare to Mrs Layard, wife of the British Ambassador. Outlaw*, Radium*, Crosbie*, Fitz* and Talal* were all imported from Egypt. Talal*, a chestnut horse foaled in 1931, had been bred by Mr Trouncer. Talal's* sire Ibn Rabdan, was to be much used in new Egyptian breeding, and his dam Hegazieh of Nejd, is recorded as being one of the four favourite horses who accompanied Sherif Hussein of Makkah when he went to Cyprus following his abdication in favour of his son, Emir Ali, brother to Feisul and Abdullah.

Gali*, another related horse to come to England, but bred at the Inshass Stud of King Farouk in 1953, has an interesting pedigree which goes back in a number of lines to Sheykh Obeyd horses including Jamil, Ghazieh and Ghadia. It is no doubt a loss to England that these Egyptian lines were mostly disregarded. Not until 1974, with the arrival of Fakhr el Kheil*, were horses again imported from Egypt.

▲ *Crosbie.*

▲ *Fitz.*

▼ Feluccas on the Nile, *etching by Charles W. Cain.*

Horses of the Desert Tribes

The majority of the horses imported came directly from the Desert of Arabia, bred by the princes and the sheikhs of the Anazeh and Shammar tribes. The great confederation of northern Bedouin, known as the Anazeh, includes many of the horse breeding tribes from whence came the Original Horses, sought and collected throughout the centuries from the time of King David to Abbas Pasha I, Count Rzewuski and Wilfrid Scawen and Lady Anne Blunt.

The Fedaan, a large and warlike tribe, was, during the latter part of the nineteenth century under the nominal leadership of Sheikh Jedaan. Both Upton and the Blunts were to meet this man and his war horse. Proximo* was eventually to be bought from Abdur Rahman by Wilfrid Blunt, in India. The leading family of this tribe were the Ibn Sbeyni of the Mehed who were famed for their Seglawieh Jedraniehs. The legendary Zobeyni of Abbas Pasha I's Collection came from them, and the Blunts' Kars* was of this strain and from the tribe. Fedaan*, the beautiful grey stallion obtained by H.V.M. Musgrave Clark in the 1930s was another Seglawi Jedran of Ibn Sbeyni, and named after the tribe.

The Sebaa, and in particular that section of this wealthy tribe known as the Gomussa, were visited by Major Upton in 1875 and by Wilfrid and Lady Anne Blunt some years later. Both were able to select a number of their finest horses and mares from this tribe. Through the good offices of J.H. Skene, Major Upton met Sheikh Suleyman Ibn Mershid, who helped him to obtain Kesia* and his other 1875 imports. It was from Beteyen Ibn Mershid, cousin to Suleyman, that the Blunts were to buy the Queen of Sheba* after months of uncertainty. Keren-Happuch*, being of the same strain as the Queen and from the same camp, was no doubt related to her and Haidee* also came from Beteyen. Ibn Hemsi, of the Gomussa tribe, bred Rataplan* and Dahma*, whose sire was related to the Queen of Sheba*. The Managi Sbeyel, Atesh* and two of Homer Davenport's desert purchases, Haleb and Gomusa of the same strain, all came from the camp of the Gomussa.

Azrek*, the grey stallion celebrated among the tribes, was bred by Sheikh Mashlab Ibn ed Derri of the Resallin, related to the Gomussa tribe of the Sebaa, Anazeh and Neddi Ibn Derri, father of Mashlab, also bred the Seglawiehs, Pharaoh* and a white mare, dam of Basilisk*. Berghi, brother to Neddi, owned Pharaoh's dam. And bred his half-sister Meshura*. The chestnut mare of uncertain temper, named Rodania* by the Blunts, had been the war mare of Sheikh Sotamm Ibn Shaalan of the Roala. This powerful tribe was later to support Emir Hussein in the Arab cause during the First World War. T.E. Lawrence writes of Nuri Shaalan, the great Emir of the Roala, and his eldest son Nawwaf, who came with a mare for Feisal in *Seven Pillars of Wisdom*.[70]

In the 1840s the Roala were renowned for their Seglawieh Jedrans of Ibn Sudan and they were avidly collected by Abbas Pasha I for his stud. Indeed, it is said he bought up all that were to be had until none of that strain remained in the desert. Abbas Pasha I also got mares of the Managhieh strain from the Roala. The Shammar of Mesopotamia were the owners of mares, and from this large

◀ *Bedouin.*

tribe came El Emir*, the Blunts' Ferida*, and Abbas Pasha Hilmi II's Venus. Many of the horses exported to India came from the district around Mosul where the Shammar and its tributary tribes pastured their stock.

The sheikhs of the Ajman, Montefik, Wuld-Ali and Muteyr were all famous for their Arab horses. Ed Duish of the Muteyr were known especially for their Krushieh, which they guarded jealously and it was their proud boast that they had never parted with one of these mares. Abbas Pasha I could not obtain one at any price, even though he sent an emissary to negotiate through the Sherif of Makkah with Watban el Duish. Many tried but with no success, including Feysul Ibn Saud and the sheikhs of the Ajman and Montefik. Although the Sauds later obtained one Krushieh mare, her descendants were lost to the Ibn Rasheeds.

Ali Pasha Sherif's records list 'Bakrah' a Kurush al Ghandour of the Beni-Khaled, neighbours to the Muteyr. The first known Krushieh to arrive in England since Burning Bush*, was Petra*, in 1923, bred by the Majali, who were to present Abdul Aziz al Saud with two mares of the same strain in 1971. Unfortunately, details of the breeding or strain of many of the horses brought out of the desert is not recorded. Thus Dwarka* is only 'from the Anazeh'. In the case of others, their pedigrees or certificates have been lost and all that can now be written is 'high-caste' or 'pure-bred'.

◀ *Dafina of the Krushieh strain.*

Desert Princes

A goodly number of the horses who appear in this book are known to have come from the great studs of the princes of Arabia. Due to the vagaries of war and the ceaseless changes in power which took place throughout the nineteenth and early twentieth centuries, the fortunes of the studs of the Sherifs of Makkah, the Ibn Rasheeds and Ibn Sauds were to wax and wane too. It is recorded that, in 1814, Abdullah Ibn Saud, the 9th Amir negotiated a truce with Tousson Pasha of Egypt and agreed to send a peace offering to Mohammed Ali, of two hundred choice mares and stallions, and in 1818 Abdullah surrendered to Ibrahim Pasha, eldest son of Mohammed Ali. The result of this action was short and sharp. Abdullah was sent to Istanbul and beheaded by the Turks and his stud acquired by Ibrahim. Later, in 1842, Prince Feysul Ibn Turki (a Saud not a Turk!), the 10th Amir, escaped from Cairo where he had been imprisoned in the Citadel with, it is said, the help of Abbas Pasha, son of Tousson. In return, Faisul helped Abbas to procure desert horses, including the famous Jellabieh 'Wazira' and Faras-Nakadan, the mare of Nakadan of the Ajman.

W.G. Palgrave was to visit the stud of Ibn Saud of Nejd in 1862 and he wrote in his book *Central and Eastern Arabia*:

> Never have I seen or imagined so lovely a collection. Their stature was indeed somewhat low; I do not think any were above 15 hands, 14 hands appeared to me about their average; but they were so exquisitely well-shaped that want of greater size seemed hardly, if at all, a defect. A little, a very little saddle-backed, just the curve that indicates springiness without weakness; a head broad above tapering down to a nose fine enough to verify the phrase of 'drinking from a pint-pot'! A most intelligent and yet singularly gentle look, full eye, sharp thorn-like little ear, legs fore and hind that seemed as if made of hammered iron, so clean and yet so well twisted with sinew; a neat round hoof, just the requisite for hard ground; a tail set on or rather thrown out at a perfect arch; coats smooth, shining and light; the mane long, but not overgrown nor heavy. The prevailing colour was chestnut or grey.

Palgrave could possibly have seen the Blunts' Sherifa* as a foal!

Whilst at Hail in 1879, Wilfrid and Lady Anne Blunt visited the stud of the Emir, Mohammed Ibn Rasheed, and Lady Anne says in her book, *A*

THE ARAB HORSE

▲ *Ibn Rasheed's stable at Hail.*

Pilgrimage to Nejd: 'Ibn Raschid's stud is now the most celebrated in Arabia, and has taken the place in public estimation of that stud of Feysul Ibn Saud's which Palgrave saw sixteen years ago at Riâd.' In her notes on the stud Lady Anne lists the following:

1. A chestnut Kehilet el-Krush with three white feet (mutlak al yemîn) 14 hands or 14 hands 1 inch, but very powerful. Her head is plainer than most here… She is Mohammed's favourite charger, and of the best blood in the Nejd. Ibn Rashid got this strain from Ibn Saoud's stables at Riâd, but it came originally from the Muteyr.

2. A bay Hamdanieh Simri, also from Ibn Saoud's collection, a pretty head, but no other distinction. NB. This mare is of the same strain as our own mare Sherifa, but inferior to her.

3. A grey Seglawieh Sheyfi, extremely plain at first sight, with very drooping quarters, and a head in no way remarkable, but with a fine shoulder. This Seglawieh Sheyfi has a great reputation here, and is of special interest as being the last of her race, the only descendant of the famous mare bought by Abbas Pasha I, who sent a bullock cart from Egypt all the way to Nejd to fetch her, for she was old.

4. A dark bay Kehilet Ajuz, quite 14 hands 2 inches… really splendid… the handsomest head and largest eye of any here. She had ideal action, head and tail carried to perfection, and recalls Beteyen Ibn Mirshid's mare [Queen of Sheba*] but her head is finer. She belongs to Hamud… [he] tells us she came from the Jerba Shammar. It surprises us to find here a mare from Mesopotamia.

Others are described, including eight stallions, 'the best is a Shueyman Sbah', and in all one hundred horses.

Charles Doughty also writes of Ibn Rasheed's Stud, which he visited in 1892: 'a very perfect young and startling chestnut mare – shapely as there are few among them'. Again: 'I saw a mare led through the town [Hail] of perfect beauty; the Emir sent her, his yearly present with the Haj [pilgrimage] to the Sherif of Mecca'. In 1917, Lady Anne Blunt was to write:

In Arabia certain studs still flourish in the hands of princes and individuals recognised as authentic. The chief of these, Ibn Raschid's at Hail, Aid el Temimi at Oneyza, Emir Ibn Khalifa, Bahrain, the Sultan of Muscat and King Ibn Saoud. Outside Arabia the only one recognised by the Arabs as authentic is that of Ali Pasha Sherif.

In 1921, Ibn Saud finally crushed the power of the Ibn Rasheed and took

THE ARAB HORSE

◀ *Facsimile of an Arab letter to Sir Gilbert Clayton, and (below) its translation.*

Sir Gilbert Clayton. ▼

In the Name of God the Compassionate the Merciful
the Empire of Hejaz and Nejd and its provinces
Palace of His Illustrious Majesty the King.

From Abd el Aziz Ibn Abder Rahman el Feysul to the most honoured Lord Sir Cle-ee-ton. After compliments we send your Excellency the horses, a stallion and a mare, and the horse is a Seglawi of the best bred of the Nejd Stock and his sire Abeyan and the mare Krush and her sire Kehilan but owing to the severe journey, I see with regret their wretched condition by reason of a whole month on the way and for the last six days, march day and night in order to arrive in time for you but on account of their purity of pedigree and that they are of the best strains bred in Nejd, I have no doubt that when then have had a rest their appearance will give you satisfaction. Sealed Abd el Aziz.

N.B. Her sire Kehilan, i.e. Kehilan of the same Kehilan el Krush strain.

into his own stud their famous white Krushieh mare. Only six years later, Dafina*, a white Keheilet el Krushieh, foaled in 1921, was presented to Lady Wentworth by King Saud, through the good offices of Sir Gilbert Clayton.[71] King Abdul Aziz al Saud gave many gifts of horses in the tradition of earlier desert rulers, including four, in 1937, to HM King George VI. Kasim* and Faras* are described in the Arabic certificate sent by Abdul Aziz (*opposite*).

The two other horses in the gift were the chestnut stallion Manak* and a grey mare Turfa*. Both have left important lines, Manak* through his association with the Bahrain mare Nuhra*, and Turfa* in America. Other recipients of horses as gifts from Ibn Saud were Kings Fouad and Farouk of Egypt, the Queen of Holland and a Syrian from the Lebanon, one Ameen Rihani.[72] He, being a close associate of the King, was sent the Managhieh mare Noura* by special messenger from Riâd to Damascus, where Rihani had her covered by a Seglawi stallion at the stud of Omar Bey Dandash in Akkar, before sending her to England in 1928. Later he moved to the USA and took the mare and her daughter with him. There they founded an important line leading to many American champions.

In 1938, Princess Alice Countess of Athlone and her husband, the Earl of Athlone (Queen Mary's brother), paid a state visit to the Middle East. On 25 February:

Jeddah: [They were met] by Emir Faisal [son of the King] in flowing robes of black and gold who conducted the visitors... to a semi-circle of golden chairs where coffee and sherbet were served... Princess Alice will wear a veil of Arab robes during her journey across Arabia.

And on 11 March:

Jeddah: The Crown Prince presented a mare and stallion, of pure Arab blood to Princess Alice and the Earl of Athlone on their departure today for Rumanhiya Wells... where he is to entertain them tomorrow with gazelle hunting... and also possibly with some hawking at bustards.[73]

During the recent visit to Saudi Arabia and Bahrain, Princess Alice and the Earl of Athlone were presented with two stallions and one mare by HM King Ibn Saud of Nejd and HH The Sheikh of Bahrain. The stallion from Nejd is a bay 2-year-old Keheilan Ajuz belonging to Ibn Sweid, one of the sheikhs of the Ajman tribe, among whom he is recognised as a thoroughbred of very old pedigree [Khaibar*]. The other stallion is from Bahrain, a bay 4-year-old. His sire a Keheilan Jellabi, one of the best known sires in Bahrain, and the dam a Keheileh al'Musinnieh [Bahrain*]. The mare, also from the Sheikh of Bahrain, is by a Keheilan

▲ *Ameen RIhani riding Noura.*

THE ARAB HORSE

Jellabi, out of a Keheileh Al'Wadneh, which is related to the Al Tabouh [Nuhra*].

This last named mare, Nuhra*, was to found a remarkable dynasty.

Since the early years of the nineteenth century, the sheikhs of Bahrain had been renowned for their stud of Arab horses. The famous Jellabiet-Feysul, an Original Mare of the Collection of Abbas Pasha I, had gone to Egypt 'from Feysul Ibn Turki, Emir of Riâd, for, it is said, £7,000, but by him obtained from Ibn Khalifeh, Sheikh of Bahrain who possessed both Kehilan Jellabi and the Dahman Shahwan strains, having got them from the Ajman tribe.'[74] Abbas Pasha I also obtained 'The Mare of Nakadan' from the same source. Such horses as Makbula*, Kasida*, and Jellabieh*, imported to England in May 1898, by the Blunts, and their little stallion, Feysul*, go back in tail-female line to the Jellabiet-Feysul of Ibn Khalifeh.

On 26 December 1907, Lady Anne Blunt bought a bay Dahmeh Shahwanieh from the Khedive of Egypt. Bred by Eissa Ibn Khalifeh, Sheikh of Bahrain, in 1898, and brought by him as a gift to the Khedive in 1903, Lady Anne was to name her, Bint el Bahreyn – the Daughter of Bahrain. This Sheikh Eissa, son of Ali, had ruled from 1869 to 1925 and it was his son HH Sheikh Hamed Bin Eissa Al-Khalifa who presented Bahrain* and Nuhra* to Princess Alice and the Earl of Athlone in 1939.

A number of interesting horses imported to this country were to come from the stud of Emir Ibn Rasheed at Hail, which the Blunts had visited in 1879. Two Managhieh mares, Nejdmieh* and Nejma* were brought home by Major G.H. Barker. Nejdmieh*, exported to Australia in 1925, was to produce a very successful family there. She, incidentally, being

◀ *Turfa at Port Said, February 1938.*

◀◀ *Bedouin with hawks.*

◀ *Another picture of Turfa.*

THE ARAB HORSE

Lalla Rookh. ▶

▲ Nimr, *drawing by Miss M.J. Stevens.*

Nissr. Dam – Lalla Rookh, sire – Nimr. ▶

91

THE ARAB HORSE

An Arabian Horse, *oil painting by Baron Antoine Jean Gros (1771-1835).*

bred by Sheikh Moubarek of the Sebaa, may well have been closely related to the Managhi stallion Atesh*, also bred by the Sebaa, though later used as a charger by Enver Pasha, before he too came to England. The Emir Abdullah Ibn Rasheed is recorded as the breeder of the flea-bitten grey mare Lalla Rookh*, later presented by him to HH The Sherif Ali Haidar, the late King of Makkah. Lalla Rookh was imported to England in 1923 in foal to Mersud*, and later produced a filly for H. Musgrave Clark. Later she was put to the desert stallions Fedaan* and Nimr*.

The brown Seglawi Jedran named Nimr* had been bred by Prince Mohuiddin, son of the late Sherif of Makkah.

In 1919, Sherif Hussein, the King of the Hejaz had presented the 7-year-old black stallion, Soueidan*, to HM King George V and Soueidan el Saghir* (the younger), to HRH the Prince of Wales. The extended pedigrees of both these

▼ *Soueidan, black Arab stallion presented to HM King George V by King Hussein of the Hejaz in 1919.*

Ctesiphon Arch, etching by Charles W. Cain. ▶

THE ARAB HORSE

horses given in Volume 1 of the AHS Stud Book, are of interest in that they demonstrate clearly the extent to which horses had passed from one great stud to another. Soueidan* goes back to a mare known as El-Batrana Saada and her dam was 'from the personal stud of the well-known Mohammed Ibn Rasheed'. (The same who the Blunts visited in Hail in 1879.) Soueidan el Saghir* foaled in 1915 and the son of Soueidan* was out of the mare Fureiha, who can be traced back in tail-female line to Qafza, whose dam 'is one of my great uncle Abdulla's mares, presented to him by Ibn Saud.'

In 1914, a British Expeditionary Force from India had moved against the Turks in Mesopotamia. Shortly after this, the British in Cairo were to take an active interest in the Arab Revolt led by Sherif Hussein in Makkah. In the event, it took the British until March 1917 to get beyond Kut and the Ctesiphon Arch to Baghdad. Once more, serving officers in yet another theatre of war learnt to admire the qualities of the little desert horses they met with and some were later brought back to England. The white horse Ibn Kuhailan*, owned by Colonel P.C. Joyce,[75] who at the time served as Senior British Advisor to King Feisal of Iraq, had been bred by Sheikh Fahd Bey al Khadhal and the dam of Ibn Kuhailan* had been the property of the Al-Zoba tribe.[76]

A number of mares came out of Iraq – the bay Jamila I* (the Beautiful), Tura'a*, Mahawiliyah*, Mandilah* and El Melha* (Evelyn). The last, formerly owned by Ali Ibn Hussein had won races in Iraq, including the Baghdad Plate, Tigris Handicap and Champion Plate in the Iraq Stakes.[77]

◀ Baghdad – Entrance to Kazimain Mosque, *etching by Charles W. Cain.*

The Great Arab Revolt and the Last Desert Horses

The Great Arab Revolt during the First World War united many of the Anazeh tribes in their struggle against the Turks. Under the leadership of Sherif Hussein's sons Abdullah and Feisul, their forces rode north and took with them Arab horses from the Hejaz.[78] Some of these mares and horses were to become the foundation stock of the studs of King Feisal of Iraq and King Abdullah of Transjordan, and further additions came in the form of gifts or purchases from the desert tribes.

One such was the white horse Mirage*, a Seglawi Jedran, famed throughout the tribes. Bred by the Sebaa Anazeh and bought from them as a 2-year-old by General Haddad Pasha for King Feisal, he was imported to England and sent to Tattersall's Sales in 1923. There, Lady Wentworth purchased him and used him at stud, but not being acceptable to the GSB, she eventually sold this lovely horse to R. Selby of Ohio in 1930. 'There, [Mirage*] sired twenty-six foals [thirteen colts and thirteen fillies] and founded a dynasty of champions.' He was a great loss to England.

In the year previous to Mirage's* importation, King Feisal had presented a fine chestnut horse, Shwaiman*, to Lord Hartington. Ridden by R. Summerhays, this horse took part in the AHS Endurance Test held in September 1922. Three hundred miles at sixty miles a day for five consecutive days was quite a test and Shwaiman* received the Gold Medal, having come second to Shahzada.

In 1958, the stud of King Feisal II – grandson of Feisal – disappeared in the bloody aftermath of the assassination of the Royal Family of Iraq, and only one horse of this breeding is known to have survived. His name was Mehrez. Mehrez, although bred by Daoud Pasha Al Daghestani, goes back to horses from the Hejaz, and he has a fascinating history which was told me by Tamara Al Daghestani.

General Muhammad Pasha, father of Daoud, was killed in battle about the year 1918 and his war mare, Wanda, carried his body back to Baghdad. Her mission fulfilled, Wanda fell dead. Fortunately, she had left a daughter, named Wanda II, to continue this great family and her filly foal, named Daghestania was the dam of Mehrez. He died aged 31 years in 1988 at the Royal Jordanian Stud, who have some precious sons and daughters of the famous old horse.

Emir Abdullah, like his father before him, was to send gifts of horses to many kings and rulers. He sent a stallion, Abdullah* and a mare, Jordania* to HM King George V in 1922. The stud he had established with the mares and horses from the Hejaz, and with further gifts from the Da'aja, Aduane and Majali tribes, suffered a severe setback following Abdullah's assassination in 1951.

Happily, HM King Hussein decided to collect together once again his grandfather's Arab horses. Some were with the Royal Mounted Guards, but others had been dispersed and proved more difficult to locate. The Krushieh mare, Gazella, was found pulling a plough. Once again disaster seemed near when the Arab/Israeli war threatened Shuna where the stables were located, close to the River Jordan. During the hours of darkness, Santiago

◀ *The Arab Revolt. Emir Feisal and Emir Abdullah.*

THE ARAB HORSE

Sherif Hussein in Makkah.

Arab mare at the plough.

Shwaiman with R.S. Summerhays.

H M King Feisal of Iraq.

Mirage.

◀ Emir Feisal in Damascus *by James McBey, 1918.*

Lopez, the Master of the King's Horse, his wife Ursula and the grooms took the horses on the hazardous mountain journey to Amman to safety. The Royal Jordanian Stud now numbers some two hundred horses and is housed in delightful stables a short distance from Amman.

In November 1958, further gifts of horses were sent by HM King Hussein of Jordan to HM The Queen. The Muniqi Shamikh* (Pride), was kept at Windsor in 1962 and Princess Anne rode him regularly. The mare, El Yamama* (Dove), produced a filly in December at Sandringham who the Queen named Muna. El Yamama, being of the Um Arkoub strain, is related to the horses of the same strain in the Royal Jordanian Stud. Nasseb, the foundation mare of that strain, was owned by HM King Abdullah, but had been bred by Dlewan Pasha al Majali, Sheikh of the Majali tribe. This tribe situated near Karak, a town dominated by the ruins of a great Crusader fortress, was a prominent Jordanian tribe whose sheikhs had bred horses for many generations. The Majali were also to present gifts of horses to rulers abroad. Some went to Ibn Saud and others were received by HM The Queen in July 1960.

From Habis el Majali came the stallion Comar* (who died in July 1961), and the mare Shams*, given to Sir Dudley Forwood in 1964 and represented by a strong family today.[79] One of the last true desert mares to be imported to this country was Shammah*. Bred by Dlewan Pasha al Majali and given as a yearling to HM King Talal, she was to come into the possession of Santiago Lopez eventually, who sent her to England. A story of this mare, told me by Santiago, well illustrates the courage of the Arab. Whilst in Jordan she foaled twin fillies and these were attacked by two wolves. Shammah* killed both wolves. She herself died at 24 years of age in 1974. I hope that some of her children and grandchildren have inherited her indomitable spirit and lionheart.

Many imports from other countries of the world have, of course, taken place, most notably that of the famous white Polish stallion Skowronek. Later in the 1950s and 1960s further Polish invasions took place, and over the years other imports from Europe, Russia, America, Australia and the Middle East have arrived here. These imports far outnumber those direct from the Desert of Arabia, and such imports continue, often encouraged by fads and fashion for the 'Straight Egyptian' or 'Straight Russian'!

H M King Abdullah of Jordan. ▶

Shammah and filly foal at 4 hours old. ▼

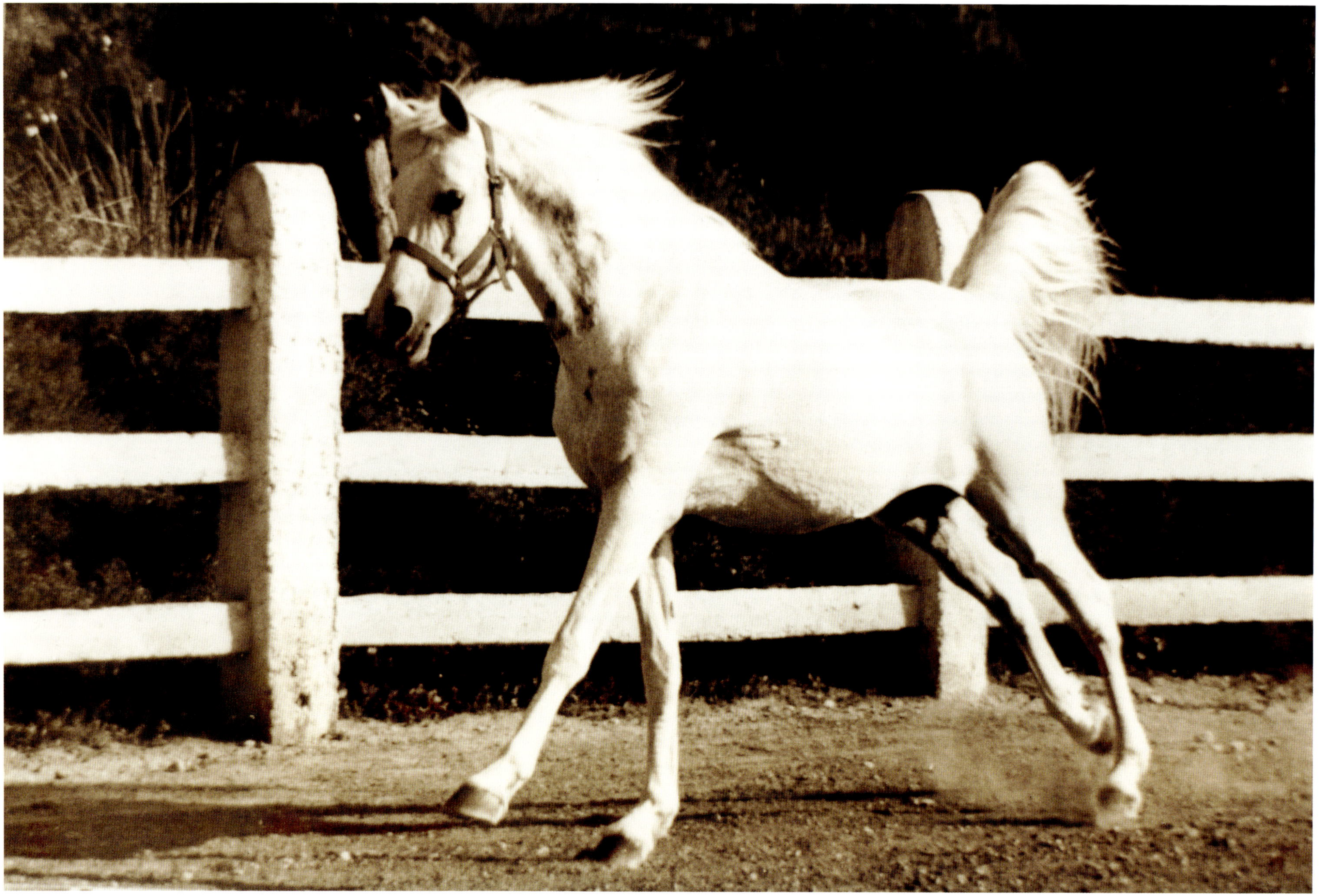

▲ *Mehrez*

THE ARAB HORSE

◀ *Wanda I, great-granddam of Mehrez.*

▼ *Adeebah, drawing, 1986.*

◀ *Karak Castle, engraving by P. Upton.*

THE ARAB HORSE

Dlewan Pasha el Majali. ▶

Dlewan Pasha el Majali on his warhorse. ▼

The Desert – The Source

In talking of English, Polish and Egyptian horses, we must remind ourselves that nearly all this stock goes back originally to the same source – the Desert of Arabia. Many of these horses have, however, been bred independently for a number of generations and so provide a new vigour and useful re-addition to our lines. Those seeking the blood of the Stud of Abbas Pasha I, would do well to remember that most horses of Crabbet breeding carry a greater percentage of that blood than do present-day Egyptians who, in any case, get most of their Abbas Pasha blood through Blunt horses from Sheykh Obeyd and the 1920 Crabbet imports.

Notable exceptions to the 'English' saturation can be found in Poland, Spain, America, Egypt and Jordan where some lines go back to completely fresh desert sources, though these are, by now, largely intermixed with 'English' lines. But one matter which is beyond doubt is the greater likelihood of authenticity of the horses imported direct from the Desert of Arabia, or known to have been bred among the tribes and by the Desert Princes. Two World Wars were to bring about changes that affected the place of honour so long held by the horse in desert life for ever. Palgrave wrote: 'In Nejd is the true birthplace of the Arab steed – the primal type, the authentic model.' Lady Wentworth was to write much later: 'The Arabian should be sought for in Arabia – he belongs especially to the tribes of Bedouins of the interior which have the best, and none other, but Arabians.'

In the horses which came to England and which are described in this book, we have a heritage beyond price. No words express more clearly why such imports of Arab horses have taken place, for hundreds of years, than those with which I conclude: 'First let us obtain the pure-bred and perfect horse, then let us take care to keep his future generations pure.'

▼ Mare and Falcon, *sketch by Peter Upton.*

Bedouin horsemen. ▼

NOTES

1. Asterisk indicates a horse imported into Great Britain.
2. From Markham's Maister-Peece (1599).
3. From John Cheney, *An Historical List or Account of all the Horse Matches run and of all the Plates and Prizes run for in England (of the Value of £10 upwards) in 1727.*
4. Roger Upton lists 186 oriental horses and thirty-three mares in his book *Newmarket and Arabia,* '…which were employed, more or less, in the formation of the English Stud from the time of James I until about the end of the eighteenth century.'
5. The Royal Stud at Weil was founded in 1817 by King William I of Württemberg. It was located in the Neckar valley about seven miles south of Stuttgart. 'Neptune' writing in the *Sporting Magazine* in 1838 under the heading 'Remarks on foreign studs and horses etc.' describes the King's Stud: 'ninety-six mares, thirty-six with foals and about thirty fillies. Most are Mecklenburg or Hungarian crossed with English Thoroughbreds. All had been put to the Arab stallions. These stallions were a weedy lot, and not one would have fetched £20 at Tattersall's. I strongly suspect that many of the mares, which they called Arabians and thoroughbred, were not so in fact, but had a cross of an old grey Persian horse which had covered in His Majesty's stud for many years and whom I saw, though a fine looking horse, certainly did not possess the appearances of pure blood which the small Arabians shewed. Their stock [therefore] will have become contaminated from this source, but they do not keep any pedigree with exactness.'
6. The stud was sold by Messrs Tattersall in the paddocks at Hampton Court on Wednesday 25 October 1837; and drew together an immense concourse including many influential noblemen and gentlemen connected with the turf, agents from France, Germany, Russia and Prussia etc. The bay stallion, sold for 440 guineas to France, the white mare was bought for 105 guineas by P.D. Pauncefoot-Duncombe, Esq., brother-in-law to Sir Tatton Sykes, the purchaser at 150 guineas of the 'flea-bitten' mare.
7. The Imaum or Sultan of Muscat, Syed Said, reigned from 1806 to 1856, and sent many genuine specimens of the Arab horse to England.
8. From *The Sporting Magazine*, Vol. XIII, Second Series, No. 75 July 1836. I have quoted at some length from this article for the descriptions of the horses are most apt and indeed very relevant, even if the horses in question were to play no part in the furtherance of the breed.
9. The horses presented by the King of Oude were probably the two grey stallions who were at the Royal Stud at Hampton Court in 1837. By 1878 Nawab Ikbálet Dowlah, the former King of Oude, was living in exile in Baghdad, where he was visited by Wilfrid Scawen and Lady Anne Blunt.
10. The second stud of Arab horses appears to have been that started by Charles Holte Bracebridge, probably in 1855, following his return from the Crimean War. His wife Selina, a remarkable and beautiful woman, was a close friend to Florence Nightingale. Both were well-known travellers and Charles Bracebridge (who liked to trace their descent from Lady Godiva), had a passion for liberty and dressed picturesquely. He had brought Arab horses from the East which he bred at Atherstone Hall, near Coventry. From Woodham-Smith, *Biography of Florence Nightingale* (Constable, 1950).
11. See Haidee* in the Tables of Descent.
12. Hussar's* foals were seen by the Blunts when they visited Poland in 1884.
13. *The Sporting Magazine*, March 1837, p. 413. 'Inquiry respecting Arab Stallions' – 'Several first-rate Arabian horses such as Buckfoot, Harlequin, Champion, Muscat, Paragon, Orelio etc., have been imported into England within these few years.'
14. Two Arab horses to arrive in England about 1816 were from France – Napoleon's favourite charger, the white stallion Marengo* and another of his horses named Jaffa*. Marengo*, who had been imported from Egypt as a 6-year-old in 1799, was brought to England by Lord Petre after the Battle of Waterloo. Only 14 hands 1 inch, he stood at stud for a fee of 10 guineas near Ely, for his owner General J. Angerstein until his death in 1831. Marengo's skeleton is in the United Services Museum. Jaffa also died at a great age and was buried at Cranbrook, Kent.
15. Vonolel* was buried in the garden of the Royal Hospital, Dublin and Lord Roberts had the following words cut on his tombstone:

   There are men both good and great
   Who hold that in a future state
   Dumb creatures we have cherished here below
   Will give us joyous greeting as we pass the Golden Gate.
   Is it folly if I trust it may be so?

16. From Colonel T.A. St Quentin late 8th-10th Hussars, *Chances of Sports of Sorts* (1912).
17. Lord Roberts sent a telegram form Kandahar on 1 September at 6 p.m.: 'Ayub Khan's army was today defeated… our casualties are … 72nd Highlanders: Lieutenant-Colonel Brownlow.'
18. *Pall Mall Gazette*, 31 March 1884. 'A telegram received at the War Office from General Graham states that the 10th Hussars, a battery of Royal Artillery, the York and Lancaster Regiment and the Royal Irish Fusiliers embarked on Saturday in the *Jumna*.'
19. If 19 years old in 1884, Maidan* would have been foaled in 1865 and not c. 1869.
20. T.B. Drybrough, *Polo* (1898).
21. Volume 1 of the AHS was not published until 1919 (twenty-five years later).
22. Major Roger Dawson Upton, born 1827, served in the British Army from 1851-61. In 1855 he joined the 9th Lancers, who were stationed in India and he served there for six years. Although a Captain when he left the army, in 1877 he was gazetted an Honorary Major. He married Sophie Turner on 21 June 1854, and they were to have two daughters and five sons. An authority on the Arab Horse, Major Upton was to champion its cause in the three books he published, the two more important being *Newmarket and Arabia* (1873) and *Gleanings from the Desert of Arabia* published posthumously in 1881.

    Although conflicting ideas exist regarding the number of visits made to the desert by Major Upton, fresh evidence enables me to state that he made two journeys to the Desert of Arabia, the first in 1874 and the second a year later, commissioned to procure Arab horses. His eldest son, Roger Hope Edward Upton (1856-1907) went to New South Wales, Australia and was employed by A.A. Dangar at his stud. He travelled with his father to the desert and then returned to Australia, where he remained with the Dangars until 1886.
23. This letter appears in an article '*From Needham Market to Oyster Bay*' by Thornton Chard, published in *The Horse* in May/June 1942.
24. This note of Upton's, quoted in Vidal's letter, would appear to have been written in 1874, as he states that No 1., the chestnut stallion Yatagan is 4 years old, and the GSB gives the horse's age as 7 years in 1877.
25. The Dangars were originally a Cornish family who had emigrated to Australia. As well as importing the two desert horses, they later bought Purple Stock* and Francolin* at the 1st Crabbet Auction held on 2 July 1882 for £115 and 10 shillings and £126 respectively. The Blunts had purchased these two desert mares for £65 (Francolin*), and £72 (Semiranis, later

renamed Purple Stock*). Lady Anne Blunt noted on 18 November 1883: 'Francolin and Purple Stock have both had fillies [by Pharaoh* and Kars*] much to the satisfaction of Mr Dangar.'

26 This is according to *Impecuniosus'* of *The Field*. This writer knew Sandeman very well and had often ridden Yataghan* during 1875 in Hyde Park.

27 Vidal suggests that Sandeman lost heart after Upton's death in January 1881 and 'handed over' Naomi to him.

28 W.S. Blunt had written on 2 February 1885 in reply to Vidal's proposal to exchange Naomi for a Crabbet mare, but nothing came of it.

29 The Honourable Henry Chaplin (1840-1923). Born 22 December 1840, eldest son of the Reverend Henry Chaplin, vicar of Rhyall in the county of Rutland. Educated at Eton and Christ Church Oxford, he succeeded to the estates of his uncle, Mr Charles Chaplin of Blankney, in 1859. This gentle-man left him not only one of the best cultivated and finest estates in mid-Lincolnshire, but a huge fortune.

Mr Chaplin began following hounds as soon as he could bestride a pony, receiving his lessons with the Cottesmore. At Oxford, he diligently hunted with the neighbouring packs, albeit when he left the Alma Mater. He carried with him the reputation of being a scholarly gentleman in a day when young men of means were usually expected to 'lark'. After a big-game tour of Upper India, Mr Chaplin returned to England and astonished the world of racing by giving the then quite unprecedented price of 11,000 guineas to Mr l'Anson of Malton for two racehorses – Bredalbane and Broomielaw to wit. It created quite a furore! Special commissioners were sent to interview l'Anson, who was so besieged with applications to view the equine wonders that tickets of admission were issued to debar *profanum vulgus* from entering the sacred stable.

Mr Chaplin's Turf career is ably dealt with in, *The Turf and the Men who made it*, where his sagacity as a breeder and the wonderful triumphs of the 'all rose' cap and jacket are described. He succeeded Doneraile as Master of the Burton Hounds in 1866. This establishment was carried through in first-class style and there was nothing in England to surpass it. Mr Chaplin bred his hunters from the grand Thorough-bred stallions in his racing stud whom he mated with great hunting mares. Riding something like 18 stone, a notable judge once said, 'He rides so light that he might only be a 12-stone man!'

In March 1870, the Prince of Wales stayed with Mr Chaplin at Blankney. In 1877 Mr Chaplin became Master of the Blankney. By 1881, finding the calls of politics too many, he then induced Major Tempest to assume the role of acting MFH. In 1885 Lord Lonsdale took the hounds for £3,600 from Mr Chaplin (a new pack was formed by Major Tempest), and Mr Chaplin bought back fourteen couples of the original pack.

30 Keren-Happuch* was barren to Joktan* in 1876 and to Ishmael* in 1884. Kesia* produced a colt to Joktan* in 1877, a chestnut filly to Hermit in 1878 and a chestnut colt to Ishmael* in 1881 (Hermit was the winner of the Derby in 1867 for Mr Chaplin).

31 Mameluke* was an Arab stallion imported by Lord Herbrand Russell, cousin to Lord Cecil.

32 Wilfrid Scawen Blunt (1840-1922). A romantic and poet, devoted to the pursuit of the passionate. His homes were Newbuildings Place and Crabbet Park in Sussex. In 1869 he married Lady Anne Noel-King, granddaughter of the poet Lord Byron.

Lady Anne Blunt *1837-1917). An accomplished artist, having been taught painting by Ruskin. She was also a language scholar.

Together she and Wilfrid travelled to the deserts of Arabia, Egypt and India, and founded the Crabbet Arabian Stud in 1878 with the horses they bought on their journeys. Blunt purchased all of the early horses and paid the main expenses of the stud, until after 1893, when Lady Anne came into her inheritance. She bought most of the Ali Pasha Sherif horses and from then on paid a share of stud costs. Wilfrid and Lady Anne separated in 1906 and Blunt handed over the management of the stud to Lady Anne. Their daughter, Judith, later Lady Wentworth, born in 1873, married the Honourable Neville Lytton in 1899 and they moved to Crabbet. Blunt lived on at Newbuildings until his death in 1922 and Lady Anne spent her last years at Sheykh Obeyd, near Cairo.

Those interested in learning more about the Blunts and their daughter would do well to read, *The Authentic Arabian Horse* by Lady Wentworth, *Lady Anne Blunt – Journals and Correspondence 1878-1917* by Rosemary Archer and James Fleming, *The Crabbet Arabian Stud – Its History and Influence and Influence* by Rosemary Archer, Colin Pearson and Cecil Covey, and at least one of the biographies of Wilfrid Blunt – *A Pilgrimage of Passion* by Elizabeth Longford, or *Wilfrid Scawen Blunt: A Memoir by his Grandson* by the Earl of Lytton; *Lady Anne Blunt*: a biography by H. Winstone.

33 This partnership was to include Lady Anne's brother, Lord Wentworth, though he only contributed £1,000, which the Blunts later repaid. Skene, already beset with financial difficulties, could do no more than introduce the Blunts to the Anazeh and buy horses for them.

34 Seyd Akmet (Ahmet), was Sheikh of the Hanadi, a tribe settled near Jedaide, east of Aleppo. Upton visited the tribe in late 1874 and met the son of the old Sheikh Hadji Batran. This son, the nephew of Seyd Akmet, whom the Blunts also met, was probably Eissa.

35 Doughty, in *Wanderings in Arabia*, describes the firing of Rahyel's mare, lame in a hind leg, but firing was used by the Bedouin, as a cure for all ills.

36 The Zoba were the breeders of the stallion El Emir* owned by the Honourable Miss Dillon.

37 In reading about the horses in Lady Anne Blunt's journals and books, care must be taken in regard to names. They often changed their names and there were indeed two Sherifas and two Tamarisks.

38 Beteyen Ibn Mirshid, cousin to Suleyman, the Great Sheikh.

39 Beteyen's mare had cost him fourteen camels, which, at an average price of £5, each equalled £70 plus £20 in money. Whoever holds the bridle half has the right to purchase the rest of the mare for half the sum already paid. She would, therefore, have cost no more than £135. Skene eventually purchased her for the Blunts for £265.

40 The Blunts did not purchase Dahma* until 1881.

41 Mrs Digby, successively Lady Ellenborough, Baroness Venningen, Countess Theotaky and wife of the Sheikh Mijuel el Mesrab, was a romantic who craved adventure. Read her biography in *The Wilder Shores of Love* by Lesley Blanch, or *Passion's Child* by Margaret Fox Schmidt.

42 Wilfrid Blunt makes it very clear as to the original intention of importing Arabs to England in an article which appeared in the *Pall Mall Gazette* of 16 July 1889:

I had the idea originally of breeding for speed, but have abandoned it; not that it would be impossible to develop racing excellence, but that it would take too long… I now restrict myself to keeping the breed pure and developing the peculiar qualities of the Arab, which are:

1. Perfect soundness, especially in the legs and feet, where English horses are most defective.
2. Good temper.
3. Beauty.
4. Staying Power.

He [the Arab Horse] is very useful as a hack, but you must not suppose that he is not capable of carrying very heavy weights in that capacity. Then he is a very bold performer across country and will carry a lightweight with the best English horses. He is a perfect ladies' hunter. He is perhaps still better adapted to light carriage work, owing to the excellence of his feet which will stand any amount of wear and tear. He is a good trotter… he has also the great advantage of a light and pleasant mouth. The special characteristics of the Arab may be traced to the circumstances and necessities of Bedouin life. The great intellectual development, if I may use the word, and the great docility of temper, clearly come from selection by breeders who live in daily companionship with their horses… Again, great hardness of constitution is necessary in a country which is subject to droughts etc. … The bedouin system of warfare, which is the purpose to which they are put, accounts for their enormous staying-power. It consists of long forced marches often as much as 500 miles, where they would be obliged to do as much as fifty to eighty miles a day, on no better feed than which chances to come their way and often without water. Then at the end they must have sufficient courage and spirit left to be able to manoeuvre in Arab lance fighting and to carry their masters back … The introduction of firearms has tended to diminish the stock [of horses]. A fleet horse is no longer a fortune to its possessor.

43. Lady Anne was eager to get Mohammed Jirro's Hadbeh Enzahi, as well as Beteyen's mare. In the event, Skene was unable to buy Jirro's.
44. Lady Anne Blunt continually mentions their dislike of the colour grey. This suggests that those greys they did choose, must have been especially good horses.
45. Major Upton stated in *Gleanings From the Desert of Arabia* that 'it is not uncommon for Arab horses to stand back, more or less, at the knees.'
46. This is an interesting comment in regard to her earlier one about the horses of the Fedaan, their recent visits to the stud of Ali Pasha Sherif and the general consensus of opinion that horses were fast disappearing among the Anazeh.
47. Three years later Rataplan* suffered a similar fate, when he perished at sea on his way to Egypt.
48. *See* Note 28.
49. It seems surprising that after eulogising so about Shahwan, just two years after buying him they put him up for sale at £350.
50. The chestnut filly was, in fact, by Aziz ex Makbula, half-sister to Kasida.
51. Of the 17 listed, the Blunts eventually bought nine – Nos. 1, 4, 5, 6, 7, 9, 11, 14 and 17. They also bought a further nine horses bred by Ali Pasha Sherif, but not listed above.
52. Of these horses, Lady Anne eventually procured Bint Horra with her foal, A'zz*, Jamil and Johara*.
53. Aziz died on 22 December 1899.
54. Kasida* was by the bay Dahman Shahwan, Nasr, half-brother to A'zz*. Nasr by Aziz ex Bint A'zz, was one of the horses on Ali Pasha Sherif's sales list in 1889, with Mesaoud*, Merzuk* and Khatila*, and he could have been bought by the Blunts for £150. Nasr died 'of the eye'. His only descendants were Kasida*, Manokta and a colt ex Makbula.
55. Jellabieh's* dam is given as Bint Jellabiet-Feysul, the dam also of 'El Argaa' and of Merzuk*. However, if Feysul was own brother to Jellabieh, being by Ibn Nura and from the lame Jellabieh (El Argaa) as stated by Lady Anne Blunt, then Jellabieh is the daughter of El Argaa, not sister to her. Incidentally, the Crabbet Stud Book records Bint Jellabiet-Feysul as a white mare, whereas the Sheykh Obeyd Stud Books give her as chestnut. I believe she was chestnut.
56. Sahab, bought by Lady Anne, sired two fillies who were to prove of great importance in Egyptian breeding, namely Zareefa and Serra.
57. Mesaoud, Merzuk, Shahwan, (Ibn) Mahruss, Abu Khasheb, Feysul, Ibn Nura, Jamil, Sahab, Anta, Sherif, Khatila, Sobha, Safra, Bint Helwa, Ghazala, Bint Horra, Ghazieh, Fulana, Badiaa, Johara, Bint Nura II, Makbula, Jellabieh, Kasida, A'zz, Yemama, Manokta, Fasiha, Bint Fereyha, Bint Bint Jamila, Bint Jamila, Jamila and Aziza. In total, the Blunts bought ninety-nine Arab horses from the desert and Egypt between 1877 and 1913, and they imported fifty of them – thirty-three mares, fifteen stallions and two geldings.
58. He, like most horses of Crabbet blood lines, although four or five generations removed from the original Imported Horses, was a 50/50 mix of Desert and Ali Pasha Sherif blood; 25 per cent Mesaoud.
59. Sir William is sometimes given as Sir George Clay.
60. Doughty writes in *Wanderings in Arabia* about the sale of horses to India: 'Abu Nejm was a horse-broker for the Indian market … the horse brokers take up young stallions in the Arab tribes. We found Abu Nejm's few sale horses … in a field among the last palms north of the town [Aneyza near Boreyda] … each horse is tethered by a hind foot to a peg driven in the ground. Their fodder is green vetches (jet) and this is their diet since they were brought in lean from the desert, through the summer weeks, until the time when the monsoon blows in the Indian seas. Then the broker's horse droves pass the long northern wilderness, with camels bearing their water, in seventeen marches to Kuweyt, where they are shipped to Bombay.
61. The other principle dealers were Ibn Kurtass, Ibn Bedr, Ali Ibn Amr and Aid ed Termini, though possibly the last was only in the employ of Kurtass.
62. No wonder Jamsetjee is a very old man, for he is the same who had sent the gift of four highbred Arabs to Queen Victoria in October 1845.
63. Shere Ali was no doubt named after the Amir of Afghanistan (1868-1907) who fled Kabul leaving his son Yabuk Khan as Regent when Major-General Roberts advanced on Kabul. There was also a nephew of Shere Ali, one Abdur Rahman, not to be confused with the Bombay dealer Abdul Rahman, sometimes written as Abder Rahman or Abd er Rahman.
64. Hermit, a grey stallion, 15 hands 'of perfect beauty'. Purchased in Bombay 1857. Unbeaten race record in Bengal, but second to Greylag at Mysore. In February 1862 he won the Trades Cup beating the English Thoroughbred, Votige.
65. Hadeed sired two fillies ex Kesia II.
66. The Muntifiq were a powerful tribe inhabiting the right bank of the River Euphrates below Hillah in Iraq. Their sheikh was Ibn Saadun.
67. Mr Broadwood was later to visit the Blunt's Sheykh Obeyd Stud in Egypt.
68. According to Spencer Borden, Kesia II had three fillies by Mameluke – Mimosa, chestnut, 1893; Shabaka, chestnut, 1894 and another chestnut in 1895.
69. Vizier is not Ali Pasha Sherif's Wazir, but a bay horse foaled in 1879 at Urie by Posta, bought by Mr Baird in Egypt, ex Aida, the property of Mr Baird.
70. T.E. Lawrence was made an Honorary Member of the AHS.
71. Colonel Gilbert Clayton (later General) was Political Officer in Palestine and Military Supervisor of the Arab Bureau.
72. Ameen Rihani wrote a number of books about the Saouds and Arabia, and lived at one time in Earl's Court, London.
73. The stallion was Khaibar* mentioned later, and the mare Hannah* a flea-bitten grey Keheilet Ajuz.
74. Sheikh Mohammed Ibn Khalifa (1813-1890). In 1843 he drove out his great uncle Abdulla, and became ruler of Bahrain. His brother, Ali, was, in turn, to force him to flee the island, but only reigned for one year. Mohammed and his followers fought a battle at Rufa in which Ali was killed in an effort to regain power.
75. Colonel P.C. Joyce had earlier served as General Staff Officer, attached to the forces of Sherif Hussein of Mecca, with T.E. Lawrence.
76. The same tribe who had earlier bred El Emir* and Abbas Pasha Hilmi II's 'Venus'.
77. Ali Ibn Hussein, eldest son of King Hussein of Mecca, who, on the abdication of his father in 1924, reigned for some months before leaving Mecca to live in Baghdad.
78. Sheikh Jweibar, standard bearer to King Abdullah, writes in a memo to HM King Hussein of Jordan: 'As for the horses which came from the Hedjaz with us there were many of them (approximately seventy mares and stallions), and they were pure-bred Arabian horses.'
79. Lieutenant-General Habis El-Majali. Commander-in-Chief, Jordan Armed Forces was with King Abdullah when he was assassinated in the Great Mosque at Jerusalem on 20 July 1951.
80. This is why I have not included recent Egyptians and Jordanians as desert-bred horses, for although the Jordan horses in particular are 'of the desert', all contain the blood of imported stock.
81. Major Roger Upton, *Newmarket and Arabia* (1873).

Lists of the Horses Imported by the Blunts 1878-1910

Bold type indicates existing lines

Mares

Imported

1878	**Hagar**	Bay, 1872, Keheilet Ajuz (GSB Volume 14).
1878	**Dajania**	Bay, 1876, Keheileh Dajanieh (GSB Volume 14).
1878	**Sherifa**	White, c. 1862, Hamdanieh Simrieh (GSB Volume 14).
1878	**Jerboa**	Bay, 1874, Maneghieh Hedrujieh (GSB Volume 14).
1878	Tamarisk	Chestnut, c. 1867, Saadeh Tokan (GSB Volume 14). Sold at 2nd Crabbet Sale 1884 to Austria/Hungary.
1878	**Wild Thyme**	Bay, 1876, Keheilet Ajuz of Ras el Fedawi (GSB Volume 14).
1878	Burning Bush (Zenobia)	Chestnut, c. 1869, Keheilet el Krush (GSB Volume 14). Given away in 1884 to Honourable Miss Dillon.
1878	Damask Rose	Chestnut, 1873, Seglawieh el Abd (GSB Volume 14). Sold at 1st Crabbet Sale in 1882 to Viscount Hardinge.
1878	Purple Stock (Semiramus)	Bay, 1874, Keheilet Ajuz (GSB Volume 14). Sold at 1st Crabbet Sale in 1882 to Mr Danger, Australia.
1878	Bablonia	Bay, (Blot) 1875, Managhieh (GSB Volume 14). Died 1878.
1878	**Basilisk**	White, 1876, Seglawieh Jedranieh of Ibn ed Derri (GSB Volume 14).
1879	**Queen of Sheba**	Bay, 1875, Abeyeh Sherrakieh (GSB Volume 14).
1879	Francolin (Ferha)	Grey, 1875, Saadeh Tokan (GSB Volume 14). Sold at 1st Crabbet Sale in 1882 to Mr Dangar, Australia.
1881	**Meshura**	Bay, 1872, Seglawieh Jedranieh of Ibn ed Derri (GSB Volume 14).
1881	**Jedrania**	Bay, 1875, Seglawieh Jedranieh of Ibn Sbeyni (GSB Volume 14).
1881	**Dahma**	Bay, 1876, Dahmeh om Aamr (GSB Volume 14).
1881	**Rodania**	Chestnut, c. 1869, Keheileh Rodanieh (GSB Volume 14).
1881	Zefifia	Grey, 1873, Kabeysheh Zefifieh (GSB Volume 14). Sold at 4th Crabbet Sale in 1888 to Mr Harrison.
1881	Canora	Chestnut, 1874, Keheilet Ajuz of Nowak (GSB Volume 14). Sold at 1st Crabbet Sale in 1882 to Sir Donald Currie.
1888	**Jilfa**	Bay, 1884, Jilfeh Stam el Bulad (GSB Volume 17). Exported to Tunis.
1891	**Sobha**	White c. 1879, Hamdanieh Simrieh (GSB Volume 17). Exported to Russia. 1899.

Imported

1891	Safra Grey, 1885, Hamdanieh Simrieh (GSB Volume 17). Died 1893.
1891 (*in utero*)	Sefina Grey, 1892, Hamdanieh Simrieh. Dam – Safra*; sire – Mesaoud*. Sold 1901, repurchased and given away 1906.
1891	Khatila Chestnut, 1887, Keheileh Jellabieh (GSB Volume 17). Given away in 1909 to Mr Ruxton.
1891 (*in utero*)	(Unnamed) Chestnut, 1892, Keheileh Jellabieh. Dam – Khatila*; sire – Merzuk*;. Died at 1 month.
1891	**Ferida** Bay, 1886, Maneghieh Hedrujieh (GSB Volume 17).
1891 (*in utero*)	Fezara Chestnut, 1892, Maneghieh Hedrujieh. Dam – Ferida*; sire – Mesaoud*. Sold at 11th Crabbet Sale 1899 and exported to Russia..
1897	**Bint Helwa** White, 1887, Seglawieh Jedranieh of Ibn Sudan (GSB Volume 19).
1897	**Johara** Chestnut, *c.* 1880. Seglawieh Jedranieh of Ibn Sudan (GSB Volume 19).
1897	**Fulana** Brown, 1893, Seglawieh Jedranieh of Ibn Sbeyni (GSB Volume 19).
1897	**Bint Nura es Shakra** Chestnut, 1885, Dahmeh Nejiba (GSB Volume 19).
1897	Badiaa Chestnut, 1884, Dahmeh Nejiba (GSB Volume 20). Given away in 1903 to R. Gregory.
1898	**Makbula** White, 1886, Keheileh Jellabieh (GSB Volume 19). Exported to Russia.
1898	**Kasida** Chestnut, 1891, Keheileh Jellabieh (GSB Volume 19).
1898	**Jellabieh** White, 1892, Keheileh Jellabieh (GSB Volume 19; AHS Volume 1).
1898 (*in utero*)	Timsa Chestnut, 1899, Keheileh Jellabieh. Dam – Jellabieh; sire – Antar. Exported to Portugal. 1904
1909	**Ghazala** White, 1896, Seglawieh Jedranieh of Ibn Sudan (GSB Volume 22). Exported to USA.
1910	'Azz White, *c.* 1895, Dahmeh Shahwanieh (GSB Volume 22). Died 1916.

Note: All of these mares, with the exception of Bablonia, Timsa and the unnamed chestnut filly of Khatila's, were incorporated into the Crabbet breeding programme. Some proved infertile, and other lines died out.

THE ARAB HORSE

Stallions

Imported

1878		**KARS** Bay, 1874, Seglawi Jedran of Ibn Sbeyni (GSB Volume 14). Exported to Australia.
1878		DARLEY Bay, 1876, Keheilan Ajuz of Ras el Fedawi (GSB Volume 14). Sold at 1st Crabbet Sale in 1882 (gelded).
1878		SAOUD Grey, 1878, Hamdani Simri, imported with dam – Sherifa* (GSB Volume 14). Sold at 1st Crabbet Sale in 1882, exported to South America.
1878 (*in utero*)		PURPLE EMPEROR Bay, 1879, Keheilan Ajuz. Dam – Purple Stock*; sire – Kehilan Nowag. Sold at 1st Crabbet Sale in 1882 to H.C. Stephens
1879		**PHARAOH** Bay, 1876, Seglawi Jedran of Ibn ed Derri (GSB Volume 14). Exported to Russia.
1879		FARIS Grey, 1879, Sadan Tokan. Dam – Francolin*; sire – Kars*. Foaled in Egypt and imported with dam. Sold at 1st Crabbet Sale in 1882 to C.E. Tebbutt.
1881 (*in utero*)		JAMSHYD Bay, 1881, Seglawi Jedran of Ibn Sbeyni. Dam – Jedrania*, sire – Abeyan el Khudr. Sold at 2nd Crabbet Sale in 1884 to R. Broadwood.
1884		**RATAPLAN** Brown, *c.* 1874, Dahman om Aamr (GSB Volume 15). Imported from India. Exported to Egypt
1884		**HADBAN** Bay, 1878, Hadban Enzeyhi (GSB Volume 15). Imported from India. Exported to Australia.
1884		PROXIMO Bay, 1875, Kehilan Ajuz of Ibn Koreyssan (GSB Volume 15). Imported from India. Exported to Russia. Given away in 1887 to Count Joseph Potocki.
1884		ABEYAN Bay, 1869, Abeyan Sherrak (GSB Volume 16). Exported to Ireland 1885.
1888		**AZREK** Grey, 1881, Seglawi Jedran of Ibn ed Derri (GSB Volume 16) Exported to South Africa.
1888		**ASHGAR** Chestnut, 1883, Seglawi Obeyran of Saekh Tribe (GSB Volume 16). Exported to Gibraltar.
1891		**MESAOUD** Chestnut, 1887, Seglawi Jedran of Ibn Sudan (GSB Volume 17). Exported to Russia.
1891		**MERZUK** Chestnut, 1887, Keheilan Jellabi (GSB Volume 17). Exported to Africa.
1892		**SHAHWAN,** White, 1887, Dahman Shahwan (GSB Volume 17). Exported to USA
1892		RADBAN Grey, 1886, Seglawi. Gelded.
1892		EL TAFUK Chestnut. Gelded
1897		**(IBN) MAHRUSS** Chestnut, 1893, Dahman Nejib (GSB Volume 19). Exported to Ireland.
1898		ABU KHASHEB (Ibn Bint Nura) Grey, 1894, Dahman Nejib (GSB Volume 19). Full brother to (Ibn)Mahruss. Sold 13th Crabbet Sale 1901, and exported to India.
1898		IBN MESAOUD Chestnut, 1892, Keheilan Ajuz (GSB Volume 19). Dam – Saada. Sold in 1900 to R. Beddington, exported to South Africa.
1904		**FEYSUL** Chestnut, 1894, Keheilan Jellabi (GSB Volume 20).
1904		**IBN YASHMAK** Chestnut, 1902, Keheilan Jellabi (GSB Volume 20; AHS Volume 1). Exported to Egypt, 1920.
1904		IBN YEMAMA Bay, 1902, Keheilan Jellabi (GSB Volume 20). Sire – Feysul*. Sold to Colonel F.D. Murray – Baillie.

Note: The majority of these stallions, except Saoud, Purple Emperor, Jamshyd, Abu Khasheb, Ibn Mesaoud and Ibn Yemama, were used at Crabbet, but some proved infertile, others were considered not good enough, or sold on.

Lists of the Horses Imported by Other Persons 1830-1960

★ indicates a royal gift

Mares

Imported

1832		Fatima
1832		Sawyer's Ayesha
c. 1835		Sawyer's Seidee
1836	★	'The Flea-bitten Grey Mare' Presented by the Imaum of Muscat to HM King William IV.
1836	★	The Grey Mare 'The White Arabian Mare' Presented by the Imaum of Muscat to HM King William IV. Purchased at the Hampton Court Stud Sale in 1838 by Mr Pauncefoot-Duncombe, renamed 'Blood Royal'.
1839		Araby's Daughter Brown. Imported from Smyrna.
1840		The Boyd 'Venus' Pure Nejdi.
1842	★	Tsafelelts Mare Presented by the Sultan of Morocco to HM Queen Victoria.
1847	★	(4 Mares) From Egypt, presented to HM Queen Victoria.
1850	★	Dark Iron Grey Mare Thoroughbred, supposed to be from the desert. A gift from the Sultan of Morocco to HM Queen Victoria.
	★	Small Grey Mare Supposed to be from the Desert of Angad. Prized as of the desert breed. A gift from the Sultan of Morocco to HM Queen Victoria.
	★	Light Chestnut Mare Supposed to be from the Desert of Angad. Prized as of the desert breed. A gift from the Sultan of Morocco to HM Queen Victoria.
	★	A fourth Mare A gift from the Sultan of Morocco to HM Queen Victoria.
1862	★	Sultana Bay. Presented by the Maharaja of Mysore to HM Queen Victoria.
1862	★	Zuleika Bay. Presented by the Maharaja of Mysore to HM Queen Victoria.
1864		Two Arab Mares Imported from Aleppo by John Johnstone Esq. of Annandale.
1874		**Haidee** Chestnut, 1869, Maneghieh Hedrujieh (GSB Volume 13). Bought by Mr Skene, Consul of Aleppo, for Mr A. Sandeman.
1874		Zuleika Bay, 1870, Maneghieh Hedrujieh (GSB Volume 13). Bought by Mr Skene, Consul of Aleppo, for Mr A. Sandeman.
1875	★	'Flora' and 'Alma', two mares presented by the King of Italy to HM Queen Victoria.
1875		**Kesia** Bay, 1865, Kehileh Nowakieh (GSB Volume 13). Bought in Arabia by Major R. Upton for the Honourable H. Chaplin.
1875 *(in utero)*		**Kesia II** Bay, 1876, Kehilieh Nowakieh (GSB Volume 17). Dam – Kesia*; sire – Seglawi el Abd.
1875		Keren-Happuch Chestnut, 1866, Abayeh Sherrakieh (GSB Volume 13). Bought in Arabia by Major R. Upton for the Honourable H.Chaplin.
1875		Jemima Bay, c. 1870, Kehilieh Nowakieh. Bought in Arabia by Major R. Upton for Mr A. Dangar. Exported to Australia, 1875.
		Spiers Arab Imported by Lady Anne Spiers and sold to Mr Dangar. Exported to Australia.
c.1876		**Ishtar** White, 1871 (GSB Volume 15). Imported by Sir William Clay.
		Aida Bay, 1873, Hamdanieh Simrieh (GSB Volume 14). Bred by Ali Pasha Sherif and bought by Mr Baird. Dam – Mahroussa; sire – Wazir. Exported to Cadiz, 1881.
1881		Belkis Bay, 1874, Hamdanieh Simrieh (GSB Volume 14). Imported by Captain Tryon. Purchased at Aleppo.
1881		'Arabian Mare' (GSB Volume 16) Presented by the Khedive of Egypt to Mrs Layard, wife of the British Ambassador. Sold by her to Mr H. Lambton who imported her to England in 1881.
1881		'Arab Mare' Dark chestnut, Hamdanieh Simrieh. Bought in Cairo from a eunoch of Halim Pasha's, in foal, to Vizier. Given to Baron Leopold de Rothschild by Mrs Oppenheim.
		Sultana '1882' Abyenn-el-Rhodder Dam – Abyenn el Achmar (bay); sire – Kylann Gernook.
c.1885		'Polly' White, 1873 (PPSB Volume 4). Purchased by Mr S. Bennett in 1885, as a pure Arab. 14 hands. Later owned by the Keynsham Stud Company.

Imported

1896		'Abjar' Bay, 1887, Hamdanieh Simrieh (GSB Volume 20; PPSB Volume 2). Purchased through Pallanjee Hormusjee in Bombay in 1892 by Colonel E. Henriques. 13 hands 2¹/2 inches. Imported with her 2-year-old daughter Dilkushi.
1896		'Dilkushi' Grey, 1894, Hamdanieh Simrieh (GSB Volume 20. PPSB Volume 4). Dam – Abjar*; sire – The Tweedie Arabian. Imported with her dam.
1896		**Shakra** Chestnut, 1888, Kehilet Ajuz (GSB Volume 20). Purchased through Pallanjee Hormusjee by Colonel E. Henriques who imported her. Bred in Arabia. Prizes in 1903 and 1904. 14 hands 2 inches.
		'Grey Wings' A flea-bitten grey, aged (PPSB Volume 8). Prizes in 1903 and 1904. 14 hands 2 inches. Owned by Reverend D. Montefiore.
		'Ladybird' A pure-bred Arab. Imported from India by Colonel de Gallais, military secretary to the Governor of Bombay.
1901		'Farha' Chestnut, Wadneh Khursanieh. 14 hands 1 inch. Imported by Lieutenant-Colonel P.J. Melvill. In foal to a Ma'anaki Hedruj stallion.
1901		'Zuleika' (Norah) Chestnut, 1890, Maneghieh Hedrujieh. Dam – Rose, Chestnut 13 hands 3 inches by Shahab – a very handsome Arab ex a Beloochi mare.
1913	★	'Grey Tick' Grey, 1902 (NPS Volume 14). Imported from India. Purchased from the 10th Hussars in 1913 and owned by HRH Prince of Wales KG. 14 hands 1³/4 inches. Played polo in India and England.
		'Whiteface' Brown, 1901 (NPS Volume 14). Eastern bred. 14 hands 2 inches. Owned by Mrs Beal.
1921		**Mejamieh** Bay, 1912 (AHS Volume 2). Bred in the Hauran and imported by General Lance.
1921		**Libnani** Bay, 1919 (AHS Volume 2). Imported with her dam Mejamieh*.
1922	★	Jordania Grey. Presented by HM King Abdullah of Jordan to HM King George V.
1923		Petra Bay, 1919, Kehilet el Krush (AHS Volume 3). Bred by El Majali of Kerak and presented to Emir Abdullah. Given to Major General Sir H. Tudor. Destroyed 1930.
1923		'Lalla Rookh' Flea-bitten grey, 1913, Saadeh Togan (AHS Volume 3). Bred by Ibn Raschid and presented to Sherif Ali Haidar, late King of Mecca. 14 hands 2 inches. Died 1931. Imported at the same time as Nimr* and Atesh*.
1923		Shabaka Bay, 1923, Saadeh Togan (AHS Volume 3). Imported *in utero*. Dam – Lalla Rookh*. Sire – Mersud a Hamdani Simri.
c.1923		**Nejdmieh** Grey, 1914, Managieh Sbeyli. (AHS Volume 3). Bred by Sheikh Moubarak, Sebaa. Exported to Australia, 1925.
c.1923		**Nejma** Chestnut, 1914, Managieh Sbeyli (AHS Volume 3). Bred by Emir Ibn Raschid. Purchased by Major Parker in Constantinople.
1925	★	'A Grey Mare' Presented by the Sheikh of Bahrain.
1925		El Melha 'Evelyn' Grey, 1918, Kehilieh Dahareh (AHS Volume 4). Imported from Baghdad. Owned by Ali Ibn Hussein.
1927		Saileh Bay, 1922, Kehilet Ajuz (AHS Volume 4). Dam – Samrah by Hardan el Seglawi ex Najma; sire – Jacefni, Kehilan Ajuz.
1927		**Dafina** Grey, 1921, Kehilet el Krush (AHS Volume 5). Imported by Sir G. Clayton for Lady Wentworth from Ibn Saoud.
1928		**Noura** Bay, 1916, Maneghieh Hedrujieh (AHS Volume 4). Imported by Ameen Rihani. Bred at Ibn Saoud's stables. Exported to USA.
1928		**Muha** Bay, 1928, Maneghieh Hedrujieh (AHS Volume 4). Imported *in utero*. Dam – Noura*; sire – a Seglawi Jedran. Exported to USA.
		Negina
c.1930		Kohaila Bay, 1923, Kehilieh Kahtan (AHS Volume 4). Presented to Mrs F. Holmes by Ibn Saoud. Bred in Nejd. Sire – Shawaff.
c.1930		Husn Chestnut, 1927, Kehilieh Sweitieh (AHS Volume 4). Bred by Ibn Saoud. Sire – Hamdani Ghayran.
1934		Mandilah Bay, 1926, Kehilieh Junathniah (AHS Volume 5). Bred by Mohammed Al Barghash, Karkhiyah, Saniyah, Shahraban in North Iraq. Dam – Keh Junathniah of the Shammar; sire – Keh-Nowag.
c.1935		**Jamila I** Bay, 1927, Kehilet (AHS Volume 5). Bred by Sabhar Mohammed of Khraison in Iraq. Sire – Seglawi.
c.1937		**Warda al Badia** Chestnut, 1924, Seglawieh (AHS Volume 5). Bred by Sheikh Ali Karim of the Khurassa, Shammar. Dam – White Seglawieh; sire – Bay Keheilan.
1937	★	**Turfa** Flea-bitten grey, 1933, Kehilet al Khorma (AHS Volume 6). Presented by Emir Saoud to HM King George VI. Exported to USA.
1937	★	'Faras' Bay, 1927, Kehilet el Krush (AHS Volume 6). Presented by Emir Saoud to HM King George VI. Sire – Kehilan (AHS incorrectly states Abayan). A mare of exceptional quality. Later owned by Miss Lyon. Died 1941.
c.1937		'Attiyat Shammar' Bay, 1930, Kehilet al Wadaj (AHS Volume 5). From Khilil Ibrahim Jaddwe, Shammar. Sire – Seglawi.

Imported

c.1939		**Mahawiliyah** Grey, 1935, Kehilet Ajuz (AHS Volume 6). Bred by Sheikh of Ali Yisar, Hilla, Iraq. Sire – Managhi.
c.1939		**Takritiyah** Chestnut, 1935, Juaithneh Hamad (AHS Volume 6). Bred by Sheikh of Abu Nissar.
1939		**Nuhra** Bay, 1936, Kehilet Wadna Khursan (AHS Volume 6). Presented to the Earl of Athlone and bred by the Sheikh of Bahrain.
1939		Hannah Flea-bitten grey, 1934, Kehilet Ajuz (AHS Volume 6). Presented to the Earl of Athlone on 11 March 1938 by the Crown Prince of Saoudi Arabia.
c.1946		'Tura'a' Flea-bitten grey, 1930, Jilfa (AHS Volume 7). Bred by Sayid Salmon Ibn Sayid Ahmed of Baghdad. Sire – Managhi. Owned by S.F. Smith.
c.1951		'Sabahia' (Bright and Swift) Chestnut, 1950, (AHS Volume 8). Bred by Sheikh Abdul Rezak in Baghdad. Desert bred. At the age of only 22 months she was ridden 70 miles to be given as a present to Mrs Beardmore.
c.1952	★	Karakesh Chestnut, 1940, Kubaisha (AHS Volume 8). Presented to HM The Queen by El Mejali, Mayor of Kerak. Sire – Shainan. Faza'at Unwan Managieh. Dam – A Ma'anagiyah mare; sire – Al'ahel.
c.1955		**Shammah** Grey, 1950, Kubeysha (AHS Volume 8). Bred by Dlewan Pasha Al Majali in Jordan. Imported by Mr Santiago Lopez.
c.1958		**Nawagiyat at Furat** 'Desert Song' Grey, 1944, (AHS Volume 9). Bred by Muhammed Said al Rashid Hussay, Falluja in Iraq. Dam – Nowagiyah; sire – King of Orient. Owned by Captain R. Sheekshanks.
1958	★	**El Yamama** 'Dove' 1953, Um Arkoub. Bred in Jordan and presented by HM King Hussein of Jordan to HM the Queen. Dam – Lo'ba; sire – Ubayan.
1958	★	**Princess Muna** Grey, 1958, Um Arkoub (AHS Volume 9). Imported *in utero*. Dam – 'Dove'*; sire – Samih.
c.1958		**Thrayat Hamid** Bay, 1953, Keheileh (AHS Volume 10). Bred at Latifiyah by Kudhai yir Rashid and imported from Baghdad by the Honourable A.J. Watson.
1960	★	**Shams** Grey, 1955, Muniqieh (AHS Volume 10). Presented by Lieutenant-Colonel Habis el Majali to HM Queen Elizabeth, the Queen Mother. Dam – Mi'Enaqia; sire – Abu Argub.

Note: Other mares including Aida, Zuleika, Keren-Happuch, Lalla Rookh and Jemima were used in breeding pure-Arabs, but their lines have died out.

Stallions

Imported

c. 1830		**PADISCHAH** Grey, 1826. A gift from the Sultan of Turkey. Exported to Germany, 1838.
1830		ORELIO Bay. From Nejd. Bred by a Wahabi sheikh and procured through the Sheikh of Bahrain by a Bombay prince. Imported by Colonel Short.
c. 1830		ELGIN ARABIAN
c. 1830		PADAN ARAN
c. 1830		ATTWOOD'S GREY ARABIAN
c. 1830		ATTWOOD'S CHESTNUT ARABIAN
		PARAGON 1820. Imported from India.
		BOXKEEPER Grey, 1825. Imported from India. Ran in thirty-three races and won twenty-one.
		FITZ ORELIO Bay, 1826.
		BUCKFOOT Grey, 1827. Imported from India. Winner of races. 14 hands 2 inches.
		SIGNAL Fleabitten grey 1825/8. Imported from India and sent by Captain Maclean of 13 Light Dragoons to his friend the Honourable Arthur Cole, Scotland. The winner of numerous races in Madras. 14 hands.
c 1830	★	(2 stallions) A chestnut and a dark chestnut. Presented by the King of Oude to HM King William IV.
		HONESTY Imported from India.
		HAMDANIEH Imported from India. 14 hands 2 inches.
		HARLEQUIN
		CHAMPION
		MUSCAT
		FAIR PLAY
		MAHOMED 'Palmerston's grey Arab'
c 1833		BIJOUX Grey Arab, owned by Mr C. Turner.
1836	★	(HORSES) A gift from the Imaum of Muscat to HM King William IV.
1836	★	SULTAN 'The Black Arabian' Black. A gift from the Imaum of Muscat to HM King William IV. Exported to the Weil Stud of the King of Württemberg, Germany in 1837.
1836	★	'THE BAY ARABIAN' Bay. A gift from the Imaum of Muscat to HM King William IV. Exported to France, 1837.
1836	★	'CHESTNUT COLT' Chestnut, 1836. Imported *in utero* ex 'the flea-bitten mare', Imaum to King William IV. Sold to Mr Rigg.
c 1837		ABEIAN Bay Colt, 1836. Abayan. Bred by Mohammed Ibn 'Aoun, Sherif of Mecca, in Cairo. Dam: El Abeieh, a white mare from Mecca. Sire: Gerboa, a white horse of Abbas Pasha I. Imported by Colonel Vyse.
1838	★	(6 HORSES) A gift from the Imaum of Muscat to HM Queen Victoria. Sent via Bombay.
1839	★	(HORSES and FOALS) A gift from the Imaum of Muscat to HM Queen Victoria.
		ABDALLAH White. An Arab horse of purest caste, owned by Mr P.D. Pauncefoot Duncombe of Brickhill Manor, Bucks.
1840	★	IMAUM White. A gift from the Imaum of Muscat to the Prince Consort.
1840	★	MUSTAPHA Bay. A gift from the Imaum of Muscat to the Prince Consort.
1840	★	(HORSES) A gift from the Imaum of Muscat to HM Queen Victoria.
c. 1840		HECTOR Grey. Arab.
c. 1842		GAZELLE
	★	TAJAR Grey. Owned by the Prince Consort.

Imported

1845	★	KHORSEED	White. A gift from Sir Jamsetjee Jejeebhoy of Bombay to HM Queen Victoria.
1845	★	SERAB	White. A gift from Sir Jamsetjee Jejeebhoy of Bombay to HM Queen Victoria.
1845	★	(HORSE)	White. A gift from Sir Jamsetjee Jejeebhoy of Bombay to HM Queen Victoria.
1845	★	(HORSE)	White. A gift from Sir Jamsetjee Jejeebhoy of Bombay to HM Queen Victoria.
	★	JEMSCHEED	Grey, 1840 (possibly one of the above). A gift from India to HM Queen Victoria. Exported to the Weil Stud, Germany, 1847.
1845	★	SIR ROBERT GILLESPIE'S small grey Arab. Imported from Calcutta, India, to England, a gift to the Prince Regent.	
1846	★	(7 HORSES) A gift from the Bey of Tunis to HM Queen Victoria.	
1846	★	(HORSES) A gift from Mehmet Ali to HM Queen Victoria.	
1847	★	(8 HORSES) A gift from the Imaum of Muscat to HM Queen Victoria.	
1847	★	(4 HORSES) A gift from Egypt to HM Queen Victoria.	
1847	★	ABDALLAH Grey, 1843. A Gift from the Pasha of Egypt to HM Queen Victoria.	
c. 1847		ALIWAL Black/bay. Sir Harry Smith's charger.	
c. 1849		THE CRAWSHAY BAILEY ARABIAN owned by Mr Crawshay Bailey. Merthyr Tydfil.	
		SIR EDWARD Grey. The property of John Whyte Melville.	
c. 1849	★	IMAUM Grey, 1844. A gift from the Imaum of Muscat to HM Queen Victoria.	
1849	★	IBRAHIM Grey, 1844. A gift from the Imaum of Muscat to HM Queen Victoria.	
1849	★	ZANZIBAR Grey, 1844. A gift from the Imaum of Muscat to HM Queen Victoria.	
1849	★	MUSCAT Chestnut, aged. A gift from the Imaum of Muscat to HM Queen Victoria.	
1850		(5 STALLIONS and 4 MARES) A gift from the Sultan of Morocco to HM Queen Victoria. (see Mares list).	
c. 1850		**SAJDEN** Chestnut horse bred in the desert and imported to England. Purchased with Beduin by Count W. Branicki from Aschton a dealer in London and exported to Balocerkiew, Poland 1850.	
c. 1850		BEDUIN Grey horse bred in the desert and imported to England. Purchased with Sajden by Count W. Branicki from Aschton a dealer in London and exported to Balocerkiew, Poland 1850.	
1850	★	(4 GREY STALLIONS) 2, 1845; 2, 1846. A gift from the Imaum of Muscat to HM Queen Victoria.	
c. 1850		**INDJANIN** White. Bought from the Viceroy of India. Exported to Poland, 1855.	
1852	★	SAID Brown, 1846. A gift from the Imaum of Muscat to the Prince Consort. Exported to the Weil Stud, Germany, 1857.	
1852	★	(GREY STALLION) A gift from the Imaum of Muscat to the Prince Consort.	
c. 1854		WHITE BOY Grey Turkish Arab, 1850. Purchased in Constantinople, 1854. Died aged 21.	
c. 1855		**NIZAM** (Indjanin II) Grey horse bred in the desert and exported to India. Imported to England and purchased in London for Slawuta, Poland in 1859, under the name Indjanin. Sold to the Branicki's, who renamed him NIZAM to avoid confusion with the other Indjanin (see above).	
c. 1856		OMAR PASHA Bay horse of 15 hands. Imported after the Crimean War by Sir Richard Airey, who had been presented with the horse by the Turkish General. Omar Pasha. Later Airey sold him to Lord Spencer, who after standing him at Althorpe, gave him to Mr J. Noble Beasley of Pitsford House.	
c. 1856		COLONEL KENT'S CHARGER. Bay, c. 1839. Imported after the Crimean War.	
c. 1859		SEGLAVI III ('Black Arabian') Imported from India to England, then sold to Slawuta, Poland in 1859.	
c. 1860		**MAHMOUD MIRZA** Dark bay 1851 Seglawi Jedran. Bred by the Anazeh. Exported to India, then to England where he was purchased by Count Bathyani for Babolna, Hungary 1866.	
c. 1860		OPAL Grey. Won a prize at Islington, 1862.	
c. 1862		A Bay Arab 1854. Bred by a Sheikh of the Wahabees and purchased in Baghdad by Sir Henry Rawlinson KCB. Exhibited in London 1864. 14 hands 3 inches.	
c. 1862		A Grey Arab of the purest Nejd breed, purchased in India. Exhibited in London 1864 by Mrs H. Turnbull. 14 hands 3 inches.	

Imported

c.1864		ARAB Grey. Owned by James Henry Legge Dutton, 3rd Baron of Sherborne.
c.1867		FARHAN Bay Arab Stallion, 1862. Bred by the Anazeh and purchased through the British Consul in Damascus. Exhibited in London 1869 by Lady Anne Spiers and won first prize. Later purchased by Mr Dangar and exported to Australia. 14 hands 3 inches.
c.1867		A Black Arab, owned by Major Adrian Hope and exhibited in London 1869. "His pedigree traced from a filly once ridden by the Prophet Mohammed". 14 hands 2 inches.
1867	★	KOUCH Grey, c.1860, Seglawi Jedran (GSB Volume 17). A gift from the Sultan of Turkey to the Prince of Wales, 9 September 1867, from the desert between the towns of Baghdad and Mosul.
1867	★	ILDERIM A gift from the Sultan of Turkey to the Prince of Wales.
1867	★	DERWICH A gift from the Sultan of Turkey to the Prince of Wales.
1867	★	KAPLAN A gift from the Sultan of Turkey to the Prince of Wales.
c.1870		MAGDALA Grey Arab, imported from Egypt, by Mr J. Clayworth of Birmingham, who exhibited him in London 1872. 14 hands 3 inches.
c.1870		MINUET A celebrated Calcutta Arab race-horse. Imported by John Johnstone of Annandale c.1870. Hunted with Sir Watkin Wynn's Hounds. J. Johnstone also imported two Arab mares in 1864 (see Mares list).
1871	★	ALEP A bay horse, acquired by M. Kent, the British Consul in Aleppo for the Prince of Wales. Purchased in 1877 by Count Konstanti Branicki for Uzin, Poland.
1874		**YATAGAN** Chestnut, 1870, Kehilan (GSB Volume 13). Purchased by Mr Skene, Consul of Aleppo, and imported by Mr A. Sandeman.
1874		GREY COLT Grey, 1870, Managhi Hedruj. Purchased by Mr Skene, Consul of Aleppo, and imported through Major R. Upton.
1875	★	ESSED Chestnut, 1869.
	★	DIARBEKER Chestnut, 1869. Two stallions a gift from the King of Italy to HM Queen Victoria (see Mares list).
c.1875	★	AKBAR Bay horse bred in the desert. Imported to England from India by the Prince of Wales. In 1879 he was purchased by Prince Roman Sanguszko the Younger for Slawuta, Poland.
1875		GOLD DUST A red gold chestnut Arab, 1871. Imported from India by Colonel Montgomery-Moore, who had bought him from Colonel T.A. St. Quintin of 8/10 Hussars for 800 rupees. Sold at Tattersall's Sales in 1891.
1875		ALIF Brown, 1871. Purchased in Arabia by Major R. Upton for Mr Dangar. Exported to Australia, 1875.
1875		JOKTAN Bay, 1871, Kehilan Tamri (GSB Volume 13). Imported by Major R. Upton for the Honourable H. Chaplin.
1875		ISHMAEL Bay, 1873, Seglawi Jedran (GSB Volume 13). Imported by Major R. Upton for the Honourable H. Chaplin.
c.1875	★	**HUSSAR** chestnut. A gift from India to the Prince of Wales. Exported to Poland, 1878.
c.1878		NOBBLER Grey, c.1868, Kehilan. Owned in India by the Honourable Algernon Moreton of 15. Hussars, and sold to Captain Fletcher of 12. Hussars. Later in the ownership of Sir William Gordon during the Crimean War, who sold him to General Laurenson, who imported him at 20 years old to England. Later he was sold to the Duke of Liechtenstein.
c.1880		GARRON A white Arab (PPSB Vol. 1) Imported.
c.1880		SELIM An Arab (PPSB Vol.3) owned by Mr Hulton-Harrop.
c.1880		POSTA Chestnut, 1867/8 (GSB Volume 14). Bought by Mr Baird in Egypt from General Stanton.
1880		**EL EMIR** Bay, c.1873, Managhi (GSB Volume 15). Bred by Dehemed Ibn Zoba of Shammar. Imported by the Honourable Miss Dillon from Algeria.
c.1880		CALIPH Dark bay. Desert-bred. Imported from India. Owned by the Honourable Miss Dillon. Exported to South Africa, 1889/90.
c.1881	★	HALEBI A Kehilan Nowag. A gift from Ali Pasha Sherif to the Prince of Wales.
1881		KING PIPPIN Dark bay 1875 (GSB Volume 16. PPSB Volume 2). Sire - Kehilan. An Arab imported to Ireland in 1881 by General Magenis, having purchased him in Bombay in 1879 from Abdul Rahman Minée Byculla. Owned by J. Stuart MD. Ballymena.
1881		CHERUB Flea-bitten grey, Kehilan (GSB Volume 16). Bred in Nejd by chief of Kahatan tribe and sent to Abdul Rahman in Bombay. Owned by Sir R.D. Cunyngham, 1885. 14 hands 2 inches.

THE ARAB HORSE

Imported

1881		ASIL Bay, 1881, Hamdani Simri. Imported in utero. Dam – Belkis; sire – Blunt's Abeyan. Purchased in Aleppo by Captain Tryon.
		MAHOMET Grey (GSB Volume 15). Presented by the Khedive to Lady Rivers Wilson.
		GIMCRACK Flea-bitten grey (GSB Volume 15). Bought at Tattersall's by Mr F. Barne.
		AMEER Bay (GSB Volume 1). A very well bred Arab, imported from India by Captain Little of the 9th Hussars. 13 hands 3 inches. Owned by W.L. Pilkington.
		ARABI Brown, aged (PPSB Volume 1). Imported. Winner of several races. 14 hands. Owned by E.A. Warren, County Meath.
1883		EUPHRATES Chestnut. Imported by Mr Kennedy from Bombay in 1883 and purchased of Abdul Rahman for 1,000 rupees. Sold in 1885 to Mr Baird of the 10th Hussars.
		ALI BABA Grey. 14 hands.
1884		EL DORADO Chestnut, 1878 (GSB Volume 15). Imported by the Honourable Miss Dillon. Bought in 1882 from Abdul Rahman of India. Sold in 1888.
1884		**KISMET** Chestnut, 1877 (GSB Volume 16). Imported by Mr Broadwood from India. Bred by the Muntifiq. Sold to Sir R.D. Cunyngham.
1884		DICTATOR Bay, 1878, Abeyan. Imported by Abdul Rahman of Bombay. Sent from Shammar, said to have been sold at the 2nd Crabbet Sale in 1884 to Mr Brown.
c.1884		KARA KOUCH Black. Of the Sultan's breed. Owned by Lord Strathnairn.
c.1884		WANDERER Bay. Owned by Major McCall.
c.1885		KHALIF Bay, 1879 (GSB Volume 16). Brought from Nejd by Yazoom bin Feyde to Abdool Rezak's, Bombay, in November 1884. Owned by Sir R.D. Cunyngham, 1885.
1885		HADBAN II Brown (GSB Volume 17). Imported by Mr J. Hallan, General Superintendent of Horse Breeding Operations, India. Dam – an Anazeh mare; sire – a Hadban.
1885		HAMDANI Brown (GSB Volume 17). Imported by Mr J. Hallan. Dam – Anazeh mare (cousin to Hadban's dam); sire – a Humdassi.
1885	★	YILDIZ Grey (GSB Volume 17). A gift from the Sultan of Turkey to George, Prince of Wales. Stood at Sandringham and Cumberland Lodge.
c.1886		ARAB A brown Arab (PPSB Volume 6). Owned by Mr Henry, Kylemore Castle, County Galway. 15 hands.
c.1886		ESAU Grey, 1882, Kehilan Ajuz (GSB Volume 16). In Mr Vidal's Stud. Sold at the 5th Crabbet Sale in 1889.
1886	★	ABEYAN A gift from the Sultan of Muscat to HM Queen Victoria.
1886	★	TERRAFI A gift from the Sultan of Muscat to HM Queen Victoria.
1886	★	SHOO-AF-AN A gift from the Sultan of Muscat to HM Queen Victoria.
1886	★	JESSCAN A gift from the Sultan of Muscat to HM Queen Victoria.
1886	★	TERRASSAN Bay, 1879 (PPSB Volume 1). A gift from the Sultan of Muscat to HM Queen Victoria and presented by her to the Congested Districts Board of Dublin. 14 hands 2 inches.
1886		MAGIC Grey, 1881 (GSB Volume 17; PPSB Volume 1). Imported by Captain M. Hayes from India. Dam – high-caste Nedj Arab. 14 hands. Magic won races in India, and 15 races in Britain. 3rd Hurlingham 1891 and 1st Liverpool. A very good Polo pony, in the winning County Cup Team 1889. Owned by W.S. Walker.
1886/7		UMPIRE Chestnut, aged, 1885, Kehilan (GSB Volume 17; PPSB Volume 3). From Anazeh to Bombay in 1886 by Ali bin Amir. Colonel Wise bought him from Mr T.S. Kennedy and sent him to UK. 14 hands 1 inch. Very good Polo pony. Purchased from Earl of Harrington by N. Haig.
1887		**MAIDAN** Chestnut, c.1869 (GSB Volume 16). Imported from India. Bought from Abdul Rahman of Bombay. 15 hands.
1887		PEDETENTIM Chestnut, 1884 (PPSB Volume 1). Imported from India. Winner of races. In 1892 to Ireland with Captain G. Wynne, Royal Irish Rifles. Later owned by Mrs Gore-Booth, County Sligo. 13 hands 2 inches.
1887		JEBEL SHAMMAR Chestnut, Kehilan Krush (GSB Volume 17). Imported by Mr J.H.B. Hallan from India. 14 hand $3^{1}/_{2}$ inches.
1887		KEHILAN ABEYEH Bay, Kehilan um Arqub (GSB Volume 17). Imported by J.H.B. Hallan. Bought from Mohammed bin Shamlan. Dam – Kehilet um Argoob; sire – Abeyen Sherrak.

Imported

1887		SHAMMAR Chestnut (GSB Volume 17). Imported by Mr J.H.B. Hallan. Bred by the Shammar. Of high caste.
c.1888		**MAMELUKE** chestnut, c.1884 (GSB Volume 17). Imported by Lord Herbrand Russell from India.
1888		SINBAD Grey. Imported from Cairo by Mr J.R. Walker in 1888, after a fifteen-day journey across the desert from Syria.
1888		SALADIN Chestnut. Imported from Cairo in 1888 and owned by Mr P. Hargreaves.
		SOLOMON Imported from Egypt and owned by Mr R. Walker
1888		GREY DAWN Grey, c.1884 (GSB Volume 17; PPSB Volume1). Imported by Colonel F.J. Wise, for Mr J.S. Kennedy, from India. Arab of high caste. 14 hands 1 inch. Owned by the Earl of Harrington.
1888		SIR ROBERT White, 1878 (PPSB Volume 1). Imported from India. Winner of flat and races over country. 14 hands 2 inches. Owned by Sir Hide Trafford Bart.
c.1888		ACKBAR An Arab stallion, sire of the grey Welsh GREYFRIARS 16 ex a pure-bred Arab (WSB Volume 1. Section B).
c.1889		AZARET Grey, 1885 (PPSB Volume 2). A Syrian Arab bought by J.H. Stock MP, in North Africa, 1889. 14 hands. Very good Polo pony and capital hack.
		FIREFLY Grey, aged (PPSB Volume 2). An Arab owned by Major A. Green-Thompson, 6th Dragoons. 14 hands 1 inch.
c. 1889		ISMAIL Dark bay, aged (PPSB Volume 2). Imported from Egypt. 14 hands. Owned by B.R. Glover.
c.1889		PRIMUS Grey, aged (PPSB Volume 3). Imported from Egypt. Purchased from Captain Whitla. 14 hands 1 inch. Owned by Tresham Gilbey.
1890		STARLIGHT Grey. Imported from India by Mr Rawlinson in 1890. Purchased by HRH The Duke of Clarence. Winner of many races in India and played polo. A high-caste Arab.
1890		RAINBOW Imported from India by Mr Rawlinson in 1890. a high-caste Arab.
c.1890		BLITZ (Lightning) White. Imported from India by Lord William Beresford. Later exported back to India. 13 hands.
c.1890		THE BEY Bay, 1886, Tahawi bred (PPSB Volume 3). Bred in Arabia. Played Polo. 14 hands ½ inch. Owned by G. Norris Midwood.
c.1890		Arab Stallion owned by Sir Pryse Pryse Bart. Sire of a bay Welsh mare 1892 (WSB Volume 1. section A).
c.1890		ST MIRIN Bay, 1885 (PPSB Volume 2). Imported from India. Pure-blood Arab. 13 hands 3 inches. 3rd Polo Derby Madras 1889. Played Polo. Owned by The Lady Susan Brown.
c.1890		SULTAN Dark chestnut, aged (PPSB Volume 2). Imported from Egypt. Bought by Captain le Gallais in Cairo. 14 hands 1¾ inches. A good Polo pony.
c.1890		ALGIERS (Bledah) Grey, aged (PPSB Volume 2). Imported from Algiers but bred in Syria. Owner, Lord Charles Bentinck. A well-known polo pony. 14 hands 1 inch.
		TANGIERS Grey (PPSB Volume 2). A Syrian, well-known polo pony. Owner, Lord Charles Bentinck. 14 hands 1 inch.
		PEREGRINE Grey, 1886 (PPSB Volume 3). Imported from India. An Arab and winner of races. 13 hands 3 inches. Owned by F.W. Evans.
c.1890		DESERT BORN Bay, 1885 (PPSB Volume 1). Dam – Kehilet Ajuz mare; sire – Arab. A good polo pony owned by the Congested Districts Board, Dublin. 14 hands.
c.1890		BOMBAY CHIEF Bay (PPSB Volume 1). An Arab imported from Egypt. 15 hands.
c.1890		THE KHAN Brown, 1888 (PPSB Volume 5). A pure-bred Arab imported by HRH The Duke of Connaught. 13 hands.
1891		**MOOTRUB** Chestnut, 1887 Seglawi Jedran (GSB Volume 20; PPSB Volume 1; AHS Volume 1). Imported from Calcutta by Mr R.S. Henderson, who bought him from General Sir John Hills RE. Bred in Arabia. 14 hands.
		PPC Imported Arab (WSB Volume 1 Section B). Sire of 308 Emlyn Beauty (HSB 1487).
		ORA Bay. Imported.
c.1891		MARQUIS Grey, 1883 (PPSB Volume 1). Imported from Bombay. Bred by Abdulla bin Faris, a native of Arabia. 14 hands. True desert-bred pony. Won over 30 races in Bombay 1888-90. 1st Ranelagh 1891.
c.1891		SUSPENSE Bay. 1889 (PPSB Volume 1). Imported from India. Winner of races, including hurdle and steeplechases. 13 hands 3 inches. Good polo pony, owned by J.H. Hampson.
c.1891		THE PRIEST Grey (PPSB Volume 1). Arab owned by E.D and G.A. Miller.

Imported

	SCIMITAR Grey, 1885 (PPSB Volume 3). Imported from Bombay. Pure Arab of Montefik bedouin sent to Bombay in 1889. Owner, Sir R.D. Cunyingham Bart. 14 hands 2 inches.
	SUNSHINE Chestnut, 1885 (PPSB Volume 3). Imported. Landed in Bombay from Arabia in 1889. Formerly owned by HH Aga Khan. Owner, Sir R.D. Cunyingham Bart. 14 hands 1½ inches.
c.1891	THE SYRIAN Bay, 1885 (PPSB Volume 3). Bred in the East (in Highland pedigrees). 14 hands 1½ inches. Owned by J.H. Munro-Mackenzie, Isle of Mull.
c.1891	WHITE ROSE Grey, aged (PPSB Volume 3). An Arab purchased by Captain le Gallais of the 8th Hussars and from him got by W.R. Court. 14 hands.
1892	KAHELAT Grey, 1887, Kehilan al Musanah (GSB Volume 17). Brought from the Ateba to Nejd by Sulaiman bin Jamas. Purchased of Abdul Rahman Badar from Ali bin Amer's stables, by Mr J. Hallan, for Sir W. Gilbey.
1892	HUZZOR Chestnut, 1887 (PPSB Volume 1). An imported Arab. 14 hands 1 inch. Owned by T.E. Brandt.
1892	ORION Bay, 1889 (PPSB Volume 4). Bred in Arabia. Owned by A. Mitchell.
1892	MUSCAT Chestnut, (PPSB Volume 4). An Arab. 14 hands.
	NIMR Arab.
1893	VONOLEL White, 1875 (GSB Volume 18). From the Nejd. Purchased from Abdul Rahman of Bombay in 1877 by Lord Roberts.
1893	SHALUFZAN Bay, 1889 (GSB Volume 18). Purchased by the Maharanee of Dholpur in Bombay in 1892. Imported by Lord Roberts in 1893.
1893	SAHOWLEE Bay, aged (PPSB Volume 2). An Arab. 14 hands ½ inch. Owned by A.D. Hussey-Freke.
c.1893	ARABI PASHA Light bay, 1886 (PPSB Volume 1). An Arab imported from Ceylon by Mr Campbell of the Gordon Highlanders. Exceptionally fast, good polo pony, owned by R.A. Richardson, County Antrim.
1893	KHALIFA Imported c.1893 by Mr Drybrough.
1893	THE RAKE Bay. Imported in 1893 by Mr Drybrough.
1893	BIMBASHI Grey. Imported in 1893 by Mr Drybrough.
1894	STAR OF INDIA Bay, 1888 (GSB Volume 18; PPSB Volume 2). A pure-bred Arab. Imported in May 1894 by Captain N. Franks who bought him in 1892 from Ali bin Amir of Bombay, and sold him to Sir R.D. Cunyingham. 14 hands 2 inches.
1894	SODA Iron Grey, 1889 (PPSB Volume 2). Imported from Cairo in October 1894 by F.S. Cayzer, 7th Dragoons. 14 hands 1½ inches. Owned by F.C. Muriel.
c.1894	ELIJAH Chestnut. A Polo pony in the 12th Lancers Club. Ridden by Mr F. Wormald.
c.1894	SEAGULL White, aged (P&RPS Volume 7). An Arab of the highest caste. Imported from Cairo by Colonel Bannister. Winner of races in Egypt. Played Polo in Inter-Regimental Tournaments in 1894/5. Ridden by Captain Wise. Owned by Reverend T. Powell. 14 hands 1 inch.
	EL EMIR Chestnut (PPSB Volume 3). Major P.T. Gascoigne.
	GREYFRIARS Grey, 1890 (WSB Volume 1). Dam – pure-bred Arab; sire – Ackbar. 13 hands 1 inch.
1895	TRUE BLUE IV Grey, 1886 (GSB Volume 18). From the stables of Ommer Jamal in Bombay, for Sir Charles Pritchard who sold him to the Aga Khan, who sold him to Mr Burder, who imported him. 14 hands 2 inches.
1895	STREET ARAB Chestnut, 1889 (PPSB Volume 3). Imported by H. Jasper Selwyn in April 1895 from Bombay. 13 hands 3 inches.
c.1895	HAPPY LAD White, aged (P&RPS Volume 8). Owned by Captain Renton, 17th Lancers in India and sold on 11 March 1890 for R 1,550. 14 hands 2 inches. Later owned by Arthur Tree.
c.1896	OSMOND Grey Arab Pony. 13 hands 3 inches.
c.1896	Grey Arab owned by Captain Douglas Haigh, having been presented to him by Sir Pertab Singh. Played Polo at Ranelagh in 1897 ridden by No 2. Kumwar Dokhul Singh.
1896	NAHILA Iron Grey, 1892 (PPSB Volume 4). Dam – Abjar*; sire – An Arab imported with dam by Colonel E. Henriques (see Mares list).

Imported

c.1897	MECCA	Grey, aged (P&RPS Volume 7). Pure Arab. Played Polo in India and also raced. Owned by C.D. Miller. No. 2. All Ireland Polo Cup 1897. Sold to F.W. Chance. 14 hands 1½ inches.
c.1897	MODENA	Chestnut Arab. Played Polo in India. Owned by C.D. Miller.
c.1898	KHALIFA (SULTAN)	Grey, 1891 (PPSB Volume 5). Syrian Arab. Ridden by Sir W. Gateacre in the Egyptian Campaign. Bought, Cairo and sold to the Lords Cecil. 14 hands 2 inches.
1899	CUNNINGHAM	Grey, aged (P&RPS volume 9). Purchased at 4 years old by General Cunningham as a charger. Bought by Colonel Gorringe in 1894 and ridden in Dongola and Soudan Expeditions, 1897/8. Exported from Khartoum. Owned by Sir Walter Gilbey. 14 hands 2 inches.
c.1899	MAHARAJAH	White. Imported from Egypt c.1899 by General J. Seely and used as his charger from 1899 to 1901 in the South African Wars.
c.1899	KHALID	Grey, aged (P&RPS Volume 7). An Arab. Winner of races in India and Egypt. Sold to Captain Alex Campbell. 14 hands 1 inch.
1900	**ROHAN**	black. 1890/2 (GSB Volume 20; P&RPS Volume 7; AHS Volume 1). Presented by Messrs Schwimmer of Budapest to Mr Calthrop. Sent to the Sultan of Turkey in 1898 from the Province of Baghdad.
1900	MARZOUK	Grey, c.1893 (GSB Volume 20; P&RPS Volume 10; AHS Volume 1). Bred in Mosul in the sub-tribe of Shammar from a famous mare of Sheikh Abu Osman of the Al-Hai. Sire – Shimar desert-bred. Imported by Mr Calthrop. Sold to Radowce of the Austro-Hungarian Government in 1907. 14 hands 2 inches.
1900	YAKOUB	Chestnut, 1894 (P&RPS Volume 11). Bred by Abdul Raman Pasha of Mecca, Damascus. Owned by Robert Crane. 14 hands 1½ inches.
1900	SULTAN	Dark chestnut (PPSB Volume 6). Arab imported to Bombay c.1896. Winner of races. Hollow on forehead. Owned by James Heap. 13 hands.
1900	ABAYAN KOHEILAN	Chestnut, 1894 (P&RPS Volume 7). Bred by Anasi Hamdaur Symbi Nagd. Dam – Djemmah (bay, 14 hands, by Abou Harkoub, chestnut, 14 hands 1½ inches); sire – Derwiche (chestnut, 14 hands 1 inch). Owned by J.R. Dixon. 14 hands 2 inches.
1900	ARNAB SACLAWI	Chestnut, 1895 (P&RPS Volume 7). Winner of races in Egypt 1899 – 1900. Owned by J.R. Dixon. 14 hands 1 inch.
1900	TAALEB GEBALAWI	Grey, 1896 (P&RPS Volume 7). Purchased from a bedouin in Egypt. Owned by J.R. Dixon. 14 hands 1 inch.
1900	BLUE BLOOD	Arab of highest caste, owned by Captain C.R. Burn (also owned Seagull).
1900	RAJAH	Chestnut, Owned by Mr G. Hardy.
	JOSS	Chestnut. Imported by General Davis. Found in circus in Cairo. Owned by Mr J. Watson MFH.
1900	SATCHEDON	Chestnut. Given to Mr Bulkre by Lord Charles Beresford. All his stock grey.
1900	BEDOUIN	Chestnut. Owned by Mr W.H. Walker.
c.1900	MAGIC SPELL	Bay horse brought from Bombay by Mr F. Graham. Taken as a Polo Pony by W.J. Drybrough.
c.1900	SHABA	Grey polo pony owned by Mr C. Adamthwaite.
1901	**DWARKA**	Bay, c.1892 (GSB Volume 25; P&RPS Volume 7; AHS Volume 1). Bred in the Arabian desert by Clan Anazai. Imported to India in 1897. 14 hands 1½ inches.
c.1901	BASHOM (The Fox)	Dark chestnut, 1892 (P&RPS Volume 7). Sire and dam, high caste Arabs. Bred by Ibn Alre Rashid, Sheikh of the north branch of the Roala tribe. Wounded at Omdurman. Galloped 50 miles out afternoon with dispatches. First rate Polo pony. Imported from Egypt in August 1901 by Captain W. Smythe VC. Queen's Bays. Owned by Honourable Mrs Ives.
1901	GHATAS	Grey horse, January 1901 (iiu) (P&RPS Volume 10). Wadnan Khursan. Dam – Farha*; sire – Ma'anaki Hedruj-white (see Mares list). Owned by Lieutenant-Colonel Melvill. 14 hands 1½ inches.
1901	EL HAKEEN	Chestnut, 1896 (P&RPS Volume 7). Syrian Arab purchased from Hassan Mohsen Bey in Alexandria. Owned by Dr. R. Lang. 14 hands ½ inch.
1901	MUTAPPAH	Brown, 1892 (P&RPS Volume 7). Pure-bred Arab imported by Captain C.L. Graham, 4th Hussars. 13 hands 3 inches.
1901	PARAHK	Chestnut (P&RPS Volume 7). Brought from India by Captain Honoré de Montmorency VC during the Soudan campaign. Owned by F.W. Barling. 14 hands.

Imported

	MAHMUD Chestnut, 1892 (P&RPS Volume 8). Purchased in Damascus. Went through Atbara, Omdurman and three years in South Africa, never sick or lame. Owned by the Marques of Tullibardine, Scotland. 14 hands 2 inches.
	KISMET Bay, 1897 (P&RPS Volume 8). Imported from Cairo by 'The Bays'. Good polo pony. 14 hands 1½ inches.
	HADBAN Brown (P & RPS Volume 8). Commended, Eastern Sires, 1903 P&RPS London Show. Owned by A. Alexander. 14 hands 1 inch.
	MARENGO White, aged (P & RPS Volume 8). Dam – Arab; sire – Arab. 3rd, Eastern Sires, 1904, London Show. Owned by Mr Heaton. 14 hands.
	MUSTAPHA Grey, 1896 (P & RPS Volume 8). Pure-bred Arab imported by Viscount Helmsley from Bombay, said to have been bred at Aleppo. Played polo. 14 hands ¼ inch.
1902	**NEJDRAN** chestnut, 1896, Seglawi Ubayran. Imported from the desert by Captain Gainsford. Exported to USA, 1904.
1902	BRIGAND Bay, 1896 (P & RPS Volume 9). Imported from India. Bred by Ali bin Taleb of Jeddah, Arabia. Winner of fourteen races. Owned by J. Scott. 13 hands 3 inches.
	HADBAN Grey, 1899 (P&RPS Volume 9). Imported from Egypt for Major G.T.G. Edwards, 20th Hussars. 14 hands 1½ inches.
c.1903	ARAB The Duke of Connaught's. Left two sons on Exmoor.
1906	RADIUM Chestnut, 1901 (AHS Volume 1). Purchased from Ibrahim Bey Sultan, in Cairo, 1905. Raced as a 4 year-old. Owner R.B. Colton Fox. Died 1928.
1906	ALADDIN Bay, 1900 (P & RPS Volume 10). An Arab pony 1st, Eastern Sires, London Show, 1908, beating Lal-i-Abdar, Astraled and Feysul*. Owned by Colonel A. Bailward. 14 hands 2 inches.
	SOUDAN Bay, aged (P & RPS Volume 10). Bred by the Sultan of Morocco and presented to one of his ministers, who sold him to Lord Aberdour at Gibraltar. 14 hands 2 inches.
	BARINGI Grey, aged (P & RPS Volume 11). Bred in Egypt. Won prizes in Cairo. Owned by D. Haward Evans. 14 hands 2 inches.
	THE TURK Flea-bitten grey, 1897 (P & RPS Volume 12). Reputed to be a pure Syrian Arab. Imported from Cairo. Played in Inter-Regimental Polo at Hurlingham 1906-8. Registered as Welsh Section C Stallion (Volume 10). Owned by A.E. Hamar, Shropshire. 14 hands 2 inches.
	CLAREMONT Grey, 1902 (P & RPS Volume 11). Bred in Arabia. Imported into Bombay by Ali bin Taleb. Owned by F. Graham. 14 hands 2 inches.
	VINO TINTO Chestnut, 1900 (P & RPS Volume 11). Imported from Aleppo in 1903. Polo player and winner of races in Malta and Egypt. Owned by Rear Admiral C. Cradock RN. 14 hands.
1908	**MUSKET** Bay, 1900 (P & RPS Volume 11; AHS Volume 1). Imported from India by Lieutenant-Colonel H.M. Abud. Winner of races in India. 1st Arab Stallions, Bombay, 1906. 3rd, Eastern Stallions, London, 1909. Owned by Lieutenant-Colonel H.M. Abud. 13 hands 2¼ inches.
c.1910	**ZOOWAR** Grey, aged (P & RPS Volume 12; AHS Volume 1). Imported from India. Bred in Arabia. Won races in India. 14 hands 1 inch.
1911	FANTASIA White, 1901 (P & RPS Volume 12). Bred in Egypt imported in June 1911. Winner of six races. 1st, Khartoum, 1911. 3rd, London, 1912. Stood in Pembrokeshire. Owned by Captain H. Thwaites. 14 hands 2½ inches.
1911	SALADIN II Bay, Hamdani (GSB Volume 22). Bred by Shammar Toga Tribe and purchased by Crabbet in 1911 from Mr T. Learmouth who brought him from Damascus. Exported to Egypt in 1913.
1912	★ NEPAL Chestnut, Imported from India.
c.1912	EL ZOBA Bay, Hamdani, Arab owned by Captain J. Straker. Carried 14 stone hunting. Very fast, good stayer. Ridden with troops. Stud fee 3 guineas. 14 hands 2 inches.
	NEW MINISTER Flea-bitten grey, aged (NPS Volume 13). Pure-bred Arab. Bought from Major-General H.H. Sir Pertab Singh, Maharajah of Idar. Won several races and prizes. Owned by the Earl of Minto. 14 hands 2 inches.
1914	SAHARA Grey, 1909 (NPS Volume 15). Bought in Morocco in 1914, but from Algeria in 1912. Owned by Mrs D. Aldridge. 14 hands 3¼ inches.

Imported

*c.*1915		LITTLE CHIEF Arab.
*c.*1915		**CROSBIE** Grey, 1908 (NPS Volume 14; AHS Volume I). Bred by an Arab in Syria and brought to Cairo. Won races, 1913-14. 14 hands 2 inches.
1916		CHANDI (Silver or Moonlight) Grey, 1911 (NPS Volume 14; AHS Volume 1). Imported from India. Desert bred. Called by the Arabs 'Azil Glat' (Of the first water). Owned by Mrs F.G. Atkinson, leased by Mr Musgrave-Clark. 14 hands 1½ inches.
		ARAB Flea-bitten grey, aged (NPS Volume 15). 15 hands.
*c.*1918		AKBAR Dark bay. Imported by General J. Seely. Frank Seely, his son, used him as a charger during the First World War.
		FITZ Bay, 1908 (AHS Volume 1). Imported from Egypt by Major G.T. Williams.
1919	★	SOUEIDAN Black, 1912 (AHS Volume 1). Bred by HH King Hussein of the Hedjaz and presented to HM King George V.
1919	★	SOUEIDAN EL SAGHIR Black, 1915 (AHS Volume 1). Presented by HH King Hussein of the Hedjaz to the Prince of Wales.
1919	★	KOWEIT Bay, 1914 (AHS Volume 2). Presented by Sheikh Ahmed Ibn Jabir of Kuwait to HM King George V.
*c.*1920		POLESTAR White, Desert Arab. Owned by Miss Bright, Oxfordshire.
*c.*1920		NORTHSTAR Imported Arab.
1920	★	SHEIKH Bay. Presented by Sheikh of Kuwait to the Prince of Wales.
1922	★	ABDULLAH Bay. Presented by HM King Abdullah of Jordan to HM King George V.
		EMIL FEISUL Flea-bitten grey, 1912, Managhi Hedruj (AHS Volume 2). Sire – Dahman Shahwan. Presented to the Marchioness of Salisbury by HH Emir Feisul, King of Iraq. Bred by the Al-Issa Tribe.
1922		SHWAIMAN Chestnut, 1913 (AHS Volume 2). Imported by King Feisal of Iraq and presented to Lord Hartington. Dam – Al Shwaima; sire – Seglawi Jedran. Later given to Lady Wentworth.
1922		KOHEILAN Flea-bitten grey, 1912, Kehilan Wati (AHS Volume 3). Bred by Emir Ibn Raschid of Nejd. Presented to HH Sherif Prince Abdul Mejid and sold to Major G.H. Barker.
*c.*1923		**MIRAGE** White, 1919, Seglawi Dalia. Bred by the Anazeh and bought from the Denadsha tribe by King Feisal of Iraq. Exported to USA, 1930.
*c.*1923		**ATESH** Chestnut, 1913, Managhi Sbeyl (AHS Volume 3). Bred by the Gomussa tribe of Sebaa Anazeh and given to Enver Pasha.
*c.*1923		**NIMR** Brown, 1914, Seglawi Jedran (AHS Volume 3). Bred by Prince Mohuiddin, son of Sherif of Mecca.
		MABROUD Grey, 1907 (NPS Volume 18). Imported from India by N.W. Muir. Played polo. 14 hands 2 inches.
1924		FELUJA Brown, 1916, Seglawi Jedran (AHS Volume 3). Bred by Fedaan, Anazeh. Purchased in Feluja. Owned by Major G.H. Barker.
*c.*1924		MENEBHI Black, 1910. Imported from Tangiers. Bred by Sidi Mehdi el Menebhi. Owned by Major S.A. Medcalf TD.
1925	★	'BAY' STALLION Presented by the Sheikh of Bahrain, and given to Lord Lonsdale.
*c.*1926		**FEDAAN** White, 1913, Seglawi Jedran (AHS Volume 3). Bred by Ibn Sbeyni of the Fedaan. Bought in Damascus.
*c.*1927		**OUTLAW** Liver chestnut, 1915, Kehilan Ajuz (AHS Volume 4). Imported from Cairo by E.W. Sheffield.
1928		MASOUD Bay, 1923, Hamdani Simri (AHS Volume 4). Imported by Ameer Rihani who was sent the horse by Ibn Saoud from Haïl to Damascus.
*c.*1929		GUERGOUR Grey, 1922. Imported from Algeria. Bred by Amor Bey Thadj, Malkomak, Constantine. Dam – Khadia; sire – Agha. Owned by Mrs M.A. Bromwich.
1930		IBN KUHAILAN White, 1919, Dahman Amr (AHS Volume 4). Bred by Sheikh Fahd Beg al Khadhal. Dam – mare owned by Dhari, Sheikh of Zauba; sire – Kuhailan. Imported by Colonel P.C. Joyce. Exported Kenya.
1935		IBN SAUD Bright chestnut, 1932. A desert-bred Arab, owned by Mr Bernard Dixon.
*c.*1936		MOONSHINE Chestnut with silver mane and tail, 1933. Dam – Molly – Arab pedigree untraced; sire – Mamaluke – a desert-bred Arab. Bred by M. Borak, Mena, Cairo.
1937	★	**MANAK** chestnut, 1928, Hamdani (AHS Volume 6). Presented to HM King George VI by Emir Saoud, son of King Ibn Saud.
1937	★	**KASIM** Bay, 1934, Seglawi (AHS Volume 6 incorrectly lists him as Abayan). Sire – Abeyan. Presented to HM King George VI by Emir Saoud. Bred by Ibn Sweid of the Ajman.

Imported

	TALAL Liver chestnut, 1931, Kehilan el Ayala (AHS Volume 6). Bred by Mr Trouncer in Egypt. Dam – Hegazieh of Nejd originally the property of Emir Hussein of Mecca. Taken to Cyprus and later exported to Egypt; sire – Ibn Rabdan, liver chestnut, 1917. Owned in UK by Miss P. Ismay.
c.1938	An Arab Stallion Chestnut. Imported from India by Sir James Marshall, Cornwall. 14 hands 3 inches.
c.1938	**RESH al BADIA** Chestnut, 1928, Seglawi (AHS Volume 7).
c.1938	ENIGMA Grey, 1928, Abeyan (AHS Volume 5). Bred by Sheikh Ead Ibrahim abu Irgayig of the Tayaha tribe and sold to Mr A. Bertrand, late French Consul of Jaffa. Dam – Abeyeh; sire – Kehilan-Ajuz.
c.1938	SURGAN Grey, 1928, Kehilan Ajuz (AHS Volume 6). Imported after racing and polo in Egypt and India. Bred by a bedouin tribe of Arabia. Owned by Captain H. Priestley, King's Dragoon Guards.
1939	KHAIBAR Bay, 1934, Kehilan Ajuz (AHS Volume 6). Presented to the Earl of Athlone by Emir Saoud on 11 March 1938. Dam – a Kehilet Ajuz of Abdul 'Ala, Chief of the Al Asama of Oteybeh. Owned by Brigadier W. Anderson CBE, and later by the Barton Stud.
1939	BAHRAIN Bay, 1936, Kehilan Al Musannieh (AHS Volume 6). Presented to the Earl of Athlone by the Sheikh of Bahrain. Sire – Kehilan Jellabi. Owned by Brigadier W. Anderson CBE, and later Mrs W. Noble.
c.1945	EL WAHID Red chestnut, 1934, Seglawi Jedran (AHS Volume 7). Dam and sire desert-bred. Owner Mrs J. Monk.
c.1945	JORDAN Chestnut, 1938, Seglawi Jedran (AHS Volume 7). Bred by Sheikh Abou Sarar of Kerak of the Majalieh tribe. Owned by Miss M. Broderick, Wales.
c.1945	RAQI al HUSSUM White, 1936, Seglawi el'Abd (AHS Volume 8). Bred in Baghdad. Sire – Hadban Abu. Owned by Miss de Beaumont.
c.1945	ACRE PASHA Bay, 1939, Seglawi Jedran (AHS Volume 7). Bred by the Governor of Palestine. Dam – Selma DB; sire – Mash'Hur.
1952	★ MLOLSHAN A Stallion presented to HM Queen Elizabeth for her Coronation, by the Emir of Bahreyn, Sulman Bin Hamed Al Khalifa.
c.1953	SAHIL Chestnut, 1942, Neget (AHS Volume 8). Gelded. Owned by Mrs D. Mackay.
c.1953	FORMIDABLE Grey, 1945, Hamdani (AHS Volume 8). Bred by Muhamed al Gatie of the Albu 'Assaf tribe. Sire – Managhi Sbaili. Owned by Miss M. Bright.
	SAHAB II Grey, 1946.
c.1953	SABAH Grey, 1946 (AHS Volume 8). Bred by the Sheikh of Amara in Baghdad. Gelded. Owned by Mrs T. Banks.
1958	AMAL al SIBAQ 'Arganout' Bay, 1944 (AHS Volume 9). Bred by Hadi al Hindi, Mahmudiyah, Iraq. Dam – Kuhaileh; sire – Violence. Gelded. Owned by Mrs R. Wright.
	★ SURPRISE 'Mufaja' Presented to HM The Queen.
	ABU 'Redoubtable' Bay, 1957. Ma'anagi. Imported in utero. Dam – Faza'at Unwan*; sire – Formidable*. Owned by Captain A. Large. (see Mares list). Gelded.
1958	★ SHAMIKH 'Pride' 1955, Manakhi. Presented to HM The Queen by HM King Hussein of Jordan. Dam – M'enakeya; sire – Ik'heilan.
c.1960	GALI Bay, 1953 (AHS Volume 10). Bred by the Inshass Stud in Egypt. Dam – Galia; sire – Hammam.
1960	★ COMAR Chestnut, 1954 (AHS Volume 9). Presented to HM Queen Elizabeth, the Queen Mother by Lieutenant-General Habis el Majali, C in C Jordanian Armed Forces. Dam – DB; sire – Saglaowi.
1960	★ **SHAMYL** Grey, 1961, Muniqi (AHS Volume 10). Imported in utero. Dam – Shams*; sire – Qaied. Presented to HM Queen Elizabeth, the Queen Mother by Lieutenant-General Habis el Majali. (see Mares list).
Note:	Other stallions such as Sultan, Beduin, Kouch, Akbar, Vonolel, Ackbar, Marzouk, Yildiz, Posta and Chandi were used at stud for the breeding of pure Arabs, but their lines have since died out.

EXISTING LINES

These written descriptions are based on the Crabbet Stud Books compiled by Lady Anne Blunt, in the case of the Blunts' Horses, and on entries in the General Stud Book, National Pony Society and Arab Horse Society Stud Books, in the case of the Other Horses.

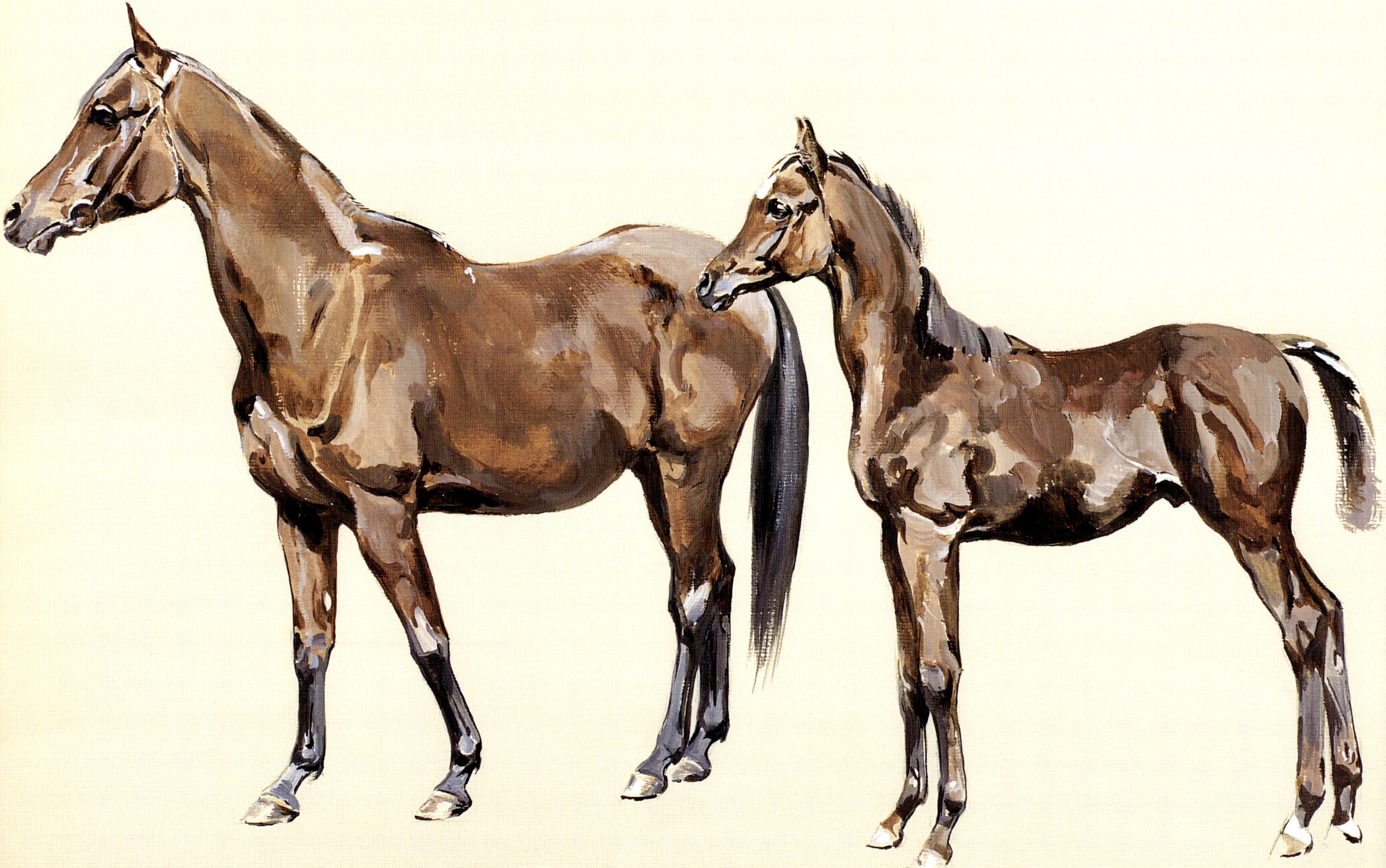

The Blunts' Original Mares

JEDRANIA

A Seglawieh Jedranieh of Ibn Sbeyni's strain.

A bay mare foaled in 1875.

Bred by Ali Agha, a Kurd of Deyr, who purchased her dam from Aslan Pasha, then Governor of Deyr, to whom Abd er Rajak Jerba gave her as a bribe.

Dam	A grey Seglawieh Jedranieh of Ibn Sbeyni's strain of the Mehed tribe of the Fedaan Anazeh.[1] She was captured with thirty-four other mares about the year 1866 by Abd er Rajak Jerba. This was at the time of Aslan Pasha to who Abd er Rajak gave the thirty-five mares. The Pasha sold them all and, at the sale, Ali Agha, formerly of El Melieh and now of Deyr Hafa, bought the grey Seglawieh. He has her still. She is now twenty-five years old (foaled in 1856) and can only eat Ajim (dough). She has produced three foals while in the present owner's possession.
Sire	A bay Kehilan Nowag of the Jarweyzi of the Moayaja tribe of the Sebaa, Anazeh.
Sale	Purchased with her bay colt foal [Jamshyd] at 12 days old, from her breeder Ali Agha, on 20 April 1881, at Aleppo, for £244.
Description	A bay mare with black points, no white except for a small star, fine large head well set on, magnificent shoulder, long neck, quarter like Kars.
Height	14 hands 2 ½ inches.
Girth	70 ¼ inches.
Below knee	7 ¼ inches.

Jedrania was imported in 1881, sold at the 3rd Crabbet Sale in July 1886 to the Honourable Miss Dillon for 95 guineas and given by her to H.C. Stephens, Esq. in 1898.

Jedrania is one of the few remaining specimens of Ibn Sbeni's strain of Seglawieh Jedranieh. Sahij Ibn Sbeni, the head of the family and his brother Hauran, who have their tents together, have three mares and a two-year-old colt. Jamshyd, (her colt) foaled April 8 1881 at Deyr, by an Abayan El Khuddr of Ibn Goblan, of the Weldi tribe.

◄ *Jedrania with colt foal Jengis Khan*

GSB Volume 14
Imported 1881

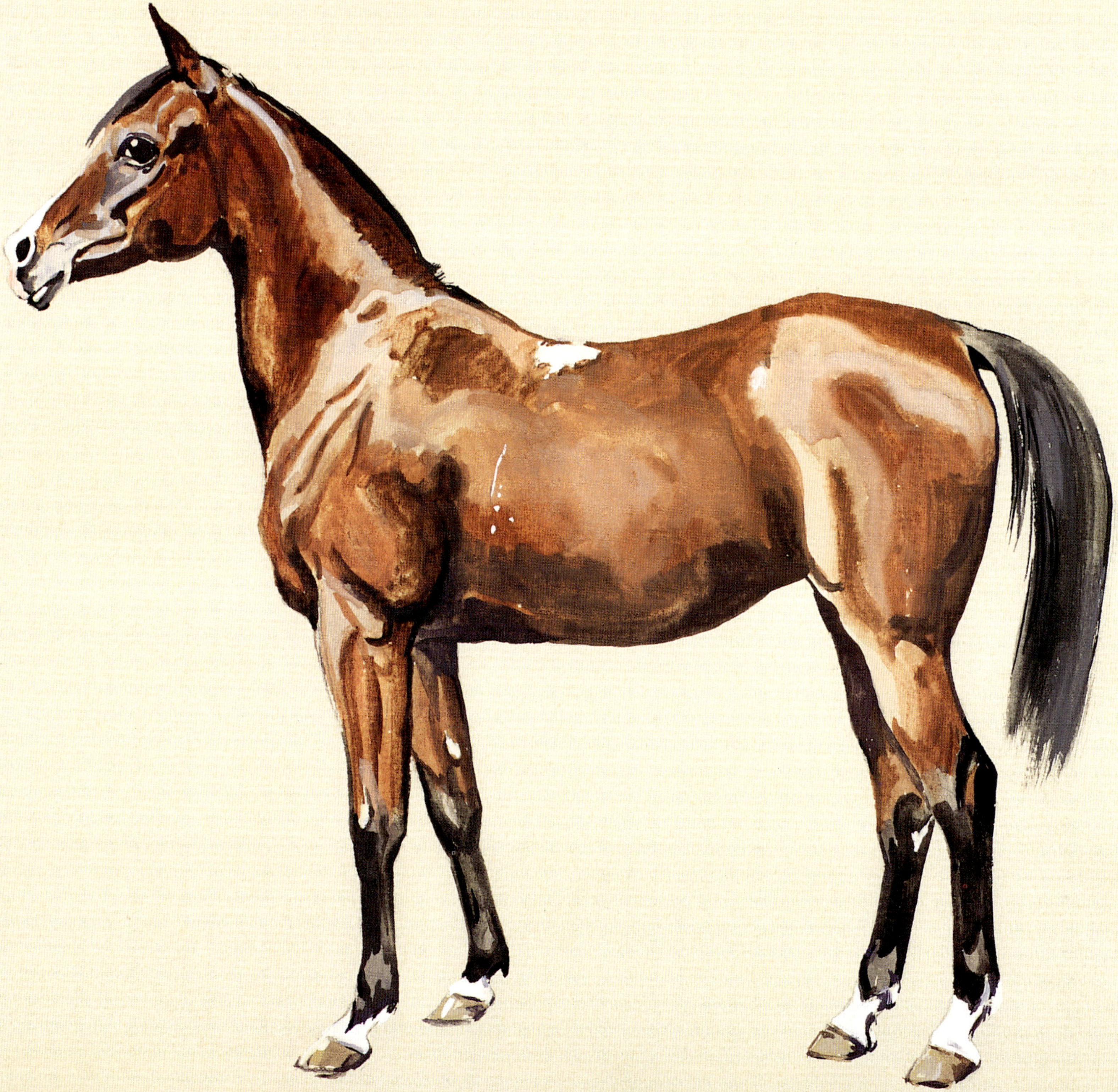

MESHURA (HAJEYLA)

A Seglawieh Jedranieh of Ibn ed Derri's strain.[2]

A bay mare foaled in 1872.

Bred by Sheikh Berghi Ibn ed Derri of the Resallin, related to the Gomussa tribe of Sebaa Anazeh.

Dam   A bay Seglawieh Jedranieh of Ibn ed Derri's strain belonging to Sheikh Berghi of that family.

Sire   A bay Managhi Hedruj of Ibn Sbeyel's strain. A celebrated horse.

Sale   Purchased by Ali Pasha, then Governor of Deyr, from her breeder, in 1879, on the Euphrates, then purchased from him in 1881, at Aleppo, for £240. Half-sister to Pharaoh through the dam. Ali Pasha had her pedigree written out, and attested by the seals of her breeder and other prominent personages of his tribe, for several generations, including mention of the mare purchased by Abbas Pasha I, Viceroy of Egypt. Mr Henderson, Consul of Aleppo, wrote of her as 'Sheikh Fadel's celebrated mare', the mare being sister to the stallion (Pharaoh) bought for us and a very great beauty and as having been purchased lately by the Governor of Deyr for £Turkish 100 and 40 camels, a ridiculous price [more than £600].[3] Afet and Meshur both say Ali Pasha's mare is better than the chestnut (Azrek's dam).

Description   A bright bay mare with four white feet and blaze ... a well-shaped head and fine eye and a beautiful crest. Remarkable carriage of tail. A celebrated mare of great reputation among the Bedouin.

Height   14 hands 1 inch.

Girth   67 inches.

Below knee   7 1/4 inches.

Meshura was imported in spring 1881. She was shot in March 1899.

◀ *Meshura*

GSB Volume 14
Imported 1881

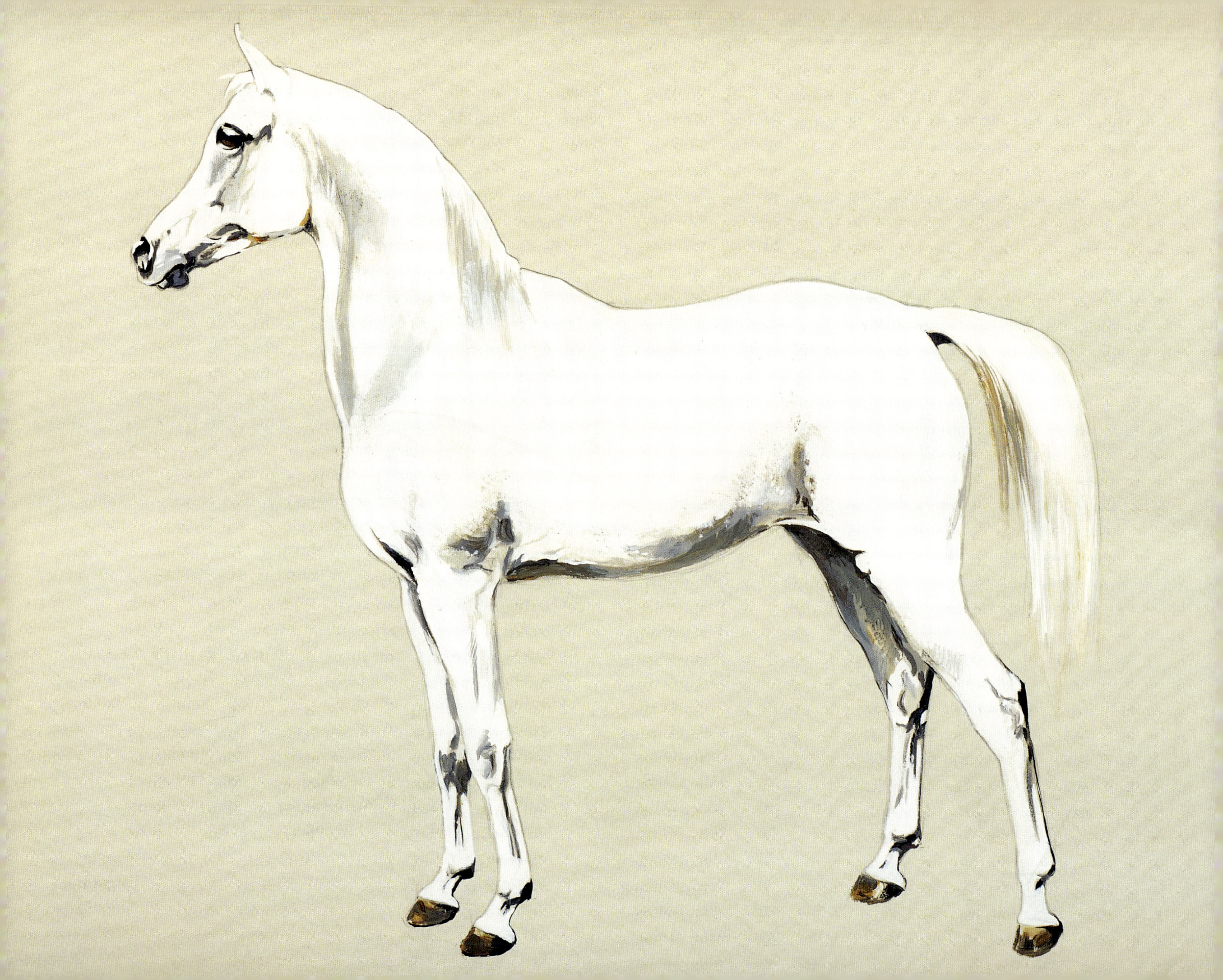

BASILISK

A Seglawieh Jedranieh of Ibn ed Derri's strain.

A white mare foaled in 1876.

Bred by Abd el Jadir of Deyr (Euphrates).

Dam   A white Seglawieh Jedranieh of Ibn ed Derri, stolen, in 1873, from a bedouin of the Abadat tribe of the Sebaa, to whom Neddi Ibn ed Derri had sold her on shares, by Faris Assat who sold her to Abd el Jadir. Neddi Ibn ed Derri of the Resallin, Gomussa said that this was so.

Sire   Said to be a bay Seglawi Jedran of the same strain.

Sale   Purchased by Mr Skene from her breeder, in February 1878, for £75.

Description   Grey with black skin and hoofs, then white and finally flea-bitten. Great power, up to any weight, good head and small muzzle, very fine shoulder, drooping quarter but tail carried like a feather in the air. Lady Anne often likened other horses to Basilisk – in India 1883: 'I liked Fairy King a flea-bitten white with wonderful head, jibbah especially, the smallest of muzzles – like Basilisk in general aspect', or at Ali Pasha Sherif's Stud in 1888: 'the white one like Basilisk which really seems the pick of the whole. White horse Seglawi Jedran by Wazir's son Ibn Nadir ... very perfect and strong. Head also fine.'

Height   14 hands 1 inch.

Basilisk was imported in 1878. She was sold on 5 September 1884 to the Duke of Westminster for 100 guineas. She died of liver disease in 1895/6.

GSB Volume 14
Imported 1878

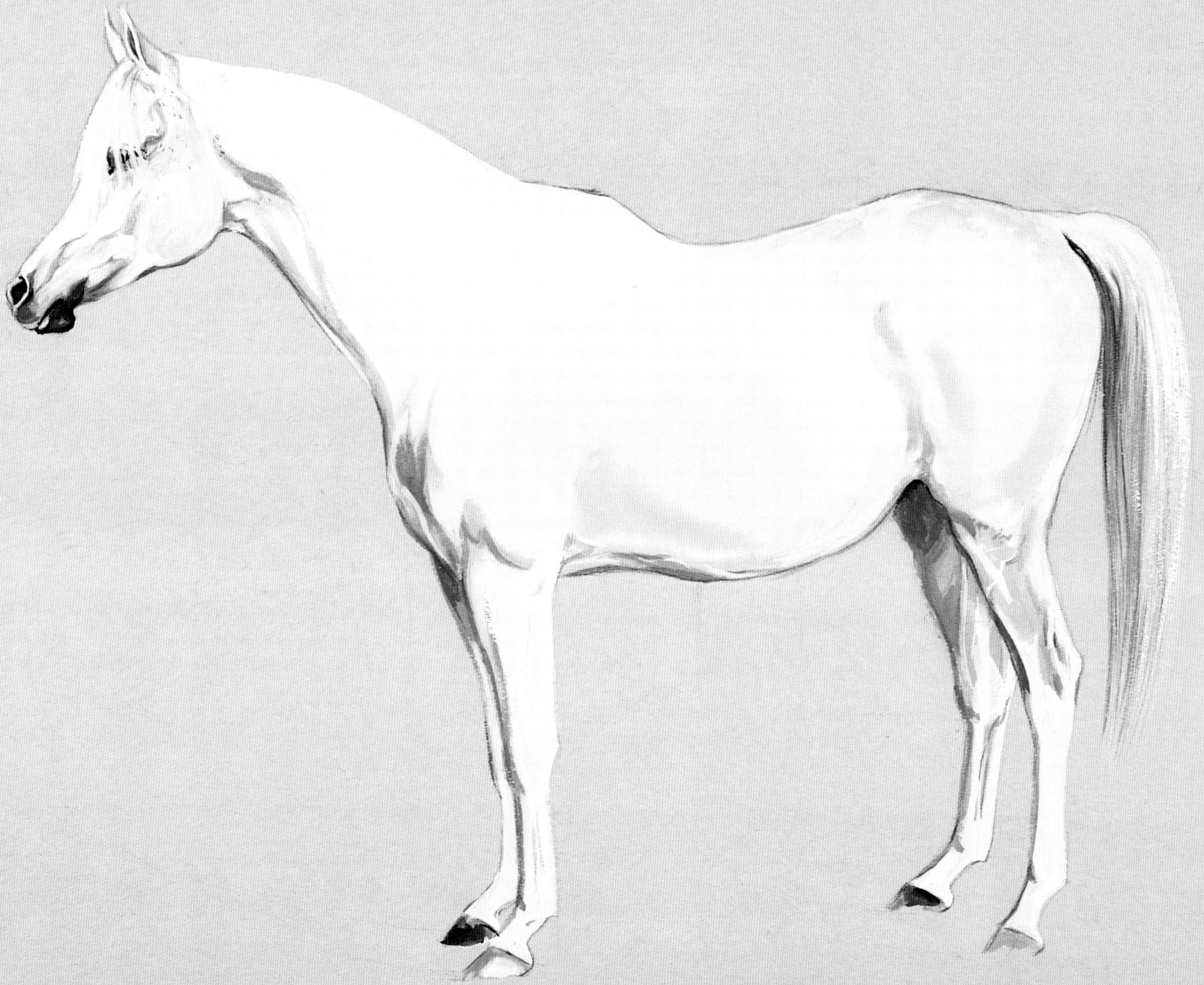

SHERIFA (MECCA)

A Hamdanieh Simrieh.

A white mare foaled c. 1862.

Bred by Saud Ibn Saud – Emir of Riâd (Nejd).

Dam	A Hamdanieh Simrieh belonging to Ibn Saud Emir of Riyadh in Nejd.
Sire	Said to be a bay Hamdani Simri.
Sale	Purchased by Mr Skene on 8 March 1878, in Aleppo, for £38. This mare was presented by Saud to Takeddin Pasha, Governor of Makkah, and by him, who brought her to Aleppo, to Sheikh Takha of that town on whose death, in 1878, she was purchased for Mr Blunt. Mr Skene 'brought a new mare got in exchange for the Nowag and 22 Turkish pounds – very cheap. She has no fault but that her colour is white. She was white as a 3-year-old and is now rising 8 [in fact, 16].' [4] He, Skene, has known her since she was that age, but lost sight of her. Captain Upton wanted to buy her but the owner, Sheikh Takha, chief Ulema of Aleppo, refused his offer of £150 and asked £500. The Sheikh died lately and Mr Skene heard from Mehemet Ali [his former canvas] that the mare would be sold cheap, as the heirs were selling off everything as fast as they could, to divide the property... As the Nowag only cost 32 Napoleons she is absurdly cheap. She is said to be in foal to the chestnut Hamdani Simri of the Mehed.
Description	White with black skin, off hoofs black, near ones white. Scar of spear wound on near quarter, slightly back at the knee. Her style of going is that on an old-fashioned hunter. Her head surpasses any that we saw in Arabia.[5]
Height	14 hands 2 inches.
Girth	65 3/4 inches
Below knee	7 1/8 inches.

Sherifa was imported to England in 1878 with her colt foal. She lived until the autumn of 1892 when she was shot. Her head (the skull) was in the Jubilee Room at Newbuildings, 1899.

◀ *Sherifa*

GSB Volume 14
Imported 1878

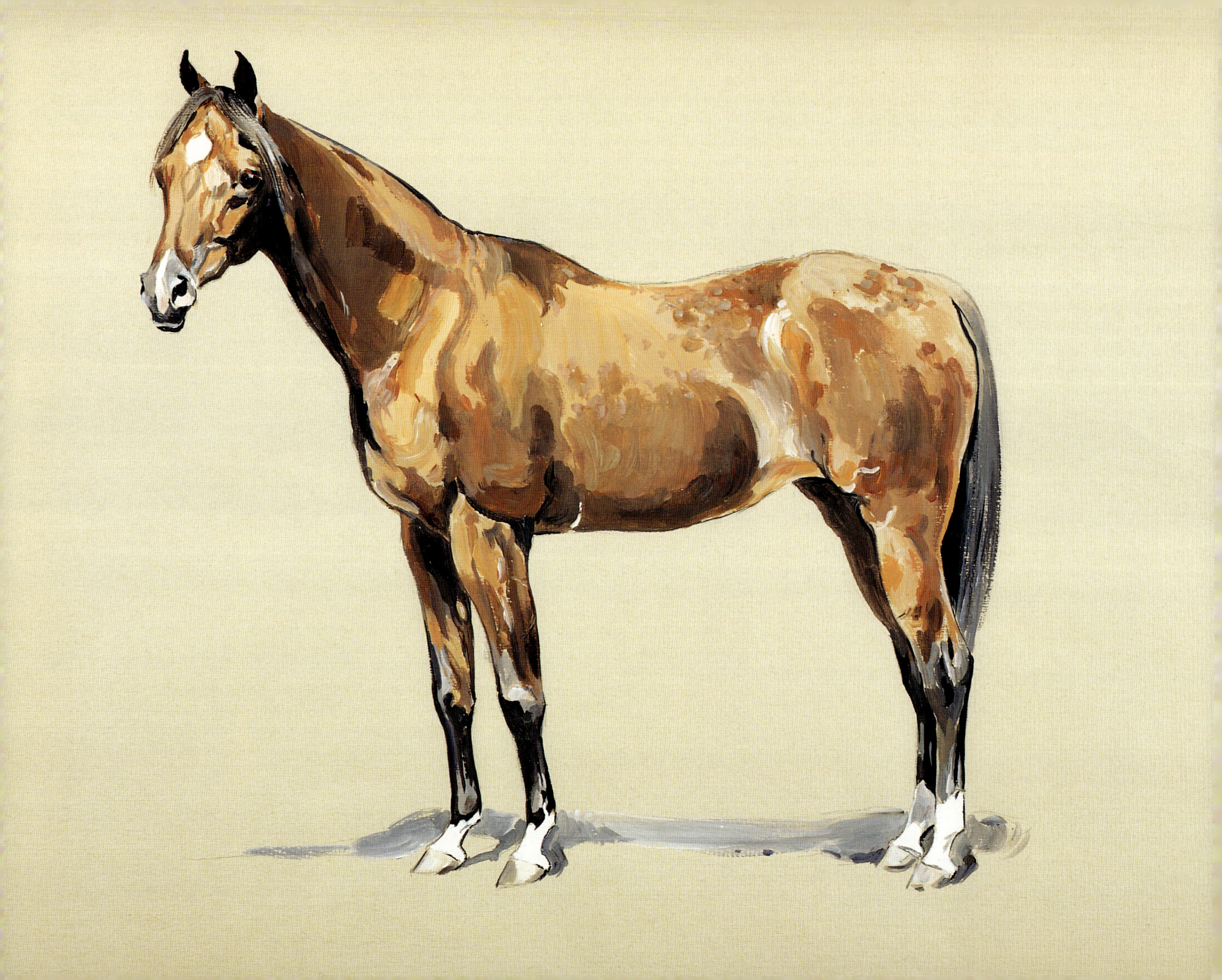

QUEEN OF SHEBA

An Abeyeh Sherrakieh.

A dark bay mare foaled in 1875.

Bred by Erheyen Ibn Alian of the Gomussa tribe of the Sebaa, Anazeh.

Dam — A bay Abeyeh Sherrakieh belonging to Erheyen Ibn Alian of the Gomussa. Four white feet and a blaze. Magnificent style of going. Quite small and narrow in the quarter [seen by the Blunts on 2 April 1881].

Sire — A Managhi Hedruj of Ibn Gufeyfi of the Gomussa.

Sale — Purchased by Mr Skene from Beteyen Ibn Mirshid, Supreme Sheikh of the Gomussa, in the autumn of 1878, for £265.[6] Beteyen Ibn Mirshid had purchased her on shares, buying the bridle half in 1877. For the half, he paid fourteen camels, average for a camel being £5. This gives £70 plus £20 in money. For the remaining half, if he chooses to buy it, he would have to pay a third, that is seven camels. The person who 'holds the bridle', that is the one who has the riding of the mare, has the right to purchase the whole ownership. Beteyen would, in this case, have to pay £135 altogether. We first saw her at his tent in April 1878 and determined to buy her [they all agreed that she surpassed anything they had yet seen]. Wilfrid Blunt wrote a letter to Skene: 'We wish to have Jirros and Beteyen's (Queen of Sheba) because we know them. The former is Lady Anne's special pony, the latter mine. As you know, I consider her far the finest animal I saw in the country', [their eventual purchase of Beteyen's Mare caused 'quite a sensation in the desert'].

Description — Bay or brown with four white feet and very small star and snip. Her head, the first point an Arab looks to, is a good one, though I have seen finer, but it is perfectly set on and the mitbeh would give distinction to any profile. Her neck is light and well arched, the wither high, the shoulder well sloped, and the quarters so fine and powerful that it is impossible she should be otherwise than a very fast mare. Her length of limb above the hock is remarkable, as is that of her pastern. She carries her tail high, as all well-bred Arabians do, and there is neatness and finish about every movement, which remind one of a fawn or a gazelle. She is celebrated in the desert.

Height — 15 hands.   Girth   69 ½ inches.   Below knee   7 ¼ inches.

Queen of Sheba was imported to England, in the spring of 1879, from Cairo, where she had been sent with Pharaoh and Francolin. She was shot on 8 March 1901, the last of the Original Imported Mares.

◀ *Queen of Sheba*

GSB Volume 14
Imported 1879

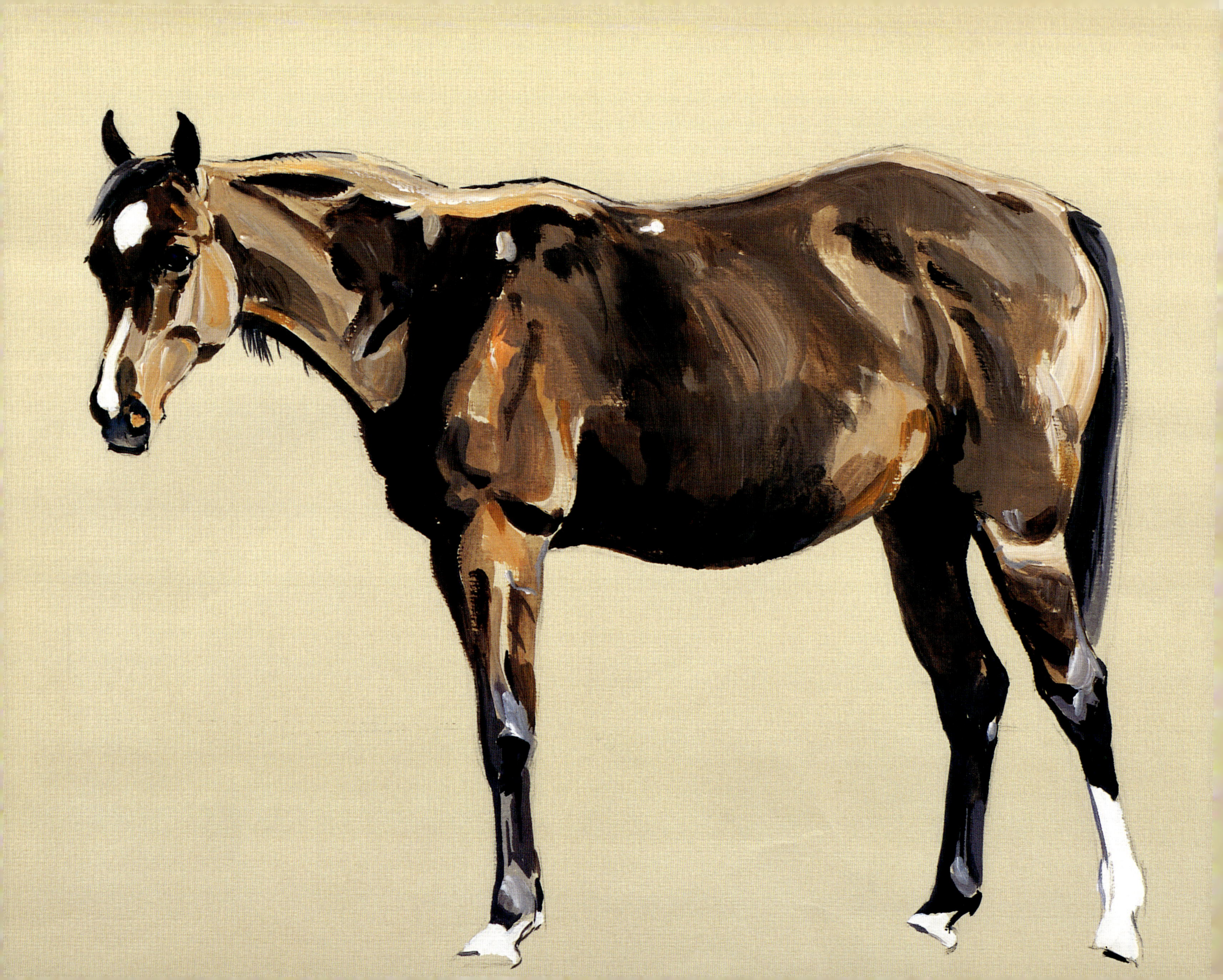

DAHMA

A Dahmeh Om Aamr of Ibn Hemsi's strain.

A bay mare foaled in 1876.

Bred by Ibn Hemsi of the Gomussa tribe of Sebaa, Anazeh.

Dam	A bay Dahmeh Om Aamr derived from a Dahmeh Shahwanieh – celebrated among the tribes 'all bays and dark bays'.
Sire	A bay Abeyan Sherrak of the Gomussa (related to the Queen of Sheba).
Sale	Purchased from Oheynan Ibn Said of the Gomussa on 11 April 1881, in the desert, for £240. Oheynan had purchased her from Ibn Hemsi. Paid down 50 French pounds, to pay 250 more sending the sum from Aleppo with revolver and cloak.
Description	A dark bay with four white feet – near hind stocking, fine shoulder, good quarters and beautiful head. A star a little to the off side of forehead and a snip. A lump under the left jaw. Very like the Queen of Sheba. Very fine mare – eyes are good. Two white marks from saddle. A well-known mare, known among the Gomussa as 'the Dahma'.
Height	14 hands 3 inches.
Girth	71 inches.
Below knee	7 3/4 or 7 1/2 inches.

Dahma was imported in 1881. She was sold at the 4th Crabbet Sale in 1888 to Mr H.C. Stephens MP and exhibited by him at the Crystal Palace Horse Show, June 1897, where she was 2nd in the Arab Class to Mesaoud. Heard in 1898 that Dahma was dead.

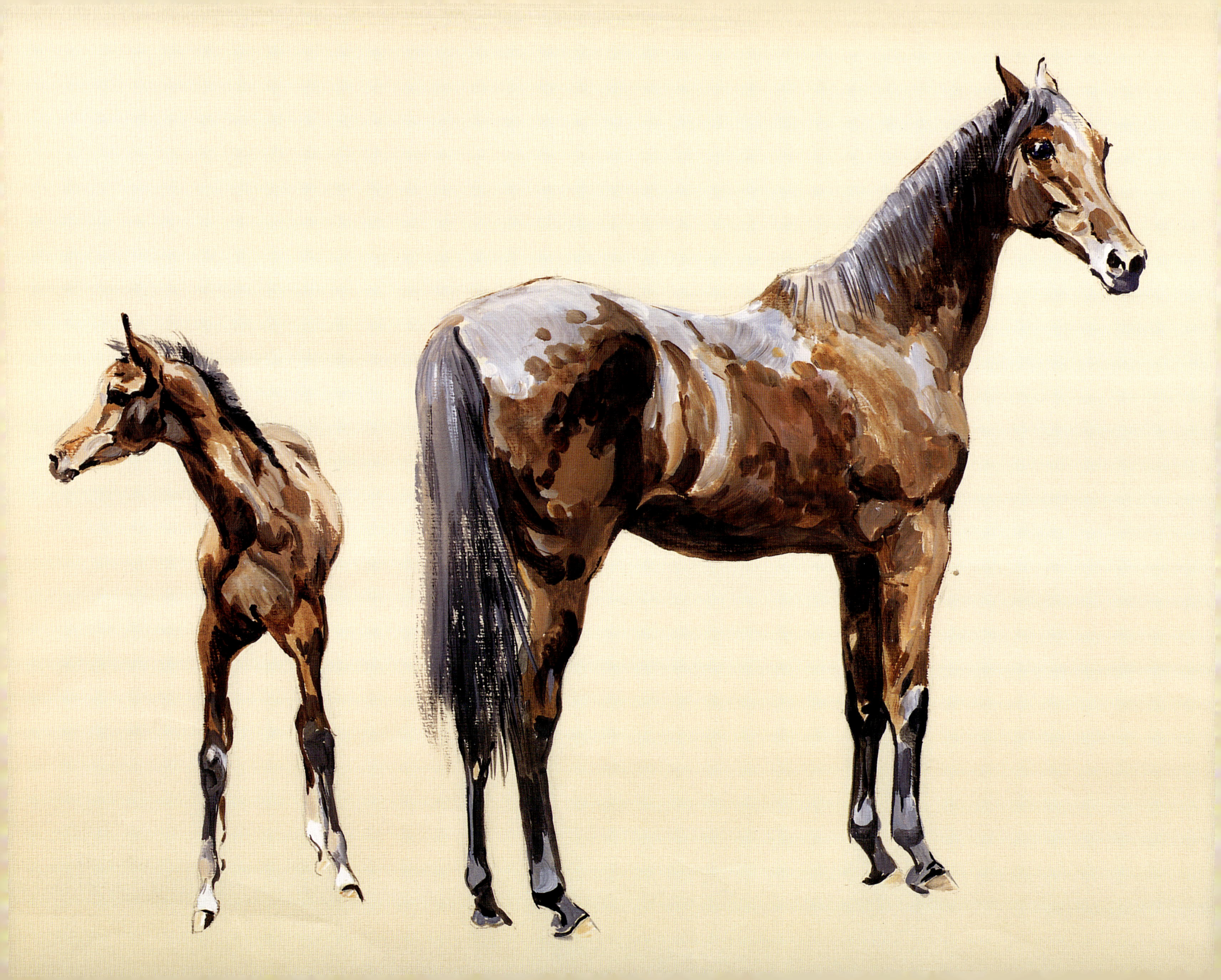

HAGAR (PALMYRA)

A Kehilet Ajuz.

A bay mare foaled in 1872.

Said to have been bred by Suleyman Jelaleh of the Sebaa, Anazeh.

Dam	Stated to be a Kehilet Ajuz belonging to and bred by Suleyman Jelaleh.
Sire	Of the same blood.
Sale	Purchased on 4 January 1878, at Aleppo, for £52, from an Arab of the Moali, who had recently brought her from the Roala. They had taken her, in war, from the Sebaa in the winter of 1877/8. [Brought to the Blunts by Seyd Ahmet] she was in foal to a Dahman om Amr horse.
Description	A dark bay mare with black points, no white. Large prominent eyes and well-placed nostrils, fine shoulder, legs good and remarkably sound, tail well placed. Fine mover especially galloping. Fired on each side of muzzle and two lines on body. She was not remarkably handsome, being ewe-necked, and having a strange, wild head; but her depth of girth and her long muscular hind-quarters gave promise of what she really possessed in a wonderful degree, speed and staying power.
Height	15 hands without shoes.
Girth	71 5/8 inches.
Below knee	7 1/4 inches.

Hagar was imported to England in 1878. She was sold, in September 1886, to the Honourable Miss Dillon for 150 guineas, and finally given by Miss Dillon to H.C. Stephens, Esq., MP, in 1898. She was shot in July 1899.

◀ *Hagar with filly foal Harik*

GSB Volume 14
Imported 1878

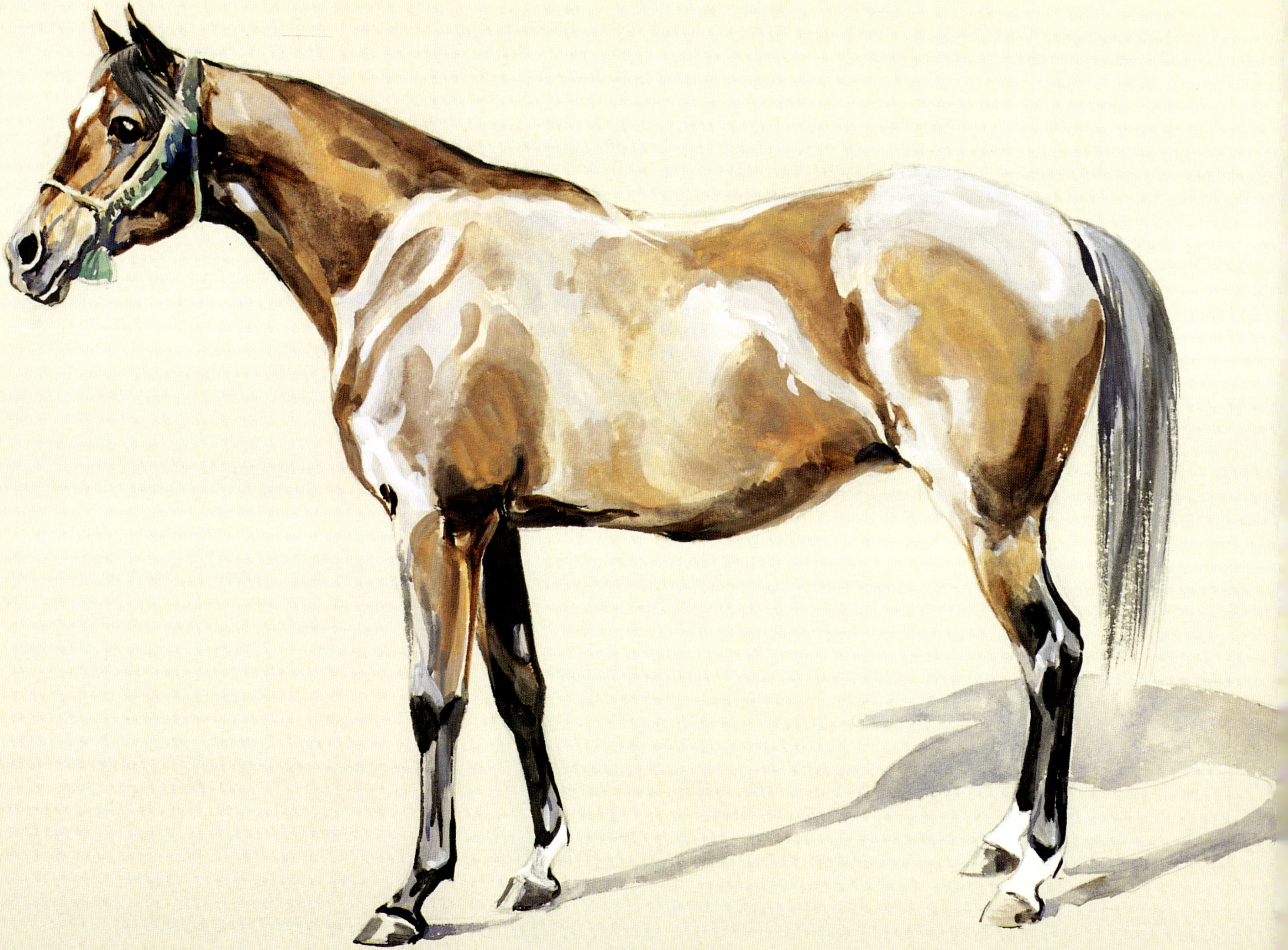

DAJANIA (JESSAMINE, LADY HESTOR OR HESTER)

A Kehilet Ajuz of the Dajani strain or Kehileh Dajanieh.

A bay mare foaled in 1876.

Bred by Mohammed Pasha, a Turkoman Chief.

Dam	A Kehilet Ajuz of the Dajani strain (or Kehileh Dajanieh) of the Sebaa, Anazeh, stolen from them by Mohammed Pasha.
Sire	A Kehilan Nowak.
Sale	Purchased on 25 December 1877, at Aleppo, for £35.[7] Among the mares and horses Seyd Ahmet brought was a filly come from the Gomussa tribe, Kehilet Dajanieh and lovely. We soon settled on her. Dajania was stolen from Mohammed Pasha and brought to Sheikh Ahmet of the Hannadi tribe; now settled at Haggla near Aleppo.
Description	A golden bay with enormous eyes, very black points, three white feet, two hind and off fore (mutlak es shemal), a star and snip. Good head, rather short neck, fine ears, short back wonderfully strong, a fair shoulder, perfect legs, fine action and carriage of tail. A lovely little thing, not so very small either.
Height	14 hands 3 inches.
Girth	70 inches.
Below knee	7 inches-plus.

Dajania was imported in 1878. She produced only one pure-bred filly – Nefisa. Sold after the 3rd Crabbet Sale in 1886, to H.E. Rustem Pasha, Turkish Ambassador, for 120 guineas.

◀ *Dajania*

GSB Volume 14
Imported 1878

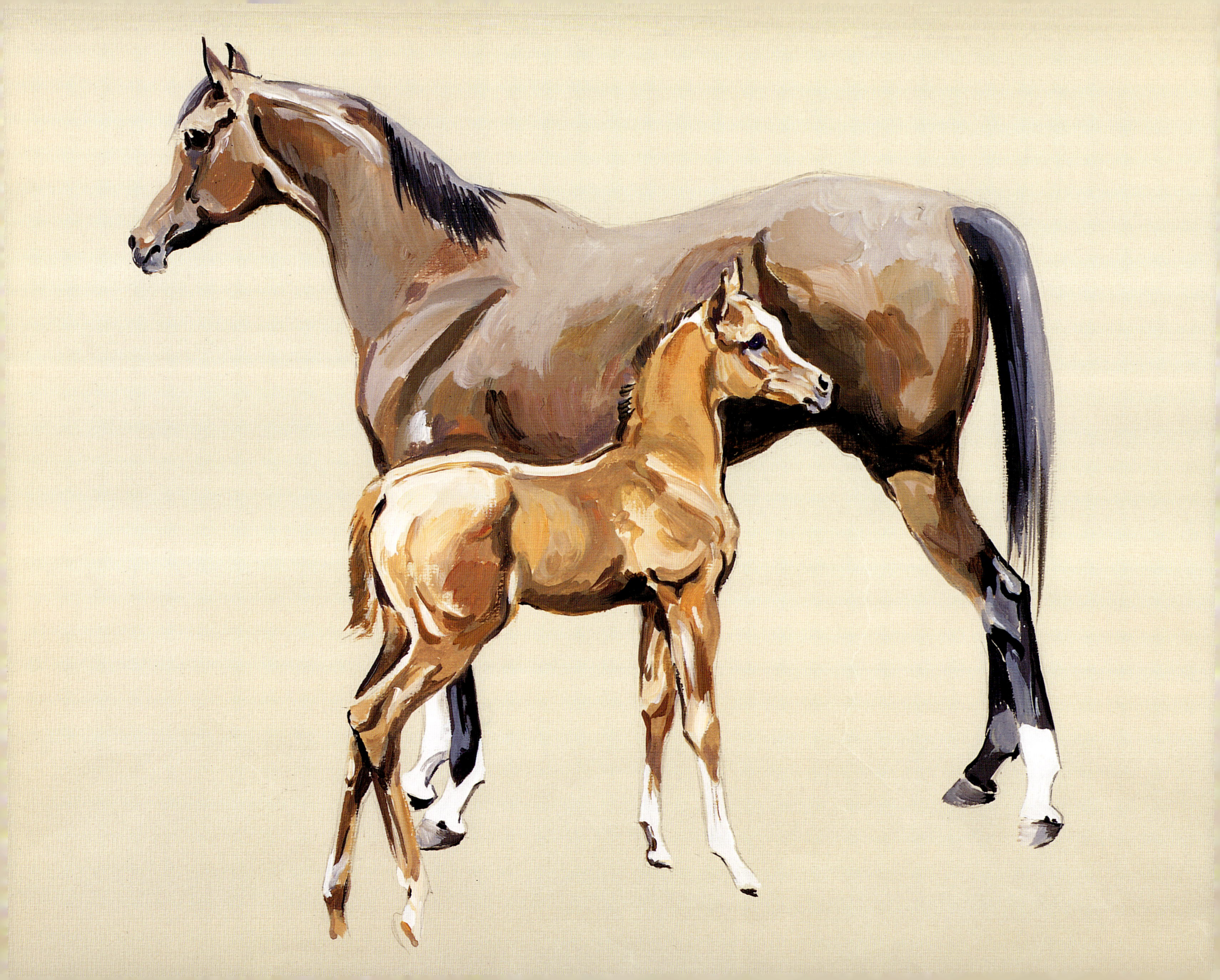

JERBOA

A Maneghieh Hedrujieh.

A bay mare foaled in 1874.

Bred by Othman el Abd of the Obeyd Tribe, in the neighbourhood of Deyr, on the Euphrates.

Dam	A bay Maneghieh Hedrujieh mare belonging to Othman el Abd of the Obeyd tribe. Long, low and very worn, old and thin.
Sire	A Managhi Ibn Sbeyl of the Gomussa.
Sale	Purchased on 24 January 1878, at Deyr, from Othman el Abd of the Obeyd tribe of Taouf Anazeh, south of the Muntifiq, for £65. The owner had originally asked £120, he now came down to £71. Wilfrid thought it rather a long price, but on seeing her again, they, Wilfrid and Skene, both liked her. I fancy her particularly – she gallops well.
Description	A bright bay, three white feet, near hind foot and both forefeet and a star. She is the only one of the 1878 importations that shows temper, being inclined to bite and kick in the stable, though perfectly quiet when out. Head showing breeding though not handsome, eye large and flashing. Splendid action trotting and fast. A good mover.
Height	14 hands 2 ½ inches.
Below knee	7 inches.

Jerboa was imported in 1878. She was shot in the autumn of 1893.

◀ *Jerboa with filly foal Jamila*

GSB Volume 14
Imported 1878

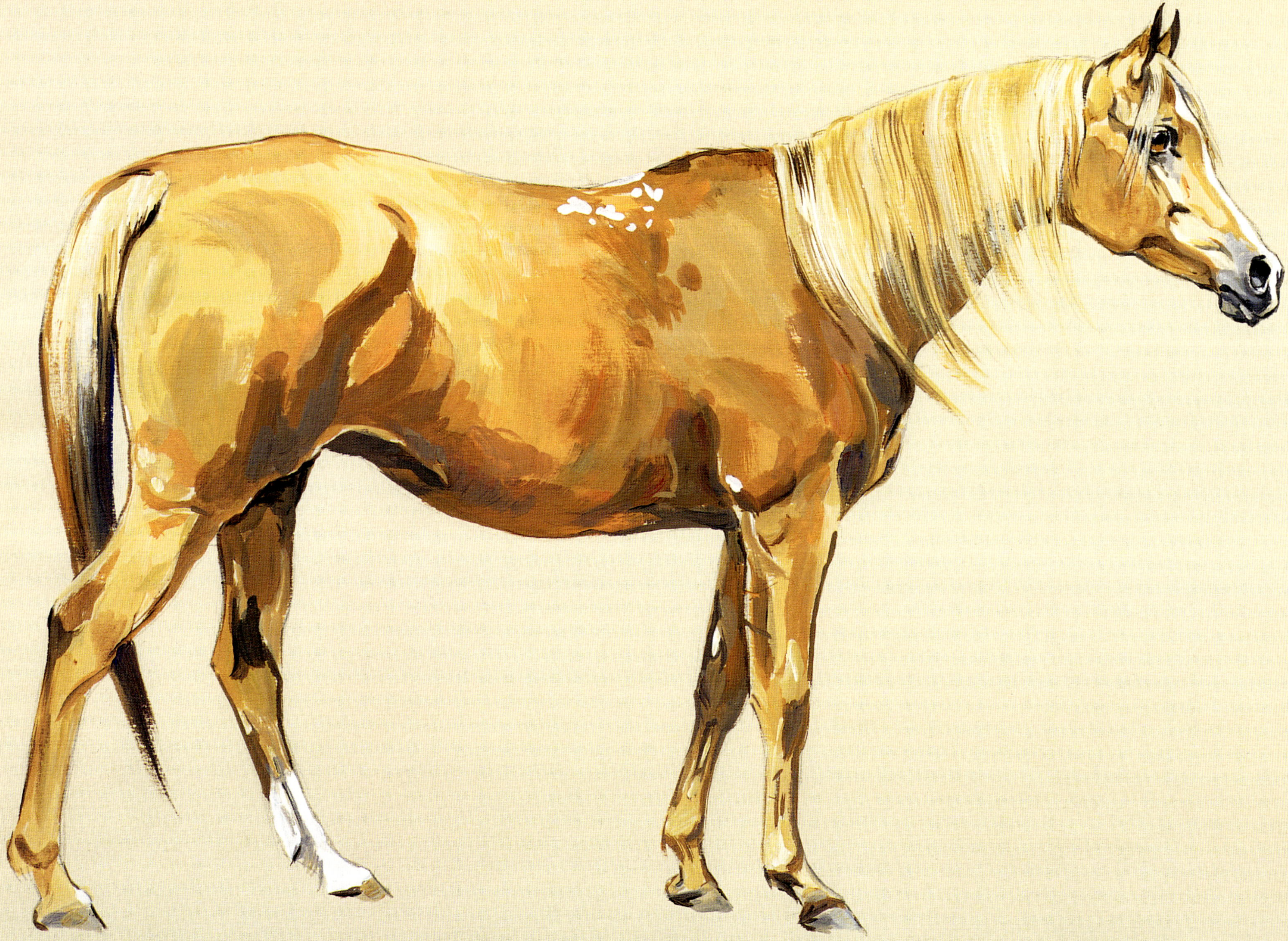

RODANIA

A Kehilet Ajuz of Ibn Rodan's strain.

A chestnut mare foaled c. 1869.

Bred by Ibn Rodan of the Roala tribe and taken in war from their Sheikh Sotamm Ibn Shaalan, in 1880, by Taïs Ibn Sharban of the Gomussa. An old and celebrated mare, formerly the property of Beneyeh Ibn Shaalan, and the cause of a feud between him and his kinsman Sotamm.[8]

Dam   A Kehilet Ajuz of Ibn Rodan's strain of the Roala tribe.

Sale   Purchased from her owner Taïs Ibn Sharban on 12 April 1881, in the desert, near the wells of Abu Fayal, for £124.

Description   Chestnut, with near hind foot white to above fetlock, blaze to mouth, pink on upper lip, deep jowl, eyes showing white like human eyes, splendid shoulder, extraordinary strength. Wounded on the quarter, belly and chest, probably sustained in a ghazu. A somewhat uncertain temper.[9]

Height   14 hands 2 inches.

Rodania was imported to England in 1881. She became sick and wretched and was shot in the winter of 1889/90.

◀ *Rodania, as an old mare*

GSB Volume 14
Imported 1881

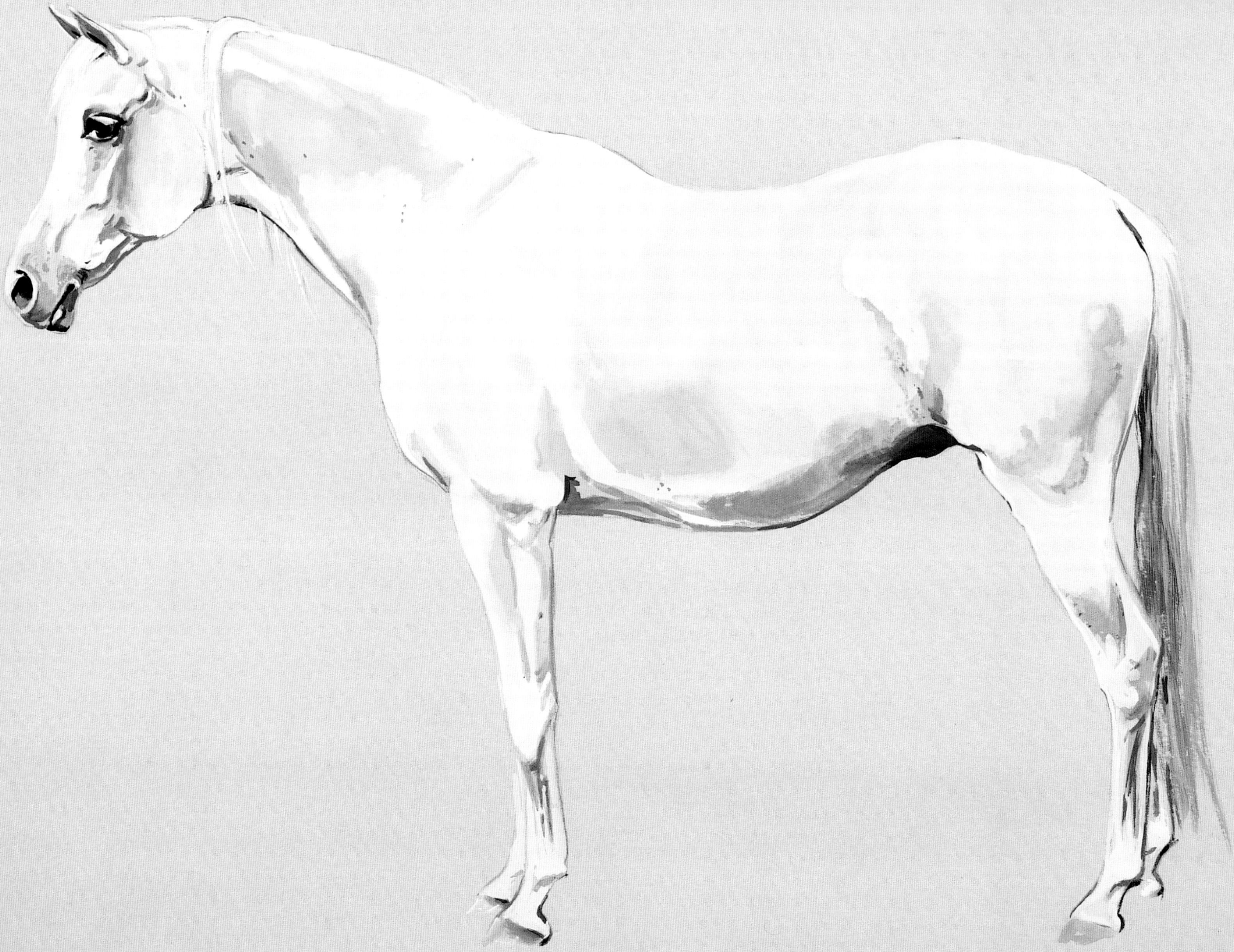

SOBHA

A Hamdanieh Simrieh.

A white mare foaled in 1879.

Bred by Mahmud Bey in Cairo.

Dam — Selma, a Hamdanieh Simrich purchased by Mahmud Bey with his brother Suleyman Bey at Ismael Pasha's Sale of the mares collected by Abbas Pasha I c. 1868. Mahmud and Suleyman Bey, being 'Mamluks' of Ali Pasha Sherif, their horses were kept with his. Mahmud survived Suleyman, still being with Ali Pasha Sherif in 1891.

Sire — Wazir, the celebrated white Seglawi Jedran of Ibn Sudan's strain. Bred by Ali Pasha Sherif.

Sale — Purchased by W.S. Blunt from Mahmud Bey in 1891. The cost of £220 included Sobha, her daughter Safra by Shueyman and two foals – Sobha's colt, Antar and Safra's colt who died – both by Aziz.

Description — White with black skin. Very like Sherifa, less fine head and less good shoulder, also I hope less in age – we think 20, they say 15 [in fact only 12] – if she has foals age does not matter. At any rate, these two mares and Khatila are mazbût of mazbût.

Height — 14 hands ½ inch.

Sobha was imported in 1891 with her daughter Safra.[10] She was sold after the 11th Crabbet Sale of 8 July 1899, to Colonel Alexandre de Sdanovitch, for 200 guineas for the Russian Government Stud at Derkoul.

◀ *Sobha*

GSB Volume 17
Imported 1891

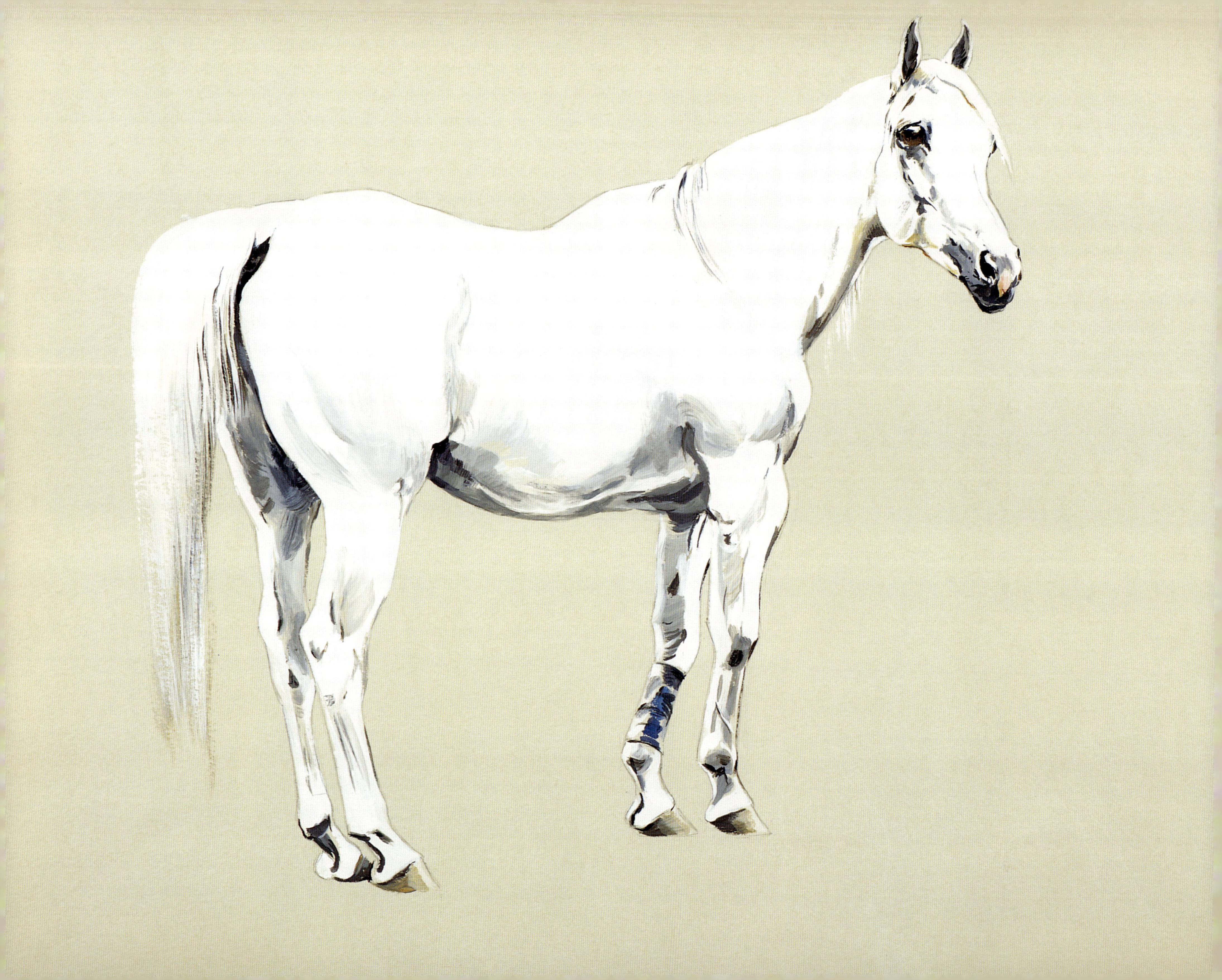

BINT HELWA

A Seglawieh Jedranich of Ibn Sudan's strain.

A white mare foaled in 1887.

Bred by Ali Pasha Sherif in Cairo.

Dam — Helwa, a white Seglawieh Jedranieh of Ibn Sudan's strain, bred by Ali Pasha Sherif, her dam – Horra[11] (own sister to Wazir), white – by Zobeyni white Seglawi Jedran, Original Horse, brought by Abbas Pasha I from Ibn Sbeyni – out of Ghazieh (zerka), grey Seglawieh Jedranieh, Original Mare brought by Abbas Pasha I from Ibn Sudan of the Roala; her sire – Shueyman by Jerboa, Original Horse out of Shueyma, Original Mare.

Sire — Aziz, a chestnut Dahman Shahwan bred by Ali Pasha Sherif c. 1877, his dam – Aziza, a grey Dahmeh Shahwanieh by Samhan, ex Bint Faras-Nakadan (Mare of Nakadan Original Mare); his sire Harkan, a grey Kehilan Ajuz of the Harkan strain, by Zobeyni, white Seglawi Jedran from Ibn Sbeyni, out of Harka, Original Mare imported by Abbas Pasha I.

Sale — Purchased from Ali Pasha Sherif, on 14 December 1896, for £80 with filly foal, about six months old by Ibn Sherara (Ghazala).

Description — White, reddish tint on near side from wither to girth, small pink patch between lower ends of nostrils also narrow pink strip up muzzle from between upper ends of nostrils towards eyes. Black hoofs. Rather old but a beautiful mare in spite of rather weak back – fine head and style.

Imported to England in May 1897, Bint Helwa met with a terrible accident in June of that year, breaking her off foreleg in two places. She continued breeding until 1906. Very infirm in 1907, unable to rise. Supposed to have rheumatism and shot in May.

GSB Volume 19
Imported 1897

◄ *Bint Helwa*

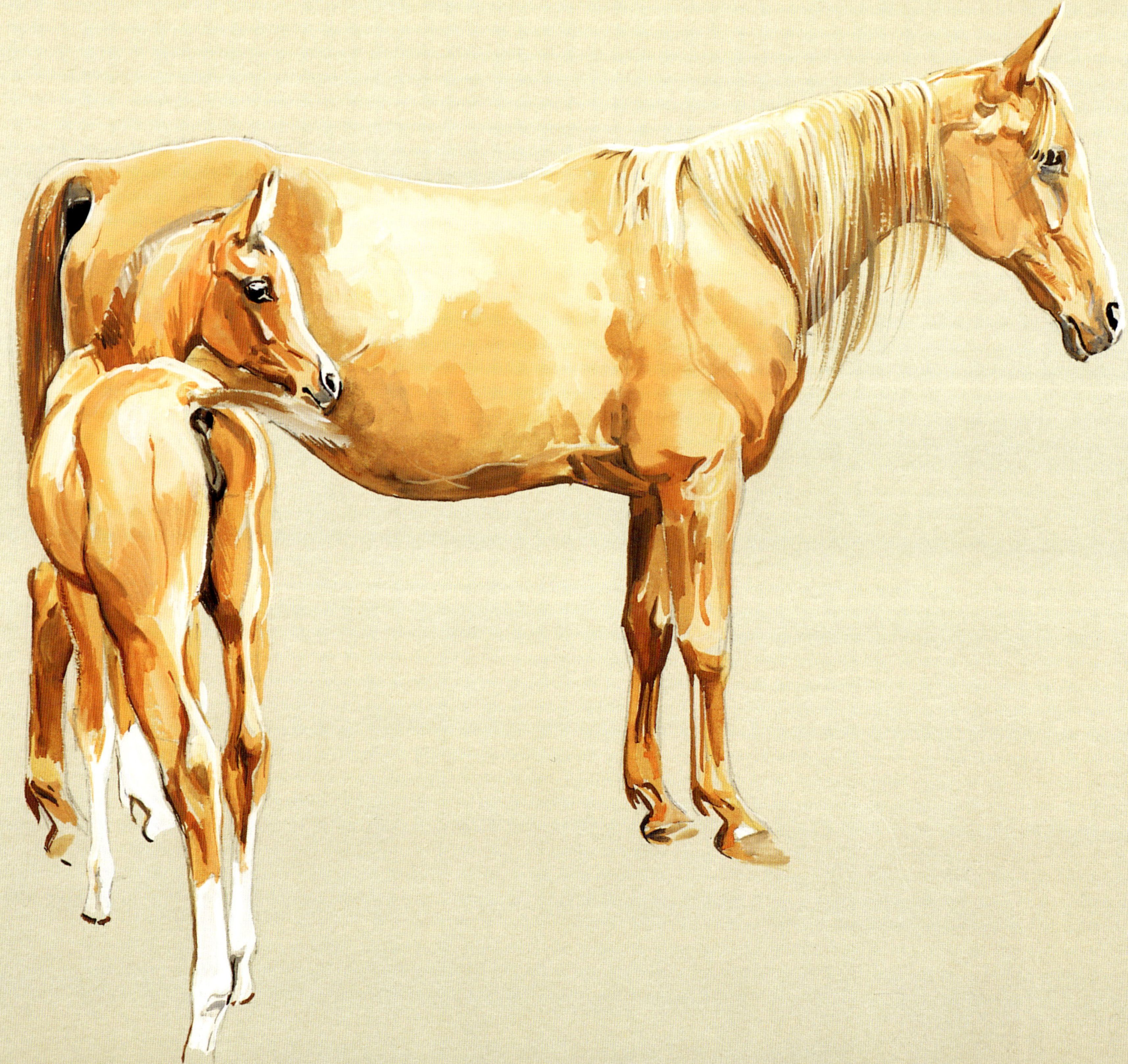

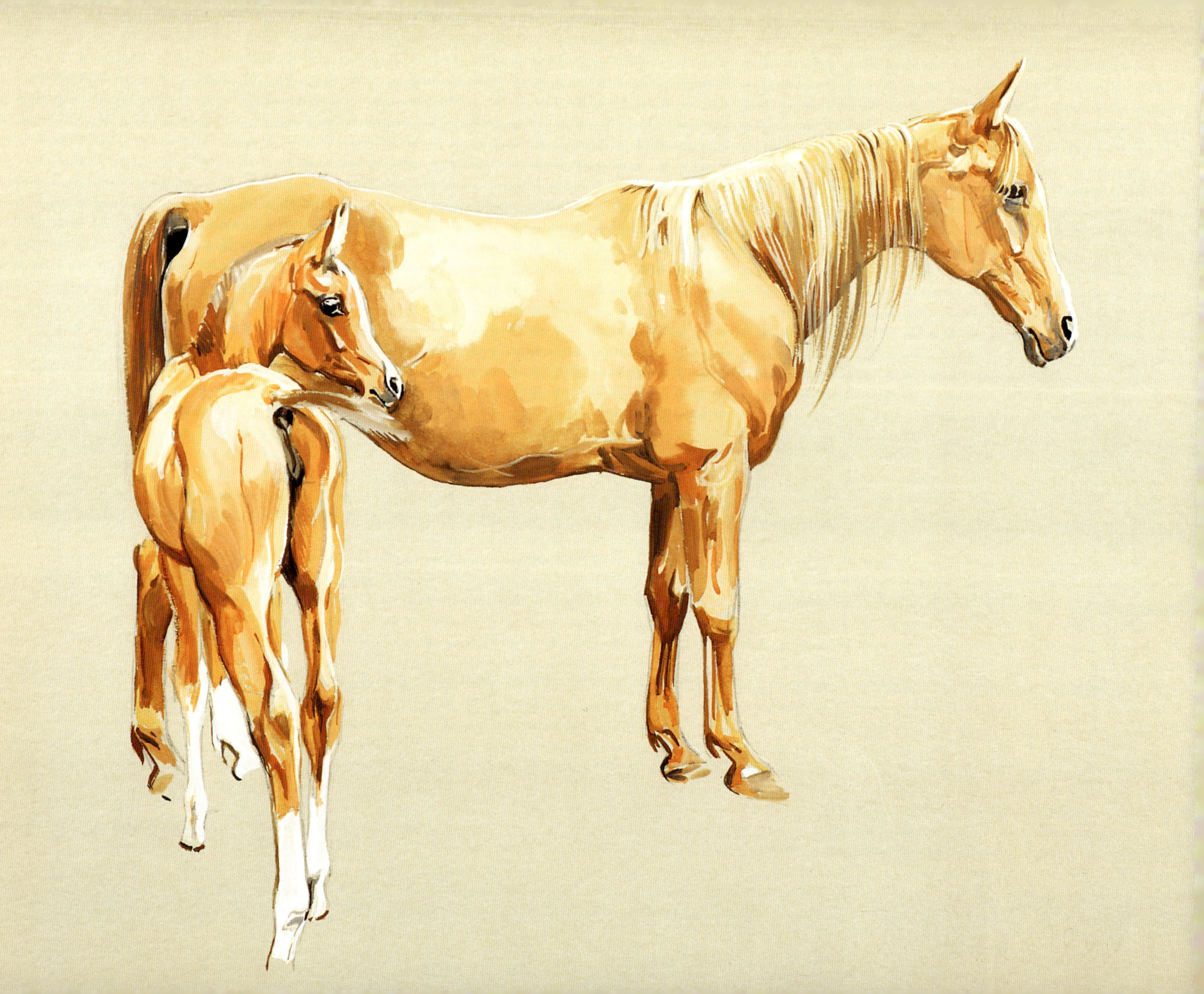

JOHARA (BINT HELWA ES SHAKRA)

A Seglawich Jedranieh of Ibn Sudan's strain.

A chestnut mare foaled c. 1880. (Full sister to Bint Helwa.)

Bred by Ali Pasha Sherif in Cairo.

Dam	Helwa, a white Seglawieh Jedranieh of Ibn Sudan's strain, bred by Ali Pasha Sherif, her dam – Horra, white Seglawieh Jedranieh bred by APS [Ali Pasha Sherif], by Zobeyni ex Ghazieh; her sire – Shueyman, white Shueyman Sabah by Jerboa ex Shueyma.
Sire	Aziz, a chestnut Dahman Shahwan bred by Ali Pasha Sherif, his dam – Aziza, grey Dahmeh Shahwanieh, her great-granddam – the mare of Ibn Nakadan – Original Mare; his sire, Harkan – grey by Zobeyni, out of Harka.
Sale	Purchased from Ibrahim Bey Sherif, on 19 April 1897, for £120. Ibrahim Bey had bought her at the auction on 26 March for £80.[12] This mare is own sister to Bint Helwa.
Description	Chestnut, near hind foot white to one-third up cannon bone, small splotch (size of shilling) of white outside off hind foot above hoof, and blaze from just below ears to lower level of nostrils. She is beautiful. Covered by Ibn Bint Nura es Shakra – a white horse with a fine head by Ibn Sherara.
	Imported in 1897. She was given in October 1903 to Mrs Pearce of Harrow on the condition that she did not breed from her or part with her.

◀ *Johara, as an old mare, with filly foal Jalmuda*

GSB Volume 19
Imported 1897

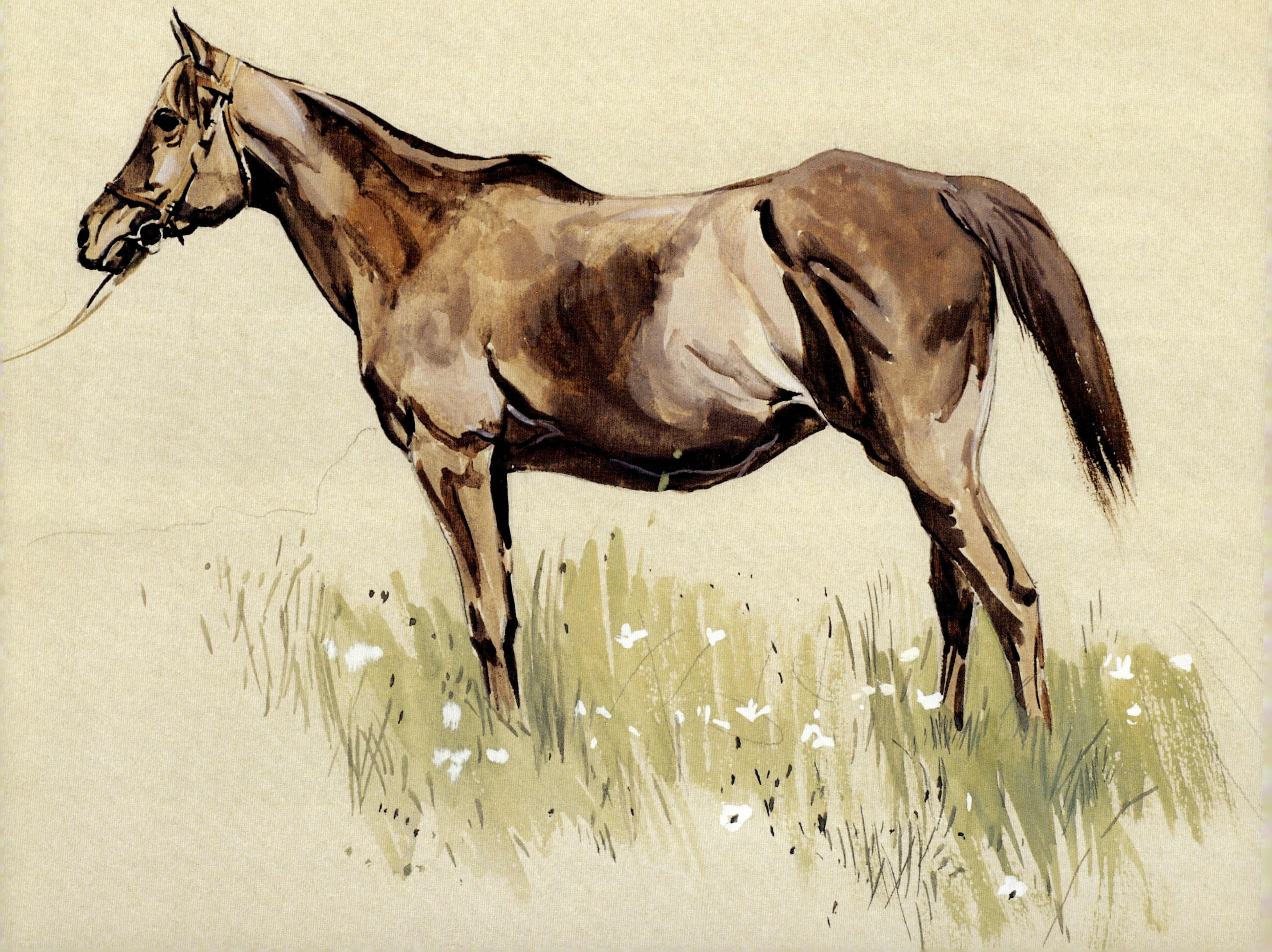

FULANA (BINT BINT FEREYHA ES SAGHIRA)

A Seglawieh Jedranieh of Ibn Sbeyni's strain.

A brown mare foaled in 1893.

Bred by Ali Pasha Sherif in Cairo.

Dam — Bint Fereyha, a flea-bitten white Seglawieh Jedranieh of Ibn Sbeyni's strain, bred by Ali Pasha Sherif in 1884. Seen in 1896, an old but a fine mare, her dam – Fereyha a white Seglawieh Jedranieh of Ibn Sbeyni; her sire – Aziz, a chestnut Dahman Shahwan. Fereyha by Jerboa out of Samha, Original Mare. Jerboa's dam – the bay Dahmeh Nejiba of Ibn Aweyde, Original Mare.

Sire — Ibn Nura, a flea-bitten white Dahman Nejib, bred by Ali Pasha Sherif c. 1876, his dam – Bint Nura, a bay daughter of the Original Mare, Nura, a Dahmeh Nejiba; his sire – Sottam, a flea-bitten grey Dahman Nejib by Sueyd, a flea-bitten grey Seglawi Jedran, Original Horse, from Ibn Sudan of the Roala, out of the white Dahmeh Nejiba Original Mare of Khalil el Hajry.

Sale — Purchased from Ali Pasha Sherif, on 14 December 1896, for £50.

Description — Dark brown with off hind foot white and on near fore a small ring of white. Great depth. Head moderately good.

Imported to England in May 1897. To Crabbet on division of the stud in 1906. She was shot in 1908.

◀ *Fulana*

GSB Volume 19
Imported 1897

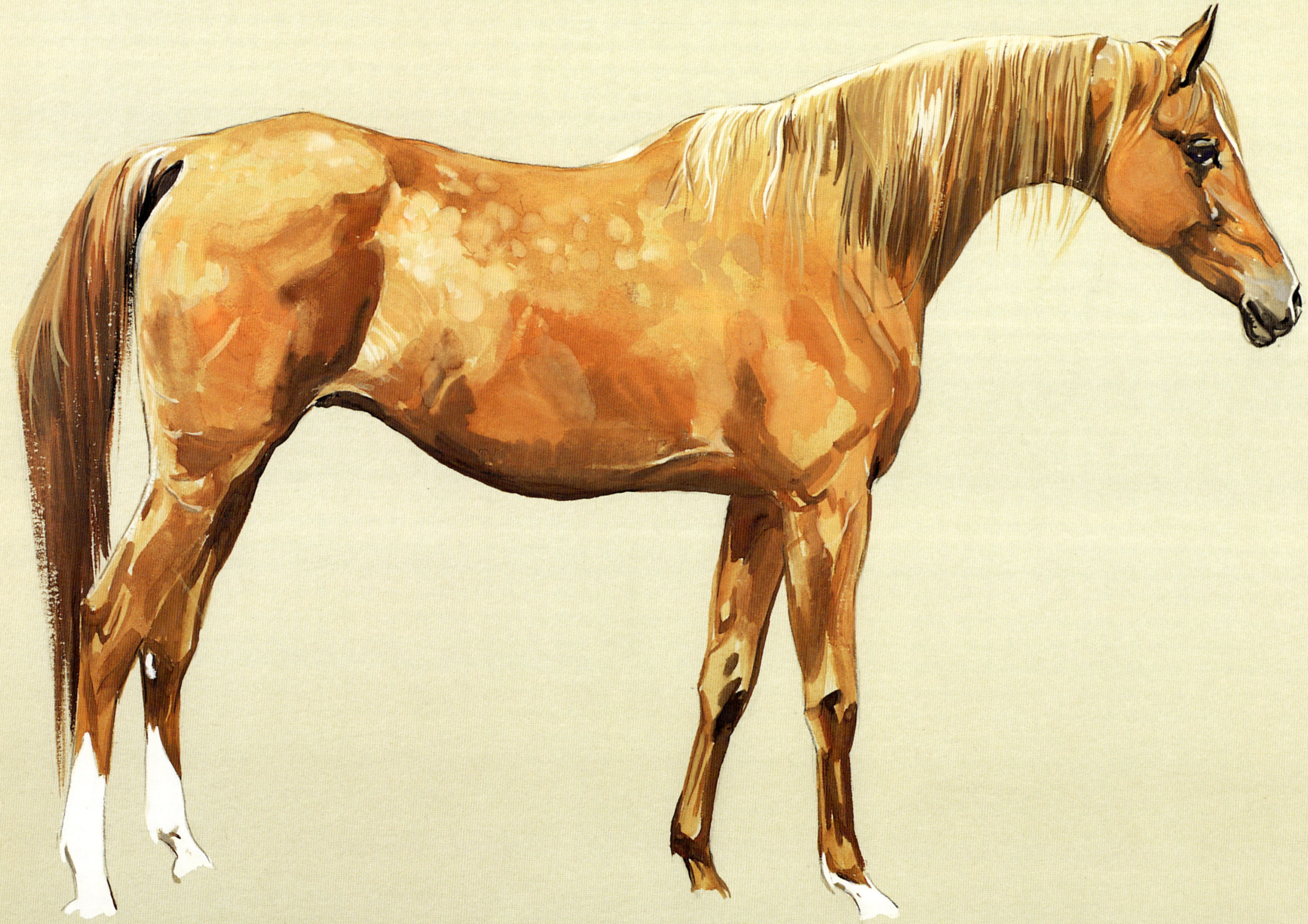

BINT NURA ES SHAKRA (SHOULD BE BINT BINT NURA)

A Dahmeh Nejiba.

A chestnut mare foaled in 1885.

Bred by Ali Pasha Sherif in Cairo.

Dam — Bint Nura, a grey Dahmeh Nejiba bred by Ali Pasha Sherif, her dam – Nura, a grey (zerka) Dahmeh Nejiba; her sire – Zobeyni, the white Seglawi Jedran of Ibn Sbeyni's strain, Original Horse bought by Abbas I. Nura was probably the Original Mare. According to Mohammed Salame, the old Syce Basha, this mare was obtained from or through one Mustafa Effendi Nuri, and so called 'Nura'; not yet discovered whether Mustafa got her from Abbas I's Collection or whether the Collection got her through him.

Sire — Aziz, a chestnut Dahman Shahwan bred by Ali Pasha Sherif c. 1877, his dam – Aziza, a grey Dahmeh Shahwanieh by Samhan out of Bint Faras-Nakadan (that is 'the daughter of the mare of Nakadan' the Original Mare); his sire – Harkan, grey Kehilan Ajuz of the Harkan strain, by Zobeyni, white Seglawi Jedran, Original Horse from Ibn Sbeyni, out of Harka, a Kehilet Ajuz of Harkan, Original Mare.

Sale — Purchased from Daïra of the late Ali Pasha Sherif, at the auction on 26 March 1897, for £E 106.

Description — Bright chestnut, three white feet (mutlak es shemâl) the hind ones to about one-third up cannon bone, the off fore to below fetlock in front and extending to top of joint behind. Star above eyes and snip slanting to near nostril. Very fine mare.

Imported to England in May 1897. She won 2nd prize for Arab Brood Mares at Crystal Palace on 28 May 1898 (Rosemary, 1st). She went to Crabbet at division of the stud in 1906. She was shot in 1912.

◀ *Bint Nura es Shakra*

GSB Volume 19
Imported 1897

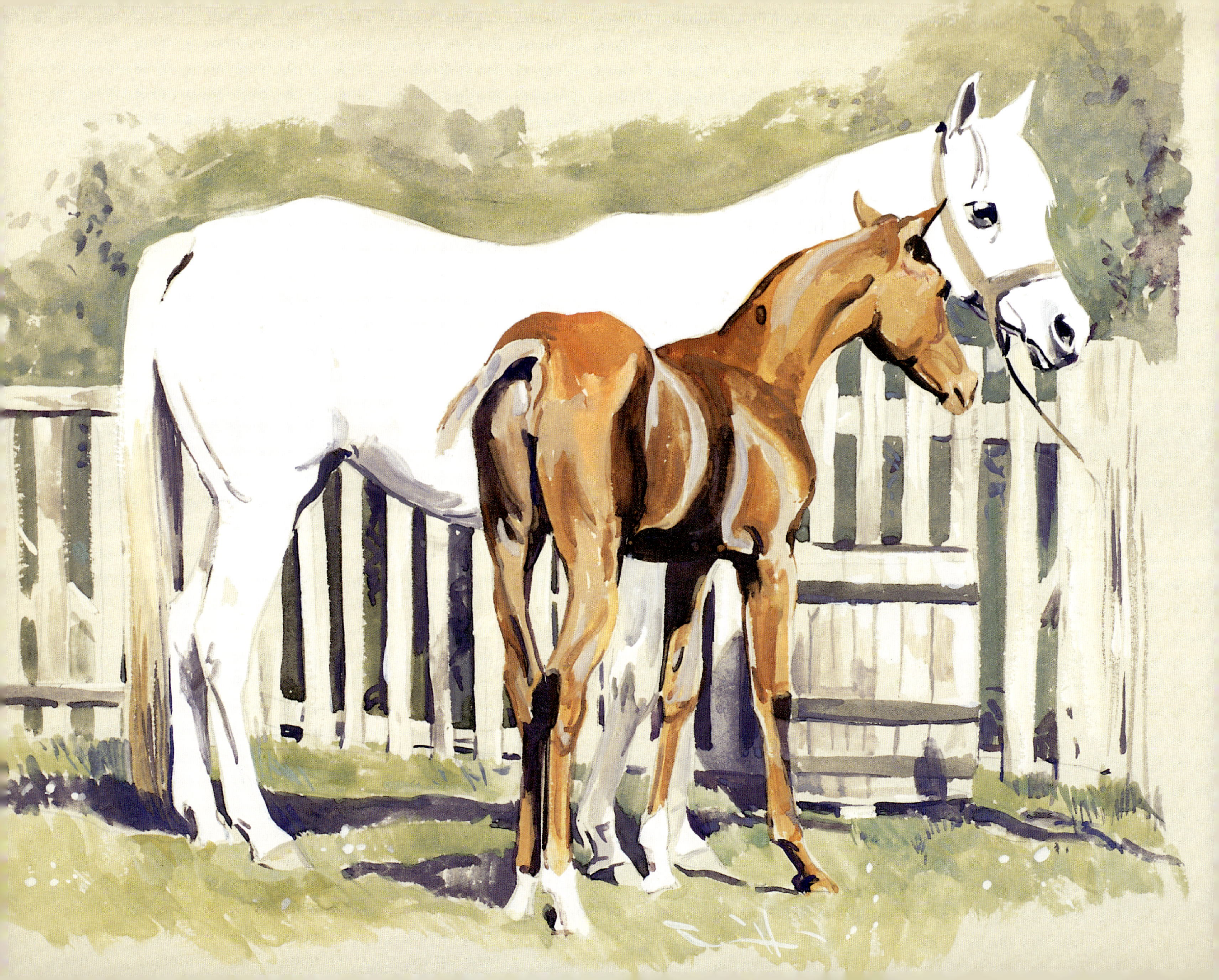

MAKBULA (SHOULD BE BINT MAKBULA)

A Kehilet Ajuz of the Jellabi strain or Kehileh Jellabieh (belonging to Ibn Khalifa of Bahrain).

A white mare foaled in 1886.

Bred by Ali Pasha Sherif in Cairo.

Dam   Makbula, a chestnut [?] [Mohammed Salame says white], Kehilet Ajuz of the Jellabi strain, her dam – Bint Bint Jellabiet-Feysul, daughter of the mare of Feysul Ibn Turki, Emir of Riâd, Original Mare; her sire – Shueyman, by Jerboa[13] out of Shueyma, Original Mare, a Shueymah S'bah. Both sire and dam bred by Ali Pasha Sherif.

Sire   Wazir, a white Seglawi Jedran of Ibn Sudan's strain, bred by Ali Pasha Sherif, his dam Ghazieh (Zerka), a white Seglawieh Jedranieh, Original Mare from Ibn Sudan of the Roala, bought by Abbas I; his sire – Zobeyni, white Seglawi Jedran, Original Horse brought by Abbas I from Ibn Sbeyni of the Mehed-Fedaan.

Sale   Purchased from Ali Pasha Sherif, on 14 December 1896, for £100.

Description   White, a few reddish spots, black hoofs, except part of near hind hoof white. In foal to Aziz. Covered by Aziz again in December 1897. [See Kasida, her daughter.]

Imported into England, in May 1898, Makbula was sold at the Paris International Horse Show in 1900, to Count Strogonoff, for 400 guineas. In April 1901 heard that Makbula had died.

◀ *Makbula with filly foal Kibla*

GSB Volume 19
Imported 1898

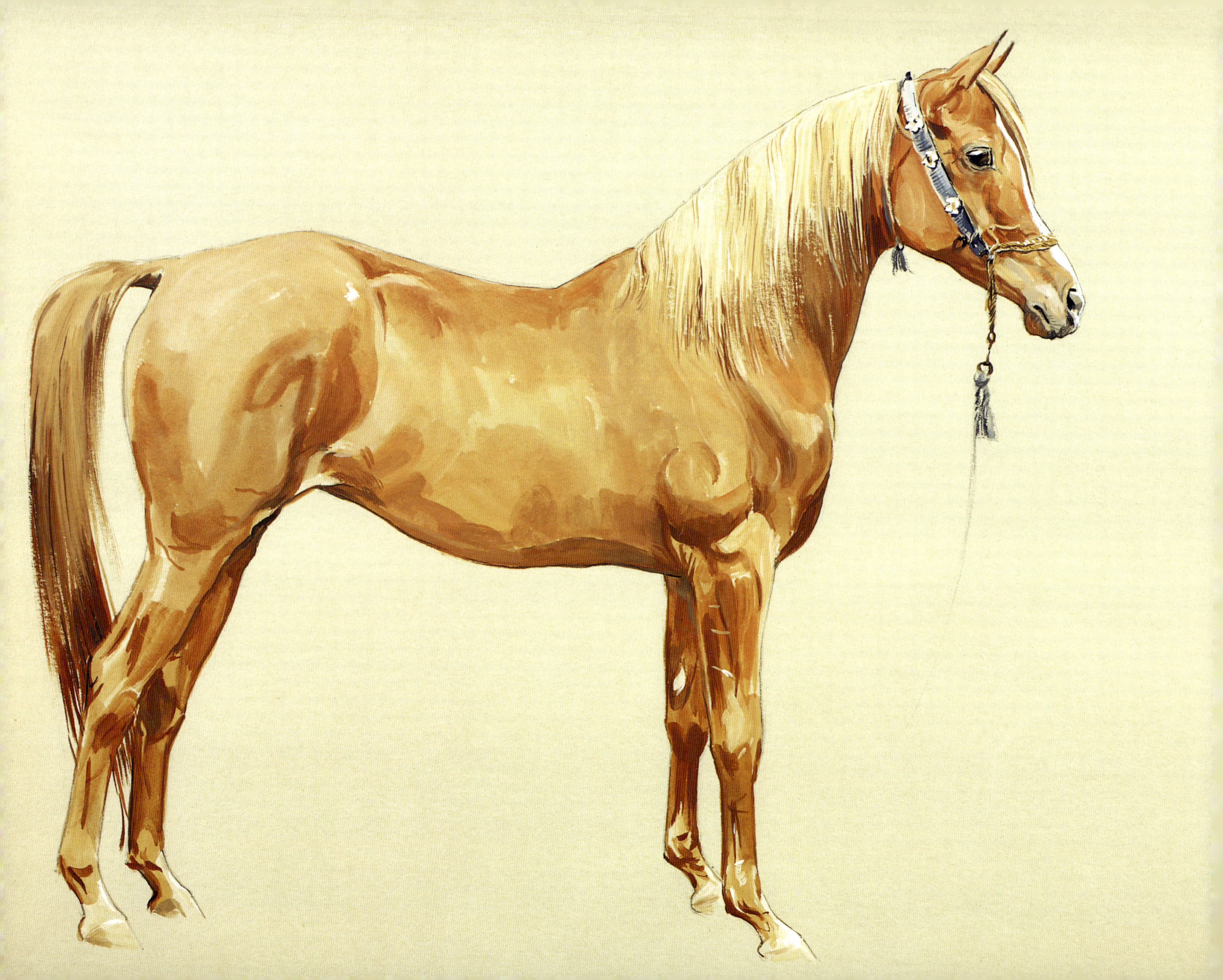

KASIDA (BINT MAKBULA ES SHAKRA)

A Kehilet Ajuz of the Jellabi strain or Kehileh Jellabieh, the strain belonging to Ibn Khallfeh of Bahrain.

A chestnut mare foaled in 1891.

Bred by Ali Pasha Sherif in Cairo. Sold on 26 March 1897 by the Daïra of Ali Pasha Sherif, after his death, to Maitre Léon Cléry, for £E260. Taken to France in April 1897, brought back to Egypt in the winter of 1897-8.

Dam   Makbula [should be Bint Makbula, daughter of Makbula], a white Kehilet Ajuz of the Jellabi strain bred by Ali Pasha Sherif, her dam – Makbula; her sire – Wazir.

Sire   Nasr, a bay Dahman Shahwan bred by Ali Pasha Sherif in 1886, his dam – Bint-Azz,[14] white by Wazir out of Azz (the daughter of the mare of Ibn Nakadan, Original Mare); his sire Aziz. Nasr, died of 'the eye', i.e. fell dead one day when being ridden out. This happened on the bridge. His only descendants were Kasida, Manokta and a colt ex Makbula.

Sale   Purchased from Maitre Cléry on 2 March 1898, in Cairo, for £200.

Description   Chestnut with white blaze and pale mane. Two white rope scars on off front leg, one a ring round the pastern over a spot just above the knee. Also, one tiny scar spot outside near fetlock joint and one in front of cannon bone of near hind leg. The blaze narrow ending pink, in shape above like a star joined to 'seyal'.

Imported to England in May 1898. Kasida went to Crabbet on the division of the stud in 1906. She was barren for eight years. Aged before her time (found to have 17 ribs). She was shot on 12 September 1913.

◀ *Kasida*

GSB Volume 19
Imported 1898

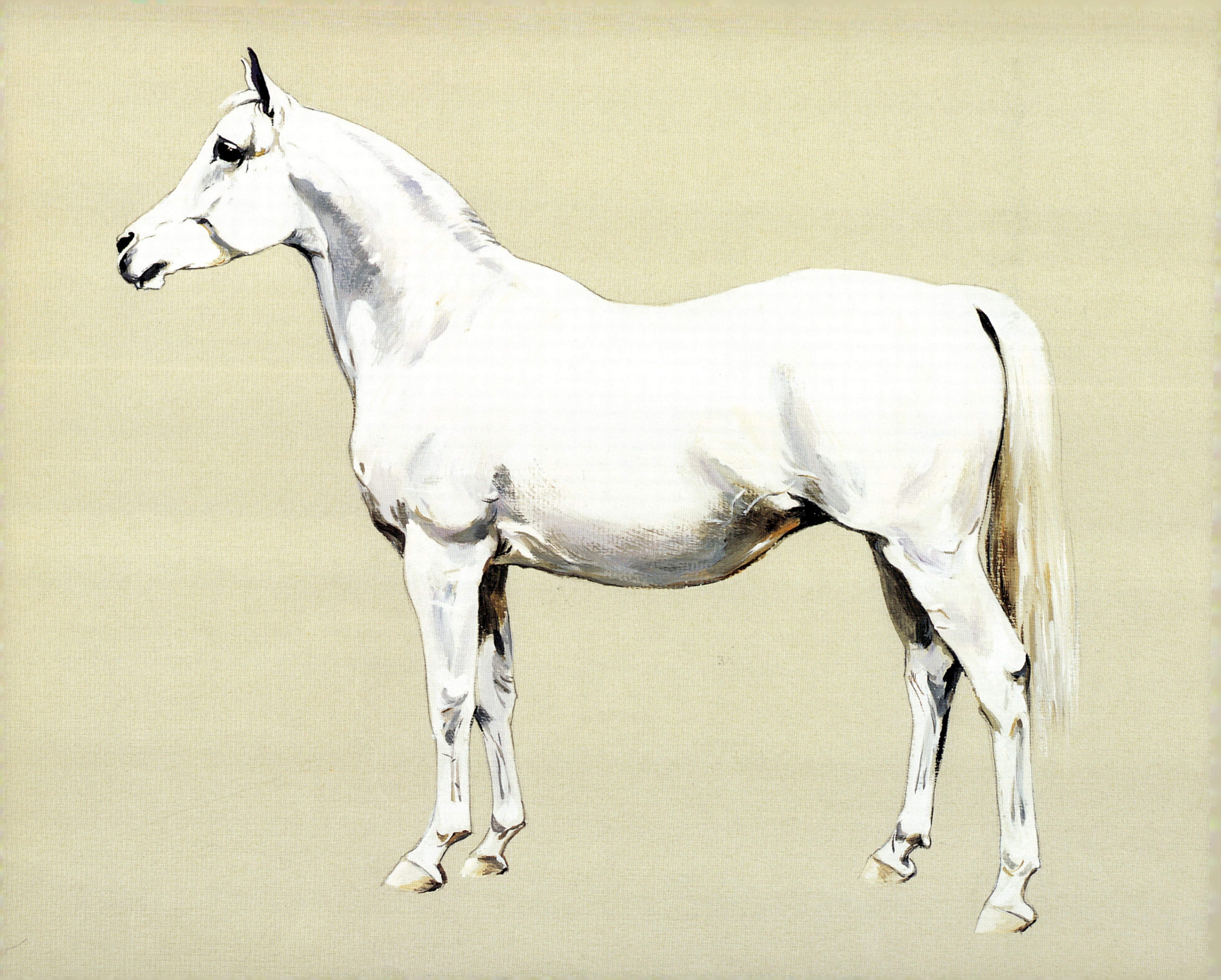

JELLABIEH (BINT BINT JELLABIET-FEYSUL)

A Kehilet Ajuz of the Jellabi strain or Kehileh Jellabieh.

The strain belonging to Ibn Khalifeh, Sheikh of Bahrain.

A white mare foaled in 1892.

Bred by Ali Pasha Sherif in Cairo.

Dam — Bint Jellabiet-Feysul, a chestnut Kehilet Ajuz of the Jellabi strain belonging to Ibn Khalifeh of Bahrain from whom Feysul Ibn Turki, Emir of Riâd obtained her dam. From Feysul she passed to the stud of Abbas Pasha I.

Sire — Ibn Nura, a white flea-bitten Dahman Nejib bred by Ali Pasha Sherif c. 1876, his dam – Bint Nura; his sire – Sottam, a Dahman Nejib.

Sale — Purchased from Ayub Bey, on 10 December 1897, for £E60, the sum Ayub Bey had paid Ali Pasha Sherif for her on 22 Rejeb 1313. Received with the mare the Hojja given at that time by her breeder.

Description — A white mare, with black hoofs, later flea-bitten, very small but strong. I like her immensely.

Imported to England in May 1898. She was sent to Lord Lovelace in the autumn of 1903 and remained at Ashley Combe, Somerset till his death in 1906, when she was returned to Crabbet. Sold to H.V.M. Clark in March 1912 with her bay filly by Berk for 30 guineas. The foal met with an accident after being weaned, when being led by Mr Clark, and was destroyed. Barren 1913 and 1914 and shot.

◄ *Jellabieh*

GSB Volume 19
AHS Volume 1
Imported 1898

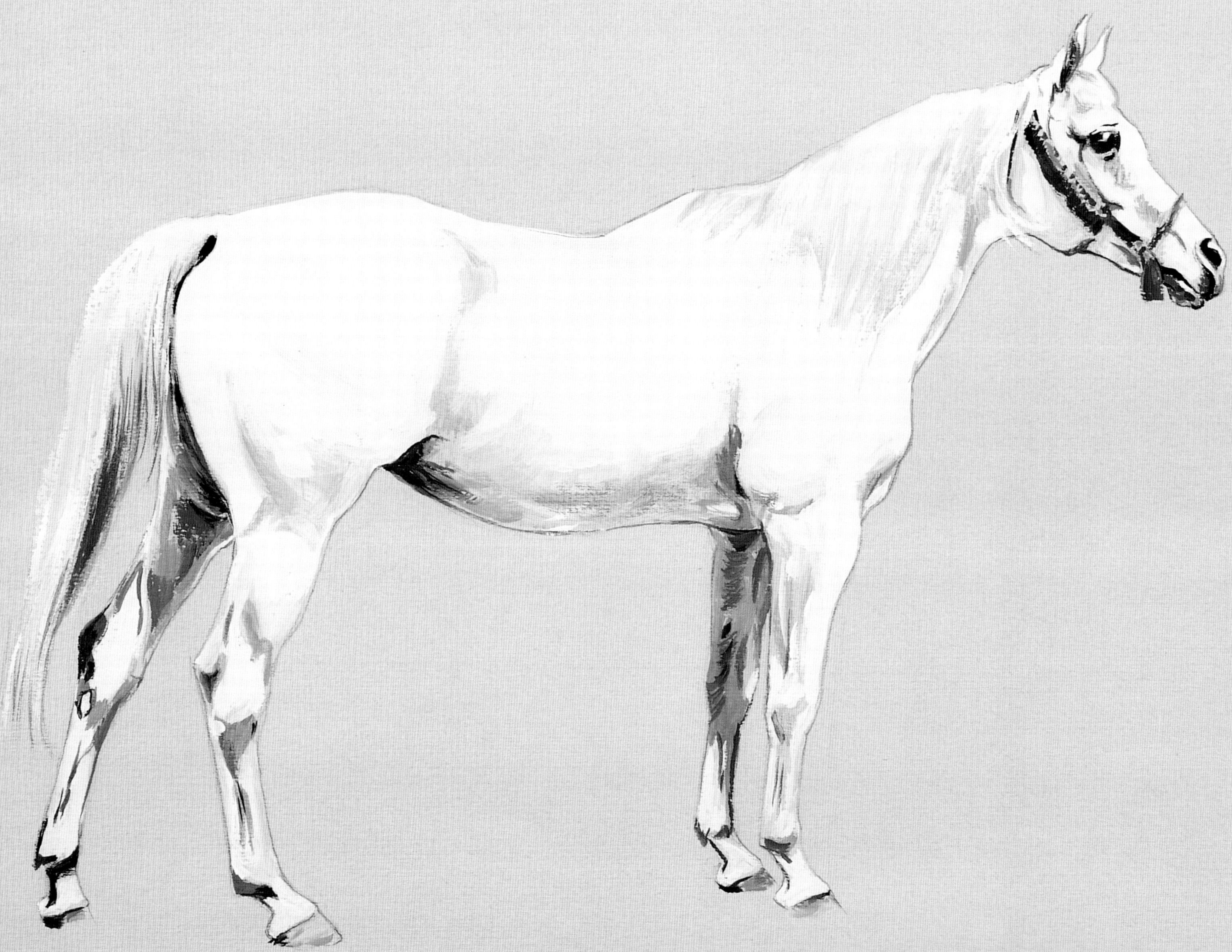

GHAZALA (BINT BINT HELWA)

A Seglawieh Jedranieh of Ibn Sudan's strain.

A grey mare foaled in May or June 1896.

Bred by Ali Pasha Sherif in Cairo.

Dam — Bint Helwa, a white Seglawieh Jedranieh of Ibn Sudan's strain bred by Ali Pasha Sherif, her dam – Helwa, a white Seglawieh Jedranieh bred by Ali Pasha Sherif; her dam – Horra (own sister to Wazir). Horra, white Seglawieh Jedranieh, by Zobeyni, Original Horse, white Seglawi Jedran brought by Abbas Pasha I from Ibn Sbeni, her dam – Ghazieh, Original Mare, grey (Zerka) Seglawieh Jedranieh bought by Abbas Pasha I from Ibn Sudan of the Roala. Helwa's sire was Shueyman, a white Shueyman Sabah bred by Ali Pasha Sherif, his dam – Shueyma, Original Mare, a Shueymah Sabahich; his sire – Jerboa, a... Dahman Nejib by ... out of the Dahmet el Hamra (bay Dahmeh Nejiba), Original Mare of Ibn Aweyde.
Bint Helwa's sire – Aziz, a chestnut Dahman Shahwan bred by Ali Pasha Sherif (c. 1877); his dam – Aziza, grey Dahmeh Shahwanieh by Samhan, a ... out of Bint Faras Nakadan (Faras Nakadan or Mare of Nakadan, Original Mare). His sire Harkan, a grey Kehilan Ajuz of the Harkan strain or Kehilan Harkan by Zobeyni, Original Horse white Seglawi Jedran of Ibn Sbeni, ex Harka, Original Mare imported by Abbas Pasha I.

Sire — Ibn Sherara,[15] a white Kehilan Ajuz of the Jellabi strain (or Kehilan Jellabi), from Ibn Khalifa and bred by Ali Pasha Sherif. His dam – Sherara, grey; his sire – Sottam, grey flea-bitten Dahman Nejib, by Sueyd, Original Horse, grey flea-bitten Seglawi Jedran bought by Abbas I from Ibn Sudan of the Roala, out of the white Dahmeh Nejiba of Khalil el Hajry. Ibn Khalifeh got both the Kehilan Jellabi and Dahman Shahwan strains from the tribes of East Arabia and Feysul Ibn Turki got the mare from him.

Sale — Purchased with her dam, Bint Helwa, from Ali Pasha Sherif on 14 December 1896.

Description — Grey mawardi, off hind leg white and blaze narrow above and vaguely spreading on muzzle ending pink. Became perfectly white.

Ghazala was sold in September 1909, to Colonel Spencer Borden, for 200 guineas for exportation to Fall River, Massachusetts. She was shipped to Liverpool on 19 October and from there forwarded by White Star 'Cymric' to USA, in foal to Jamil. In GSB Volume 22, Ghazala is recorded as having been imported in 1909 by Lady Anne Blunt and sent to USA.

◀ *Ghazala*

GSB Volume 22
Imported 1909

WILD THYME

A Kehilet Ajuz of the Ras el Fedawi strain.

A bay mare foaled in 1876.

Dam	Stated to have been bred by the Baggara tribe.
Sire	A Kehilet Ajuz of the Ras el Fedawi strain said to have been bred by the Baggara tribe.
Sale	Purchased by Mr Skene from Hamid el Abbas of the Beni Jamil, a branch of the Baggara tribe from the left bank of the Euphrates, in 1878, for £68. 16s. Mr Skene was buying for W.S. Blunt.
Description	Bay, no white except a star, leggy and light. Wilfrid Blunt wrote: 'No style, plain head, good shoulder. Paces and action easy. Temper perfect.'
Height	14 hands 3 1/2 inches.
Girth	71 inches.
Below knee	7 3/8 inches.

Wild Thyme was imported in 1878.[16] In the autumn of 1887 she as given to C.E. Tebbutt, Esq., with the agreement that should her Rataplan foal be a filly it should belong to the Crabbet Arabian Stud. The foal was the filly 'Wild Bee', who arrived at Crabbet on 3 November 1888.

GSB Volume 14
Imported 1878

JILFA

A Jilfeh Stam el Bulad of Abu Jedda.

A bay mare foaled in 1884.

Bred by Khashman el Kasab of the Moahib of the Sebaa, Anazeh, who obtained her granddam from Abu Jedda of the Shammar tribe in Mesopotamia.

Dam	A Jilfeh Stam el Bulad of Abu Jedda of the Shammar.
Sire	A Seglawi.
Sale	Purchased from her breeder, in the summer of 1887, near Tell el Ghorab, for £70. The witness of sale was Mutlak Ibn Hedeb of the Moayaja tribe of Sebaa.
Description	Description A strong bay, with a star.
Height	14 hands 1 inch.

Jilfa was imported in 1888 for Egypt, having been taken there with Azrek and Ashgar, by Zeyd Saad who had been sent to buy them. She was given to the Honourable Terence Bourke in August 1896 for exportation to Tunis and fetched away on 13 October 1896.

GSB Volume 17
Imported 1888

FERIDA

A Managhieh Hedruzieh of the strain of Ibn Sbeyel or Managhieh Sbeyelieh.

A bay mare foaled in 1886.

Dam	Bred by the Shammar tribe.
Sire	A Managhieh of the strain of Ibn Sbeyel.
Sale	Purchased by W.S. Blunt from Mohammed Khuddr Jemal el Din, Egypt, on 21 January 1891, for £35. Mohammed Khuddr, the Syrian, had brought her from Deyr on the Euphrates, where she had been purchased for him by his nephew from a Turkish Bey, an official there.
Description	All bay, about three white hairs on forehead. Good head and eye – small muzzle, light neck, excellent shoulder, good style and carriage of tail – small of bone, but short cannons and some windgalls on forefeet – a mark of firing round the body behind the girth. The mare resembles Jerboa.
Height	14 hands 1 ½ inches.

Ferida was imported in 1891. She was given to J.A.D. Lytton in 1907 and a home found for her.

GSB Volume 17
Imported 1891

The Blunts' Original Stallions

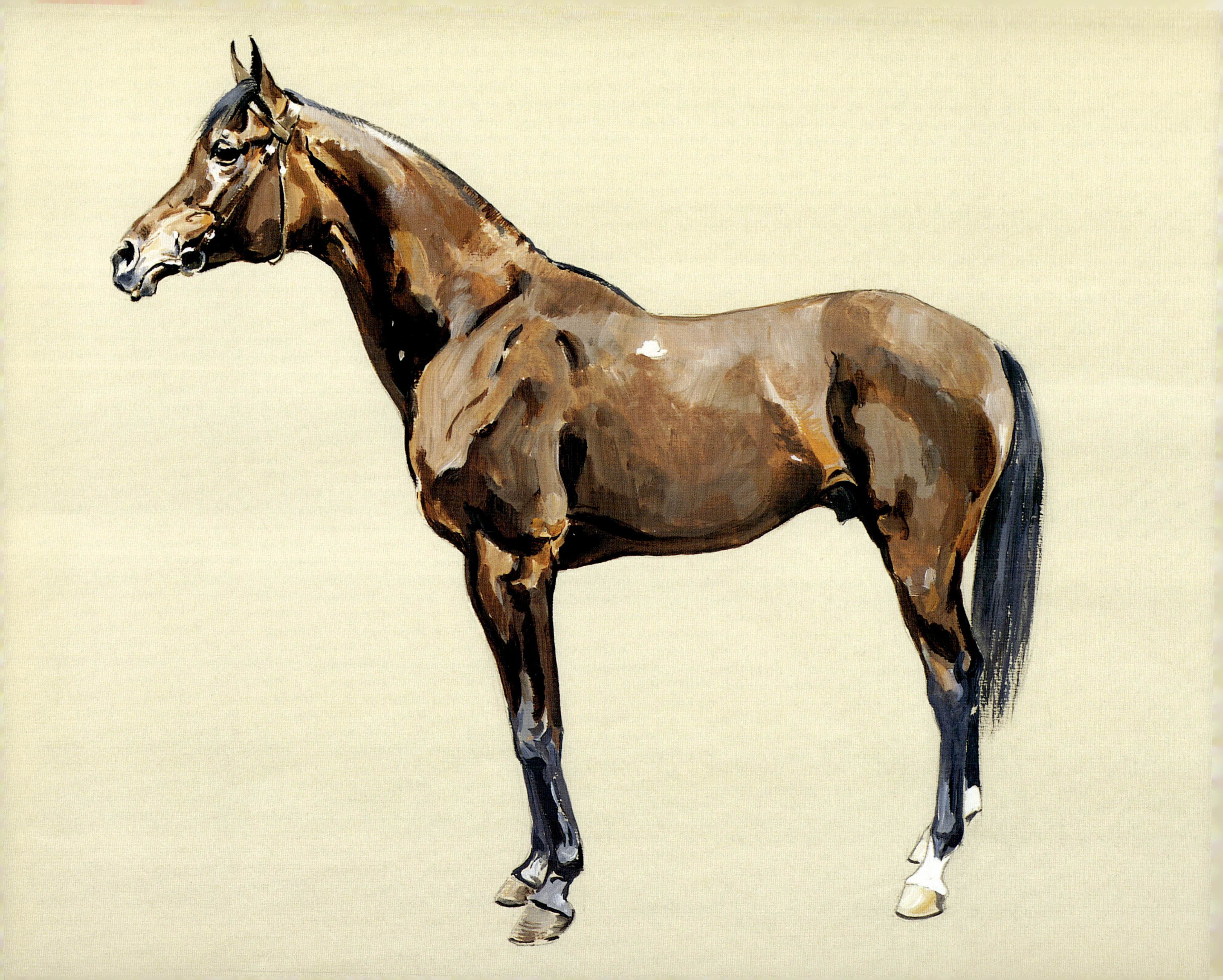

KARS

A Seglawi Jedran of Ibn Sbeyni's strain of the Mehed tribe of Fedaan Anazeh.

A bay horse foaled in 1874.

Bred by Ibn Sbeyni of the Mehed.

Dam	A Seglawieh Jedranieh of Ibn Sbeyni's strain.
Sire	Stated to have been a Seglawi Jedran.
Sale	Purchased from Haj Mahmud Aga, a Kurdish chief of Irregular Cavalry, on 5 January 1878, at Aleppo, for £69. Mahmud Aga obtained him as a 2-year-old from the Fedaan Anazeh and rode him to the war in Armenia in 1877, where nearly every other horse perished. Mahmud Aga was a Kurd of the Keydekani min Barazan tribe. He and his brother Mohammed went to the war with one hundred Khayal – fifty returned. Kars was hit twice by bullets, once on the near shoulder and once on the off leg below the knee inside. This brought blood and knocked him and Mahmud Aga over and several yards off. On the journey home, Kars was so ill that they took his bridle off and left him behind. When he saw that he was left, he got up and followed. Mahmud Aga did not buy Kars direct from the bedouin, but from an Agheyl. Mahmud was, however, positive that the Agheyl showed clearly that he was Seglawi Jedran of Ibn Sbeyni.
Description	A bright strong bay with black points, hind feet white to fetlocks, small star on forehead, fine head with deep jowl (mitbeh) and prominent forehead (jibbah), large nostrils, small muzzle, magnificent shoulder, high wither, great depth in front of girth, rather light of barrel, powerful quarter but rather drooping, tail however, well carried when galloping, perfect hocks and knees and a mark-a-dent on near side of neck (prophet's thumb mark). A brilliant fencer, well up to 13 stone with hounds. He is magnificent – just enough action and a good stride with his legs well under him. In short, he leaves nothing to be desired as to shape, action, colour, and temper.
Height	14 hands 2 $\frac{1}{2}$ inches.
Girth	63 $\frac{1}{2}$ inches.
Below knee	7 $\frac{1}{2}$ inches.

Kars was imported in 1878 and sold to D. MacKay Esq., of New South Wales, in June 1885, for 250 guineas. 'In July 1900, heard from H.C. White, Esq., that Kars is still living.'

GSB Volume 14
Imported 1878

◀ *Kars*

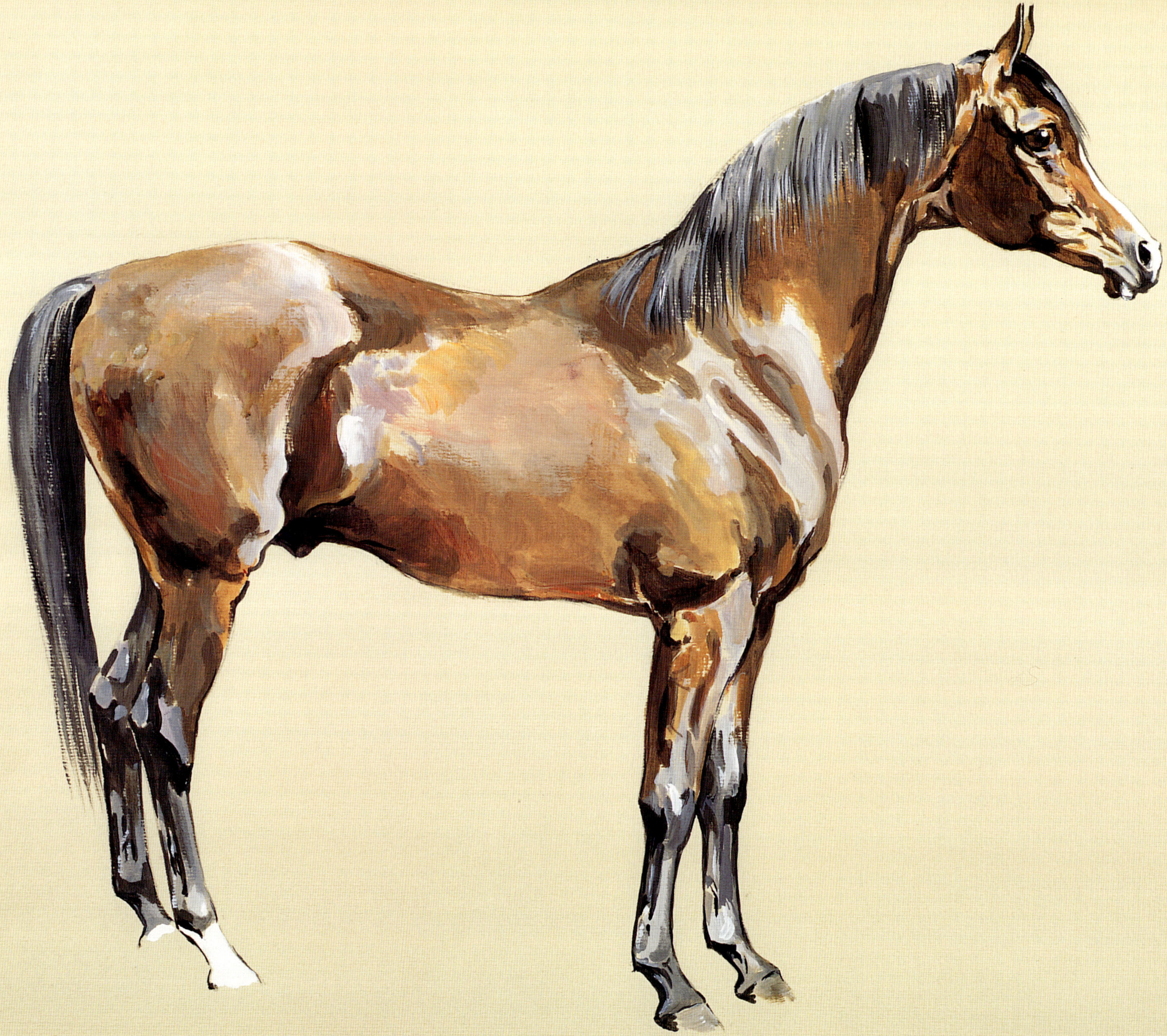

PHARAOH

A Seglawi Jedran of Ibn ed Derri's strain.

A dark bay horse foaled in 1876.

Bred by Neddi Ibn ed Derri of the Resallin, related to the Gomussa tribe of Sebaa Anazeh.

Dam	A bay Seglawieh Jedranieh, her sire – a Seglawi Jedran of Obeyd el Belasi of the Ibn Majil section of the Roala.
Sire	A bay Kehilan Ajuz belonging to Jemaat, of the portion of the Gomussa tribe under the supreme Sheikh Beteyen Ibn Mirshid.
Sale	Purchased by Mr J.H. Skene from Neddi Ibn ed Derri of the Resallin in October 1878, at the camp of Beteyen Ibn Mirshid near Palmyra, at a cost of £275 (£125 in gold, the rest being the value of a mare given). Mr Skene was buying for Mr Blunt.
Description	A dark rich bay with black points, hind feet white to just below the fetlocks, narrow blaze and strip of white (seyal) from the forehead above the eyes down to the lip, fine head with deep jowl, very beautiful ears, eyes showing white like human eyes, splendid carriage of tail at all times, never forgets himself, nor slouches. A fine mover galloping.
Height	14 hands 3 inches.
Girth	67 inches.
Below knee	7 3/4 inches.

Pharaoh was imported in 1879 and sold at the 1st Crabbet Sale in 1882, to Count Joseph Potocki for 500 guineas, for export to Russian Poland. 'We sold the horse too soon but £500 was a large price, and indeed the mistake at Crabbet was not have more Pharaoh foals before he left – we had three years to do it and yet only have now one pure Pharaoh mare, viz. Bozra who is the pick of the stud. There is Shelfa, of course, too, who is granddaughter through Jeroboam. Count Potocki sold Pharaoh three years later and the horse became the principal stallion in the Emperor of Russia's private stud. In 1891 an enquiry was made with a view to the re-purchase (Azrek being sold) of Pharaoh, but Count Potocki wrote: "il n'y a pas question de le racheter", that if there were he would be the first to do it. The letter says, "Pharaoh quite unattainable – he is much valued and all his stock are good, strong and beautiful." In 1899 head from Colonel de Sdanovitch that Pharaoh was at the Derkoul stud.'

◀ *Pharaoh*

GSB Volume 14
Imported 1879

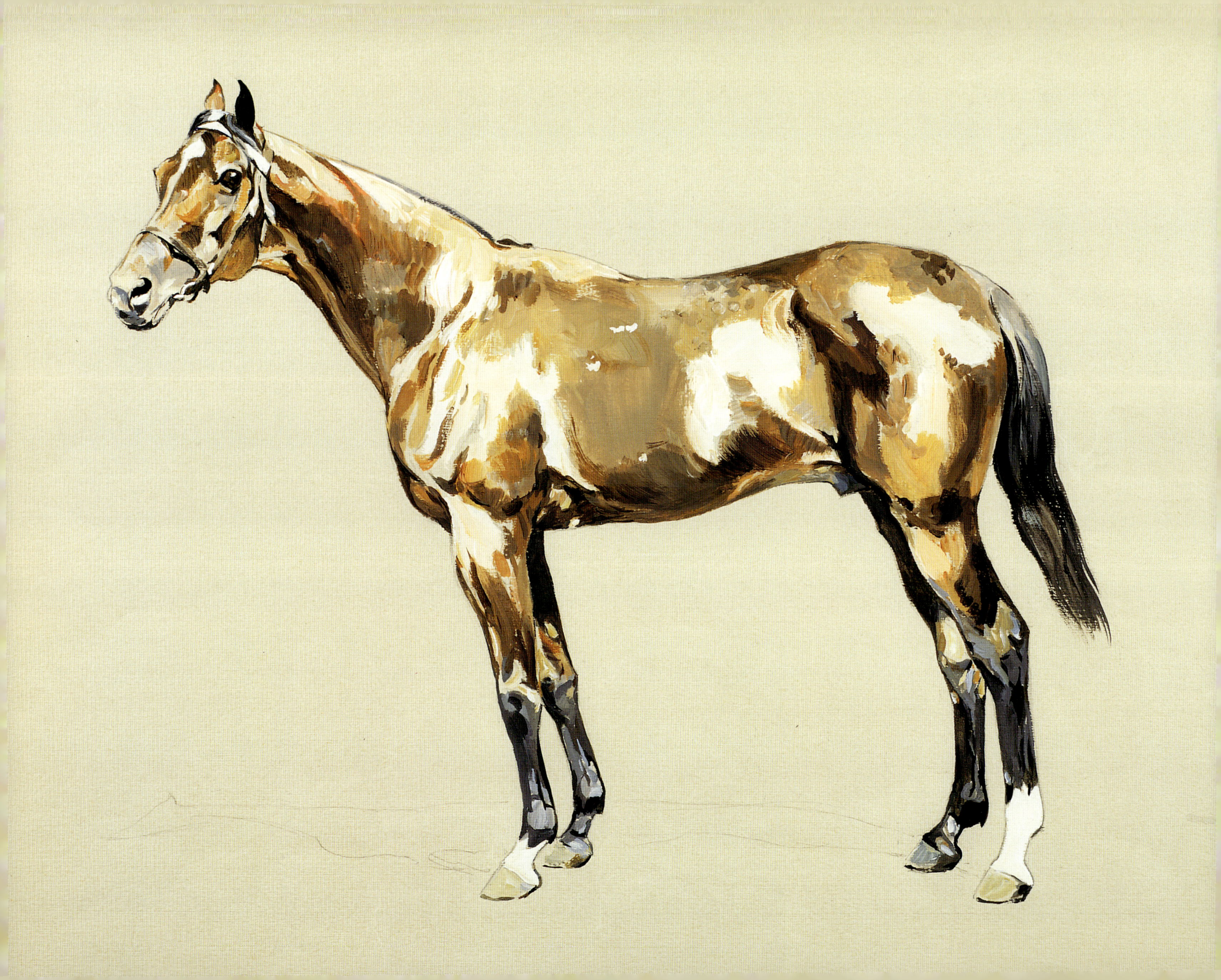

RATAPLAN

A Dahman Om Aamr of Ibn Hemsi's strain.

A brown horse foaled c. 1874.

Bred by Ibn Hemsi of the Gomussa. From the Gomussa he passed through a certain Khalaf of Baghdad to Abdul Mehsin Ibn Bedr of the Erfuddi tribe of Ibn Haddal Anazeh. He brought the horse over to India and sold him to Abder Rahman Minni of Shakra and Bombay.

Sale — Purchased from Abder Rahman Minni on 17 February 1884, at Bombay, for £250. A winner of races at Mysore, Poona, Bangalore, Wellington and Baroda.

Description — A rich brown with very black points, near feet white to under fetlock joints and star. Good head with prominent forehead [Wilfrid did not admire his head as much as Lady Anne], well set on a light neck. Fine forehand and fine shoulder, great depth, powerful quarter, tail carried well, perfect paces walking, trotting, galloping. Very quiet and gentle, yet with hounds a hard puller. We shall name him Ambar.

Height — 14 hands 2 1/2 inches.

Girth — 62 inches.

Below knee — 7 1/2 inches.

Imported on 4 April 1884. He came third in the two-mile race on 2 July 1884 at Newmarket. He perished at sea on the way to Egypt in October 1887.

GSB Volume 15
Imported 1884

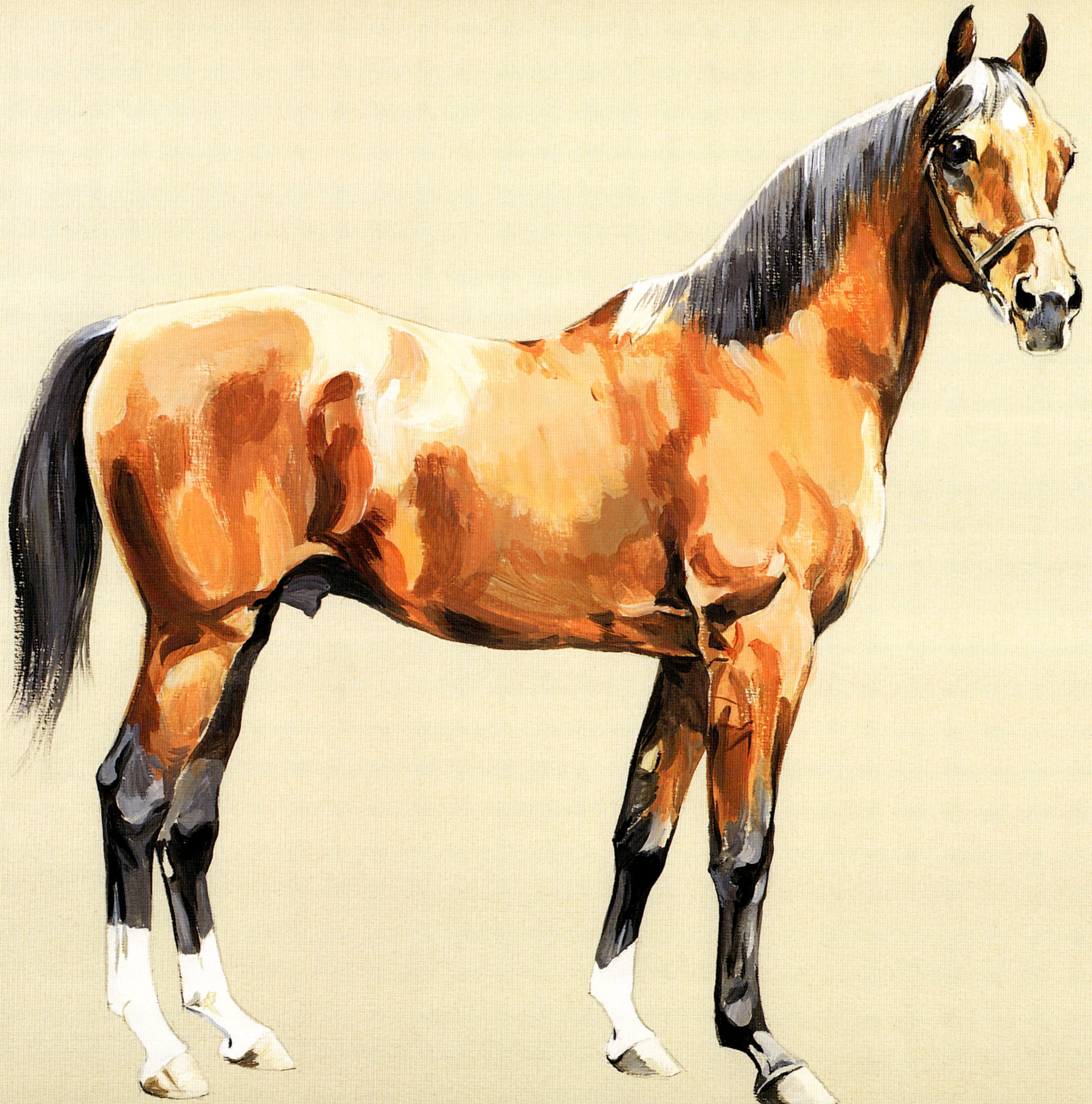

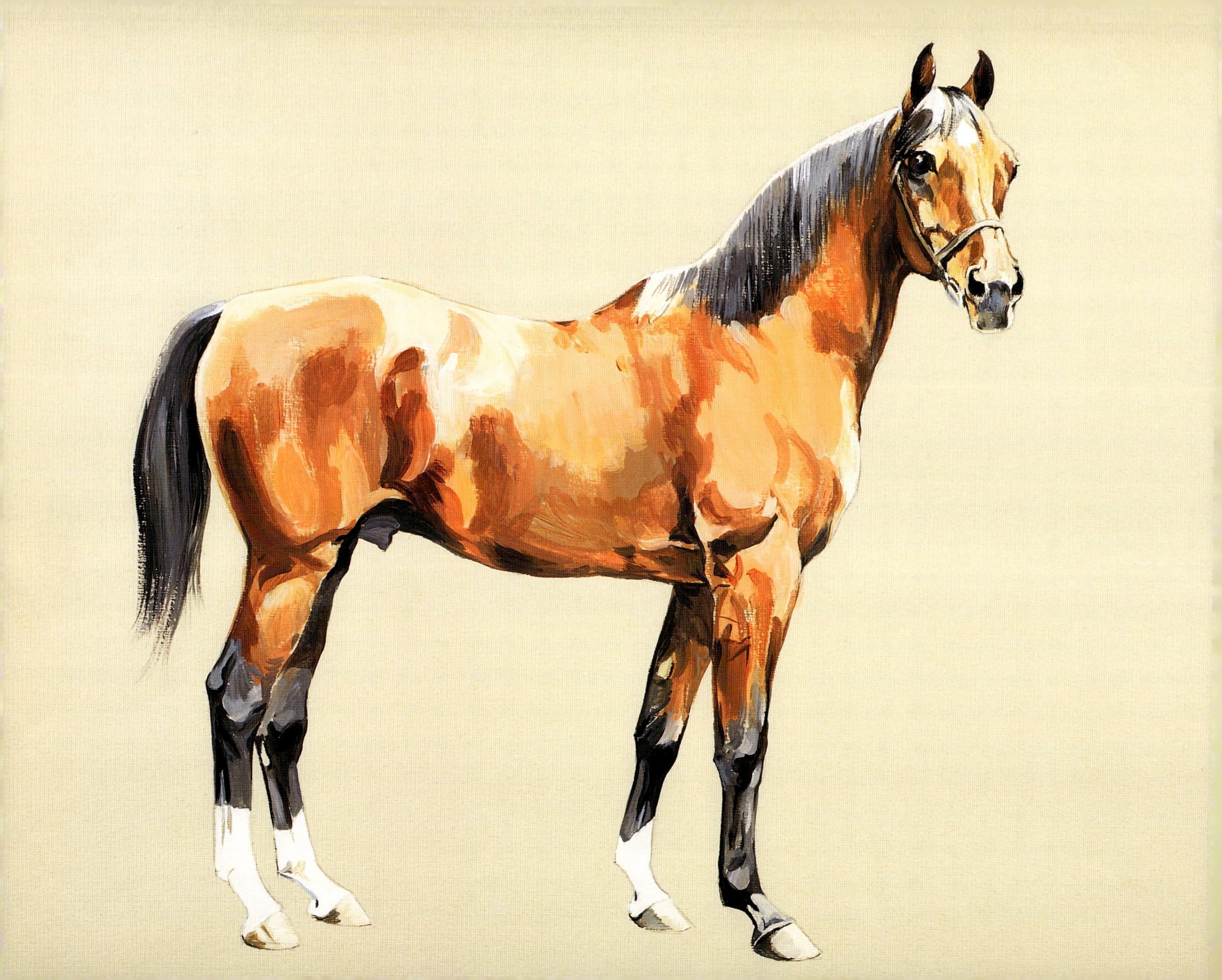

HADBAN

A Hadban Enzeyhi of the Oteybeh tribe.

A bay horse foaled in 1878.

Bred by Jakin Ibn Aghil, Sheikh of the Daajini tribe of Oteybeh, a tribe of Western Nejd, from whom he was purchased, as a 5-year-old, by Ali Ibn Amr of Bussora and Bombay, for 500 rials, and exported to Bombay in the autumn of 1883.

Sale	Purchased from Ali Ibn Amr on 13 December 1883, soon after being landed at Bombay, for 1217 rupees [just over £100].
Description	A bright bay with three white feet, hind feet and near forefeet (mutlak al yemin) and star. Splendid head with prominent forehead (jibbah), small muzzle, neck a trifle short but well placed, good shoulder, pasterns rather too long, fine carriage of tail. A fine trotter in harness and a grand mover galloping. Defect – stands slightly back, also bone lighter than some, but quality of sinews appears wirey and shape and style shows perfect blood. Masbut in the tribe. He has a fine temper. First seen on 13 December 1883. A splendid horse.
Height	14 hands 2 1/2 inches.
Girth	68 inches.
Below knee	7 3/4 inches, rather over than under.

Imported on 4 April 1884 and sold to D. Mackay, Esq., of New South Wales for 120 guineas for export to Australia. In view of the excellence of the mares by Hadban it is to be regretted that there were so few of his stock. Still alive in 1895.

Wilfrid Blunt wrote of him: 'Hadban is, next to Mesaoud, the most important sire we imported, being numerously represented in the Stud Book through Rose of Sharon and Nefisa, his two best daughters and our two most valuable brood mares.'

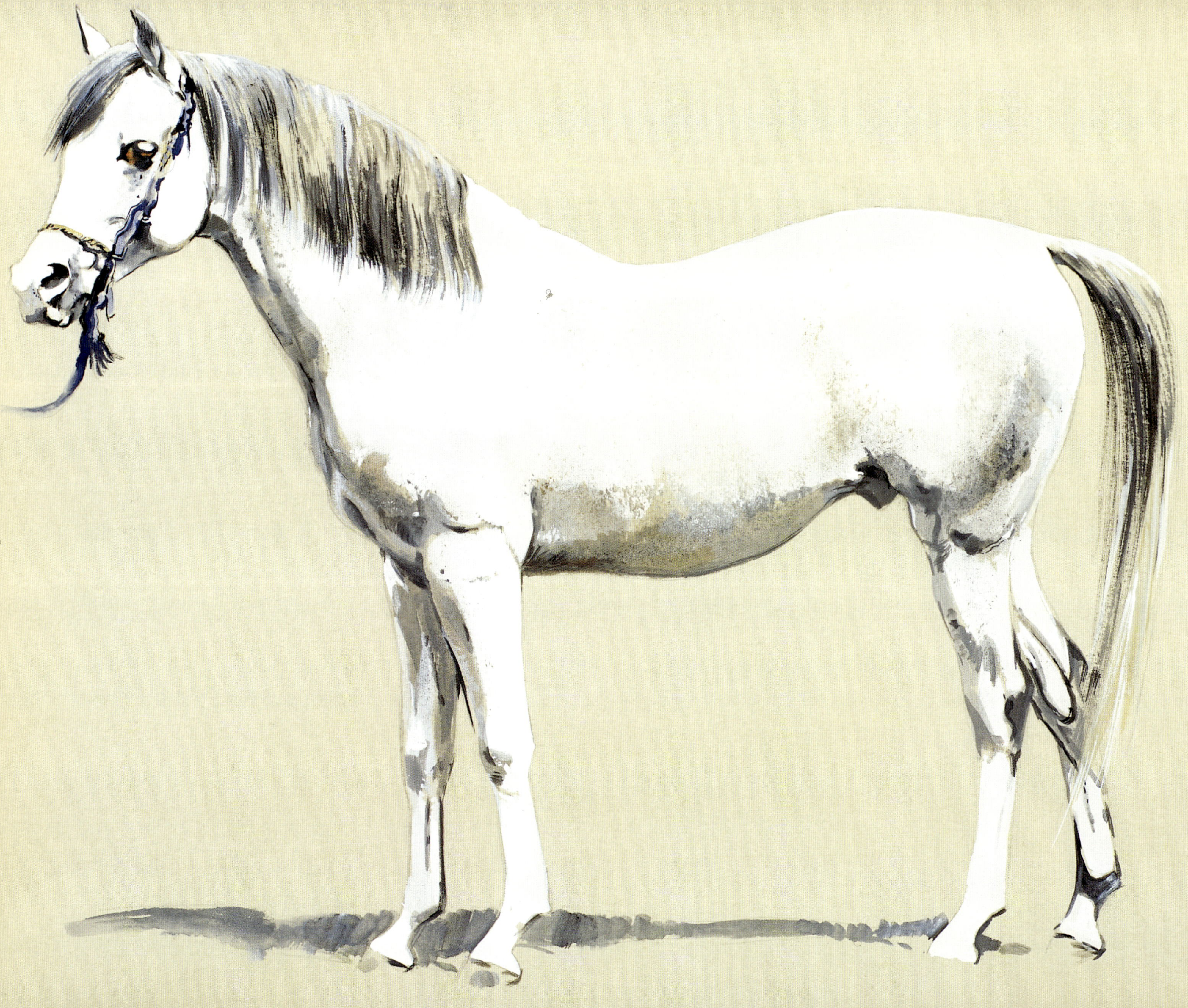

AZREK

A Seglawi Jedran of Ibn ed Derri's strain.

A grey horse foaled in 1881.

Bred by Sheikh Mashlab Ibn ed Derri of the Resallin, related to the Gomussa tribe of the Sebaa Anazeh.[17]

Dam — A chestnut Seglawieh Jedranieh, half-sister to Pharaoh. [Seen by the Blunts in Meshur's camp on 8 April 1881 when they tried to buy her.] Very small, fine carriage of tail, off knee scarred, no white except for blaze, sire – a Hadban. With her a bay yearling colt (will be grey) [Azrek] extremely handsome – will be a wonderful horse.

Sale — Purchased from his breeder in the desert in the summer of 1887 for W.S. Blunt by Zeyd Saad el Muteyri, who was sent, via Beyrout and Damascus, in March 1887, expressly to purchase this grey horse of Ibn ed Derri's. The Seglawi was bought for 500 rials – about the price Zeyd told us – namely, £110 English. He was brought by land – with Ashgar and Jilfa – to Egypt. A celebrated stallion among the tribes both for his speed and as a sire. Seen as a foal at Ibn ed Derri's in the spring of 1881.

Description — A grey with very black points and black mane and tail (at 7 years). Afterwards, became white and flea-bitten. A magnificent horse in every way, grand head and neck, powerful shoulder with unrivalled trotting action, seen approaching at a trot, one saw underneath the hoof. Enormous strength of back and quarter up to any weight. Tail set very high and splendidly carried; legs absolute perfection, the sinew literally like steel to touch. Great speed and impossible to tire. His stock superior to any other sire yet in this stud in 1891. Azrek is excited at the sight of a white mare – his own colour.

Height — 14 hands 2 inches.

Below knee — 7 1/8 inches.

Imported to England early in 1888, with Ashgar and Jilfa. Azrek was sold in the autumn of 1891 to the Honourable Cecil Rhodes, through his agent Mr Thompson, for 400 guineas, for export to the Cape. It is impossible not to feel a pang of regret at the departure of a horse such as Azrek whose stock are so satisfactory, while the stud remains with yet untried sires. There should be a good many worthy sires to represent him; but they are still young, the oldest, a 2-year-old.

GSB Volume 16
Imported 1888

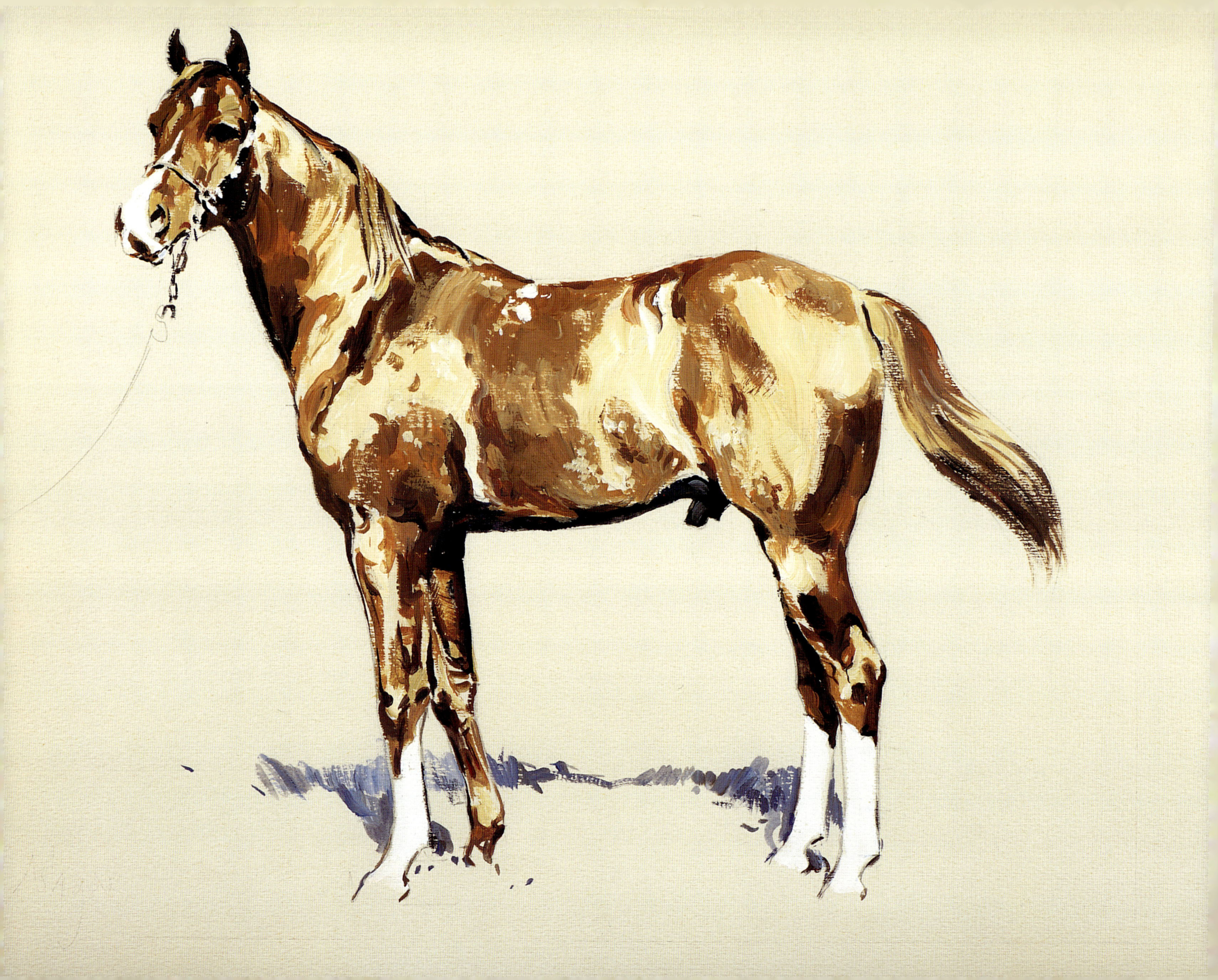

ASHGAR

A Seglawi Obeyran of the Saëkh tribe.

A dark chestnut horse foaled in 1883

Bred by Othman el Ibrahim el Akeyli of Deyr on the Euphrates.

Dam	A Seglawieh Obeyrieh of the Saëkh tribe of the Shammar in Mesopotamia.
Sire	An Abeyan Sherrak.
Sale	Purchased from his breeder in 1887 by Mr W.S. Blunt, who had sent Zeyd Saad el Muteyri to the Resallin tribe of the Sebaa, in order to purchase the grey horse of Ibn ed Derri's [Azrek*], and two other colts, or a colt and a mare, or two mares. He had not to give a large price for any horse, but the celebrated grey of Ibn ed Derri. He was to take £150 with him. Zeyd returned to Egypt with three horses – Azrek*, Ashgar* and the mare Jilfa*.
Description	A very dark chestnut with some grey hairs on the barrel. Three white feet, hind feet and near front foot (mutlak al yemin), star and snip so joined as to make almost a blaze. Good and fast trotter, excellent in single harness and untiring.
Height	c. 14 hands.

Imported in 1888. Ashgar was sold in September 1890 to Lieutenant Cecil Taylor RA for 120 guineas for exportation to Gibraltar.

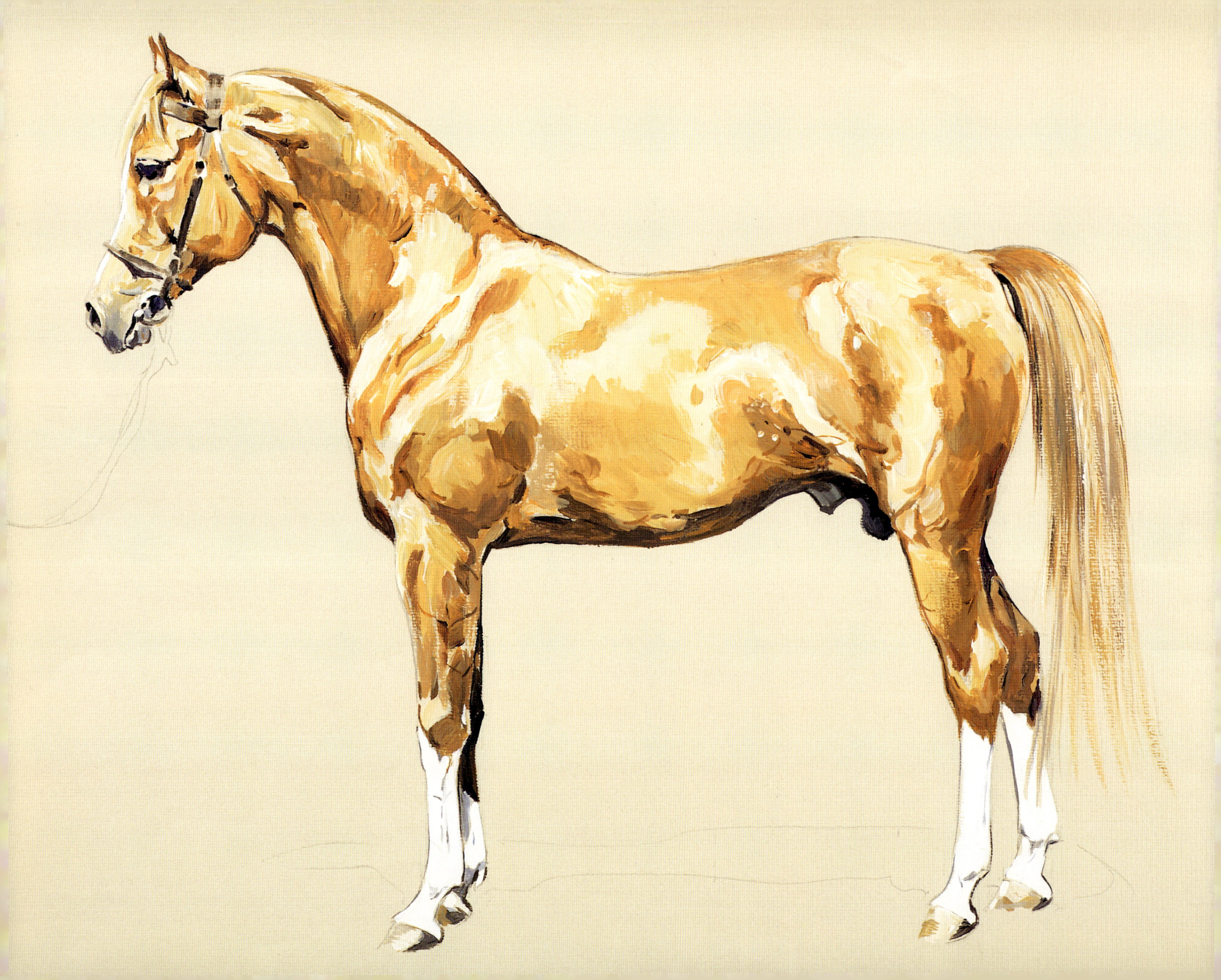

MESAOUD

A Seglawi Jedran of Ibn Sudan's strain.

A chestnut horse foaled on 3 January 1887.

Bred by Ali Pasha Sherif.

His strain formerly belonged to Ibn Sudan of the Roala, but no longer exists in the desert, for Abbas Pasha I bought up all that he could hear of till none were left, and all that Abbas Pasha's stud possessed, passed into the hands of Ali Pasha Sherif.

Dam — Yemameh, a grey Seglawieh Jedranieh of Ibn Sudan's strain, her dam – Bint Ghazieh by Zobeyni, Original Horse; her sire – Shueyman.

Sire — Aziz, a chestnut Dahman Shahwan, bred by Ali Pasha c.1877, whose dam, Aziza, was granddaughter to the 'mare of Nakadan', Original Mare, a Dahmeh Shahwanieh from the stud of Feysul Ibn Turki, Emir of Riâd, but originally from Ibn Khalifeh of Bahrain. [Aziz was a first much criticized by Lady Anne for his bad hocks, although otherwise considered good. However, she later described him as a handsome, very showy horse and the hocks altogether improved. Rather long in the head with fine long well-arched neck. At 20 years old, Lady Anne described him as glorious.]

Sale — Purchased from Ali Pasha Sherif, on 27 January 1889, priced at £60. [Merzuk and Khatila were purchased at the same time. Lady Anne noted: '...the pick is, of course, the Seglawi Soudani, son of Aziz. He is four white legged and high up to the knee but surprising handsome. For a defect there is a certain lightness of hock inherited from Aziz but nothing wrong.']

Description — A bright chestnut with four white feet and a blaze, a mark of white under the chin, also a group of white specks under the jowl. Beautiful head and ears, very fine shoulder, great depth in front of girth, powerful quarters, large hocks and knees and remarkably deep-cut sinews. Tail set on very high and carried magnificently. Dark line along back. Fine mover, fast walker and trotter.

Height — 14 hands 2 1/2 inches.   Girth   69 inches.   Below knee   7 3/4 inches.

Mesaoud was imported to England in 1891, and was sold, in June 1903, to Wladislas Kliniewski, 'a Niezdow près Opole Royaume de Pologne Empire de Russia', for 240 guineas, and taken away, in July, a few days after the 15th Crabbet Sale of 4 July 1903.

Wilfrid Blunt wrote: 'Mesaoud was by far the most important of our imported sires, and nearly all our best mares are descended from him. Indeed, he may be considered as the foundation in the male line of our stud, for neither Kars, nor Pharaoh, nor Azrek were at all to be compared to him as a sire.'

◄ *Mesaoud*

GSB Volume 17
Imported 1891

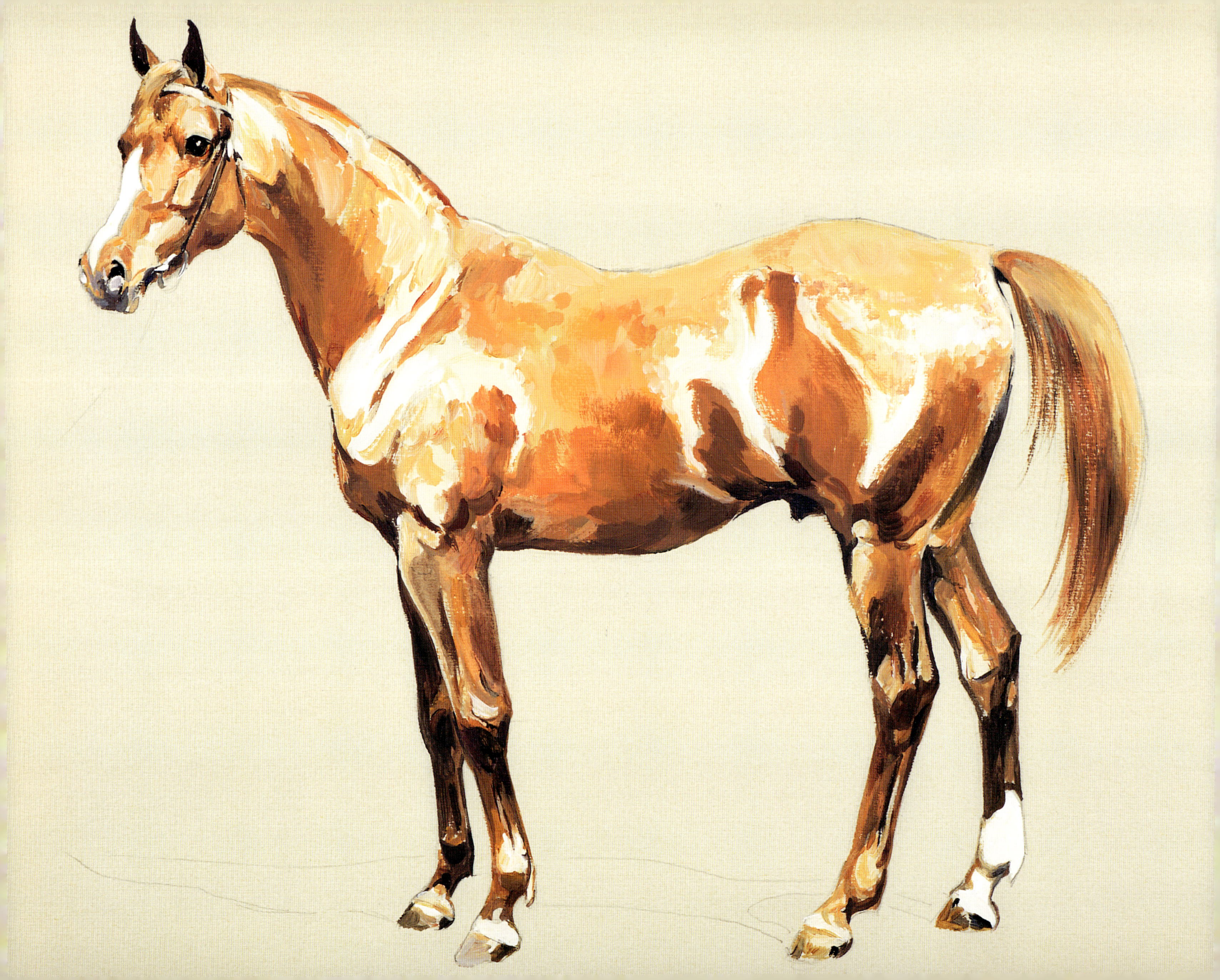

MERZUK

A Kehilan Ajuz of the Jellabi strain or Kehilan Jellabi.

A chestnut horse foaled in February 1887.

Bred by Ali Pasha Sherif.

A Kehilan Jellabi of the strain procured by Abbas Pasha I from Ibn Khalifeh, the Sheikh of Bahrain and afterwards possessed by Ali Pasha Sherif.

Dam	A chestnut Kehileh Jellabieh.
Sire	Wazir, the celebrated white stallion, a Seglawi Jedran of Ibn Sudan's strain – a strain no longer existing in the desert. [In 1888, Lady Anne noted that: 'Wazir... seems well in spite of his great age, 26 years.']
Sale	Purchased from Ali Pasha Sherif, on 27 January 1889, priced at £100.
Description	A strong chestnut with two white feet, off hind and near fore, and a speck of white on near hind foot and narrow crooked blaze. Very broad forehead and prominent eyes, short ears very pricked, strong back well ribbed up, remarkably good legs and especially fine hocks. Very handsome and full of fire.
Height	14 hands 2 ½ inches.

Merzuk (also known as the Jelaby colt, Marzouk and Merzug), was imported in 1891, and sold during the summer of 1891 to Sir Henry Loch, Governor of the Cape, for 200 guineas for export to Basutoland. A horse that would have been valuable to keep, but a promise had been given to find a horse for the Cape. In 1893, after having been the sire of about forty foals, Merzuk fell a victim to the African horse-sickness.

Wilfrid Blunt noted: 'There is no doubt that Merzuk ought to have remained in this stud. His value is evident from the excellence of the one mare (Ridaa) by him.'

◄ *Merzuk*

GSB Volume 17
Imported 1891

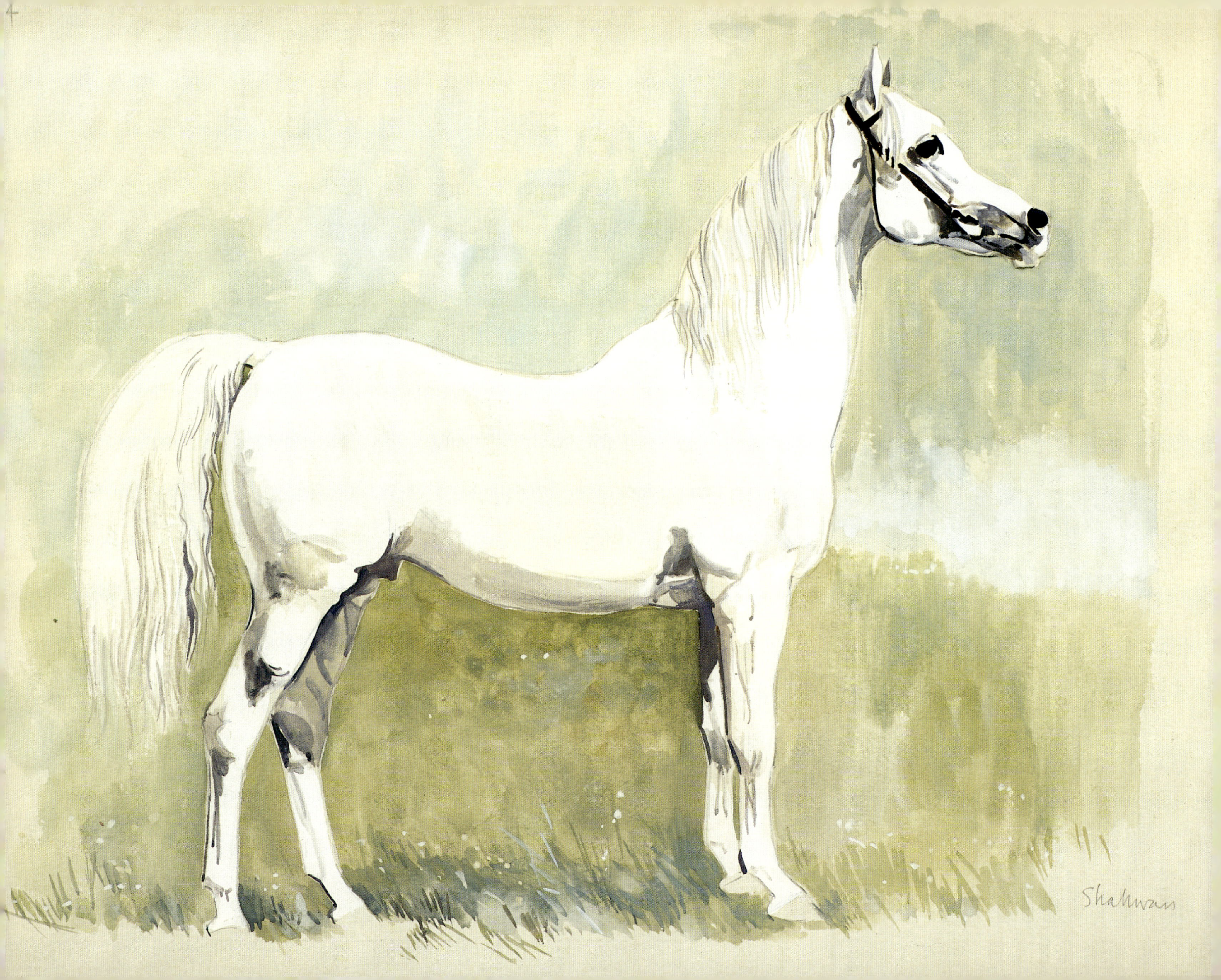
Shahwan

SHAHWAN

A Dahman Shahwan of the strain of Ibn Khalifeh, Sheikh of Bahrain.

A white horse foaled on 12 January 1887.

Bred by Ali Pasha Sherif, but foaled in the possession of Mohammed Sadyk Pasha to whom Ali Pasha Sherif gave the dam in foal.

Dam	A grey Dahmeh Shahwanieh, dam's granddam - the mare of Ibn Khalifeh.
Sire	Wazir, the celebrated white Seglawi Jedran bred by Ali Pasha Sherif, his dam - Ghazieh, white Seglawieh Jedranieh, Original Mare; his sire - Zobeyni, the white Seglawi Jedran of Ibn Sbeyni, Original Horse. [This horse was described by Lady Anne Blunt as, 'fine all round', and she preferred him above all others, remarking that he combines the Ibn Sudan and Ibn Sbeni strains. His head reminded her at different times of Kars, Basilisk and Sherifa.]
Sale	Purchased from Mohammed Sadyk Pasha, on 23 January 1892, for £62.
Description	White with black hoofs, about the ears and tail are still (in 1892) traces of the horse having been foaled chestnut. Fine style and surprising carriage of tail; great strength of back and quarters and free shoulder action. The off knee blemished, said to have been done when a foal. The more we see the more we like him.
Height	14 hands 1 inch.
Girth	64 ½ inches.
Below knee	7 inches.

Shahwan was imported in April 1892. He was sold in September 1895 to J.A.P. Ramsdell of America for 250 guineas down with 50 more to follow on success at a show. Exported to USA. Winner of prizes in England - 2nd, Hurlingham, 1894; 3rd, Ranelagh, 1894 - and in America.

Wilfrid Blunt wrote of him: 'Shahwan was a splendid type of white Arab, very beautiful and very powerful. As, however, his colour was very little in request, he was used sparingly at the stud. We made a great mistake in this, but many of his mares proved barren and his stock was less than first rate. We have an important strain of his blood in Ibn Yashmak, where his dam Yashmak was sired by him at Sheykh Obeyd.

◀ *Shahwan*

GSB Volume 17
Imported 1892

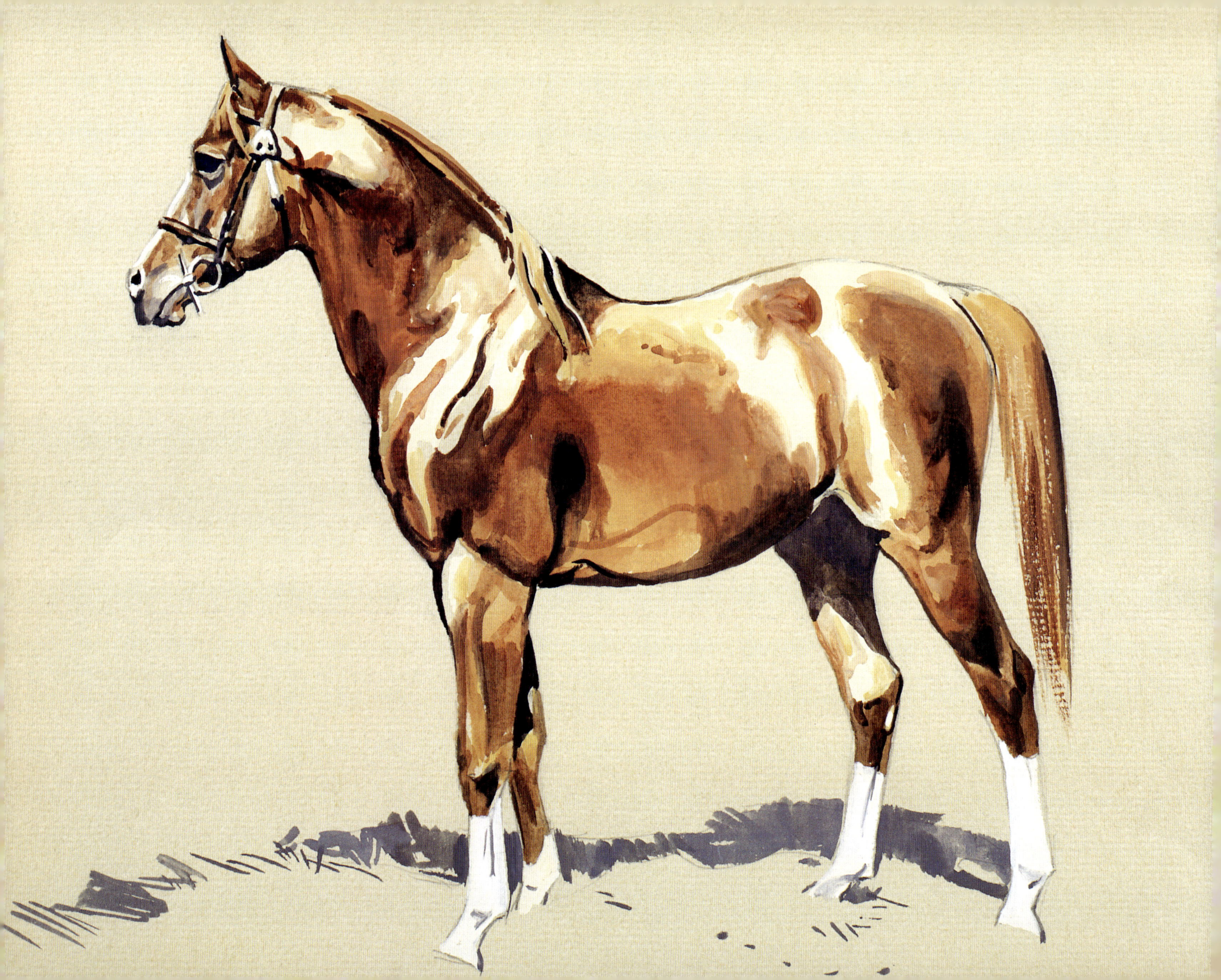

MAHRUSS (SHOULD BE IBN MAHRUSS)

A Dahman Nejib.

A chestnut horse foaled in 1893 (22 Ramadan 1313 or 6 Ramadan 1310).

Bred by Ali Pasha Sherif.

Dam	Bint Nura (should be Bint Bint Nura), a chestnut Dahmeh Nejiba bred by Ali Pasha Sherif, her dam – Nura (should be Bint Nura); her sire – Aziz.
Sire	Mahruss, a grey Wadnan Kursan bred by Ali Pasha Sherif, his dam – the grey mare, daughter of the 'black' mare of Bender Ibn Saadun, Original Mare; his sire – Wazir, the celebrated white Seglawi Jedran of Ibn Sudan's strain. [Mahruss died in Cairo in 1895.
Sale	Purchased from Ali Pasha Sherif, on 17 January 1896, for £50.
Description	A bright strong chestnut with four white feet, three of them stockings, the off fore only to above pastern. Star rather high and to off side of forehead and joined to it by very narrow white line, a snip ending between nostrils.
Height	14 hands 1 ½ inches.
Below knee	7 ¾ inches.

Mahruss was imported in May 1897. He was sold on 20 June 1900 to J. Hamilton Leigh, Esq., of Brinnington Mount, Stockport for 200 guineas.

Wilfrid Blunt wrote of him: 'Mahruss was a good horse, strong and handsome but not first rate and with defective action. He was put to stud in 1898 but used sparingly and [mares] proving mostly barren to him, he was sold. His sole stock remaining with us, Rijm, however, gives him a place of honour here. He has proved a successful stock getter in his new owner's hands in Ireland having been purchased of W. Leigh for only £84.'

Abu Khasheb, full brother to Mahruss was also imported to England. A grey, bred by Ali Pasha Sherif in 1894, he was purchased for £40. He was sold at the 13th Crabbet Sale, on 6 July 1901, to Sir John Watson KCB, for 280 guineas, for exportation to India.

◀ *(Ibn) Mahruss*

GSB Volume 19
Imported 1897

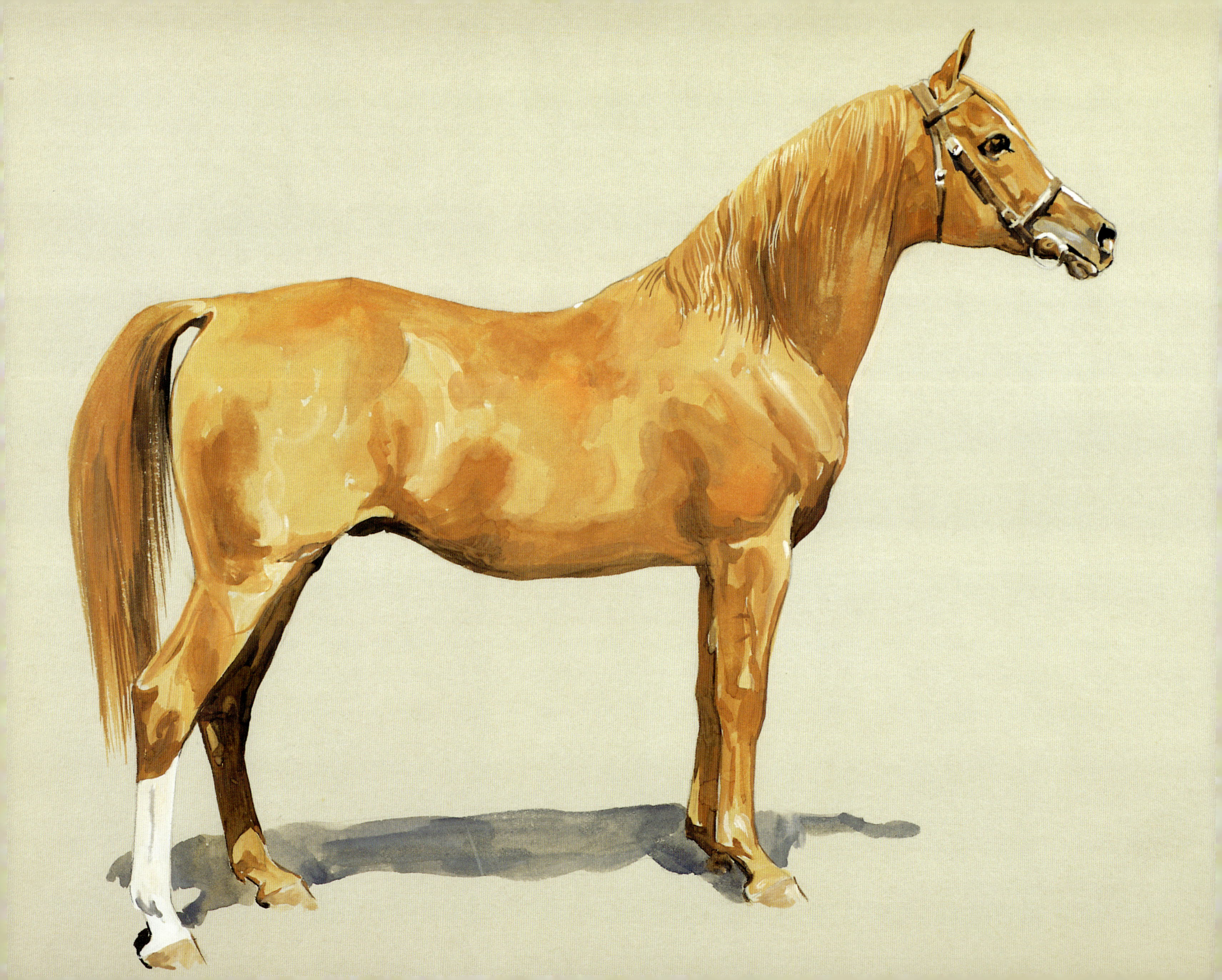

FEYSUL

A Kehilan Ajuz of the Jellabi strain or Kehilan Jellabi.

A chestnut horse foaled in 1894.

Bred by Ali Pasha Sherif in Cairo.

Dam — 'Bint Bint-Jellabiet-Feysul' (i.e. Feysul Ibn Turki – Amir of Riâd) a chestnut/white[?] Kehileh Jellabieh also called 'the Lame' from having broken a front leg, bred by Ali Pasha Sherif, her dam - Bint-Jellabiet-Feysul, a Kehileh Jellabieh... out of Jellabiet-Feysul, a Kehileh Jellabieh, Original Mare brought to Egypt by Abbas Pasha I, Viceroy of Egypt (for, it is said, £7,000!) from Feysul Ibn Turki, Emir of Riâd.

Sire — Ibn Nura, a flea-bitten white Dahman Nejib, bred by Ali Pasha Sherif [owned by WSB and AINB], his dam – Bint Nura, a bay Dahmeh Nejiba by Zobeyni, Original Horse, out of Nura, a grey Dahmeh Nejiba, Original Mare, (Query, was 'Nura' the daughter of the Dahmeh Nejiba of Khalil el Hajry?); his sire – Sottam, a grey flea-bitten Dahman Nejib by Sueyd, a flea-bitten grey Seglawi Jedran, Original Horse, from Ibn Sudan out of the white Dahmeh Nejiba, Original Mare, of Khalil el Hajry. 'Ibn Nura is magnificent.'

Sale — Purchased from Seyyid Mohammed Fathi, son of Ahmed Fathi, 'Katim son' Wakib of the Daïra of the late Ali Pasha Sherif on 7 December 1898, in exchange for Atwa, the bay Nowakieh (Sheykh Obeyd), 15 years old, and £15 cash. Mohammed Fathi had bought him from Saleh Bey Sherif, his purchaser at the 2nd auction of March 1897, when Saleh had purchased him from the Daïra.

Description — A chestnut, very strong colour, off hind foot white and seyal (narrow blaze), fine shoulder, arched neck, head set on like Ibn Nura's and same way of turning it. Short legged, a good mover. Feysul, though small, is magnificent.

Height — 13 hands 3 3/8 inches.

Girth — 65 inches.

Below knee — 7 3/4 inches.

Feysul [first called Arûs] was imported to England in September 1904 and arrived at Crabbet on 22 September.

Lady Wentworth noted: 'Sold in 1915 to Mr D. Fenton for £25. Later exchanged for Riyal – seized by Mr Blunt at the death of Lady Anne in 1917 and shot.'

GSB Volume 20
Imported 1904

◄ *Feysul*

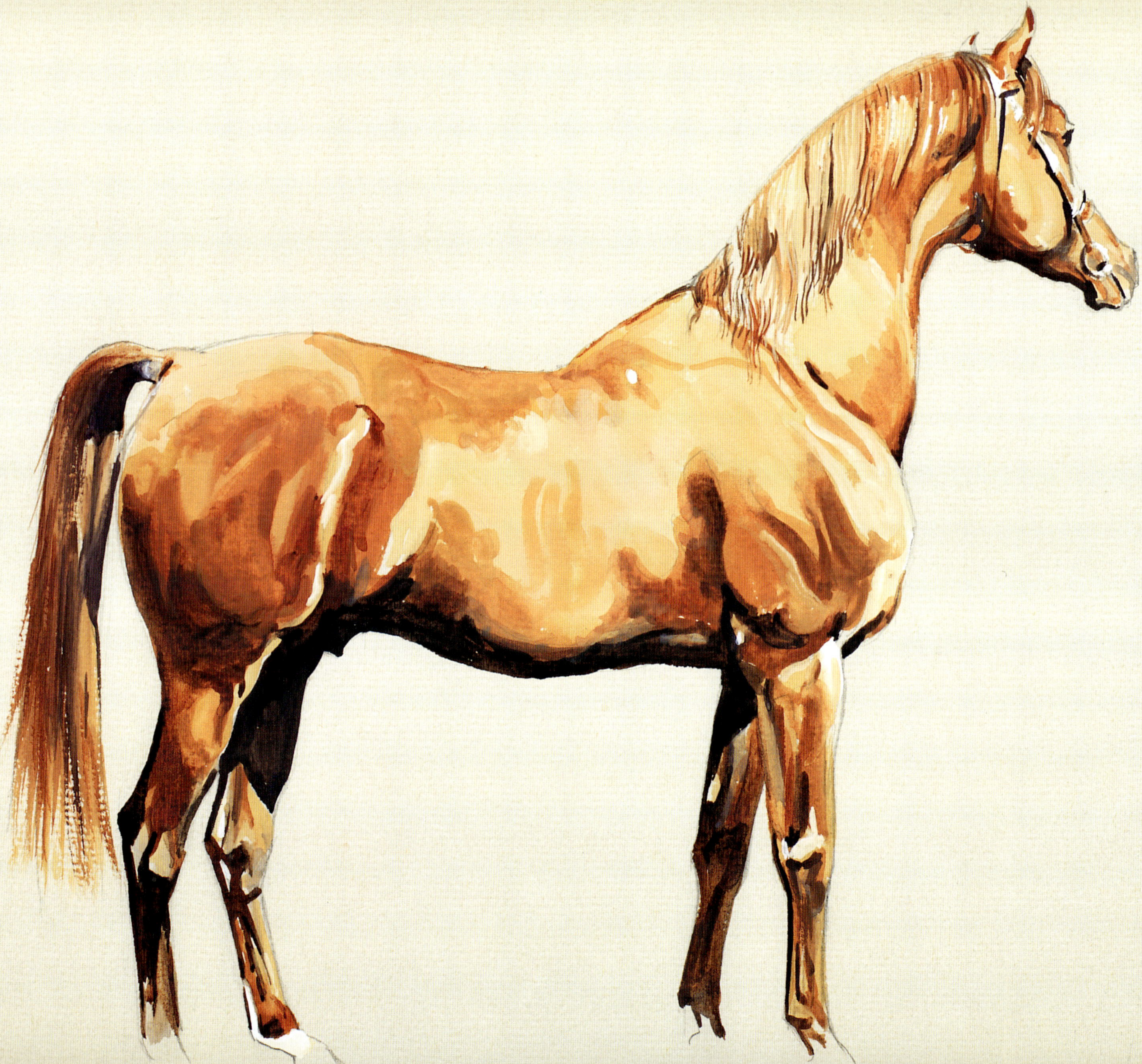

IBN YASHMAK

A Kehilan Ajuz of the Jellabi strain or Kehilan Jellabi.

A Chestnut horse foaled on 14 February 1902.

Bred at Sheykh Obeyd Stud in Egypt by Wilfrid and Lady Anne Blunt.

Dam — Dam Yashmak, a white Kehileh Jellabieh bred at Sheykh Obeyd in 1893, her dam – Yemama, a bay Kehileh Jellabieh foaled in 1885, bred by Ali Pasha Sherif and sold by him to Moharrem Pasha from whom she was purchased in 1893. [The intermediary, however, gave a very wrong account of the mare, describing her as an 'Abeyeh' brought to Moharrem Pasha through certain tribes from Arabia but without details as to her origin and this account was only discovered to be incorrect when Moharrem Pasha himself came to visit Sheykh Obeyd Stud and Yashmak was identified as the daughter of his Kehileh Jellabieh from Ali Pasha Sherif.] Yashmak's sire was Shahwan, the white Dahman Shahwan. 'Yashmak foaled just after midnight last night, a colt. He appears to be a chestnut that intends to turn grey. A very well bred head, profile excellent, rather remarkable blaze.'

Sire — Feysul, a chestnut Kehilan Jellabi.

Description — Golden chestnut, near feet white and blaze. A good mover.

Height — About 14 hands 2 inches.

Below knee — 7 ½ inches.

Ibn Yashmak was imported to England on 22 September 1904. He was sold to the Royal Agricultural Society of Egypt in 1920. He died in 1927.

◀ *Ibn Yashmak*

GSB Volume 20
AHS Volume 1
Imported 1904

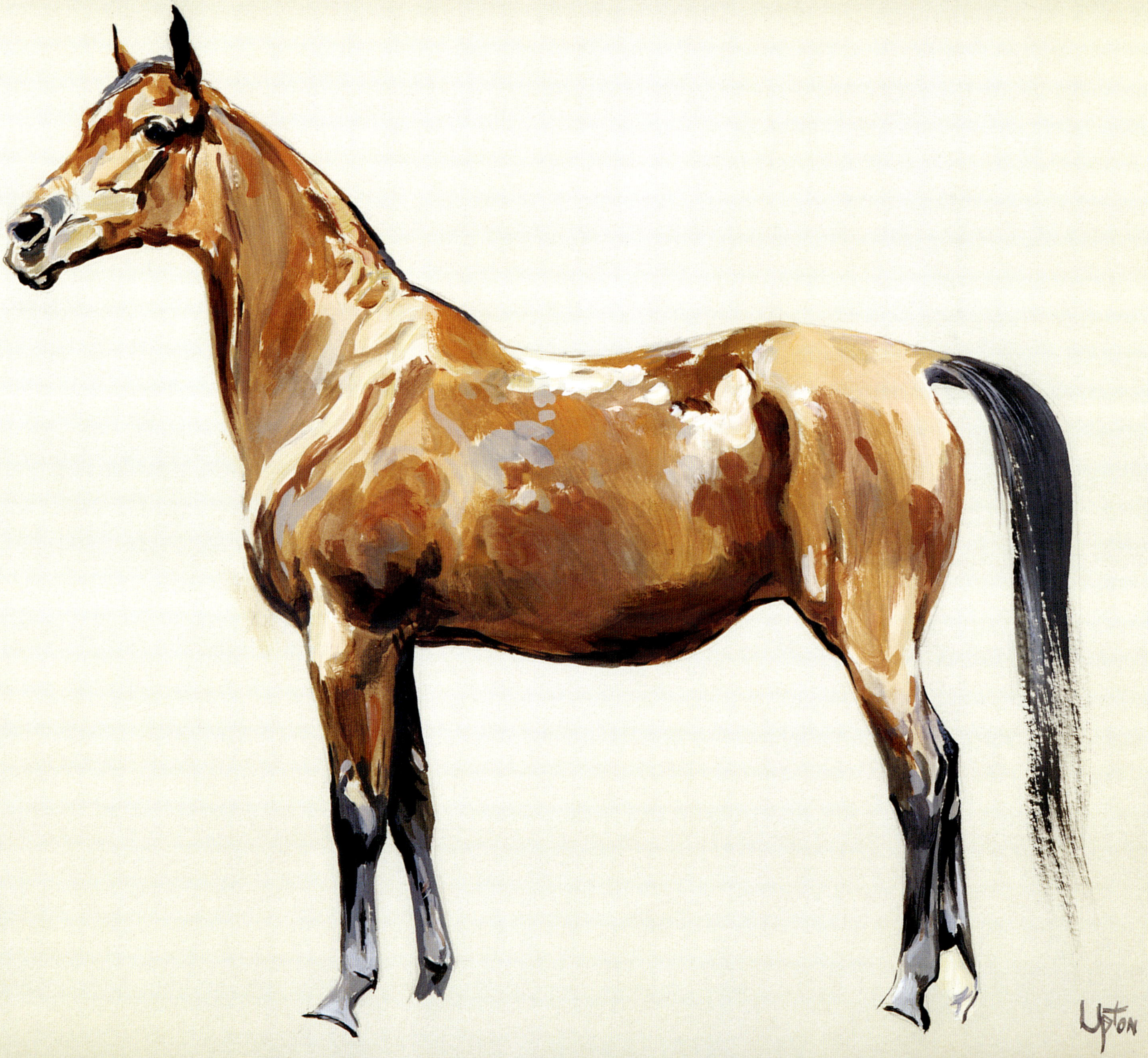
Upton

Other Original Mares

MEJAMIEH

A bay foaled in 1912.

Bred in the Hauran by the Guzzawieh, a bedouin horse breeding tribe.[18] She was captured in North Palestine after General Allenby's defeat of the Turks in 1918.[19] One Arab who had been sniping was ridden down and captured on the edge of a ravine and brought in with his mare. The man was executed the next day and the mare was bought from the British Government by General Lance, when hostilities ceased. She was brought to England with a filly to which she had given birth (see Libnani). Until she was actually on board ship, she had to be strictly guarded day and night as more than one warning was given that the owner's family were following her to regain her.

Description   Bay. Off hind coronet white.

Owned by Brigadier-General F.F. Lance. She was 1st in the Brood Mare Class at Ranelagh in 1922, 1st at the Royal, Bath and West, and London in 1923 and 1926 and 2nd Brood Mares at the NPS Show in 1926. She died in 1927 after slipping her foal.

◂ *Mejamieh*

AHS Volume 2, page 131
Imported 1921

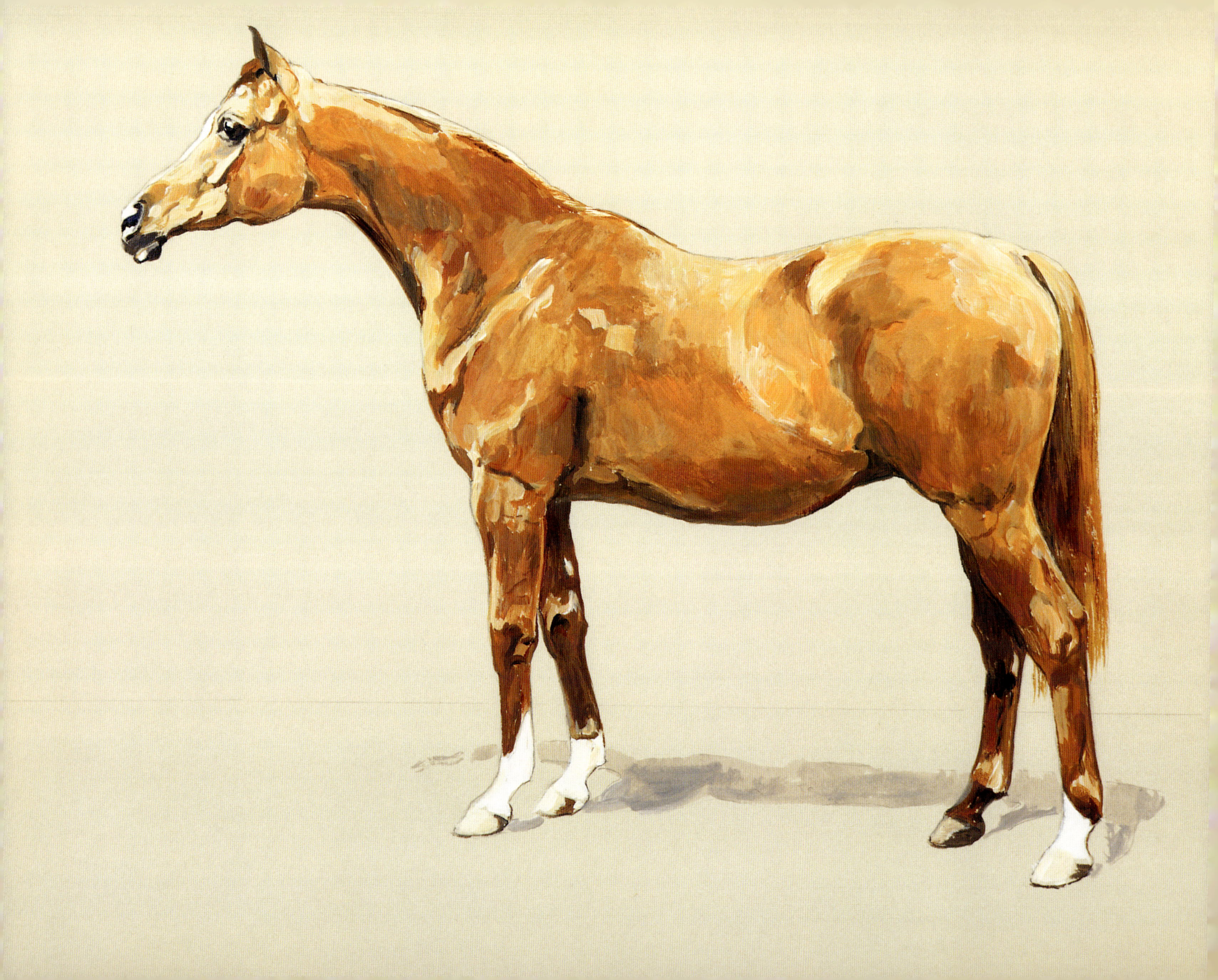

NEJMA

A Managhieh Ibn Sbeyeli

A chestnut mare foaled in 1914.

Bred by the Emir Ibn Raschid of Haïl, Nejd. Nejma, and the grey mare Nejdmieh were presented to Talaat Pasha for HM the late Mohammed Rashad Khan, by the Emir. Major G.H. Barker purchased both mares in Constantinople and exported them to England. Considered by the Arabs to be two of their best mares.

Sale Purchased by C.W. Hough c.1924. 1st and Champion Brood Mare NPS London Show, 1924. 1st in 1926 and 2nd in 1925.

Description Chestnut with blaze and snip. Both fore and near hind fetlocks white.

◀ *Nejma*

AHS Volume 3, page 118
Imported *c.* 1923

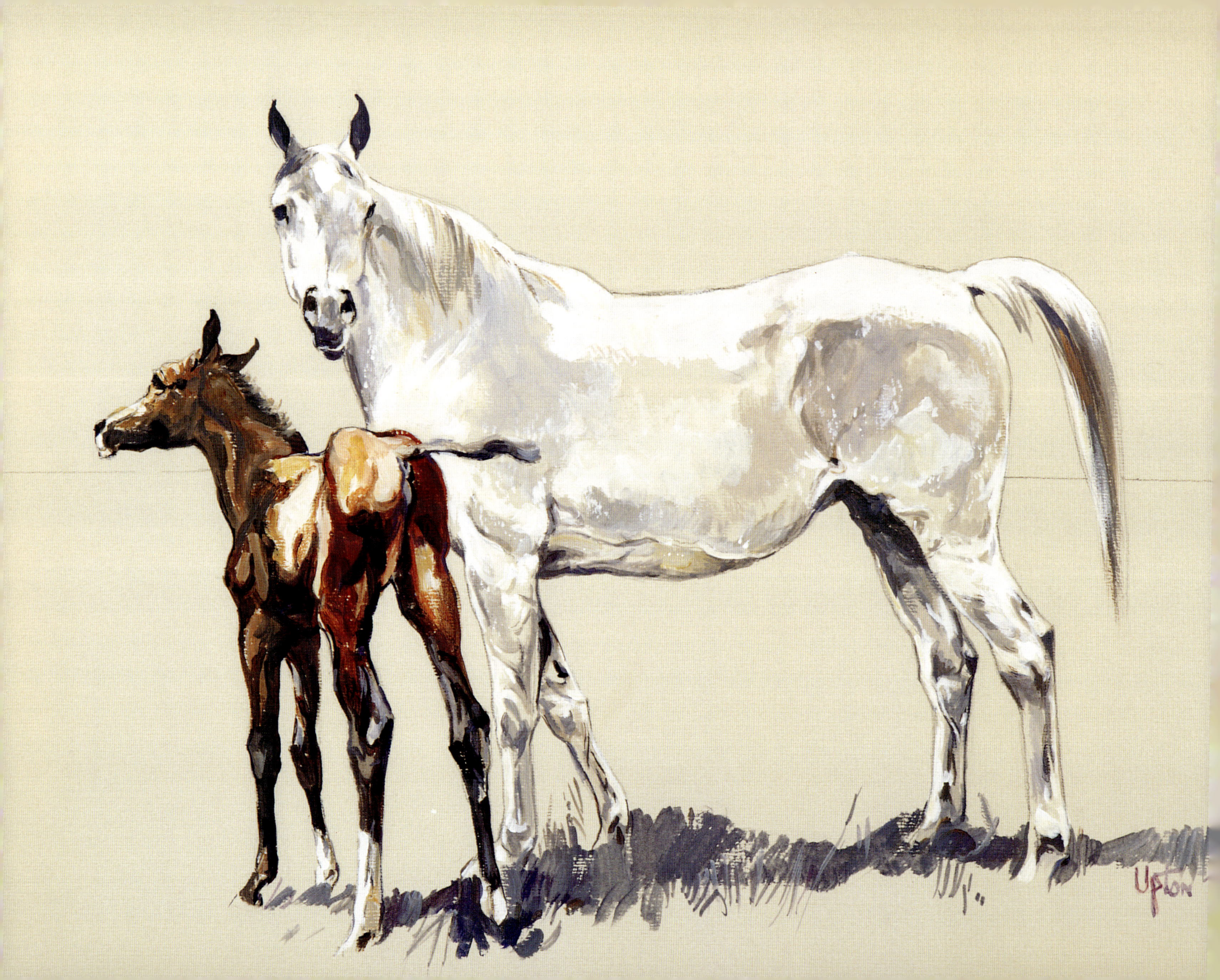
Upton

DAFINA

A Keheilet el Krush.

A white mare foaled in 1921.

Bred in the Nejd by the Muteyr tribe.

Dam   A Keheilet el Krush of King Feysul Ibn Saud.

Sire   A Horse of King Feysul Ibn Saud, a Keheilan el Krush (Krushan).

Imported through King Ibn Saud, in June 1927, by Sir Gilbert Clayton, for Lady Wentworth.

Reserve Arab Brood Mares, NPS Show, 1936. She was sold to Mrs Elm in 1936 and her last registered foal was born in 1947 (Dafina then 26 years old).

The mare, a grey of rare beauty, is of the inaccessible Krush strain, which was the property of the Muteyr tribe, and no money would induce them to sell a mare.

◀ *Dafina with foal*

AHS Volume 5, page 123
Imported 1927

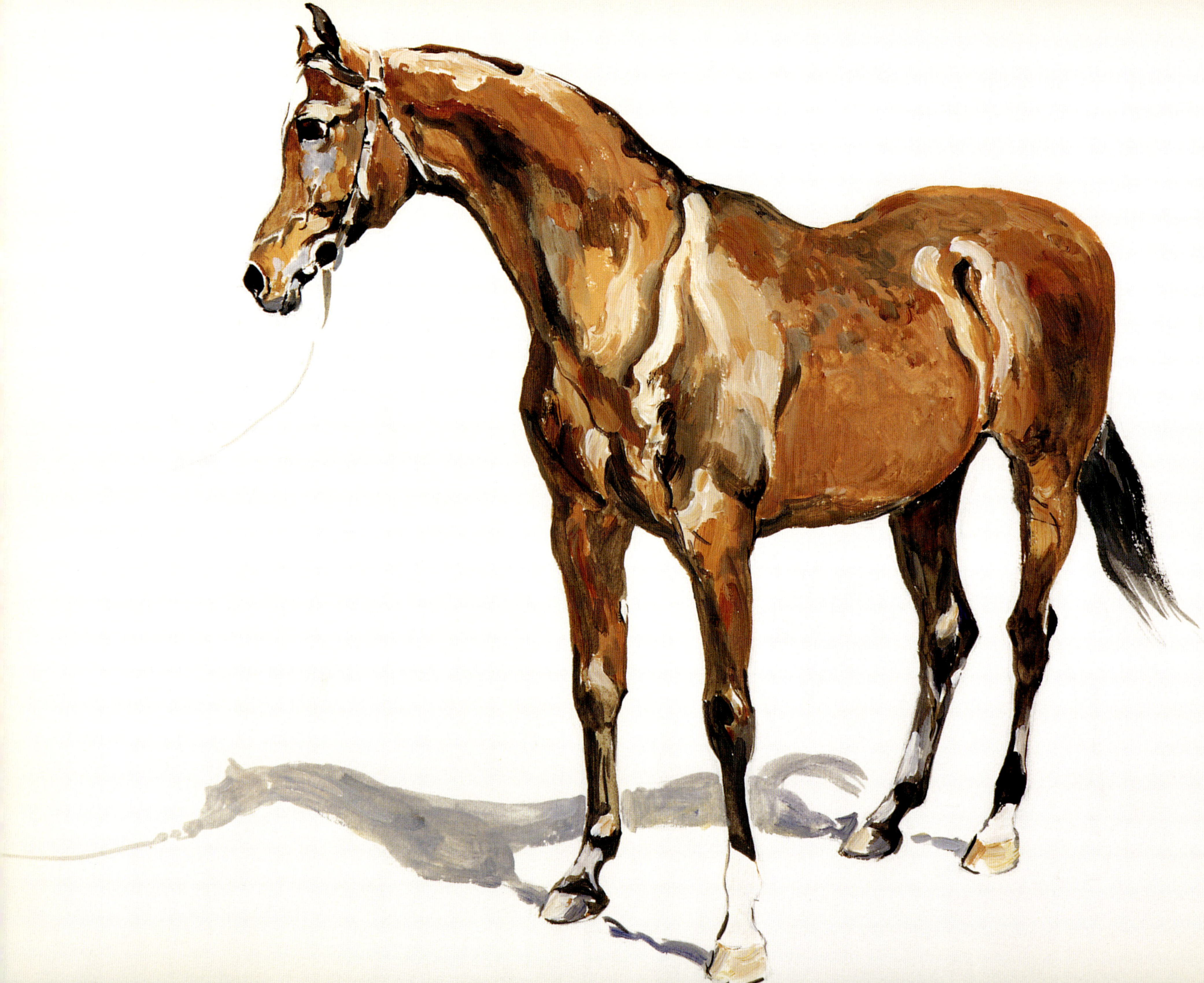

NOURA

A Maneghieh Hedrujieh.

A bay mare foaled in 1916/17.

Bred at the stables of King Ibn Saud, Riyadh. Noura was sent to Ameen Rihani with a special messenger from King Ibn Saud, from Riyadh to Damascus, a distance of about eight hundred miles.[20]

Description   A bay with star, race and snip. Near hind coronet white, near fore and near hind feet partly white.

Imported by Ameen Rihani in 1928 and later exported with her daughter, Muha, to USA

◀ *Noura*

AHS Volume 4, page 157
Imported 1928

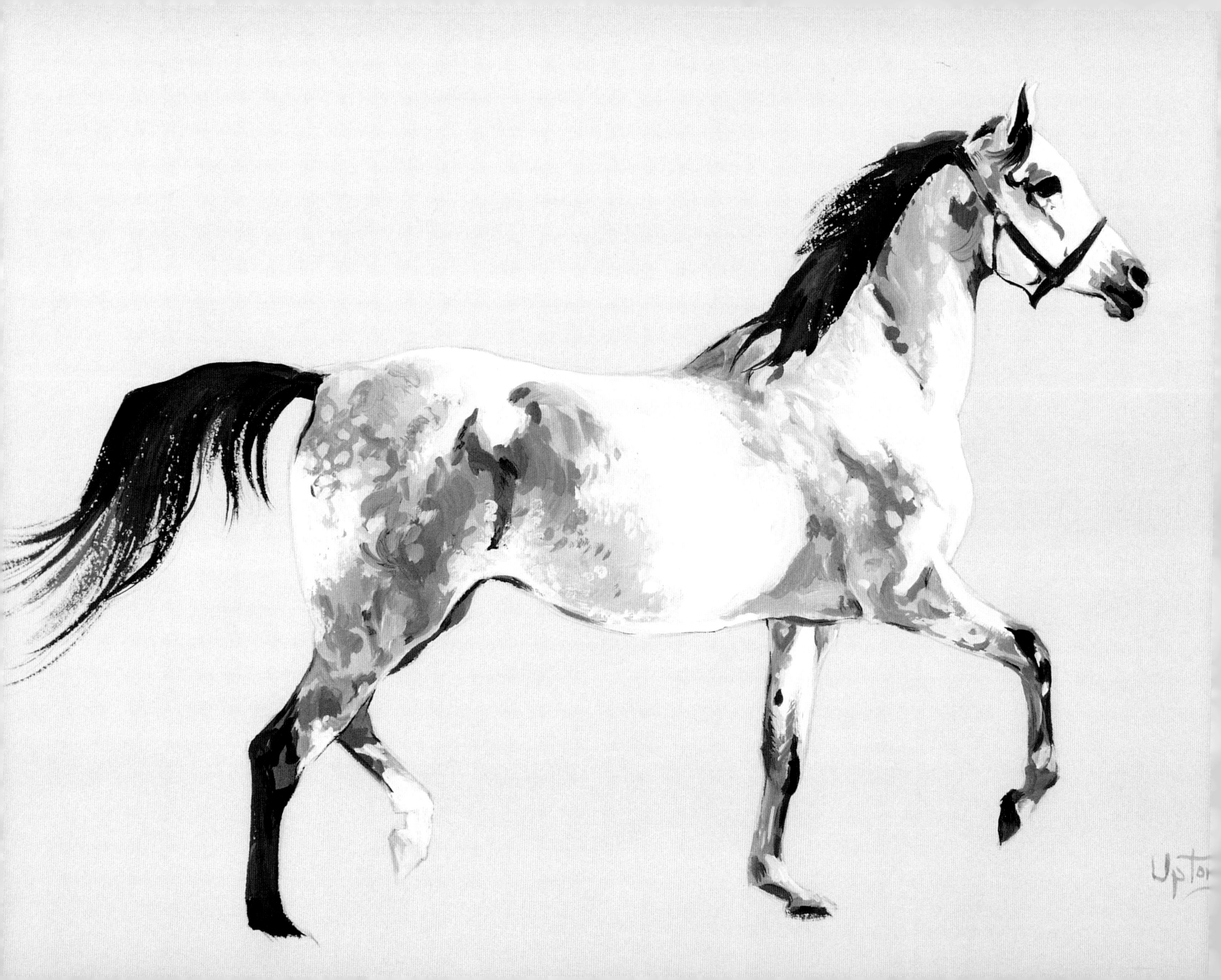

TURFA

A Keheilet Al Khorma.[21]

A flea-bitten grey mare, foaled in 1933.

Bred by King Ibn Saud in Riyadh.

Dam   A Keheilet Al Khorma.

Sire   An Abayan Al Hamra.

Presented as a Coronation Gift to HM King George VI by King Ibn Saud, in December 1937, with three other Arabians, Manak, Kasim and Faras, in appreciation for the hospitality received by Abdul Aziz Al Saud, the King's son.

Description   Grey with a flesh mark above and running into near nostril, a faint flesh mark right of centre of upper lip and along border of lower lip. Both fore and near hind pasterns light grey or white with black patches on coronets, off hind heel and back of pasterns white.

Imported in 1937. Brigadier W.H. Anderson, Secretary of the AHS, acquired Turfa and broke her to ride, 'A grey of great quality and a nice mover'. At the outbreak of the Second World War it was decided that several Arabians, including Turfa, would be sent to Canada for safe-keeping. Whilst there, she was seen by Mr Henry Babson, who arranged to purchase her in 1941, now 8 years old.

Turfa had been covered in England by the stallion, Hilal, and so Ibn Hilal was exported in utero. At Babson farm, Turfa was bred exclusively to Fadl and she had three colts and three fillies. Homer Watson, manage of Babson Farms, described Turfa as, 'A very intelligent and friendly mare that loved people. She was also very spirited and energetic under saddle and brilliant action and presence.'

◀ *Turfa*

AHS Volume 6, page 321
Imported 1937

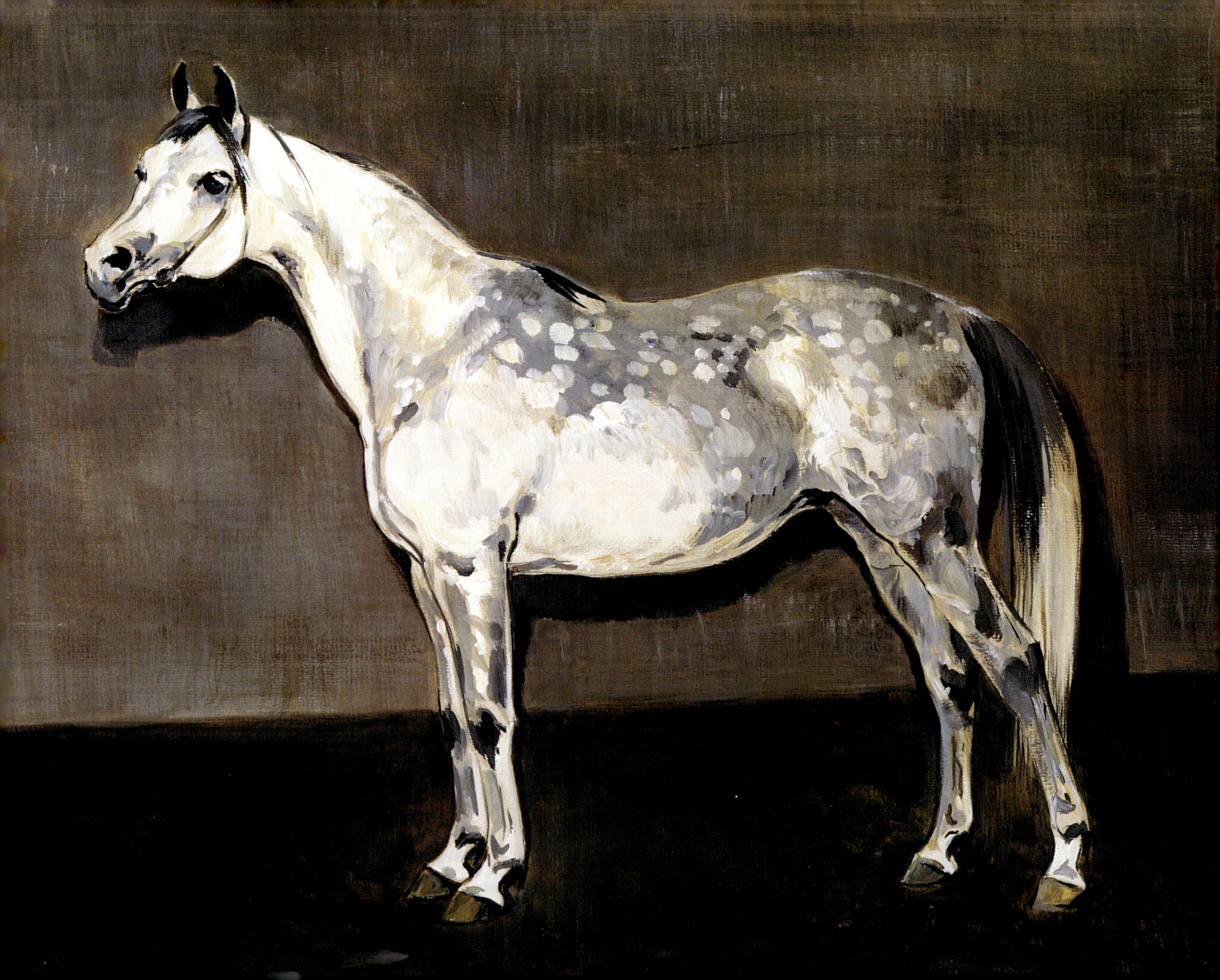

MAHAWILIYAH

A Keheilet Ajuz.

A grey mare foaled in 1935.

Bred by Abdul Kadim Jabbar, Sheikh of the Ali Yisar, Hillah.[22]

Dam — A Keheileh, desert-bred of Abdul Khadim Jabbar of the Ali Yisar Mahawil, Hillah, by a Seglawi of Husain al Dhiban of the Albutaif, out of a Keheileh of Abdul Khadim Jabbar, Sheikh of the Yisar.

Sire — A Managhi desert-bred of Haji Fayadh, Sheikh of the Abu Amr, Yusufiyah.[23]

Description — Grey with star, stripe into off nostril and upper lip partly. Flecks around orbits and sides of face. Off fore fetlock and hoof, off hind pastern with hoof striped on outside.

First owner – J. Spence, second owner – J.C. Sword.

◀ *Mahawiliyah*

AHS Volume 6, page 225
Imported *c.* 1939

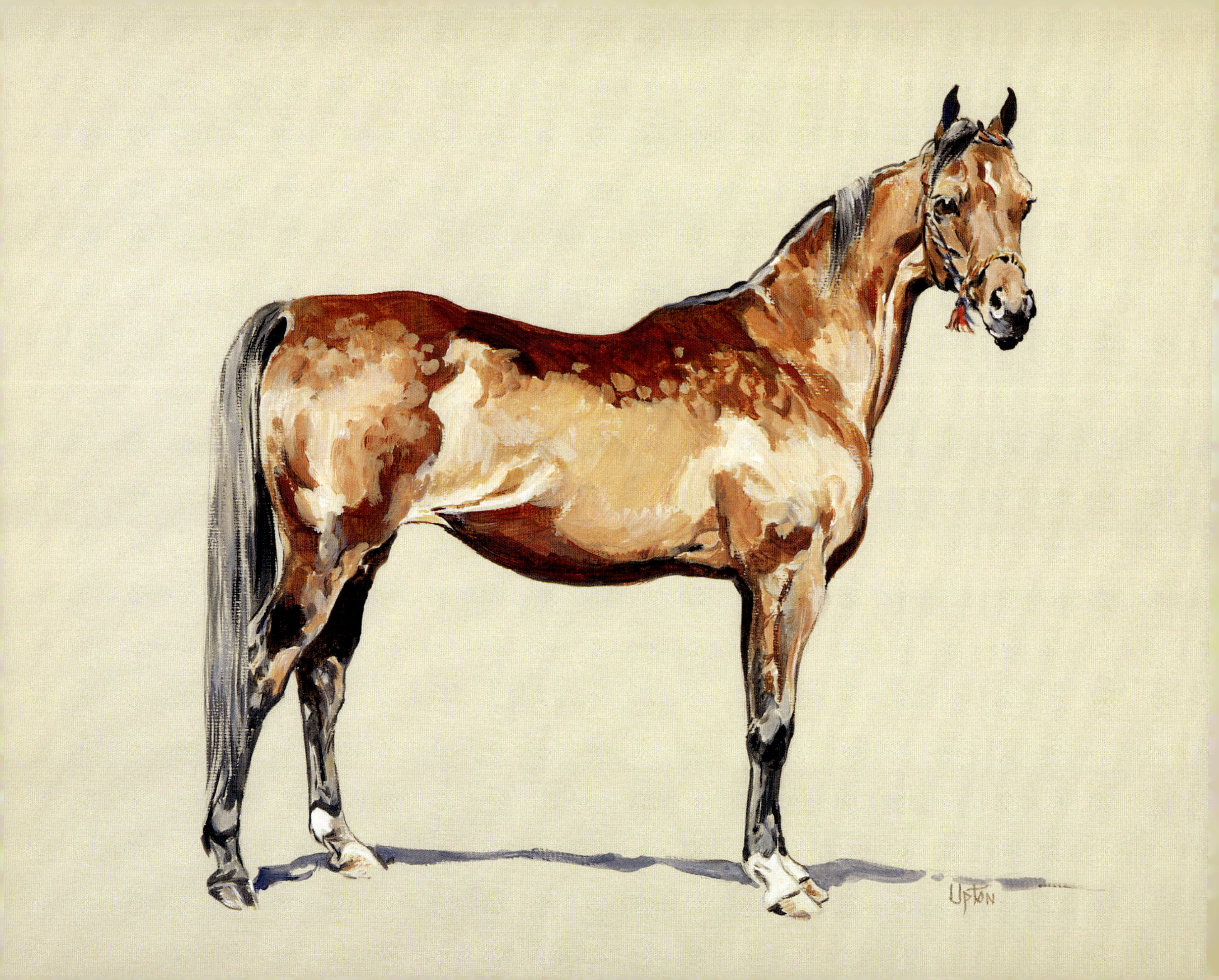
Upton

NUHRA

A Wadnah Khursanieh.

A bay mare foaled in 1936.

Bred in the desert, Bahrain.

Dam   A Keheilet el Wadna Khursanieh by a Keheilan Obeyan, out of a Keheilet el Wadna Khursanieh (which is related to al Tabouh).

Sire   A Keheilan Jellabi by a Keheilan Jellabi, out of a Keheileh Jellabieh.

Description   Bay with star. Near fore coronet partly, off fore pastern, near hind pastern and fetlock partly.

Presented to Major-General the Right Honourable the Earl of Athlone KG, by HH Sheikh Hamed Bin Eissa Al-Khalifa, the Sheikh of Bahrain, in 1939.

Nuhra is half-sister to the horse Bahrain.

◀ *Nuhra*

AHS Volume 6, page 254
Imported 1939

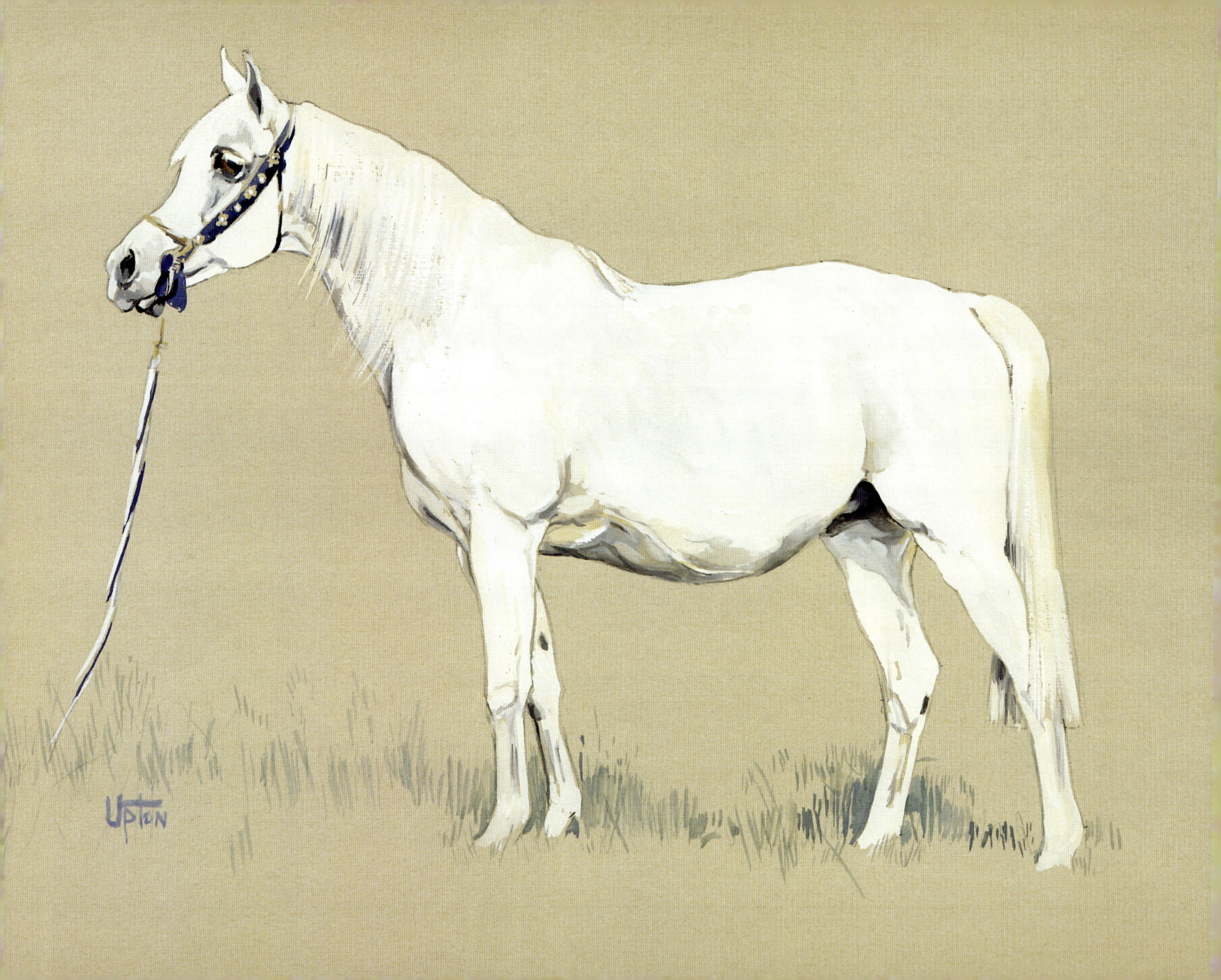
UPTON

SHAMMAH

A Kubeysha.

A grey mare foaled in 1950.

Bred by Dlewan Pasha Al-Majali of Rabbah, north-east of Kerak, Sheikh of the Al Majali tribe.

Dam — Al Karkhieh (possibly Karakesh, the chestnut Kubeysha mare, foaled in 1940 and presented to HM The Queen c.1952, by Dlewan Pasha Al-Majali). [See AHS Volume 8.].

Sire — Abu Arqub an iron grey horse owned by Nazzal el Armiti of Menja, Jordan.

Presented by Dlewan Pasha al-Majali, in 1951, to HM King Talal (father to HM King Hussein). Talal, in his turn, gave her to Haji Mustafa Abdo Tabash, known as Abu Salim, the Prime Minister. According to Santiago Lopez, whilst in Jordan, this mare foaled twin fillies, which were attacked by two wolves, which Shammah killed. Shammah eventually came into the possession of 'The Master of the King's Horses', Santiago Lopez, and was sent by him to England. In 1964, Mrs du Boulay saw the mare and offered to look after her, though she was described as of uncertain temper and thought to be barren.[24] Shammah was to produce five pure-bred foals before she died, at 24 years of age, in 1974.

◀ *Shammah*

AHS Volume 8, page 88
Imported *c.* 1955

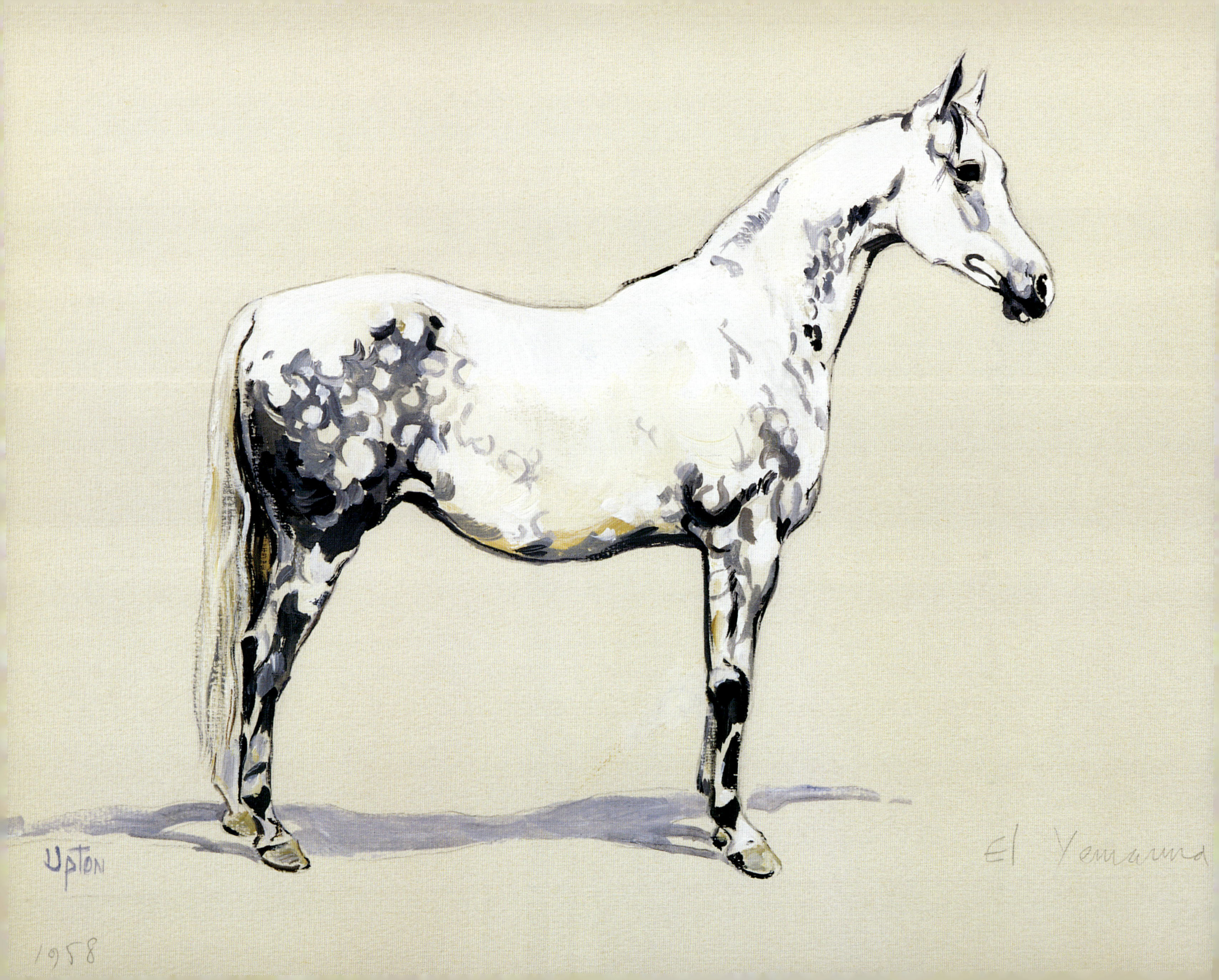
Upton
1958
El Yemama

EL YAMAMA (DOVE)

An Um Arkoub

A grey mare foaled in 1953.

Bred at the Royal Stud, Jordan.

Dam   Lo'ba [Lurbi I (RJS Volume 1)] a chestnut mare of the Um Argub strain. Her sire – Selman, a grey Dahman Shahwan, bred at the RAS Egypt in 1933, and presented to King Abdullah of Jordan in 1940. Selman's sire, Mansour by Gamil Manial ex Nafaa el Saghira, and dam, Sabah by Mabrouk Manial ex Bint Obeya.

Lo'ba's dam – Sabal I, a chestnut mare of the Um Argub strain. Her sire Kehilan, a desert-bred horse, and her dam Al Johara by Hamdani desert-bred, ex Nasseb, bred by Dlewan Pasha Al Majali, Sheikh of the Al Majali tribe, Karak, Jordan. Nasseb was presented by Al-Majali to HM King Abdullah of Transjordan.

Sire   Ubayan.

Presented to HM Queen Elizabeth by HM King Hussein of Jordan in 1958. El Yamama was in foal to Samih, at the time of her importation.

◀ *El Yamama*

Imported 1958

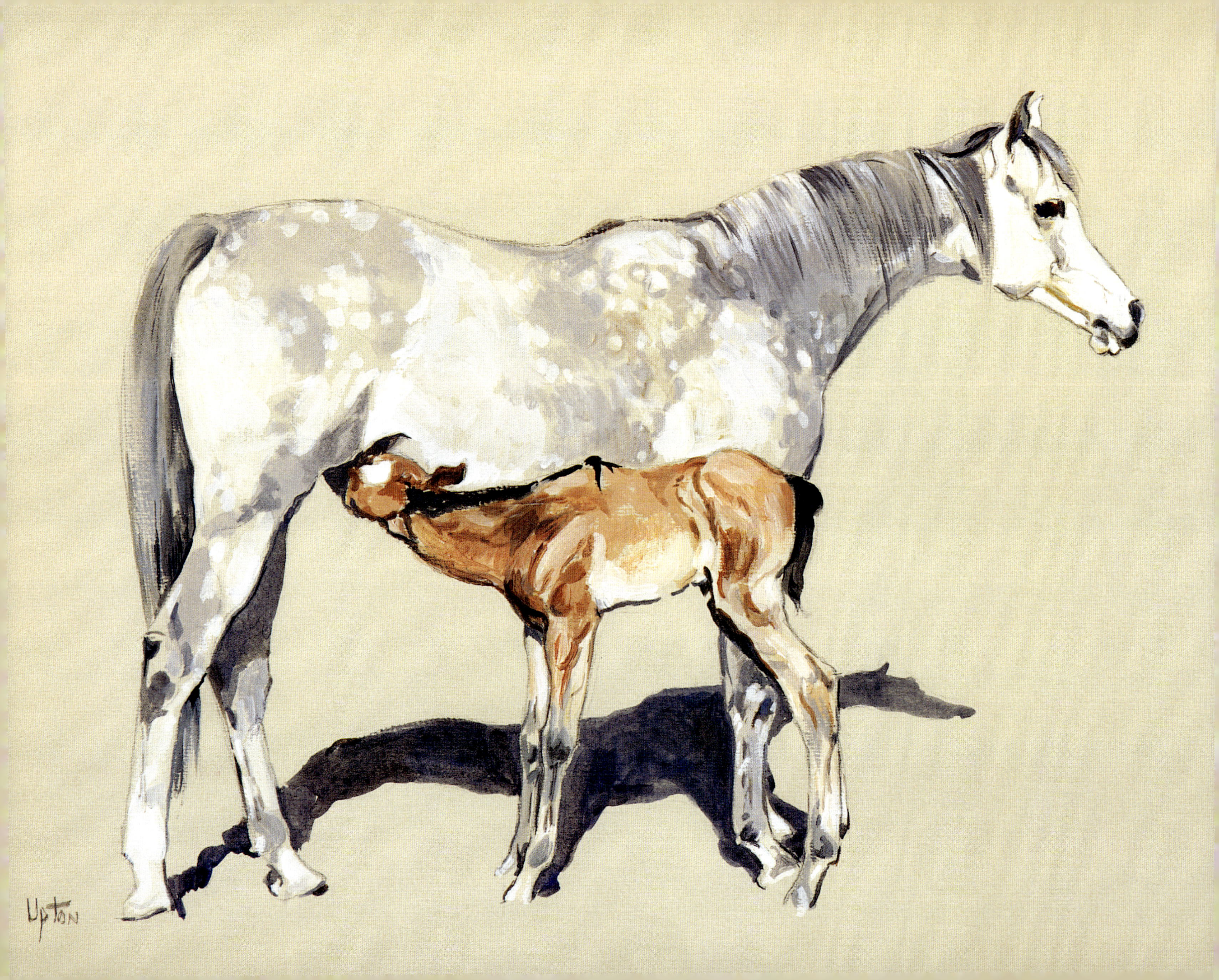
Upton

PRINCESS MUNA

An Um Argub.

A grey mare, foaled at Sandringham, in 1958.

Bred in Jordan.

Dam	El Yamama* (Dove), by Ubayan ex Lo'ba.
Sire	Samih (Kind and Generous).[25]
Description	Grey; irregular blaze covering off eye, narrowing and continuing to cover whole of near nostril and near half of upper lip, under lip. Near hind fetlock behind, off hind fetlock.

Named Muna by HM The Queen on 28 February 1962. The prefix 'Princess' was added to her name in March 1962, when she was registered with the AHS.

Loaned to, or owned by Mrs S.A. Nicholson, County Meath, Eire. Then to George Alexander, Duke of Mecklenburg, and lastly to Mr J.G. Roberts.

Muna's last foal was born in 1970.

◀ *Princess Muna with foal*

AHS Volume 9, page 118
Imported *in utero* 1958

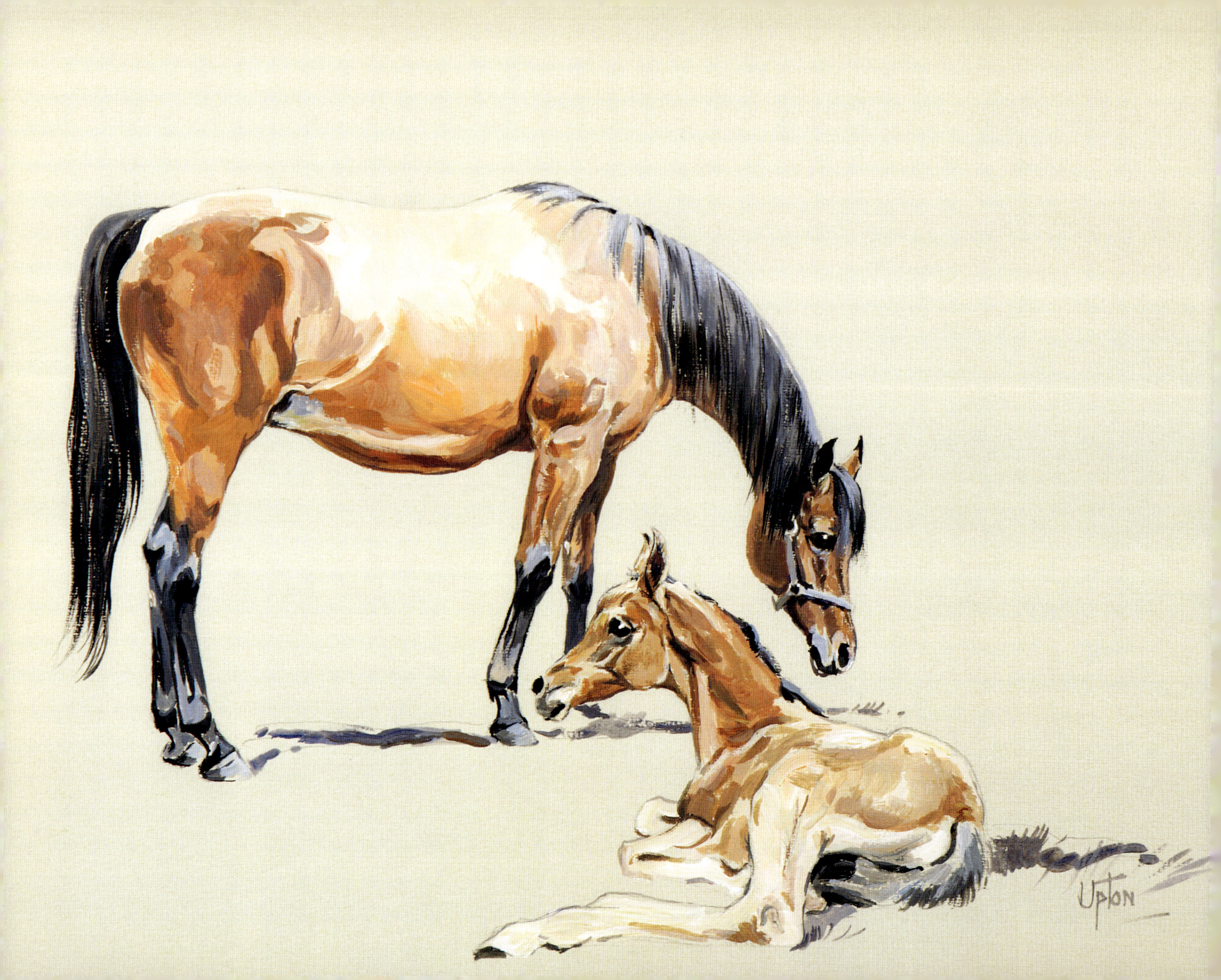
Upton

THRAYAT HAMID

A Keheilet Ajuz.

A bay mare foaled in 1953.

Dam   Qadisiyah (Keheileh).

Sire   Violence (bred at Latifiyah by Kudai yir Rashed).

Description   Bay with black points, small elongated star, short stripe above muzzle. Tiny snip below off muzzle.

Imported from Baghdad by the Honourable A.J. Watson. Being rather too hot for polo, she was sold to Mr and Mrs Adam Bell. Mr Bell hunted her in the West Country and then took her to Ireland. The mare was then given to Mrs W.B.R.B. Somerville of County Wicklow, when the Bells emigrated to Australia. Mrs Somerville described her in a letter to the author:

> She stood approximately 14 hands and 3 inches high and was the most beautiful golden bay, with very black points and black dorsal stripe. Her mane and tail were very thick and long, the texture being rather coarser than one expects in English-bred Arabians, consequently when she galloped they didn't fly in the wind! Head, rather plain, better from the front, prominent nasal bones which made her muzzle look rather large, eyes very large and prominent, sweet expression. Straight neck and shoulders with unusually prominent withers, girth average, fairly short back. A very leggy mare. Croup short... She was tremendously tough, very sweet tempered if hot. As far as I was concerned her colour was very eye-catching but she was not 'out of the top drawer'.

◀ *Thrayat Hamid with foal*

AHS Volume 10, page 151
Imported *c.* 1958

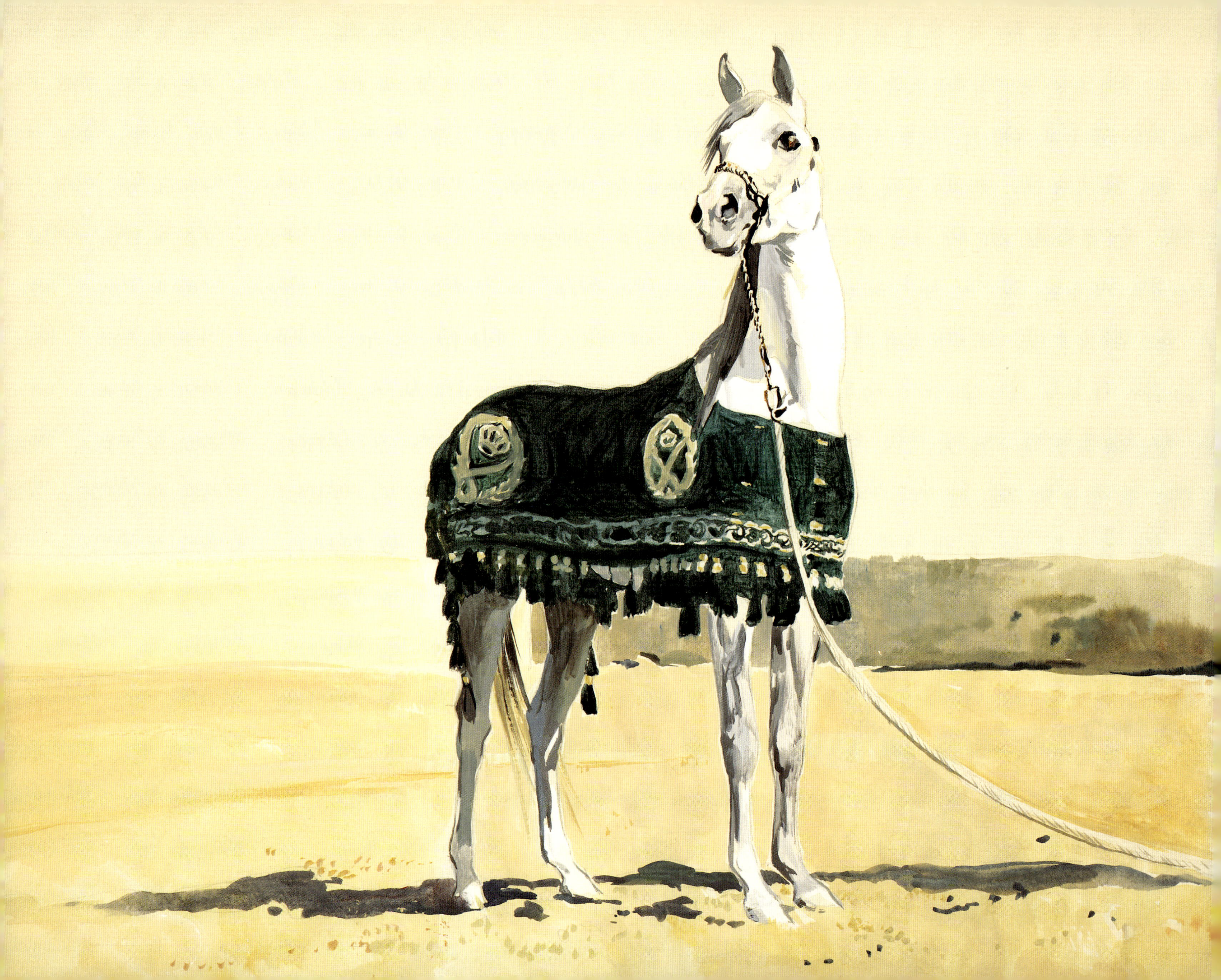

SHAMS

A Muniqieh Sbeyli.

A grey mare foaled on 22 September 1955.

Bred by Lieutenant-General Habis El-Majali, Commander-in-Chief, Jordan Armed Forces.

Dam Mi'Enaqia (Muniqieh), Royal Racing Club, Amman, Jordan. Certificate Horse Number 79.

Sire Abu Argub (possibly Abu Arqub of the Royal Jordanian Stud, his dam – Al Yamama I [RJS Volume 1, page 25]; his sire – Selman.

Description Grey with flesh coloured snip down centre of muzzle. 'The ancestors of this pure-bred Arab mare have been in the Majali family for over two centuries. The Majali's are a prominent tribe living in the Karak area of the Hashemite Kingdom of Jordan.'

Bred at Karak. Shams was imported, in foal, to Qaied (Kaid).[26] She was presented by Lieutenant-General Habis El-Majali to HM Queen Elizabeth, The Queen Mother, in 1960. On the advice of The Crown Equerry, Lieutenant-Colonel Sir John Miller, The Queen Mother was pleased to loan the mare to Sir Dudley and Lady Forwood. Transferred – AHS, 5 May 1964.

◀ *Shams*

AHS Volume 10, page 151
Imported 1960

HAIDEE

A Maneghieh Hedrujieh of Ibn Sbeyel's strain.[27]

A chestnut mare foaled in 1869 (GSB Volume 15).

Bred by Sheikh Suleyman Ibn Mirshid of the Gomussa tribe, Sebaa, Anazeh.

Dam   A Maneghieh Hedrujieh.

Sire   A Managhi Hedruj.

Sale   Purchased by Mr Skene, Consul of Aleppo, from Beteyen Ibn Mirshid, cousin to Suleyman.

Description   Chestnut, 'Noted for speed and bottom – not selected for her shape'.

Height   14 hands 3 inches.

Imported to England by Mr Albert Sandeman in 1874. She foaled a filly, Naomi, by Yatagan, in 1877, at Brightwell Park, Oxfordshire. There is no account of her from 1877 to 1881. Barren 1882 and 1883. Sold to Mr J.C. Macdona's Stud in 1883. Not covered in 1883 or 1884. Haidee died c.1887. (Recorded in GSB Volume 16, 1888).

GSB Volume 13
Imported 1874

KESIA

A Keheilet Nowagieh.

A bay mare foaled in c.1865.

Bred by Debbe Ibn Nowag of the Gomussa tribe of Sebaa, Anazeh.

Dam	A Keheilet Nowagieh.
Sire	A Nowag horse of the Debbe family. Both sire and dam of the Debbe Nowag family in the Gomussa tribe of Sebaa, Anazeh.
Sale	Purchased for the Honourable Henry Chaplin in the summer of 1875, by Major R.D. Upton, in the camp of the Gomussa, from Suleyman Jelaleh Ibn Mirshid.
Description	A red bay. Major Upton wrote:

> A very good specimen of the Arabian mare; she stood about 14 hands 1½ inches in height. She was much disfigured by saddle marks and by having been fired. She was of a fine frame and a roomy mare. She had a fine and noble head; a magnificent eye; a nostril not to be surpassed for delicacy, for beauty of form, sharpness of outline and capability of expression. She was excessively fine at the muzzle, with the under lip small and compressed; her jaws were very deep and set very wide apart; very perfect ears; a fine neck with a good mitbeh. She had the most perfect shoulders, elevated withers, a fine haunch, and her tail was well set on. She was square and broad across the haunch; her hocks were good, but without any striking development at the os calcis, so often to be observed. Her arms were long and very good.

Kesia was covered in the desert in 1875 by the Hedud, Seglawi el Abd, bred by the Roala tribe, Anazeh, but then in the possession of the Sebaa, Anazeh.

Imported to England in 1875, she went to Blankney Hall, Lincolnshire the home of the Honourable Henry Chaplin. Lady Anne Blunt wrote in 1878: 'Wilfrid called on Mr Weatherby who had just returned from Blankney and seen Mr Chaplin's Arabians and said Kesia, the older mare had a foal this year,[28] that she would probably have no more and that the first foal she had in England by a horse in the desert (Seglawi el Abd), is a very fine one and will be over 15 hands high (Kesia II).' Kesia was destroyed in 1881.

GSB Volume 13
Imported 1875

KESIA II

A Keheilet Nowagieh.

A bay mare foaled in 1876.

Bred by the Gomussa tribe of Sebaa, Anazeh.

Dam — Kesia*, a Keheilet Nowagieh, bred by Debbe Ibn Nowag of the Gomussa, imported in 1875.

Sire — The Hedud Seglawi el Abd, bred by the Roala tribe, Anazeh, but then in the possession of the Sebaa, Anazeh.[29]

Description — Bay. 'A fine one', (Mr Weatherby).

Height — 15 hands-plus.

Imported in utero in 1875 and foaled at Blankney Hall, Lincolnshire in April 1876.

Purchased by Lord Arthur Cecil, c.1885. Kesia II's best known son was Imamzada, and two of her daughters, Mimosa and Shabaka, were sired by Mameluke* [the imported stallion owned by Cecil's cousin, Lord Russell]. Miss Dillon purchased Shabaka, with her dam, Kesia II, in 1894, and when Wilfrid Blunt saw her on a visit in that year he described her as, 'Kesia, a fine old ruin'. In 1895 Kesia II had her last foal, a filly named Borak. She died after foaling.

GSB Volume 17
Imported *in utero* 1875

ISHTAR

A white mare foaled in 1871.

Sale — Purchased by Sir William Clay in 1876 and imported to England by him.[30] Lady Anne Blunt noted: 'Undoubtedly pure-bred, but her pedigree has been lost through frequent changes of ownership.' Given, on the death of Sir William c.1878, to Mr Raymond, and bought by the Honourable Ethelred Dillon in 1884 (or March 1885).[31] Sold in 1889 at the 5th Crabbet Sale, by Miss Dillon to Mr Weatherby for 110 guineas. [Notes on the Sale give Ishtar as, 'Grey mare aged, imported by Sir George (William) Clay. Pedigree lost.] owned by a Mr John Gretton, Burton-on-Trent, from 1890. Ishtar produced her last foal – a filly by El Emir – in 1891, slipped twins in 1892 and was destroyed 1893.

GSB Volume 15
Imported *c.* 1876

SHAKRA

A Keheilet Ajuz.

A chestnut mare foaled in 1888.

Bred in Arabia.

Sent as a gift, in 1892, from Arabia to a Bombay Parsee, in recognition of services rendered to the tribe. She is described in the Maharajah of Patiala's Stud Certificate, as being of the highest caste.

Sale · Purchased through Pallanjee Hormusjee in Bombay. Imported by Colonel E.N. Henriques in 1896. Foaled to Mootrub in 1913, when 25 years old.

GBS Volume 20
Imported 1896

LADYBIRD

A pure-bred Arab.

Imported from India by Colonel de Gallais, military secretary to the Governor of Bombay.

Owned by Mr Everard R. Calthrop.

AHS Volume 1
Imported 1896

LIBNANI

A bay mare foaled in 1919 at Baalbek, Syria.[32]

Dam · Mejamieh* (imported). [See page 193]

Description · Bay with star and black points.

She was brought to England with her dam, in 1921, by Brigadier-General F.F. Lance. In 1925 she was Champion Brood Mare at the Bath and West. In 1926 she was exported to the Duke of Veragua, Spain.

AHS Volume 2, page 127
Imported 1921

NEJDMIEH

A Managhieh Ibn Sbeyel.

A grey mare foaled in 1914.

Bred by Sheikh Moubarek Ibn Sebagh (Sebaa) in Nejd, and presented to Enver Pasha, the Turkish General, by the late Emir Ibn Raschid of Haïl, and bought of the successors of Enver Pasha by Major G.H. Barker, who imported her to England.

Description Grey with pink spots round eyes and mouth [markings favoured by the Arabs].

Sale Purchased by S.G. Hough c.1924.

2nd, Arab Mares, RAS Show, 1924 and Reserve Arab Mares NPS London Show, 1925. She was exported to A.E. Grace, New South Wales, Australia, in 1925.

AHS Volume 3, page 116
Imported *c.* 1923

MUHA

A Maneghieh Hedrujieh.

A bay mare foaled in 1928.

Dam Noura* (imported), a bay Maneghieh Hedrujieh. [See page 199]

Sire A Seglawi Jedran, bred at the stud of Omar Bey Dandash in Akkar. 'This stallion was presented to General Goureaux, the French High Commissioner for Syria and Lebanon and is now in the Etablissement Hippique de Levant. His dam, a Seglawieh Jedranieh, is still in the possession of Dandash Bey of the Dandashah House of Akkar. The Dandashah of Akkar keep in their studs only the pure desert blood.'

Description A bay with star, race and snip and lower lip. Off fore fetlock partly white.

Imported in utero by Ameen Rihani and exported with her dam, Noura, to USA.

AHS Volume 4, page 149
Imported *in utero* 1928

JAMILA I

A Keheileh.

A bay mare foaled in 1927.

Bred by Sabhar Mohamed of Khraisan, Arabia.

Dam	A Keheileh.
Sire	A Seglawi.
Description	Bay with star and race into near nostril, off nostril partly and upper and lower lips partly. Wither marks. Near hind sock and off hind fetlock.
Height	14 hands 3 ½ inches.

Imported from Baghdad, Iraq. Raced in Iraq by Mr Webster, Director of Agriculture, and later sold to Judge Pritchard, and by him to present owner, Miss Claudia Phillips (later Mrs C.E. Barling).

AHS Volume 5, page 138
Imported *c.* 1935

WARDA AL BADIA

A Seglawieh.

A chestnut mare foaled in 1924.

Bred by Sheikh Ali Karim of the Khurasa tribe of the South Sinjarah, Shammar.

Dam	A white Seglawieh, the property of Sheikh Ali Karim of the Khurasa.
Sire	A bay Keheilan, the property of HH The Sheikh of Mohammerah.

Entered in the Arabian Horse Stud Book of Iraq at Baghdad, where she was raced as a 2-year-old.

Description	A chestnut with blaze white lower lip. Near fore and near hind stocking and off hind sock.

Imported into England by Miss Browning (later Mrs Powell) and later owned by Miss H.I. Barr and Mrs G.E. Atkinson (1940).

AHS Volume 5, page 205
Imported *c.* 1937

TAKRITIYAH

A Juaithnieh (Keheileh Juwayhi).

A chestnut mare foaled in 1935.

Bred by Haji Daham Haji Daud, Sheikh of the Abu Nissar.

Dam   Juaithnieh of the Abu Nissar.

Sire   Juaithni Abu Jabir.

Description   Chestnut with star, short stripe and snip between nostrils and small patch upper lip. Tattoo - I - on upper gums. Saddle marks. Near hind sock and inside off hind fetlock partly on outside, spots on coronet.

First owner - Major H. Sanford, second owner - L.W. Cutler.

AHS Volume 6, page 320
Imported *c.* 1939

NAWAGIYAT AL FURAT (DESERT SONG)

A Keheilet Nowagieh.

A grey mare foaled in 1944.

Bred by Muhammed Said al Rashid Hussay of Falluja, Iraq.[33]

Dam   Nowagiyah.

Sire   King of Orient.

Description   Grey mare with no markings.

Owner - Captain R.J. Sheepshanks, Dragoon Guards.

AHS Volume 9, page 115
Imported *c.* 1958

Other Original Stallions

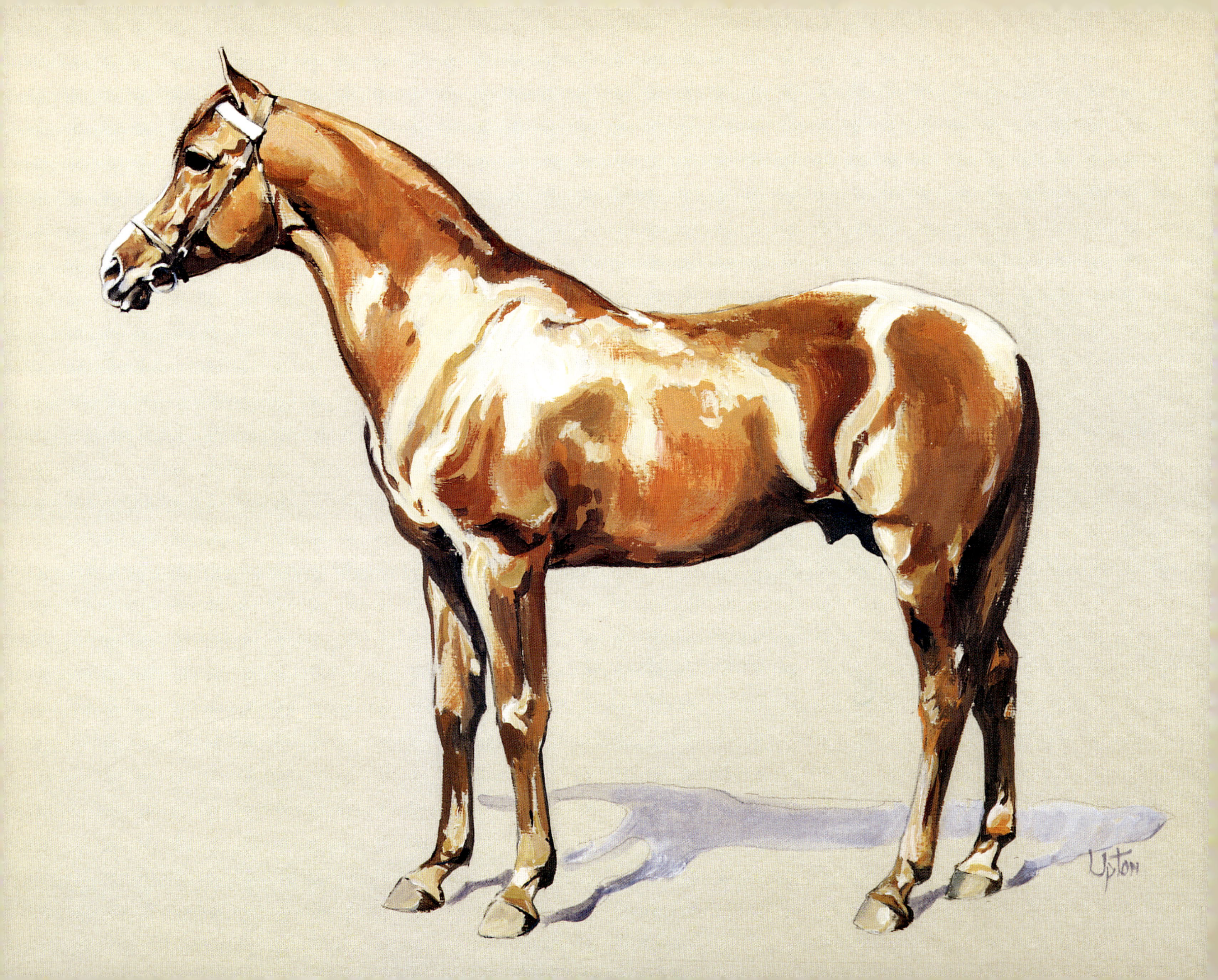
Upton

YATAGAN

A Kehilan Jurayban.

A chestnut horse foaled in 1870.

Bred by Sheikh Suleyman Ibn Mirshid of the Gomussa tribe of Sebaa-Anazeh.

Dam — A mare of the Juraybah (Greban) family taken from the Heissa-Anazeh.

Sire — A famous horse of the Kehilan Halawi (Hellawee) family of the Shammar tribe.[34]

Sale — Purchased by Mr Skene, Consul at Aleppo, and imported by Mr A. Sandeman MP, in 1874.

Height — 14 hands 2 inches.

In a note, Upton states: 'The Kehilan Hellawi, sire of the chestnut colt, is preferred to any Seglawi Jedran stallion for covering mares. On account of the constant success of his progeny, colts got by him are always sought after. All horses bear the name of the breed of the dams and the Keheilan Jeeban is, therefore, considered first class, as that is one of the best varieties of the Keheilan Adjooz breed. The Hellawi strain is also a branch of the Keheilan Adjooz – but not in general so much thought of as the sire of this chestnut colt is in particular.'

◀ *Yatagan*

GSB Volume 13
Imported 1874

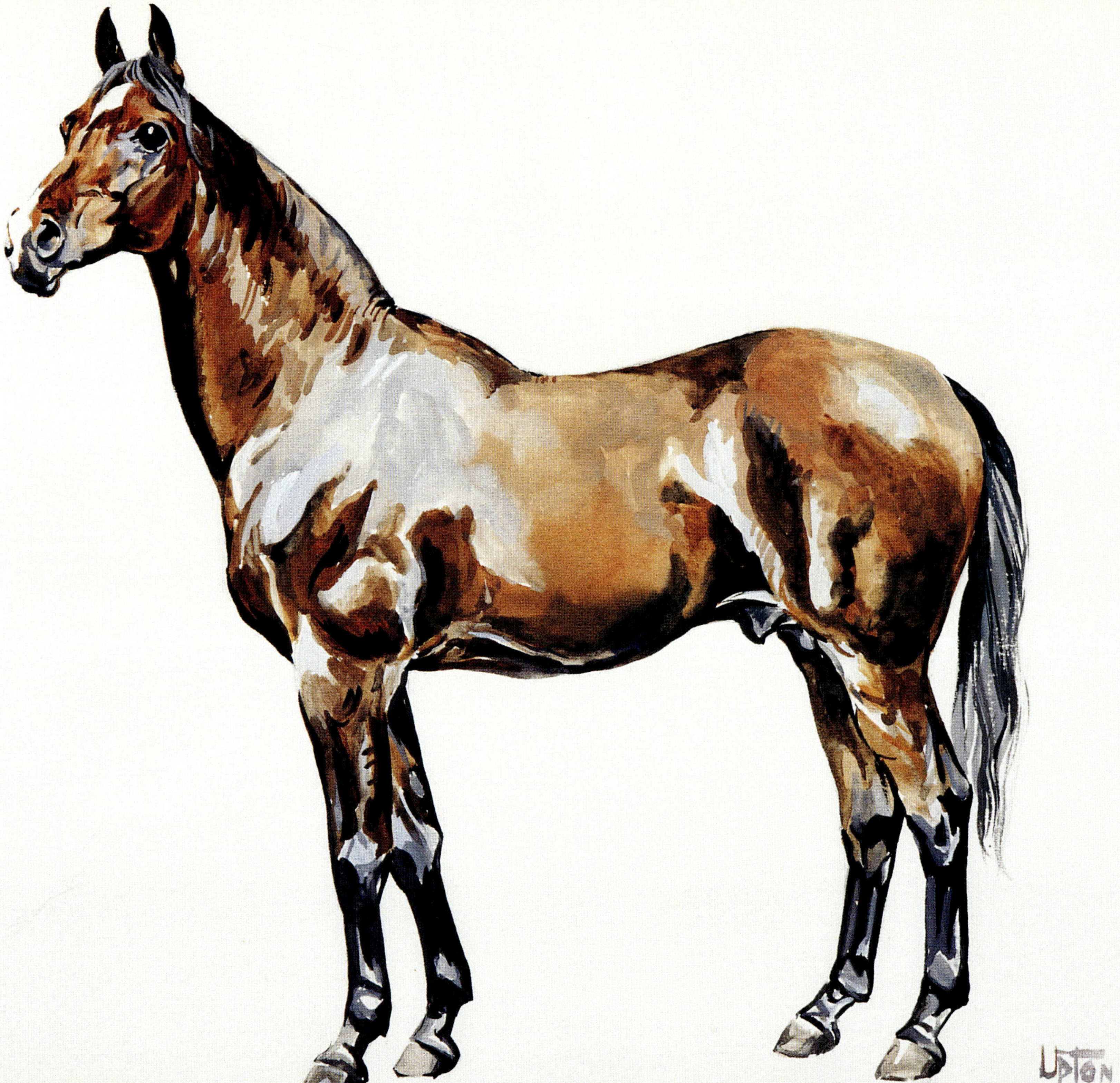
UPTON

EL EMIR (SANAD)

A Managhi Ibn Sbeyel.

A bay horse foaled c.1873.

Bred by Dehmedi Alzoba Ibn Amoud (Sheikh el Hamoud of the Al Zoba tribe, allies of the Shammar).[35]

Dam   A bay Managhieh Ibn Sbeyeli

Sire   A grey Kohel Cheyti (Kehilan Sueyti).

Description   A dark bay with star and snip.[36]

Height   14 hands 2 ½ inches.

El Emir is believed to have been exported to Algiers in November 1877, and was sold to the horse dealer Mr Charles Masne. He eventually became the property of Don Carlos Waetgin y Arango. The Honourable Miss Dillon purchased the horse from Mr John Legard who had bought him from Don Carlos. A very well-known horse in Algiers. Imported to England by the Honourable Miss E. Dillon in July 1880. El Emir was shipped out to India to join her in the autumn of 1883 and was entered for a race at Poona. He was placed second. He died in 1897.

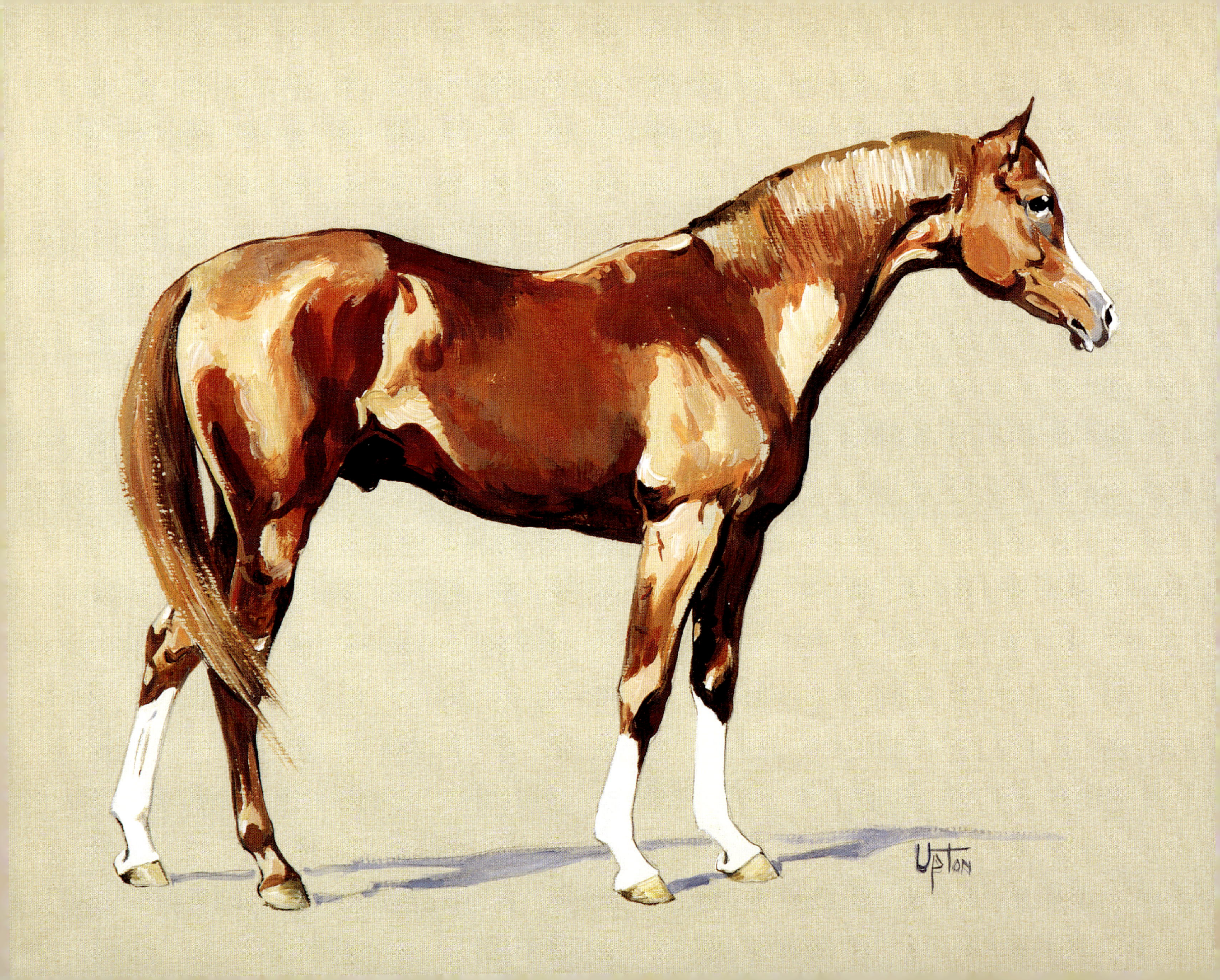
Upton

KISMET

A Kehilan of the Muntifiq.

A dark chestnut horse foaled in 1877.

Bred by the Muntifiq and sent from Arabia to Abdul Rahman of Bombay in October 1882.

Sale — Purchased by Lieutenant R.S. Broadwood of the 12th Lancers. [He visited the Blunts at Sheykh Obeyd, Egypt.] Put into racing, Kismet won the Mysore Cup on 12 July 1883, the Mysore Purse on 14 July 1883, the Deccan Handicap on 22 November 1883, the Bombay Derby on 12 February 1884 and four of the Aga Khan's Plates from 1883-84. His total winnings for those two seasons in India amounted to £30,000 and he never lost a race.

Description — Dark liver chestnut, three white legs, both forelegs and near hind and a blaze.

Height — 14 hands 3 inches.

Imported in April 1884 by Mr Broadwood. After running in the Newmarket 2-mile race on 2 July, and a 1-mile race at Sandown on 22 July, Kismet was sold to Sir R.D. Cunyingham VC, for whom he won matches in England, including Sandown Park in July 1886 where he beat the horse Asil over 2 miles.[37] Sir R.D. Cunyngham sold him to the Honourable John Corbett MP of Impney, Droitwich for 90 guineas. He was then sold to the Reverend F.F. Vidal at the Crabbet Sale, in the spring of 1890, for £30. Vidal stood him at stud until 1891, when he leased him to Mr Randolph Huntington of USA at £200 per annum. The agreement for leasing Kismet, involved Mr Huntington taking all risks and paying all expenses of transport, as well as the premium on insurance, in principle, an amount of £1,000. It also provided that the horse should be limited to twenty mares in any one year. Kismet sailed for New York on board the SS Canada on 24 October 1891, and was nineteen days at sea, reaching Long Island on 11 November 1891. The cost of the trip was £176.12.6. Kismet died of pneumonia one hour after completion of his voyage to New York.

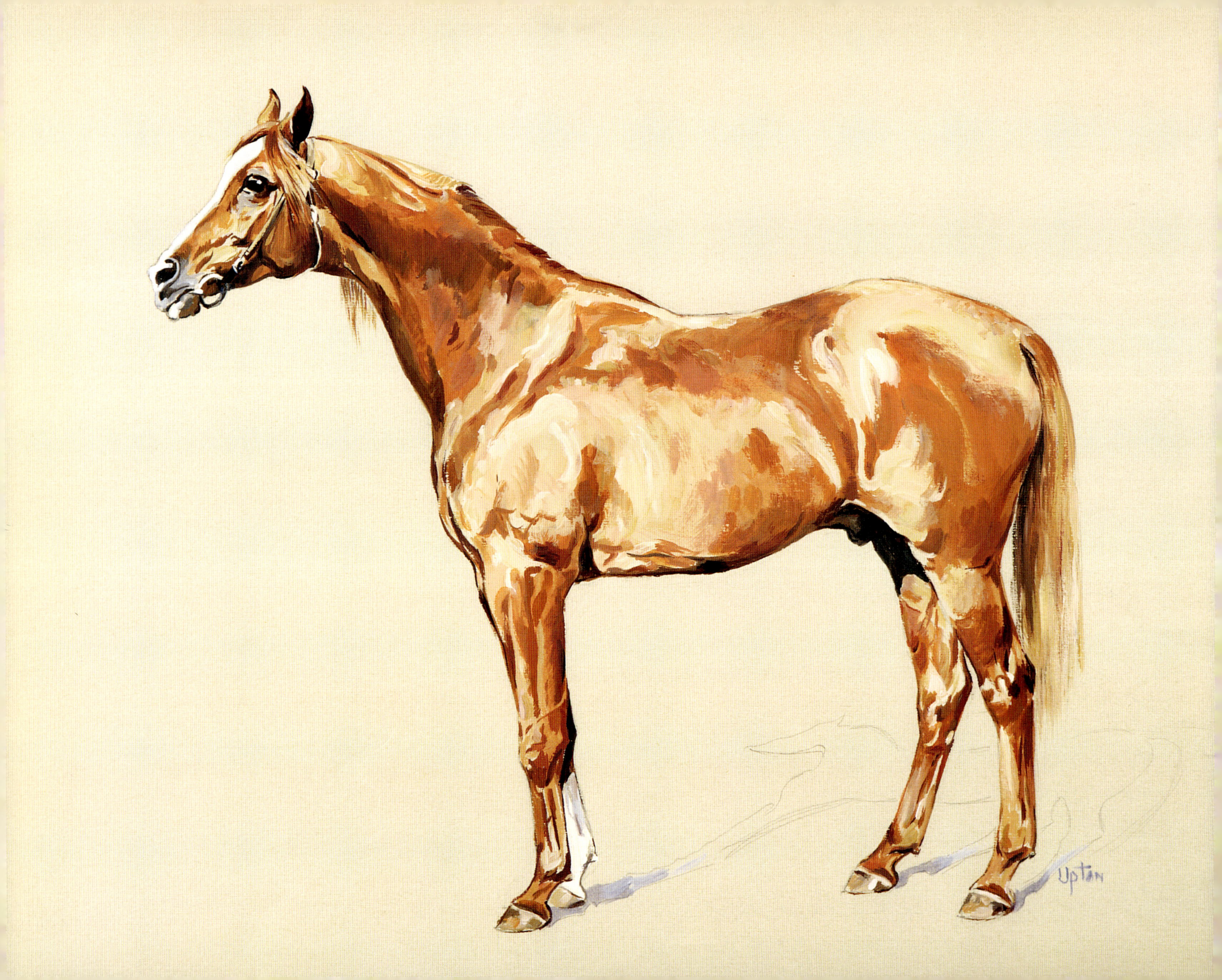
Upton

MAIDAN

A chestnut horse foaled c.1869.

Sale — Purchased by Colonel Brownlow in 1871 and Abd er Rahman of Bombay, or purchased by Captain Johnstone from Abd er Rahman and sold to Lieutenant-Colonel Brownlow of the 72nd Highlanders. Brownlow received a certificate from Abd er Rahman who vouched for the horse's origin. Maidan was ridden as a charger in campaigns through India and Afghanistan until Lieutenant-Colonel F. Brownlow was killed on 1 September 1880 commanding his troops at Kandahar at the end of Lord Robert's famous march of 300 miles from Kabul. Major Brough then bought the horse but sold him on to Captain Fisher. For three years between 1881 and 1884, Maidan won many races including the Ganges Hog Hunt Cup and a 4-mile steeplechase. He also won the Kadir Cup [the Blue Ribbon of Pigsticking in India]. Maidan was then purchased by Lord Airlie, who put him in racing again. Then he was sold to the Honourable Eustace Vesey who bought him to take to England.

Description — A chestnut with white sock on off fore and a narrow blaze. Good head, jaw deep, girth and shoulder good. [Seen by Lady Anne Blunt: 'Far more beautiful than Kismet.']

Height — 15 hands.

Below knee — 8 inches.

Imported in 1887. He was shipped to England on the troopship Jumna, but at Suez, the ship was pressed into service to carry troops to Massawah, going to the relief of Suakim. Maidan reached Marseilles after 100 days of travel. He won a race at Pau and was successfully raced in England. At the death of Vesey, Maidan was purchased by the Honourable Miss Dillon in 1889. He was hunted in Suffolk during the winter of 1889/90 and won a steeplechase at 22 years of age. Then in 1892, at 23 years, he slipped and broke a leg whilst at exercise and had to be destroyed.

◀ *Maidan*

GSB Volume 16
Imported 1887

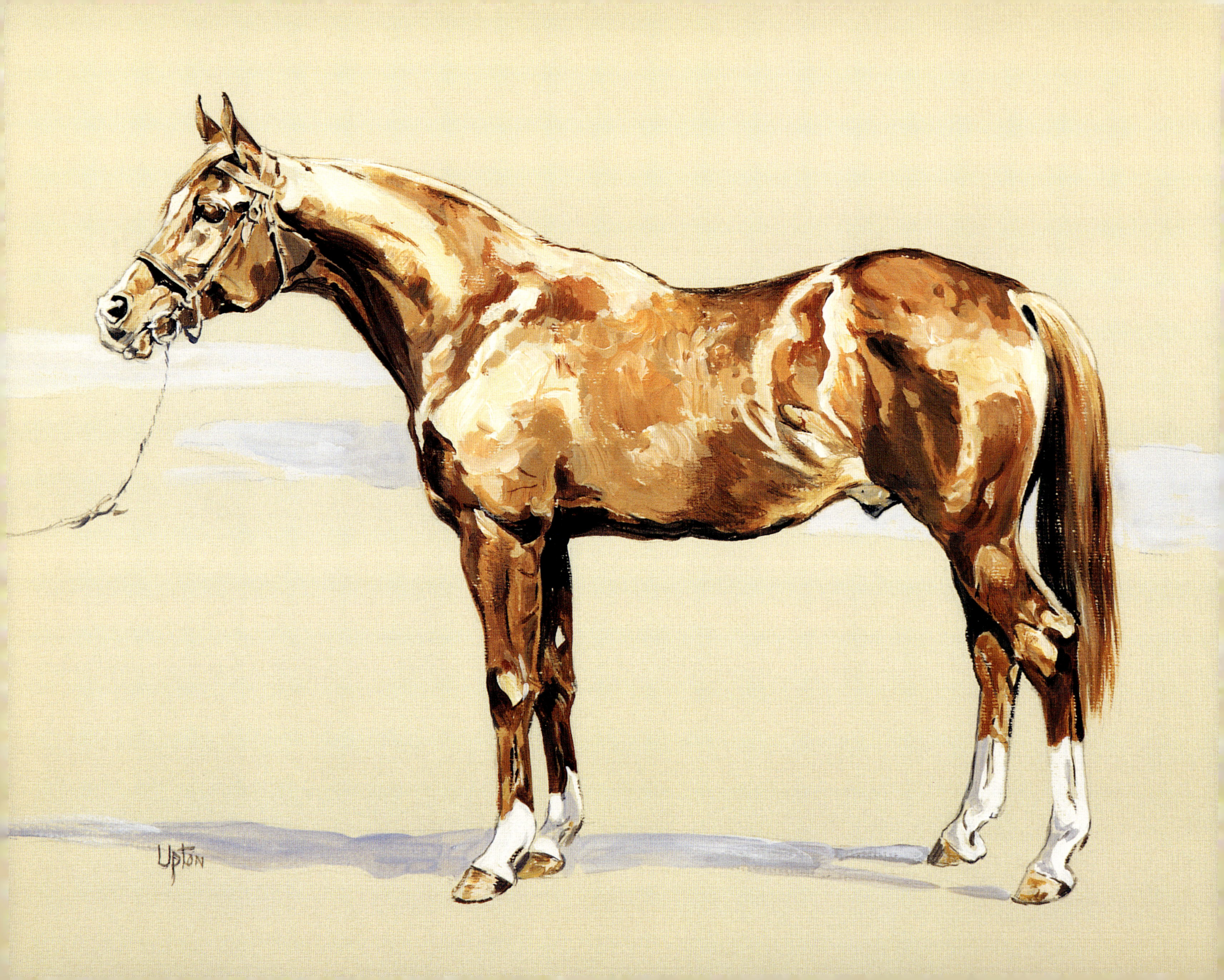
Upton

MOOTRUB

A Seglawi Jedran.

A chestnut horse foaled in 1887 [1884 according to P & RPS Volume 1].

From Nejd, Central Arabia.

Sale — Purchased by General Sir John Hills RE, in India, soon after he arrived from Arabia. He won races in India and was purchased from General Hills by Mr R.S. Henderson.

Description — Chestnut with star, race and four white socks.

Height — 14 hands ½ inch.

Imported from Calcutta in 1891 by Mr R.S. Henderson. Mootrub won 1st prize in the Pony Stallion Class at Hurlingham in 1893.

He was bought by Mr Stewart Foster who sold him in 1899. Later owners were Reverend D.B. Montefiore, Colonel E.N. Henriques and Henry C. Stephens, Esq. He was 1st Eastern Sires of the National Pony Show 1904 and 1905, and 1st Eastern Sire, RASE 1903 and 1904.

GSB Volume 20
P&RPS Volume 1, Number 32
AHS Volume 1, page 131
Imported 1891

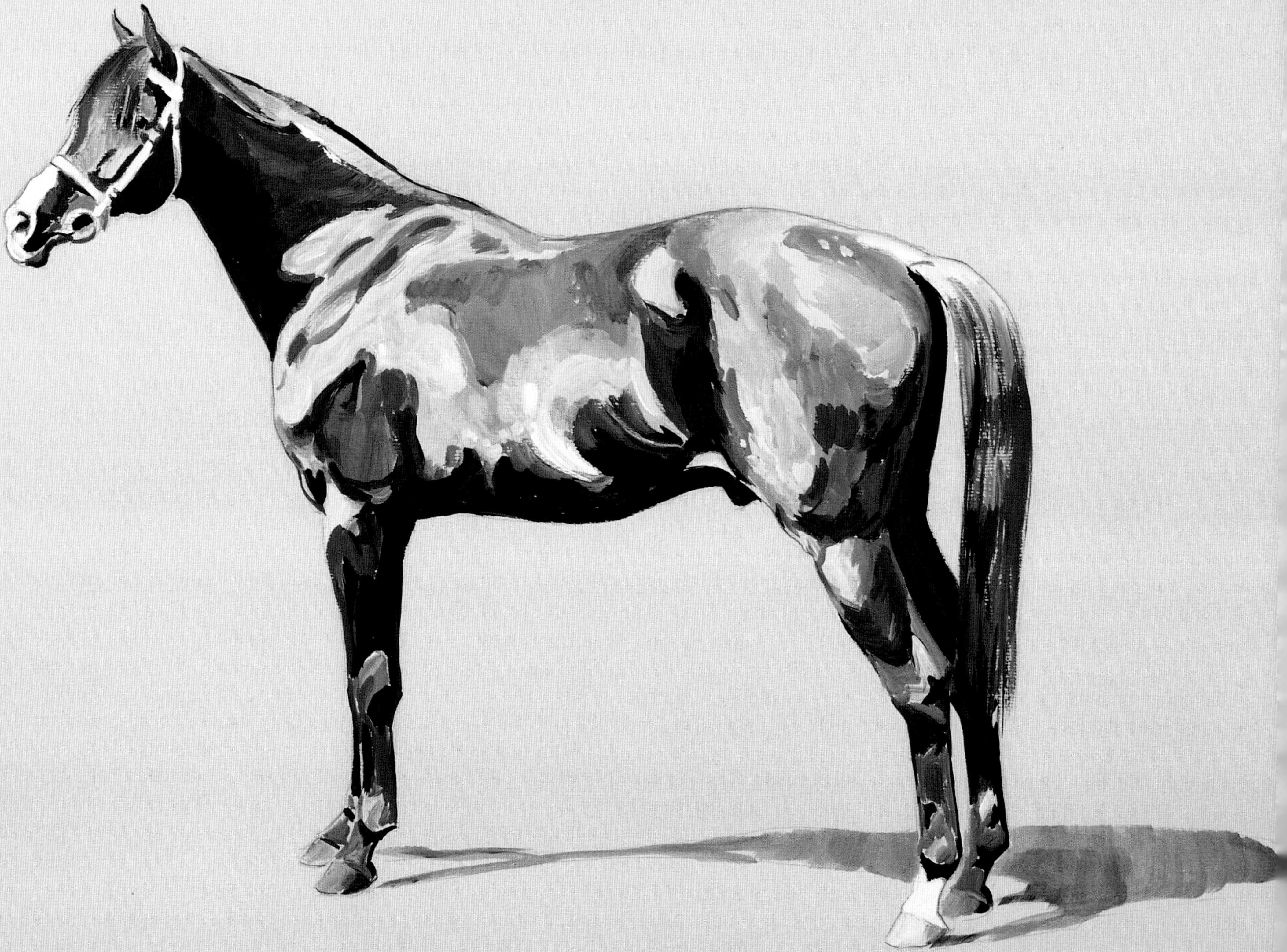

ROHAN

A black horse foaled c.1890.

Bred at Rishan in the Vilayet of Baghdad.

Sire — Bohar the famous, celebrated as the male horse of Abu Ridwan of the same sub-tribe, among the tribe of Ali-Haï of the Shammar.

It is stated that in 1898, Rohan was sent to H.I.M the Sultan of Turkey from the Province of Baghdad. At the command of His Majesty, and in recognition of the high quality of Hungarian horses supplied to the Turkish Government during the late Turko-Greek war, he, Rohan was presented to Messrs. Schwimmer of Budapest by his Excellency Haki Pasha, Aide-de-Camp to H.I.M the Sultan. A special Iradé being given by His Majesty to authorise his exportation from Constantinople.

In November 1900, Rohan was presented by the Messrs. Schwimmer to Mr. E.R. Calthrop.

Description — Black with a blaze widening over both nostrils. Near hind pastern white.

Shot 5 August 1917.

◄ *Rohan*

GSB Volume 20
P&RPS Volume 7
AHS Volume 1
Imported November 1900

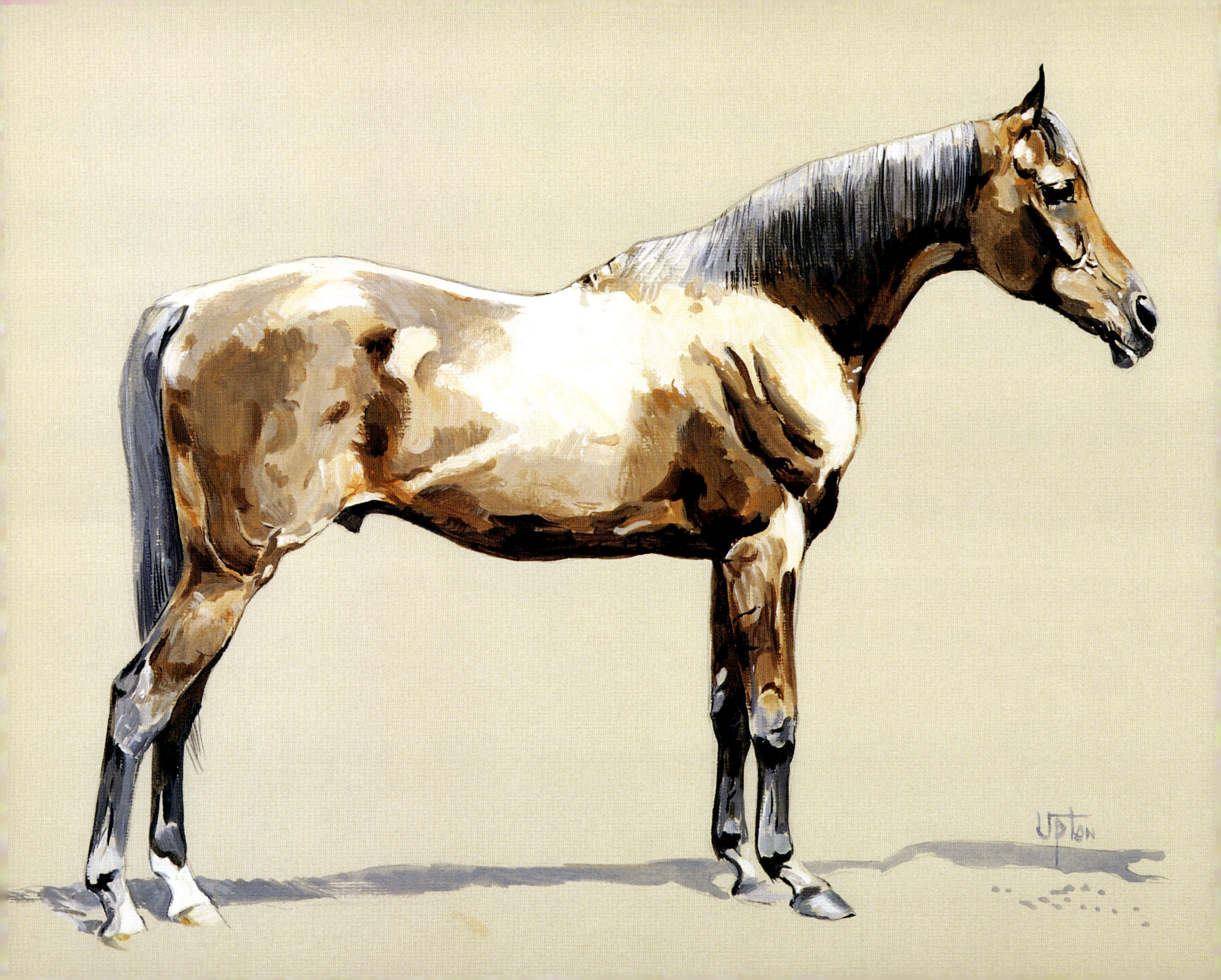
Upton

DWARKA (DEWARKA)

	A bay horse foaled c. 1892.
Sale	Chosen especially by a friendly Arab sheikh in the heart of the Anazeh country for General Ralph Broome, Director of Remounts, India, who took him to India in 1897. An extract from Volume 8 of the P-RPSSB reads: 'Dewarka is of the highest caste and most aristocratic strain of Arabian. Imported into India for racing purposes and especially chosen by Major Ralph Broome, Remount Agent for the Government of Bombay. Winner of twelve out of fifteen events on the flat including the Hurricane Stakes at the Rawal Pindi Spring Meeting, 1898, where he did the mile in 1 minute 53 seconds easily. He has also won numerous gymkana races and other events; and was considered the best Arab of his day in India.' 1st prize for Ladies Hacks 1898, Broome described him as: 'the most beautiful Arab I have ever seen'.
Description	A bay with black points, a small star, some white on near hind pastern and coronet and on off hind coronet. Rope mark on poll, white dots behind girth. [Note in margin NPS Volume 14 – 'Dwarka – defective action'.]
Height	14 hands 1 ½ inches.
Below knee	7 ¾ inches.

Imported to England in 1901 having been purchased by Mrs Atkinson from Major-General Broome, Dwarka carried Mrs Atkinson with the Burghley and Fitzwilliam Packs where he earned for himself the title of the 'Marvel'. He was a brilliant hunter under side-saddle with twenty-six different packs in Northumberland, Durham, Leicestershire and Devon. His stud work was carried out in the intervals between the last day's hunting and the first day's club hunting each year. For some years Dwarka was owned by Captain W.A. McDougall AVD, of The Scaurs, Jedburgh. In 1916 he was sold or leased to the Prince of Wales to stand at his Tor Royal Stud, Devonshire. Dwarka was destroyed at Tor Royal in 1921 and his bones are in the British Museum (seventeen ribs and six lumbar vertebrae).

◀ *Dwarka, as an old horse*

GSB Volume 25
P&RPS Volume 7, Number 217
AHS Volume 1, page 39
Imported 1901

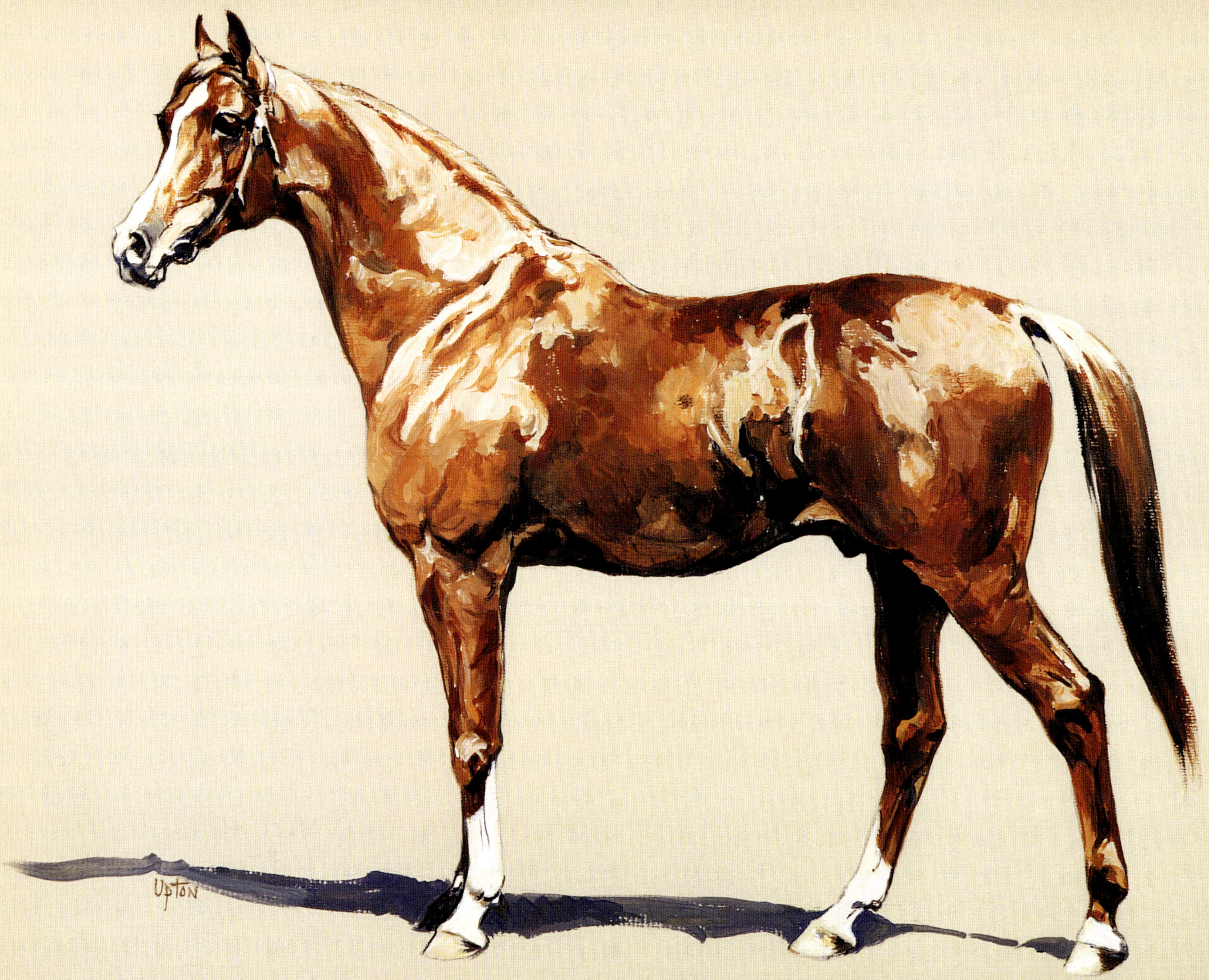
Upton

NEJDRAN

A Seglawi Ubayran.

A chestnut horse foaled in 1896.

Bred in the desert, from the Nejd.

Description | A chestnut with blaze and two white socks on near fore and hind and a white mark around the pastern of the off hind.

Imported to England in 1902, as a 6-year-old, by Captain Gainsford, Nejdran was exported to the USA, in 1904, and bought by Homer Davenport. He wrote, in a letter to Lady Anne Blunt, in June 1908: 'Five years ago I bought on landing here from England a very pretty sorrel Arab horse that was supposed to be brought out of the desert by a Captain Gainsford.' Albert W. Harris wrote in The Blood of the Arab – the World's Greatest War Horse, published in 1941: 'In 1904 Homer Davenport secured from Captain Gainsford of the English Army, a chestnut stallion, he had imported from the Arabian desert, of the Seglawi Jedran family, bred in 1896. He played in the International Polo Match in Ireland in 1903... his name was Nejdran. He was as beautiful a horse as probably ever came from the desert... Horsemen commented on his perfection.' Of three offspring born in the USA only one bred on.

◀ *Nejdran*

Imported 1902

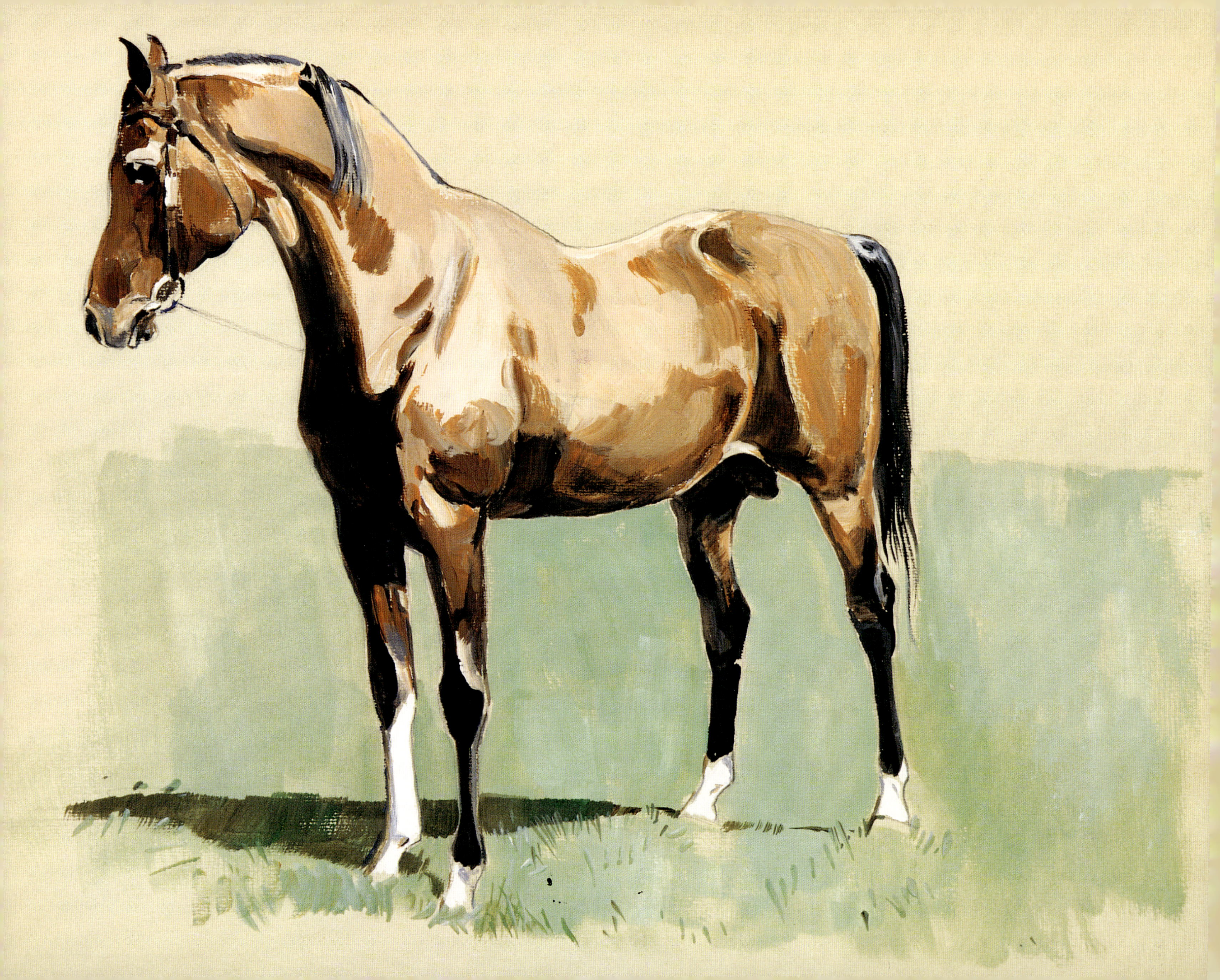

MUSKET

A bay horse foaled in 1900.

Bred in the desert of Arabia.

Imported from Bombay, India by Lieutenant-Colonel H.M. Abud in 1908.

Description Bay with a star, and socks, off fore and hind legs.

Height 13 hands 2 $\frac{1}{4}$ inches.

A winner of races in India. 1906, 1st Arab Stallions, Bombay Horse Show. 1909, 3rd Eastern Stallions, London Show.

Owned by Mr Everard R. Calthrop.

Died 1914.

◀ *Musket*

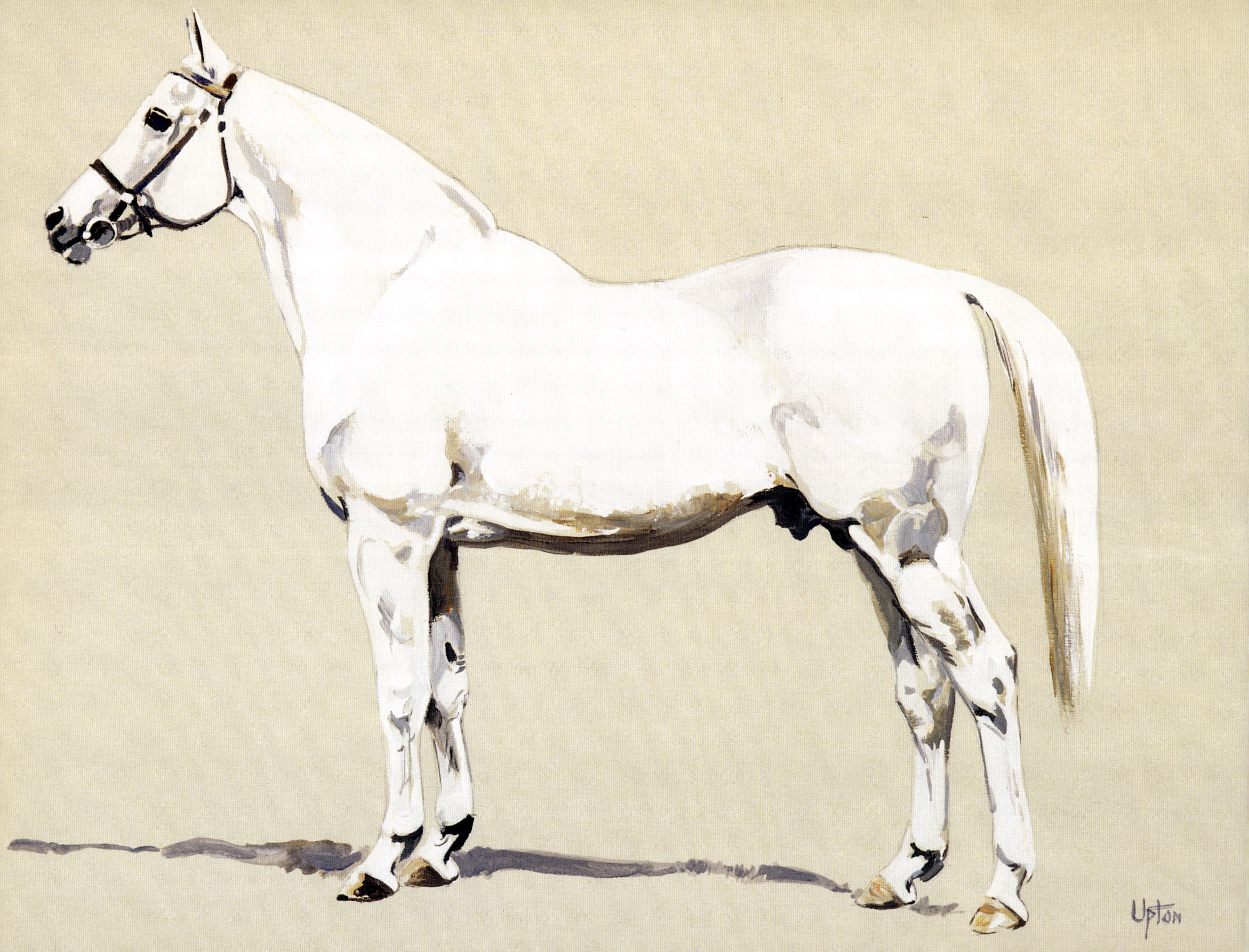
Upton

ZOOWAR

A grey horse.

Bred in Arabia.

Sold to India where he won the Punjab Army Cup and Handicap Steeplechase in 1907 and many other races on the flat and over hurdles.

Description Grey; scar on withers.

Height 14 hands 1 inch.

Imported from India to England by Major G.B. Ollivant of the 12th Royal Lancers and sold to Captain the Honourable George Savile. (Registered by the Board of Agriculture and Fisheries, on or after 1 November 1911.) He was 1st Eastern Sires P-RPS, London Show 1912. Zoowar was destroyed in 1920.

◀ Zoowar

P&RPS Volume 12, Number 513
AHS Volume 1, page 79
Imported *c.* 1910

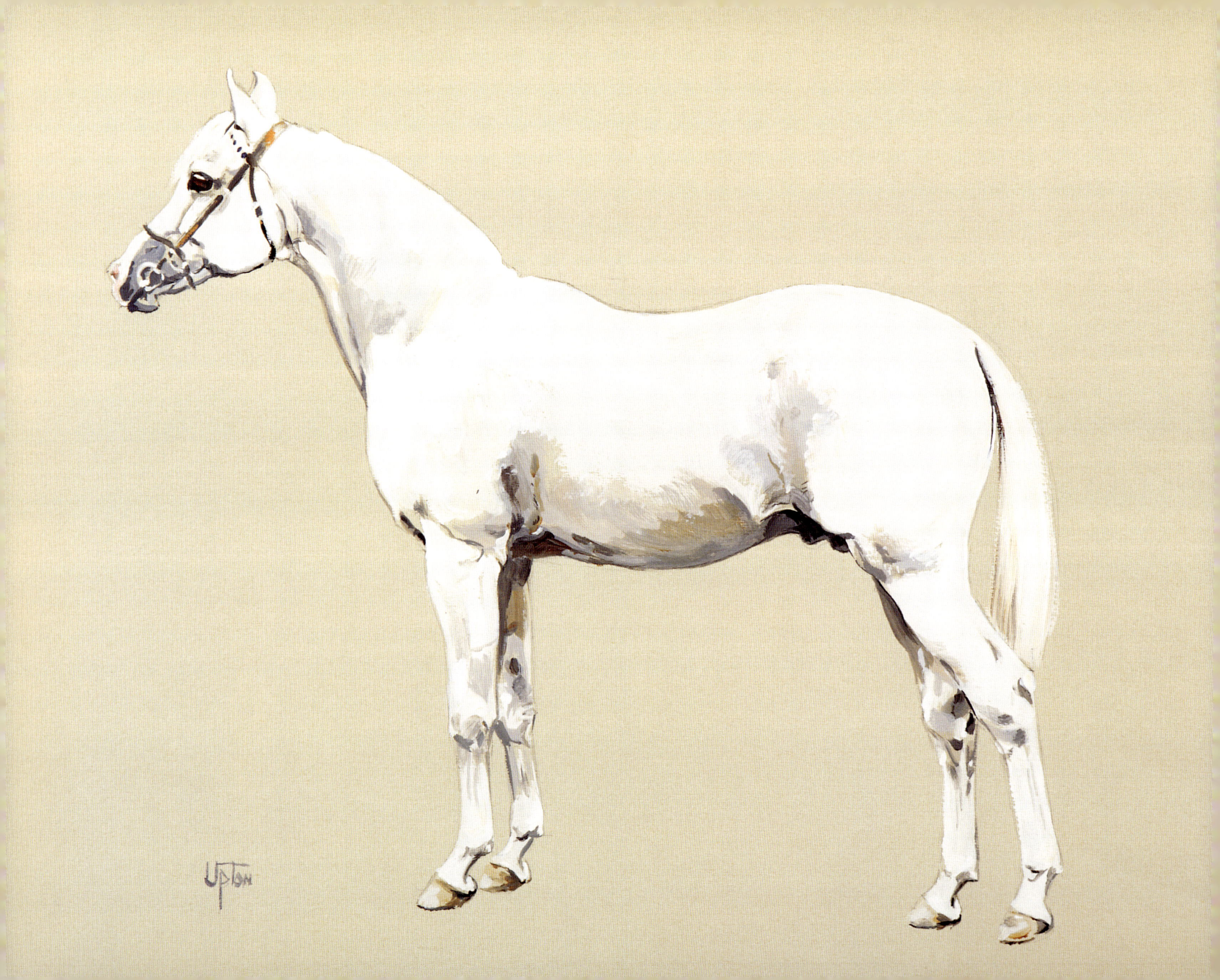
UPTON

CROSBIE

A grey horse foaled in 1908 [1910 according to NPS 1921 catalogue].

Bred by the Dursi tribe in the Arabian desert, Syria.

Brought to Abassia, Egypt, where he was purchased by Lieutenant-Colonel Patrick D. Stewart, DSO. He was a winner of many races [six or seven] in Cairo, including the Municipal Cup, Alexandria 1913 [1 ½ miles].

Description   Grey, white muzzle, part white lower lip. Aged.

Imported to England after 1914, Crosbie was 1st Eastern Sires, NPS London Show, 1916 and 1920 (2nd, Skowronek), and 1st Arab Stallions, NPS London Show, 1924 and 1925.

◀ *Crosbie*

P&RPS Volume 14, Number 760
AHS Volume 1, page 36
Imported after 1914

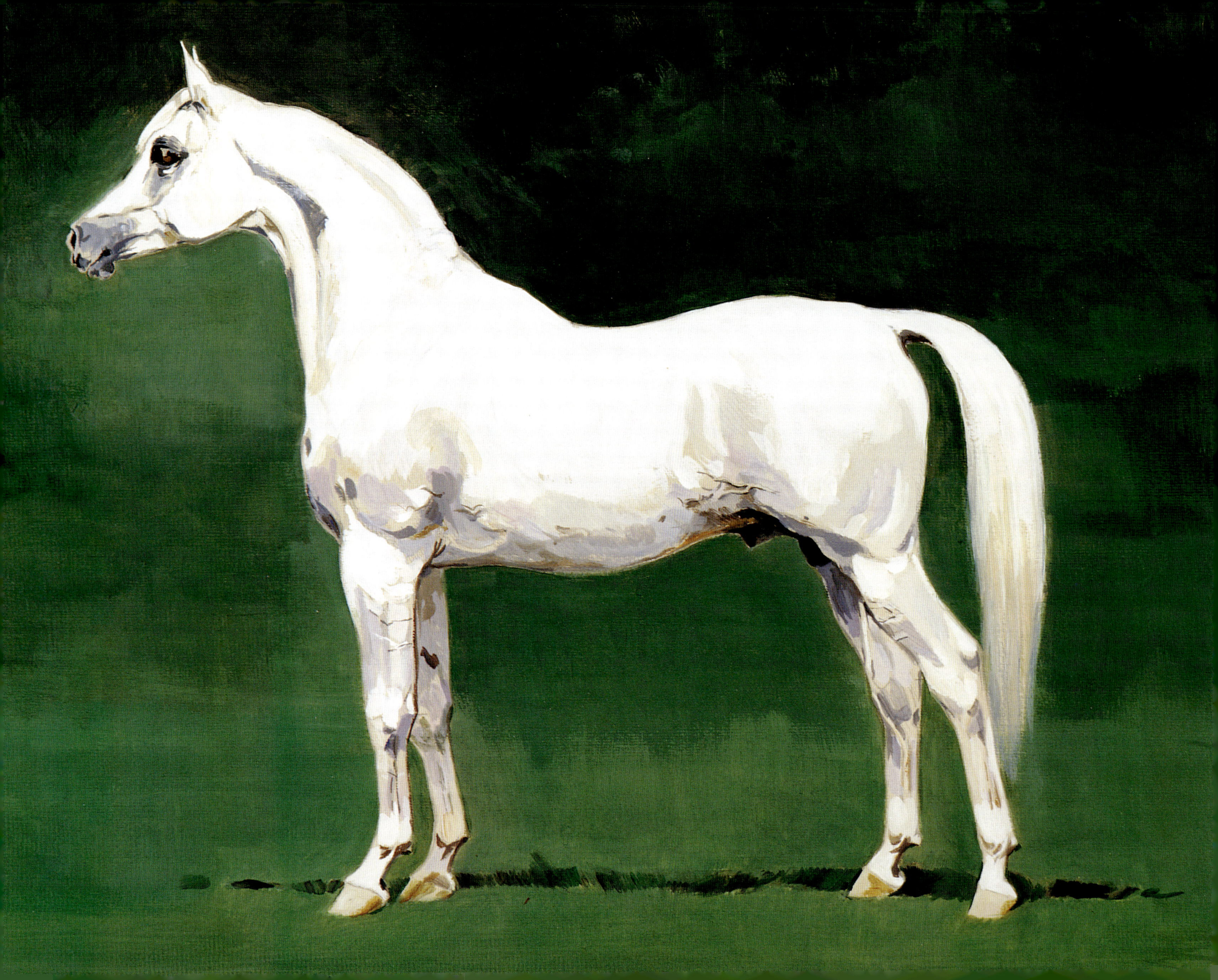

MIRAGE (CALLED 'FERHAN' IN ARABIA)

A Seglawi Jedran Dalia.

A white horse foaled in 1919 [Lady Wentworth gives 1914 and Roger Selby, 1909].

Bred by the Sebaa-Anazeh.

Dam — A Seglawieh Jedranieh of Dalia.

Sire — A Kehilan Ajuz of the Denadsha strain.

Sale — Bought for King Faisal of Iraq from the Denadsha tribe of Sebaa-Anazeh, by General Haddad Pasha. The translation of the Arabic Certificate reads: 'We the undersigned certify that the white stallion is 9 years old. A Seglawi Jedran of Dalia bred by the Sebaa-Anazeh. He is pure bred and the Denadsha tribe bought him and sold him to General Haddad Pasha in the name of His Majesty the King of Iraq – Faisal I. His dam – a Seglawieh Jedranieh; his sire – a Kehilan Ajuz of the Anazeh. Baghdad, 1 June 1927, Director of the Royal Stables' [El Mahasshami].

Description — White, 'A handsome level-backed horse of much beauty and iron legs. Exceptional front and girth and beautiful cantering style. Very fine trotting action and is a beauty under saddle. He reminds me of Azrek who came from the same district. The Denadsha were originally from Nejd but have now moved to Mesopotamia.' [Lady Wentworth]. A horse famed throughout the tribe. His head is a glory and his great eyes express high but gentle spirit and gracious personality.

Height — 14 hands 2 inches [Lady Wentworth states 14 hands 3 ½ inches].   Below knee   8 inches.

'He was brought to France and presented as a first choice of imported horses to Signor de Martino, the Italian Ambassador, who, when he was ordered to China in 1923, sent the horse to be sold at Tattersall's (London). I purchased him just before the auction from Senor Ricci for... guineas and he was withdrawn, immensely to the indignation of Messrs Clark and Hough and others who followed the horse in motor cars and stopped my man in the street to find out who had got him, and finally went to Victoria station to examine the labels on the horse box. He was identified by General Haddad Pasha who had paid £500 to the tribe on behalf of King Feysul and knew the horse well and complimented me on having secured him. He was, he said, the pick of all the horses sent over, the next best being the one given to Lord Hartington (Shueyman), a chestnut for which the King gave £700, a fancy price, said the General. Shueyman was 2nd in the 30-mile English race at Lewis, 1923 and was regularly hunted by Lord Hartington, until he broke down and he gave him to me, but he was not good enough for my stud. Naheis Bey visited the Stud in October 1924 and again identified the horse as one he had travelled six days to see with the Anazeh by whom he was bred and much valued as a sire.' [Lady Wentworth]

Champion Arab at Richmond Royal Show, 1926 Mirage was sold, in 1930, to Mr R. Selby of Ohio and exported to USA. He was Champion Arab Stallion at the National Arabian Show, USA, 1934 and sired twenty-six foals in the USA.

◀ *Mirage*

Imported 1923

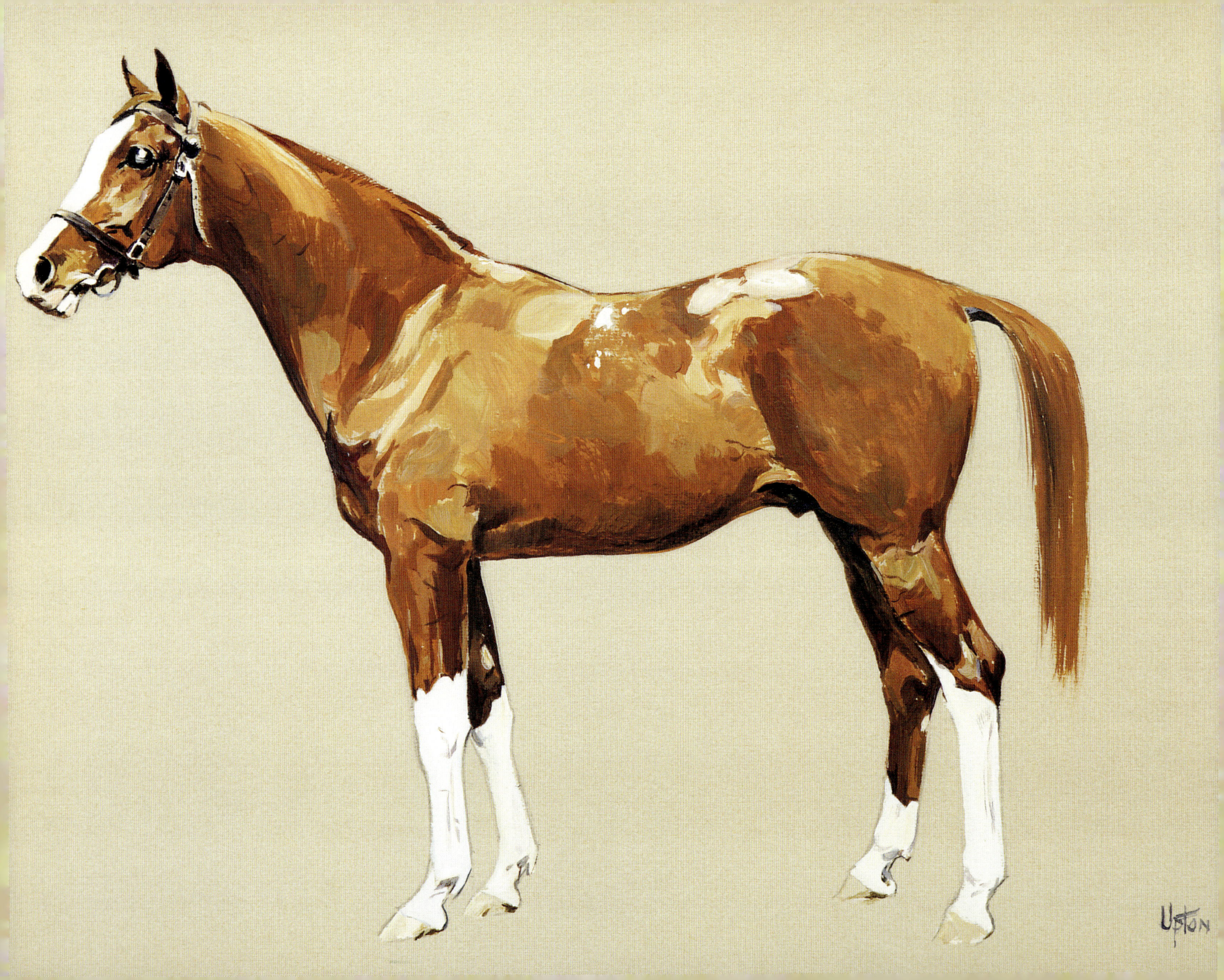
UPTON

ATESH

A Managhi Ibn Sbeyel.

A chestnut horse foaled in 1913.

Bred by the Gomussa tribe of Sebaa-Anazeh and given as a colt by them to the late Enver Pasha (Turkish Commander-in-Chief and leader of the 'Young Turks'). Enver Pasha used him as a charger during the Great War. He later raced successfully in Egypt, winning nine races.

Description   A chestnut with wide blaze and four white stockings, near fore to well above knee, off fore to the knee, near hind to inside of hock and off hind one-third up cannon bone. White saddle marks.

Height   14 hands 3 ½ inches.

Imported at the same time as Nimr and Lalla Rookh and owned by H.V. Musgrave Clark c.1923.

His last foal was born in 1938.

◀ *Atesh*

AHS Volume 3, page 26
Imported *c.* 1923

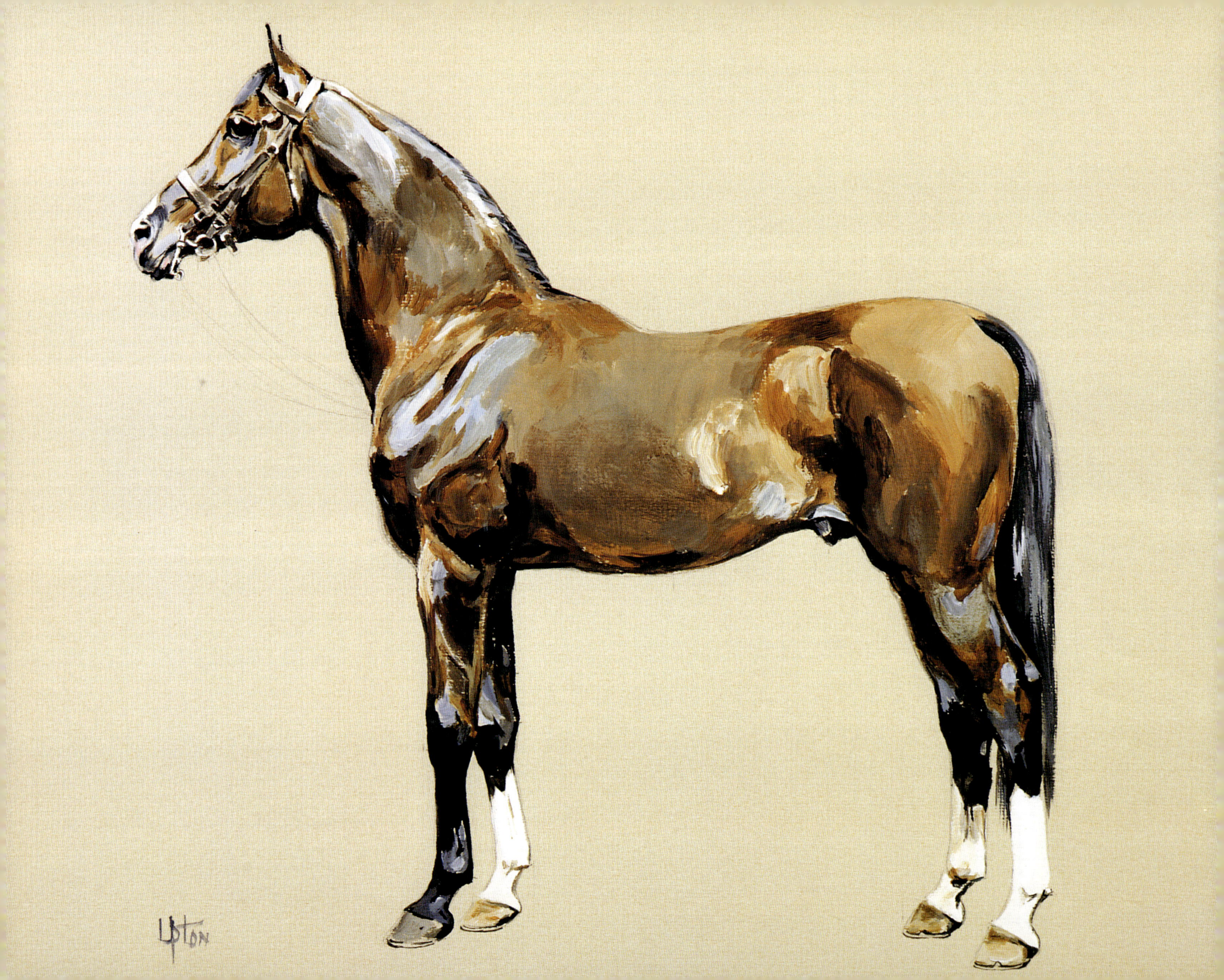
Upton

NIMR

A Seglawi Jedran

A brown horse foaled in 1914.

Bred and owned by Prince Mohuiddin, son of the late Sherif of Makkah and ridden by him as his war horse.[38]

Dam — Yaz, a Seglawieh Jedranieh. Her original owner was Sheikh Ul Mashaeikh of the Anazeh, who gave her to Hazim Bey, Governor of Baghdad. Hazim Bey took her to Constantinople where he sold her to Sherif Ali Jaffer, who gave her to Prince Mohuiddin.

Sire — A Seglawi Jedran belonging to the late Abdul Hamid II, Sultan of Turkey.

Description — Brown with blaze, off fore and both hind white socks. Written pedigree from Prince Mohuiddin. Eighteen ribs and five lumbar vertebrae.

Height — 15 hands

Imported c.1923 and owned by H.V. Musgrave Clark c.1923.

'I have paid £750 for a big brown imported horse from Arabia' (extract from a letter to Mrs D. Maclean, Fenwick, Australia from Mr Musgrave Clark).

Imported at the same time as Atesh* and Lalla Rookh*. 'A Magnificent type of Arab'. Lady Wentworth noted: 'A good imported horse was Nimr – well authenticated'.

Died 1931.

◀ *Nimr*

AHS Volume 3, page 51
Imported *c.* 1923

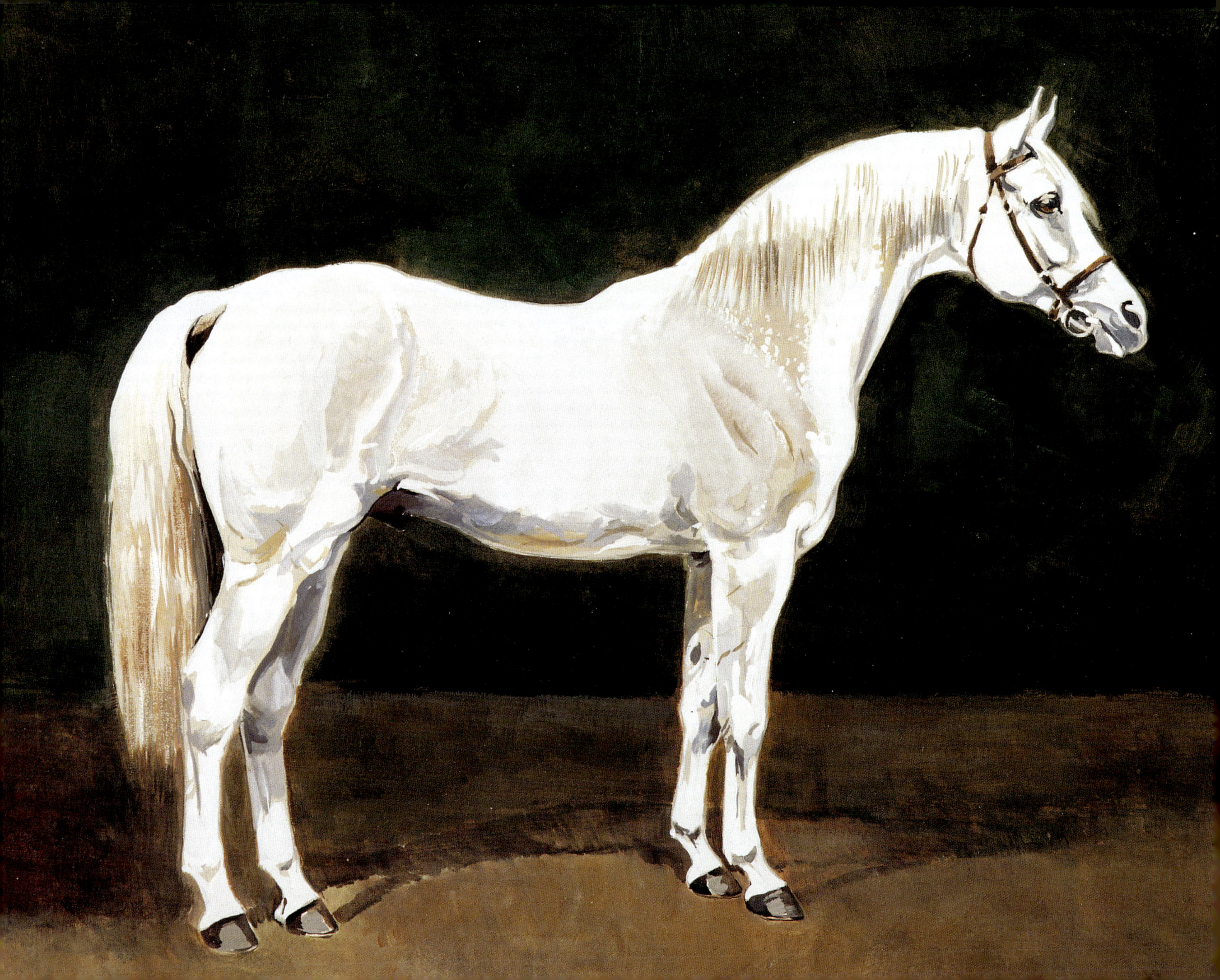

FEDAAN

A Seglawi Jedran of Ibn Sbeyni.

A white horse foaled in 1913.

Bred by the Ibn Sbeyni family of the Mehed tribe of Fedaan Anazeh.

Dam	Nejmeh by Ibn Sheefi ex Hadidieh.
Sire	Rashad.
Sale	Fedaan was brought to Damascus by Abdur Rahman Pasha, as a foal, with his dam, during the War. The mare was seized by the Germans and sent to Germany. The colt, was raised in Damascus, and Captain R.W. Brierley, late 21st Lancers, acquired him as a charger. He won races with him and brought him to England.
Description	White [Lady Wentworth noted: 'A beautiful white horse – well authenticated.']
Height	15 hands.

Imported c.1926, Captain Brierley showed Fedaan at the NPS Shows of 1926 and 1927. He was purchased by Mr Musgrave Clark in 1927 and he won several prizes and races – 1st in the Riding Class for Arabs, NPS Show 1928, 1st in the Arabian Stakes 1928 and 1929 at 1 1/4 miles and 2nd at 1 1/2 miles in 1929. 'Mr Clark placed him above Skowronek'.

His last recorded foal was born in 1939.

◂ *Fedaan*

AHS Volume 3, page 33
Imported *c.* 1926

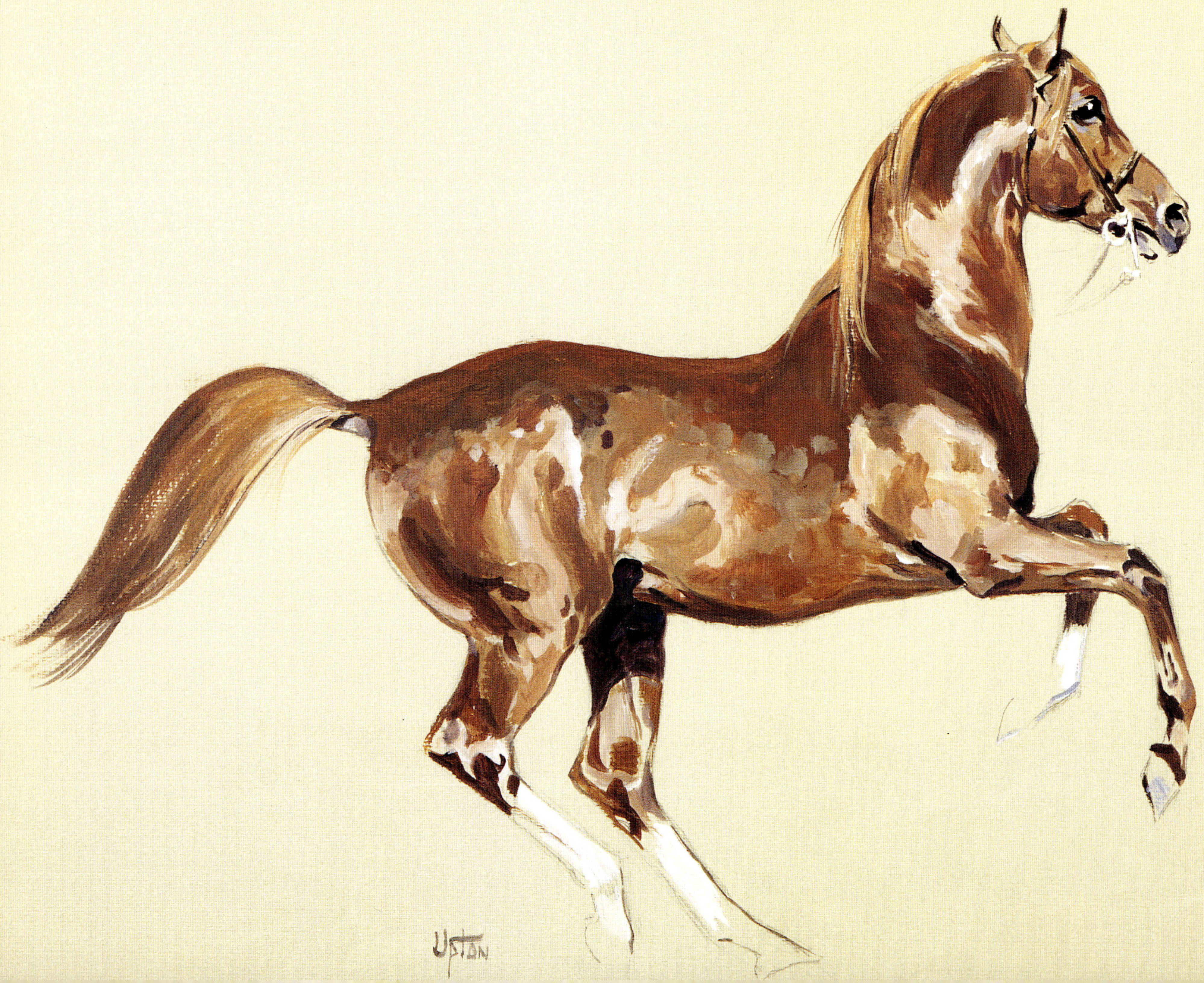
Upton

OUTLAW

A Kehilan Ajuz, possibly of the Jellabi strain.

A chestnut horse foaled in 1915.

Bred in Arabia.

Dam   Jellabieh, a Kehilet Ajuz.

Sire   Sheihan.

Sale   Owned by E.W. Sheffield, Sharia, El Manakh, Cairo.

Description   A liver chestnut with blaze, near fore and both hind white socks. [Lady Wentworth noted: 'Outlaw is a good-looking horse.']

Imported to England c.1927 by E.W. Sheffield and shown successfully in 1927 and 1930 when 1st in Ridden Arabs. He stood 2nd to Fedaan in 1928 in the Riding Class for Arabs, NPS Show. He had stood 2nd to Sainfoin in the Stallion Class in 1927 and 1928. Purchased by Miss G. Spencer c.1929 and later (c.1930), owned by Colonel J. Cookson, Outlaw ran 3rd to Fedaan and Sainfoin in the Arab Stakes at Northolt Park on 21 August 1929. He died c.1936.

◀ *Outlaw*

AHS Volume 4, page 68
Imported *c.* 1927

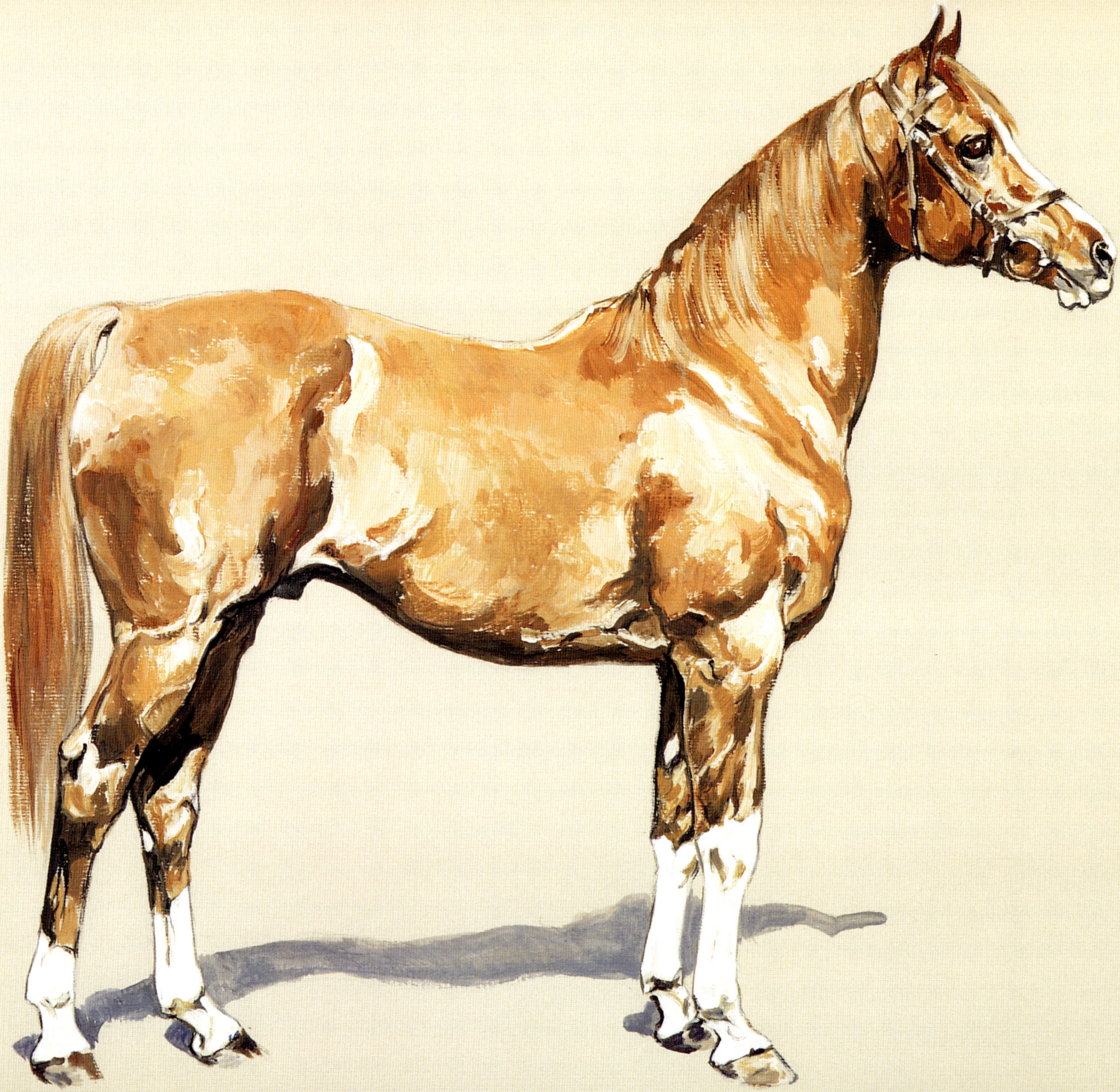

MANAK

A Kehilan Hamdani of Ibn Ghayam.

A chestnut horse foaled in 1928.

Bred in Arabia.

Presented by the Emir Saud, son of HM King Ibn Saud to His Majesty King George VI, as a token of friendship and in appreciation of the hospitality given to him at the coronation.

In December 1937, four Arab horses, and four camels were unloaded from the liner 'Mantola' at the Royal Albert Docks, London. The contingent consisted of two stallions and two mares – Manak*, Kasim* a bay horse (see page 260), Turfa* a grey mare (see page 201) and Faras* a bay mare (see page 113).

Description Chestnut with wide blaze and four white socks. A very masculine type of exceptional quality, good bone, strong loins, quarters and hocks. A fine mover. He carries his head and 'flag' [tail] like an aristocrat. He is a horse of perfect temperament.

Height 14 hands 2 inches.

Imported in 1937, Manak was lent by His Majesty the King to the Arab Horse Society to stand at stud at Colonel J. Anderson's Upend Stud, Newmarket. He died in 1947.

◀ *Manak*

AHS Volume 6, page 85
Imported 1937

PADISCHAH

A grey horse, bred in the desert in 1826 by the Muntifiq tribe. Taken from them in battle by Daoud Pasha, Governor of Baghdad, and given by him to Mr Macdonald, the British Ambassador to the Persian Court.

Sire   Atlas

In 1838 Padischah was purchased in England for export to the Weil Stud, Germany. This Royal Stud had been founded in 1817 by King William I of Württemburg. He was used at stud until 1842.

Imported *c.* 1830

INDJANIN

A grey horse, bred in the desert, and taken to India, where he had belonged to the Governor General. Sent to England, he was purchased in 1853 by Count Wladyslaw Branicki for Szamrajowka Stud, Poland.[39]

Imported *c.* 1850

SAJDEN

A chestnut horse, desert-bred and imported to England. Purchased in London, with Beduin* by Count Wladyslaw Branicki from Aschton, a dealer.[40] Sent in 1850 to the Bialocerkiev Stud, Poland.

Imported *c.* 1850

INDJANIN (NIZAM)

A white horse of high nobility and breeding, black mane and tail. Bred in the desert and exported to India. Imported to England from Calcutta by the Viceroy of India. Purchased in 1859 in London for Slawuta, Poland. Sold the same year to Count Branicki, for Bialocerkiev, who re-named him Nizam to avoid any confusion with the Indjanin imported six years earlier to Szamrajowka.

Imported *c.* 1855

MAHMOUD MIRZA

A dark bay Seglawi Jedran, foaled in 1851.

Bred by the Anazeh and exported to India later sent to England, where he was purchased in 1866 by Count Bathyani for Babolna, Hungary.

Imported *c.* 1860

HUSSAR

A chestnut horse bred in the desert in c.1872.

He had been given as a gift to the Prince of Wales (Edward VII) whilst on his tour of India in 1875. Purchased in 1878, it is said, at the London Show, Islington for Count Branicki and exported to Poland. Used at all the Bialocerkiew Studs until 1890 when he was sold to the Streleck Stud, Russia.

Described by Borowiak as 'very noble, distinguished and of outstanding conformation.'

The Blunts saw two foals by Hussar in 1884 - a grey colt ex Epopeja, and a grey colt ex Yagoda.

Imported *c.* 1875

MAMELUKE

A chestnut [?] horse foaled c.1884.

A high-caste Arabian, desert bred.

Sale — Purchased by Lord Herbrand Russell (later 11th Duke of Bedford), in India. Russell took up his appointment as aide-de camp to the Viceroy, Lord Dufferin, in 1884 and returned to England with his wife in 1888.

Mameluke was imported to England c.1888.[41] He was used as a stallion by Lord Arthur Cecil, cousin to the 11th Duke, in 1893 and 1894. The result of the 1893 covering was Shabaka ex Kesia II.[42]

GSB Volume 18
Imported *c.* 1888

KASIM

A Seglawi [AHS lists Abayan].

A bay horse foaled in 1934.

Bred by Ibn Sweid of the Ajman tribe.

Dam   A Seglawieh [AHS lists Abeyeh].

Sire   An Abeyan.

Presented to HM King George VI by Emir Saud, son of King Ibn Saud of Nejd, through the offices of Sir Gilbert Clayton. In December 1937, four Arab horses and four camels were unloaded from the liner 'Mantola' at the Royal Albert Docks, London. Presented to His Majesty by King Ibn Saud, as a token of friendship and in appreciation of the hospitality given to his son at the King's Coronation.

The contingent consisted of the stallions Kasim* and Manak* (see page 257) and the mares Turfa* (see page 201) and Faras* (see page 113).

Description   Bay with star, streak and snip into both nostrils. Near fore stocking and both hind fetlocks white. A horse of quality and a very good mover.

Height   14 hands 3 inches

Lent to the Arab Horse Society. He stood at the Nant Fawr Stud of D.E. Neale in South Wales.

AHS Volume 6
Imported 1937

RESH AL BADIA (OR RECH)

A Seglawi.

A chestnut horse foaled in 1928.

Bred in Arabia.

Dam · A Seglawieh.

Sire · A Seglawi.

Description · A chestnut with a star, race and snip into off nostril, near hind stocking.

Imported c.1938, he was owned by Mrs G.E. Atkinson.

AHS Volume 7, page 220
Imported *c.* **1938**

SHAMYL

A Muniqi.

A grey horse foaled in 1961.

Bred by the Commander-in-Chief Jordan Armed Forces, Lieutenant-General Habis El Majali.[43]

Dam · Shams* by Abu' Arqub ex M'ienaqia [Managieh], presented to HM Queen Elizabeth, the Queen Mother by Lieutenant-General Habis El Majali. The mare is foal to Qaied.

Sire · Qaied [Kaid] by a Sherif Nasser Arab that belonged to King Abdullah and came from the Hejaz, ex a Mienaquia Aribi [Managieh].

Description · A grey, foaled red roan.

AHS Volume 10, page 146
Imported *in utero* **1960**

NOTES

1. The fact of this grey mare being taken from the Fedaan fifteen years ago was corroborated by Ibn Sbeyni.
2. All the Ibn ed Derri's were first thought to be Obeyrans but, in fact, all were found to be Jedrans.
3. Even at this price she was not obtained without some pressure. Ibn ed Derri had refused to sell her, but the Pasha had set his heart upon possessing a mare already famous among the tribes. He seized an opportunity to negotiate with her owner when the latter, suspecting nothing, had encamped with a section of his tribe near the riverbank at a spot where they could be hemmed in by soldiers. This having been effected, the Governor sent word that unless the mare was delivered up he would order the troops to open fire. Berghi had no choice but to yield; the Pasha, however, was an honest man and did not propose to take the mare for nothing. He wanted to pay and was prepared to give a handsome price, more especially as it did not come altogether out of his own pocket. The forty-four camels conveniently at hand were Government property seized from the Shammar bedouins in payment of taxes claimed by the Government. Ali Pasha showed his delight at his new acquisition by pampering her with all sorts of dainties and decorating her with a chain halter of solid silver. Once, too, he lost his temper with her because she was fidgeting when he rode out, and he put her under arrest in irons for three days. But his bargain, according to gossip in Deyr and Aleppo, brought him no luck. While in his stable, Meshura did not produce a foal, and before two years were out the Pasha's affairs were so involved that he was forced to part with the whole of the stud he had collected.
4. First called Mecca, later Shereefa, then Sherifa.
5. 'An extraordinary head, very broad forehead, very small muzzle, very deep jowl, broad hollow between the jaws, beautiful ears like a gazelle's, large eyes showing some white, long nostril lying very flat when in repose; with crinkles round the upper end, muzzle very black, except small pink snip on lip, and quite bare of hair in summer (nearly up to the eyes) eyes surrounded by bare black skin (in summer).'
6. £265, a rifle and a cloak.
7. The Blunts' first Arab purchase.
8. We had heard of this mare two years before we saw her on our journey through Nefud to Nejd beyond Joff in January 1879 at the well of Shaqiq, where we met a son of Beneyeh Ibn – Shaalan. We were told about the quarrel between Beneyeh and his cousin Sotamm Ibn Shaalan, on account of this chestnut mare which Sotamm insisted on having and managed to take by force, failing to get her by fair means. Beneyeh then had left Sotamm to fight his own battles with the Sebaa, in the course of which, last summer, Sotamm lost the mare for whose possession he had sacrificed a valuable alliance, who was taken from him by Taïs Ibn Sharban of the Gomussa in 1880.
9. She strikes with her forefeet and kicks too. Her strange temper may possibly be the result of having been knocked about and especially the severe firing she had undergone.
10. Lady Anne Blunt considered that the Hamdanieh mare 'Muniet el Nefous', owned by Sennari, was full sister to Sobha.
11. Lady Anne Blunt saw Horra on 19 December 1888: 'The old old Seglawieh Jedranieh and a beautiful mare she must have been!'
12. With the purchase of this mare Lady Anne Blunt was to remark: '… and now the stud is complete'.
13. Jerboa's dam – the Original Mare Dahmeh el Hamra of Ibn Aweyde.
14. Bint Azz was bought at the 1st Auction, on 15 January 1897, by the dealer Amato, for £E 40 and exported to Russia (22 years old). In July 1899, Colonel de Sdanovitch stated that Bint Azz, who was bought by Prince Sanguszko, had one foal and is now dead. Prince Sanguszko wrote that she had met with an accident, a broken leg, and died at Slawuta without leaving any produce.
15. December 1896 – Ibn Sherara, white, also fine and very old (hind toes turned in) like Upton's frontispiece horse.
16. Known as the Darley filly.
17. Mashlab, son of Neddi Ibn ed Derri.
18. Hauran is in North Jordan.
19. Supported by the Great Arab Revolt
20. Ameen Rihani, a Syrian from the Lebanon, known to Ibn Saoud, was the author of books on Arabia and the Ibn Saouds. His address, for some time, was Earl's Court, London.
21. Khorma – a town east of Mecca, where one of the Saoudi Studs was situated.
22. Hillah – a town on the Euphrates, south of Baghdad.
23. Abu Amr – a low tribe, visited by the Blunts at Hurnabat on 10 February 1878. Sheikh Mohammed Yusufiyah Canal is half-way between Baghdad and Hillah.
24. Shammah had had a foal previously by the Thoroughbred stallion Cintrist.
25. Samih is, in all probability, Saameh (Jabao), a bay stallion foaled in 1941 and bred in Spain by Don José Maria de Ybarra y Gomez Rull. He was presented to HM King Abdullah and imported to Jordan in 1948/9, his dam – Uganda, a bay by Sawah II an Egyptian horse ex Sada Yama, from France; his sire – Ilustre, a grey by Seanderich DB ex Divina by Wan Dyck ex Navin.
26. The resulting foal, imported *in utero*, was a grey colt named Shamyl*, 1961. On 14 April 1964, Shams produced Shamanto, a chestnut filly by Manto. Both offspring are recorded as bred by HM Queen Elizabeth, The Queen Mother.
27. A note by Major Upton states. 'The Managhi Hedruj is highly esteemed as a breed, and those of the family of Ibn Sbeyel of the Gomussa tribe are known as the best strain of that blood though not always so handsome as some other breeds.'
28. Her 1878 foal had been a chestnut filly by Hermit (Winner of The Derby in 1867 for Henry Chaplin). Barren in 1879 and 1880, Kesia had her last foal, a chestnut colt by Ishmael* in 1881.
29. He-dud – well-bred.
30. Spencer Borden states that Ishtar was a white mare, one of the first bought in the desert by the Blunts!
31. Lady Wentworth notes in 1889, 'Miss Dillon's underbred (pretended Arab) mare has been bought by old Mr Weatherby.'
32. Baalbek is now in the Lebanon, thirty-five miles north of Damascus.
33. Falluja – situated on the Euphrates, about forty miles west of Baghdad.
34. Halawi was an accepted strain, according to Lady Anne Blunt, and confirmed by the Muteyr tribe, but listed as 3rd-class Kehilan by Major Upton.
35. The Zoba tribe were met by the Blunts, south of Ramady, on 10 February 1878.
36. Lady Anne Blunt described El Emir in 1890: 'his want of quality is so apparent, moreover he is very narrow in the quarter, does not hold his tail and has an extremely plain head.' However, she does not question his Arab authenticity.

THE ARAB HORSE

37 Kismet was in fact beaten in races by several Indian Arabs, including Dictator and Rataplan and in 1884, he was beaten by Asil at Newmarket.
38 Prince Mohuiddin was the son of Sherif Ali Haidar, who was installed by the Turks as Sherif in Medina, not Mecca. This was in retaliation to the growing independence of Emir Hussein, Sherif of Mecca, leader of the Arab Revolt, proclaimed on 10 June 1916 (9th day of Sha'ban).
39 The Branicki Stud situated at Bialocerkiev, South of Kiev, was founded c.1775 and disappeared during the Revolution of 1917. Count Branicki according to The Druid, in his book *Silk and Scarlet*, 'has a large stud of 700 brood mares and has spent an immense sum over his hobby of importing Arab stallions.' He also imported British Thoroughbred stallions, many of them supplied by the English Agent, Ashton.
40 Mr Ashton (spelt Aschton in Russia and Poland) was an English Agent who held the Government Commission, from 1827 when he succeeded a Mr. Walkden, to purchase Thoroughbred and Arab stallions for Tsar Nicholas of Russia, and for Count Branicki.
41 In 1888 Lord Russell bought Halfa – a chestnut mare, 7 years old, by Kars ex Hagar, at the 4th Crabbet Sale on 28 July, for £80. It was noted that she was 'quiet to ride and drive'.
42 Borden states that Kesia II had three fillies by Mameluke - 'Mimosa in 1893, Shabaka in 1894 and another chestnut in 1895.
43 The Majali tribe from the area around Karak, Jordan.

The Hamdanieh, drawing by Peter Upton.

263

TABLES OF DESCENT

These tables do not include all of the offspring of any one mare or stallion, but a selection of the more important lines.

To read the tables:

* = imported to the UK from the Desert of Arabia

Upper case = stallion

Lower case = mare

Each indentation from the left = one generation

e.g.:

Jedrania* b. – An imported bay mare.
    JEZAIL b. 1888. (El Emir*) – A bay son of Jedrania, foaled 1888 by El Emir (imported)
        HAURAN b. 1897. (Hagar*) – A bay son of JEZAIL, foaled 1897 ex Hagar (imported)
            Nessa b. 1905. (Raschida) – A bay daughter of HAURAN, foaled 1905 ex Raschida
            Bathsheba b. 1913. (Butheyna) – A bay daughter of HAURAN, foaled 1913 ex Butheyna
                Bazrah b. 1919. (Rodan) - A bay daughter of Bathsheba, foaled 1919 by Rodan
                    BAZLEYD ch. 1928. (Abu Zeyd) – A chestnut son of Bazrah, foaled 1928 by Abu Zeyd
    Yasimeen br. 1896 (Imamzada) – A brown daughter of Jedrania* foaled in 1896 by Imamzada

THE BLUNTS' MARES

Jedrania

Jedrania* b.1875. Imp. 1881. Sold 1886
    JAMSCHYD* b. 1881. (Abeyan el Khudr). Imp. *In utero*
    Jebel Druz b. 1884. (Kars*)
    Juniper b. 1885. (Kars*)
    JEDRAN b. 1888. (El Emir*)
    JEZAIL b. 1893. (Imam)
        HAURAN b. 1897. (Hagar*). Exp. USA 1910
            Nessa b. 1905. (Raschida). Exp. USA 1905
                Bathsheba b. 1913. (Butheyna)
                    Bazrah b. 1919. (Rodan)
                        BAZLEYD ch. 1928. (Abu Zeyd)
                            Habiba ch. 1935. (Nafud)
                                Binni ch. 1940. (Gulastra)
                                    BINIS ch. 1944. (Islam)
                            Gayza gr. 1933. (Gulnare) [*see* Ghazala*]
                            Gara gr. 1935. (Gharifet)
                    Bakmal ch. 1933. (Rahas)
                    Bazvan b.1925. (Rizvan)
                  Bazikh ch. 1927. (Abu Zeyd)
    Yasimeen br. 1896. (Imamzada)

Meshura

Meshura* b. 1872. Imp. 1881. Shot 1899
    Meroe b. 1885. (Kars*)
        Moallaka b. 1896. (Mesaoud*)
            Desdemona ch. 1904. (Mootrub*)
    Mansura b. 1890. (Ashgar*)
        MAREB b. 1896. (Mesaoud*)
        MIREED b. 1911. (Ibn Yemama*)
    Mabruka b. 1891. (Azrek*)
        MUBARAK b. 1897. (Mesaoud*)
        Mazna b. 1906. (Astraled)
            SHER-I-KHURSHID b. 1911. (Lal-i-Abdar)
        Marhaba b. 1911. (Daoud)
            MABROUK BLUNT ch. 1916. (Ibn Yashmak*). Exp. Egypt 1920
            Minsa b. 1919. (Sotamm)
                Maasreh gr. 1923. (Crosbie*)
                      Matara gr. 1933. (Algol)
            MIRZAM ch. 1925. (Rafeef). Exp. USA 1928
            MENZIL b. 1929. (Nureddin II). Exp. USA 1932

Meshura cont.

    Mabsuta b. 1892. (Mesaoud*)
        MUSTAPHA KAMEL b. 1906. (Feysul*)
        Malaka b. 1911. (Rijm)
            MERSA MATRUH b. 1916. (Ibn Yashmak*)
            Moubarek b. 1917. (Ibn Yashmak*)
            MANSOUR b. 1918. (Rustem)
            Mouraffa b. 1920. (Ibn Yashmak*)
    Merjana b. 1896. (Mesaoud*)
    Maisuna b. 1898. (Mesaoud*)
        Mulaika ch. 1902. (Rejeb)
        Markisa b 1905. (Narkise). Exp. USA 1906
        EL BORAK b. 1914. (Nadir). Exp. Egypt 1920
        JOSEPH b. 1917. (Nadir)
            MANASSEH b. 1937. (Aatika)
                DARGEE ch. 1945. (Myola)
                AL BURAK b. 1947. (Algoletta). Exp. S. Africa 1951
        Beryl b. 1940. (Belkis II)
            BLENHEIM ch. 1953. (Rheoboam)
            BEND OR b. 1959. (Rheoboam)

Basilisk

Basilisk* gr. 1876. Imp. Sold 1884
    Bozra gr. 1881. (Pharaoh*)
        Bushra br. 1889. (Azrek*). Exp. USA 1900
            IBN MAHRUSS ch. 1901. (Ibn) Mahruss*). Exp. USA 1900 *in utero*
            EL JAFIL ch. 1909. (Sheba)
                EL SABOK ch. 1916. (Narkeesa)
                    STAMBUL gr. 1926. (Morfda)
        Sira b. 1909. (Hamrah DB)
            Sabot ch. 1913. (Euphrates DB)
    BEDR b. 1891. (Azrek*). Exp. USA 1893
    Bukra gr. 1896. (Ahmar)
        Baylis gr. 1902. (Seyal)
        BERK b. 1903. (Seyal). Exp. USA 1918
        HAZZAM B. 1911. (Hilmyeh)
        Safarjal br. 1915. (Somra I) [*see* Sobha*]
        Ramim b. 1915. (Rim). Exp. USA [*see* Rodania*]
        Rissla ch. 1917. (Risala) [*see* Rodania*]
        RIBAL b. 1920. (Rijma)
        HARIR b. 1911. (Hamasa). Exp. Australia 1913
    Battla gr. 1915. (Razaz). Exp. USA 1918

THE ARAB HORSE

Basilisk cont.
  Bozra
    Bukra
      Battla
        Babirah ch. 1922. (Nafia)
          Baribeh ch. 1927. (Ribal)
            Banna gr. 1935. (Nasr)
              Rabanna gr. 1947. (Rasik)
        Bahreyn* br. 1924. (Rizvan). Imp. *in utero* 1924 and exp. USA 1926
          RONEK gr. 1931. (Raseyn)
      Bereyda gr. 1898. (Ahmar)
        Belkis gr. 1902. (Seyal)
          Butheyna b. 1904. (Seyal). Exp. USA 1908
            Bathsheba b. 1913. (Hauran)
              Bazrah b. 1919. (Rodan)
                BAZLEYD ch. 1928. (Abu Zeyd)
                  Habiba ch. 1935. (Nafud)
                    Binni ch. 1940. (Gulastra)
                      BINIS ch. 1944. (Islam)
                Gayza gr. 1933. (Gulnare) [*see* Ghazala]
                Gara gr. 1935. (Gharifet) [*see* Ghazala]
              Bakmal ch. 1933. (Rahas)
                LUTAF ch. 1943. (Alyf)
              Bazvan b.1925. (Rizvan)
              Bazikh ch. 1927. (Abu Zeyd)
              Rahika ch. 1936. (Rahas)
                Natta b. 1940. (Farana)
                  Vans Natta b. 1943. (Alla Amarward)
                    Fer-Natta gr. 1950. (Fertif)
                    Hi-Natta gr. 1951. (Fertif)
                  EL NATTALL b. 1944. (Alla Amarward)
      Belka gr. 1912. (Rijm)
        Bekr b. 1926. (Nimr*)
          Bozra II ch. 1933. (Fedaan*)
            Dil Kushi gr. 1947. (Rangoon)
          Belkis II b. 1934. (Sainfoin)
            Beryl b. 1940. (Joseph)
              BLENHEIM ch. 1953. (Rheoboam)
              BEND OR b. 1959. (Rheoboam)
          Bussora b. 1935. (Atesh*)
            Karim gr. 1943. (Ruskov)
              Tarim gr. 1949. (Rukaban I)
          Balis II b. 1936. (Sainfoin)
          Baranova b. 1938. (Sainfoin)
            BENJAMIN b. 1946. (Champurrado)
          BENDIGO gr. 1927. (Atesh*)
          Ruth II b. 1943. (Rahab)
        Betina gr. 1935. (Fedaan*)
          BOAZ gr. 1940. (Joseph). Exp. S. Africa 1946
          BAHRAM ch. 1946. (Sainfoin)
      Baraza b. 1915. (Razaz). Exp. USA 1918

SHERIFA

Sherifa* gr. 1862. Imp. 1878. Shot 1892.
  Shehrezad gr. 1880 (Kars*)
  Shiraz gr. 1881. (Kars*)
    Shicha gr. 1889. (Azrek*)
      SHANFARA gr. 1902. (Seyal)
        KAFTAN gr. 1911. (Kibla)
  Shemse gr. 1883. (Pharaoh*)
    BEN AZREK gr. 1892. (Azrek*)
    Ruth Kesia gr. 1903. (Borak)
      SHAHZADA gr. 1913. (Mootrub*). Exp. Australia 1922
      Rizada b. 1924. (Riz)
        Aatika ch. 1933. (Algol)
          MANASSEH b. 1937. (Joseph)
            DARGEE ch. 1945. (Myola)
      RAZADA gr. 1925. (Ranya). Exp. Spain 1926
        NANA SAHIB gr. 1934. (Jalila)
        Famula gr. 1942. (Sara)
          MAQUILLO ch. 1949. (Gandhy)
            UZACUR gr. 1956. (Veranda)
        Egina b. 1941. (Saboya)
          JAECERO gr. 1946. (Barquillo)
          MALVITO b. 1949. (Gandhy)
        Kantista gr. 1947. (Morayma)
          ALHABAC gr. 1956. (Caireh)
            Ispahan gr. 1965. (Chavali)
              AN MALIK gr. 1970. (Galero)
      IFNI gr. 1937. (Reyna)
        USHAAHE gr. 1942. (Duquesa). Exp. Jordan 1947
          BAHAR gr. 1952. (Sabal I)
          Gazella gr. 1958. (Emira I)
          Sabal II gr. 1959. (Lurbi I)
            Huseima gr. 1965. (Madrid)
          Samiha gr. 1961. (Farha)
            BAHAREIN ch. 1967. (Bahar)
            Sarra gr. 1979. (Huseima)
  NURI PASHA gr. 1920. (Nureddin II). Exp. USA 1924
  Almas gr. 1924. (Amida)
    ALUF gr. 1932. (Barkis)
      Rafeena gr. 1940. (Ranya II)
        RIKHAM gr. 1945. (Rissam). Exp. Australia 1948
        IRIDOS gr. 1951. (Irex)
        Rexeena gr. 1948. (Irex)
          Sirikit ch. 1961. (Alexus)
            LUDREX ch. 1961. (Ludo)
              DONAX ch. 1971. (Dargemet)

Sherifa cont.
  Shemse
    BEN AZREK
      Ruth Kesia
        NURI PASHA
          Almas
            ALUF
              Rafeena
                COUNT RAPELLO ch. 1954. (Count D'Orsaz)
              Rufeiya I b. 1938. (Ranya II)
                Rosheiya b. 1942 (Rosh)
                  Roshnara ch. 1949. (Hassan II)
                    Roshina ch. 1962. (Count Roland)
                      Russallka ch. 1968. (Gold Rex)
              Zarifet gr. 1938. (Roglemar Zarad)
      Sheeba b. 1903. (Riad)
        NURI SHERIF b. 1920. (Nureddin II)
        Nurschida ch. 1930. (Razina)
          Namilla ch. 1937. (Algol)
            MIKENO ch. 1949. (Rissalix)
          Manzana b. 1938. (Naufal)
          Rikitea ch. 1942. (Rissalix)
          Sulka ch. 1934. (Naseem). Exp. Holland
    Shiboleth gr. 1884. (Kars*)
    Shelfa gr. 1887. (Jeroboam)
      Shohba gr. 1893 (Shahwan*). Exp. Greece 1903
        Shibine ch. 1899 (Mesaoud*). Exp. USA 1905/9
        Shebaka b. 1892 (Merzuk*). Exp. S. Africa 1892

QUEEN OF SHEBA

Queen of Sheba* b. 1875. Imp. 1879. Shot 1901
  AHMAR b. 1890. (Azrek*). Exp. Java 1901
    Selma II gr. 1894. (Sobha*) [see Sobha*]
    Siwa gr. 1896. (Sobha*) [see Sobha*]
    Bukra gr. 1896. (Bozra) [see Basilisk*]
    Bereyda gr. 1898. (Bozra) [see Basilisk*]
    Hilmyeh b. 1899. (Bint Helwa*) [see Bint Helwa*]
  Asfura b. 1891. (Azrek*)
    Abla b. 1899. (Mesaoud*)
      Arusa b. 1915. (Rustem)
        Amusheh b. 1922. (Rasim)
          Niskha b. 1926. (Aldebaran)
            Nusi b. 1935. (Sainfoin)
      Amra b. 1906. (Feysul*). Exp. USA 1909
    Ajramieh ch. 1901. (Mesaoud*)
      AJMAN ch. 1906. (Feysul*). Exp. S .America 1910
      Amida ch. 1913. (Ibn Yashmak*)
        ALDEBARAN ch. 1919. (Dwarka*). Exp. Canada 1929
          HOUBARAN b. 1923. (Arusa). Exp. Holland 1924
          Myra ch. 1924. (Rangha)
          ALGOL ch. 1928. (Rangha)
            Algoletta ch. 1935 (Rythma)
              AL BURAK b. 1947. (Manasseh). Exp. S. Africa 1951

Queen of Sheba cont.
  Asfura
    Ajramieh
      Amida
        ALDEBARAN
          ALGOL
            Namilla ch. 1937. (Nurschida)
              MIKENO ch. 1949. (Rissalix)
            Aatika ch. 1933. (Rizada). Exp. Siam
              MANASSEH b. 1937. (Joseph)
                DARGEE ch. 1945. (Myola)
                AL BURAK b. 1947. (Algoletta)
            SHIHAB ch. 1935. (Almas)
            Shabryeh b. 1932. (Seriya)
              Shabrette b. 1950. (Rissalix)
                Farette b. 1954. (Rifari)
                  FARI II b. 1965. (Blue Domino)
            Myola b. 1937. (Rythma)
              DARGEE ch. 1945. (Manasseh)
                Dargemet ch. 1961. (Bint Yasimet)
                  DONAX ch. 1971. (Ludrex)
                Sirella ch. 1953. (Shalina)
                  HANIF gr. 1962. (Silver Vanity)
                DARJEEL ch. 1962. (Rajjela)
              Zahri ch. 1962. (Zirree el Wada)
            Myolanda ch. 1948. (Manasseh)
              ALGOLSON ch. 1952. (Myolanda)
                Cinders ch. 1959. (Yateemah)
                  SOLE HOPE ch. 1953. (Heart's Desire)
          BARKIS ch. 1929. (Rangha)
            ALUF gr. 1932. (Almas)
          SAHBAN ch. 1930. (Seriya)
          The Lady Roxane ch. 1943. (Dil Fireb)
        KALAT gr. 1941. (Kehefe)
        DURRAL b. 1941. (Fa-Durra)
        BAAROUF gr. 1941. (Maaroufa)
          ROUF ch. 1945. (Fa-Deene)
          MAIROUF b. 1958. (Mailatrah)
        Zabba gr. 1941. (Fa-Saana)
          ZAB gr. 1945. (Fay el Dine)
      Ana b. 1920. (Dwarka*). Exp. USA 1924
    Almas gr. 1924. (Nuri Pasha)
      Alika gr. 1937. (Nazar)
        Almanak br. 1946. (Manak*)
      Aziza Ann gr. 1939. (Joseph)
        Arabian Dawn gr. 1947. (Jair)
          Arabian Moonshine b. 1951. (Shihab
            Shirabia ch. 1960. (Shifari)
              Kashmira ch. 1967. (Kami)
    Astrella ch. 1929. (Raseem)
    Ariffa gr. 1936. (Raftan)
      RIFFAYAL gr. 1942. (Fayal). Exp. Australia 1950
      Riffila gr. 1949. (Drusilla) [see Dafina*]
    Astrab ch. 1939. (Radi)
      Astreelia ch. 1948. (Jaleel). Exp. USA 1959
        Bint Astreelia ch. 1952. (Blue Domino)

THE ARAB HORSE

Queen of Sheba cont.

Asfura
  Ajramieh
    Amida
      Astrella
        Asrab
          Astreelia
            Bint Astreelia
              Oriole gr. 1975. (Ormonde)
          ORAN ch. 1940. (Riffal)
            Mifaria ch. 1947. (Rithyana)
              GRAND ROYAL ch. 1947. (Sharima). Exp. Australia 1959
              SILVER VANITY gr. 1950. (Silver Gilt). Exp. USA 1962
                SINDH ch. 1958. (Silfina) Exp. Australia 1961.
                HANIF gr. 1962. (Sirella)
                INDIAN KING ch. 1953. (Indian Pride)
                NORAN ch. 1956. (Nerina)
            Rubiania b. 1942. (Riffal)
              Misery b. 1950. (Rithan)
                Consuella b. 1962. (Magnet)
                  Angelica ch. 1966 (General Grant)
                  Fanya b. 1964. (Fancy Shadow)
              Blue Dawn gr. 1963. (Blue Grotto)
    Ajjam ch. 1915. (Ibn Yashmak*)
    Antika ch. 1902. (Mesaoud*). Exp. USA 1906
      RAZZIA ch. 1907. (Harb). Exp. USA *in utero* 1906
    Andarina ch. 1908. (Rijm). Exp. S. Africa
  ANBAR b. 1893. (Mesaoud*). Exp. Russia 1896
  ASTRALED br. 1900. (Mesaoud*). Exp. USA 1909
    Riyala ch. 1905. (Ridaa) [*see* Rodania*]
    Rokhama b. 1906. (Rabla) [*see* Rodania*]
    RUSTEM b. 1908. (Ridaa). Exp. Egypt 1920 [*see* Rodania*]
    Rim ch. 1910. (Ridaa) [*see* Rodania*]
    SOTAMM br. 1910. (Selma II) [*see* Sobha*]
    GULASTRA ch. 1924. (Gulnare) [*see* Ghazala]

DAHMA

Dahma* b. 1876. Imp. 1881. Sold 1888
  Dahna br. 1883 (Kars*). Exp. Australia 1891
    Abdul b. 1904. (Rafyk)
      MINARET b. 1916. (Zubeir)
    Dinarzade b. 1887. (Rataplan*). Exp. Russia 1899
      El Lahr 1899. (Imamzada). Exp. Australia 1901
        Al Caswa 1903. (Rafyk)
          Kufara gr. 1921. (Khamasin)
            Sir Aatika gr. 1938. (Sirdar)
              ALADDIN gr. 1943. (Kataf)
                Alaga Maid gr. 1946. (Anaga)
                  Hestia gr. 1952. (Jedran)
                    AETHON gr. 1963. (Spindrift)

Dahma cont.

Dahna
  Dinarzade
    El Lahr
      Al Caswa
        Mecca II gr. 1924. (Khamasin)
          Salome gr. 1935. (Ishmael)
          Cazada ch. 1938. (Sirdar)
          Caswa ch. 1937. (Sirdar)
          Kassie ch. 1944 (Kataf)
        Dijleh br. 1889. (Ashgar*). Exp. Russia 1899
  Sherifa II gr. 1893. (Rafyk)
    Labadah (Mahboub)
      Khadijah 1905. (Faraoun)
        Alcouza (Khamasin)
          Deryabar (Khamasin)
            Matoufa gr. 1937. (Indian Light)
              Medina gr. 1946. (Rakib)
              Meliha ch. 1939. (Indian Light)
Debora b. 1888. (Roala)

HAGAR

Hagar* b. 1872. Imp. 1878. Sold 1886
  Harik b. 1884. (Kars*)
  Harra b. 1888. (Rataplan*)
    Howa I b. 1892. (Azrek*)
      Hagar II b. 1909. (Daoud)
        Hubara b. 1924. (Rasim)
          Hammami b. 1928. (Almulid)
          Hameeshé b. 1930. (Almulid)
          Hada b. 1939. (Nigm Essubh)
            Halfina b. 1949. (Rafi)
              Rusala ch. 1954. (Rasul)
              Harima b. 1956. (Naseel's Nephew)
                Hamu b. 1962. (Indian Fakir)
          Howa II b. 1941. (Nigm Essubh)
          Heart's Desire b. 1943. (Faris)
          Harra II b. 1951. (Irex)
      Hanna b. 1911. (Rijm)
      HUSEYNI gr. 1924. (Skowronek). Exp. Palestine
  Zem Zem br. 1889. (El Emir*)
    Zimrud b. 1896. (Jamrood)
      FIRUSEH ch. 1906. (Nejef)
      UNS EL WUJOOD ch. 1914. (Kabila)
        Kateefah ch. 1922. (Jawi Jawi)
          KATAF ch. 1928. (Outlaw*). Exp. Australia 1935
          ALADDIN gr. 1943. (Sir Aatika)
            Alaga Maid gr. 1946. (Anaga) [*see* Dahma*]
    Husn-u-gul ch. 1907. (Lal-i-Abdar)
    Shejret Eddur b. 1913. (Zoowar*)
      Sant ch. 1921. (Uns el Wujood)
      Kirat b. 1926. (Sher-i-Khurshid)
      HILAL b. 1924. (Uns el Wujood)

Hagar cont.
  Zem Zem
    Zimrud
      Husn-u-gul
        Baida I gr. 1914. (Zoowar*)
          Jasmeen gr. 1923. (Uns el Wujood)
            Mish Mish I b. 1932. (Joseph). Exp. Holland 1937
              Ritla II b. 1939. (Rythal)
                Dewi ch. 1945. (Karusen)
                  Fathia ch. 1950. (Haji I). Exp. S. Africa
              Moonbeam gr. 1936. (Hilal). Exp. Holland 1937
                Aatifa b. 1948. (Karusen)
            Bint Yasim ch. 1940. (Manak*)
              Yasimet ch. 1949. (Grey Owl). Exp. S. Africa
                Bint Yasimet ch. 1954. (Blue Domino)
                  Dargemet ch. 1961. (Dargee)
                    DONAX ch. 1971. (Ludrex)
              ZINGARI b. 1959. (Zahir)
      Rose of Persia ch. 1908. (Lal-i-Abdar)
        JERUAN ch. 1920. (Nureddin II). Exp. Russia 1936
  HAÏL b. 1892. (Jamrood). Exp. USA 1905
    Riad b. 1897. (Raschida)
      Sheeba b. 1903. (Ben Azrek)
        NURI SHERIF b. 1920. (Nureddin II)
        Nurschida ch. 1930. (Razina)
          Namilla ch. 1937. (Algol)
            MIKENO ch. 1949. (Rissalix)
          Manzana b. 1938. (Naufal)
            Moraea b. 1950. (Irex)
          Sulka ch. 1934. (Naseem). Exp. Holland
            NIZAR ch. 1953. (Nizzam)
            Fatma b. 1951. (Nizzam)
  HAURAN b. 1897. (Jezail). Exp. USA 1910
    Bathsheba b. 1913. (Butheyna)
      Bazrah b. 1919. (Rodan)
        BAZLEYD ch. 1928. (Abu Zeyd)
        Habiba ch. 1935. (Nafud)
          Binni ch. 1940. (Gulastra)
            BINIS ch. 1944. (Islam)

DAJANIA

Dajania* b. 1876. Imp. 1878. Sold 1886
  Nefisa b. 1885. (Hadban*)
    NEJRAN b. 1891. (Azrek*)
      Rish b. 1903. (Rabla) [see Rodania*]
    Nejiba gr. 1892. (Azrek*)
    Narghileh b. 1895. (Mesaoud*)
      Narda ch. 1902. (Rejeb). Exp. USA 1909/10
        CRABBET ch. 1909. (Rijm). Exp. USA 1909
      Noam ch. 1911. (Rijm)
        Nusara ch. 1919. (Abu Zeyd)

Dajania Cont.
  Nefisa
    Narghileh
      NASIK b. 1908. (Rijm). Exp. USA 1926
        Rokhsa b. 1915. (Rokhama). Exp. USA 1918 [see Rodania*]
        Ranya b. 1916. (Riyala) [see Rodania*]
        RAFEEF ch. 1917. (Riyala) [see Rodania*]
        Fantana ch. 1922. (Ferda) [see Ferida*]
        FARANA b. 1929. (Farasin) [see Ferida*]
        RIFNAS ch. 1932. (Rifla)
        SIKIN b. 1933. (Farasin) [see Ferida*]
        Nafara b. 1931. (Farasin) [see Ferida*]
      Nessima b. 1909. (Rijm)
        NAFIA ch. 1916. (Ibn Yashmak*). Exp. USA 1918
        NAHRAWAN gr. 1926. (Skowronek). Exp. Brazil 1930
        Naxina gr. 1927. (Skowronek)
          GREY OWL gr. 1934. (Raseem)
          NASEEL gr. 1936. (Raftan)
          Raxina gr. 1938. (Raktha)
            RAYAL gr. 1942. (Fayal)
              XAYAL b. 1947. (Rubana)
              Berlanta gr. 1950. (Roshara)
                Roxanta ch. 1956. (Count D'Orsaz)
            GHAILAN gr. 1943. (Fayal)
              The Lady Heloise ch. 1948. (The Lady Roxane)
                The Lady Idar gr. 1951. (Idar)
                Lhotse gr. 1955. (Disa)
                Silver Velvet gr. 1955. (Sapphire) [see Crosbie*]
        Samsie b. 1940. (Riffal)
          GENERAL GRANT ch. 1945. (Raktha)
      NUREDDIN II ch. 1911. (Rijm). Exp. USA 1933
        NURI PASHA gr. 1920. (Ruth Kesia). Exp. USA 1924 [see Sherifa*]
        NURI SHERIF b. 1920. (Sheeba) [see Sherifa*]
        SHAREER b. 1923. (Selima). Exp. Russia 1936 [see Sobha*]
        Rishna ch. 1923. (Rish) [see Rodania*]
        FARIS ch. 1924. (Fejr) [see Ferida*]
        Sardhana b. 1924. (Selima). Exp. Poland 1928 [see Sobha*]
        Ramayana ch. 1924. (Riyala). Exp. Russia 1936 [see Rodania*]
        Ruellia ch. 1926. (Riyala). Exp. Russia 1936 [see Rodania*]
        FERDIN ch. 1927. (Ferda). Exp. USA *in utero* 1926 [see Ferida*]
        Neraida gr. 1928. (Nasifa). Exp. Russia 1936
      NAJIB br. 1914. (Rustem)
      NAUFAL br. 1916. (Sotamm)
        RIFFAL b. 1936. (Razina). Exp. Australia [see Rodania*]
    NAAMAN b. 1897. (Mesaoud*). Exp. Russia 1899
    NARENK b. 1898. (Mesaoud*). Exp. India 1901
    NARKISE b. 1899. (Mesaoud*)
      Kasima b. 1905. (Kasida*) [see Kasida*]
    NEJEF b. 1900. (Mesaoud*)
    NADIR b. 1901. (Mesaoud*)
      JOSEPH b. 1917. (Maisuna) [see Meshura*]
      RISHAN b. 1922. (Rish) [see Rodania*]
    Ninawa b. 1904. (Mesaoud*)
    NAWAB b. 1905. (Astraled). Exp. Egypt 1920

Dajania Cont.
  Nefisa
    Nasra b. 1908. (Daoud)
      Nisreen b. 1919. (Nureddin II)
        Nasirieh gr. 1923. (Skowronek). Exp. Australia 1935
          Nisyana ch. 1927. (Raseem)
            Naama ch. 1933. (Astralis)
        Incoronata gr. 1925. (Skowronek). Exp. USA 1936
        Indaia b. 1927. (Raseem). Exp. USA 1936
          INDRAFF gr. 1938. (Raffles)
          INDRAGE gr. 1934. (Mirage*)
          INDY gr. 1947 (Raffles)
        INDIAN GOLD ch. 1934. (Ferhan)
          Silver Gilt gr. 1943. (Silver Fire) [see Sobha*]
          Rissiletta ch. 1943. (Rissla)
          Gleaming Gold ch. 1952. (Risira)
        Indian Crown ch. 1935. (Raseem)
          INDIAN MAGIC gr. 1944. (Raktha)
          Incoronetta ch. 1954. (Dargee)
        Indian Pride ch. 1938. (Irex)
          Indian Glory ch. 1950. (Dargee)
          INDIAN KING ch. 1953. (Oran)
      Nashisha b. 1920. (Rasim). Exp. Russia 1936
        Sharima ch. 1932. (Shareer)
          Sharfina ch. 1937. (Rytham)
            Silfina ch. 1944. (Indian Gold)
              ELECTRIC SILVER gr. 1948. (Raktha). Exp. Australia 1950
              Silindra ch. 1950. (Raktha)
              Silent Wings ch. 1954. (Oran)
              SINDH ch. 1958. (Silver Vanity). Exp. Australia 1961
            Serafina ch. 1945. (Indian Gold)
              SERAFIX ch.1949. (Raktha). Exp. USA 1953
              SILVER DRIFT gr. 1951. (Raktha). Exp. USA 1963
            Shades of Night ch. 1946 (Rissam). Exp. USA 1957
            Shalina ch. 1948. (Rissam)
              Sirella ch. 1953. (Dargee)
                HANIF gr. 1962. (Silver Vanity)
          Grey Royal gr. 1942. (Raktha). Exp. USA 1963
            Serafire gr. 1950. (Indian Magic)
          Crown Royal ch. 1945. (Oran)
            GRAND ROYAL ch. 1947. (Oran). Exp. Australia 1959
      Nasira br. 1921. (Nadir)
        Nuralina br. 1929. (Hazzam). Exp. Australia 1936
        Nautch Girl br. 1940. (Sainfoin)
          NIMROD b. 1952. (Champurrado). Exp. USA 1958
      NASEEM gr. 1922. (Skowronek). Exp. Russia 1936
        Silver Fire gr. 1926. (Somra) [see Sobha]
        IREX ch. 1927. (Rissla) [see Rodania*]
        RISSAM ch. 1928. (Rim) [see Rodania*]
        Rissletta ch. 1930. (Risslina). Exp. USA 1936 [see Rodania*]

Dajania Cont.
  Nefisa
    Nasra
      NASEEM
        RAKTHA gr. 1934. (Razina). Exp. S. Africa 1951 [see Rodania*]
        Sulka ch. 1934. (Nurschida). Exp. Holland [see Hagar*]
        NEGATIW gr. 1945. (Taraszcza)
          NABOR gr. 1950. (Logodna)
            ARGOS gr. 1957. (Arfa)
            GWALIOR gr. 1961. (Gwadiana)
            ARAMUS gr. 1962. (Amneris)
          SUVENIR gr. 1957 (Sonata)
          PATRON ch. 1957. (Provincia)
          SALON gr. 1959 (Sonata)
            MUSCAT ch. 1971. (Malpia)
          BANDOS gr. 1964. (Bandola)
          Negotka gr. 1967. (Bigotka)
            NEGATRAZ b. 1971. (Bask)
              MONOGRAMM ch. 1985. (Monogramma)
        NOMER gr. 1943. (Oaza)
        Napraslina gr. 1948. (Plotka)
          Nasmeshka gr. 1965. (Semen)
          Naadirah gr. 1966. (Aswan). Exp. Australia 1970
        Nera ch. 1948. (Rezeda II)
        Nitochka gr. 1948. (Taraszcza)
        Nagrada gr. 1938. (Rixalina)
        Naturalistka ch. 1937. (Rissalma)
        Nomenklatura b. 1943. (Mammona)
      NISSAR b. 1923. (Nadir)
      Nasifa gr. 1924. (Skowronek). Exp. Russia 1936
        Neraida gr. 1928. (Nureddin II). Exp. Russia 1936
          Niseyra ch. 1935. (Rissam)
            CHAMPURRADO ch. 1940. (Irex)
              BENJAMIN b. 1946. (Baranova)
              RAZAZ II ch. 1949. (Rahab). Exp. Australia 1955
              NIMROD b. 1952. (Nautch Girl). Exp. USA 1958
              SHAMMAR gr. 1955. (Somra II)
          Tehoura ch. 1946. (Radi)
            BLUE DOMINO ch. 1947. (Rissalix)
      NAZIRI gr. 1925. (Skowronek)
        Risira gr. 1939. (Risslina) [see Rodania*]
        SALADIN II gr. 1940. (Starilla)
          BURKAN gr. 1964. (Biruta)
            WHITE LIGHTNING gr. 1967. (Latawica)
              CARMARGUE gr. 1979. (Velvet Shadow)
      Nezma b. 1926. (Rafeef)
        Nazziria b. 1940. (Naziri)
        NIZZAM b. 1943. (Rissam). Exp. Holland and USA 1960
          Fatima ch. 1949. (Mishka)
          Fatma b. 1951. (Sulka)

JERBOA

Jerboa* b. 1874. Imp. 1878. Shot 1893
    JEROBOAM b. 1882. (Pharaoh*). Exp. Egypt 1887
        Rosemary b. 1886. (Rodania*) [see Rodania*]
        Shelfa gr. 1887. (Sherifa*) [see Sherifa*]
    Jerud b. 1883. (Pharaoh*)
        JAMROOD. b.1888. (Maidan*)
        HAÏL b. 1892. (Hagar*). Exp. USA 1905 [see Hagar*]
        Zimrud b. 1896. (Zem Zem)
    Jamila ch. 1887. (Roala). Exp. USA 1893
    Jeneyna b. 1891. (Azrek*). Exp, Russia 1899
        JOHAR b. 1895. (Mesaoud*). Exp. S. Africa 1899
        Jemeyza ch. 1896. (Mesaoud*)

RODANIA

Rodania* ch. 1869. Imp. 1881. Shot 1889
    Rose of Jericho b. 1883. (Kars*). Exp. Australia 1891
        Rose Diamond b. 1890. (Azrek*)
            Rose of Hind b. 1902. (Rejeb)
                RAZAZ b. 1907. (Astraled). Exp. Egypt 1920
                Rudeyna b. 1916. (Daoud)
                Rasima ch. 1917. (Daoud). Exp. USA 1926
                    Jalila gr. 1922. (Skowronek). Exp. Spain 1931
                        Rose of France gr. 1926. (Raswan). Exp, USA 1930
                        Rasmina ch. 1928. (Shareer). Exp. USA 1930
                        NANA SAHIB gr. 1934. (Razada)
                            Famula gr. 1942. (Sara)
                                MAQUILLO ch. 1949. (Gandhy)
                            Egina b. 1941. (Saboya)
                                MALVITO b. 1949. (Gandhy)
                            Kantista gr. 1947. (Morayma)
                                ALHABAC gr. 1956. (Cairel)
                                    Ispahan gr. 1965. (Chavali)
                Rossana gr. 1921. (Skowronek). Exp. USA 1926
            LAL-I-ABDAR 'Abu Zeyd' ch. 1904. ((Mesaoud*). Exp. USA 1910
            BAZLEYD ch. 1928. (Bazrah) [See Basilisk*]
        Domow b. 1913. (Wadudda DB)
            TABAB b. 1921. (Deyr DB)
            Monica b. 1926. (Sankirah)
                Moneyna gr. 1937. (Raseyn)
                    FERNEYN gr. 1944. (Ferseyn)
                  MONEYN gr. 1934. (Raseyn)
        Larkspur b. 1912. (Onrust)

Rodania cont.
    ROALA b. 1884. (Kars*)
        Jamila ch. 1887. (Jerboa). Exp. USA 1893
    Rose of Sharon ch. 1885. (Hadban). Exp. USA 1905
        RAFYK b. 1890. (Azrek*). Exp. Australia 1891
        Ridaa ch. 1892. (Merzuk*)
        Risala ch. 1900. ((Mesaoud*)
            RASIM ch. 1906. (Feysul*). Exp. Poland 1924
            Nashisha b. 1920. (Nasra) [see Dajania*]
                RASEEM ch. 1922. (Rim). Exp. Russia 1936
        Rijma ch. 1911. (Rijm). Exp. USA 1918
        Riz b. 1916. (Razaz)
            Rizada b. 1924. (Shahzada)
                Aatika ch. 1933. (Algol)
                    MANASSEH b. 1937. (Joseph)
                        DARGEE ch. 1945. (Myola)
                Naomi I b. 1938. (Joseph)
            REGISTAN gr. 1927. (Skowronek). Exp. Egypt 1936
                Kasbana b. (Serra)
                    Mahasin gr. 1942. (Sheikh el Arab)
            RIZVAN ch. 1919. (Ibn Yashmak*) [Exp. in utero. USA 1918]
            Bahreyn b. 1924. (Battla)
                RONEK gr. 1931. (Raseyn)
            Gharifet gr. 1927. (Gulnare)
                Gara gr. 1935. (Bazleyd) [see Ghazala*]
                Gutne gr. 1932. (Bazleyd)
        RIBAL ch. 1920. (Berk)
        Bint Sedjur gr. 1935. (Sedjur)
            Bint Sahara gr. 1942. (Farawi) [see Ferida*]
        Raad ch. 1922. (Sidi)
            RAHAS ch. 1928. (Gulastra)
                RABIYAS ch. 1936. (Rabiyat)
                    ABU FARWA ch. 1940. (Rissletta)
    Rythma b. 1914. (Berk)
        Ruanda br. 1926. (Najib). Exp. Russia 1936
            Raduga b. 1937. (Rytham)
                Kreatura b. 1941. (Kann)
                Plaska ch. 1941. (Priboj)
        Myola b. 1937. (Algol)
            DARGEE ch. 1945. (Manasseh)
                Sirella ch. 1953. (Shalina)
                    HANIF gr. 1962. (Silver Vanity)
                Dargemet ch. 1961. (Bint Yasimet)
                    DONAX ch. 1971. (Ludrex)
                Zahri ch. 1962. (Zirree el Wada)
                    DARJEEL ch. 1962. (Rajjela)
                        RIAZ ch. 1974. (Razehra)
        Algoletta ch. 1935. (Algol)
            AL BURAK b. 1947. (Manasseh). Exp. S. Africa 1951
        RYTHAM ch. 1929. (Shareer). Exp. Russia 1936
            Sharfina ch. 1937. (Sharima)
                Shalina ch. 1948. (Rissam)
                    Sirella ch. 1953. (Dargee)

THE ARAB HORSE

Rodania cont.
  Rose of Sharon
    Ridaa
      Risala
        Rythma
          RYTHAL br. 1933. (Shareer). Exp. Holland 1937
        Rissla ch. 1917. (Berk)
          Rifala gr. 1922. (Skowronek). Exp. USA 1928
            RAFFLES gr. 1926. (Skowronek). Exp. USA 1932
              INDRAFF gr. 1938. (Indaia)
                Sahra Su gr. 1946. (Fa Rahna)
                  SYNBAD gr. 1955. (Julep)
              RAPTURE b. 1946. (Rafla)
              GEYM gr. 1942. (Rageyma)
                SOTEP gr. 1953. (Zareyna)
              INDY gr. 1947. (Indaia)
              RAFFERTY gr. 1953. (Masrufa)
              BAMBY b. 1947. (Bambina)
              Bambina b. 1942. (Rihani)
              AZRAFF gr. 1949. (Azja IV)
                Azleta gr. 1961. (Phleta)
                  GAI PARADA gr. 1969. (Ferzon)
              HANRAFF ch. 1943. (Chrallah)
              RIFRAFF gr. 1947. (Rafissa)
              RAFFI gr. 1946. (Imagida)
              AARAF ch. 1943. (Aarah)
                LA FLAG ch. 1957. (Flaiga)
            IMAGE ch. 1933. (Mirage*)
            Ragala gr. 1935. (Mirage*)
            RIFAGE gr. 1936. (Mirage*)
            PHANTOM gr. 1941. (Image)
          Reyna gr. 1925. (Skowronek). Exp. Spain 1930
          IFNI gr. 1937. (Razada)
            USHAAHE gr. 1942. (Duquesa). Exp. Jordan 1948
              BAHAR gr. 1952. (Sabal I)
              Gazella gr. 1958. (Emira I)
              Mashalla II gr. 1958. (Farha)
              Sabal II gr. 1959. (Lurbi I)
              Samiha gr. 1961. (Farha)
        Risslina ch. 1926. (Rafeef)
          Risira gr. 1939. (Naziri)
            Nerina ch. 1950. (Rissalix)
              Nerinora ch. 1954. (Oran)
                INDIAN FLAME II ch. 1964. (Indian Magic)
                INDIAN STAR ch. 1962. (Indian Magic)
              NORAN ch. 1956. (Oran)
            Risseefa ch. 1943. (Faris)
              Silver Ripple gr. 1960. (Silver Vanity)
            Gleaming Gold ch. 1952. (Indian Gold)
              GOLD REX ch. 1960. (Alexus)
              Dreaming Gold ch. 1963. (Blue Domino)

Rodania cont.
  Rose of Sharon
    Ridaa
      Risala
        Rissla
          Risslina
            RIFARI ch. 1941. (Faris)
              Farette b. 1954. (Shabrette)
            Rissletta ch. 1930. (Naseem). Exp. USA 1936
              ABU FARWA ch. 1940. (Rabiyas)
          IREX ch. 1927. (Naseem)
          Indian Pride ch. 1938. (Nisreen)
            INDIAN KING ch. 1953. (Oran)
            CHAMPURRADO ch. 1940. (Niseyra) [see Dajania*]
            ALEXUS ch. 1949. (Aletta)
            GREATHEART ch.1951. (Garance)
            IRIDOS gr. 1951. (Rafeena)
          Rixalina ch. 1929. (Raseem). Exp. Russia 1936
            KOREJ ch. 1939. (Kann)
              KNIPPEL ch. 1954. (Parfumeria)
              KANKAN gr. 1954. (Nagrada)
            Nagrada gr. 1938. (Naseem)
          Rissalma ch. 1932. (Shareer). Exp. Russia 1936
            Florencia ch. 1936. (Faris). Exp. Russia 1936
              Parfumeria ch. 1945. (Piolun)
                KNIPPEL ch. 1954. (Korej)
            PRIBOJ ch. 1944. (Piolun)
              POMERANETS ch. 1952. (Mammona)
              Monopolia. 1956. (Mammona)
                MAGNAT gr. 1966. (Aswan)
          RISSALIX ch. 1934. (Faris)
            Pale Shadow ch. 1944. (Shamnar)
              BRIGHT SHADOW ch. 1948. (Radi)
            COUNT D'ORSAZ ch. 1945. (Shamnar). Exp. USA 1959
            BLUE DOMINO ch. 1947. (Niseyra)
              LUDO ch. 1953. (Rithyana)
              Dreaming Gold ch. 1963. (Gleaming Gold)
              FARI II b. 1965. (Farette)
            MIKENO ch. 1949. (Namilla)
              RAJMEK ch. 1961. (Rajjela)
            Shabrette b. 1950. (Shabryeh)
              Farette b. 1954. (Rifari)
                FARI II b. 1965. (Blue Domino)
          Rissiletta ch. 1943. (Indian Gold). Exp. USA 1956
        Rafina ch. 1919. (Rustem) Exp. Australia 1925
        Razieh 'Bint Risala' ch. 1920. (Ibn Yashmak*). Exp. Egypt 1920
          IBN MANSOUR gr. 1931. (Mansour). Exp. Saudi Arabia 1939
          Kateefa gr. 1938. (Shahloul)
            Bint Kateefa ch. 1954. (Sid Abouhom)
              KAISOON gr. 1958. (Nazeer). Exp. Germany 1963
          MOFTAKHAR gr. 1946. (Enzahi)
          ALAA EL DINE ch. 1956. (Nazeer)

Rodania cont.
　Rose of Sharon
　　Ridaa
　　　Risala
　　　　Razieh
　　　　　Kateefa
　　　　　　ALAA EL DINE
　　　　　　　FARAZDAC gr. 1966. (Farasha). Exp. USA 1974
　　　　Yashmak b. 1941. (Sheikh el Arab)
　　　　Om el Saad gr. 1945. (Shahloul)
　　　Riyala ch. 1905. (Astraled)
　　　　Ranya I b. 1916. (Nasik). Exp. Spain 1926
　　　　　Ranya II b. 1922. (Redif)
　　　　　　Roxana gr. 1932. (Ruskov)
　　　　　　　Roshara gr. 1944. (Harab)
　　　　　　　　MARINO MARINI gr. 1961. (Mikeno)
　　　　　　　Bint Roxana gr. 1957. (Greatheart)
　　　　　　　　ROXAN gr. 1964. (Count Roland)
　　　　　　　　Roxira gr. 1966. (Gold Rex)
　　　　　　Rafeena gr. 1940. (Aluf)
　　　　　　　RIKHAM gr. 1945. (Rissam). Exp. Australia 1948
　　　　　　　　RALVON PILGRIM ch. 1969. (Trix Silver)
　　　　　　　IRIDOS gr. 1951. (Irex)
　　　　　RAZADA gr. 1925. (Shahzada). Exp. Spain 1926
　　　　　NANA SAHIB gr. 1934. (Jalila)
　　　　　Egina b. 1941. (Saboya)
　　　　　　JAECERO gr. 1946. (Barquillo)
　　　　　　MALVITO b. 1949. (Gandhy)
　　　　　Famula gr. 1942. (Sara)
　　　　　　MAQUILLO ch. 1949. (Gandhy)
　　　　　　UZACUR gr. 1956. (Veranda)
　　　　　Kantista gr. 1947. (Morayma)
　　　　　　ALHABAC gr. 1956. (Caireh)
　　　　　　Ispahan gr. 1965. (Chavali)
　　　　　　　AN MALIK gr. 1970. (Galero). Exp. USA 1972
　　　　　IFNI gr. 1937. (Reyna)
　　　　　　USHAAHE gr. 1942. (Duquesa). Exp. Jordan c.1947
　　　　　　BAHAR gr. 1952. (Sabal I)
　　　　　　Gazella gr. 1958. (Emira I)
　　　　　　Sabal II gr. 1959. (Lurbi I)
　　　　　　　Huseima gr. 1965. (Madrid)
　　　　　　Samiha gr. 1961. (Farha)
　　　　　　　BAHAREIN ch. 1967. (Bahar)
　　　　　　　　Sarra gr. 1979. (Huseima)
　　　　RAFEEF ch. 1917. (Nasik) Exp. Argentina.
　　　　Risama 'Bint Riyala' b. 1920. (Nadir). Exp. Egypt 1920
　　　　　Bint Bint Riyala. 1924. (Gamil Manial)
　　　　　　Malaka (Eg) gr. 1941. (Kheir)
　　　Razina ch. 1922. (Rasim)
　　　　RADI b. 1925. (Rishan)

Rodania cont.
　Rose of Sharon
　　Ridaa
　　　Riyala
　　　　Razina
　　　　　RADI
　　　　　　BRIGHT SHADOW ch. 1948. (Pale Shadow)
　　　　　　　GREYLIGHT gr. 1959. (Royal Radiance). Exp. Australia
　　　　　　　BRIGHT WINGS ch. 1965. (Silent Wings). Exp. Belgium 1968
　　　　　　　　Odessa ch. 1973. (Serinda)
　　　　　　　　　PADRON ch. 1977. (Patron)
　　　　　　　　　　PADRON'S PSYCHE ch. 1988. (Kilika)
　　　　　　Tehoura ch. 1946. (Niseyra)
　　　　　Nurschida ch. 1930. (Nuri Sherif)
　　　　　　Namilla ch. 1937. (Algol)
　　　　　　　MIKENO ch. 1949. (Rissalix)
　　　　　　　Umatella ch. 1945. (Oran)
　　　　　　　Iorana b. 1942. (Radi). Exp. USA 1953
　　　　　　Manzana b. 1938. (Naufal)
　　　　　　　Moraea b. 1950. (Irex). Exp. USA 1960
　　　　　　　Yamain ch. 1942. (Rissalix)
　　　　　　　　Yatagan gr. 1947. (Rangoon)
　　　　　　　　Yatima gr. 1953. (Iran)
　　　　　Rikitea ch. 1942. (Rissalix)
　　　　　　Garance gr. 1946. (Grey Owl)
　　　　Sulka ch. 1934. (Naseem). Exp. Holland [see Hagar*]
　　　RAKTHA gr. 1934. (Naseem). Exp. S. Africa 1951
　　　　INDIAN MAGIC gr. 1944. (Indian Crown)
　　　　　ELECTRIC STORM gr. 1952. (Silfina). Exp. USA 1956
　　　　　INDIAN SILVER gr. 1970. (Dalika). Exp. USA 1976
　　　　　SILVER MOONLIGHT gr. 1949. (Silver Fire). Exp. Australia 1951
　　　　GENERAL GRANT ch. 1945. (Samsie)
　　　　ELECTRIC SILVER 1948. (Silfina). Exp. Australia 1950
　　　　SERAFIX ch. 1949. (Serafina). Exp. USA 1953
　　　　SILVER DRIFT gr. 1951. (Serafina). Exp. USA 1962
　　　　RITHAN ch. 1941. (Rishna)
　　　RIFFAL b. 1936. (Naufal). Exp. Australia 1947
　　　　ORAN ch. 1940. (Astrella)
　　　　　GRAND ROYAL ch. 1947. (Sharima). Exp. Australia 1959
　　　　　Mifaria ch. 1947. (Rithyana)
　　　　　SILVER VANITY gr. 1950. (Silver Gilt). Exp. USA 1962
　　　　　INDIAN KING ch. 1953. (Indian Pride)
　　　　Nerinora ch. 1954. (Nerina)
　　　　NORAN ch. 1956. (Nerina)
　　　Shamnar ch. 1939. (Naziri)
　　　　COUNT D'ORSAZ ch. 1945. (Rissalix). Exp. USA 1959
　　Ramayana ch. 1924. (Nureddin II). Exp. Poland 1937
　　Ruellia ch. 1926. (Nureddin II), Exp. Russia 1936
　　　Rezeda II ch. 1939. (Rytham)
　　　　Nera ch. 1948. (Nomer)
　　　　　Nerpa ch. 1957. (Priboj)

Rodania cont.
  Rose of Sharon
    Ridaa
      RUSTEM br. 1908. (Astraled). Exp. Egypt 1920
        Ferda b. 1913. (Feluka). Exp. USA 1926 [see Ferida*]
        Rayya br. 1915. (Riada) [see Rosemary]
        MEKDAM b. 1932. (Bint Bint Dalal)
          Obeya gr. 1940. (Abla)
            ANTAR ch. 1946. (Hamdan)
      Rim ch. 1910. (Astraled)
        Ramim b. 1915. (Berk). Exp. USA 1918
          REHAL ch. 1923. (Sidi)
            Rabiyat b. 1926. (Rokhsa) [see Rosemary]
        Rifla ch. 1920. (Rasim). Exp. USA 1926
        RASWAN gr. 1921. (Skowronek). Exp. USA 1926
          FERHAN ch. 1925. (Fejr). Exp. Russia 1936 [see Ferida*]
          Rose of France gr. 1926. (Jalila). Exp. USA 1930
          Star of the Hills br. 1927. (Selima). Exp. Russia 1936 [see Sobha*]
        RASEEM ch. 1922. (Rasim). Exp. Russia 1936
          Indaia b. 1927. (Nisreen). Exp. USA 1928
            INDRAFF gr. 1938. (Raffles)
            INDRAGE ch. 1934. (Mirage*)
          Rixalina ch. 1929. (Rissla). Exp. Russia 1936
            KOREJ ch. 1939. (Kann)
              KNIPPEL ch. 1954. (Parfumeria)
              KANKAN gr. 1954. (Nagrada)
            Nagrada gr. 1938. (Naseem)
          Astrella ch. 1929. (Amida)
            ORAN ch. 1940. (Riffal)
          Indian Crown ch. 1935. (Nisreen)
            INDIAN MAGIC gr. 1944. (Raktha)
          Starilla b. 1935. (Star of the Hills)
          GREY OWL gr. 1934. (Naxina)
        RAHAL ch. 1924. (Nureddin II). Exp. USA 1933
        Rimini gr. 1925. (Skowronek). Exp. USA 1933
        GREY OWL gr. 1934. (Naxina)
        NAHARIN gr. 1941. (Gulastra)
        RIX ch. 1927. (Mirage* or Iram) [see Dafina*]
        RISSAM ch. 1928. (Naseem)
          Niseyra ch, 1935. (Neraida) [see Dajania*]
          Rizala ch. 1943. (Ghezala). Exp. Australia 1947
          NIZZAM b. 1943. (Nezma). Exp. Holland 1950 and exp. USA 1960
          RIKHAM gr. 1945. (Rafeena). Exp. Australia *in utero* 1945
          Shalina ch. 1948. (Sharfina)
          Rishyana ch. 1939. (Rishna)
    RIJM ch. 1901. (Ibn Mahruss*). Exp. Spain 1910
      RODAN II ch. 1908. (Rakima)
      NASIK b. 1908. (Narghileh). Exp. USA 1926 [see Dajania*]
      Nessima b. 1909. (Narghileh)
      NUREDDIN II ch. 1911. (Narghileh). Exp. USA 1933 [see Dajania*]
    Rumeliya ch. 1902. (Rejeb). Exp. USA 1906
    RODAN ch. 1906. (Harb). Exp. *In utero* USA 1905
      Gulnare gr. 1914. (Ghazala*) [see Ghazala*]
      Bazrah b. 1919. (Bathsheba) [see Basilisk*]
      GHAZI gr. 1925. (Guemara) [see Ghazala*]

Rodania cont.
  Rose of Sharon
    Rosa Rugosa ch. 1907. (Imamzada)
      SIDI ch. 1917. (Khaled)
        REHAL ch. 1923. (Ramim)
          NEJAL ch. 1928. (Larkspur)
            Nafud b. 1931. (Hazna)
              ISLAM ch. 1939. (Gulastra)
                BINIS ch. 1944. (Binni)
Rosemary b. 1886. (Jeroboam)
  REJEB ch. 1897. (Mesaoud*)
    Rose of Hind b. 1902. (Rose Diamond)
    Jiwa ch. 1902. (Jalmuda) [see Johara*]
    Narda ch. 1902. (Narghileh) [see Dajania*]
  Rakima ch. 1898. (Mesaoud*)
    RODAN ch. 1908. (Rijm)
  Rabla b. 1899. (Mesaoud*)
    Rish b. 1903. (Nejran)
      RISHAN b. 1922. (Nadir)
        RADI b. 1925. (Razina)
      Rishna ch. 1923. (Nureddin II)
        Rishyana ch. 1939. (Rissam)
          Rithyana ch. 1943. (Raktha)
            Mifaria ch. 1947. (Oran)
            Lilac Domino ch. 1952. (Blue Domino)
            LUDO ch. 1953. (Blue Domino)
          RITHAN ch. 1941. (Raktha). Exp. USA 1951
          Rafika gr. 1943. (Ruskov)
            Fafika gr. 1952. (Fayal)
              HARWOOD ASIF ch. 1967. (Zeus II)
                Anna Rose ch. 1972. (Charlotte Rose)
                  KASADI ch. 1977. (Taqah)
        Marishna ch. 1950. (Manasseh)
          Mafari ch. 1962. (Shifari)
            Sheer Magic gr. 1967. (Scindian Magic). Exp. Australia
  Rokhama b. 1906. (Astraled)
    Rokhsa b. 1915. (Nasik). Exp. USA 1918
      Rabiyat b. 1926. (Rehal)
        RABIYAS ch. 1936. (Rahas)
          ABU FARWA ch. 1940. (Rissletta)
    Roshana b. 1920. (Berk)
      Raaf b. 1925. (Rodan)
  Rangha b. 1911. (Berk)
    ALGOL ch. 1928. (Aldebaran)
      Shabryeh b. 1932. (Seriya) [see Sobha*]
      Myola b. 1937. (Rythma)
        DARGEE ch. 1945. (Manasseh)
    Namilla ch. 1937. (Nurschida)
      MIKENO ch. 1949. (Rissalix)
    Rahab b. 1931. (Sainfoin)
      RAZAZ II ch. 1949. (Champurrado). Exp. Australia 1955
      Ruth II b. 1943. (Bendigo)
    RHEOBOAM ch. 1936. (Sainfoin)
  Raida gr. 1922. (Skowronek). Exp. USA 1926

Rodania cont.
  Rosemary
    Rosetta ch. 1903 (Mesaoud*). Exp. USA 1906
    Riada br. 1904. (Mesaoud*)
      Rayya br. 1915. (Rustem)
        RASEYN gr. 1923. (Skowronek). Exp. USA 1926
          FERSEYN gr. 1937. (Ferda) [see Ferida*]
          SUREYN gr. 1940. (Crabbet Sura) [see Sobha*]
          RONEK gr. 1931. (Bahreyn)
          MONEYN gr. 1934. (Monica)
          Moneyna gr. 1937. (Monica)
  REDIF B. 1906. (Daoud)
  Rueyda ch. 1908. (Daoud)

WILD THYME

Wild Thyme* b. 1876. Imp. 1878. Given away 1887
  Wild Honey 'Raschida' b. 1883. (Kars*)
    Riad b. 1897. (Hail)
      Sheeba b. 1903. (Ben Azrek)
        NURI SHERIF b. 1920. (Nureddin II)
        Nurschida ch. 1930. (Razina)
          Namilla ch. 1937. (Algol)
            MIKENO ch. 1949. (Rissalix)
          Manzana b. 1938. (Naufal)
          Moraea b. 1950. (Irex)
          Sulka ch. 1934. (Naseem). Exp. Holland
            NIZAR ch. 1953. (Nizzam)
            Fatma b. 1951. (Nizzam). Imp. UK 1970
    Rakusheh b. 1889. (El Emir*). Exp. USA 1893
    Nessa b. 1905. (Hauran). Exp. USA 1905
      Tahdik – 1920 (Berk)
        Santa Fe – 1927 (Raas)
          Fe Gama – 1950 (Gamhuri)
            Zakieh b. 1959 (Fa-abi)
              Afhar Rahza - - (Al-Marah Radames)
                Katahza - - (Aza Destiny)
                  Little Liza Fame b. 1987 (Fame VF)
                    MARWAN AL SHAQAB b. 2000 (Gazal al Shaqab)
  Mahal b. 1904. (Imamzada). Exp. USA 1905

JILFA

Jilfa* b. 1884. Imp. 1888. Given away 1896
  Jamusa b. 1890. (Azrek*)
    Mareesa b. 1902. (Mareb)
      Alfarouse ch. 1917. (Berk)
        ALMULID gr. 1923. (Skowronek)
        Rasana gr. 1928. (Razina)
          Ghezala gr. 1934. (Faris). Exp. S. Africa 1946
            Amanda b.1941. (Raktha). Exp. USA 1951
              Rizala ch. 1943. (Rissam). Exp. Australia 1947
          Hameeshe b. 1930. (Hagar II). [see Hagar*]
        AJEEB gr. 1925. (Skowronek). Exp. Hungary 1930
          203 Ajeeb-4 gr. 1933. (18 Izis)
          205 Ajeeb-2 gr. 1934. (5 Koheilan IV-1). Exp. Poland c1945
          AJEEB I gr. 1931. (5 Koheilan IV-1)
      Alfila b. 1928. (Nuri Sherif)
      AZYM ch. 1929. (Sher-i-Khurshid)
    Yaquta b. 1923. (Rasim)
      Rasheeqa ch. 1937. (Azym)
        Muna b. 1942. (Yassb)
          Munariffa b. 1955. (Shariff)
            Mariposa ch. 1973. (Gold Moidore)
        Fauna b. 1946. (Fayal)
          Elizabeth ch. 1952. (Larkspur)
        Rakud ch. 1947. (Aaron)
          Noora b. 1955. (Tummundar)
          Saadyah b. 1951. (Manasseh)
        Resique b. 1948. (Aaron)
          Amirat b. 1956. (Rashid). Exp. Holland 1962

SOBHA

Sobha* gr. 1879. Imp. 1891 and exp. Russia 1899
  Safra* gr. 1885. (Shueyman). Imp. 1891
    SHERIF gr. 1887. (Ibn Nadir)
    ANTAR (SO) gr. 1890. (Aziz)
    Selma II gr. 1894. (Ahmar)
      Simrieh b. 1903. (Seyal)
        Selmnab b.1920. Exp. USA 1930
          IDOL gr. 1939. (Mirage*)
          SELMAGE b. 1941. (Image)
          Imna ch. 1942. (Image)
        Shemma b. 1923. (Muskro)
          Falha b. 1935. (Rishan)
            Fuwasa b. 1945. (Kasim*)
    Selima br. 1908. (Astraled)
      SHAREER b. 1923. (Nureddin II). Exp. Russia 1936

THE ARAB HORSE

Sobha cont.
Selma II
  Selima
    SHAREER
      Sharima ch. 1932. (Nashisha)
        Sharfina ch. 1937. (Rytham)
          Serafina ch. 1945. (Indian Gold)
            SERAFIX ch. 1949. (Raktha). Exp. USA 1953
            SILVER DRIFT gr. 1951. (Raktha). Exp. USA 1962
          Silfina ch. 1944. (Indian Gold)
            ELECTRIC SILVER gr. 1948. (Raktha). Exp. Australia 1950
            ELECTRIC STORM gr. 1952. (Indian Magic). Exp. USA 1956
            Silent Wings ch. 1954. (Oran)
          Shalina ch. 1948. (Rissam)
            Sirella ch. 1953. (Dargee)
              HANIF gr. 1962. (Silver Vanity)
        GRAND ROYAL ch. 1947. (Oran). Exp. Australia 1959
      Sardhana b. 1924. (Nureddin II). Exp. Poland
        Crabbet Sura gr. 1928. (Skowronek). Exp. USA 1936
          SUREYN gr. 1940. (Raseyn)
          SURF gr. 1955. (Jubilema)
      Rasima br. 1943. (Rasim I)
      Star of the Hills br. 1927. (Raswan). Exp. Russia 1936
        Starilla b. 1935. (Raseem)
          Krona ch. 1939. (Kann)
            Taktüka b. 1943. (Taki Pan)
              Platina. 1950. (Priboj)
                Panel. 1960. (Nil)
                  PALAS gr. 1968. (Aswan)
    SELMIAN gr. 1929. (Naseem). Exp. USA 1932
  SOTAMM br. 1910. (Astraled). Exp. Egypt 1920
  KAZMEEN b. 1916. (Kasima). Exp. Egypt 1920 [see Kasida*]
  NAUFAL b. 1916. (Narghileh) [see Dajania*]
  Bint Serra b. 1923. (Serra). Exp. USA 1932 [see Ghazala*]
Siwa gr. 1896. (Ahmar)
  Soleyma gr. 1907. (Daoud)
    Selinga ch. 1911. (Feysul*)
      Meliha I b. 1918. (Dwarka*)
  Somra gr. 1908. (Daoud)
    Safarjal br. 1915. (Berk)
      SAINFOIN b. 1923. (Rasim)
      Belkis II b. 1934. (Bekr)
        Beryl b. 1940. (Joseph)
          BLENHEIM ch. 1953. (Rheoboam)
          BEND OR b. 1959. (Rheoboam)
        RHEOBOAM ch. 1936. (Rangha)
        Baranova b. 1938. (Bekr)
          BENJAMIN b. 1946. (Champurrado)
        Nautch Girl br. 1940. (Nasira)
          NIMROD b. 1952. (Champurrado). Exp. USA 1953

Sobha cont.
Siwa
  Somra
    Safarjal
      SAINFOIN
        BAHRAM ch. 1946. (Betina)
      Sukr b. 1926. (Atesh*)
      Somra II gr. 1932. (Fedaan*)
        Siwa II gr. 1043. (Rheoboam)
      SHAMMAR gr. 1955. (Champurrado)
  Seriya gr. 1921 (Skowronek).
    Sahra ch. 1925. (Crosbie*)
      Algola ch. 1935. (Algol)
        Araby gr. 1940. (Jellaby)
          Sapphire gr. 1950. (Indian Magic)
            Silver Velvet gr. 1955. (Ghailan)
      Sahmana ch. 1943. (Manak*)
    Shabryeh b. 1932. (Algol)
      Shabrette b. 1950. (Rissalix)
        Farette b. 1954. (Rifari)
          FARI II b. 1965. (Blue Domino)
          Farenta gr. 1975. (Magenta)
    Serena b. 1943. (Mabruk II)
  Silver Fire gr. 1926. (Naseem)
    Somara gr. 1930. (Nureddin II)
      Senga gr. 1936. (Rangoon). Exp. USA
      Silver Crystal gr. 1937. (Rangoon). Exp USA 1951
        Silwa gr. 1950. (Raktha). Exp. USA 1957
          SILWAN gr. 1954. (Dargee). Exp. Australia 1958
        MUJAHID gr. 1954. (Sureyn)
      Silsilla gr. 1949. (Rithan). Exp. S. Africa 1951
        CHEZ NOUS SHAH RUKH gr. 1953. (Al Burak)
    Silver Gilt gr. 1943. (Indian Gold)
      SILVER VANITY gr. 1950. (Oran). Exp. USA 1962
        HANIF gr. 1962. (Sirella)
    Silver Grand gr. 1951. (Grand Royal). Exp. USA 1957
      SPINDRIFT gr. 1957. (Silver Drift). Exp. Australia 1959
    Royal Radiance gr. 1955. (Royal Diamond). Exp. Australia 1958
      GREYLIGHT gr. 1959. (Bright Shadow). Exp. Australia *in utero* 1958
        RASHAM gr. 1975. (Sparkle)
    Silver Grey gr. 1957. (Royal Diamond)
    Silver Sheen gr. 1962. (Bright Shadow)
    Silver Shadow gr. 1946. (Oran)
      SILVER MOONLIGHT gr. 1949. (Indian Magic). Exp. Australia 1951
    Silka b. 1929. (Nureddin II). Exp. Russia 1936
  Sarama b. 1910. (Daoud)
    Simawa b. 1915. (Rustem). Exp. USA 1918
      KATAR b. 1929. (Gulastra)
SEYAL gr. 1897. (Mesaoud*)
  BERK b. 1903. (Bukra). Exp. USA 1918 [see Basilisk*]

FERIDA

Ferida* b. 1886. Imp. 1891. Given away 1907
    Fezara ch. 1892. (Mesaoud*). Exp. Russia 1899
    Feluka ch. 1899. (Mesaoud*)
        Fejr ch. 1911. (Rijm)
            Felestin ch. 1916. (Ibn Yashmak*). Exp. USA 1918
                Kishta gr. 1940. (Akil)
                Fasila ch. 1923. (Rasim). Exp. Poland 1927
                    SULEJMAN gr. 1934. (Fetysz)
                    RASIM PIERWSZY b. 1937. (Rasim III)
                        Elza b. 1942. (El Zabibe)
                          Celina b. 1949. (Witraz). Imp. UK 1959
                FARIS ch. 1924. (Nureddin II)
                    RISSALIX ch. 1934. (Rissla) [see Rodania*]
                    RIFARI ch. 1941. (Risslina)
                FERHAN ch. 1925. (Raswan). Exp. Russia 1936
                  INDIAN GOLD ch. 1934. (Nisreen) [see Dajania*]
                  Silver Gilt gr. 1943. (Silver Fire) [see Sobha*]
                FAYAL ch. 1927. (Mirage* or Iram)
                  RAYAL gr. 1942. (Raxina)
                  RIFFAYAL gr. 1942. (Ariffa). Exp. Australia 1950
                  Fayella gr. 1942. (Dafina*) [see Dafina*]
                  GHAILAN gr. 1943. (Raxina)
                  Taima br. 1944. (Naomi I)
                  Fafika gr. 1952. (Rafika)
    Ferda b. 1913. (Rustem). Exp. USA 1926
        Farasin b. 1920. (Rasim). Exp. USA 1926
            FARANA b. 1929. (Nasik)
                FARAWI b. 1936. (Ghazawi)
                Bint Sahara gr. 1942. (Bint Sedjur)
                Fersara gr. 1947. (Ferseyn)
                  FERZON gr. 1952. (Ferneyn)
                    FERDINE gr. 1958. (Gadina)
                      GAI PARADA gr. 1969. (Azleta)
                    GAZON b. 1955. (Scheraff)
                    GAIZON gr. 1957. (Gajala)
                    DUNES gr. 1956. (Ferneyn)
                    THE REAL McCOY gr. 1960. (Aarief)
                FADJUR b. 1952. (Fadheilan)
                  Jurneeka b. 1958. (Fadneeka)
                    KHEMOSABI b. 1967. (Amerigo)
              SIKIN b. 1933. (Nasik)
                Gazya b. (Rabiyat)
                  ZADIR ch. 1952. (Faronek)
            Nafara b. 1931. (Nasik)
              NARZIGH ch. 1939. (Ghazi)
              Rabna ch. 1946. (Rabkhal)
                AURAB ch. 1957. (Aulani)
        Fantana ch. 1922. (Joseph)
            Dil Fireb ch. 1933. (Joseph)
                The Lady Roxane ch. 1943. (Sahban)
                    The Lady Heloise ch. 1948. (Ghailan)
                        The Lady Idar gr. 1951. (Idar)

Ferida cont.

    Feluka
        Ferda
            Fantana
                Dil Fireb
                    The Lady Roxane
                        The Lady Euridice ch.1949. (Sitaab)
                            Blue Sophonisba ch. 1962. (Blue Domino)
                    The Lady Lucretia ch. 1946. (Fayal)
                Firefly b. 1940. (Mabruk II)
            Josepha ch. 1929. (Joseph)
        FERDIN ch. 1927. (Nureddin II). Exp. In utero USA 1926
            Ferdirah gr. (Sankirah)
                ERRABI ch, 1949 (Arabi Kabir) [see Mirage*]
        FERSEYN gr. 1937. (Raseyn)
            FERNEYN gr. 1944. (Moneyna)
                FERZON gr. 1952. (Fersara)
            Fersara gr. 1947. (Bint Sahara)
            Saki gr. 1950. (Ferdia)
                FADI gr. 1960. (Fadjur)
                    Heritage Labelle gr. 1964. (La Donna)
                        Heritage Memory b. 1971. (El Magato)
                            ALI JAMAAL b. 1982. (Ruminaja Ali)
                AMERIGO gr. 1962. (Syarya)
                  KHEMOSABI b. 1967. (Jurneeka)
    Fasiha gr. 1920. (Skowronek)
        Fantasia I ch. 1927. (Atesh*)
            Fashoda ch. 1947. (Sainfoin)
            Farida II ch. 1945. (Sainfoin)
                Fitnah b. 1955. (Rashid I). Exp. USA 1960
    Feluka II b. 1928. (Nimr*)
        Sherezada gr. 1942. (Hazzal)

BINT HELWA

Bint Helwa* gr. 1887. Imp. 1897. Shot 1907
    Ghazala* gr. 1896 (Ibn Sherara). Imp. 1909 and exp. USA 1909 [see Ghazala*]
    Hilmyeh b. 1899. (Ahmar)
        HALIM b. 1906. (Astraled). Exp. USA 1908
        Hamida ch. 1908. (Daoud). Exp. USA 1923
            Josephine b. 1920. (Joseph)
            Hama I b. 1921. (Joseph). Exp. USA 1923
        HAZZAM b. 1911. (Berk)
        Hafra ch. 1941. (Berk)
        Hilwe br. 1920. (Najib). Exp. USA 1930
            AGWE gr. 1936. (Mirage*)
                JASPRE gr. 1945. (Roda)
    Hamasa ch. 1902. (Mesaoud*)
        HARIR b. 1911. (Berk). Exp. Australia 1913
        Hazna b. 1914. (Razaz). Exp. USA 1918
            Nafud b. 1931. (Nejal)
                Habiba ch. 1935. (Bazleyd)

Bint Helwa cont.

    Hamasa
        Hazna
            Nafud
                Habiba
                    Binni ch. 1940. (Gulastra)
                        Habina b. 1957. (Hallany Mistanny)
                ISLAM b. 1939. (Gulastra)
                  BINIS ch. 1944. (Binni)
            Ghazayat ch. 1926. (Rehal)
                Yatana b. 1936. (Farana)
                Ghazeyna gr. 1937. (Raseyn)
        HAMRAN b. 1915. (Berk). Exp. Egypt 1920
        Bint Dalal gr. 1926. (Dalal)
            HAMRAN II ch. 1930. (Durra)
                Helwa gr. 1940. (Bint Farida)
        Halima I b. 1916. (Razaz)
    HARB ch. 1901. (Mesaoud*)
        RODAN ch. 1906. (Rose of Sharon). Exp. *In utero* USA [*see* Rodania*]
            Gulnare gr. 1914. (Ghazala*) [*see* Ghazala*]

FULANA

Fulana* br. 1893. Imp. 1897. Destroyed 1908
    Fadila b. 1898. (Mesaoud*). Exp. Australia 1909
        FAND. 1904. (Daoud). Exp. S. Africa 1911
        FARAOUN b. 1899. (Mesaoud*). Exp. Australia 1901
    Zarif (Rabi)
        Gadara b. 1925. (Harir)
            Barada II b. 1934. (Raisuli)
                Baksheesh gr. 1946. (Rakib)
                    Electricia b. 1953. (Electric Silver)
                        Trix Silver ch. 1958. (Royal Domino)
    Zahr gr. 1947. (Rabi)
        Akabah II ch. 1926. (Harir)
    Khadijah (Labadah)
        Alcouza (Khamasin)
        Deryabar (Khamasin)

JOHARA

Johara* ch. 1880. Imp. 1897. Given away 1903
    Jalmuda ch. 1898. (Mesaoud*)
        Jiwa ch. 1902. (Rejeb)
            Jawi Jawi ch. 1912. (Rijm)
                Kateefah ch. 1922. (Uns-el-Wujood) [*see* Hagar*]
                NIGM ESSUBH ch. 1926. (Uns-el-Wujood)
                    Hada b. 1939. (Hameeshé)
                    Howa II b. 1941. (Hameeshé) [*see* Hagar*]
                JALEEL ch. 1927. (Naseem)
                    Rose du Sable gr. 1943. (Nisan) Exp. Australia 1951
                        Zirree el Wada gr. 1948. (Naseel)
                            ZEUS II gr. 1957. (Silver Vanity)
                            Zilati gr. 1958. (Silver Vanity)
                            Zahri ch. 1962 (Dargee)
                    Astreelia ch. 1948. (Astrab)
                Gileem ch. 1924. (Uns-el-Wujood). Exp. USA 1938
                Shalimar b. 1921. (Yakoot). Exp. Spain 1928

BINT NURA ES SHAKRA

Bint Nura es Shakra* ch. 1885. Imp. 1897. Shot 1912
    (IBN) MAHRUSS* ch. 1893. (Mahruss). Imp. 1897
        RIJM ch. 1901. (Rose of Sharon). Exp. Spain 1910 [*see* Rodania*]
    ABU KHASHEB* gr. 1894. (Mahruss). Imp. 1898 and exp. India 1901
    DAOUD ch. 1899. (Mesaoud*)
        Nasra b. 1908. (Nefisa) [*see* Dajania*]
        Somra gr. 1908. (Siwa) [*see* Sobha*]
        Hamida ch. 1908. (Hilmyeh). Exp. USA 1923 [*see* Bint Helwa*]
        Sarama b. 1910. (Siwa) [*see* Sobha*]
        Marhaba b. 1911. (Mabruka) [*see* Meshura*]
        Rasima ch. 1917. (Rose of Hind) [*see* Rodania*]
    REDIF b. 1906. (Rosemary)
        Ranya II b. 1922. (Ranya I) [*see* Rodania*]

MAKBULA

Makbula* gr. 1886. Imp. 1898 and exp. Russia 1900
    Kasida* 1891. (Nasr). Imp. 1898 [see Kasida*]
        Kerima ch. 1897. (Aziz)
        Kibla gr. 1900. (Mesaoud*)
            Kabila ch. 1906. (Feysul*)
                Julnar ch. 1911. (Lal-i-Abdar)
                      Kiyama ch. 1926. (Rafeef). Exp. USA 1930
                      Kareyma gr. 1927. (Naseem). Exp. USA 1928
                          Rageyma gr. 1936. (Mirage*)
                            GEYM gr. 1942. (Raffles)
                            Gajala gr. 1943. (Raffles)
                            GALIMAR ch. 1945. (Gaysar)
                            SKORAGE ch. 1947. (Gaysar)
                      ARABI KABIR ch. 1942. (Image)
            UNS EL WUJOOD ch. 1914. (Firuseh)
            Kateefah ch. 1922. (Jawi Jawi)
                KATAF ch. 1928. (Outlaw*). Exp. Australia 1935
                    ALADDIN gr. 1943. (Sir Aatika)
                        Alaga Maid gr. 1946. (Anaga)
                            Hestia gr. 1952. (Jedran)
                                AETHON gr. 1963. (Spindrift)
                Jasmeen gr. 1923. (Baida I)
                    Mish Mish I b. 1932. (Joseph). Exp. Holland 1937
                      Ritla II b. 1939. (Rythal)
                    Bint Yasim ch. 1940. (Manak*)
                      Yasimet ch. 1949. (Grey Owl)
                          Bint Yasimet ch. 1954. (Blue Domino)
                            Dargemet ch. 1961. (Dargee)
                                DONAX ch. 1971. (Ludrex)
                            Luda ch. 1967. (Ludo)
                            Parthia ch. 1959. (Shifari)
                            Oranet ch. 1962. (Oran)
            HILAL b. 1924. (Shejret Eddur)
                IBN HILAL ch. 1942. (Turfa*). Exp. in utero USA 1941
                Zobeide ch. 1943. (Guliran)
                Nouronnihar ch. 1945. (Guliran)

KASIDA

Kasida* ch. 1891. Imp. 1898. Shot 1913
    Kantara ch. 1901. (Mesaoud*)
        Kerbela ch. 1911. (Ibn Yashmak*). Exp. USA 1918
        KARUN ch. 1915. (Rustem). Exp. Egypt 1920
    Kasima b. 1905. (Narkise). Exp. USA 1918
        KAZMEEN 'Kazmeyn' b. 1916. (Sotamm). Exp. Egypt 1920
        Bint Samiha b. 1925. (Samiha)
            Samha gr. 1931. (Baiyad)
                Kamla gr. 1942. (Sheikh el Arab)

Kasida cont.

Kasima
    KAZMEEN
        Bint Samiha
            Samha
                Kamla
                    HADBAN ENZAHI gr. 1952. (Nazeer). Exp. Germany 1955
    NAZEER gr. 1934. (Mansour)
        HADBAN ENZAHI gr. 1952. (Kamla). Exp. Germany 1955
        IBN FAKHRI 'Korayem' gr. 1952. (Helwa)
        GHAZAL gr. 1953. (Bukra). Exp. Germany 1955
        MORAFIC gr. 1956. (Mabrouka). Exp. USA 1965
            SHAKER EL MASRI ch. 1963. (Zebeda). Exp. Germany
                EL SHAKLAN gr. 1975. (Estopa) [see Indjanin]
            IBN MONIET EL NEFOUS gr. 1964. (Moniet el Nefous)
            THE EGYPTIAN PRINCE gr. 1967. (Bint Mona)
            SHAIKH AL BADI gr. 1969. (Bint Maisa el Saghira)
                RUMINAJAA ALI gr. 1976. (Bint Ma Gidaa)
                    ALI JAMAAL b. 1982. (Heritage Memory)
                        THEE MINSTRIL b. 1984. (Bahila)
                            THEE DESPERADO b. 1989. (AK Amiri Asmarr)
        ALAA EL DIN ch. 1956. (Kateefa)
            Hanan br. 1967. (Mona)
                ASFOUR gr. 1984. (Malik). Exp. Australia
                SALAA EL DINE gr. 1985. (Ansata Halim Shah)
                    KAMAR AL ZAMAN gr. 1992. (Kamar). Exp. Qatar
                                          then Jordan
                HLAYYIL RAMADAN gr. 1996. (Haboub)
            JAMIL gr. 1975. (Madkour I)
        MOHAWED gr. 1963. (Rafica)
        FARAZDAC gr. 1966. (Farasha). Exp. USA 1974
        IKHNATOON gr. 1974. (Bint Om el Saad)
    TALAL gr. 1957. (Zaafarana). Exp. USA 1967
    Bint Moniet el Nefous ch. 1957. (Moniet el Nefous). Exp. USA 1958
    Bint Bukra gr. 1957. (Bukra). Exp. USA 1964
    ANSATA IBN HALIMA gr. 1958. (Halima). Exp. USA 1959
    ASWAN 'Raafat' gr. 1958. (Yosreia). Exp. Russia 1963
    KAISOON gr. 1958. (Bint Kateefa). Exp. Germany 1963
    Bint Mabrouka gr. 1958. (Mabrouka). Exp. USA 1959
    Bint Zaafarana gr. 1958. (Zaafarana). Exp. USA 1959
    FAYEK gr. 1958. (Fayza II). Exp. USA 1970
    Bint Mona gr. 1958. (Mouna). Exp. USA 1964
    Bint Maisa el Saghira b. 1958. (Maisa). Exp. USA 1962
    FAKHER EL DIN ch. 1960. (Moniet el Nefous). Exp. USA 1967
    GALAL ch. 1960. (Farasha)
Bint Sabah b. 1925. (Sabah)
    Layla ch. 1929. (Ibn Rabdan)
        SID ABOUHOM gr. 1936. (El Deree DB)
            Elwya gr. 1950. (Zareefa)
                SEEF gr. 1959. (Mashour)
            Mouna ch. 1954. (Moniet el Nefous)
                Fayrouz ch. 1965. (Alaa el din)

Kasida cont.

Kasima
  KAZMEEN
    Bint Sabha
      Layla
        SID ABOUHOM
          Mouna
            Bint Mouna gr. 1958. (Nazeer). Exp. USA 1964
          Mabrouka ch. 1951. (Moniet el Nefous)
          Bint Kateefa ch. 1954. (Kateefa)
            KAISOON gr. 1958. (Nazeer). Exp. Germany 1963
          Sanaaa gr. 1961. (Yashmak)
            HOSSNY gr. 1966. (Ansata Ibn Halima)
    Bint Bint Sabah b. 1930. (Bayyad). Exp. USA 1932
      Fa Saana gr. 1937. (Fadl)
        Aana gr. 1945. (Fay el Dine)
      Fa Habba b. 1947. (Fadl)
        HAROD br. 1959. (Nimrod)
      Faaba ch. 1949. (Fadl)
      FABAH b. 1950. (Fadl)
        Maarqada gr. 1963. (El Maar)
          ANSATA EL ARABI gr. 1971. (Ansata Ibn Halima)
        THE SHAH br. 1966. (Bint Fada). Imp. UK 1968
  SHEIKH EL ARAB gr. 1933. (Mansour)
    Wanisa ch. 1941. (Medallela)
      Moniet el Nefous ch. 1946. (Shahloul)
        Mabrouka ch. 1951. (Sid Abouhom)
          MORAFIC gr. 1956. (Nazeer). Exp. USA 1965
          Bint Mabrouka. 1958. (Nazeer). Exp. USA 1959
        Bint Moniet el Nefous ch. 1957. (Nazeer). Exp. USA 1958
        FAKHER EL DIN ch. 1960. (Nazeer). Exp. USA 1967
        TUHOTMOS b. 1962. (El Sareei). Exp. USA 1973
      Yashmak b. 1941. (Bint Risala)
        Om el Saad gr. 1945. (Shahloul)
        RASHAD IBN NAZEER b. 1955. (Nazeer). Exp. USA 1958
      Mahasin gr. 1942. (Kasbana)
        Muneera gr. 1951. (Sid Abouhom)
      Kamla gr. 1942. (Samha)
        HADBAN ENZAH I gr. 1952. (Nazeer). Exp. Germany 1955
      Yosreia gr. 1943. (Hind)
        ASWAN 'Raafat' gr. 1958. (Nazeer). Exp. Russia 1963
      El Bataa b. 1944. (Medallela)
      Halima b. 1944. (Ragia)
        Moheba b. 1951. (Sid Abouhom)
        ANSATA IBN HALIMA gr. 1958. (Nazeer). Exp. USA 1959
      Bukra gr. 1942. (Shahloul)
        GHAZAL gr. 1953. (Nazeer). Exp. Germany 1955
        Bint Bukra gr. 1958. (Nazeer). Exp. USA 1964
    Zareefa b. 1927. (Durra)
      Badia b. 1934. (Ibn Rabdan)
      Bint Zareefa gr. 1936. (Balance)
      EL SAREEI b. 1942. (Shahloul)
    Bint Farida gr. 1933. (Farida)
  IBN FAYZA b. 1930. (Fayza)

JELLABIEH

Jellabieh* gr. 1892. Imp. 1898. Sold 1912
  TIMSA* gr. 1889. (Antar). Imp. *in utero* 1898
  Jerawa gr. 1908. (Berk). Exp. Sweden 1916
  Jask gr. 1910. (Berk). Exp. Brazil/Equador 1921
    JELLAL b. 1919. (Riyal)
  Jezabel b. 1912. (Berk)

GHAZALA

Ghazala* gr. 1896. Imp. 1909 and exp. USA 1909
  Ghadia 'Radia' fl. gr. 1904. (Feysul)
    Bint Radia fl. gr. 1920. (Mabrouk Manial)
      SHAHLOUL gr. 1931. (Ibn Rabdan)
        Kateefa gr. 1938. (Bint Risala)
        MASHOUR br. 1941. (Bint Rustem)
        Bukra gr. 1942. (Bint Sabah)
        EL SAREEI b. 1942. (Zareefa)
          TUHOTMOS b. 1962. (Moniet el Nefous). Exp. USA 1973
        Om el Saad gr. 1945. (Yashmak)
        Moniet el Nefous ch. 1946. (Wanisa)
          Mabrouka ch. 1951. (Sid Abouhom)
            MORAFIC gr. 1956. (Nazeer). Exp. USA 1965
            Ansata bint Mabrouka gr. 1958. (Nazeer). Exp. USA 1959 (*see* Bint Mabrouka)
              ANSATA SHAH ZAMAN gr. 1968. (Morafic)
          Mona ch. 1954. (Sid Abouhom)
          Bint Moniet el Nefous ch. 1957. (Nazeer). Exp. USA 1958
          FAKHER EL DIN ch. 1960. (Nazeer). Exp. USA 1967
          IBN MONIET EL NEFOUS gr. 1964. (Morafic)
      RADWAN gr. 1934. (Ibn Rabdan)
      Samira gr. 1935. (Ibn Rabdan)
      Zaafarana gr. 1946. (Balance)
        TALAL gr. 1957. (Nazeer). Exp. USA 1967
        Ansata Bint Zaafarana gr. 1958. (Nazeer). Exp. USA 1959 (*see* Bint Zaafarana)
      HAMDAN gr. 1936. (Ibn Rabdan)
        ANTAR ch. 1946. (Obeya)
        Hafiza b. 1949. (Mahfouza)
    Zarifa gr. 1911. (Sahab)
      Bint Zareefa gr. 1926. (Hadban)
        EL MOEZ gr. 1934. (Ibn Fayda)
        Abla gr. 1920. (El Zafer)
          Obeya gr. 1940. (Mekdam)
  GHADIR gr. 1905. (Feysul*)
  Jemla 'Jamila' gr. 1906. (Jamil)
    Serra gr. 1915. (Sahab)

Ghazala cont.
GHADIR
Jemla 'Jamila'
  Serra gr. 1915.
    Kasbana b. (Registan)
      Mahasin gr. 1942. (Sheik el Arab)
    Bint Serra b. 1923. (Sotamm). Exp. USA 1932
      FAY EL DINE gr. 1934. (Fadl)
      FA SERR bl. 1947. (Fadl)
  Maamouna gr. 1922. (Ibn Obeya)
Guemura gr. 1912. (Segario)
  GHAZI gr. 1925. (Rodan)
    Ghazawi ch. 1931. (Gharifet)
      FARAWI b. 1936. (Farana)
        Bint Sahara gr. 1942. (Bint Sedjur)
          FADJUR b. 1952. (Fadheilan)
          Fersara gr. 1947. (Ferseyn)
            FERZON GR. 1952. (Ferneyn)
      Rahzawi ch. 1935. (Rahal)
        HANRAH ch. 1939. (Hanad)
      NARZIGH ch. 1939. (Nafara)
      Rabna ch. 1946. (Rabkhal)
        AURAB ch. 1957. (Aulani)
Gulnare gr. 1914. (Rodan)
  GULASTRA ch. 1924. (Astraled)
    RAHAS ch. 1928. (Raad)
      RABIYAS ch. 1936. (Rabiyat)
        ABU FARWA ch. 1940. (Rissletta)
      Rahika ch. 1936. (Bazikh)
        Natta. 1940. (Farana)
          EL NATTAL b. 1944. (Alla Amarward)
      AZKAR gr. 1935. (Aziza)
    KATAR b. 1929. (Simawa)
    KOLASTRA ch. 1928. (Kola)
    IBN GULASTRA ch. 1935. (Loilo)
    ISLAM b. 1939. (Nafud)
      BINIS ch. 1944. (Binni)
    JULEP gr. 1939. (Aziza)
      SYNBAD gr. 1955. (Sahra-Su)
    NAHARIN gr. 1941. (Rimini)
    Binni ch. 1940. (Habiba)
      BINIS ch. 1944. (Islam)

Ghazala cont.
Gulnare
  Gharifet gr. 1927. (Rizvan)
    Ghazawi ch. 1931. (Ghazi)
      FARAWI b. 1936. (Farana)
        Bint Sahara gr. 1942. (Bint Sedjur)
    Gara gr. 1935. (Bazleyd). Imp. UK 1937
      HARAB gr. 1940. (Jellaby)
        Hisan ch. 1944. (Gayza*)
      Roshara gr. 1944. (Roxana)
        MARINO MARINI gr. 1961. (Mikeno)
  GHADAF ch. 1929. (Ribal)
  GHAWI ch. 1930. (Ribal)
  Gayza gr. 1933. (Bazleyd). Imp. UK 1937
    GHARBI ch. 1937. (Nejal)
    Nisan gr. 1940. (Jellaby)
      Rose du Sable gr. 1943. (Jaleel)
        Zirree el Wada gr. 1948. (Naseel)
          ZEUS II gr. 1957. (Silver Vanity)
          Zilati gr. 1958. (Silver Vanity)
          Zahri ch. 1962. (Dargee)
    Nasam gr. 1947. (Shihab)
      Nasim gr. 1951. (Jair)
        Velvet Shadow b. 1965. (Bey Shadow)
          ROSTAM gr. 1970. (White Lightning)
            CARMARGUE gr. 1979. (White Lightning)
        White Lace gr. 1973. (White Lightning)
  Hisan ch. 1944. (Harab)
  Sea Pearl ch. 1952. (Dargee)

The Sheikh, drawing by Peter Upton.

THE BLUNTS' STALLIONS

KARS

KARS* b. 1874. Imp. 1878 and exp. Australia 1885
    Shehrezad gr. 1880. (Sherifa*) [see Sherifa*]
    Shiraz gr. 1881. (Sherifa*) [see Sherifa*]
    Dahna br. 1883. (Dahma*). Exp. Australia 1891 [see Dahma*]
    Rose of Jericho b. 1883. (Rodania*). Exp. Australia 1891 [see Rodania*]
    Wild Honey 'Raschida' b. 1883. (Wild Thyme*) [see Wild Thyme*]
    ROALA b. 1884. (Rodania*) [see Rodania*]
    Harik b. 1884. (Hagar*) [see Hagar*]
    Jebel Druz b. 1884. (Jedrania*) [see Jedrania*]
    Meroe b. 1885, (Meshura*) [see Meshura*]
    GOMUSSA ch. 1884. (Naomi)
    Kushdil b. 1886. (Naomi)
        GARAVEEN b. 1892. (Kismet*). Exp. USA 1893 [see Haidee*]

PHARAOH

PHARAOH* b. 1876. Imp. 1879 and exp. Russia/Poland 1882
    Bozra br. 1881. (Basilisk*) [see Basilisk*]
    JEROBOAM b. 1882. (Jerboa*). Exp. Egypt 1887 [see Jerboa*]
    Shemse gr. 1883. (Sherifa*) [see Sherifa*]
    Jerud b. 1883. (Jerboa*) [see Jerboa*]
    MOHORT br. 1884. (Precjosa)
        Mlecha I gr. 1895. (Mlecha)
            DZELFI-MLECHA b. 1910. (Dzelfi)
                Sahara ch. 1916. (Zulejka)
                      Ugra ch. 1935. (Kuhailan-Kruszan DB). Exp. USA 1938
                          Gumniska b. 1940. (Czubuthan)
        Mlecha III b. 1897. (Mlecha)
            ALMANZOR b. 1909. (Athos)
        Gruzinka bl. 1923. (Sahra)
    Podolanka. 1885. (Precjosa)
        ATHOS b. 1899. (Abu-Argub DB)
            ALMANZOR b. 1909. (Mlecha III)
                Przepiorka ch. 1935. (Jaskolka II). Exp. USA 1937
                    Panay gr. 1942. (Nasr)

Pharaoh cont.

    Podolanka
        ATHOS
            ALMANZOR
                Przepiorka
                    Guda ch. 1946. (Czubuthan)
                  ROZMARYN ch. 1935. (Dziewanna)
                    Fregata ch. 1957. (Fanfara)
                        Fama gr. 1963. (Nabor)
                Druchna ch. 1957. (Darda)
                  Druzba gr. 1964. (Nabor)
            Elokwencja ch. 1957. (Ela)
                Elekcja ch. 1965. (Comet)
        Rozeta b. 1936. (Kamea)

RATAPLAN

RATAPLAN* b. 1874. Imp. 1884 and exp. Egypt 1887
    Dinarzade b. 1887. (Dahna) [see Dahma*]
    Harra b. 1888. (Harik) [see Hagar*]

HADBAN

HADBAN* b. 1878. Imp. 1884 and exp. Australia 1885
    Rose of Sharon ch. 1885. (Rodania*). Exp. USA 1905 [see Rodania*]
    Nefisa b. 1885. (Dajania* [see Dajania*]

THE ARAB HORSE

AZREK

AZREK* gr. 1881. Imp. 1888 and exp. South Africa 1891
    Shieha gr. 1889. (Shiraz) [see Sherifa*]
    Bushra br. 1889. (Bozra) [see Basilisk*]
    SHAH gr. 1889. (Shehrezad). Exp. Spain 1892
    AHMAR b. 1890. (Queen of Sheba*). Exp. Java 1901 [see Queen of Sheba*]
    Rose Diamond b. 1890. (Rose of Jericho) [see Rodania*]
    RAFYK b. 1890. (Rose of Sharon). Exp. Australia 1891 [see Rodania*]
    Jamusa b. 1890. (Jilfa*) [see Jilfa*]
    Asfura b. 1891. (Queen of Sheba*) [see Queen of Sheba*]
    Mabruka b. 1891. (Meshura*) [see Meshura*]
    NEJRAN b. 1891. (Nefisa) [see Dajania*]
    Jeneyna b. 1891. (Jerboa*). Exp. Russia 1899 [see Jerboa*]
    RASHAM gr. 1891. (Rose of Sharon)
    Nejiba gr. 1892. (Nefisa) [see Dajania*]
    Howa b. 1892. (Harra) [see Hagar*]
    BEN AZREK gr. 1892. (Shemse) [see Sherifa*]

ASHGAR

ASHGAR* ch. 1883. Imp. 1888. Exp. Gibraltar 1890
    Dijleh br. 1889. (Dahna). Exp. Russia 1899 [see Dahma*]
    Nahla b. 1889. (Nefisa)
    Mansura b. 1890. (Meshura*) [see Meshura*]
        MAREB b. 1896. (Mesaoud*)
            Mareesa b. 1902. (Jamusa) [see Jilfa*]
                Alfarouse ch. 1917. (Berk)
                      ALMULID gr. 1923. (Skowronek)
                      AJEEB gr. 1925. (Skowronek). Exp. Hungary 1930
    JOKTAN ch. 1891. (Jamila)

MESAOUD

MESAOUD* ch. 1887. Imp. 1891 and exp. Russia 1903
    Mabsuta b. 1892. (Meshura*) [see Meshura*]
    Fezara ch. 1892. (Ferida*). Exp. Russia 1899 [see Ferida*]
    ANBAR b. 1893. (Queen of Sheba*). Exp. Russia 1896 [see Queen of Sheba*]
    Narghileh b. 1895. (Nefisa) [see Dajania*]
    JOHAR b. 1895. (Jeneyna). Exp. S. Africa 1899 [see Jerboa*]
    Moallaka b. 1896. (Meroe) [see Meshura*]
    MAREB b. 1896. (Mansura) [see Meshura*]
    Merjana b. 1896. (Meshura*) [see Meshura*]
    Jemeyza ch. 1896. (Jeneyna) [see Jerboa*]
    SEYAL gr. 1897. (Sobha*) [see Sobha*]
    NAAMAN b. 1897. (Nefisa). Exp. Russia 1899 [see Dajania*]
    REJEB ch. 1897. (Rosemary) [see Rodania*]
    Maisuna b. 1898. (Meshura*) [see Meshura*]
    NARENK b. 1898. (Nefisa). Exp. India 1901 [see Dajania*]
    Fadila b. 1898. (Fulana*). Exp. Australia 1909 [see Fulana*]
    Jalmuda ch. 1898. (Johara*) [see Johara*]

Mesaoud cont.

    Rakima ch. 1898. (Rosemary) [see Rodania*]
    Abla b. 1899. (Asfura) [see Queen of Sheba*]
    FARAOUN b. 1899. (Fulana*). Exp. Australia 1901 [see Fulana*]
    NARKISE b. 1899. (Nefisa) [see Dajania*]
    Rabla b. 1899. (Rosemary) [see Rodania*]
    Feluka ch. 1899. (Ferida*) [see Ferida*]
    DAOUD ch. 1899. (Bint Nura II*) [see Bint Nura II*]
    Shibine ch. 1899. (Shohba). Exp. USA 1909 [see Sherifa*]
    ASTRALED br. 1900. (Queen of Sheba*). Exp. USA 1909 [see Queen of Sheba*]
    NEJEF b. 1900. (Nefisa) [see Dajania*]
    Risala ch. 1900. (Ridaa) [see Rodania*]
    Kibla gr. 1900. (Makbula*) [see Makbula*]
    HARB ch. 1901. (Bint Helwa*) [see Bint Helwa*]
    Kantara ch. 1901. (Kasida*) [see Kasida*]
    Ajramieh ch. 1901. (Asfura) [see Queen of Sheba*]
    NADIR b. 1901. (Nefisa) [see Dajania*]
    Hamasa ch. 1902. (Bint Helwa*) [see Bint Helwa*]
    Antika ch. 1902. (Asfura). Exp. USA 1906 [see Queen of Sheba*]
    Rosetta ch. 1903. (Rosemary). Exp. USA 1906. [see Rodania*]
    LAL-I-ABDAR 'ABU ZEYD' ch. 1904. (Rose Diamond). Exp. USA 1910 [see Rodania*]
    Riada br. 1904. (Rosemary) [see Rodania*]
    Ninawa b. 1904. (Nefisa) [see Dajania*]

MERZUK

MERZUK* ch. 1887. Imp. 1891 and exp. S. Africa 1891
    Ridaa ch. 1892. (Rose of Sharon) [see Rodania*]
    Shebaka b. 1892. (Shelfa). Exp. S. Africa 1892

SHAHWAN

SHAHWAN* gr. 1887. Imp. 1892 and exp. USA 1895
    Yashmak gr. 1893. (Yemama)
        IBN YASHMAK* ch. 1902. (Feysul*) [see IBN YASHMAK*]
    Shohba gr. 1893. (Shelfa) [see Sherifa*]
    RABIAH gr. 1896. (Rakusheh)
    Nonliker gr. 1898. (Nejdme DB)
        Onrust gr. 1903. (Garaveen)
            Larkspur b. 1912. (Abu Zeyd) [see Haidee*]
                NEJAL cg. 1928. (Rehal) [see Kesia*]

(IBN) MAHRUSS

(IBN) MAHRUSS* ch. 1893. Imp. 1897. Sold 1900
    RIJM ch. 1901. (Rose of Sharon) [see Rodania*]
    IBN MAHRUSS ch. 1901. (Bushra). Exp. in utero USA 1900

Feysul

FEYSUL* CH. 1894. Imp. 1904. Destroyed 1917
    IBN YASHMAK* ch. 1902. (Yashmak). Exp. Egypt 1920 [see IBN YASHMAK*]
    IBN YEMAMA* ch. 1902. (Yemama). Imp. 1904
        MIREED b. 1911. (Mansura)
    Ghadia 'Radia' gr. 1904 (Ghazala*). Given to RAS Egypt [see Ghazala*]
    Kabila ch. 1906. (Kibla) [see Makbula*]
    RASIM ch. 1906. (Risala). Exp. Poland 1924 {see Rodania*]
    MUSTAPHA KAMEL b. 1906. (Mabsuta) [see Meshura*]
    Amra b. 1906. (Abla). Exp. USA 1909 [see Queen of Sheba*]
    AJMAN ch. 1906. (Ajramieh) [see Queen of Sheba*]
    RAS AL HADD ch. 1907. (Risala). Exp. Egypt 1911

Ibn Yashmak

IBN YASHMAK* ch. 1902. Imp. 1904 and exp. Egypt 1920
    Kerbela ch. 1911. (Kantara). Exp. USA 1918 [see Kasida*]
    Amida ch. 1913. (Ajramieh) [see Queen of Sheba*]
    Ajjam ch. 1915. (Ajramieh) [see Queen of Sheba*]
    MABROUK BLUNT ch. 1916. (Marhaba). Exp. Egypt 1920 [see Meshura*]
    MERSA MATRUH b. 1916. (Malaka) [see Meshura*]
    Felestin ch. 1916. (Fejr). Exp. USA 1918 [see Ferida*]
    NAFIA ch. 1916. (Nessima). Exp. USA 1918 [see Dajania*]
    Moubarek b. 1917. (Malaka) [see Meshura*]
    RIZVAN ch. 1919. (Rijma). Exp. in utero USA 1918 [see Rodania*]
    Razieh 'Bint Risala' ch. 1920. (Risala). Exp. Egypt 1920 [see Rodania*]

Mesaoud, drawing by Peter Upton

OTHER MARES

HAIDEE

Haidee* ch. 1869. Imp. 1874
  Naomi ch. 1877. (Yataghan*). Exp. USA 1888
    GOMUSSA ch. 1884. (Kars* or Kouch*)
    Kushdil ch. 1886. (Kars*)
      GARAVEEN b. 1892. (Kismet*). Exp. USA 1893
        Onrust gr. 1903. (Nonliker)
          Larkspur b. 1912. (Abu Zeyd)
            NEJAL ch. 1928. (Rehal)
              Nafud b. 1931. (Hazna)
                ISLAM b. 1939. (Gulastra)
                  BINIS ch. 1944. (Binni)
              Roglemar Zarad ch. 1933. (Kola)
              GHARBI ch. 1937. (Gayza). Imp *in utero* UK
        Ophir gr. 1917. (Segario)
      Najine gr. 1899. (Nejdme DB)
        SARGON ch. 1918. (Segario)
      Nanda b. 1905. (Nejdme DB)
        KEMAH gr. 1925. (Nuri Pasha)
      YIMA gr. 1902. (Nonliker)
        Slipper gr. 1921. (Sabot)
          Pera gr. 1933. (Mirage*)
  Naama b. 1887. (El Emir*)
  Nazli ch. 1888. (Maidan*). Exp. USA 1893
    NIMR ch. 1891. (Kismet*). Exp. USA 1893
      SEGARIO ch. 1902. (Shabaka)
        Guemura gr. 1912. (Ghazala*)
          GHAZI gr. 1925. (Rodan)
            Ghazawi ch. 1931. (Gharifet)
              FARAWI b. 1936. (Farana)
                Bint Sahara gr. 1942. (Bint Sedjur)
                  FADJUR b. 1952. (Fadeilan)
                    Jurneeka b. 1958. (Fadneeka)
                      KHEMOSABI b. 1967. (Amerigo)
                Fersara gr. 1947. (Ferseyn)
                  FERZON gr. 1952. (Ferneyn)
                  THE REAL McCOY gr. 1960. (Aarief)

Haidee cont.
Naomi
  Nazli
    NIMR
      SEGARIO
        Guemura
          GHAZI
            Ghazawi
              FARAWI
                Bint Sahara
                  Sahara Rose gr. 1958. (Ferseyn)
                  Sahara Dawn gr. 1959. (Ferseyn)
                  Sahara Queen gr. 1960. (Ferseyn)
        SARGON ch. 1918. (Najine)
      Ophir gr. 1917. (Onrust)
        Mirza gr. 1923. (Nejran Jr.)
          ZEM ZEM b. 1929. (Kemah)
            KARNAK gr. 1937. (Mershid)
        Hira ch. 1926. (El Sabok)
        Kerak gr. 1937. (Kemah)
    KHALED ch. 1895. (Naomi)
      SIDI ch. 1917. (Rosa Rugosa)
        REHAL ch. 1923. (Ramim)
          NEJAL ch. 1928. (Larkspur)
      SINBAD ch. 1908. (Shabaka)
    Nazlet ch. 1900. (Nazli)
  Naomi II ch. 1896. (Naomi)
  NAAMAN ch. 1896. (Anazeh)
  Nazlet ch. 1900. (Khaled)
ANAZEH ch. 1890. (Leopard DB)
  NEJD ch. 1894. (Naomi)
  Narkeesa ch. 1897. (Naomi)
    EL SABOK ch. 1916. (El Jafil)
      Hira ch. 1926. (Ophir)
  Nareesa ch. 1898. (Naomi)
NEJD ch. 1894. (Anazeh)
KHALED ch. 1895. (Nimr)
Naomi II ch. 1896. (Nimr)
Narkeesa ch. 1897. (Anazeh)
  EL SABOK ch 1916. (El Jafil)
Nareesa ch. 1898. (Anazeh)

Kesia and Kesia II

Kesia* b. *c.*1865. Imp. 1875
   Kesia II* b. 1876. (Seglawi el Abd). Imp. *in utero*
      Nowagieh ch. 1887. (Hadeed)
         IMAMZADA b. 1891. (Imam). Exp. USA 1905
         Hamada b. 1896. (Hagar*)
            El Lahr 1899. (Dinarzade). Exp. Australia 1901
               Al Caswa. 1903. (Rafyk)
                  Kufara gr. 1921. (Khamasin)
                     Sir Aatika gr. 1938. (Sirdar)
                        ALADDIN gr. 1943. (Kataf)
                           Alaga Maid gr. 1946. (Anaga)
                              Hestia gr. 1952. (Jedran)
                                 AETHON gr. 1963. (Spindrift)
                 Mecca II gr. 1924. (Khamasin)
               Rosa Rugosa ch. 1907. (Rose of Sharon)
                 SIDI ch. 1917. (Khaled) [*see* Haidee*]
                 REHAL ch. 1923. (Ramim)
                    NEJAL ch. 1928. (Larkspur)
                       Nafud b. 1931. (Hazna)
                          ISLAM b. 1939. (Gulastra)
                             BINIS ch. 1944. (Binni)
                          Habiba ch. 1935. (Bazleyd)
                             Binni ch. 1940. (Gulastra)
                                BINIS ch. 1944. (Islam)
        Dabeh ch. 1892. (Hadeed)
        Mimosa ch. 1893. (Mameluke*)
        Shabaka ch. 1894. (Mameluke*). Exp. USA 1898
            SEGARIO ch. 1902. (Nimr) [*see* Haidee*]
            SINBAD ch. 1908. (Khaled)
      Borak 1895. (Boanerges)
         Ruth Kesia gr. 1903. (Ben Azrek)
            SHAHZADA gr. 1913. (Mootrub*). Exp. Australia 1925
               HELWAR gr. 1923. (Hamida I)
                  Rizada b. 1924. (Riz)
                       Naomi I b. 1938. (Joseph)
               RAZADA gr. 1925. (Ranya I). Exp. Spain 1926
                  NANA SAHIB gr. 1934. (Jalila)
                     Egina b. 1941. (Saboya)
                          JAECERO gr. 1946. (Barquillo)
                             MALVITO b. 1949. (Gandhy)
                  Famula gr. 1942. (Sara)

Kesia cont.
Kesia II*
   Borak
      Ruth Kesia
         SHAHZADA
            RAZADA
               NANA SAHIB
                  Famula
                     MAQUILLO ch. 1949. (Gandhy)
                        UZACUR gr. 1956. (Veranda)
                  Kantista gr. 1947. (Morayma)
                     ALHABAC gr. 1956. (Caireh)
                        Ispahan gr. 1965. (Chavali)
                           AN MALIK gr. 1970. (Galero). Exp. USA 1972
               Morayma ch. 1933. (Reyna)
            IFNI gr. 1937. (Reyna)
               USHAAHE gr. 1942. (Duquesa). Exp. Jordan *c.* 1948
                  BAHAR gr. 1952. (Sabal I)
                     Farida ch. 1969. (Farha)
                     Bint Kerima ch. 1977. (Kerima)
                  Gazella gr. 1958. (Emira I)
                     Asila gr. 1967. (Bahar)
                     Mahbuba gr. 1973. (Bahar)
                  Sabal II gr. 1959. (Lurbi I)
                     Huscima gr. 1965. (Madrid)
                  Samiha gr. 1961. (Farha)
                     BAHAREIN ch. 1967. (Bahar)
                     Sarra gr. 1979. (Huseima)
            PRINCE NEJD gr. 1928. (Nejdmieh*) [*see* Nejdmieh*]
         Tatima gr. 1929. (Sa'id)
            Tarney gr. 1952. (Zarney)
               Argency gr. 1965. (Argent)
       SIRDAR gr. 1930. (Nejdmieh*) [*see* Nejdmieh*]
   NURI PASHA gr. 1920. (Nureddin II). Exp. USA 1924
   Almas gr. 1924. (Amida)
      ALUF gr. 1932. (Barkis)
      Rufeiya I b. 1938. (Ranya II)
         Rosheiya B. 1942. (Rosh)
            Roshnara ch. 1949. (Hassan II)
               Russallka ch. 1968. (Gold Rex)
      Zarifet gr. 1938. (Roglemar Zarad)
         ZETHAN gr. 1946. (Rithan)
   Rafeena gr. 1940. (Ranya II)

THE ARAB HORSE

Kesia cont.
    Kesia II
        Borak
            Ruth Kesia
                NURI PASHA
                    Almas
                      ALUF
                          Rafeena
                              RIKHAM gr. 1945. (Rissam). Exp. Australia *in utero* 1945
                                  RALVON PILGRIM ch. 1969. (Trix Silver)
                            Rexeena gr. 1948. (Irex)
                                Sirikit ch. 1961. (Alexus)
                                    LUDREX ch. 1965. (Ludo)
                                        DONAX ch. 1971. (Dargemet)
                        IRIDOS gr. 1951. (Irex)
                          Nimet gr. 1967. (Indian Snowflake)
                          KAMI ch. 1957. (Kabara)
                          COUNT RAPELLO ch. 1954. (Count D'Orsaz)
                SHIHAB ch. 1935. (Algol)
            KEMAH gr. 1925. (Nanda)
                ZEM ZEM b. 1928. (Mirza) [*see* Haidee*]
                    KARNAK gr. 1937. (Mershid)
            Kaukab. (Hira)
            KASIM ch. 1937. (Simawa)
            Kerak gr. 1937. (Hira)
                Mistana gr. 1955. (Rithan)
                    COMANCHE ch. 1963. (Komsul)
        KAIBAB gr. 1929. (Bazran)
            KHYBER ch. 1934. (Fath)
        KHALIL gr. 1927. (Ophir)
        KHALID ch. 1934. (Simawa)
        MOOTRUB II b. 1909. (Mootrub*)
        Krim gr. 1922. (Nureddin II)
        Yetima gr. 1944. (Shibab)
            Yet Again gr. 1962. (K of K)
                Pomona ch. 1968. (Iridos)
                Yirene gr. 1969. (Iridos)
            Kasimet b. 1950. (Azym)
                KASIMDAR b. 1954. (Tummundar)
                K of K b. 1957. (Kalfa)

ISHTAR

Ishtar* gr. 1871. Imp. *c.* 1876
    IMAM b. 1886. (El Emir*)
        IMAMZADA b. 1891. (Kesia II*). Exp. USA 1905
        Yasimeen br. 1896. (Jedrania*)
        Hamada b. 1896. (Hagar*)
        El Lahr b. 1899. (Dinarzade). Exp. Australia 1901 [*see* Kesia*]
        Rosa Rugosa ch. 1907. (Rose of Sharon) [*see* Kesia*]
    JEZAIL b. 1893. (Jedrania*)
        HAURAN b. 1897. (Hagar*). Exp. USA 1910 [*see* Jedrania*]

Ishtar cont.
    BOANERGES. 1889. (El Emir*)
        Borak 1895. (Kesia II*)
            Ruth Kesia gr. 1903. (Ben Azrek)
                MOOTRUB II b. 1909. (Mootrub*)
                SHAHZADA gr. 1913. (Mootrub*). Exp. Australia 1925
                    HELWAR gr. 1923. (Hamida I)
                    SHELOOK ch. 1922. (Queen Shakra). Exp. Natal [*see* Shakra*]
                    Nezza ch. 1924. (Nejma) [*see* Nejma*]
                    RAZADA gr. 1925. (Ranya I). Exp. Spain 1926 [*see* Kesia*]
                    PRINCE NEJD gr. 1928. (Nejdmieh*) [*see* Nejdmieh*]
                    Tatima gr. 1929. (Sa'id) [*see* Kesia*]
                    SIRDAR gr. 1930. (Nejdmieh*) [*see* Nejdmieh*]
                NURI PASHA gr. 1920. (Nureddin II). Exp. USA 1924 [*see* Kesia*]
            Krim gr. 1922. (Nureddin II) [*see* Kesia*]

SHAKRA

Shakra* ch. 1888. Imp. 1896
    Queen Shakra ch. 1911. (Mootrub*)
        Maid of the Moot gr. 1921. (Shahzada). Exp. Holland 1932
            Bakoorah ch. 1934. (Karusen)
            RAGHIBAH b. 1936. (Karusen)
        SHELOOK ch. 1922. (Shahzada). Exp. Natal 1927
            Shelfa gr. 1929. (Almas)
            Kassida ch. 1930. (Khadijah Kesia)
                HASSAN I b. 1935. (Nazar)
                JOTHAM ch. 1937. (Jaleel)
                AUDA b. 1940. (Hilal)
                SAYYID b. 1941. (Hilal)

LADYBIRD

Ladybird* Imp. 1896
    Robirda I b. 1907. (Rohan*)
        MUSKRO b. 1915. (Musket*)
            Shemma b. 1923. (Simrieh) [*see* Sobha*]
        Tava b. 1918. (Muskro)
    Robirda II bl. 1910. (Rohan*)
        Vaga b.1918 (Muskro)
    Marladi gr. 1907. (Marzouk*)
        MUSKMAR br. 1915. (Musket*)

Mejamieh and Libnani

Mejamieh* b. 1912. Imp. 1921. Died 1927
    Libnani* b. 1919. Imp. 1921 and exp. Spain 1926
        Awalani b. 1923. (Rasim). Exp. Spain 1926
            Fedora b. 1930. (Razada)
            DJEZZAR ch. 1923. (Razada)
        MEJDIL gr. 1921. (Skowronek)
        AJLUN b. 1923. (Rasim). Exp. Spain 1926
        Zahle gr. 1926. (Crosbie*)
            Shthora ch. 1931. (Outlaw*)
            Jenin gr. 1935. (Kataf)
            ZERKA gr. 1936. (Ruskov). Exp. Tanganyika 1936
            Bekaa gr. 1947. (Raftan)

Nejdmieh

Nejdmieh* gr. 1914. Imp. *c.* 1923 and exp. Australia 1925
    Khadijah Kesia gr. 1924. (Nuri Pasha). Exp. Holland 1935
        Kassida ch. 1930. (Shelook) [*see* Shakra*]
    Nejd Sherifa. 1925. (Nuri Sherif). Exp. *in utero* Australia 1925
        SHAH SHERIFA b. 1930. (Shahzada)
        RUKUBAN II b. 1945. (Kataf)
        Rifa ch. 1937. (Sirdar)
            Falka ch. 1942. (Kataf)
                Riffalka ch. 1950. (Riffal)
    BEDOUIN ch. 1926. (Shahzada)
    PRINCE NEJD gr. 1928. (Shahzada)
        Hilwa gr. 1934. (Sa'id)
        HUKUM gr. 1934. (Akabah II)
        Sayif ch/gr. 1935. (Salama)
        Warda ch/gr. 1935. (Gadara)
        JEDRAN gr. 1935. (Salama)
            HERMES gr. 1951. (Buraida)
            Hestia gr. 1952. (Alaga Maid)
                AETHON gr. 1963. (Spindrift)
        ZADARAN gr. 1936. (Yenbo)
            Atlanta ch. 1951. (Salama)
                ATILLA ch. 1959. (Count Manilla)
            Lady Blunt b. 1958. (Scherzade)
            Tuema gr. 1956. (Medina)
    Salome I ch. 1929. (Shahzada)
    SIRDAR gr. 1930. (Shahzada)
        Sir Aatika gr. 1938. (Kufara)
            ALADDIN gr. 1943. (Kataf)
            Iona gr. 1955. (Sala)
                DELOS gr. 1961. (Spindrift)

Nejdmieh cont.
    SIRDAR
        Sir Antika
            JUNO gr. 1950. (Sala)
        DARINTH gr. 1936. (Judith)
            Daralga gr. 1950. (Siralga)
                ZARIFE ch. 1960. (Sala)
            Darani gr. 1950. (Caswa)
            Darella ch. 1957. (Siralga)
                ABDULLAH ch. 1963. (Spindrift)
        Grace Kesia ch. 1934. (Miriam I)
        THE SHAH gr. 1935. (Judith)
        Makeda ch. 1936. (Miriam I)
        Anaga gr. 1936. (Judith)
            Alaga Maid gr. 1946. (Aladdin)
                Hestia gr. 1952. (Jedran)
                    AETHON gr. 1963. (Spindrift)
            Alaga Girl gr. 1948. (Aladdin)
                Demeter ch. 1955. (Sala)
                BABYLON ch. 1958. (Razaz)
        Caswa ch. 1937. (Mecca II)
            Kassie cg. 1944. (Kataf)
        Cazada ch. 1938. (Mecca II)
            ARGUS gr. 1959. (Sala)
        Buraida gr. 1941. (Salome)

Nejma

Nejma* ch. 1914. Imp. *c.* 1923
    Nezza ch. 1924. (Shahzada)
        NEBUCHADNEZZAR b. 1928. (Nuri Sherif)
        NAZAR b. 1930. (Nuri Sherif). Exp. Australia 1937
        HASSAN I b. 1935. (Kassida I)
        Alika b/gr. 1937. (Almas)
            Almanack br. 1946. (Manak*)
    Najadie ch. 1925. (Shahzada). Exp. Holland 1935

Dafina

Dafina* gr. 1921. Imp. 1927
    Ryama gr. 1931. (Nureddin II). Exp. Russia 1936
        Neamis gr. 1938. (Naseem)
            Orientacia gr. 1943. (Ofir)
                Knopka ch. 1950. (Korej)
                    Kapel ch. 1959. (Pomeranets)

Dafina cont.

 Dafinetta gr. 1935. (Naziri)
  Drusilla gr. 1939. (Rix)
   Russilla gr. 1946. (Rangoon)
    Riffilla gr. 1949. (Riffayal)
     Blue Fantasy gr. 1963. (Blue Domino)
      INDRANI ch. 1967. (Indriss)
      Istashra gr. 1968. (Indriss)
    Nefudi b. 1952. (Risheel)
   Doonyah gr. 1941. (Raftan)
    Dragonfly gr. 1949. (Saladin II)
    DARZEE gr. 1952. (Saladin II)
    Dorelia gr. 1954. (Saladin II)
    Darthula gr. 1955. (Saladin II)
     Shazla gr. 1962. (Shazda)
      Ziba gr. 1980. (Dancing Magic). Exp. Jordan 1983
    Daifa ch. 1964. (Mikeno)
     Datura gr. 1969. (Burkan). Exp. Sweden 1974
   Dura b. 1942. (Raftan)
    Durr el Zaman b. 1961. (Rimini)
     DEEPAK b. 1977. (Banat). Exp. Jordan 1984
   Damask Rose b. 1943. (Saladin II)
    Dawn ch. 1950. (Naseel)
   Doniazad gr. 1944. (Saladin II)
    Little Sheba of Yeomans ch. 1953. (Robagol)
   Darfil gr. 1946. (Saladin II)
    Damaris ch. 1961. (Kami)
     Delphine gr. 1966. (Rimini)
      Devyani gr. 1977. (Barkos)
   Dryad gr. 1949. (Saladin II)
   Daphne I gr. 1950. (Saladin II)
   Daffodil gr. 1952. (Saladin II)
  REYNALTON gr. 1937. (Algol)
  HAZZAL gr. 1938. (Algol)
   Sherezada gr. 1942. (Fand)
    SHAZDA gr. 1949. (Shariff)
    Zaduban gr. 1947. (Rukuban I)
  Yarzeena gr. 1940. (Yassb)
   FLAME of REYNALL ch. 1946. (The Amir Al Omrah)
   Yaronda b. 1950. (Flame of Reynall)
  YASSIF gr. 1941. (Yassb)
  Fayella gr. 1942. (Fayal)
   Fiona b. 1948. (Aaron). Exp. USA 1960
    Zilfe b. 1953. (Naidarus)
     Furzey Amanda b. 1956. (Naidarus)
  Aafina gr. 1943. (Aaron). Exp. Australia
  Daronda gr. 1945. (Aaron)

NOURA AND MUHA

Noura* b. 1916. Imp. 1928 and exp. USA
 Muha* b. 1928. (A Seglawi Jedran). Imp. *in utero* 1928 and exp. USA
  Rihani b. 1933. (Saoud*)
   Joharah b. 1939. (Mirage*)
    My Bonnie Nylon ch. 1946. (Raffles)
     TSALI ch. 1953. (Ibn Hanad)
      TSATYR b. 1957. (Imamura)
       Hillcrests Bint Tsatyr b. 1961. (Drissanne)
        IVANHOE TSATAN b. 1968. (Czortan)
     AMBASSADOR b. 1959. (Imafara)
     Kamocli ch. 1964. (Kamoctin)
      Kalima gr. 1968. (Ansata Ibn Halima)
     KAMIM b. 1969. (Ansata Ibn Halima)
     LEWISFIELD AMIGO ch. 1964. (Griffin)
    Sunny Acres Tammie ch. 1957. (Ibn Hanad)
    Melody ch. 1951. (Tuk Ankh Amen)
    MELNAD ch. 1955. (Ibn Hanad)
   Bambina b. 1942. (Raffles)
    BAMBY ch. 1947. (Raffles)
    Wadeya b. 1948. (Raffles)
    Gebina b. 1951. (Fa el Gemar)
     GAGE b. 1958. (Image)
   Raffani b. 1944. (Raffles)
    RAMIK ROGUE gr. 1956. (Ibn Rogue)
   Sel Hani b. 1948. (Selmage)
    Bel Lindah gr. 1958. (Jamil el Hirzez)
     HALIN gr. 1965. (Ansata Ibn Halima)
  DEBIR ch. 1934. (Mahomet)
  Miralai ch. 1935. (Asil)

JAMILA

Jamila* b. 1927. Imp. *c.* 1935
 AIN SAHIB AL MUNTAFIQ ch. 1936. (Ruskov)
 Guliran ch. 1938. (Algol)
  Zobeide ch. 1943. (Hilal)
   Jamila II gr. 1947. (Rukuban)
   JADY ch. 1948. (Rifari)
   Zahrawiyah ch. 1949. (Shibab)
   Maid Marian ch. 1951. (Rithan)
  Nouronnihar ch. 1945. (Hilal)
   Suleena ch. 1951. (Irex). Exp. S. Africa
    Rasheeda ch. 1969. (Zingari)

Jamila cont.
    Guliran
        Nouronnihar
            Ramara ch. 1952. (Irex)
        Zarifah b. 1946. (Ash Kar)
        ROBIN ADAIR of KINGSHOLME 'AL BURAK' ch. 1948. (Rithan)
        ROBIN HOOD of KINGSHOLME ch. 1951. (Rithan)
        Gail of Kingsholme ch. 1955. (Robin Adair of Kingsholme)
            HURRICANE ch. 1968. (Akram)
            SHARZAN ch. 1969. (Akram)
            OPHAAL ch. 1971. (Risslan)
    Safie ch. 1943. (Hilal)
    Zohorab Bostan b. 1944. (Hilal)
        ROBAGOL b. 1949. (Algol)
    Falha el Muntafiq ch. 1945. (Shariff)
        Magic Moments b. 1956. (Ash-Kar)
            Shimagic ch. 1966. (Shihab Kid)
                KING SHIHAB ch. 1967. (Shihab Kid). Exp. Denmark 1967
        Golden Dream ch. 1961. (Robin Adair of Kingsholme)
            ABADAN gr. 1971. (Rexana)
    AIN SAHIB B. 1946. (Shariff)

WARDA AL BADIA

Warda Al Badia* ch. 1924. Imp. *c.* 1937
    Shem el Nassim ch. 1941. (Rech Al Badia*)
    Nemisia ch. 1946. (Nigm Essubh)
        Falha ch. 1953. [Formerly 'Primula'] (Rech Al Badia*)
            Bluehayes Tezra ch. 1970. (Magnet)
                NIALL ch. 1978. (Orion)
                Blue Sierra gr. 1979. (Abba Blue)
                Starlight Blue Dancer gr. 1980. (Abba Blue)
                Kezzia ch. 1981. (Brandreth)
            Zarissa ch. 1977. (Taqah)

TURFA

Turfa* gr. 1933. Imp. 1937 and exp. USA 1941
    IBN HILAL ch. 1942. (Hilal). Exp. *in utero* USA 1941
    Turfada ch. 1943. (Fadl)
    Bint Turfa b. 1944. (Fadl)
    IBN FADL gr. 1946. (Fadl)
        Habbana gr. 1954. (Bint Habba)
            Sharbana b. 1964. (Negem)
        Fadaa gr. 1962. (Maedae)
    Turfara b. 1948. (Fadl)
        Bint Turfara gr. 1959. (Sirecho)

Turfa cont.
    Turfara
        Bint Turfara
            Bint Bint Turfara 1967. (Ibn Fadl)
            Fara Fadl ch. 1969. (Ibn Fadl)
        Al Asmar ch. 1960. (Ibn Fadl)
        IBN SIRECHO ch. 1961. (Sirecho)
    FA TURF gr. 1952. (Fadl)
        FA RAAD gr. 1961. (Raada)
        Raafada gr. 1962. (Raada)
    TARFF gr. 1954. (Fadl)

MAHAWILIYAH

Mahawiliyah* gr. 1935. Imp. *c.* 1939
    JABBAR b. 1941. (Nuri Sherif)
    Sharaya gr. 1944. (Sharaf)
        Tar Asman gr. 1948. (Rakan)
            Samia gr. 1955. (Rustem Bey)
                Samantha gr. 1964. (Manto)
                SHASAR b. 1966. (Grojec)
        Sharon br. 1949. (Aaron)
        Rexaya gr. 1952. (Irex)
            Rexbaya b. 1961. (Ibn Irex)
                Vanessa b. 1965. (Magic Fire)
                Abigail ch. 1968. (Halma)
                Estrella ch. 1969. (Halma)
                    AURELIAN ch. 1981. (Ben Rabba)
                Rexalla b. 1966. (Halma)
    Rixiliyah gr. 1946. (Shimrix)
        Rexan Shemara b. 1960. (Zethan)
        El Kardomah gr. 1961. (Zethan)
        Myrilla b. 1962. (Myrex)
            Starlight Shadow b. 1970. (Bey Shadow)
                Yakouta ch. 1976. (Shades of Silver)
        Zethari gr. 1965. (Zethan)
    Marah gr. 1949. (Rakan)
    Bangle b. 1950. (Sahban)

TAKRITIYAH

Takritiyah* ch. 1935. Imp. *c.* 1939
    Takrithan ch. 1940. (Rithan)
    HAJI I ch. 1944. (Jaleel)
        Fathia ch. 1950. (Dewi). Exp. S. Africa
    Sayyeda b. 1945. (Rizaab)
        Sayrayal ch. 1950. (Rayal)

THE ARAB HORSE

Takritiyah cont.
    TAKAMIR ch. 1946. (The Amir al Omrah)
    Court Maiden ch. 1948. (Rithan)
    Tarriff ch. 1949. (Riffayal)
        Fabiola ch. 1964. (Mikardo)
            Dancing Princess ch. 1967. (Radfan)
        Gaytariff ch. 1954. (Algayam)
        TARRA ch. 1956. (Rizaab)
        Myrtle b. 1966. (My Man)
            Regal Lady b. 1971. (Zehros)
                Zona bl. 1979. (Luxor). Exp. Jordan 1984
    RIFFYAH gr. 1950. (Riffayal)
    TAKOMEGA ch. 1952. (Xayal)
    Rizza gr. 1955. (Rizaab). Exp. Australia
        Hazia gr. 1965. (Count Hamish)
            Velvet Haze ch. 1973. (Crystal King)
            Shakana gr. 1979. (El Shaklan)
            DON CARLOS gr. 1974. (Crystal King). Exp. Australia 1980
        Geneva gr. 1969. (General D'Orsaz)

NUHRA

Nuhra* b. 1936. Imp. 1939
    Nurmahal b. 1943. (Manak*)
        Hedba b. 1950. (Rheoboam)
            Helga b. 1955. (Manasseh)
        Buseyna ch. 1952. (Rheoboam)
        Assarkha b. 1956. (Blue Domino)
    Taj Mahal b. 1945. (Manak*)
    Nurmana ch. 1946. (Manak*)
        Zehraa ch. 1951. (Irex)
            Razehra ch. 1955. (Rashid)
                Kazra ch. 1961. (Mikeno)
                      Muzri cg. 1967. (Indriss)
                          Muneera ch. 1976. (Fakhr el Kheil)
                              MALEIK EL KHEIL gr. 1979. (El Shaklan)
                        Muzehra ch. 1980. (Riaz)
                    Kazminda ch. 1970. (Indriss)
                      Kalilah ch. 1978. (St Simon)
                      Khamala ch. 1979. (El Shaklan)
                Kazamah gr. 1974. (Indian Silver)
                Kazaba gr. 1979. (Saab)
                Kazra el Saghira gr. 1977. (Shakhs)
                PERSIMMON b. 1978. (St Simon)
            Alzehra ch. 1957. (Count D'Orsaz)
                MEHZEER ch. 1979. (Mehriz)

Nuhra cont.
    Nurmana
        Zehraa
            ZEHROS gr. 1964. (Argos)
                Autumn Copper Beech ch. 1971. (Autumn Velvet)
            Zaian ch. 1973. (Al Malik)
                Riazana ch. 1984. (Riaz)
    Rediaa b. 1948. (Rheoboam)
        Khamisa ch. 1954. (Champurrado)
            Khamilla ch. 1966. (General Grant)
                MYROS ch. 1972. (Song of India)
    Nuhajjela ch. 1951. (Irex)
        Rajjela ch. 1957. (Grand Royal)
            RAJMEK ch. 1961. (Mikeno)
            DARJEEL ch. 1962. (Dargee)
                RIAZ ch. 1974. (Razehra)
    Rabiha ch. 1952. (Rheoboam)
        Orilla ch. 1960. (Oran)
            DORIAN ch. 1971. (Darjeel)
        Sheeba gr. 1961. (Silver Vanity)
        RAGOS gr. 1964. (Argos)
        RABIDAN ch. 1970. (Darjeel)
        Meera ch. 1975. (Rajmek)
    Alexa ch. 1953. (Manasseh)
        Calexa ch. 1959. (Champurrado)
            Arcadia ch. 1965. (Argos)
                DADIA ch. 1970. (Darjeel)

SHAMMAH

Shammah* gr. 1950. Imp. *c.* 1955
    Fara gr. 1966. (Azan)
    EUPHRATES gr. 1968. (Marino Marini)
    Shahiya gr. 1969. (Marino Marini)
        Blue Sabha ch. 1975. (Blue Ludo)
        Shima gr. 1977. (Fakhr el Kheil)
        Sahfiya ch. 1979. (El Shaklan)
        Nafisa el Shaakirah ch. 1982. (Donax)
    Shanina gr. 1971. (Rustem Pasha)
        Shabana ch. 1976. (Banat)
        SHEBOOTH ch. 1977. (Blue Ludo)
        SHISHAK gr. 1978. (Blue Ludo)
        La Sombra gr. 1979. (Procyon)
        Sirena gr. 1980. (Procyon)
        Blue Sapphire gr. 1982. (Blue Ludo)

Nawagiyat al Furat 'Desert Song'

Nawagiyat al Furat* gr. 1944. Imp. *c.* 1958
    Cressida roan. 1961. (Shifari)
    Electra gr. 1964. (Tummundar)
        Arabella Minette gr. 1968. (Scindian Magic)
            Minifette Silvan gr. 1972. (Hanif)
                SYLVAN SHADOW gr. 1982. (Cranleigh Red Shadow)
        Estella Arabella gr. 1969. (Scindian Magic)
            Elmwood Geinine ch. 1972. (Grenadier). Exp. Cyprus 1979
        PRINCE CASPIAN gr. 1970. (Sha'ir)

Thrayat Hamid

Thrayat Hamid* b. 1953. Imp. *c.* 1958
    Rossana b. 1968. (Samson). Exp. Australia 1978
        AKRAN b. 1974. (Wasel Gerwazy)
        LUBEK gr. 1975. (Wasel Gerwazy)
        Hakima gr. 1976. (Farif)
        Bint Rossana gr. 1977. (Kheir Allah)
        CARLO ch. 1978. (Kheiralla). Exp. Australia 1978
    Deraiya b. 1970. (Samson)
        EMIR RAPERIO b. 1975. (Count Raperio)
        Maeve b. 1980. (Shamyl*)

El Yamana and Princess Muna

El Yamana* 1953. Imp. 1958
    Princess Muna* gr. 1958. (Samih). Imp. *in utero* 1958
        ACHMED gr. 1964. (Naseel)
        MUNTASSER gr. 1966. (Zeus II)
        GENJO ch. 1970. (Genji)

Shams

Shams* gr. 1955. Imp. 1960
    SHAMYL* gr. 1961. (Kaid). Imp. *in utero*
        Cuan Mylindra b. 1967. (Fayalindra)
        Maeve b. 1980. (Deraiya)
    Shamanto ch. 1964. (Manto)
        Rajanto ch. 1970. (Rajmek)
    SHAMDAR gr. 1968. (Darjeel)
    SHEELAR ch. 1970. (Darjeel)
    ABU SHAMMEK gr. 1971. (Rajmek)
    Hermosura gr. 1973. (Darjeel)

OTHER STALLIONS

Padischah

PADISCHAH* gr. 1826. Imp. *c.* 1830 and exp. Germany 1838
    Czebessie V 1840. (Czebessie IV)
        Czebessie VI (Zarif DB)
            Hedba. 1886. (Hedban II)
            Hamdany V 1853. (Amurath 1829)
                Hamdany VI gr. 1859. (Zarif DB)
                    SEGLAVI gr. 1864. (Bournu)
                      Sabine gr. 1872. (Kereja VI)
                        Dueba gr. 1879. (Djerid DB)
                          DYNAMIT gr. 1902. (Souakim)
                  Selma V gr. 1871. (Kereja VI)
                    Koheil III gr. 1876. (Mehemed Ali)
                      AMURATH gr. 1881. (Tajar 1873)
                        Amurath gr. 1901. (Malta)
                          Koalicja gr. 1918. (Koheilan IV)
                            ENWER BEY gr. 1923. (Abu Mlech)
                              Taraszcza gr. 1937. (Gazella II)
                              TRYPOLIS gr. 1937. (Kahira)
                                Carmen II gr. 1942. (Wilga)
                                  COMET gr. 1953. (Abu Afas)
                                    FAHER gr. 1953. (Ferha)
                                      EL AZRAK br. 1960. (Ellora)
                                        BANAT b. 1967. (Bandola).
                                              Imp. UK
                                  Biruta gr. 1955. (Bika). Imp. UK
                                    BURKAN gr. 1964. (Saladin II)
                                Nawarra gr. 1957. (Najada). Imp. UK
                                Trypolitanka b. 1958. (Eleonora). Imp. UK
                                Canaria b. 1942. (Saga)
                                    Cantata b. 1963. (Litaur)
                            HALEF b. 1937. (Kasztelanka)
                            HALADIN. 1952. (Jadine)
                    MIECZNIK gr. 1931. (Fetysz)
                      Panika gr. 1941. (Imatra)
                        Bika gr. 1948. (Wielki Szlem)
                          Biruta gr. 1955. (Trypolis). Imp. UK
                    MARABUT ch. 1942. (Maja)

Padischah cont.

Czebessie V
  Hamdany V
    Hamdany VI
      SEGLAVI
        Selma V
          Koheil III
            AMURATH
              Amurath
                Koalicja
                  MIECZNIK
                    MARABUT
                        Gastronomia b. 1946. (Ofirka)
                          GROJEC b. 1960. (Comet). Imp. UK
                          Gomora gr. 1959. (Comet)
                            GOKART gr. 1975. (Partner)
                    DOKTRYNER gr. 1950. (Blaga)
                        GERWAZY gr. 1955. (Gwara). Imp. UK
                        Barcelona gr. 1955. (Brussa). Imp. UK
                  AQUINOR gr. 1951. (Amneris)
                      EXCELSJOR gr. 1963. (Eleonora)
                      TRYPTYK gr. 1965. (Tryncza)
                      ELKIN gr. 1966. (Ellenai)
                      Elkana gr. 1969. (Estebna)
                      PARTNER gr. 1970. (Parma)
                Lafirynda gr. 1954. (Lala). Imp. UK
            Niezgoda gr. 1932. (Fetysz)
      AMURATH II b. 1907. (Fatme DB)
        AMURATH SAHIB gr. 1932. (Sahiba)
          Lala gr. 1938. (Elsissa)
            Lafirynda gr. 1954. (Miecznik). Imp. UK
              Lalage gr. 1963. (Gerwazy)
                ALADDIN b. 1979. (Nureddin)
          Ela gr. 1951. (Miecznik)
            ESPARTERO gr. 1960. (Nabor)
        Balalajka gr. 1941. (Iwonka III)
          Arfa b. 1947. (Witraz)
            ARGOS gr. 1957. (Nabor). Imp. UK
          Bandola gr. 1948. (Witraz)
            BANDOS gr. 1964. (Negativ)
          BASK b. 1956. (Witraz)
      Arwila gr. 1947. (Wilga)
        ARAX b. 1952. (Angora)

Padischah cont.

    Czebessie V
        Hamdany V
            Hamdany VI
                SEGLAVI
                    Selma V
                      Koheil III
                          AMURATH
                              AMURATH II
                                  AMURATH SAHIB
                                      ARAX
                                          Magnolia b. 1960. (Mammona)
                                          Karta b. 1962. (Kapella)
                                          Nashmeshnik b. 1963. (Neposeda)
                                            NABEG b. 1966. (Nomenklatura)
                                              MENES b. 1977. (Metropolia)
                                                  BALATON ch. 1982. (Panagia)
                                GWARNY gr. 1953. (Gwara)
        Sabal gr. 1872. (Hamma I)
            Selma gr. 1883. (Djerid DB)
                SELIM gr. 1896. (Amurath 1881)
                    NANA SAHIB I gr. 1907. (Smyrna DB)
                      Sahiba gr. 1924. (Donka)
                          AMURATH SAHIB gr. 1932. (Amurath II)
                            Amneris gr. 1940. (Elsissa)
                                AQUINOR gr. 1951. (Miecznik)
                                ARAMUS gr. 1962. (Nabor)
                          Darda gr. 1950. (Brda)
                          Gwadiana gr. 1952. (Gwarna)
                          Estokada gr. 1952. (Saga)
            Saida gr. 1884. (Djerid DB)
                Sylphide I gr. 1892. (Amurath 1881)
                    Soldateska gr. 1911. (Souakim DB)
                      Jatta gr. 1933. (Jasir)
                          Haita gr. 1952. (Halef)
                          Hathor gr. 1955. (Halef)
                          Hajar gr. 1956. (Halef)
                          Sahmet gr. 1957. (Hadban Enzahi)
            Saoud. 1885. (Djerid DB)
                Savona gr. 1896. (Amurath 1881)
                    Sardine gr. 1908. (Souakim DB)
                      Carmen b. 1915. (Dardziling)
                          Caesarea b. 1927. (Koheilan IV)

Padischah cont.

    Czebessie V
        Hamdany V
            Hamdany VI
                SEGLAVI
                    Sabal
                        Saoud
                            Savona
                                Sardine
                                    Carmen
                                      Caesarea
                                          Jena gr. 1944. (Jasir)
                                              Haifa br. 1952. (Halef)
                            Doris gr. 1916. (Dardziling)
                              Dinarsad gr. 1928. (Dynamit)
                                Jadine gr. 1947. (Jasir)
                                  HALADIN gr. 1952. (Halef)
                                    Masarrah gr. 1957. (Moheba)
                                      Mamsahi gr. 1964. (Ghazal)
                                        MELCHIOR gr. 1974.
                                              (Mameluke).Imp UK
                Winarsad b. 1949. (Wind)

INDJANIN

INDJANIN* gr. Imp. *c.* 1850 and exp. Poland 1855
    JARZMO Sold to the Sultan of Turkey
    INAK Sold to the Sultan of Turkey
    Joasia — (Ismena)
        Hamleta — (Hami)
            HAMDANI II ch. 1896. (Hamdani I)
    JUNAK
        INKAS (Maska) Sold to the Sultan of Turkey
        Irena (Najada)
            Arabella gr. 1898. (Vasco de Gama)
        C-sse Julie
            VASCO DE GAMA gr. 1885. (Woltyzer)
                WANDYK gr. 1898. (Hela). Exp. Spain 1908
                    Varsovia ch. 1913. (Bint)
                        ECO gr. 1919. (Scanderich DB)
                        Divina gr. 1918. (Navin)
                          ILUSTRE gr. 1923. (Scanderich DB)
                            CONGO gr. 1941. (Triana)

THE ARAB HORSE

Indjanin cont.
    JUNAK
        INKAS
            C-sse Julie
                VASCO DE GAMA
                    WANDYK
                        Divina
                            ILUSTRE
                                CONGO
                                    TABAL gr. 1952. (Hilandera)
                                        Estopa gr. 1965. (Uyaima). Exp. Germany 1971
                                            EL SHAKLAN gr. 1975. (Shaker el Masri).
                                    JACIO gr. 1968. (Teorica)
                                Transjordania gr. 1952. (Nubia II)
                                ZANCUDO ch. 1958. (Yaima)
                                    GALERO gr. 1965. (Zalema)
                        SAAMEH 'Jabao' b. 1941. (Uganda). Exp. Jordan 1948/9
                          Chocolata ch. 1955. (Advania)
                            Samha gr. 1967. (Reemer)
                  Rabina ch. 1930. (Baghdad DB)
                      BARQUILLO gr. 1938. (Eco)
                          JAECERO gr. 1946. (Egina)
                          ORIVE gr. 1951. (Galatife)
                          Teorica gr. 1955. (Galatife)
                          Uyaima ch. 1956. (Imelina)
                              Estopa gr. 1965. (Tabal). Exp. Germany 1971
              Facina gr. 1920. (Motasen)
                Triana gr. 1932. (Ursus)
                    CONGO gr. 1941. (Ilustre)
                      Zalema gr. 1958. (Galatife)
                      Alhama III gr. 1959. (Galatife)
        VAMPIRE (Elfa)
            Flora ch. 1916. (Jurta)
                TUAREG ch. 1931. (Rasim)
                      DERAZNE gr. 1938. (Mattaria). Exp. *in utero* USA 1937

SAJDEN

SAJDEN* chestnut imp. *c* 1850. Exp. Poland 1850
    Jadwiga – (Miranda)
        Kastylya – (Kodeks)
    SZAMIL
        Szansa – (Tajemnica)
            Euterpe – (Ernani)
                Hela b. – (Hamdani I)
                    WANDYK gr. 1898. (Vasco de Gama). Exp. Spain 1908 [*see* Indjanin*]
        Kandija
            Nawarra – (Normi DB)
                Tajemnica – (Tengi)
                    Szansa – (Szamil)
        SOLFERINO – (Kaskada)

Sajden cont.
    SZAMIL
        SOLFERINO
            Semiramida – (Purytanka)
                EL TALI gr. 1880. (El Nissr al Abiad DB)
        Teofanja – (Samarytanka)
        Alpaka – (Allach)
            Halka – (Hussar*)

NIZAM

NIZAM* (Indjanin II) grey. Imp. *c*. 1855. Exp. Poland 1859
    NAIB
        Negressa
            HAMDANI I ch. 1882. (Hussar*)
                Hagar gr. 1894. (Elzusia)
                    URSUS b. 1908. (Dahman Umir DB). Exp. Spain 1912
            HAMDANI II ch. 1896. (Hamleta)
            Hela b. – (Euterpe)
                WANDYK gr. 1898. (Vasco de Gama). Exp. Spain 1908
    Najada – *c*. 1861. (Hillaryta)
        Irena gr. 1887. (Inkas)
    Nadsada – (Miranda)
        Tamiza – (Taib DB)
            Halina – (Hamat)

MAHMOUD MIRZA

MAHMOUD MIRZA* dark bay 1851. Seglawi Jedran. Imp. *c*. 1860. Exp. Hungary 1866
    MEHEMED-ALI ch. 1868. (104 Koreishan)
        Koheil III gr. 1876. (Selma V)
            AMURATH gr. 1881. (Tajar 1873)
                35 AMURATH II b. 1907. (186 Fatme DB)
                    AMURATH SAHIB gr. 1932. (Sahiba)
                        25 Amurath-Sahib 2 gr. 1952. (221 Kuhailan-Zaid 4)
                            3 Siglavi-Bagdady VI-6 gr. 1967. (Siglavy-Bagdady VI)
                                204 Ghalion ch. 1976. (Ghalion)
                                    216 Ibn Galal 1-8 ch. 1980. (Ibn Galal I)
                Sylphide I gr. 1892. (Saida)
                Soldateska gr. 1911. (Souakim DB)
                Jatta gr. 1933. (Jasir)
            Savona gr. 1895. (Saoud)
                Sardine gr. 1908. (Souakim DB)
                    Carmen b. 1915. (Dardziling)
                        Caesarea b. 1927. (Koheilan IV)
                            Jacaranda gr. 1933. (Jasir)
                    Doris gr. 1915 (Dardziling)
                      Dinarsad gr. 1928. (Dynamit)
                          JASON gr. 1933. (Jasir)
                            Jadine gr. 1947. (Jasir)

Mahmoud Mirza cont.
MEHEMED-ALI
    Koheil III)
        AMURATH
            Amourette gr. 1887. (Dueba)
                Amadine gr. 1895. (Padischah II)
                    DOLMATSCHER 'Arab' gr. 1901. (Doge). Imp. UK c.1918
JUSSUF br. 1869. (113 Aghil-Aga)
    37 Jussuf gr. 1889. (60 Adjuze DB)
        MERSUCH I gr. 1904. (Mersuch DB)
    91 Jussuf gr. 1874. (61 El-Delemi)
        KOHEILAN II gr. 1887. (Koheilan-Adjuze DB)
        KOHEILAN IV gr. 1904. (124 O'Bajan)

YATAGAN

YATAGAN* ch. 1870. Imp. 1874
    Naomi ch. 1877. (Haidee*). Exp. USA 1888 [see Haidee*]

HUSSAR

HUSSAR* ch. Imp. c. 1875 and exp. Poland 1878
    HAMDANI I ch. 1882 (Negressa)
        Hela b. (Euterpe/Szansa)
            WANDYK gr. 1898. (Vasco di Gama). Exp. Spain 1908 [see Indjanin*]
        HERON ch. 1896. (Hawanna)
            Hami – 1902. (Harda)
        HAMDANI II ch. 1896. (Hamleta)
            HUSSAR II ch. 1907. (Halina)
        Hela b. 1905. (Altonia)
        Halka ch. 1893. (Helwetka)
        Hagar ch. 1894. (Elzusia)
            URSUS b. 1908. (Dahman Amir DB). Exp. Spain 1912
                Meca ch. 1923. (Siria)
                    Barakat gr. 1932. (Fondak)
                        Bonita ch. 1945. (Carauan)
                GANDHY gr. 1931. (Gomara)
                  TETUAN gr. 1938. (Teutonica)
                    ORNIS ch. 1945. (Fifinella)
                      Hilandera gr. 1942. (Abisinia)
                        TABAL gr. 1952. (Congo)
                            Estopa gr. 1965. (Uyaima). Exp. Germany 1971
                            JACIO gr. 1968. (Teorica)
                  Galatife gr. 1943. (Veracruz)
                    ORIVE gr. 1951. (Barquillo)
                    Teorica gr. 1955. (Barquillo)
                    Zalema gr. 1958. (Congo)
                    Alhama III gr. 1959. (Congo)
            HABIENTE ch. 1944. (Veranda)

Hussar cont.
HAMDANI I
    Hagar
        URSUS
            GANDHY
                HABIENTE
                    Paita gr. 1952. (Jaecera)
                        Chavali ch. 1959. (Ornis)
                            Ispahan gr. 1965. (Alhabac)
                Imelina gr. 1945. (Verana)
                    Uyaima ch. 1956. (Barquillo)
                        Estopa gr. 1965. (Tabal). Exp. Germany 1971
            Impedida gr. 1945. (Veralina)
                MALVITO gr. 1949. (Egina)
                    ZURICH b. 1956. (Extranjera)
                    Casiopea ch. 1959. (Transjordania)
                        PROCYON gr. 1972. (Saludo). Imp. UK
                            Fianza gr. 1983. (Farenta)
                MAQUILLO ch. 1949. (Famula)
                    SALUDO ch. 1954. (Jacobita)
                    UZACUR gr. 1956. (Veranda)
            LEBRIJANO bl. 1931. (Lebrijana)
            Triana gr. 1932. (Facina)
                CONGO gr. 1941. (Ilustre)
                    TABAL gr. 1952. (Hilandera)
                        Estopa gr. 1965. (Uyaima)
                        JACIO gr. 1968. (Teorica)
                  Transjordania gr. 1952. (Nubiall)
                  ZANCUDO gr. 1958. (Yaima)
                      GALERO gr. 1965. (Zalema)
                Zalema gr. 1958. (Galatife)
                Alhama III gr. 1959. (Galatife)
Hajwa
    Elfa 1892. (Eljan)
        VAMPIRE (Vasco de Gama)
            Flora ch. 1916. (Jurta)
                TUAREG ch. 1931. (Rasim)
                    DERAZNE gr. 1938. (Mattaria). Exp. in utero USA 1937
Hebe. (Alhambra)
    DZELFI I ch. 1895. (Druid)
        DZELFI-MLECHA b. 1910. (Mlecha I)
            Sahara ch. 1916. (Zulejka)
                Ugra ch. 1935. (Kuhailan Kruszan DB). Exp. USA 1938
                    Gumniska b. 1940. (Czubuthan)
                        GANDUR b. 1946. (Kenur)
Janczarka ch. 1886. (Swietna)
    NOWIK ch. 1904. (Sultan DB)
Halka – (Alpaka)
    Elzusia – (Ernani)
        Hagar ch. 1894. (Hamdani I)
            URSUS b. 1908. (Dahman Amir DB)

THE ARAB HORSE

EL EMIR

EL EMIR 'Sanad*' b. *c.*1873. Imp. 1880. Died 1897
    IMAM b. 1886. (Ishtar*) [*see* Ishtar*]
    Naama b. 1887. (Naomi) [*see* Haidee*]
    Rommia b. 1887. (Raschida)
    HAFIZ. 1888. (Hagar*)
    JEDRAN b. 1888. (Jedrania*)
    BOANERGES. 1889. (Ishtar*) [*see* Ishtar*]
    Zem Zem br. 1889. (Hagar*)
        Zimrud b. 1896. (Jamrood)
            FIRUSEH ch. 1906. (Nejef)
                UNS EL WUJOOD ch. 1914. (Kabila)
                    Kateefah ch. 1922. (Jawi Jawi)
                        KATAF ch. 1928. (Outlaw*). Exp. Australia 1928/35
                            ALADDIN gr. 1943. (Sir Aatika)
                                Alaga Maid gr. 1946. (Anaga)
                                  Hestia gr. 1952. (Jedran)
                                      AETHON gr. 1963. (Spindrift)
                          Kassa ch. 1942. (Nasirieh)
                            Khalasa b. 1950. (Riffal)
                                Leila b. 1954. (Sirhan)
                                  Tamara b. 1961. (Rami)
                                    Dimity (Banderol)
                      HILAL b. 1924. (Shejret Eddur)
                        IBN HILAL ch. 1942. (Turfa*). Exp. *in utero* USA 1941
                        Nouronnihar ch. 1945. (Guliran)
                Husn-u-Gul ch. 1907. (Lal-i-Abdar)
                    Shejret Eddur b. 1913. (Zoowar*)
                        Sant ch. 1921. (Uns el Wujood)
                        Kirat b. 1926. (Sher-i-Khurshid)
                    Baida I gr. 1914. (Zoowar*) [*see* Zoowar*]
    Rakusheh b. 1889. (Raschida). Exp. USA 1893
    Aziza b. 1891. (Raschida)

KISMET

KISMET* ch. 1877. Imp. 1884 and exp. USA 1891. Died 1891
    NIMR ch. 1891. (Nazli). Exp. USA 1893 [*see* Haidee*]
    GARAVEEN b. 1892. (Kushdil). Exp. USA 1893 [*see* Haidee*]

MAIDAN

MAIDAN* ch. *c.* 1869. Imp. 1887. Destroyed 1892
    JAMROOD b. 1888. (Jerud)
        HAÏL b. 1892. (Hagar*). Exp. USA 1905
            Riad b. 1897. (Raschida)
                Sheeba b. 1903. (Ben Azrek)
                    NURI SHERIF b. 1920. (Nureddin II)

Maidan cont.
    JAMROOD
        HAÏL
            Riad
                Sheeba
                    NURI SHERIF
                        Nurschida ch. 1930. (Razina)
                            Sulka ch. 1934. (Naseem). Exp. Holland
                                NIZAR ch. 1953. (Nizzam)
                                Fatma b. 1951. (Nizzam)
                                    Cora b. 1972. (Achim)
                        Namilla ch. 1937. (Algol)
                            MIKENO ch. 1949. (Rissalix)
                                RAJMEK ch. 1961. (Rajjela)
                                EL MELUK ch. 1959. (Mifaria)
                        Manzana b. 1938. (Naufal)
                            Moraea b. 1950. (Irex). Exp. USA 1960
                    Rosanna gr. 1942. (Rose of the Sea)
    Zimrud b. 1896. (Zem Zem)
        FIRUSEH ch. 1906. (Nejef)
    Rose of Persia ch. 1908. (Lal-i-Abdar)
    Nazli ch. 1888. (Naomi). Exp. USA 1893 [*see* Haidee*]
    Raksh b. 1893. (Rakusheh). Exp. USA 1898

MAMELUKE

MAMELUKE* ch. *c.* 1884. Imp. *c.* 1888
    Shabaka ch. 1894. (Kesia II*). Exp. USA 1898 [*see* Kesia*]

MOOTRUB

MOOTRUB* ch. 1887. Imp. *c.* 1891
    Cleopatra ch. 1903. (Raheita)
    Desdemona ch. 1904. (Moallaka)
    MOOTRUB II b. 1909. (Ruth Kesia)
    Queen Shakra ch. 1911. (Shakra*) [*see* Shakra*]
    KIMAREE b. 1911. (Maisuna)
    SHAHZADA gr. 1913. (Ruth Kesia). Exp. Australia 1925 [*see* Kesia*]

ROHAN

ROHAN* Black *c.* 1890. Imp. 1900
    Robirda I b. 1907. (Ladybird*) [*see* Ladybird*]
        Rorobird ch. 1913. (Rohan*)
    Robirda II br. 1910. (Ladybird*)
    ROMAR II – (Ladybird*)
    Rorobird ch. 1913. (Robirda I)

MUSKET

MUSKET* bay 1900. Imp. 1908
  MUSKRO b. 1915. (Robirda I) [see Ladybird*]
    Shemma b. 1923. (Simrieh) [see Sobha*]
      Falha b. 1935. (Rishan)
  MUSKMAR br. 1915. (Marladi)

DWARKA

DWARKA* b. *c.* 1892. Imp. 1901. Destroyed 1921
  Meliha I b. 1918. (Selinga)
  ALDEBARAN 'ALDEBAR' ch. 1919. (Amida). Exp. Canada 1929 and USA 1940
    HOUBARAN b. 1923. (Arusa). Exp. Holland 1924
    Myra ch. 1924. (Rangha)
      Meccana b. 1940. (Riffal)
        Mocha b. 1945. (Ruskov)
      Misma ch. 1941. (Ruskov)
    ALGOL ch. 1928. (Rangha)
      Shabryeh b. 1932. (Seriya)
        Shabrette b. 1950. (Rissalix)
          Farette b. 1954. (Rifari)
            FARI II b. 1965. (Blue Domino)
      Aatika ch. 1933. (Rizada). Exp. Siam *c.* 1939
        MANASSEH b. 1937. (Joseph)
          DARGEE ch. 1945. (Myola)
            SERADIN ch. 1962. (Silindra)
      Algoletta ch. 1935. (Rythma)
      Alsita b. 1935. (Sita). Exp. Holland
        SAOUD b. 1946. (Houbaran)
      SHIHAB ch. 1935. (Almas)
      Namilla ch. 1937. (Nurschida)
        MIKENO ch. 1949. (Rissalix)
      Myola b. 1937. (Rythma)
        DARGEE ch. 1945. (Manasseh)
          ROYAL CRYSTAL gr. 1952. (Grey Royal). Exp. S. Africa
          Dancing Sunlight ch. 1952. (Shades of Night)
          Sirella ch. 1953. (Shalina)
            HANIF gr. 1962. (Silver Vanity)
          Dargemet ch. 1961. (Bint Yasimet)
            DONAX ch. 1971. (Ludrex)
          Zahri ch. 1962. (Zirree el Wada)
          DARJEEL ch. 1962. (Rajjela)
        Myoletta ch. 1946. (Manasseh)
        Myolanda ch. 1948. (Manasseh)
      Guliran ch. 1938. (Jamila*) [see Jamila*]
        HAZZAL gr. 1938. (Dafina*) [see Dafina*]
      AARON b. 1938. (Rythma)
        ALGOLSON ch. 1952. (Myolanda)
          Cinders ch. 1959. (Yateemah)

Dwarka cont.
  ALDEBARAN 'ALDEBAR'
    ALGOL
      ALGOLSON
        Cinders
          Serinda ch. 1969. (Seradin)
            Odessa ch. 1973. (Bright Wings)
              PADRON ch. 1977. (Patron)
      SOLE HOPE ch. 1953. (Heart's Desire)
    BARKIS ch. 1929. (Rangha)
      ALUF gr. 1932. (Almas) [see Kesia*]
        KIT br. 1936. (Karoosha)
    SAHBAN ch. 1930. (Seriya)
      RANA b. 1942. (Ranya II)
      RUKUBAN I gr. 1942. (Roxana)
        SHAITAN gr. 1949. (Guliran)
      The Lady Roxane ch. 1943. (Dil Fireb)
      The Lady Heloise ch. 1948. (Ghailan)
    KALAT gr. 1941. (Kehefe)
      PADISHAH III ch. 1945. (Koreish)
    DURRAL br. 1941. (Fa-Durra)
    BAAROUF gr. 1941. (Maaroufa)
      ROUF ch. 1945. (Fa-Deene)
      ZAROUF gr. 1957. (Wadi-Sirhan)
      MAIROUF b. 1958. (Mailatrah)
    Zabba gr. 1941. (Fa Saana)
      ZAB gr. 1945. (Fay el Dine)
  Ana b. 1920. (Amida). Exp. USA
    Kholey gr. 1929. (Nuri Pasha)
      Kamseh gr. 1942. (Bakir)
        Hillcrests Bint Imaraff gr. 1959. (Imaraff)
          IVANHOE TSULTAN b. 1971. (Ivanhoe Tsatan)
  Karoosha b. 1921. (Rangha)
    Karaka b. gr. 1933. (Akal)
    Kalfa b. 1938. (Joseph)
      K of K b. 1957. (Kasimdar)
  THE LEAT b. 1918. (Blackdown) [Dartmoor]

NEJDRAN

NEJDRAN* ch. 1896. Imp. 1902 and exp. USA 1904
  NEJDRAN JR ch. 1906. (Sheba)
    Dawn b. 1914 (Rhua)
      Horma ch. 1927. (Nuri Pasha)
        Kedem gr. 1935. (Katar)
          Ur ch. 1939. (Nasr)
    Sabigat b. 1928. (El Sabok)
      Sinai ch. 1940. (Gulastra)
      Shangri-La gr. 1942. (Rodasr)
      Siyasa b. 1946. (Warsaw)

THE ARAB HORSE

Nejdran cont.

NEJDRAN JR
- Sultana ch. 1917. (Rhua)
  - Medinah gr. 1922. (El Bulad)
    - Gitthera gr. 1927. (Nuri Pasha)
      - Urga gr. 1938. (Nasr)
        - GUIMARAS ch. 1945. (Gulastra)
        - Ganyma ch. 1946. (Czubuthan)
      - Karubah gr. 1935. (Nuri Pasha)
- Gamelia b. 1918. (Saaida)
- Zamora b. 1922. (Saaida)
  - Zara gr. 1931. (Nuri Pasha)
    - Gariba b. 1942. (Katar)
- Mirza gr. 1923. (Ophir) [see Haidee*]
- ALCAZAR ch. 1924. (Rhua)
  - BAKIR b. 1932. (Bint Yildiz)
    - Kamseh gr. 1942. (Kholey) [see Dwarka*]
  - KATUN ch. 1939. (Nufoud)
    - KULUN gr. 1944. (Mershid)
  - KHALDI ch. 1945. (Khalilla)

ZOOWAR

ZOOWAR* gr. Imp. *c.* 1910. Destroyed 1920
- RAJAH I gr. 1911. (Rose of Persia)
- YAKOOT gr. 1912. (Husn-u-Gul)
- Shejret Eddur b. 1913. (Husn-u-Gul)
  - Sant ch. 1921. (Uns el Wujood)
  - HILAL b. 1924. (Uns el Wujood)
    - IBN HILAL ch. 1942. (Turfa*). Exp. *in utero* USA 1941
    - Zobeide ch. 1943. (Guliran)
    - Nouronnihar ch. 1945. (Guliran) [see Jamila*]
  - Kirat b. 1926. (Sher-i-Khurshid). Exp. Spain 1928
- Baida I gr. 1914. (Husn-u-Gul)
  - Jasmeen gr. 1923. (Uns el Wujood)
    - Mish Mish I b. 1932. (Joseph). Exp. Holland 1937
      - Ritla II b. 1939. (Rythal)
        - Dewi ch. 1945. (Karusen)
          - HAJI II ch. 1951. (Jaleel). Exp. S. Africa
          - Fathia ch. 1950. (Haji I). Exp. S. Africa
    - Moonbeam gr. 1936. (Hilal). Exp. Holland 1937
      - Aatifa b. 1948. (Karusen). Exp. New Zealand
    - Bint Yasim ch. 1940. (Manak*)
      - Yasimet ch. 1949. (Grey Owl). Exp. S. Africa
        - Bint Yasimet ch. 1954. (Blue Domino)
          - Dargemet ch. 1961. (Dargee)
            - DONAX ch. 1971. (Ludrex)
              - Luda ch. 1967. (Ludo)
            - Parthia ch. 1959. (Shifari)
              - BORAK ch. 1960. (Shifari)
            - Oranet ch. 1962. (Oran)

Zoowar cont.

Baida I
- Jasmeen
  - Bint Yaseem
    - Yasimet
      - ZINGARI b. 1959. (Zahir)
- ELMAS b.gr. 1927. (Sher-i-Khurshid)
- ZABARJID ch.gr. 1928. (Sher-i-Khurshid)
- JIDDAN b. 1930. (Sher-i-Khurshid). Exp. S. Africa 1938
- MABRUK II b. 1937. (Hilal)
  - Firefly b. 1940. (Fantana)
    - Farida ch. 1954. (Un-named by Raktha/Indian Diamond)
      - Ecurb Rinarida ch. 1965. (Ringing Gold)
        - Ringing Derida ch. 1975. (El Shinder)
          - Ringing Enchantress gr. 1979. (Silver Sword)
- Baqubah b. 1938. (Hilal)

CROSBIE

CROSBIE* gr. *c.* 1908. Imp. 1914
- SOHRAB ch. 1920. (Selinga)
- MIZAN 'NIZAM' gr. 1921. (Rose of Persia). Exp. Palestine. Gelded 1931
- Maasreh gr. 1923. (Minsa)
  - MAJID gr. 1930. (Almulid)
  - KARUSEN b. 1924. (Arusa). Exp. Holland 1926
    - Bakoorah ch. 1934. (Maid of the Moot)
    - Dewi ch. 1945. (Ritla)
      - Fathia ch. 1950. (Haji I). Exp. S. Africa
      - HAJI II ch. 1951. (Jaleel). Exp. S. Africa
    - Karit b. 1947. (Ritla)
    - Aatifa b. 1948. (Moonbeam)
- Sahra ch. 1925. (Seriya)
  - Shagra ch. 1933. (Azym)
  - Algola ch. 1935. (Algol)
    - Araby gr. 1940. (Jellaby I)
      - D'Lorb ch. 1947. (Kairouan)
      - Fajr ch. 1946. (Kairouan)
        - Sapphire gr. 1950. (Indian Magic)
          - Silver Velvet gr. 1955. (Ghailan)
            - Silmana gr. 1964. (Manalix)
              - Radsilla gr. 1969. (Radfan)
          - Indian Trinket gr. 1958. (Crystal Fire)
            - Crystal Clear gr. 1964. (Bright Shadow)
              - CRYSTAL KING gr. 1969. (Indian King). Exp. Brazil
    - Amina ch. 1952. (The Chief)
  - Sahmana ch. 1943. (Manak*)
    - SAHRAN gr. 1948. (Rangoon)
    - Rumana gr. 1951. (Rukuban I)
- Zahle gr. 1926. (Mejamieh*) [see Mejamieh*]
- Khashbi b. 1928. (Petra*)

MIRAGE

MIRAGE* gr. 1919. Imp. 1923 and exp. USA 1930
    Zahra ch. 1924. (Rose of Persia)
    Eastern Rose ch. 1925. (Rose of Persia)
    RASEEL ch. 1925. (Rafina)
    RIX ch. 1927. (Rim) [or sire Iram]
        SHIMRIX ch. 1939. (Rishima)
        Drusilla gr. 1939. (Dafinetta) [see Dafina*]
    Black Bunny gr. 1927. (Battla). Exp. India
    FAYAL ch. 1927. (Fejr) [or sire Iram] [see Ferida*]
        RAYAL gr. 1942. (Raxina) [see Dajania*]
        RIFFAYAL gr. 1942. (Ariffa). Exp. Australia 1950 [see Queen of Sheba*]
        Fayella gr. 1942. (Dafina*) [see Dafina*]
        GHAILAN gr. 1943. (Raxina) [see Dajania*]
        Taima br. 1944. (Naomi I)
        Shamal b. 1944. (Rizada)
        The Lady Lucretia ch. 1946. (Dil Fireb)
        RUSTEM BEY ch. 1948. (Rithyana)
        Oriana gr. 1948. (Rimiana)
        Fafika gr. 1952. (Rafika) [see Rodania*]
        Fayalindra ch. 1952. (Naxindra)
    Peraga gr. 1932. (Slipper)
    Pera gr. 1933. (Slipper)
    IMAGE ch. 1933. (Rifala)
        Imagida ch. 1939. (Ourida)
            IMARAFF b. 1945. (Raffles)
                Imamara b. 1953. (Bint Abu)
                      TSATYR b. 1957. (Tsali) [see Noura*]
            RAFFI gr. 1946. (Raffles)
                Gaffi gr. 1964. (Galatina)
                      GAFFIZON gr. 1970. (Ferzon)
        PHANTOM gr. 1941. (Rifala)
            Galena b. 1949. (Balena)
                NIGA bl. 1957. (Nitez)
            Guzida gr. 1953. (Rafaia)
                GRANDE DUKE gr. 1967. (Ferzon)
        SELMAGE b. 1941. (Selmnab)
        Sel Hani b. 1948. (Rihani) [see Noura*]
    ARABI KABIR ch. 1941. (Kareyma)
        ERRABI ch. 1949. (Ferdirah)
            BAY ABI b. 1957. (Angyl)
                BAY EL BEY b. 1969. (Naganka)

Mirage cont.
IMAGE
    ARABI KABIR
        ERRABI
            BAY ABI
                BAY EL BEY
                    HUCKLEBERRY BEY b. 1976. (Taffona)
                        DESPERADO V b. 1986. (Daraska)
                    BEY SHAH b. 1976. (Star of Ofir)
                      FAME VF b. 1982. (Raffoleta-Rose)
    Imna ch. 1942. (Selmnab)
    Sebba gr. 1947. (Rafflette)
    IMAGIN gr. 1950. (Rafina)
        GYN b. 1959. (Geymna)
        MEHEMET ALI gr. 1962. (Sah Mirada)
    El Hacene gr. 1951. (Bahia)
        RAFFENE b. 1955. (Raffey)
        TAKARA RAFFON br. 1967. (Raffon)
    Sange gr. 1951. (Santee)
    IMAGINATION gr. 1953. (Rafina)
        FACINATION gr. 1962. (Gusherri)
    Imaja gr. 1956. (Nimja)
        GAGE b. 1958. (Gebina)
        ZELIMAGE ch. 1959. (Merzel)
INDRAGE b. 1934. (Indaia)
NAMIR gr. 1934. (Namilla)
    Komir ch. 1950. (Komyrah)
        KOMSUL ch. 1956. (Sulejman)
            COMANCHE ch. 1963. (Mistana)
Ragala gr. 1935. (Rifala)
    Lakshmi gr. 1956. (Rapture)
        FIRE BOLT b. 1967. (Bask)
AGWE ch. 1936. (Hilwe)
    APOLLO gr. 1939. (Roda)
    Rodetta gr. 1940. (Roda)
    JASPRE gr. 1945. (Roda)
RIFAGE gr. 1936. (Rifala)
    GAYSAR ch. 1942. (Ralouma)
        GALIMAR ch. 1945. (Rageyma)
        SKORAGE ch. 1947. (Rageyma)
            PULQUE ch. 1957. (Rahanna)
    Gay Negma gr. 1951. (Fay Negma)
        OZEM bl. 1961. (Fa-Serr)

Mirage cont.
    RIFAGE
        Rishima gr. 1952. (Ishmia)
        Rominna gr. 1953. (Dominica)
        Rageyma gr. 1936. (Kareyma) [see Makbula*]
            GEYM gr. 1942. (Raffles)
                Geynima ch. 1956. (Nima)
            Gajala gr. 1943. (Raffles)
                GAIZON gr. 1957. (Ferzon)
                Ga-Rageyma ch. 1958. (Ferzon)
                Ga-Gajala b. 1962. (Ferzon)
            GALIMAR ch. 1945. (Gaysar)
            SKORAGE ch. 1947. (Gaysar)
        Romira gr. 1936. (Rose of France)
            Raffira gr. 1943. (Raffles)
        YAMAGE gr. 1938. (Kiyama)
        IDOL gr. 1939. (Selmnab)
        IBN MIRAGE gr. 1939. (Kareyma)
            MIRFEY gr. 1954. (Rafeyma)
            Rafleyga gr. 1954. (Rafleyma)
        ADONIS ch. 1939. (Curfa)
        Kae gr. 1939. (Keturah)
            SHIRIK gr. 1952. (Indraff)
            Fae gr. 1950. (Indraff)
                IBN JULEP gr. 1955. (Julep)
        Joharah b. 1939. (Rihani)
            My Bonnie Nylon ch. 1946. (Raffles) [see Noura*]

Atesh

ATESH* ch. 1913. Imp. *c.* 1923
    Sukr b. 1926. (Safarjal)
        Selma III ch. 1943. (Rissam)
            Salambo ch. 1952. (Rheoboam)
            Salote ch. 1954. (Champurrado). Exp. USA 1960
        Sheba's Queen b. 1946. (Champurrado)
    BENDIGO gr. 1927. (Belka)
        Ruth II b. 1943. (Rahab)
            Rosina b. 1950. (Saoud). Exp. S. Africa
            Rosemary II b. 1959. (Champurrado)
                Rosemaria ch. 1977. (Samhan)
    SHEM b. 1927. (Safarjal). Exp. Brazil 1931
    Fantasia I ch. 1927. (Fasiha)
        Farida II ch. 1945. (Sainfoin)
            Fitnah b. 1955. (Rashid I). Exp. USA 1960
        Fashoda ch. 1947. (Sainfoin)
    Ruth I ch. 1934. (Rangha). Exp. USA 1940
    Bussora b. 1935. (Bekr)
        Karim gr. 1943. (Ruskov)
            Tarim gr. 1949. (Rukuban I)
    SOLOMON gr. 1937. (Somra II)
    FEZ gr.1938. (Fand)

Nimr

NIMR* br. 1914. Imp. *c* 1923
    SHADRACH br. 1924. (Safarjal). Exp. Spain 1934
    NISSR gr. 1925. (Lalla Rookh*)
    SAOUD b. 1925. (Safarjal)
        RASHID I b. 1938. (Safarjal)
            Razehra ch. 1955. (Zehraa) [see Nuhra*]
                Kazra ch. 1961. (Mikeno)
        Rosina b. 1950. (Ruth II). Exp. S. Africa
    Bekr b. 1926. (Belka)
        Bozra II ch. 1933. (Fedaan*)
            Dil Kushi gr. 1947. (Rangoon)
        Belkis II b. 1934. (Sainfoin)
            Beryl b. 1940. (Joseph)
                BLENHEIM ch. 1953. (Rheoboam)
                BEND OR b. 1959. (Rheoboam)
        Bussora b. 1935. (Atesh*) [see Atesh*]
        Balis II b. 1936. (Sainfoin). Exp. USA 1940
            Bessarabia b. 1940. (Joseph)
        Baranova b. 1938. (Sainfoin)
            BENJAMIN b. 1946. (Champurrado)
            BASHOM b. 1949. (Champurrado)
        Barada I b. 1940. (Sainfoin)
    SAHAR b. 1927. (Shabaka)
    Shaara b. 1927. (Shemma)
    SALADIN I br. 1928. (Safarjal)
    Feluka II b. 1928. (Fasiha)
    Fand gr. 1931. (Fasiha)
        Sherezada gr. 1942. (Hazzal) [see Dafina*]
            Banzada gr. 1948. (Rukuban I)
            Sherie b. 1950. (Shariff)
    Rachel I b. 1932. (Rangha)

Fedaan

FEDAAN* gr. 1913. Imp. *c.* 1926
    Fedala br. 1928. (Lalla Rookh*)
    MANEEFAH gr. 1928. (Maasreh)
    FAZARAH b. 1929. (Lalla Rookh*)
    SELIM II br. 1929. (Safarjal)
    FEYD gr. 1929. (Fasiha)
    Somra II gr. 1932. (Safarjal)
        Siwa II gr. 1943. (Rheoboam)
            Sesame gr. 1950. (Champurrado)
            Sabrina ch. 1956. (Rheoboam)
                ST SIMON b. 1973. (Benjamin). Exp. Brazil 1977
                SAMHAN b. 1961. (Bahram)
                Solome IV gr. 1969. (Blenheim)
                    Signorinetta gr. 1978. (Samhan)
            Selima gr. 1961. (Bahram)
            Sappo ch. 1971. (Blenheim)

Fedaan cont.
    Somra II
        Siwa II
            Selima
                Sceptre gr. 1977. (Blenheim)
        SHAMMAR gr. 1955. (Champurrado)
    Bozra II ch. 1933. (Bekr) [see Nimr*]
        Dil Kushi gr. 1947. (Rangoon)
    REUBEN ch. 1933. (Rangha). Exp. Colombia 1938
    SISERA b. 1933. (Safarjal)
    Betina br./gr. 1935. (Belka)
        BAHRAM ch. 1945. (Sainfoin)
    Rhoda b. 1939. (Rahab)

OUTLAW

OUTLAW* ch. 1915. Imp. *c.* 1927. Died *c.* 1933
    KATAF ch. 1928. (Kateefah). Exp. Australia 1928/35
        Kassa ch. 1942. (Nasirieh) [see El Emir*]
        ALADDIN I gr. 1943. (Sir Aatika)
            Alaga Maid gr. 1946. (Anaga) [see Nejdmieh*]
                Hestia gr. 1952. (Jedran)
                      AETHON gr. 1963. (Spindrift)
            Alaga Girl gr. 1948. (Anaga)
        Falka ch. 1942. (Rifa) [see Nejdmieh*]
            Riffalka ch. 1950. (Riffal)
                Hebe II ch. – (Grand Royal)
        Mira ch. 1943. (Melika)
        Kassie ch. 1944. (Caswa) [see Nejdmieh*]
        Semna ch. 1943. (Caswa)
            Sparkle br. 1954. (Silver Sparkle)
        RUKUBAN II b. 1945. (Nejd Sherifa) [see Nejdmieh*]
    Safari b. 1931 (Rayya) Exp. West Indies
    Mish Mish II ch. 1938 (Ruskov)
    Shthora ch. 1931 (Zahle)

MANAK

MANAK* ch. 1928. Imp. 1937. Died 1947
    SARAFAN b. 1939. (Seriya). Exp. Canada
    SIRIUS ch. 1939. (Myra)
    RAKAN b. 1939. (Ranya II)
        Tar Asman gr. 1948. (Sharaya)
        Cheran ch. 1959. (Simiha)
        Algella b. 1962. (Simiha)
            El Arabella ch. 1968. (El Meluk)
                NAXOR b. 1970. (Roxan)
        Rudena gr. 1963. (Rosanna)
            PAQUERRA ch. 1969. (Mikeno)

Manak cont.
MANAK
    Bint Yasim ch. 1940. (Jasmeen) [see Zoowar*]
    Syria ch. 1942. (Myra)
    Sahmana ch. 1943. (Sahra) [see Crosbie*]
    Nurmahal b. 1943. (Nuhra*) [see Nuhra*]
    Taj Mahal b. 1945. (Nuhra*) [see Nuhra*]
    Nurmana ch. 1946. (Nuhra*) [see Nuhra*]
    Almanak br. 1946. (Alika)

RESH AL BADIA

RESH AL BADIA* ch. 1928. Imp. *c.* 1938
    Shem el Nassim ch. 1941 (Warda al Badia*)
    Falha II [formerly Primula] ch. 1953 (Nemisia) [see Warda al Badia*]

KASIM

KASIM* bay 1934. Imp. 1937
    Freyha b. 1942. (Falha)
    Fuwasa b. 1945. (Falha) [see Sobha*]
    KAHTAN b. 1946. (Falha)

SHAMYL

SHAMYL* gr. 1961. Imp. *in utero* 1960
    CuanMylindra b. 1967 (Fayalindra)
        Lady Mylindra ch. 1970. (Alyosha)
            MALIK MYLINDRA b. 1971. (Bright Pearl)
            SHALINDRA OF WEATHEROAK ch. 1973. (Indian Blizzard)
    Maeve b. 1980 (Deraiya) [see Thrayat Hamid*]

THE ARAB HORSE

Stallion, drawing by Peter Upton

APPENDIX 1

Origins and Strains

The origins of the Arab horse are inextricably linked with the bedouin, 'The Children of Shem'. Indeed, Baz, who lived in Yemen *c.* 3200 BC and whose father, Omaim, was the son of Lud (son of Shem), possessed a mare known to us only as the 'Mare of Baz'. The traditions of *The Days of Ignorance* include the history of some early Arab horses, and they were first recorded in AD 876, by El Kelbi, a writer of the time of Haroun-al-Raschid. He wrote of a famous stallion of the Beni Azd, named 'Zad-el-Rakib', reputed to have been given by Salaman (*c.* 1630 BC). The Beni Taghlib used 'Zah-el-Rakib' at stud and produced 'Hojeys' (Young Lion). The Beni Bekr, closely related to the Beni Taghlib, also bred a stallion of this male line, a son of 'Hojeys', named 'El Dinari' (Golden Coin), and the Beni 'Amr mated their mare 'Sabal' with 'El Dinari'. 'Sabal' was the daughter of 'Sawadeh' (the Dark One) and 'Qannas' (the Hunter). 'Sawadeh's' dam 'Qasameh' (the Oath), and sire 'Fayed' (Overflowing), both belonged to the Beni Jadeh. 'Fayed's' sire was of the blood of 'Hoshabeh' and 'The Mare of Baz' and it is possible that 'Qasameh' was full sister to 'Fayad'.

The tribes of Taghlib and Bekr descend from Jadailah, brother to Anazeh, ancestor of the Anazeh tribes of Central Asia [*see* Appendix 2]. Rabiah 'al Faras' (of the horse), grandfather to Anazeh and Jadaileh, is known to have owned 'the horses of his ancestors', which no doubt descended from the five Keheilet mares of Salaman Ibn Nabet al Ishmael. These five mares were, I believe, the original 'Al Khamseh' from which the strains were to develop, for it is said that all strains originate in Keheilet Ajuz, the generic term for 'pure-bred'. Over the intervening centuries the strains have grown far beyond the original five.

'Sabal', the mare who belonged to the Beni Amr, produced, in time, two colts both sired by 'Sahab'. They were named 'Awaj I' of the Beni Ghani and 'Awaj II' of the Beni Helal. The Beni Ghani descended from Quays Ibn Ailan, brother to Al Yas, son of Modar and brother to Rabiah 'Al Faras'. Al Yas is an ancestor of the Koreish tribe, from whom descend 'The Prophet' Mohammed, the Hashemite Sherifs of Makkah and HM King Hussein of Jordan. Although these traditions offer us a fascinating glimpse into, and indeed evidence of, the early ancestors of the Arab horse before the time of Islam, we must turn to nineteenth century records for more details.

The main sources, or records of the genealogies of the Arab horse, appear to be the fragments of the original Abbas Pasha I manuscript, which Lady Anne Blunt was to transcribe and study. Later, Prince Mohammed Ali published some of the same material, but that translation is often muddled and difficult to follow. However, there is no doubt that we owe most of our knowledge of the Arab horse, and in particular those of the Collection of Abbas Pasha I, to the meticulous research and collection of records by Lady Anne Blunt. Through her, we know the names and strains of a number of the Original Horses and Mares collected by Abbas Pasha I, who appear in the pedigrees of the horses bought by the Blunts from the stud of Ali Pasha Sherif. Undoubtedly, many other lines were lost when the major part of Ali Pasha Sherif's stud was decimated by the Horse Plague.

Some of these Original Horses can be traced back still further by the study of the Abbas Pasha manuscripts. The Original Mare, the bay Dahmeh el Hamra of Ibn Aweyde, great granddam of Mesaoud's dam Yemameh, was given by her breeder, Mubarak Ibn Khalifa, to Mishwat Ibn Shab'aan ibn Aweyde of the Qahtan, and her female line is recorded for a further seven generations. Incidentally, it also shows how the Dahmeh Nejiba strain evolved from the Shahwanieh.

Dahmeh el Hamra of Ibn Aweyde, OM

1 ex Dark Bay Dahmeh Nejiba, owned by Mubarak Ibn Khalifa on shares with Shafi Ibn Shab'aan, uncle to Mishwat (her sire a Keheilan Amr of Qahtan).
2 ex Dahmeh Nejiba, bought by Abdallah Ibn Khalifa of Bahrain.
3 ex Grey Dahmeh Nejiba, bought by Turki Ibn Saud (her sire an Abeyan Sherrak).
4 ex Dahmeh Nejiba, bought on shares by El Nejib of the Beni Huseyn.
5 ex Dahmeh (named after the black ass her foster mother) bought by Ibn Azeyran of the Ajman.
6 ex Dahmeh of Ibn Fursan of the Qahtan.
7 ex Dahmeh Shahwanieh of Ibn Hallal of the Qahtan.

THE ARAB HORSE

The Original Mare, Ghazieh, a white Seglawieh Jedranieh of Ibn Sudan of the Roala, can be traced back to a chestnut Seglawieh, known as 'Awdah' (the old and well-trained mare). She was owned by Mansour Ibn Sudan, who had bought her from the Sheikh of the Sebaa. 'Awdah's' history, as related by the Sheikhs of the Gomussa is as follows.

Awdah (her Sire, a Keheilan Ajuz)

1 ex   Bay Seglawieh, owned by Sheikh Faysal Ibn Sha'lan of the Roala (her sire a Keheilan al Khurs).
2 ex   Chestnut Seglawieh of Ibn-Qufayfah.
3 ex   Chestnut Seglawieh (her sire Hamdani of Jad'ah)
4 ex   Chestnut Seglawieh, owned by Ibn Sudan (her sire a Hamdani Simri of Al Jasim).
5 ex   Chestnut Seglawieh, owned by Mutliq Ibn Rushud (her sire a Rabdah Khashibi of 'Unayzan).
6 ex   Chestnut Seglawieh, owned by Ali Ibn Sudan (her sire a Seglawi Jedran of the Buhayyim strain owned by Su'ud).
7 ex   The Seglawieh of Ibn Jedran, left with Beni-Huseyn.

According to some records, the sire of Ghazieh's dam was the famous stallion, 'Al Araj' (the Lame), a chestnut Seglawi, also known as 'Al Mahyubi'. He and his full brother, the grey 'Horse of Jadib', appear again and again in the Abbas Pasha manuscripts. Both were bred by Jadib of the Duish. It is also worth noting in the records of both 'Dahmeh el Hamra' and 'Awdah', that, where the sires are known, they are, in almost every case, of a different strain to the dam, which does not support any breeding-within-the-strain theory.

This early history, often confusing and difficult to follow, and the matter of strains, led some to believe that there was more than one breed of Arab horse in the desert. Major Upton was the first to state clearly in his book *Newmarket and Arabia*, that the Arab is *one* breed with a number of distinguished families, including Keheilan, Seglawi, Abeyan, Hadban and Hamdani. He lists the Maneghi as a first-class sub-division of the Keheilan. Later, after visiting some of the Anazeh tribes, Upton was to review some of his original thoughts on the matter of Arab strains. In an article in *Frazer's Magazine* in September 1876 entitled 'Arabian Horses studied in the Native Country 1874-5', Major Upton has this to say as regards strains:

> There is but one breed of Arabian horses, and it is to be found in the highest perfection among the Anazeh tribes, and that certain tribes of this people are possessed of better horses and are more particular in breeding than others... I have heard people assert they could tell to which of the five families any individual horse belonged, but I feel sure this must be taken with great reservation. The general characteristics and features among Arabian horses are the same. It would be wrong to say all are equally beautiful or all are equally perfect and there is, of course, individuality of character and expression to be seen among animals bred by the same person and from the same strain.

Many and conflicting are the theories regarding strains. Abbas Pasha I was said to have valued the Dahmeh strain most, but the bedouin tribes prized the Seglawieh Jedranieh above all others. The Muteyr, however, were justly proud of their Krushiehs, the Gomussa renowned for horses of the Nowagieh strain, whilst the Ajman and the Khalifa's of Bahrain prized their Jellabiehs. Whatever the relative merits, correctly or incorrectly attributed to certain strains, there are some matters which are quite clear.

Strains should not be confused with breed or type. Special prepotent mares or 'lines' may breed consistently true and, in the past, the development of strains was due to selection based on the ideals of a breeder and the name continued in tail-female line from the 'founding' mare. Certainly, some strains gained favour and became known throughout the desert and beyond, as did certain famous individual horses. The sheikhs and their tribes guarded their mares jealously, for not only did they carry them in war, but the were the providers of future generations and so certain strains often became associated with a particular tribe. The Seglawieh Jedraniehs of Ibn Sudan of the Roala were eagerly sought after by Abbas Pasha I, and also those of Ibn Sbeni of the Mehed, Fedaan.

Originally, there would have been little problem in associating a certain type with a strain name. There were, after all, almost as many strains as there were well-known breeders and those breeders gave their names to the strains. Inevitably, particular strains gained prominence and this 'handful' of names was recognised by bedouins and recited when enquiries were made of them. The first who were to write of the Arab horse therefore assumed – as the sheikh counted off the strains on his fingers – some magical 'five' (Al Khamsa), though not all listed the same five strains. Indeed, 'Al Khamsa' was eventually to appear in an infinite variety of guises, in the writings of General Daumas and Abd-el-Kader, including the ultimate translation by Carl Raswan, from 'Al Khamsa' to 'Al Thalatha' (the three) – a strain-related-to-type theory, with no basis in bedouin history.

Lady Anne and Wilfrid Blunt, no doubt influenced by their discussions regarding the strains with Mr Skene, Consul at Aleppo, and the Emir Abd-el-Kader, who they met in Damascus, at first supported the 'Al Khamsa' theory. Wilfrid Blunt records in *Bedouin Tribes of the Euphrates*, the names of 'Al Khamsa', or Five Great Strains of Blood (originally Awaj and possibly all Keheilan) as follows: 1 – Keheilan, 2 – Seglawi, 3 – Abayan, 4 – Hamdani, 5 – Hadban, but besides these he lists a further sixteen 'breeds' – Managhi, Saadun, Dahman, Shueyman, Jilfan, Toessah, Samhan, Wadnan, Risheh, Kubeysha, Melekhan, Jereybah, Jeytani, Ferejan, Treyfi and Rabdah. It is of interest that he should describe the Managhi as: 'plain and without distinction, have coarse heads', yet on 26 March 1881, Lady Anne noted in her journal: '[saw a] Managyeh mare – a lovely white mare (head something like Sherifa)'!

Later, the Blunts were to revise some of their ideas as regards strains and in 1916 Lady Anne wrote:

> [Particular] families [of horses] occasionally go through periods of renown owing to remarkable exploits in war of individual mares. But there has never been one [strain] that permanently retained a superior rank, nor indeed is there any strain kept separate – very rarely are both parents of a foal of the same family. The family name, corresponding to a surname with human beings – is given by the mare, according to Arab custom. And all families or strains go back to, or in other words originate in 'Keheilan Ajuz'.

There is no longer any mention of 'al Khamsa'. The strain name was both a useful method, when no written records were kept, of recognising a particular female line or stud, and a natural way of referring to the family of a brood-mare. Even today, many of our most successful studs have been founded on one special brood-mare, and her daughters and granddaughters will be much sought after, as were certain 'strains' in the past. How should we view strains today and are they still relevant? It is no longer possible to ascribe type to a strain name. We are too far from the original concept of the breeder of that strain, and in the majority of cases the prepotency of a particular female can no longer be an influential factor. Naturally, we may have a Keheileh Rodanieh, for example, who breeds true to her type, but her type may not necessarily be that of another Keheileh Rodanieh. What we now have are new strains or family-lines developing, as indeed they have been doing over the years.

So, strains are an important pointer to the family and the stud or tribe from which the horses originated. Any horse of the Wadnah al Khursan strain in this country, almost certainly traces to the imported mare Nuhra* and most Krushiehs will go back to Dafina*. Breeding within a strain, however, has little or no merit, although breeding within a family, or line-breeding, may well be valuable in fixing desirable characteristics, but it needs to be used judiciously. Listed below are the strains, where known, of the horses who appear in this book.

The White Stallion, drawing by Peter Upton.

The Arab Strains

(Female)	(Male)	(Female)	(Male)
Keheileh or Keheilet	Keheilan	Kubeysha	Kubeyshan
Keheilet Ajuz	Keheilan Ajuz		
Keheilet Akhras	Keheilan Akhras	Maneghieh	Maneghi
Keheilet Al Korma	Keheilan Al Korma	Maneghieh Hedrujieh	Maneghi Hedruj
Keheilet Al Krushieh	Keheilan Al Krush	Maneghieh Ibn Sbeyli	Maneghi Ibn Sbeyli
Keheilet Al'Musinnieh	Keheilan abu Musin		
Keheileh Dajanieh	Keheilan Dajani	Rabdah	Rabdan
Keheileh Jellabieh	Keheilan Jellabi		
Keheileh Jereybah	Keheilan Jereyban	Risheh	Rishan
Keheileh Juaithnieh	Keheilan Juaithni		
Keheileh Nowagieh	Keheilan Nowag	Sa'dah Togan	Sa'dan Togan
Keheileh Ras el Fedawi	Keheilan Ras el Fedawi		
Keheileh Rodanieh	Keheilan Rodan	Seglawieh	Seglawi
Keheileh Sueyti	Keheilan Sueyti	Seglawieh el Abd	Seglawi el Abd
Keheileh Tamrieh	Keheilan Tamri	Seglawieh Jedranieh	Seglawi Jedran
Keheileh Wadneh Khursanieh	Keheilan Wadnan Khursan	Seglawieh Obeyreh	Seglawi Obeyran
		Seglawieh Semmeh	Seglawi Semma
Abayeh	Abayan	Seglawieh Sheyfi	Seglawi Sheyfi
Abayeh Sherrakieh	Abayan Sherrak		
		Samheh	Samhan
Dahmeh	Dahman		
Dahmeh Om'Aamr	Dahman Abu'Aamr	Shueyma S'bah	Shueyman S'bah
Dahmeh Nejiba	Dahman Nejib		
Dahmeh Shahwanieh	Dahman Shahwan	Toessah	Toessan
Hadbeh	Hadban	Um Argub	Abu Argub
Hadbeh Enzahieh	Hadban Enzahi		
Hamdanieh	Hamdan		
Hamdanieh Simrieh	Hamdan Simri		
Hamdanieh Ibn Ghayam	Hamdan Ibn Ghayam		
Jilfeh	Jilfan		
Jilfeh Stam el Bulad	Jilfan Stam el Bulad		

Jeytani and Melekhieh (mentioned by Blunt)

(This list is by no means all strains and sub-strains. It however includes the main strains and the strains mentioned in the book). As usual in translation from Arabic, there are an infinite variety of spellings for each word!

The Strains of Horses Imported by the Blunts
(whose lines exist today)

Keheilet Ajuz: Hagar
Keheilet Jellabieh: FEYSUL; MERZUK; IBN YASHMAK; Makbula; Kasida; Jellabieh
Keheileh Dajanieh: Dajania
Keheileh Rodanieh: Rodania
Keheilet Ajuz of Ras el Fedawi: Wild Thyme
Seglawieh Jedranieh of Ibn Sbeyni: KARS; Jedrania; Fulana
Seglawieh Jedranieh of Ibn ed Derri: PHARAOH; AZREK; Meshura; Basilisk
Seglawieh Jedranieh of Ibn Sudan: MESAOUD; Bint Helwa; Johara; Ghazala
Seglawieh Obeyran: ASHGAR
Dahmeh Shahwanieh: SHAHWAN
Dahmeh Nejiba: (IBN) MAHRUSS; Bint Nura II
Dahmeh om Aamr: RATAPLAN; Dahma
Hadbeh Enzahi: HADBAN
Hamdanieh Simrieh: Sherifa; Sobha
Abeyeh Sherrakieh: Queen of Sheba
Jilfeh Stam el Bulad: Jilfa
Managhieh Hedrujieh: Jerboa, Ferida

The Strains of Other Imported Horses
(whose lines exist today)

Keheilet Ajuz: KISMET; OUTLAW; Shakra; Jamila I; Mahawiliyah; Thrayat Hamid
Keheilet al Khorma: Turfa
Keheileh Juaithnieh: Takritiyah
Keheileh Jurayban: YATAGHAN
Keheilet el Krush: Dafina
Keheileh Nowagieh: Kesia; Kesia II; Nawagiyat al Furat
Seglawieh: RESH al BADIA; Warda al Badia
Seglawieh Jedranieh: MOOTRUB; FEDAAN; NIMR; MIRAGE; MAHMOUD-MIRZA; KASIM
Seglawieh Obeyran: NEJDRAN
Hamdanieh Ibn Ghayam: MANAK
Kubeysha: Shammah
Managhieh Hedrujich: Noura; Muha
Managhieh Ibn Sbeyli: EL EMIR; ATESH; SHAMYL; Haidee; Nejdmieh; Nejma; Shams
Um Argoub: El Yamama; Princess Muna
Wadneh Khursanieh: Nuhra

Horses of Strain Unknown

Mejamieh; Libnani; Ishtar; Ladybird; PADISCHAH; INDJANIN; SAJDEN; NIZAM; HUSSAR; MAMELUKE; MAIDAN; DWARKA; ZOOWAR; CROSBIE; ROHAN; MUSKET

Horses* of the Same Strain Imported by Lady Anne and W.S. Blunt

The Seglawieh Jedranieh of Ibn Sudan

1. Ghazieh, white, OM of Abbas Pasha I
   Bint Ghazieh, white, *c.* 1858 (Zobeyni OH)
   Yemameh, grey, *c.* 1872 (Shueyman)
   <u>MESAOUD</u>*, chestnut, 1887 (Aziz)
   WAZIR, white, 1862 (Zobeyni OH)
   Horra, white, 1879 (Zobeyni OH)
   Helwa, white, *c.* 1875 (Shueyman)
   <u>Johara</u>*, chestnut *c.* 1880 (Aziz)
   <u>Bint Helwa</u>*, white, 1887 (Aziz)
   <u>Ghazala</u>*, grey, 1896 (Ibn Sherara)
2. SUEYD, flea-bitten grey, OH of Abbas Pasha I

The Seglawieh Jedranieh of Ibn Sbeyni

1. Samha, grey, OM of Abbas Pasha I
   Fereyha, white, (Jerboa)
   Bint Fereyha el Saghira, white, 1884 (Aziz)
   <u>Fulâna</u>*, brown, 1893 (Ibn Nura)
2. ZOBEYNI, white, OH of Abbas Pasha I
3. Mare stolen from Ibn Sbeyni by the Shammar
   <u>KARS</u>*, bay, 1874
4. Grey mare of Ibn Sbeyni
   <u>Jedrania</u>*, bay, 1875 (Kehilan Nowak)

The Seglawieh Jedranieh of Ibn ed Derri

1. Bay mare of Berghi Ibn ed Derri (Seglawi Jedran of Obeyd)
   <u>Meshura</u>*, bay, 1872 (Bay Managhi Sbeyel)
   <u>PHARAOH</u>*, bay, 1876 (Bay Kehilan Ajuz)
   Chestnut Mare of Neddi Ibn ed Derri (Hadban)
   <u>AZREK</u>*, grey, 1881
2. White Mare of Neddi Ibn ed Derri
   <u>Basilisk</u>*, grey, 1876 (Bay Seglawi Jedran)

The Keheileh Jellabieh

1. Jellabiet-Feysul, grey, *c.* 1845, OM of Abbas Pasha I
   Bint Jellabiet-Feysul, chestnut, *c.* 1868
   Bint Bint Jellabiet-Feysul 'El Argaa,' chestnut/white, *c.* 1875
   Makbula el Kebira, chestnut, 1880 (Shueyman)
   <u>Makbula</u>* 'Bint Makbula', white, 1886 (Wazir)
   <u>Kasida</u>*, chestnut, 1891 (Nasr)
   <u>Khatila</u>*, chestnut, 1887 (Aziz)
   <u>Jellabieh</u>*, white, 1892 (Ibn Nura)
   <u>FEYSUL</u>*, chestnut, 1894 (Ibn Nura)
   <u>MERZUK</u>*, chestnut, 1887 (Wazir)
2. Yemama, bay 1885
   Yashmak, grey, 1893 (Shahwan*)
   <u>IBN YASHMAK</u>*, chestnut, 1902 (Feysul*)
   <u>IBN YEMAMA</u>*, bay, 1902 (Feysul*)

The Dahmeh Shahwanieh

1. Faras Nakadân: 'The Mare of Sheykh Ibn Nakadân of the Ajman,' OM of Abbas Pasha I
   Bint Faras Nakadân, *c.* 1840 (Zobeyni OH)
   Aziza, grey, *c.* 1868 (Samheh)
   AZIZ, chestnut, *c.* 1877 (Harkan)
   'Azz, white, *c.* 1840
   Bint 'Azz, white, *c.* 1880 (Wazir)
   <u>A'zz</u>* 'Bint Bint 'Azz', white, *c.* 1895 (Ibn Nura)
2. Mare of Ibn Khalifeh
   Mare
   Grey mare
   <u>SHAHWAN</u>*, white, 1887 (Wazir)

THE ARAB HORSE

The Dahmeh Nejiba

1. 'Shohba', white mare of Khalil el Hajry, OM of Abbas Pasha I
    SOTTAM, flea-bitten grey, *c.* 1860 (Sueyd OH)
    Mumtaza, white, (Gharrân)
    <u>Badiaa</u>*, chestnut, 1884 (Aziz)
2. Nura, grey, OM of Abbas Pasha I
    Bint Nura, bay, *c.* 1860 (Zobeyni OH)
    IBN NURA, flea-bitten white, 1876 (Sottam)
    <u>Bint Nura es Shakra</u>* 'Bint Bint Nura', chestnut, 1885 (Aziz)
    <u>(IBN) MAHRUSS</u>*, chestnut, 1893 (Mahruss)
    <u>ABU KHASHEB</u>*, grey, 1894 (Mahruss)
3. Dahmet el Hamsa, bay mare of Ibn Awedye, OM of Abbas Pasha I
    GHARRÂN, white
    JERBOA – (Gharrân)

The Hamdanieh Simrieh

1. Selma of Abbas Pasha I
    <u>Sobha</u>*, white, *c.* 1879 (Wazir)
    <u>Safra</u>*, white, 1885 (Shueyman)
2. Mare of Ibn Saoud
    <u>Sherifa</u>*, white, *c.* 1862 (Bay Hamdani Simri)
    <u>SAOUD</u>*, grey, 1878

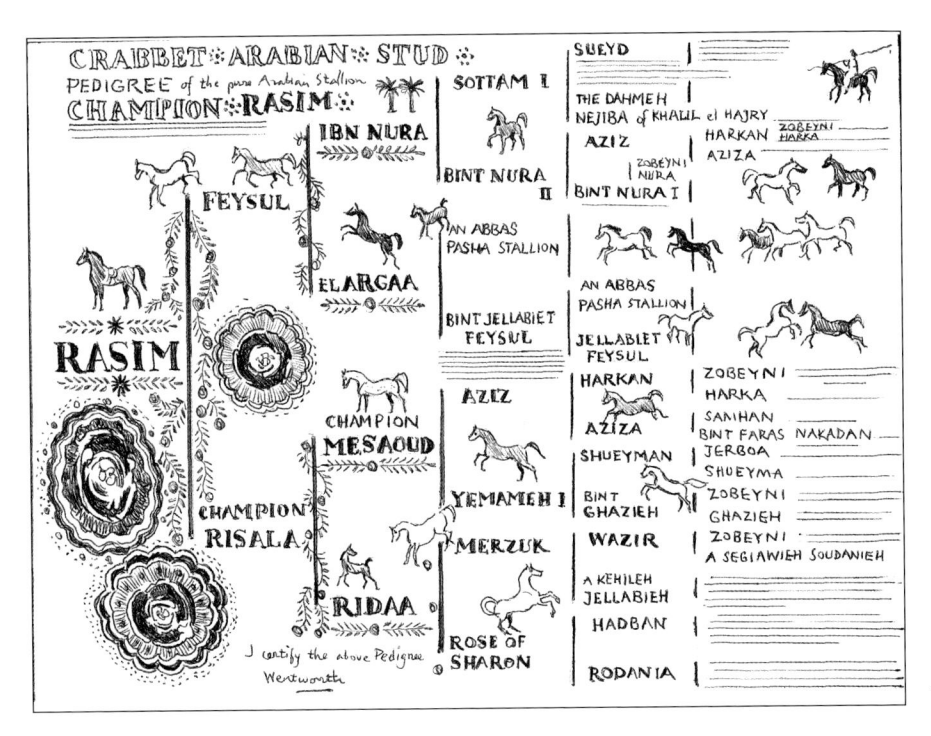

A Crabbet Pedigree, drawing by Peter

APPENDIX 2

The Tribes and their Horses

The bedouin, the noble tribes of the desert, and in particular that great confederation of tribes of central Arabia, known as the Anazeh, still trace their origins back to one Adnan through the great-grandson Rabiah al Faras whose son Asad (the Lion) fathered Anazeh and Jadailah. Adnan descends from Salaman, through his son Al Hamaisa, Al Yasa, Odad and Oddo, father of Adnan. Salaman, who lived *c* 1630 BC, was the owner of five Keheilet Mares, and the son of Nabet, son of Hamal, son of Kidar (King of Hijaz) the son of Ishmael. He, Ishmael, was born of Hajar and Ibrahim, whose descent can be traced through Peleg, brother of Kahtan (Joktan), Eber, Arphaxad and Shem to Noah, of the Ark. Through Yaarab (the Arab), son of Kahtan and father of the Arabic language, descend Hamyar and Kahlan. From Kahlan descend the Kings of Oman and through Hamyar the line traces to Balkis, thought to be the Queen of Sheba.

Anazeh was the father of the Banu Anazah who inhabited Khaibar, south of Jabal Shammar, and from there spread throughout all the central desert. Of the Banu Anazah was the Great Sheikh Wail, often called their 'First Ancestor' and from him descend Bishar, Jelas and Wahab. From Bishar come the Amarat of Ibn Haddal, the Fedaan of Ibn Muhair and the Seba'a of Ibn Mirshid. From Jelas come the great Roala tribe of Ibn Sha'alan and from Wahab come the Wuld-Ali and the family of Ibn Saud.

The major horse breeding tribes were these bedouin of the central and northern desert, the Anazeh, but by the 1870s, when Upton and the Blunts made their first journeys to Aleppo and the desert, the number of first-class horses to be found was already on the decline due to many causes. It is noticeable that the majority of good horses imported were obtained from two powerful sheikhs – the Ibn Mirshids of the Gomussa and the Ibn ed Derri of the Resallin. The Blunts found few good horses among the Shammar of Iraq, although for many years the trade in horses to India had centred about the town of Mosul.

It was from the collections of the Emirs of Arabia that many of the most valuable imports came, and, indeed, the horses imported by the Blunts from Egypt and of the Stud of Ali Pasha Sherif were of supreme importance. However, the horses which were obtained for the great studs of Arabia and Egypt were all originally purchased or taken from the bedouin tribes of the desert – the same as were visited by Major Upton and Wilfrid and Lady Anne Blunt. Zobeyni, an Original Horse of the Collection of Abbas Pasha I came from the Fedaan tribe as did Kars*, an Original Horse of the imports of the Blunts.

The Major Horse Breeding Tribes *c.*1800 (see Map)

The Anazeh A great confederation of tribes including:
- **The Roala (Ibn Shaalan)** – the most powerful tribe of the desert.
- **The Sebaa, including the Gomussa (Ibn Mirshid), the Resallin (Ibn ed Derri), the Abadat, the Moayaja, the Denadsha and the Amarat** – a wealthy tribe, possessing many of the best horses.
- **The Fedaan (Ibn Sbeyni), including the Mehed (Ibn Mehaid).**

The Wuld-Ali (Ibn Smeyr).

The Beni Sakhr (Al Faïz), including Al Guben, Al 'Amr, Al Geish, Al Koreishan and Al Ajbour.

The Shammar (Ibn Sfûk) including the Taï, the Zoba (Ibn Hamoud), the Saekh, Al-Hai, and Baggara including the Beni Jamil.

The Muntifiq (Ibn Saadun).

The Dhafir (Ibn Sueyti).

The Muteyr (Ibn Dawish).

The Ajman (Ibn Hithlain).

The Harb (Ibn Mutib).

The Oteybeh (Ibn Waeydha) including The Daajini.

The Qahtan (Ibn Hadi) – the most southern of the horse breeding tribes.

The Emir's Studs

The Ibn Al-Khalifah's of Bahrain
The Ibn Saud's of Riyadh
The Ibn Al-Rasheed's of Hail
The Sherif's of Makkah
    King Faisal of Iraq
    King Abdullah of Jordan
    The Royal Jordanian Stud
The Imaum of Muscat
The Sultan of Turkey
Abbas Pasha I of Egypt
    Ali Pasha Sherif

THE ARAB HORSE

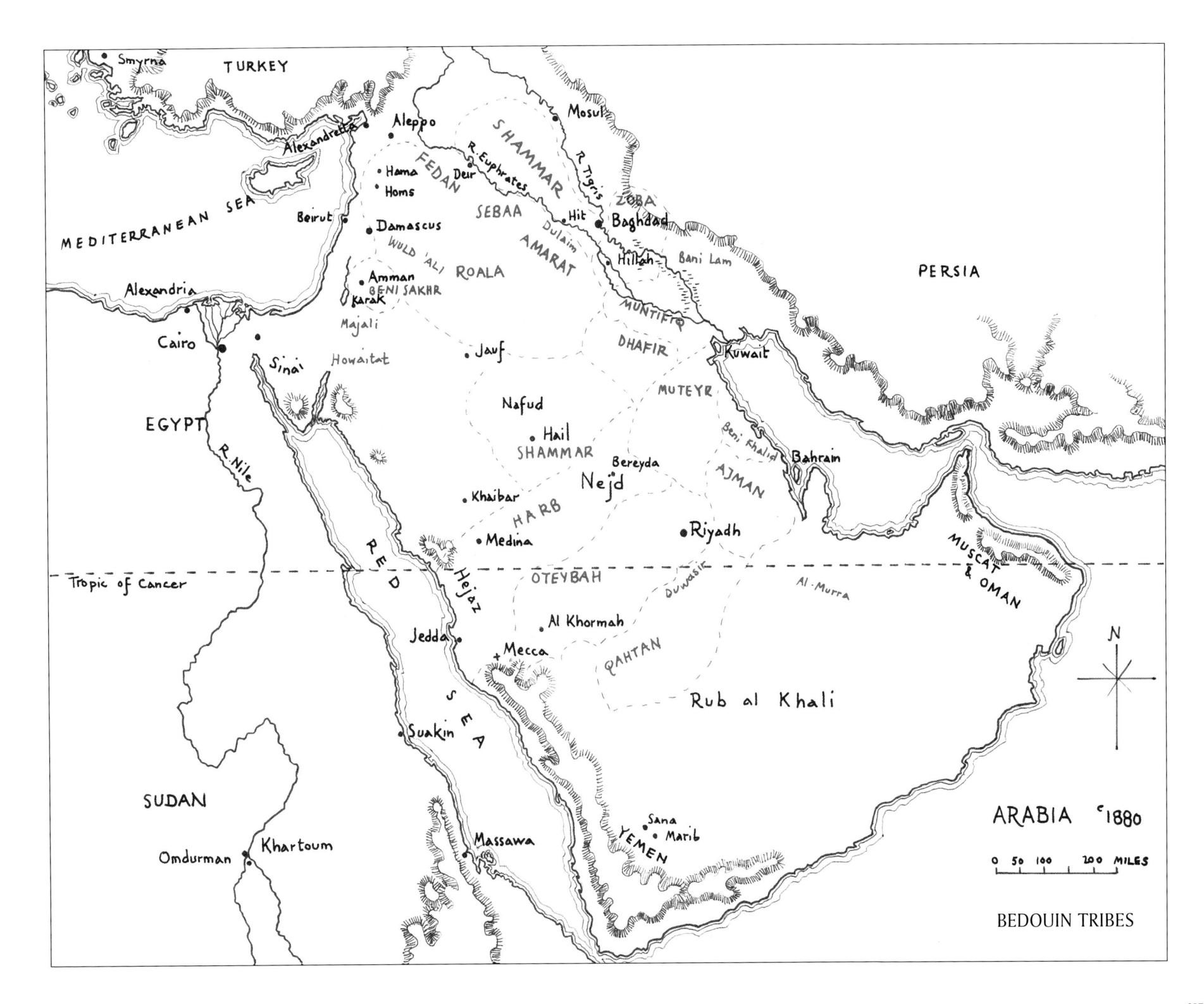

ARABIA c.1880
BEDOUIN TRIBES

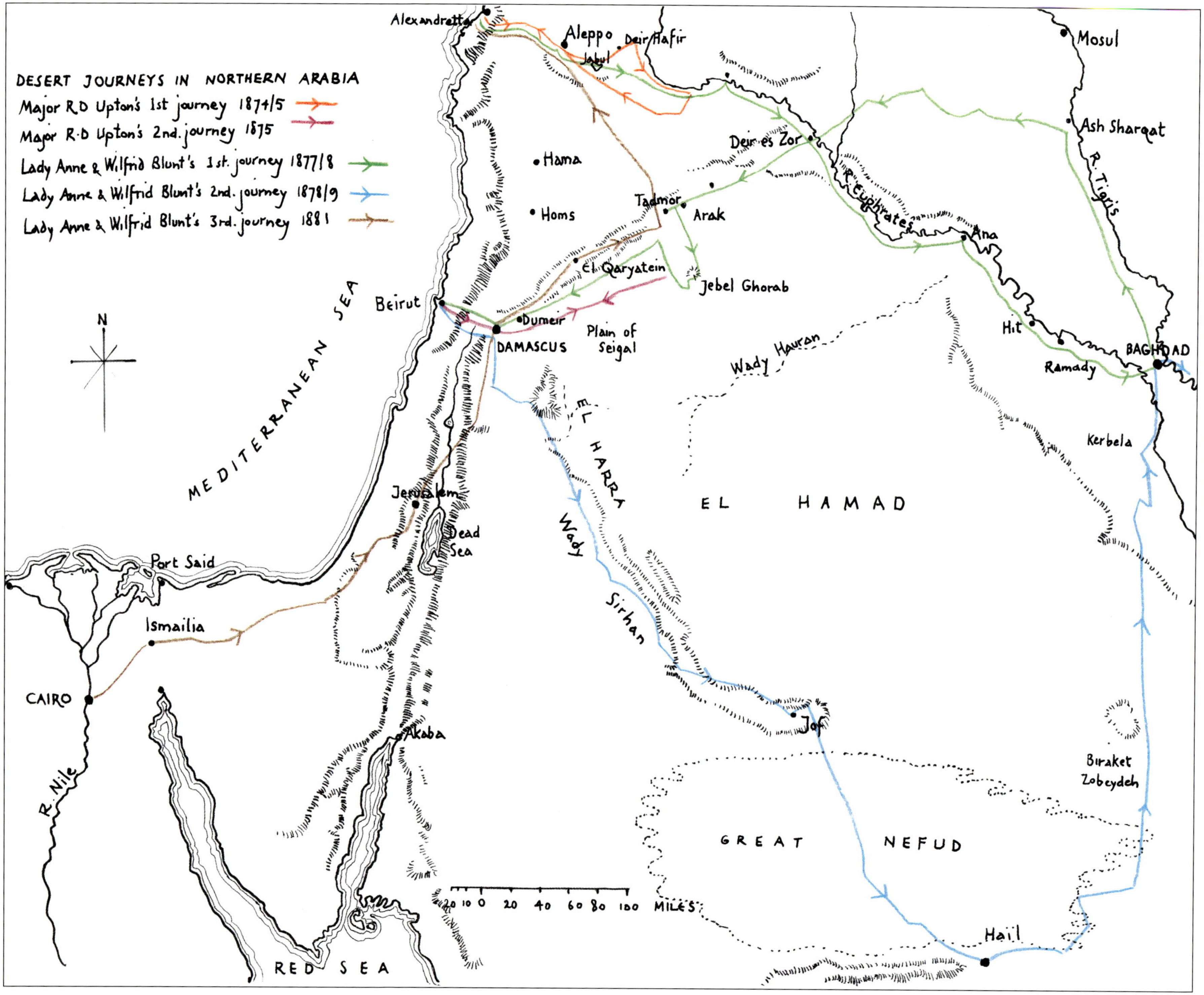
DESERT JOURNEYS IN NORTHERN ARABIA
Major R.D Upton's 1st journey 1874/5
Major R.D Upton's 2nd. journey 1875
Lady Anne & Wilfrid Blunt's 1st. journey 1877/8
Lady Anne & Wilfrid Blunt's 2nd. journey 1878/9
Lady Anne & Wilfrid Blunt's 3rd. journey 1881
N
MEDITERRANEAN SEA
Alexandretta
Aleppo
Deir Hafir
Jabul
Mosul
Ash Sharqat
R. Tigris
Deir es Zor
R. Euphrates
Hama
Homs
Tadmor
Arak
Ana
El Qaryatein
Jebel Ghorab
Beirut
Dumeir
DAMASCUS
Plain of Seigal
Wady Hauran
Hit
Ramady
BAGHDAD
Kerbela
EL HARRA
EL HAMAD
Jerusalem
Dead Sea
Wady Sirhan
Port Said
Ismailia
CAIRO
R. Nile
Akaba
Jof
Biraket Zobeydeh
GREAT NEFUD
20 10 0 20 40 60 80 100 MILES
Hail
RED SEA

The Tribes from which the Blunts' Horses Came
(Whose Lines Exist Today)

The Anazeh
   The Roala: Rodania.
   The Sebaa: Hagar (Dajania's dam).
      The Gomussa: Queen of Sheba, Dahma, RATAPLAN (via India).
      The Resallin: Meshura, PHARAOH, AZREK (Basilisk's dam).
      The Moahîb: Jilfa.
   The Fedaan
      The Mehed: KARS (Jedrania's dam).
The Shammar: Ferida.
The Baggara: Wild Thyme.
The Saekh: (Ashgar's dam).
The Oteybeh
   The Daajini: HADBAN (via India).
The Obeyd: Jerboa.

The Tribes from which the Other Horses Came
(Whose Lines Exist Today)

The Anazeh: MAHMOUD-MIRZA (via India), DWARKA (via India), MOOTRUB (via India).
   The Sebaa: Nejdmieh, MIRAGE (via Iraq).
      The Gomussa: Haidee, Kesia, Kesia II, YATAGHAN, ATESH.
   The Fedaan: FEDAAN.
The Shammar: Warda al Badia, Thrayat Hamid.
   The Zoba: EL EMIR (via Algeria).
   The Ali Yisar: Mahawiliyeh.
   The Abu Nisar: Takritiyah.
The Muteyr: Dafina (via Ibn Saud).
The Ajman: KASIM.
The Majali: Shammah, Shams, SHAMYL.
The Guzzawieh: Mejamieh, Libnani.
The Montefik: PADISCHAH (via Turkey), KISMET (via India).
The Dursi: CROSBIE (via Egypt).

Horses Imported by the Blunts, of the Stud of Ali Pasha Sherif
(Whose Lines Exist Today)

MESAOUD
MERZUK
SHAHWAN (Mohammed Sadyk Pasha)
(IBN) MAHRUSS
FEYSUL
IBN YASHMAK (The Blunts' Sheykh Obeyd)
Bint Helwa
Johara
Fulana
Bint Nura es Shakra
Makbula
Kasida
Jellabieh
Sobha (Mahmud Bey)

Horse Imported by the Blunts, of the Stud of Ibn Saud
(Whose Lines Exists Today)

Sherifa (via Sheikh Takha; Ulema at Aleppo)

Horses Imported by the Blunts, from India
(Whose Lines Exist Today)

HADBAN
RATAPLAN

THE ARAB HORSE

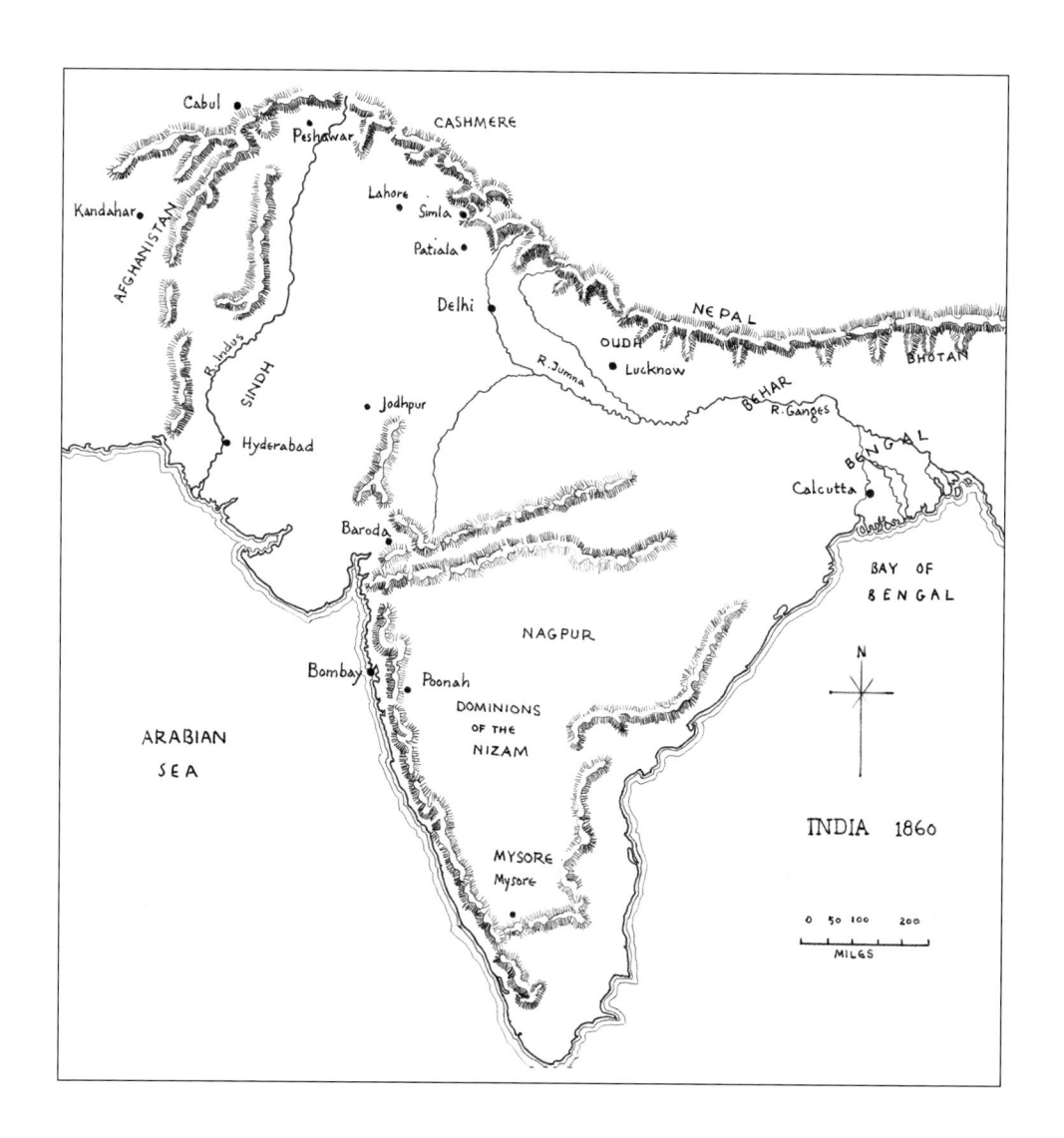

Horses Imported From the Studs of the Emirs of Arabia
(Whose Lines Exist Today)

Mecca (Prince Mohuiddin) NIMR.
Iraq (King Faisal) MIRAGE, Jamila I.
Jordan (King Hussein) El Yamama, Princess Muna.
Saudi Arabia (King Ibn Saud) KASIM, MANAK, Noura, Muha, Turfa, Dafina.
Haïl (Emir Abdullah Ibn Rasheed) Nejma.
Bahrain (Emir Hamed Bin Eissa Al-Khalifa) Nuhra.

Horses Imported From India
(Whose Lines Exist Today)

MUSKET
INDJANIN
NIZAM
MAHMOUD MIRZA
HUSSAR
KISMET
MAIDAN
MAMELUKE
MOOTRUB
DWARKA
ZOOWAR
Shakra
Ladybird

GLOSSARY

Abd	Slave.	*Husan*	Horse.
Abd-ul	The Honourable.	*Ibn (Ben)*	Son of.
Abuha	Her father.	*Ikhtara*	Raised tail when galloping.
Agha	Official, military or administrative.	*Jebel*	Mountain.
Ahmar	Red (bay) female – *hamra*).	*Jeeban*	Proven.
Akid	Military leader in the tribe.	*Jémel*	Camel.
Asfar	Yellow (white) (female – *safra*).	*Jibbah*	Prominence of forehead.
Ashgar	Chestnut (female – *shaqra*).	*Kadish (Attech)*	Impure.
Ashraf	Of noble blood.	*Khamsa*	Five.
Asil	Pure.	*Khedive*	Title of Turkish Viceroy of Egypt.
Aswad	Black/brown (Female – *saouda*).	*Kheyl*	Horses.
Azrek	Blue (grey) (female – *zerka*).	*Mahwardi*	Rose grey.
Bersim	Vetches.	*Marbut*	Strain (literally – tied).
Bey (Turkish)	Governor of district or title of respect.	*Mazbût*	Perfect.
Bint	Daughter.	*Mitbah*	Arch of throat.
Canvas	Groom, servant or attendant.	*Mohra*	Filly.
Daïra	Estate or property.	*Mutlak es Shemâl*	Three white feet, both hind and off fore.
Dakna	Flatback.	*Mutlak al Yemîn*	Three white feet, both hind and near fore.
Dalîl	Guide.	*Nafud*	Red sand desert of Arabia.
Delul	Riding camel (female).	*Nejd*	Central plain of Arabia.
Dîra	Area of desert over which a tribe travels.	*Pasha (Turkish)*	Hereditary title in Egypt.
Effendi (Turkish)	Title of respect.	*Rásan*	Strain (literally – rope).
El Kebir	The older (female – *el Kebira*).	*Rotha*	Pasture.
El Saghir	The younger, smaller (female – *el Saghira*).	*Seyal*	Blaze (literally – flowing).
Emir (Amir)	Leader.	*Shebba (Yesshebb)*	To serve, with stallion.
Fáras	Mare.	*Sherîf*	A descendant of the Prophet Mohammed.
Ghazu	Raid.	*Sultan*	Ruler of the Turkish Empire.
Haj	Pilgrimage to Mecca.	*Syce*	Groom.
Hammad	Desert.	*Ulema*	Learned man of religion.
Hedud	Well bred.	*Wâdy*	Valley.
Hellawi	Sweet.	*Wakîl*	An attorney.
Hojja	Certificate of pedigree.	*Zerka Marshusha*	Flea-bitten.

BIBLIOGRAPHY

Books

Abdy, Jane and Gere, Charlotte, *The Souls* (Sidgwick & Jackson, 1984)

Aly, Prince Mohammed, *Breeding of Pure-Bred Arab Horses* (Cairo, 1935)

Archer, Pearson and Covey, *The Crabbet Arabian Stud* (Alexander Heriot, 1978)

Bedford, John Duke of, *A Silver Plated Spoon* (Cassell, 1959).

Bell, Gertrude, *The Letters of Gertrude Bell* (S. Benn, 1927)

Blanch, Lesley, *The Wilder Shores of Love* (Abacus, 1954)

Blunt, Lady Anne, *Bedouin Tribes of the Euphrates* (John Murray, 1879)

Blunt, Lady Anne, *A Pilgrimage to Nejd* (John Murray, 1881)

Blunt, Wilfrid Scawen, *My Diaries 1888 – 1914* (Secker, 1919/20)

Blyth, Henry, *'Skittles' – The Last Victorian Courtesan* (Hart-Davis Ltd., 1970)

Borden, Spencer, *The Arab Horse* (Privately published, 1906)

Brown-Edwards, Gladys, *The Arabian – War Horse to Show Horse* (Arabian Horse Trust of America, 1969)

Buchman-Linard, Sara, *The Horse from Birth to Old Age* (Everett & Co., 1902)

Calthrop, Everard, *The Horse as Comrade & Friend* (Hutchinson & co., 1920)

Craver, Charles, *Al Khamsa Arabians* (Thrift Remsen, USA, 1983)

Doughty, Charles M., *Travels in Arabia Deserta* (Cambridge University Press, 1888)

Druid, The, *Silk and Scarlet* (Vinton & Co. 1859)

Drybrough, T.B., *Polo* (Vinton & Co., 1898)

Egremont, Max, *The Cousins* (Collins, 1977)

Fox Schmidt, Margaret, *Passion's Child: The Extraordinary Life of Jane Digby* (Hamish Hamilton, 1977)

Gazder, Dr Pesi, *Arab Horse Families* (AHS, 1964)

Greely, Margaret, *Arabian Exodus* (J.A. Allen, 1975)

Guarmani, Carlo, *Northern Najd* (Argonaut Press, 1938)

Harris, Albert W., *The Blood of the Arab, The World's Greatest War Horse* (1941)

Lawrence, T.E., *Seven Pillars of Wisdom* (Cape, 1926)

Londonderry, The Marchioness of, *Henry Chaplin a Memoir by his Daughter* (Macmillan, 1926)

Longford, Elizabeth, *A Pilgrimage of Passion, The Life of Wilfrid Scawen Blunt* (Weidenfeld & Nicolson, 1979)

Luteyns, Lady Emily, *A Blessed Girl* (Hart-Davis, 1953)

Lytton, The Earl of, *Wilfrid Scawen Blunt a Memoir by his Grandson* (MacDonald, 1961)

Maxwell, Joanna, *Spanish Arabian Horse Families 1898 – 1978* (Alexander Heriot)

Menzies, Mrs Stuart, *Lord William Beresford VC* (1917)

Miller, Capt. F.D., *Modern Polo*

Moray-Brown, J., *Riding and Polo* (Badminton Library, 1891)

Palgrave, William Gifford, *Personal Narrative of a Year's Journey Through Central & Eastern Arabia* (Macmillan, 1865)

Prior, C.M., *The Royal Studs of the 16th and 17th Centuries* (H & H, 1935)

Rihani, Ameen, *Ibn Sa'oud of Arabia*

Roberts, Field Marshall Lord, *Forty-One Years in India* (Bentley, 1897)

Sermoneta, Duchess of, *Things Past*

Sidney, S., *The Book of the Horse* (Casell, Petter & Galpin)

St Quintin, Col. T.A., *Chances of Sports of Sorts* (1912)

Trench, Richard, *Arabian Travellers* (MacMillan, 1986)

Upton, Major Roger D., *Newmarket and Arabia* (Henry S. King & Co., 1873)

Upton, Major Roger D., *Gleanings from the Desert of Arabia* (Kegan Paul & Co., 1881)

Upton, Roger C. *O For a Falconer's Voice* (Crowood, 1987)

Wentworth, Lady, *The Authentic Arabian Horse and his Descendants* (J.A. Allen, 1945)

Woodham Smith, *Florence Nightingale* (1950)

Articles

'An Interview with Mr Wilfrid Blunt', *Pall Mall Gazette*, July 1889

'The Royal Stud at Hampton Court', *The Sporting Magazine*, Volume XII, Second Series, Number 75, July 1836

Dickinson, J.M., 'Traveller's Rest Arabian Horses', A Catalog, 1939

'Egypt and the Soudan – Embarkation of Troops at Suakin', *Pall Mall Gazette*, March 1884

'Gifts of Horses to the King and Prince of Wales', *The Field*, 9 August 1919

'Horse Dealing in Syria in 1854', *Blackwoods Magazine*, Volume LXXXVI
'Impecuniosus', 'The Crabbet Park Arabs', *The Field*, 23 July 1881
'Neptune', 'Remarks on Foreign Studs and Horses', *The Sporting Magazine, 1836*
Selby, R.A., 'Arabian Horses', 1937
The Arab Horse Society: Journals and News, 1935-1988
The National Pony Society Show Catalogues, 1903-1933
Upton, Captain Roger, 'Arabian Horses Studied in Their Native Country in 1874-5', *Fraser's Magazine*, September 1876

Stud Books

Crabbet and Sheykh Obeyd
The Arab Horse Society, Volumes 1 – 15
The General Stud Book, Volumes 13 –35
The National Pony Society (formerly Polo Pony Society and Polo and Riding Pony Society), Volumes 1- 21
The Welsh Stud Book, Volumes 1 & 10
The Arab Horse Stud Books of Australia, Bahrain, Egypt, Germany, Italy, Jordan, Poland, Spain, South Africa, USA and USSR. (Russia)

THE ARAB HORSE

The Lone Horseman, Wadi Rum, *oil painting by Peter Upton.*

INDEX OF HORSES NAMES

Italic numerals denote page numbers of illustrations
*distinguishes imported horses from others of the same name
API – Abbas Pasha I; Ali Pasha Sherif – Ali Pasha Sherif;
EAO – Egyptian Agricultural Organisation; PBA – Part-bred Arab;
RAS – Royal Agricultural Society of Egypt; SO – Sheykh Obeyd; TB – British Thoroughbred

Mares

Aafina 292
Aana 282
Aatifa 271, 302
Aatika 268, 269, 273, 301
Abdul 270
Abigail 293
Abla 269, 286
Abla (EAO) 284
Adeebah 101
Afhar Rahza 277
Aida 84
203 Ajeeb-4 277
205 Ajeeb-2 277
Ajjam 287
Ajramieh 269, 286
Akabah II 280
Alaga Girl 291, 305
Alaga Maid 270, 281, 289, 291, 300, 305
Al Asmar 293
Al Caswa 270, 289
Alcouza 270, 280
Alexa 294
Alfarouse 277, 286
Alfila 277
Algella 305
Algola 278, 302
Algoletta 269, 273, 301
Alhama III 298, 299
Alika 269, 291
Al Johara 209
Al Karkhieh 207
Almanak 269, 291, 305
Almas 268, 269, 289
Alpaka 298
Alsita 301
Alzehra 294
Amadine 299
Amanda 277
Amida 269, 287

Amina 302
Amirat 277
Amneris 297
Amourette 299
Amra 269
Amurath 296
25 Amurath-Sahib 2 298
Amusheh 269
Ana 269, 301
Anaga 291
Andarina 270
Angelica 270
Anna Rose 276
Ansata Bint Mabrouka 281, 282
Ansata Bint Zaafarana 282
Antika 270, 286
Arabella 297
Arabella Minette 295
Arabian Dawn 269
Arabian Moonshine 269
Araby 278, 302
Arcadia 294
Arfa 296
Argency 289
Ariel 51, 53
Ariffa 269
Arusa 269
Arwila 296
Asfura 269, 286
Asila 289
Asrab 269
Assarkha 294
Astreelia 269, 280
Astrella 269, 276
Atlanta 291
Autumn Copper Beech 294
Awalani 291
Awdah 302
Ayesha 51
Aziza (APS) 149, 151, 155, 163, 181,
Aziza (SO) 72
Aziza Ann 269

Azleta 274
Azz 159
Azz (Bint Bint Azz)* 69, 70, 72

Babirah 268
Babylonia* 51
Badia 282
Badiaa* 68, 69, 70
Bahreyn 268, 273
Baida I 271, 300, 302
Bakmal 267, 268
Bakoorah 290, 302
Bakrah (APS) 86
Baksheesh 280
Balalajka 296
Balis II 304
Bambina 274, 292
Bandola 296
Bangle 293
Banna 268
Banzada 304
Baqubah 302
Barada I 304
Barada II 280
Barakat 299
Baranova 268, 278, 304
Baraza 268
Barcelona 296
Baribeh 268
Basilisk* 44, 45, 47, 51, 53, 57, 59, 61, 65, 84, 85, 67 268, 130, 131, 135, 148, 267
Bathsheba 267, 268, 271
Battla 267
Bay Abeyeh Sherrakieh of Erheyen Ibn Alian 135
Baylis 267
Baylis II 268
Bay Seglawieh Jedranieh of Ibn ed Derri 129
Baz, The Mare of 307
Bazikh 267, 268

Bazrah 267, 268, 271, 276
Bazvan 267, 268
Bekaa 297
Bekr 268, 304
Belka 268
Belkis 268
Belkis II 268, 278, 304
Bel Lindah 292
Bereyda 268, 269
Berlanta 271
Beryl 267, 268, 278, 304
Bessarabia 304
Beteyen's Mare, see Queen of Sheba
Betina 268, 305
Bika 296
Binni 268, 271, 280, 283, 289
Bint Astreelia 269
Bint Azz 68, 69, 159
Bint Bint Azz, see Azz
Bint Bint Fereyha, see Fasiha and Fulana
Bint Bint Horra 69
Bint Bint Jamila I 68, 69
Bint Bint Jamila II 68, 69
Bint Bint Jellabiet-Feysul (El Argaa) 68, 69, 72, 161, 189
Bint Bint Mahroussa 68
Bint Bint Nura, see Bint Nura II
Bint Bint Riyala 275
Bint Bint Sabah 282
Bint Bint Turfara 293
Bint Bukra 281, 282
Bint Dalal 280
Bint el Bahreyn 90
Bint Faras-Nakadan 149, 151, 155, 181
Bint Farida 282
Bint Fereyha 68, 153
Bint Ghazieh 181
Bint Helwa* 61, 66, 68, 69, 70, 148, 149, 151, 163, 278, 280
Bint Helwa es Shakra, see Johara

Bint Horra 70
Bint Jamila 70, 72
Bint Jellabiet-Feysul 161, 189
Bint Kateefa 274, 281
Bint Kerima 290
Bint Mabrouka, see Ansata Bint Mabrouka
Bint Maisa el Saghira 281
(Bint) Makbula, see Makbula*
Bint Makbula, see Manokta
Bint Makbula es Shakra, see Kasida
Bint Mona 281, 282
Bint Moniet el Nefous 281, 282
Bint Mumtaza, see Badiaa
Bint Nura (bay) 161, 189
Bint Nura (grey) 155, 186
Bint Nura II* see Bint Nura es Shakra
Bint Nura es Shakra, 53, 61, 68, 69, 70, 154, 155, 187, 280
Bint Obeya 209
Bint Radia 282
Bint Risala (Razieh) 274, 287
Bint Riyala (Risama) 275
Bint Rossana 295
Bint Roxana 275
Bint Sabah 281
Bint Sahara 273, 279, 283, 288
Bint Samiha 281
Bint Sedjur 273
Bint Serra 278, 282
Bint Turfa 293
Bint Turfara 293
Bint Yaseem 302
Bint Yasim 305
Bint Yasimet 271, 281, 302
Bint Yasmin 271, 281
Bint Zaafarana 281, 282
Bint Zareefa 282
Biruta 296
Black Bunny 303
Black Mare of Bender Ibn Saadun 187
Blue Dawn 270

323

THE ARAB HORSE

Blue Fantasy 292
Bluehayes Tezra 293
Blue Sabha 294
Blue Sapphire 294
Blue Sierra 293
Blue Sophonisba 279
Bonita 299
Borak 218, 289, 290
Bozra 171, 267, 285
Bozra II 268, 304, 305
Bukra 267, 269
Bukra (EAO) 282
Buraida 291
Burning Bush* 49, 51, 62, 84
Buseyna 294
Bushra 267, 286
Bussora 268, 304
Butheyna 268

Caesarea 297, 298
Calexa 294
Canaria 296
Canora 53, 54, 56, 61
Cantata 296
Carmen 296, 297, 298
Carmen II 296
Casiopea 299
Caswa 270, 291
Cazada 270, 291
Celina 279
Chavali 299
Cheran 305
Chocolata 298
Cinders 269, 301
Cleopatra 300
Consuella 270
Cora 300
Court Maiden 294
Crabbet Sura 278
Cressida 295
Crown Royal 272
Crystal Clear 302
Crystal Trinnket 302
C-sse Julie 297
Cuan Mylindra 295, 305
Czebessie V 17, 296, 297
Czebessie VI 296

Dabeh 289
Daffodil 292
Dafina* 78, 86, 89, 196, 197, 291, 292
Dafinetta 292
Daghestania
Dahma* 49, 60, 61, 86 270, 136, 137

Dahmeh el Hamra of Ibn Aweyde 153, 163, 307
Dahmeh Nejiba of Khalil el Hajry 153, 163, 189
Dahna 270, 285
Daifa 292
Dajania* 44, 51, 58, 271, 272, 140, 141
Damaris 292
Damask Rose 292
Dancing Princess 294
Dancing Sunlight 301
Daphne I 292
Daralga 291
Darani 291
Darda 297
Darella 291
Darfil 292
Dargemet 269, 271, 273, 281, 301, 302
Darley Filly, see Wild Thyme
Daronda 292
Darthula 292
Datura 292
Dawn 292, 301
Debora 270
Delphine 292
Demeter 291
Deraba 270
Deraiya 295
Deryabar 270, 280
Desdemona 300
Desert Song, see Nawagiyat al Furat
Devyani 292
Dewi 271, 302
Dijleh 270, 286
Dil Fireb 279
Dil Kushi 268, 304, 305
Dimity 300
Dinarsad 297, 298
Dinarzade 270, 285
Divina 297
D'Lorb 302
Domow 273
Doniazad 292
Doonyah 292
Dorelia 292
Doris 297, 298
Dove, see El-Yamana
Dragonfly 292
Dreaming Gold 274
Druchna 285
Drusilla 292, 303
Druzba 285
Dryad 292
Dueba 296

Dura 292
Durr el Zaman 292

Eastern Rose 303
Ecurb Rinarida 302
Egina 268, 273, 275, 289
Ela 296
El Arabella 305
El Argaa, The lame Jellabieh, see Bint Bint Jellabiet-Feysul
El Bataa 282
El Batrana Saada 94
Electra 295
Electricia 280
Elekcja 285
Elfa 299
El Hacene 303
Elizabeth 277
Elkana 296
El Kardomah 293
El Lahr 270, 289, 290
El Melha 94
Elmwood Geinine 295
Elokwencja 285
El Yamama* 98, 208, 209, 211, 295
Elwa 282
Elwya 281
Elza 279
Elzusia 299
Epoyeja 259
Estelle Arabella 295
Estokada 297
Estopa 298, 299
Estrella 293
Euterpe 298
Evelyn, see El Melha

Faaba 282
Fabiola 294
Fadaa 293
Fadila 280, 286
Facina 298
Fae 304
Fafika 276, 279, 303
Fa Habba 282
Fajr 302
Falha 277, 293, 301
Falha (Primula) 293
Falha el Muntafiq 293
Falka 291
Fama 285
Famula 268, 273, 275, 289
Fand 304
Fanya 270
Fantana 271, 279
Fantasia I 279, 304

Fara 294
Fara Fadl 293
Farasin 279
Faras* 89, 201, 257, 260
Faras-Nakadan 86
Farenta 278
Farette 269, 274, 278, 301
Farida (Jordan) 289
Farida II 279, 304
Farida III 302
Fa Saana 282
Fashoda 279, 304
Fasiha 69, 279
Fasila 279
Fathia 271, 293, 302
Fatima (bay) 272
Fatima (ch) 272
Fatma 271, 277, 300
Fauna 277
Fayalindra 303
Fayella 279, 292, 303
Fayrouz 281
Fedala 304
Fedora 291
Fejr 279
Felestin 279, 287
Feluka 279, 286
Feluka II 279, 304
Fe Gama 277
Ferda 216, 275, 279
Ferdirah 279
Fereyha 153
Ferha, see Francolin
Ferida* 166
Fer-Natta 268
Fersara 279, 283, 288
Fezara 279, 286
Fianza 299
Fiona 292
Firefly 279, 302
Fitnah 279, 304
Fleabitten Grey Mare* 19, 19
Flora 298, 299
Florencia 274
Francolin 44, 45, 47, 53, 54, 61, 80, 81, 135
Fregata 285
Freyha 305
Fulana* 68, 69, 152, 153, 280
Fureiha 94
Furzey Amanda 292
Fuwasa 277, 305

Gadara 280
Gaffi 303
Ga-Gajala 304

Gail of Kingsholme 293
Gajala 281, 304
Galatife 299
Galena 303
Gamelia 302
Ganyma 302
Gara 267, 268, 273, 283
Ga-Gajala 304
Ga-Rageyma 304
Garance 275
Gariba 302
Gastronomia 296
Gay Negma 303
Gay Tarriff 294
Gayza 267-9, 283
Gazella 268, 274, 275, 289
Gazya 267 268, 279
Gebina 292
Geneva 294
Geynima 304
Ghadia (Radia) 73, 84, 282, 287
204 Ghalion 298
Gharifet 273, 283
Ghezala 95, 277
Ghazawi 283, 288
Ghazayat 280
Ghazeyna 280
Ghazieh (SO) 84
Ghazieh (API) 149, 151, 157, 163, 185
Ghazala* 68, 73, 149, 162, 163, 282, 283, 279
Ghazu, see Zefifia
Gileem 280
Githera 302
Gleaming Gold 272, 274
Golden Dream 293
Gomora 296
Grace Kesia 291
Grey Mare* 19, 19
Grey Royal 272
Grey Seglawieh Jedranieh of Ibn Sbeyni 127
Gruzinka 285
Guda 285
Guemura 282, 288
Guliran 292, 301
Gulnare 276, 280, 283
Gumniska 285, 299
Gutne 273
Guzida 303
Gwadiana 297

Habbana 293
Habiba 267, 268, 271, 279, 289
Habina 280

Hada 270, 280
Hafiza 282
Hafra 279
Hagar* 45, 47, 48, 49, 51, 60, 80, 83 138, 139, 270, 271, 298, 299
Hagar II 270
Hagar (Polish) 298, 299
Haidee* 32, 35, 36, 37, 65, 216, 288
Haifa 297
Haita 297
Hajar 297
Hajeyla, see Meshura
Hajwa 299
Hakima 295
Halfa 81, 82, 83
Halfina 270
Halima (EAO) 282
Halima I 280
Halina 298
Halka 298, 299
Hama I 279
Hamada 289, 290
Hamasa 279, 286
Hamdany V 296
Hamdany VI 17, 296
Hameeshé 270, 277
Hami 299
Hamida 279
Hamleta 297
Hammami 270
Hamu 270
Hanan 281
Hanna 270
Harik 138, 270, 285
Harima 270
Harka 149, 151, 155, 163
Harra 270, 285
Harra II 270
Hathor 297
Hawanna 299
Hazia 294
Hazna 279
Heart's Desire 270
Hebe 299
Hebe II (Aust.) 305
Hedba 294, 296
Hegazieh of Nejd 84
Hela 298, 299
Helga 294
Helwa 149, 151, 163, 280
Heritage Labelle 279
Heritage Memory 279
Hermosura 295
Hester, see Dajania
Hestia 270, 281, 289, 291, 300, 205

Hilandera 298, 299
Hillcrests Bint Imaraff 301
Hillcrests Bint Tsatyr 292
Hilmyeh 269, 279
Hilwa 291
Hilwe 279
Hi-Natta 268
Hira 288
Hisan 283
Horma 301
Horra (Hora) 58, 65, 149, 151, 163
Howa I 270, 286
Howa II 270, 280
Hubara 270
Huseima 268, 275, 289
Husn-u-Gul 270, 300

216 Ibn Ghalal 1-8 298
Imagida 303
Imaja 303
Imamara 303
Imelina 299
Imna 277, 303
Impedida 299
Incoronata 272
Incoronetta 272
Indaia 272, 276
Indian Crown 272, 276
Indian Glory 272
Indian Pride 272, 274
Indian Trinket 302
Iona 291
Iorana 275
Irena 297, 298
Ishtar* 78, 80, 218, 290
Ispahan 268, 273, 275, 289, 299
Istashra 292

Jadine 297, 298
Jadwiga 297, 298
Jacaranda 297, 298
Jalila 273
Jalmuda 150, 280, 286
Jamila (Jemla) (RAS) 73, 142
Jamila (SO) 72
Jamila (ch) 142, 273
Jamila I* 94, 227, 292, 293
Jamila II 292
Jamusa 277, 286
Janczarka 299
Jask 282
Jasmeen 271, 281, 302
Jasmine, see Dajania
Jatta 297, 298
Jawi Jawi 280

Jebel Druz 267, 285
Jedran 300, 305
Jedrania* 58, 60, 80, 126, 127, 267
Jellabieh* 69, 72, 77, 90, 160, 161, 282
Jellabiet-Feysul 90, 157, 189
Jemeyza 273, 286
Jemima 41, 42, 43, 80
Jemla 282
Jena 297
Jeneyna 273, 286
Jenin 291
Jerawa 282
Jerboa* 44, 51, 60, 61, 142, 143, 273
Jerud 273, 285
Jessamine, see Dajania
Jezabel 282
Jilfa* 64, 165, 177, 179, 277
Jirro's Mare 51, 60
Jiwa 276, 280
Joasia 297
Johara (Bint Helwa es Shakra)* 69, 70, 150, 151, 280
Joharah* 292, 304
Jordania 95
Josepha 279
Josephine 279
Judith 80
Julnar 281
Juniper 267
Jurneeka 279, 288
37 Jussuf 299
91 Jussuf 299

Kabila 281, 287
Kae 304
Kalfa 301
Kalilah 294
Kalima 292
Kamla 281, 282
Kamocli 292
Kamseh 301, 302
Kandija 270, 298
Kantara 281, 286
Kantista 268, 273, 275, 289
Kapel 291
Karaka 301
Kareyma 281
Karim 268, 304
Karit 306
Karoosha 301
Karta 297
Karubah 302
Kasbana 273, 282
Kashmira 269

Kasida* 70, 70, 72, 74, 75, 90, 157, 158, 159, 281, 282
Kasima 271, 281
Kasimet 290
Kassa 300, 305
Kassida 290, 291
Kassie 270, 291, 305
Kastylya 298
Katahza 277
Kateefa 274, 281, 282
Kateefah 270, 300
Kaukab 290
Kazaba 294
Kazamah 294
Kazminda 294
Kazra 294, 304
Kazra el Saghira 294
Kedem 301
Kerak 288, 290
Kerbela 281, 287
Keren-Happuch* 41, 42, 43, 85
Kerima 281, 289
Kesia* 13, 35, 39, 41, 42, 43, 78, 85, 217, 218, 289, 290
Kesia II* 42, 43, 83, 217, 218, 259, 289, 290
Kezzia 292
Khadijah 270
Khadijah Kesia 291
Khalasa 300
Khamala 294
Khamilla 294
Khamisa 294
Khashbi 302
Khatila 65, 66, 67, 147, 181
Kholey 301
Kibla 156, 281, 286
Kirat 270, 300, 302
Kishta 279
Kiyama 281
Knopka 291
Koalicja 296
Koheil III 296, 298
Komir 303
Kreatura 273
Krim 290
Krona 278
Kubaysheh 58
Kufara 270, 289
Kushdil 285, 288

Labadah 270
Lady Alice 80
Lady Anne 80
Ladybird* 219, 290

Lady Blunt 291
Lady Hestor, see Dajania
Lady Mylindra 305
Lafirynda 296
Lakshmi 303
Lala 296
Lalage 296
Lalla Rookh* 91, 91, 93, 249, 251
Languish (TB) 15
Larkspur 273, 286, 288
La Sombra 294
Layla 281
Leila 300
Lhotse 271
Libnani 193, 219, 291
Lilac Domino 276
Little Liza Fame 277
Little Sheba of Yeoman's 292
Lo'ba (dam of El Yamana) 209, 211
Loo-el-Nejdi
Luda 281
Lurbi I, see Lo'ba

Maamouna 282
Maarqada 282
Maasreh 267, 302
Mabrouka 267, 282
Mabruka 286
Mabsuta 267, 286
Maeve 295, 305
Mafari 276
Magic Moments 293
Magnolia 297
Mahal 277
Mahasin 273, 282
Mahawiliyah* 94, 202, 203, 293
Mahbuba 267, 280, 289
Mahroussa 84
Maid Marian 292
Maid of the Moot 290
Maisuna 267, 286
Makbula* 68, 72, 90, 156, 157, 159, 281
Makbula I 157, 159
Makbula el Kebira see Makbula I
Makeda 291
Malaka 267
Malaka (Eg) 275
Mamsahi 97
Mandilah 94
Manokta 68, 159
Mansura 267, 286
Manzana 269, 271, 275, 277, 300
Marah 293
Marladi 290

Mareesa 277, 286
Mare of Nakadan, see Faras-Nakadan
Marhaba 267, 280, 287
Mariposa 277
Marishna 276
Markisa 267
Marladi 290
Masarrah 297
Mashalla II 274
Matara 267
Matoufa 270
Mazna 267
Meca 299
Mecca, see Sherifa*
Mecca II 270, 289
Meccana 301
Medinah 270
Medina 291
Meera 294
Mejamieh* *192*, 193, 219, 291
Meliha (Aust.) 270
Meliha I 278, 301
Melody 292
Merjana 267, 286
Meroe 267, 285
Meshura* 51, 59, *59*, 60, 85, *128*, 129, 267
Mesopotamia 51
Mi'Enaqia 215
Mifaria 78, 270, 275
Mimosa 218, 289
Minifette Silvan 295
Minsa 267
Mira 305
Miralai 292
Mirza 288, 302
Misery 270
Mish Mish I 271, 302
Mish Mish II 305
Misma 301
Mistana 290
Mlecha I 285
Mlecha III 285
Moallaka 267, 286
Mocha 301
Moheba 282
Mona (Mouna) 281, 282
Moneyna 273, 277
Monica 273
Moniet el Nefous 282
Monopolia 274
Moonbeam 271, 302
Moraea 271, 275, 277, 300
Morayama 289
Moubarek 267, 287

Mouraffa 267
Muha* 32, 199, 220, 292
Mulaika 267
Muna 277
Muna, see Princess Muna
Munariffa 277
Muneera 282
Muzehra 294
Muzri 294
My Bonnie Nylon 292, 304
Myola 269, 273, 276, 301
Myolanda 269, 301
Myoletta 301
Myra 269, 301
Myrilla 293
Myrtle 294

Naadirah 272
Naama 272, 288, 300
Nadsada 298
Nafaa El Sahira 209
Nafara 271, 279
Nafisa el Shaakirah 294
Nafud 276, 288, 289
Nagrada 272, 274, 276
Nahla 286
Najada 298
Najadie 291
Najine 288
Namilla 269, 271, 275-7, 300, 301
Nanda 288
Naomi 288, 299
Naomi I 27, 35, 36, *37*, 63, 82, 273, 289
Naomi II 288
Napraslina 272
Narda 271, 276
Nareesa 288
Narghileh 271, 286
Narkeesa 288
Nasam 283
Nashisha 272, 273
Nashmeshnik 297
Nasifa 272
Nasim 283
Nasira 272
Nasirieh 272
Nasmeshka 272
Nasra 272, 280
Nasseb 98, 209
Natta 268, 283
Naturalistka 272
Nawagiyat al Furat* (Desert Song) 252, 295
Nautch Girl 272, 278

Nawarra I 298
Nawarra II
Naxina 271
Nazlet 288
Nazli 27, 36, 288, 300
Nazziria 272
Neamis 291
Nefisa *62*, 63, 141, 175, 271, 285
Nefudi 292
Negotka 272
Negressa 298
Nejadie 291
Nejdmieh* 90, 195, 220, 291
Nejd Sherifa 291
Nejiba 271, 286
Nejma* 90, *194*, 195, 291
Nejmeh 253
Nemisia 293
Nera 272, 275
Neraida 271, 272
Nerina 274
Nerinora 274, 275
Nerpa 275
Nessa 267, 277
Nessima 271, 276
Nezma 272
Nezza 290, 291
Niezgoda 296
Nimet 290
Ninawa 271, 286
Nisan 283
Niseyra 272, 276
Niskha 269
Nisreen 272
Nisyana 272
Nitochka 272
Noam 271
Nomenklatura 272
Nonliker 286
Noora 277
Norah 58
Noura* 32, *89*, 89, *198*, 199, 220, 292
Nouronnihar 281, 292, 300, 302
Nowagieh 222, 289
Nuhra* 89, 90, *204*, 205, 294
Nuhajjela 294
Nura (Mrs Digby's) 59, 60
Nura (APS) 65, 153, 155, 189
Nuralina 272
Nurmahal 294, 305
Nurmana 294, 305
Nurschida 269, 271, 275, 277, 300
Nusara 271

Nusi 269

Obeya 276, 282
Odessa 301
Om el Saad 275, 282
Onrust 286, 288
Ophir 288
Oranet 281, 302
Oriana 303
Orientacia 291
Orilla 294
Oriole 270

Paita 299
Pale Shadow 274
Panay 285
Panel 278
Panika 296
Parfumeria 274
Parthia 281, 302
Pera 288, 303
Peraga 303
Petra* 302
Plaska 273
Platina 278
Podolanka 285
Pomona 290
Princess Muna* 98, *210*, 211, 277, 295
Przepiorka 285
Purple Stock 49, 51, *52*, 54, 61, 80
Qadisiyah (Keheileh) 213
Qafza 93
Qasameh 307
Queen of Sheba* 48, *49*, 49, 51, 53, 58, 65, 81, 85, 87, *134*, 135, 137, 269, 270
Queen Shakra 290, 300

Raad 273
Raaf 276
Raafada 293
Rabanna 268
Rabiha 294
Rabina 294
Rabiyat 276
Rabla 276, 286
Rabna 279, 283
Rachel I 304
Radsilla 302
Raduga 273
Rafeena 268, 275, 289
Raffira 304
Raffani 292
Rafika 276

Rafina 274, 276
Rafleyga 304
Ragala 274, 303
Rageyma 281, 304
Rahab 276
Rahika 268, 283
Rahzawi 283
Raida 276
Rajanto 295
Rajjela 294
Rakima 286
Raksh 300
Rakud 277
Rakusheh 277, 300
Ramara 293
Ramayana 271, 275
Ramim 267, 276
Rangha 276
Ranya I 271, 275
Ranya II 275, 280
Rasana 277
Raschida (Wild Honey) 277, 285
Rasheeda 292
Rasheeqa 277
Rasima 273, 278, 280
Rasmina 273
Raxina 271
Rayya 276, 277
Razehra 294
Razieh, see Bint Risala
Razina 275
Rediaa 294
Regal Lady 294
Resique 277
Rexalla 293
Rexan Shemara 293
Rexaya 293
Rexbaya 293
Rexeena 278, 290
Reyna 274
Rezeda II 275
Rhoda 305
Riad 271, 277, 300
Riada 183, 277, 286
Riazana 294
Ridaa 273, 286
Rifa 291
Rifala 274
Riffalka 291
Riffilla 269
Rifla 276
Rihani 292
Rijma 273
Rikitea 269, 275
Rim 270, 276

Rimini 276
Ringing Derida 302
Ringing Enchantress 302
Risala 273, 286
Risama, *see* Bint Riyala
Rish 271, 276
Rish (Beteyen's) 51
Rishima 303, 304
Rishna 271, 276
Rishyana 276
Risira 272, 275
Rissalma 274
Risseefa 274
Rissiletta 272
Rissla 267, 274
Rissletta 272, 274
Risslina 274
Rithyana 276
Ritla II 281, 302
Rixalina 274, 276
Rixiliyah 293
Riyala 270, 275
Riz 273
Rizada 268, 273, 289
Rizala 276, 277
Rizza 294
Robirda I 290, 300
Robirda II 290, 300
Rodania* 32, 60, 61, 85, *144*, 145, 273-7
Rodetta 303
Roglemar Zarad 288
Rokhama 270, 276
Rokhsa 271, 276
Rominna 300
Romira 304
Rommia 304
Rorobird 300
Rosanna 273, 300
Rosa Rugosa 276, 289, 290
Rose Diamond 273
Rose du Sable 280, 283
Rosemaria 304
Rosemary 155, 273, 276
Rosemary II 304
Rose of France 273, 276
Rose of Hind 273, 276
Rose of Jericho 273, 285
Rose of Persia 300
Rose of Sharon *62*, 63, 175, 273, 276
Rosetta 277, 286
Roshana 276
Roshina 269
Rosheiya 269, 289
Roshara 275, 283

Roshnara 269, 289
Rosina 304
Rossana 273
Rossana II 295
Roxana 275
Roxanta 271
Roxira 275
'Royal' Mares 15, 16
Royal Radiance 278
Rozeta 285
Ruanda 273
Rubiana 270
Rudena 305
Rudeyna 278
Ruellia 271, 275
Rueyda 277
Rufeiya 269
Rufeiya II
Rumana 302
Rumeliya 276
Rusala 270
Russallka 269, 289
Russilla 292
Ruth I 304
Ruth II 268, 276, 304
Ruth Kesia 268, 289, 290
Ryama 291
Rythma 273
Saadyah 277
Saaida 302
Sabah 209
Sabal 297, 307
Sabal I 209
Sabal II 268, 274, 275, 289
Sabigat 301
Sabine 296
Sabot 267
Sabrina 304
Safari 305
Safarjal 267
Safie 293
Safra* *67*, 67, 147, 277
Sahara 285, 299
Sahara Dawn 288
Sahara Queen 288
Sahara Rose 288
Sahfiya 294
Sahiba 297
Sahmana 302, 305
Sahmet 297
Sahra 302
Sahra-Su 274
Saida 297
Saki 279
Salambo 304

Salome I 270, 291
Salote 304
Samantha 293
Samarytanka
Samha (API)
Samha 153, 297, 298
Samha (Jordan)
Samia 293
Samiha 268, 274, 275, 289
Samira 282
Samsie 271
Samura
Sanaaa 282
Sange 303
Sant 270, 300, 302
Santa Fe 277
Saoud 297
Sapphire 302
Sappo 304
Sarama 278
Sardhana 271, 278
Sardine 297, 298
Sarra 268, 275, 289
Savona 297, 298
Sawadeh
Sayrayal 293
Sayif 291
Sayyeda 293
Sceptre 305
Sea Pearl 283
Sebba 303
Sel Hani 292, 303
Selima 277, 304
Selinga 278
Selma 297
Selma II 269, 277
Selma III 304
Selma V 296
Selmnab 277
Semiramida 298
Semna 305
Senga 278
Serafina 272, 278
Serafire 272
Serena 278
Serinda 301
Seriya 278
Serra 278
Sesame 304
Shaara 305
Shabaka 218, 289, 300
Shabana 294
Shabrette 268, 274, 278, 301
Shabryeh 301
Shades of Night 272

Shagra 302
Shahiya 294
Shakana 294
Shakra* 219, 290
Shalimar 280
Shalina 272, 273, 276, 278
Shamal 303
Shamanto 295
Shammah* *99*, 99, *206*, 207, 294
Shamnar 275
Shams* *98*, *214*, 215, 261, 295
Shangri-La 301
Shanina 294
Sharaya 269, 276, 278, 293
Sharbana 293
Sharfina 272, 273, 278
Sharima 272, 278
Sharon 293
Shazla 292
Shebaka 269, 286
Sheba's Queen 304
Sheeba 269, 271, 277, 300
Sheeba II 294
Sheer Magic 276
Shehrezad 268, 285, 304
Shcjrct Eddur 270, 300, 302
Shelfa 53, 171, 269, 273, 290
Shelfa II 290
Shem el Nassim 293, 305
Shemma 277, 290, 301
Shemse 268, 285
Sherara 163
Sherezada 279
Sherezada II 292, 304
Sherie 304
Sherifa* 46, 47, 49, 51, *52*, 59, 64, *65*, 65, 67, 86, 87, *132*, 133, 147, 185, 268, 269
Sherifa (Australia) 270
Shibine 269, 286
Shiboleth 269
Shicha 268, 286
Shima 294
Shimagic 293
Shirabia 269
Shiraz 268, 285
Shohba (API)
Shohba 269, 296
Shthora 291, 305
Shueyma 149, 151, 157, 163
3 Siglavi-Baghdady V1-6 298
Signorinetta 304
Silent Wings 272, 278
Silfina 272, 278
Silindra 272

Silka 278
Silmana 302
Silsilla 278
Silver Crystal 278
Silver Fire 272, 278
Silver Gilt 272, 278, 279
Silver Grand 278
Silver Grey 278
Silver Ripple 274
Silver Shadow 278
Silver Sheen 278
Silver Velvet 271, 302
Silwa 278
Simawa 278
Simrieh 277
Sinai 301
Sira 267
Sir Aatika 270, 289, 291
Sirella 269, 272, 273, 301
Sirena 294
Sirikit 268, 290
Siwa 269, 278
Siwa II 304
Siyasa 301
Slipper 288
Sobha* *65*, 67, *146*, 147, 277, 278
Soldateska 297, 298
Solome IV 304
Soleyma 278
Somara 278
Somra 280
Somra II 304
Sparkle 305
Starilla 276, 278
Starlight Blue Dancer 293
Starlight Shadow 293
Star of the Hills 276, 278
Sukr 304
Suleena 292
Sulka 269, 271, 272, 275, 277, 300
Sultana 302
Sunny Acres Tammie 292
Sylphide I 297, 298
Syria 305
Szansa 298

Tahdik 277
Taima 279, 303
Tajemnica 298
Taj Mahal 294, 305
Takrithan 293
Takritiyah* 222, 293, 294
Taktika 278
Tamara 300
Tamarisk* 26, 44, *45*, 47, 49, 51, 62

Tamarisk 49
Tamiza 298
Tar Asman 293, 305
Taraszcza 396
Tarim 268, 304
Tarney 289
Tariff 294
Tatima 289, 290
Tara 290
Tehoura 272
Teofanja 298
Teorica 298, 299
The Lady Euridice 279
The Lady Heloise 271, 279, 301
The Lady Idar 271, 279
The Lady Lucretia 279, 303
The Lady Roxane 269, 279, 301
Thrayat Hamid* *212*, 213, 295
Transjordania 289, 299
Triana 298, 299
Trix Silver 280
Truncefice* 14
Trypolitanka 296
Tuema 291
Tura'a 94
Turfa* 32, 89, *90, 200*, 201, 257, 260, 293
Turfada 293
Turfara 293

Ugra 285, 299
Umatella 275
Ur 301
Urga 302
Uyaima 298, 299

Vaga 290
Vanessa 293
Vans Natta 268
Varsovia 297
Velvet Haze 294
Velvet Shadow 283
Venus (Abbas Pasha Hilmi II) 86

Wadeya 292
Wanda 95
Wanda II 95
Wanisa 282
Warda 291
Warda al Badia* 293
Wazira, see Jellabiet-Feysul
White Dahmeh Nejiba of Khalil el Hajry, see Dahmeh Nejiba of Khalil el Hajry
White Lace 283

White Seglawi Jedranieh of Neddi Ibn ed Derri 131
Wild Bee 164
Wild Honey 277, 285
Wild Thyme 49, 51, 61, 164, 277
Winarsad 297

Yakouta 293
Yamain 275
Yaquta 277
Yaronda 292
Yarzeena 292
Yashmak 185, 191, 275, 286
Yashmak (EAO)
Yasimeen 267, 290
Yasimet 302
Yatagan 275
Yatana 280
Yatima 275
Yaz 251
Yemama 191
Yemameh 187
Yet Again 290
Yetima 290
Yirene 290
Yosreia 282

Zaafarana 282
Zabba 269, 301
Zaduban 292
Zahle 291, 302
Zahr 280
Zahra 303
Zahrawiyah 292
Zahri 269, 273, 280, 283, 301
Zaian 294
Zakieh 277
Zalema 299
Zamora 302
Zara 269
Zareefa 281, 282
Zarif 280
Zarifa 282
Zarifah 282, 293
Zarifet 269, 289
Zarissa 293
Zefifia *59*, 59, 61
Zehraa 294
Zem Zem 300
Zenobia, see Burning Bush
Zethari 293
Ziba 292
Zilati 280, 283
Zilfe 292
Zimrud 273, 300

Zirree el Wada 280, 283
Zobeide 281, 292, 302
Zohorab Bostan 293
Zona 294
Zuleika 35, 36

Stallions

Aaraf 274
Aaron 301
Abadan 293
Abd-el-Azaiz 81
Abdullah* 84, 95
Abdullah 291
Abeyan 20, 62, 64, 88
Abu Argub II ,215
Abu Farwa 273, 274, 276, 283
Abu Khasheb* 68, 280
Abu Shammek 295
Abu Zeyd, see Lal-i-Abdar
Achmed 295
Actaeon (TB) 20
Adonis 304
Aethon 270, 281, 200, 289, 291, 300, 305
Agwe 279, 303
Ahmar *73*, 73, 269, 286, 296
Ain Sahib 293
Ain Sahib al Muntafiq 292
Ajeeb 277, 286
Ajeeb I 277
Ajlun 291
Ajman 269, 287
Akran 295
Alaa el Dine 274, 281
Aladdin 291
Aladdin (Australia) 270, 281, 289, 296, 300, 305
Al Araj, see Al Mahyubi
Al Burak 267, 269, 273, 293
Alcazar 302
Alcock Arabian 14, 16
Aldebaran (Aldebar) *83*, 83, 269, 301
Alexus 274
Algol 269, 276, 301
Algolson 269, 301
Alhabac 268, 273, 275, 289
Alif 34, 36, 43
Ali Jamaal 279, 281
Almanzor 285
Al Mahyubi 308
Almulid 277, 286
Aluf 268, 269, 289, 301
Ambassador 292

Ameer 29
Amerigo 279
Amurath 1881 296, 297, 298
Amurath II 296, 297, 298
Amurath Sahib 296, 297, 298
Anazeh 288
Anbar 270, 286
An Malik 268, 275, 289
Ansata el Arabi 282
Ansata Ibn Halima 281, 282
Ansata Shah Zaman 282
Antar (SO) *67*, 67, 147, 279
Antar (EAO) 276, 282
Apollo 303
Aquinor 296, 297
Arabian Night (PBA) *32*, 32, *33*
Arabi Kabir 281, 303
Aramus 272, 292
Arax 296, 297
Argos 272, 296
Argus 291
Arundel* 14
Asfour 281
Ashgar* 26, *63*, 64, 165, 177, *178*, 179, 286, 296
Asil 81, 82
Astraled 66, 73, 270, 286, 296
Aswan 281, 282
Atesh* 85, 93, *248*, 249, 251, 304
Athos 285
Atilla 291
Atlas 258
Auda 290
Aurab 279, 283
Aurelian 293
Awaj I 307
Awaj II 307
Aziz 57, 61, 65, 68, 147, 149, 151, 153, 155, 157, 159, 163, 181, 187
Azkar 283
Azraff 274
Azrek 59, *63*, 64-6, *72*, 73, 85, 129, 165, 171, *176*, 179, 181, 247, 286
Azym 277

Baarouf 269, 301
Babylon 291
Bahar 268, 274, 275, 289
Baharein 268, 275, 289
Bahrain 89, 90, 205
Bahram 268, 278, 305
Bairaktar 17
Bakir 302
Balaton 297
Bamby 274, 292

Banat 296
Bandos 272, 296
Barkis 269, 296, 301
Barquillo 298
Bashom 304
Bashom 'The Fox' 27
Bask 296
Bay Abi 303
Bay Arabian 18, 19
Bay el Bey 303
Bazleyd 267, 268, 271, 273
Bedouin 292
Bedr 267
Ben Azrek 268, 286
Bendigo 268, 304
Bend Or 267, 268, 278, 304
Bend Or (TB) 36
Benjamin 268, 272, 278, 304
Berk 73, 161, 267, 278
Bey Shah 303
Binis 267, 268, 271, 276, 280, 283, 288, 289
Black Arabian, see Sultan
Blenheim 267, 268, 278, 304
Blitz 24-6
Blue Domino 272, 274
Boanerges 290, 300
Boaz 268
Bob 25
Bohar the Famous 235
Borak 302
Bright Shadow 275
Bright Wings 275
Burkan 272, 296
Byerley Turk* 16

Carlo 295
Carmargue 272, 283
Champurrado 272, 274
Chandi* *32*, 32
Chez Nous Shah Rukh 278
Comanche 290, 303
Comar 98
Comet 296
Congo 297, 298, 299
Count D'Orsaz 274, 275
Count Rapello 269, 290
Crabbet 271
Crosbie *84*, 84, *244*, 245, 302
Crystal King 302

Dadia 294
Daoud *66*, 66, 280, 286
Dargee 78, *79*, 267-9, 273, 276, 301
Darinth 291

Darjeel 269, 273, 294, 301
Darley 51, *52*, 61
Darley Arabian 16, 18, 49
Darzee 292
Debir 292
Deepak 292
Delos 291
Derazne 289, 299
Desperado V 303
Dictator 26, 62, 64, 81, 82
Djezzar 291
Doktryner 296
Dolmatscher 299
Donax 268, 269, 271, 273, 281, 290, 301, 302
Don Carlos 294
Dorian 294
Dunes 279
Durral 269, 301
Dwarka* 13, *31*, 31, 32, 77, 78, *83*, 83, 86, *236*, 237, 301
Dynamit 296
Dzelfi 299
Dzelfi-Mlecha 285, 299

Eco 297
El Azrak 296
El Borak 267
El Dinari 307
Electric Silver 272, 275, 278
Electric Storm 275, 278
El Emir* 13, 61, 78, 80, 86, 218, *226*, 227, 300
El Jafil 267
Elkin 296
Elmas 302
El Meluk 300
El Moez 282
El Nattall 268, 283
El Sabok 267, 288
El Sarcei 282
El Shaklan 281, 298
El Tali 298
Emir Raperio 295
Enwer Bey 296
Errabi 279, 303
Espartero 296
Euphrates 294
Excelsjor 296

Fabah 282
Facination 303
Fadi 279
Fadjur 83, 279, 283, 288

Fadl 201
Faher 296
Fakher el Din 281, 282
Fakhr el Kheil 294
Fame VF 303
Fand 280
Fa Raad 293
Farana 271, 279
Faraoun 280, 286
Farawi 279, 283, 288
Farazdac 275, 281
Farhan 80
Fari II 269, 274, 278, 301
Faris* 61
Faris 271, 279
Fa-Serr 282
Fa Turf 293
Fayad 307
Fayal 279, 303
Fayek 281
Fay el Dine 282
Fedaan* 85, 93, *252*, 253, 255, 304, 305
Ferdin 271, 279
Ferdine 279
Ferhan 276, 279
Ferneyn 273, 279
Ferseyn 277, 279
Ferzon 83, 279, 283, 288
Feyd 304
Feysul* 70, *71*, 72, 72, 91, *188*, 189, 191, 287
Fez 304
Fire Bolt 303
Firuseh 270, 300
Fitz* *84*, 84
Flame of Reynall 292

Gaflizon 303
Gage 292, 303
Gai Parada 274, 279
Gaizon 279, 304
Galal 281
Galero 289, 299
Gali 84
Galimar 281, 303, 304
Gamil Manial 209
Gandhy 299
Gandur 299
Garaveen 36, 82, *83*, 285, 300
Gaysar 303
Gazon 279
General Grant 271, 275
Genjo 295
Gerwazy 296

Geym 274, 281, 304
Ghadaf 283
Ghadir 282
Ghailan 271, 279, 303
Gharbi 283, 288
Ghawi 283
Ghazal 281, 282
Ghazi 276, 283, 288
Godolphin Arabian* *16*, 16, 18, *58*, 58
Gokart 296
Gold Rex 274
Gomusa* (Davenport) 85
Gomussa 22, 285, 288
Grand Duke 303
Grand Royal 270, 272, 275, 278
Greatheart 274
Greylight 275, 278
Grey Owl 271, 276
Grojec 296
Grosvner's Arabian 15
Guimaras 302
Gulastra 270, 283
Gwalior 272
Gwarny 297
Gyn 303

Habiente 299
Hadban* 61, 62, 63, 75, 81, *174*, 175, 285
Hadban Enzahi 281
Hadeed 81
Hadramaut 81, 82
Hafiz 300
Hail 271, 273, 300
Haji I 293
Hajji II 302
Haladin 296, 297
Haleb* (Davenport) 85
Halef 296
Halim 279
Halin 292
Hamdan 282
Hamdani I 298, 299
Hamdani II 297, 299
Hamran 280
Hamran II 280
Hanif 269, 270, 272, 273, 278, 301
Hanraff 274
Hanrah 283
Harab 283
Harb 280, 286
Harir 267, 279
Harkan 149, 151, 155, 163
Harod 282

Harwood Asif 276
Hassan I 290, 291
Hauran 267, 271290
Hazzal 292, 301
Hazzam 267, 279
Helwar 289, 290
Hermes 291
Heron 299
Hilal 201, 270, 281, 300, 302
Hlayyil Ramadan 281
Hojeys 307
Hoshabeh
Hossny 282
Houbaran 269, 301
Huckleberry Bey 303
Hukum 291
Hurricane 293
Huseyni 270
Hussar* 23, 29, 32, 63, 259, 299
Hussar 259, 299
Hussar II 299
Huzzor 29, 30

Ibn Azz Saghir 70
Ibn Bint Horra 68
Ibn Bint Jamila, see Jamil
Ibn Bint Jellabiet-Feysul, see Feysul
Ibn Bint Nura, see Abu Khasheb
Ibn Bint Nura es Shakra 68, 151
Ibn Bint Nura Kebir 70
Ibn Bint Nura Saghir 70
Ibn Fadl 293
Ibn Fakhri 281
Ibn Fayza 282
Ibn Gulastra 283
Ibn Hilal 201, 281, 293, 300, 302
Ibn Johara 69, 70
Ibn Julep 304
Ibn Kuhailan* 94
(Ibn) Mahruss* 68, *186*, 187, 286, 280, 296
Ibn Mahruss 267, 286
Ibn Makbula 70
Ibn Mansour 274
Ibn Mirage 304
Ibn Moniet el Nefous 281, 282
Ibn Mumtaza 68
Ibn Nadir 65, 68, 69, 131
Ibn Nura 68, *69*, 69, 72, 153, 161, 189
Ibn Rabdan 85
Ibn Sherara 65, 68, 69, 149, 151, 163
Ibn Sirecho 293
Ibn Yashmak* 72, 73, 77, 185, *190*, 191, 286, 287

Ibn Yemama* 72, 287
Ibn Zarifa Kebir 69
Ibn Zarifa Saghir 69
Ibrahim 20
Idol 277, 304
Ifni 268, 274, 275, 289
Ikhnatoon 281
Ilustre 297
Image 274, 303
Imagin 303
Imagination 303
Imam 290, 300
Imamzada 218, 289, 290
Imaraff 303
Imaum I* 20
Imaum II* *20*, 20
Inak 23, 297
Indian Flame II 274
Indian Gold 272, 279
Indian King 270, 272, 274, 275
Indian Magic 78, 272, 275, 276
Indian Silver 275
Indian Star 274
Indjanin* 22, 23, 32, 297, 298
Indjanin, see Nizam
Indraff 272, 274, 276
Indrage 272, 276, 303
Indrani 292
Indy 272, 274
Inkas 297
Irex 272, 274
Iridos 268, 274, 275, 290
Ishmael* 41, 42, 43
Islam 276, 280, 283, 288, 289
Ivanhoe Tsatan 292
Ivanhoe Tsultan 301

Jabbar 293
Jacio 298, 299
Jadib, Horse of 308
Jady 292
Jaecero 268, 275, 289, 298
Jaleel 280
Jamil 72, 73, 84, 163
Jamil (Germany) 281
Jamrood 273, 300
Jamschyd 127, 267
Jarzmo 23, 297
Jason 298
Jaspre 279, 303
Jedaan, see Proximo
Jedran 267, 300
Jedran (Australia) 291
Jellal 282
Jemscheed 22

THE ARAB HORSE

Jengis Khan 127
Jerboa 149, 151, 153, 157, 163
Jeroboam *61*, 61, 64, 171, 273, 285
Jeruan 271
Jesscan 20
Jezail 267, 290
Jiddan 302
Job 53
Johar 273, 286
Joktan* 41, 42, 43
Joktan II 286
Joseph 267, 271
Jotham 290
Julep 283
Junak 297
Juno 291
Jussuf 299

K of K 290, 301
Kaftan 268
Kahtan 305
Kaibab 290
Kaisoon 274, 281, 282
Kalat 269, 301
Kamar al Zaman 281
Kami 290
Kamim 292
Kankan 274, 276
Kara Kouch 81
Karnak 288, 290
Kars* 22, 44, *45*, 51, 53, 54, 57, 58, 60, 62, *63*, 64, 65, 66, 73, 80, 83, 84, 85, 127, *168*, 169, 181, 185, 285
Karun 281
Karusen 302
Kasadi 276
Kasim* 89, 201, 257, 260, 290, 305
Kasim I 286
Kasimdar 290
Kasmeyn 77, 278, 281
Kataf 270, 281, 300, 305
Katar 278, 283
Katun 302
Kazmeen, *see* Kasmeyn
Kehilan 209
Kemah 288, 290
Khaibar 89
Khaldi 302
Khaled 288
Khalid 290
Khalifa 27
Khalil 290
Khemosabi 83, 279, 288
Khorseed 22
Khyber 290

Kimaree 300
King of Orient 222
King Shihab 293
King Soloman 81
Kismet* 26, 61, 81, 82, 83, *228*, 229, 231, 300
Kit 301
Knippel 274, 276
Koheilan II 299
Koheilan IV 299
Kolastra 283
Komsul 303
Korej 274, 276
Kouch 22
Kuchkolla 81
Kulun 302

La Flag 274
Lal-i-Abdar (Abu Zeyd) 273, 286
Lebrijano 299
Leedes Arabian* 16
Lewisfield Amigo 292
Lubek 295
Ludo 274, 276
Ludrex 268, 290
Lutaf 268

Mabrouk Blunt 267, 287
Mabrouk Manial 209
Mabruk II
Magic 29, *30*
Magnat 274
Mahmoud (TB) 14
Mahmoud Mirza* 259, 298, 299
Mahomet 84
Mahruss 68, 69, *70*, 187
Maidan* 26, 27, 81, *230*, 231, 300
Mairouf 269, 301
Majid 302
Maleik el Kheil 294
Malik Mylindra 305
Malvito 268, 273, 275, 289, 299
Mameluke* 42, 82, 83, 218, 259, 300
Manak* 89, 201, *256*, 257, 260, 305
Manasseh 267, 269, 301
Maneefah 304
Mansour 209, 267
Maquillo 268, 273, 275, 289, 299
Marabut 296
Mareb 267, 287
Marino Marini 275, 278
Markham Arabian 16
'Marvel', *see* Dwarka
Marwan Al Shaqab 277
Marzouk* 290

Mashour 281, 282
Mecca 29, 47, 49
Mehemed-Ali 298, 299
Mehemet Ali 303
Mehrez 95, *100*, 101
Mehzeer 294
Mejdil 291
Mekdam 275, 282
Melchior 297
Melnad 292
Menes 297
Menzil 267
Mersa Matruh 267, 287
Mersuch I 299
Mersud 93
Merzuk* 65, 66, 73, 181, *182*,, 183, 286
Mes'ad 68, 69
Mesaoud 32, 61, 65, *66*, 73, 76, 137, 175, *180*, 181, 286
Mesenneh 84
Mieczmik 296
Mikeno 269, 271, 274-7, 300, 301
Minaret 270
Mirage *246*, 247, 303, 304
Mireed 267, 287
Mirfey 304
Mirzam 267
Mizan 302
Modena 28, 31
Moftakhar 274
Mohawed 281
Mohort 285
Moneyn 273, 277
Monogramm 272
Mootrub* 29, 78, 219, *232*, 233, 300
Mootrub II 290, 300
Morafic 281, 282
Mubarak 267
Mujahid 278
Mumtaz Mahal (TB) 14
Muntasser 295
Muscat 20, 272
Muscat (Russia)
Musket* *240*, 241, 301
Muskmar 290, 301
Muskro 290, 301
Mustapha 267
Mustapha Kamel 267, 287
Myros 294

Naaman 271, 286
Naaman (USA) 288
Nabeg 297
Nabor 272

Nadir 271, 286
Nafia 271, 287
Naharin 276, 283
Nahrawan 271
Naib 298
Najib 271
Namir 303
Nana Sahib (Poland) 297
Nana Sahib (Spain) 268, 273, 275, 273
Narenk 271, 286
Narkise 73, 271
Narzigh 279, 283
Naseel 271
Naseem 73, 272
Nasik 73, 271, 276
Nasr 68, 159
Naufal 271, 278
Nawab 271
Naxor 305
Nazar 291
Nazeer 281
Naziri 272
Nebuchadnezzar 291
Negatiw 272
Negatraz 272
Nejal 276, 286, 288, 289
Nejd 288
Nejdran* 29, 32, *238*, 301, 302
Nejdran jun. 301
Nejef 271, 286
Nejran 73, 271, 286
Niall 293
Niga 303
Nigm Essubh 280
Nimr* 82, *91*, 93, 249, *250*, 251, 304
Nimr (Vidal) 36, 288, 300
Nimrod 272, 278
Nissar 272
Nissr 91
Nizam* (Indjanin) 272, 298
Nizar 271, 277, 300
Nizzam 271, 272, 276, 277,
Nomer 272, 275
Noran 270, 274, 275
Nowik 299
Nureddin II 271, 276
Nuri Pasha 268, 271, 289, 290
Nuri Sherif 269, 271, 277, 300

Ophaal 293
Oran 76, 270, 275, 276
Orive 298, 299
Ornis 299

Outlaw* 84, *254*, 255, 305
Ozem 303

Padischah* 13, 17, 24, 32, 258, 296, 297
Padishah III 301
Padron 275, 301
Padron's Psyche 275
Palas 278
Pantaloon (TB) 15
Paquerra 305
Parahk 27
Partner 301
Patron 272
Pelham's Grey Arabian, *see* Alcock Arabian
Persimmon 294
Phantom 274, 303
Pharaoh* 51, 53, 54, 55, *56*, 59, 60, 61, 63, 66, 80, 85, 73, 129, 135, *170*, 171, 177, 181, 285
Pomeranets 274
Priboj 274
Pride, *see* Shamikh
Prince Caspian 295
Prince Nejd 289, 290, 291
Procyon 299
Proximo 48, *49*, 60, 62, 81, 85
Pulque 303
Purple Emperor 61, 81

Qaied 215, 161
Qannas 307

Rabalain 81
Rabiah 286
Rabidan 294
Rabiyas 273, 276, 283
Radi 275, 276
Radium 84
Radwan 282
Rafeef 271, 275
Raffene 303
Rafferty 274
Raffi 274, 303
Raffles 78, 274
Rafyk 273, 286
Raghibah 290
Ragos 294
Rahal 276
Rahas 273, 283
Rajah I 302
Rajmek 294, 300
Rakan 305
Raktha 272, 275

Ralvon Pilgrim 275, 290
Ramik Rogue 292
Rana 301
Raouf 73
Rapture 274
Ras al Hadd 287
Raseel 303
Raseem 273, 276
Raseyn 277
Rashad 253
Rashad Ibn Nazeer 282
Rasham 278, 286
Rashid I 304
Rasim 73, 273, 287
Rasim Pierwszy 279
Raswan 276
Rataplan* 36, *61*, 62, 64, 81, 82, 85, 164, *172*, 173, 285
Rayal 271, 279, 303
Razada 268, 275, 289, 290
Razaz 273
Razaz II 272, 276
Razzia 270
Red Rover 26
Redif 277, 280
Reformer 62, 81
Registan 273
Rehal 276, 288, 289
Rejeb 276, 286
Resh al Badia* 261, 305
Reuben 305
Reynalton 292
Rheoboam 276, 278
Riaz 273, 294
Ribal 267, 273
Rifage 274, 303
Rifari 274, 279
Riffal 271, 275
Riffayal 269, 279
Riffyah 294
Rifnas 271
Rifraff 274
Rijm 187, 286, 276, 280
Rikham 268, 275, 276
Rishan 271, 276
Rissalix 274, 279
Rissam 272, 276
Rithan 275, 276
Riyal 189
Rix 276, 303
Rizvan 273, 287
Roala 273, 285
Robagol 293
Robin Adair of Kingsholme, *see* Al Burak

Robin Hood of Kingsholme 293
Rodan 276, 280
Rodan II 277
Rohan* *234*, 235, 300
Romar II 300
Ronek 268, 273, 277
Rostam 283
Rouf 269, 300
Roxan 275
Royal Crystal 301
Rozmaryn 285
Rukuban I 301
Rukuban II 291, 305
Ruminajaa Ali 281
Rustem 270, 276
Rustem Bey 303
Rythal 274
Rytham 273

Saameh 298
Sahab 282, 307
Sahar 304
Sahara 33
Sahban 269, 301
Sahran 302
Said 20, *23*
Sainfoin 255, 278
Sajden* 298
Salaa el Dine 281
Saladin I 304
Saladin II 272
Salon 272
Saludo 299
Sameh (Samih) 209, 211
Samhan 51, 149, 155, 163, 304
Sanad, *see* El Emir
Saoud* 61
Saoud II 301
Saoud III 304
Sarafan 305
Sargon 288
Sayyid 290
Seef 281
Segario 288, 289
Seglavi 296, 297, 299
Selim 297
Selim II 304
Selmage 277, 303
Selman 209
Selmian 278
Serab 22
Seradin 301
Serafix 272, 275, 278
Seyal *73*, 73, 278, 286
Shadrach 304

Shah 286
Shahloul 282
Shah Sherifa 291
Shahwan* 66, 67, 68, *69*, 73, *184*, 185, 191, 286
Shahzada 95, 268, 288, 299, 300
Shaikh al Badi 281
Shaitan 301
Shaker el Masri 281
Shalindra of Weatheroak 305
Shalufzan 24
Shamdar 295
Shamikh 98
Shammar 272, 278, 305
Shamyl 261, 295, 305
Shanfara 268
Shareer 73, 271, 277
Sharzan 293
Shasar 293
Shazda 292
Shebooth 294
Sheelar 295
Sheihan (sire of Outlaw) 255
Sheik el Arab 282
Shelook 290
Shem 304
Shere Ali 81
Sherif (SO) 277
Sher-I-Khurshid 276
Shihab 269, 290, 301
Shimrix 303
Shirik 304
Shishak 294
Shoo-af-an 20
Shueyman *57*, 57, 61, 65, 87, 147, 149, 151, 157, 163, 181, 247
Shwaiman* 95, *97*
Sid Abouhom 281
Sidi 276, 288, 289
Sikin 271, 279
Silver Drift 272, 275, 278
Silver Moonlight 275, 278
Silver Vanity 270, 275, 278
Silwan 278
Sinbad 288, 289
Sindh 270, 272
Sir Akid
Sirdar 291
Sirius 305
Sisera 305
Skorage 281, 303, 304
Skowronek* 76, *77*, 77, 99, 245, 253
Sohrab 302
Sole Hope 269, 301
Solferino 298

Solomon 304
Sottam (APS) 153, 161, 163, 189
Sotamm (Crabbet) 270, 278
Sotep 274
Soueidan* *93*, 93
Soueidan el Saghir* 93
Spindrift 278
Stambul 267
St Simon 304
Sueyd 153, 163, 189
Sulejman 279
Sultan 17, 18, 20
Sureyn 277, 278
Surf 278
Suvenir 272
Sylvan Shadow 295
Symmetry 36
Synbad 274, 283
Szamil 298

Tabab 283
Tabal 298, 299
Takamir 294
Takara 303
Takara Raffon 303
Takomega 294
Talal* 84
Talal 281, 282
Tarff 293
Tarra 294
Terrafi 20
Terrassan 20
Tetrarch (TB) 14
Tetuan 299
The Bey 31
The Desperado 281
The Egyptian Prince 281
The Leat (Dartmoor) *31*, 32, 301
The Minstril 281
The Real McCoy 288
The Shah 282
The Shah (Australia)
The Syrian* 29
Timsa 282
Trypolis 297
Tryptyk 296
Tsali 292
Tsatyr 292, 303
Tuareg 298, 299
Tuhotmos 282

Ubayan 209, 211
Umpire 26, *27*
Uns el Wujood 270, 300
Ursus 298, 299

Ushaahe 268, 274, 275
Uzacur 268, 275, 299

Vampire 299
Vasco de Gama 297
Violence 213
Vizier (see Wazir)
Vonolel * *24*, 24, *25*, 81

Wanderer 81
Wandyk *23*, 23, 297, 298, 299
Warda al Badia 221
Wazir 57, 61, 65, 67, 68, 84, 131, 147, 149, 157, 159, 163, 183, 185, 187
White Lightning 272

Xayal 271

Yagoda 259
Yakoot 302
Yamage 304
Yassif 292
Yatagan* 32, 35, 216, *224*, 225, 299
Yaz 251
Yima 288
Young Revenge 61

Zab 269, 301
Zabarjid 302
Zadaran 291
Zad-el-Rakib 307
Zadir 279
Zancudo 298, 299
Zanzibar 20
Zarif 280
Zarife 291
Zarouf 301
Zehros 294
Zelimage 303
Zem Zem 288, 290
Zerka 291
Zethan 289
Zeus II 280, 283
Zingari 271, 302
Zobeyni 149, 151, 155, 157, 163, 181, 185, 189
Zoowar* *242*, 243, 302
Zurich 299

GENERAL INDEX

Abadat, tribe of the Sebaa 59, 131
Abassia (Abassieh) 57, 58, 245
Abbas Pasha I 58, 67, 72, 76, 84-9, 100, 129, 147, 149, 155, 157, 161, 163, 181, 183, 189
Abbas Pasha Hilmi II 85, 87, 91
Abd el Hamid Bey 69
Abd el Jadir of Deyr 131
Abd el Kader 34
Abd er Rahman Minni (Abdul Rahman, Abdur Rahman) 24, 26-7, 61, 62, 81, 85, 88, 121, 173
Abd er Rajak Jerba 127
Abdul Aziz al Saud, King 86, 87, 89
Abdul Khadim Jabbar of the Al Yissah 203
Abdullah Ibn Rasheed, Emir 90, 93
Abdullah Ibn Saud (9th Amir) 86
Abdullah, King of Jordan 95, 98, *99*, 113, 123, 209
Abdullah, great uncle to Sherif Hussein of Makkah 94
Abdul Mehsin Ibn Bedr 173
Abdur Rahman, Minni 229, 231
Abdur Rahman Pasha 62, 64, 85, 253
Abtan 60
Abu 'Amr 203
Abu Fayad Wells 145
Abu Jedda tribe, Shammar 165
Abu Nissar 222
Abu Ridwan 235
Abud, Lt. Col. H.M. 241
Aduane tribe 95
Afghanistan 27, 231
Aga Khan, HH 81, 82
Ahmed, Sheikh of the Hanadi, *see* Sayed Akmet
Aid el Temimi 87
Airlie, Lord 26, 27, 231
Ajman tribe 86, 89, 90, 260
Akid 47
Akkar 89
Akmet, Sheikh of the Hanadi, *see* Seyd Ahmed, Sheikh of the Hannadi 44
Albert, HRH Prince 22
Aleppo 14, *34*, 34-7, 43-4, 47, 49, 51, 53, 59-62, 82, 129, 133, 137, 169, 216, 225
Alexandretta 36
Algiers 227
Al-Hai, sub tribe of Shammar 235

Ali Abdullah 81
Ali Agha, a Kurd at Deyr 127
Alice, Princess, *see* Athlone, Countess of 89-90
Ali Haidar, Sherif 93
Ali Ibn 'Amr 81, 175
Ali Ibn Hussein (Emir) 84, *96*
Ali Ibn Khalifa *see* Ibn Khalifa
Ali Jaffer, Sherif 251
Al-Khalifa *see* Ibn Khalifa
Ali Karim, Sheikh of Khurasa 221
Ali Pasha, Governor of Deyr 129
Ali Pasha Sherif 43, 57, 58, 61, 65-70, 84, 86-7, 112, 117, 131, 147, 149, 151, 153, 155, 157, 159, 161, 163, 181, 183, 185, 187, 189, 191
Ali Yisar tribe 203
Allenby, General 193
Al Tabouh 90
Al Thalatha
Al-Zoba tribe 47, 80, 94, 229
Amato 69
Amman 98
Anazeh 34, 36, 43, 44, 47, 51-3, 57, 80, 83, 85, 86, 165, 169, 173, 177, 216, 217, 218, 225, 237, 247, 249, 251, 253, 259
Anazeh, brother to Jadailah 307, 314
Ancaster, 2nd Duke of 14
Anderson, Brigadier W.H. 124, 201
Anderson, Colonel J. 124
Anne, HRH Princess 98
Antoniny Stud 63
Antrim, Earl of 64
Arab Horse Society (AHS) 29, 76, 95, 257
Arab Horse Society Stud Book 94, 135, 161, 191, 193, 195, 197, 199, 203, 205, 207, 211, 213, 215, 219, 220, 221, 222, 233, 235, 237, 241, 243, 245, 249, 251, 253, 255, 257, 260, 261
Arab-Israeli War 95
Arab Revolt *95*, 95-9
Arak 47
Arango, Don Carlos y Wactgin J. *see* Wactgin
Armenia 169
Ashley Combe 161
Ashton, Mr. (or Aschton) 116
Aslan Pasha 123

Ateybeh *see* Oteybeh
Athlone, Countess of 89
Athlone, Major-General, the Rt.Hon., The Earl of 89, 90, 114, 114, 205
Atkinson, Mrs G.E. 83, 221, 237, 261
Australia 34-6, 42, 61, 63, 73, 80, 90, 99, 169, 175, 213, 220
Ayub Bey 72, 161

Baalbek, Syria 219
Babolna Stud 259
Babson, Henry 201
Baggara tribe 164
Baghdad 47, 47, 52, 53, *54*, 81, *94*, 94, 95, 213, 221, 235, 247
Bahrain 87, 89, 90, 157, 159, 161, 181, 205
Baird, Mr A. 81, 84
Bakkah Valley 36
Banu Anazah tribe
Barker, Major G.H. 90, 195, 220
Barr, Miss H.I. 221
Basutoland 183
Bathyani, Count 259
Beal, Mrs 113
Beddington, R. 110
Bedford, 11th Duke of 83
Beirut 36, 51, 177
Bell, Mr & Mrs Adam 213
Beneyeh Ibn Shaalan 145
Beni Jamil 164
Beni Khalid tribe 86
Bentinck, Lord C. 119
Beresford, Lord William 25, 119, 121
Berghi Ibn ed Derri, Sheikh of the Resallin 85
Beteyen Ibn Mirshid, Sheikh of the Gomussa 48, 51, 58, 59, 85, 87, 135, 171, 216
Bevys of Hampton, Sir 14
Bialocerkiev Stud 22, 259
Blankney Hall, Lincolnshire *42*, 42, 217, 218
Blunt, Judith, *see* Wentworth, Lady
Blunt, Lady Anne 13, 26, 32, 43, *44*, 44, 45, *51*, 52, 72, *74*, *75*, 125, 131, 135, 163, 173, 177, 181, 217, 218, 231, 239, 259
Blunt, Wilfrid Scawen 13, 22, 32, 34, 40 et seq, *43*, *54*-5, *56*-7, *68*, 76, 133, 135, 139, 143, 147, 164, 166, 171, 173, 175, 177, 179, 183, 185, 197, 189, 191, 217, 218, 259

Bombay 20, 24, 173, 175, 219, 229, 231, 237, 241
Bondyshe, Sir Thomas, Ambassador at Constantinople 14
Borden, Colonel Spencer 163
Borowiak 259
Boulay, Mme du 207
Bourke, Hon. Terence 165
Bourke, A. 81
Bradmound, King of Damascus 14
Brandt, T.E. 29, 30, 120
Branicki, Count 22, 23, 116, 118, 259
Brierley, Captain R.W. 253
Brightwell Park, Oxfordshire *36*, 36, 216
Broadwood, Lieutenant R.S. 81, 82, 229
Broome, Major-General Ralph 83, 237
Browning, Miss 221
Brownlow, Lieutenant-Colonel 26, 27, 231
Brough, Major 231
Budapest 235
Burghley Hunt 83
Bussora 175

Cairo 52, 57, 58, 61, 69, 84, 86, 94, 135, 147, 149, 151, 155, 159, 161, 163, 187, 189, 245, 255
Calcutta 22, 61, 81,
Calthrop, Everard 61, 219, 235, 241
Canada 201
Cecil, Lord Arthur 42, 83, 218, 259
Chaplin, The Honourable Henry 17, 34, 36, 40, *42*, 42, 43, 48, 51, 61, 217
Charles II, HM King 16
Chicago Exposition 36
Citadel, The 86
Clark, H.V.M. *see* Musgrave Clark
Clay, Sir William 80, 112, 218
Clayton, Sir Gilbert *88*, 89, 113, 197, 260
Cléry, Maitre Léon 72, 159
Congested District's Board, Dublin 22, 119
Connaught, HH the Duke of, 119, 122
Constantinople 14, 22-3, 195, 235, 251
Cookson, Colonel J. 255
Corbett, The Honourable John 82, 229
County Wicklow 213
Covey, Cecil 78
Crabbet

333

Park *45, 48, 51,* 53, 54, *54-55,* 57, 78, 80, 82
Sales 61, 62, 80, 82, 83, 127, 137, 141, 147, 171, 187, 218, 229
Stud 13, 40, 43, 51, 53, 61, *62,* 63-67, 72, 74, 76-8, 80, 80, 103, 153, 155, 159, 161, 164, 189
Stud Book 62, 65, 125, 175
Cromwell 14
Ctesiphon Arch *93,* 94
Cunyngham, Sir R.D. 82, 117, 118, 120, 229
Cutler, L.W. 222
Cyprus 84

Da'aja tribe 95
Daghestani, Daoud Pasha al 95
Daghestani, General Muhammed Pasha al 95
Daghestani Tamara 95
Daira of Ali Pasha Sherif 72, 155, 159, 189
Daajin tribe, Otyebeh 175
Damascus 15, 36, 37, 49, *51,* 51, 57-9, 89, 177, 299, 253
Dangar, A.A. & W.J. 34-6, 42-3, 61, 112, 117
Dar Hafar 34
Daumas, General 34
Davenport, Homer 85, 239
David, King 85
Debbe Ibn Nowag of the Gomussa 80, 217, 218
Dehmedi el Hamoud of the Zoba 80, 227
Denadsha tribe 247
Derkoul Stud, Russia 147, 171
De Sdanovitch, Colonel Alexandre 147
Deyr 44, 47, 51, 127, 129, 131, 143, 166, 179
Digby, Mrs Jane 49, *50,* 51, 59
Dillon, The Hon. Miss Ethelred 13, 27, 42, 61-2, 80, 127, 139, 218, 227, 231
Dlewan Pasha al Majali, *see* Majali
Dodd, F. 27
Doughty, Charles 87
Drybrough, T.B. 29, 120, 121
Dufferin, Lord Viceroy of India 82, 259
Dursi tribe 245

Eastern Sires 29-33
Ed Duish of the Muteyr 87
Egypt 22, 27, 29, 53, 57, 64, 65, 73, 76, 81, 84, 86, 87, 89, 90, 99, 103, 116, 124, 159, 165, 166, 173, 177, 179, 189, 191, 229
Egyptian Campaigns 27
Ein Shems 61
Eire 211
Eissa Ibn Khalifa *see* Ibn Khalifa
Elizabeth, HM The Queen 98, 114, 124
Elizabeth, HM The Queen Mother 114, 124, 207, 209, 211, 215
El Hamoud of Zoba 227

Elm, Mrs 197
El Obeid 27
Emir of Riyadh, *see* Saud Ibn Saud
Enver Pasha 93, 123, 220, 249
Euphrates, River 34, 43, 44, 47, 48, 129, 143, 164, 166, 179
Erheyen Ibn Alian of the Gomussa 135

Fahd Bey al Khadhal, Sheikh 94
Faisal, King of Iraq 94, 95, *97,* 97, 247
Faisal II, King of Iraq 85, 95
Faisal Ibn Saud, Prince *78,* 78, 87, 89, 197
Falluja, Iraq 222
Faris Assat 47, 131
Faris Ibn Sfuk, Sheikh of the northern branch of Shammar 47
Farouk, HM King of Egypt 84, 89
Fathi, Ahmed 189
  Seyyid Mohammed 198
Fathi, Sayyid Mohammed 189
Fedaan tribe 37, 44, 53, 60, 72, 85, 86, 127, 169
Fenton, D. 189
Fenwick, Sir John 16
Feysul Ibn Turki, 10th Emir of Riyadh 86, 90, 91, 157, 161, 163, 181, 189
First World War 95, 103
Fisher, Capt. 231
Fitzwilliam Hunt 83
Flemetomo (Tomo) 67
Foster, Stewart 233
Forwood, Sir Dudley 98, 215
Fouad, HM King of Egypt 89
France 27, 36, 159, 247

Gainsford, Captain 29, 122, 239
Gallais, Colonel de 113, 119, 120, 219
Gateacre, Sir W. 27
Gaye, Dr. 81
General Stud Book (GSB) 17, 22, 35, 36, 73, 80, 83, 95, 125-191, 216-219, 225, 227, 229, 231, 233, 235, 237, 259
George V, HM King *32,* 32, 90, 95, 113, 123
George VI, HM King 89, 201, 257, 260, 113, 123
Gerard 81
Germany 17, 20, 22, 253
Ghudda 37
Gibraltar 179
Gifford 34
Gomussa tribe 35, 41, 43, 44, 48-50, 80, 85, 129, 131, 137, 141, 143, 171, 173, 177, 216-18, 225, 249
Gonne, Mr 80
Goureaux, Col. de 220
Governor of Deyr, *see* Huseyn Pasha

Grace, A.E. 220
Gretton, J. 218
Guzzawieh tribe 193

Haddad Pasha, General 95, 247
Haggla 60, 141
Haig, Capt. D. *28*
Hail 52-3, 86, 87, 90, 94, 195, 220
Haj 87
Haj Mahmud Aga 169
Haji Daham Haji Daud, Sheikh of Abu Nissar 222
Haji Fayadh, Sheikh of Abu Amr 203
Haji Mustapha Abd Tabash 207
Haki Pasha, HE 235
Halim Pasha 84
Hama 49
Hamed Bin Eissa Al-Khalifa HH 90, 205
Hamid el Abbas 164
Hamidie Horses 36
Hamilton, Leigh J. 187
Hampton Court Royal Stud 17, 18, 20
Hannadi tribe 60, 141
Harb tribe 61
Harris, Albert W. 239
Hartington, Lord 95, 123, 247
Hauran 193
Hayes, Captain 29, 118
Hazim Bey 251
Heissa Anazeh 35, 225
Hejaz 88, 95
Henderson, R.S. Consul at Aleppo 47, 51, 53, 60, 62, 64, 82, 118, 129, 233
Henriques, Colonel E.N. 113, 120, 219, 233
Herring, sen, John F. 20
Hillah (Hilla) 203
Hills, Sir John 233
Hit *46,* 47
Holland, Queen of 89
Homs 49
Hormusjee, Pallanjee 219
Hough, C.W. & S.G. 195, 220, 247
Huntington, Randolph 27, 35, 36, 82, 229
Hurlingham 29
Husain al Dhiban of Albutaif 203
Hussars, 9th 29
Hussars, 11th 30
Hussein, HM King of Jordan 95, 98, 114, 124, 207, 209
Hussein, Sherif, King of the Hejaz 84, 85, 93, *96,* 123
Huseyn Pasha, Governor of Deyr 44, 47, 93, 94
Hyderabad 61, 82

Ibn Aweyde, Mishwat Ibn Shab'aan 153, 163

Ibn ed Derri of the Resallin 51, 64, 129, 131, 177, 179
  Sheikh Afet 59, 129
  Sheikh Berghi 85, 129
  Sheikh Neddi 59, 85, 131, 171
  Sheikh Mashlab 85, 177
Ibn Ernan 59
Ibn Hamoud of the Zoba 80, 227
Ibn Hemsi of the Gomussa 86, 137, 173
Ibn Ghayan 257
Ibn Khalifa, Sheikh of Bahrain 87, 157, 159, 163, 181, 183, 185
  Eissa 87, 89, 90, 91
  Ali 90
  HH Sheikh Hamed bin Eissa 90, 205
Ibn Mehaid of the Mehed 36
Ibn Mirshid of the Gomussa, Sebaa 36
  Sheikh Beteyen, *see* Beteyen Ibn Mirshid
  Sheikh Ibn Ernan, *see* Erheyen Ibn Alian
  Sheikh Meshur, *see* Meshur Ibn Mirshid
  Sheikh Suleyman, *see* Suleyman Ibn Mirshid
Ibn Nakadan 86, 90
Ibn Rasheed, Emir 86, 90, 93, 220
Ibn Rasheed, Mohammed, Emir of Haïl, *see* Mohammed
Ibn Rodan of the Roala 145
Ibn Saadun, Sheikh Bender of the Muntifiq 187
Ibn Saud, Feysul Ibn Turki (10th Emir)
  Feysul Ibn Saud, *see* Faisal Ibn Saud
  Abdullah (9th Emir), *see* Abdullah Ibn Saud
  King, *see* Abdul Aziz al Saud
Ibn Sauds 86, 87, 98, 199, 201, 260
Ibn Sbeyel of Gomussa, Sebaa 35, 44, 166, 216
Ibn Sbeyni of the Mehed-Fedaan 46, 60, 85, 127, 149, 163, 169, 185, 253
  Hauran 127
  Sahij 127
Ibn Shaalan of the Roala
  Sheikh Sotamm, *see* Sotamm Ibn Shaalan
  Sheikh Beneyeh, *see* Beneyeh Ibn Shaalan
  Sheikh Nuri, *see* Nuri Ibn Shaalan
  Sheikh Nawwaf, *see* Nawwaf Ibn Shaalan
Ibn Smeyr of the Wuld-Ali 48
Ibn Sudan of the Roala 85
  Sheikh Mansour Ibn Sudan, 149, 153, 163, 181, 183, 185
Ibn Sweid of the Ajman 89, 123, 260
Ibrahim Bey Sherif 70, 151
Ibrahim Pasha 86
Ibrahim, Prince 61
Imaum of Muscat, Syed Said 18-20, 112, 115, 116, 118
Impecuniosus 53, 54

Imperial Stud, Constantinople 22, 23
India 23, 27, 29, 48, 53-4, 61, 73, *80*, 80, 81 *et seq*, 131, 173, 187, 219, 227, 229, 231, 233, 237, 241, 243, 259
Inshass Stud 84
Iraq 94, 95
Ireland 29, 187, 213
Islington Horse Show 61
Ismael Pasha 67, 147
Istanbul 86
Italy, King of 35, 247

Jakin Ibn Aghil, Sheikh of the Daajini tribe, Oteybeh 175
James I, King 16
Java 73
Jebel Ghorab 47
Jedaan Ibn Mehaid, Sheikh of the Fedaan 37, 39, 41, 47-49, 60, 61, 85
Jeddah 57, 58, 89
Jejeebhoy, Sir Jamsetjee 22, 81
Jellabieh, strain, *see* Keheileh Jellabieh
Jemaat 171
Jerba Shammar tribe 87
Jereybah, strain *see* Keheileh
Jerusalem 58
Jirro, Mohammed 51, 59, 135
Jockey Club 81, 82
Johnstone, Captain 27, 231
Joktan 61
Jordan 98, 99, 103, 207, 209, 211, 215
Jordanian, Royal Stud 95, 98, 209
Jordan, River 58, 95
Joyce, Colonel P.C. 94
Jubul, Lake of 33
Jumna, (troopship) 27

Kabul 24, 27, 231
Kahtan, *see* Joktan
Kahtan tribe, *see* Qahtan
Kal'a, the *34*
Kandahar 231
Karak 95, *101*
Kasim 81
Kellogg, Mr 78
Kenna, Capt. *28*
Kerak 207, 215
Keydekani min Barazan tribe 169
Khalaf of Baghdad 173
Khalifa, HH Sheikh Hamed Bin Eissa *see* Ibn Khalifa
Khartoum 27
Khashman el Kasab 165
Khedive of Egypt 90
Khurassa, tribe of Shammar 221

Kliniewski, Wladislas 181
Krushieh, *see* Keheilet el Krushieh
Krush al Ghandour, *see* Keheilet el Krush
Kurd 169
Kut 94
Kuwait 53

Landseer, Sir Edwin 20
Lance, Brigadier-General F.F. 193, 219
Lancers, 12th 82, 229, 243
Lancers, 21st 28, 253
Layard, Mrs 84
Lawrence, T.E. 85
Lebanon 84, 220
Legard, John 227
Levant Company 14
Little, Captain 29
Lock, Sir Henry, Governor of the Cape 183
Lopez, Santiago 98-9, 207
Lovelace, Lord 161
Lucknow 26
Lyon, Miss 78
Lytton, J.A.D. 166
Lytton, Lady Anne 78, *79*
Lytton, Lord, Viceroy of India 53

MacDona, J.C. 36, 216
Machell, Captain 61
Mackay, D. 169, 175
Maharajah of Jodhpore 61
Maharajah of Mysore 112
Maharajah of Patiala 26, 219
Mahmud Aga 60
Mahmud Bey (Mahmud Beg) 66, 67, 147
Majali tribe 86, 95, 98
Majali, Dlewan Pasha el 99, *102*, 207
Majali, Lieutenant-Colonel Habis el 98, 215, 261
Makkah 47, 58, 94, *96*
Markham, Gervase 16
Marseilles 27, 36, 61, 231
Martino, Signor de, Italian Ambassador 247
Mashaeikh, Sheikh ul- 251
Mashlab Ibn ed Derri *see* Ibn ed Derri
Masne, C. 227
Massawah 27, 231
McCall, Major 81
McDougall, Capt. M.A. 237
Mecklenburg, Duke of 211
Mehed Fedaan tribe 86, 127, 133, 169
Mehmet Ali 133
Meshur Ibn Mirshid 49, 60, 129, 177
Mesopotamia 44, 47, 51, 80, 85, 87, 165, 179, 247
Meskene 34, 44

Midwood, Norris G,*81*
Mijuel, The Mesrab 49, 72
Miller, C.D. 29, *31*, 121
Miller, Lt.-Col. Sir John 215
Mishwat Ibn Shabaan Ibn Aweyde, *see* Ibn Aweyde
Moahib tribe of Sebaa1 65
Moali tribe 139
Moayaja tribe of Sebaa 127, 165
Mohamed Sabha 221
Mohammed Ali, The Great 86, 87
Mohammed Ibn Rasheed, Emir 52, 86, 87, 94, 195
Mohammed Khuddr Jemal el Din, Egypt 166
Mohammed Pasha 141
Mohammed Rashad Khan 195
Mohammed Sadyk Pasha 185
Mohammed Salem, Syce 155
Mohammerah, Sheikh 221
Moharrem Pasha 191
Mohuiddin, Prince 93, 251
Montefik tribe *see* Muntifiq tribe
Montefiore, Reverend D.B. 233
Montmorency, Captain Honoré de 27
Morocco 32
Mosul 47, 81, 86
Moubarek, Sheikh of the Sebaa 93, 220
Mowali tribe 34
Muhammed, Prophet 117
Muhammed Said al Rashid Hussay 114, 222
Mull, Isle of 29
Munro-Mackenzie,. J.H. 29, 120
Muntifiq tribe 86, 143, 229
Mûsa, Senior, Austrian Consul at Aleppo 60
Muscat 20, 88
  Imaum of, *see* Imaum
Musgrave-Clark, H.V.M., 78, 85, 93, 123, 161, 247, 249, 251, 253
Mustafa Effendi Nuri 155
Muteyr tribe 59, 61, 86, 87, 192
Mutlak 69, 72
Mutlaq Ibn Hedeb of Moayaja Sebaa 165
Mysore Cup 82

Naheis Bey 247
Nakadan of the Ajman 86
Napier, Lt. Gen. Sir Charles *26*
Narhar, Sheikh of Mowali tribe 34
Nasr el Mizrab 72
National Pony Society (NPS) 29, 33
  Stud Books 125
Nawwaf Ibn Shaalan, Emir of the Roala 85
Nazzal el Armiti, Menja 207
Neale, D.E. 260
Neddi Ibn ed Derri *see* Ibn ed Derri

Nejd 24, 29, 43, 52, 58, 87, 89, 103, 195, 197, 220, 233, 239, 247, 260
Nejd, town of *53*, 133, 175
Newbuildings Place 54, *65*, 70, 77, 78, *79*, 133
Newcastle, Duke of 16
Newmarket 33, 34, 44, 61, 62, 81, 82, 173, 229
New York 36, 82
Nicholson, Mrs S.A. 211
Nigm 51
Nixon, Colonel, Consul General, Baghdad 47, 53
Noel-King, Lady Anne, *see* Blunt, Lady Anne
Nuri Ibn Shaalan, Emir of the Roala 85

Obeyd tribe 143
Oheynan Ibn Said 137
Old Palace, Cairo 69
Ollivant, Major G.B. 243
Omar Bey Dandash 89, 220
Omdurman 27, 28
Oneyza 87
Oppenheim, Mr & Mrs 84
Oteybeh tribe 175
Othman Bey Sherif 72
Othman el Abd of the Obeyd tribe 143
Othman el Ibrahim el Akeyli 179
Oude, King of (Nawab Ikbálet Dowlah) 20, 47

Palermo 61
Palestine 193
Palgrave, W.G. 34, 86, 87, 103
Palmerston, Lord 20
Palmyra 51, 171
Patiala Maharajah of, *see* Maharajah
Pau 27, 231
Pauncefoot-Duncombe 112, 115
Pearce, Mrs 151
Pearce, Stephen 64, 65
Persian Gulf 53, 81
Phillips, Miss Claudia (later Mrs C. Barling) 221
Poland 22, 23, 53, 103, 259
Polo Pony Society (PPS) 29 *et seq*
Polo Pony Stud Book 22, 29
Polo and Riding Pony Society (P&RPS) 29, 29, 233, 235, 237, 241, 243, 245
Potocki, Count Joseph 61, 62, 171
Prince of Wales, HRH *see* Wales, Prince of
Pritchard, Judge 221
Prophet, The 24

Queen's Bays 27

Ramady 80
Ramsdell J.A.P. 185
Rasheed, Ibn, *see* Ibn Rasheed

Ras-el-Fedawi, strain 34, 49, 51
Raymond, Mr 218
Resallin tribe of Seb'aa 85, 129, 131, 171, 177, 179
Rhodes, The Hon. Cecil 65, 177
Rihani, Ameen *89*, 89, 199, 220
Rishan, Baghdad 235
Riyadh (Riâd) 87, 90, 133, 199-201
Roala tribe 27, 41, 49, *50*, 58, 85, 139, 145, 149, 153, 163, 181, 217, 218
Robert, J.G. 211
Roberts, Lord *24*, 24, *25*, 25, 120, 231
Rockingham, Marquis of 65
Rogay, Mohammed A. 81
Rothschild, Leopold de 84
Royal Agricultural Society, Egypt (RAS) 76, 191, 209
Royal Jordanian Stud (RJS) 95, 98
Royal Mounted Guards (Jordan) 95
Royal Stud, Tutbury 14
Rumady 47
Rumanhiya Wells 89
Russell, Lord Herbrand *82*, 83, 218, 259
Russia 66, 69, 73, 78, 79, 147, 181
Russian Stud 171, 259
Rustem Pasha, HE, Turkish Ambassador 141
Rzewuski, Count 85

Saëkh tribe 179
Saleh Bey Sherif 70
Sandeman, Albert Glas 17, 34-36, 43, 216, 225
Sanford, Major H. 222
Sandown Park 82
Sandringham 98, 211
Sanguszko, prince Roman the Younger 262
Sauds, *see* Ibn Sauds
Saud Ibn Saud, Emir of Riyadh 257, 260
Saud Ibn Saud 133
Saudi Arabia 78, 89
Savile, The Hon. George 243
Schmidt, Carl (Raswan) 78
Schwimmer, Messrs 235
Sdanovitch, Col. Alexandre de 147, 171
Sebaa tribe 36, 37, 41, 47,48, 59, 72, 80, 81, 86, 93, 95, 127, 129, 137, 139, 141, 177, 179, 216-218, 225, 249
Second World War 201
Selby, Roger 78, 95, 247

Seyd Ahmed, Sheikh of the Hannadi 44, 60, 139, 141
Shah of Persia 20
Shakra 173
Shammar tribe 34, 44, 47, 64, 80, 85, 86, 166, 177, 221, 225
Shass 34
Sheepshanks, Captain R.J. 114, 222
Sheffield E.W. 123, 255
Sherif of Makkah 86, 93, 115, 251
Sherif, Saleh Bey 189
Sheykh Obeyd 185, 189, 191, 229
Sheykh Obeyd Stud, Egypt *60*, 61, 64, 65, 68, 72, 73, 84, 103
Sheykh Obeyd Stud Book *71*
Shuna 95
Simla 56
Singh, Kumwar Bokhul *28*,
Skene, J.H., HM Consul-General at Aleppo 34 *et seq*, 40, 43, 44, 47, 49, 51, 85, 133, 135, 143, 164, 171, 216, 225
Skene, Mrs 51
Smyrna (Izmir) 34, 36, 61
Smythe, Captain W. 27
Somerville, Mrs W.B.R.B. 213
Sotamm Ibn Shaalan, Sheikh of the Roala 49, 85, 145
Soukim, *see* Suakim
'Souls', the 55
South Africa 27, 73, 177
South Down Hunt 55
Spain 23, 78, 103, 219
Spence J. 203
Spencer, Miss G. 255
Spheri 34
Stephens, H.C. 81, 127, 137, 139, 233
Stewart, Lieutenant-Colonel P.D. 245
St Quintin, Colonel T.A. 25
Strathnairn, Lord 81
Strogonoff, Count 157
Suakim 27, 231
Suares 70, 72
Sudan Campaigns 27, 28
Suez 231
Suleyman Ibn Mirshid, Supreme Sheikh of the Gomussa Sebaa 35, 37, 40, 41, 49, 85, 216, 217, 225
Suleyman Jelaleh of the Sebaa 139
Sultan Abdul Ajiz of Turkey 17, 22

Sultan of Morocco 112, 116
Summerhays, R.S. 95
Sutton, Sir Robert 14,16
Sword, J.C. 203
Sydney 80
Syria 81, 219, 220, 245
Szamrajowka Stud 258

Tais Ibn Sharbann 145
Takeddin Pasha, Governor of Makkah 133
Takha Sheikh and Chief Ulema 40, 133
Talaat Pasha 195
Talal, HM King of Jordan 99, 207
Talkat 41
Tattersall, Mr 36
Tattersall's Sales 20, 95
Taylor, Lt. Cecil 179
Tebbutt, C.E. 164
Tel el Ghorab 165
Tersk 78
Thompson, H.A. 80, 177
Thompson, Major Meysey 82
Tigris, River *46*, 47
Tor Royal Stud 83, 237
Tousson Pasha 86
Tower of Nimrod *46*, 47
Tree, A.M. 29
tribes *see* Appendix 2
Trouncer, Mr 84, 125
Tryon, Admiral G. 81, 112, 118
Tudmur 58
Tunis 165
Turks, the 86, 94, 95, 193, 235
Turkey 22
  Sultan of 235
    Abdul Hamid II 251
Turkish Porte 24
Turkish Purchasing Commission 22, 31
Turkoman 44
Tutbury Royal Stud, *see* Royal Stud

Ukraine 22
Upton, Major Roger Dawson 13, 17, 34 *et seq*, 47-51, 60, 80, 85, 133, 217, 225
Upton, Mrs R.D. (née Turner) 35
Upton, Roger Hope Edward (son of Major R.D. Upton) 34, 36, 42, 112, 117
USA 29, 73, 80, 82, 83, 85, 89, 98, 185, 199, 220, 229, 239, 247

Valensin, M. Jacques 72
Veragua, Duke of 78, 219
Vesey, The Hon. Eustace 27,
Viceroy of India 22
Victoria, HM The Queen *22*, 22, 24, 84, 112, 115, 116, 118
Vidal, Reverend F. Furze 35, 36, 63, 82, 229

Wadneh Khursan, strain, *see* al'Wadneh
Wactgin y Arango, Don Carlos 227
Wakib 69
Wales, Prince of 13, 22-3, 31-2, 42, 83, 93, 237, 259
Walker, W.H. 29, 30, 118, 121
Watban el Duish, Sheikh 86
Watson, Homer 201
Watson, The Hon. A.J. 114, 213
Watson, Sir John 121, 187
Weatherby, Mr 61, 80, 221
Weatherby's 83
Webb 70
Webster, Mr, Director of Agriculture Iraq 221
Weil Stud 17, 116
Weldi tribe 34, 127
Welled Ali tribe *see* Wuld-Ali tribe
Wentworth, Lady 13, *74*, 76, *77*, 78, 80, 85, 103, 113, 123, 189, 197, 247, 251, 253, 255
Westminster, Duke of 62
White, H.C. 169
White Star 'Cymric' 73
William IV, HM The King 18, 19, 112, 114-5
Williams, Sir J. 14
Wilson, Lady Rivers 61, 84, 118
Windsor 20, 98
Winifrid, Lady Tryon (née Lytton) 73
Woburn 83
Wood, Sir E. 20
World War I *see* First World War
World War II *see* Second World War
Wuld-Ali tribe 48, 49
Württemberg, King William I of 17, 115
Wyvil, Sir Christopher 16

Yaarab (Arab)
Yule, Lady 78

Zeyd, Saad el Muteyri 59, 61, 64, 165, 177, 179
Zoba, Dehemedi al 81, 117
Zoba tribe *see* Al-Zoba tribe

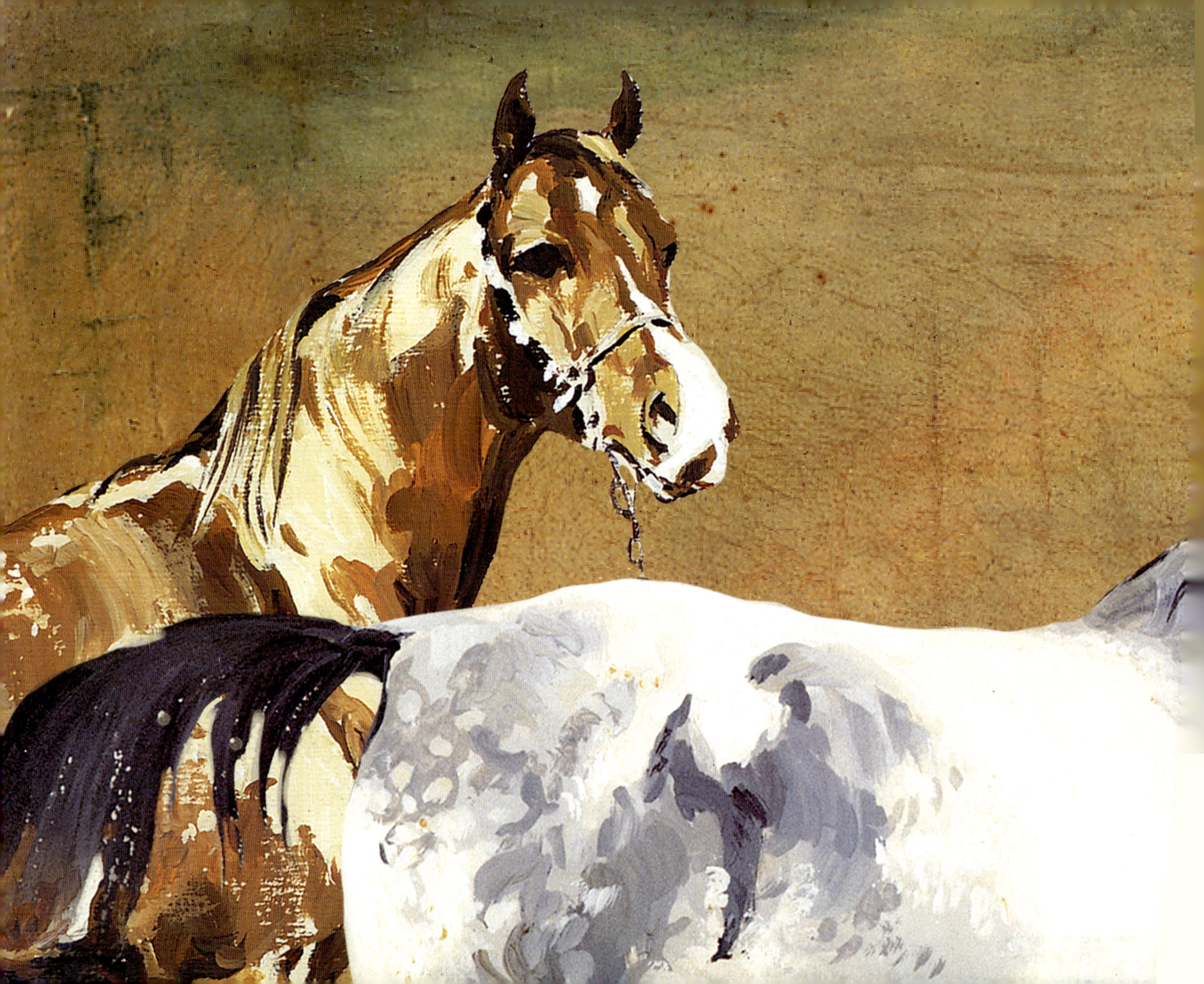